THE *ESSENTIAL* BLUE & WHITE BOOK

A TORONTO MAPLE LEAFS FACTBOOK

ANDREW PODNIEKS

GREYSTONE BOOKS

VANCOUVER/TORONTO/NEW YORK

Greystone Books
A division of Douglas & McIntyre Ltd.
2323 Quebec Street, Suite 201
Vancouver, British Columbia
Canada V5T 4S7
www.greystonebooks.com

NATIONAL LIBRARY OF CANADA CATALOGUING IN PUBLICATION DATA
Podnieks, Andrew.
   The essential blue and white book

   Previously published as a serial under title: The blue and
      white book.
   Includes index.
   ISBN 1-55054-882-4

   1. Toronto Maple Leafs (Hockey team) I. Podnieks, Andrew.
Blue and white book. II. Title.
GV848.T6P62 2001   796.962′64′09713541   C2001-911020-0

Editing by John Eerkes-Medrano
Proofreading by Neall Calvert
Cover photograph by Dave Sandford/Hockey Hall of Fame
Cover and text design by Tanya Lloyd/Spotlight Designs
All photographs courtesy of the Hockey Hall of Fame. pp. 89, 132,
   147, 332: Imperial Oil—Turofsky; pp. 106, 199: Dave Sandford;
   p. 191: Frank Prazak; pp. 253, 267, 395: London Life—Portnoy;
   p. 297: Graphic Artists
Printed and bound in Canada by Friesens
Printed on acid-free paper ∞

We gratefully acknowledge the financial support of the Canada
Council for the Arts, the British Columbia Ministry of Tourism,
Small Business and Culture, and the Government of Canada
through the Book Publishing Industry Development Program
(BPIDP) for our publishing activities.

CONTENTS

THE BIRTH OF
THE MAPLE LEAFS

THE NATIONAL HOCKEY LEAGUE (NHL) WAS
formed in 1917 and was a continuation of
the National Hockey Association. The new league
was created in part to rid the NHA of Eddie
Livingstone, the despised owner of the Toronto
Arenas. The plan worked. The Arenas were
bought by Charlie Querrie, Paul Ciceri, Frank
Heffernan, Harry Sproule, Percy Hambly, and his
brother, Fred, and continued to play out of the
same stadium at 60 Mutual Street at Shuter
Street. The building came to be known as the
Mutual Street Arena, but for many years it was
known simply as the Arena Gardens (thus the
name of the hockey club), or, even more affec-
tionately, as Andy's Igloo (in reference to the
building's manager, Andy Taylor).

The Arena Gardens was built in 1911–12 from
designs by F.H. Herbert and the firm of Ross and
MacFarlane. It was financed by a syndicate called
"The Arena Gardens of Toronto, Limited." The
president was Sir Henry Pellatt, whose more
famous house, Casa Loma, still sits on a hill on
Spadina Avenue. The Arena cost $200,000 to build
and was financed by a group of 15 businessmen:
Aemilius Jarvis, Joseph Kilgower, R.A. Smith, Hume

Blake, George W. Beardmore, Lawrence Solman, and George Horne of Toronto; R. Reford, W.I. Gear, Col. J. Carson, R.S. Logan, Hartland MacDougall, E.A. Shepherd, A.G.B. Claxton, and G.A. Ross of Montreal.

The other great Toronto arena of this era was the Ravina Gardens (also known as Ravina Rink) at 50 Rowland Avenue. Built in 1911, it was home to the Toronto Ravinas, a kind of developmental farm club for the St. Pats, successors to the Arenas, where many future NHLers apprenticed. It was also frequently used by the Arenas and St. Pats for practices, and the New York Rangers even held their 1930–31 training camp there. It was torn down in 1962.

On December 13, 1919, just prior to the start of the 1919–20 season, the Arenas hockey team was bought by Querrie, Ciceri, John Paris (J.P.) Bickell (president of McIntyre Mines), and N.L. Nathanson (managing director of the Famous Players Canadian Corporation).

Members of the Board of Directors and Executive at Maple Leaf Gardens and the Air Canada Centre

Sir John Aird, 1931–1939	Jake Dunlap, Q.C., 1983–1990
H.R. Aird, 1930–1931	E.S. Duggan, 1930–1931
J.B. Aird, 1963–1970	Lorne Duguid, 1972–1982
R.J. Amell, 1958–1970	Thor E. Eaton, 1990–1992
B. Ballard, 1972–1976	A.L. Ellsworth, 1931–1951
H. Ballard, 1961–1990	George J. Engman, 1994–197
John Bassett Jr., 1953–1970	Cliff Fletcher, 1991–1997
J.S. Beatty, 1930–1931	Arthur Gans, 1985–1989
Brian P. Bellmore, 1992–present	G.R. Gardiner, 1958–1970
Robert G. Bertram, 1994–present	P.R. Gardiner, 1941–1958
J.P. Bickell, 1930–1951	Donald Giffin, 1972–1992
E.W. Bickle, 1930–1961	George H. Gooderham, 1931–1943
J.E. Birks, 1931–1937	Scott Griffin, 1930–1931
Henry Borden, Q.C., 1965–1970	M.S. Haas, 1930–1931
N.L. Bosworth, 1977–1990	Dr. J.L. Hall, 1972–1982
J.R. Bradfield, 1966–1970	W.M. Hatch, 1958–1970
William T. Brock, 1994–1997	Sydney Hermant, 1964–1970
A. Campbell Burgess, Q.C., 1972–1989	C.B. Jackson, 1930–1931
C.F.W. Burns, 1951–1970	T.D. Jeffries, 1963–1970
P.G. Campbell, 1930–1931	Ian Johnson, Q.C., 1946–1970
King Clancy, 1970–1986	Terence V. Kelly, Q.C., 1992–1997
G.R. Cottrelle, 1931–1952	R.A. Laidlaw, 1931–1970
F.J. Crawford, 1930–1931, 1934–1965	Dale Lastman, 2000–present
J. Donald Crump, 1990–1995	Edward Lawrence, 1972–1992

The name of the club was changed to the St. Pats in the hope that the new moniker would lure Toronto's large Irish population to the rink. The Arena could seat about 8,000 people, and its ice surface was gigantic by today's NHL standards—230 x 90 feet. Under the new name, the club flourished. In 1927, Conn Smythe, who had been general manager of the New York Rangers the previous season, convinced the Toronto owners to sell the club to him. Smythe also persuaded J.P. Bickell to retain his part of the ownership by investing in the new club with associates Peter G. Campbell and Ed Bickle. On February 17, 1927, the team became the Maple Leafs (named after the World War I fighting unit, the Maple Leaf Regiment) and won its first game 4–1 over the New York Americans.

As the club continued to draw impressive crowds, Conn Smythe envisioned a grand new hockey palace in Toronto, unlike any other

S.H. Logan, 1939–1952
W.A.H. MacBrien, 1930–1970
John MacIntyre, 1997–present
Larkin Maloney, 1949–1968
George E. Mara, 1958–1970
A. Bruce Matthews, 1951–1970
Hon. R.C. Matthews, 1937–1951
T.A. McAuley, 1930–1931
Leighton McCarthy, 1931–1945
C. George McCullagh, 1937–1952
Frederick G. McDowell, 1990–1992
Harry McGee, 1931–1937
Paul McNamara, 1962–1990
Dean Metcalf, 1997–present
F.K. Morrow, 1931–1953
J.Y. Murdoch, 1931–1962
Balmer Neilly, 1953–1956
Ted Nikolaou, 1992–1997
Frank P. O'Connor, 1931–1939
W. Eric Phillips, 1952–1964
W. Frank Prendergast, 1937–1959
W. Ron Pringle, 1992–1997
Alfred Rogers, 1931–1949

Edward S. Rogers, 1990–1992
Frank A. Rolph, 1931–1941
Victor Ross, 1931–1934
Hon. W.D. Ross, 1931–1943
Douglas Roxborough, 1972–1989
Sigmund Samuel, 1932–1933, 1934–1962
Robert M. Sedgewick, Q.C., 1972–1984
R. Home Smith, 1931–1935
Conn Smythe, 1930–1966
C. Stafford Smythe, 1956–1971
Hugh Smythe, 1971–1972
Steve Stavro, 1982–present
John Stewart, 1953–1970
W.W. Stratton, 1930–1931
Larry Tanenbaum, 1996–2000
John A. Tory, 1931–1950
W.O. Twaits, 1960–1970
N.C. Urquhart, 1942–1966
J.J. Vaughan, 1937–1964
George E. Whyte, Q.C., 1992–1997
J.R. White, 1959–1960

facility in the world. He formed Maple Leaf Gardens Limited in 1930 to encourage the development of and investment in a new building. The final finances were made possible by Bickell, who used his influence with his friend Sir John Aird, president of the Canadian Imperial Bank of Commerce, to secure the necessary loan. (Bickell later became the Gardens' first president and then chairman of the board until his death in 1951.) The choicest parcel of land was bought, measuring 349 feet 10 inches x 282 feet and bounded by Carlton, Church, and Wood Streets (although a second site, at Yonge and Fleet Streets, almost won the day). Smythe acquired the land from Timothy Eaton, and the new Gardens was designed by Toronto's pre-eminent architectural firm of the twentieth century, Ross and Macdonald, also renowned for creating some of this city's finest edifices, such as College Park, Union Station, and the Royal York Hotel. Ground was broken on June 1, 1931, and just 165 days later, on November 12, 1931, Maple Leaf Gardens hosted its first NHL game, a Chicago Black Hawks 2–1 win over the Leafs.

Some facts: a daily average of 700 workers used a total of 13,500 cubic yards of concrete, 600 tons of reinforcing steel, 760 tons of structural steel, and 1.5 million bricks and tiles (the former provided by Conn Smythe's sand and gravel pits in Etobicoke). The domed roof measured 207 x 225 feet, and from street to ceiling it soared 150 feet high. No seat was farther than 65 feet from ice level, and the seating capacity was an enormous 12,500. The total cost of construction was $1.5 million.

When the Gardens opened, its amenities included a bowling alley, a billiards room, and a full gymnasium. Smythe used to keep cats in the building to ensure that rodents stayed out, and he employed two full-time painters, who used to touch up virtually every small crack or chip on a daily basis to maintain the building's pristine character.

One of the reasons the Gardens didn't take long to build was that its finest attribute was its outer appearance. Inside, it was plain and unglamorous at the start, a testament to the speed with which it was erected. Once completed, however, Smythe set about ensuring that it would be at the forefront of stadium design and the most professional building in the world. The Gardens was the first arena to have a four-faced time clock (1932); the first to use penalty clocks; the first to paint the ice surface so that fans could see the puck more clearly; the first to use a red/blue light, goal judge, and timer to determine last-second goals and announce the end of periods; the first to have separate penalty boxes (1962); the first to use Plexiglas (Herculite) above the boards (1947); the first to install an electronic system of clocking the on-ice time for each player (1947); the first to install escalators (1955); and the first to have a portable X-ray machine in the hospital room (1956). Although the Gardens did not host the first televised *Hockey Night in Canada*, the first hockey broadcasts—pay-per-view to 1,000 residents of Etobicoke—came from Maple Leaf Gardens.

By the 1990s, the NHL's landscape changed dramatically. Expansion created a league of thirty teams by the year 2000, salaries soared, and teams had to find ways to generate greater sums of money. In Toronto, the sports scene was also affected by the incoming National Basketball Association (NBA) team, the Raptors, who were building a new arena at Bay and Front Streets, just two blocks from the Hockey Hall of Fame. The Leafs sought to build their own arena and looked at sites ranging from the Armoury to the Canadian National Exhibition (CNE) grounds. All worked out perfectly when Raptors owner Allan Slaight agreed to sell the basketball team and the new arena, already under construction, to Leafs owner Steve Stavro on February 12, 1998. With the help of Tom Anselmi, senior vice-president of business, the Leafs redesigned much of the interior to accommodate the hockey club, and from a corporate perspective the longstanding MLG Ltd. gave way to Maple Leaf Sports and Entertainment (MLSE).

Construction of the Air Canada Centre (ACC) began March 12, 1997, from designs made by Brisbin Brook Beynon Architects. The exterior featured a modern glass design incorporating the old postal building (circa 1939) on the site into the structure. The ACC hoped to retain the intimacy of the Gardens in an expanded and more luxurious context. Seats were widened, concession stands offered greater varieties of food, and wider hallways maintained the history of the team through photographs and a new Maple Leafs Hall of Fame. The ACC's 18,800 capacity makes it one of the smaller new buildings, and fans are no farther from the ice than they were at the Gardens.

The final game at the Gardens took place on February 13, 1999. The Leafs played Chicago, as they had on the building's opening night some 68 years previous. To face off the opening puck, the Leafs' Red

Horner—the oldest living Hall of Famer and member of the 1931–32 Cup team—came to centre ice with Mush March, who had scored the first goal in the Gardens in 1931, as a member of the Black Hawks. In fact, March brought with him the very puck and used it for the closing ceremony. The Leafs made the theme of the transition from Maple Leaf Gardens to the Air Canada Centre "Memories and Dreams," and at game's end a special ceremony featured a parade of dozens of Leafs alumni onto the ice. They included obscure names such as Moe Morris, who would pass away a short time later, to the ever-popular Borje Salming. The final tableau of the evening saw Horner hold high a flag bearing the inscription "Memories and Dreams," a flag he would take with him to the opening of the ACC one week later.

That opening, on February 20, 1999, featured the greatest rivalry in sport—Toronto vs. Montreal—in a game won by the Leafs in dramatic fashion with a Steve Thomas goal in overtime. The next afternoon the Raptors played their first game, and the night after that the ACC's first concert took place, featuring The Tragically Hip.

Sweaters

The original St. Pats sweater, in conjunction with the nickname, was primarily green, with a white neck, white armbands at the elbows, and a band around the chest, into which the St. Pats name was integrated.

When the St. Pats became the Maple Leafs midway through the 1926–27 season (February 17, 1927), a makeshift sweater was employed for the rest of the schedule, using the same green and white sweater but with a maple leaf replacing the "St. Pats" on the chest. No photographs of this sweater are known to exist.

For the team's first season at Maple Leaf Gardens, 1931–32, the Leafs wore plain white sweaters with a maple leaf on the front. This is documented in the famous photograph of opening night, November 12, 1931.

The Leafs' first proper sweater was dark blue, with many white stripes incorporated on the arms and legs and a 48-point leaf with "Toronto Maple Leafs" inscribed therein. The road white uniforms were slightly different during these early years (1928–34). They consisted of three blue bands above and below the maple leaf, and the stockings were also limited to three stripes. One small change was made for the 1933–34 season to the blue home sweaters: the three stripes, instead of being thin-thick-thin, were of equal width.

The uniform adopted in 1934 remained almost unchanged for more than 40 years. The stockings still conformed to three sets of three stripes (thin-thick-thin), but the arms now had two stripes that were matched by two other stripes along the waist of the sweater.

In 1937, the crest was altered in two ways: the "Toronto Maple Leafs," which sloped upward like a smile, now featured the "Toronto" sloping downward and the "Maple Leafs" straight across. Also, the leaf itself became veined.

By 1942, the crest had 35 points to it, and for the 1946–47 season the familiar "C" and "A" appeared on the front of the captain's and alternates' sweaters for the first time. Also, in an experiment that lasted only for team portraits in 1947–48, the lettering of "Toronto Maple Leafs" appeared in red.

In 1960, the sweater was given six eyelets and a lace at the neck, a change that lasted until 1973. In 1961, the Leafs began to put numbers on the arms of the sweater so that players could be identified with greater ease from all angles in the Gardens and on television.

To celebrate Canada's centennial, the team significantly altered the sweater prior to the 1967 playoffs. The Leaf crest was now 11 points, the lettering inside it was modified, and the stripes on the arms and waist were reduced to one set of thin-thick-thin lines.

In 1970–71, the NHL adopted a policy that the home team wear white. The Leafs sweater was again altered. The crest, while still 11 points, changed design, and the lettering for "Toronto Maple Leafs" went straight across. The stockings now had two thick stripes, the waist had one thick band, and the dark-coloured arms extended completely from the neck to the wrist, where before just stripes existed. Between the number on the arm and the neck, a miniature maple leaf appeared on both sides. By 1978, names also appeared on the back of uniforms, both home and away.

Since the mid-1980s, patches have sometimes adorned the sweater. A patch appeared for the 1983–84 season to celebrate Toronto's sesquicentenntial; in memory of King Clancy, the 1986–87 uniform featured an armpatch shamrock; and, in 1990–91, to mark the death of then owner H. Ballard, another patch, "HEB," appeared. For the

NHL's 75th anniversary season in 1991–92, the Leafs employed two sweaters, one with a simple patch, the other (for games against Original Six opponents) featuring the dark at home and vintage crest.

A new design was introduced in 1992, blending the distant past with the recent past. The stockings reverted to the classic style that had existed for decades (three sets of thin-thick-thin stripes), while the crest from 1970 remained. The arm-length band of colour was discontinued, and above the shoulder numbers the old veined leaf in miniature was attached and two stripes were added below the numbers.

In 1995–96, two variations were introduced. One, adopted for the whole season, saw a "65th Anniversary Maple Leaf Gardens" patch sewn on the right chest of the sweater. The other, to celebrate this anniversary on November 2, 1996, saw the Leafs revert to the classic Conn Smythe version for this one game only. For 1997–98, the sweater remained the same but the style of the numbers was changed to match the letters on the Leafs logo and a mesh under-arm was incorporated. This design incorporated suggestions from Tie Domi and Nick Kypreos. For 1998–99, to acknowledge the transition from Maple Leaf Gardens to the Air Canada Centre, all players wore a special "Memories and Dreams" patch above the right breast. And, for ten games (five home, five away) the Leafs played in a 35-point crest sweater against Original Six teams.

Finally, for 2000–01 the Leafs added a black outline to the lettering and replaced the maple leaf shoulder patch with a stylized "TML" in which all letters were superimposed on each other. Again, they occasionally wore their Original Six sweater against their greatest rivals.

Leafs Draft Choices

1963 Montreal, June 5
(6th choice overall)

Round 1	6	Walt McKechnie	London Jr. B
Round 2	12	Neil Clairmont	Parry Sound Midgets
Round 3	17	Jim McKenny	Neil McNeil Jr. A
Round 4	21	Gerry Meehan	Neil McNeil Jr. A

1964 Montreal, June 11
(5th choice overall)

Round 1	5	Tom Martin	Toronto Marlie Midgets
Round 2	11	Dave Cotey	Aurora Jr. C
Round 3	17	Mike Pelyk	Toronto Marlie Midgets
Round 4	23	Jim Dorey	Stamford Jr. B

1965 Montreal, April 27
(3rd choice overall)
None selected (the Leafs passed on all rounds)

1966 Montreal, April 25
(4th choice overall)

Round 1	4	John Wright	West Clair (Toronto), Jr. B
Round 2	10	Cam Crosby	Toronto Marlies (OHA)
Round 3	16	Rick Ley	Niagara Falls Flyers (OHA)
Round 4	22	Dale MacLeish	Peterborough Petes (OHA)

1967 Montreal, June 7
(4th choice overall)

Round 2	16	Bob Kelly	Port Arthur Jrs.

1968 Montreal, June 13

Round 1	10	Brad Selwood	Niagara Falls Flyers (OHA)

1969 Montreal, June 12
(7th choice overall)

Round 1a	9	Ernie Moser	Estevan Bruins (WCJHL)
Round 2	20	Doug Brindley	Niagara Falls Flyers (OHA)
Round 3	31	Larry McIntyre	Moose Jaw Canucks (Saskatchewan Jr. A)
Round 4	43	Frank Hughes	Edmonton Oil Kings (WCJHL)
Round 5	55	Brian Spencer	Swift Current Broncos (Saskatchewan Jr. A)
Round 6	67	Bob Neufeld	Dauphin Kings (Manitoba Jr. A)

a. acquired from Detroit

1970 Montreal, June 11
(8th choice overall)

Round 1	8	Darryl Sittler	London Knights (OHA)
Round 2	22	Errol Thompson	Charlottetown Srs. (PEI)

Round 3	36	Gerry O'Flaherty	Kitchener Rangers (OHA)
Round 4	50	Bob Gryp	Boston University Terriers (ECAC)
Round 5	64	Luc Simard	Trois Rivières Dukes (QMJHL)
Round 6	78	Calvin Booth	Weyburn Red Wings (Saskatchewan Jr. A)
Round 7	91	Paul Larose	Quebec Jr.
Round 8	103	Ron Low	Dauphin Kings (Manitoba Jr. A)

1971 Montreal, June 10
(9th choice overall)

Round 1	9	traded to Flyers (Pierre Plante) with Bruce Gamble on February 1, 1971, for Bernie Parent and a 2nd-round draft choice in 1971 (Rick Kehoe)
Round 2a	22	Rick Kehoe	Hamilton Red Wings (OHA)
Round 2	23	Dave Fortier	St. Catharines Black Hawks (OHA)
Round 3	37	Gavin Kirk	Toronto Marlies (OHA)
Round 4	51	Rick Cunningham	Peterborough Petes (OHA)
Round 5	65	Bob Sykes	Sudbury Wolves (OHA)
Round 6	79	Mike Ruest	Cornwall Royals (QMJHL)
Round 7	93	Dale Smedsmo	Bemidji State University Beavers (Minnesota)
Round 7b	98	Steve Johnson	Verdun Maple Leafs (QMJHL)
Round 8	107	Bob Burns	Canadian Armed Forces (Greenwood, N.S.)

a. acquired from Flyers with Bernie Parent on February 1, 1971, for Bruce Gamble and a 1st-round draft choice in 1971 (Pierre Plante)
b. acquired from Boston

1972 Montreal, June 8
(11th choice overall)

Round 1	11	George Ferguson	Toronto Marlies (OHA)
Round 2	27	Randy Osburn	London Knights (OHA)
Round 3	43	Denis Deslauriers	Shawinigan Bruins (QMJHL)
Round 4	59	Brian Bowles	Cornwall Royals (QMJHL)
Round 5	75	Michel Plante	Drummondville Rangers (QMJHL)
Round 6	91	Dave Shardlow	Flin Flon Bombers (WCJHL)
Round 7	107	Monte Miron	Clarkson University Golden Knights (ECAC)
Round 8	123	Peter Williams	University of P.E.I. (CIAU)
Round 9	139	Pat Boutette	University of Minnesota (WCHA)
Round 9a	143	Gary Schofield	Clarkson University Golden Knights (ECAC)

a. acquired from Rangers

1973 Montreal, May 15
(4th choice overall)

Round 1	4	Lanny McDonald	Medicine Hat Tigers (WCJHL)
Round 1a	10	Bob Neely	Peterborough Petes (OHA)
Round 1b	15	Ian Turnbull	Ottawa 67's (OHA)
Round 2	20	traded to Flyers (Larry Goodenough) and the rights to Bernie Parent on May 15, 1973, for Doug Favell and a 1st-round draft choice in 1973 (Bob Neely)
Round 3	36	traded to Boston (Doug Gibson) with Jacques Plante on March 3, 1973, for a 1st-round draft choice in 1973 (Ian Turnbull) and future considerations (Ed Johnston)

Round 4	52	François Rochon	Sherbrooke Beavers (QMJHL)
Round 5	68	Gord Titcomb	St. Catharines Black Hawks (OHA)
Round 6	84	Doug Marit	Regina Pats (WCJHL)
Round 7	100	Dan Follet	Downsview Bombers
Round 8	116	Les Burgess	Kitchener Rangers (OHA)
Round 9	132	Dave Pay	University of Wisconsin (WCHA)
Round 9c	144	Lee Palmer	Clarkson University Golden Knights (ECAC)
Round 10	147	Bob Peace	Cornell University Big Red (ECAC)
Round 10	159	Norm McLeod	M & W Rangers (Ottawa)

a. acquired from Flyers with Doug Favell on May 15, 1973, for the rights to Bernie Parent and a 2nd-round draft choice in 1973 (Larry Goodenough)
b. acquired from Boston with future considerations (Ed Johnston) on March 3, 1973, for Jacques Plante and a 3rd-round draft choice in 1973 (Doug Gibson)
c. acquired from Canadiens

1974 Montreal, May 28
(13th choice overall)

Round 1	13	Jack Valiquette	Sault Ste. Marie Greyhounds (OHA)
Round 2	31	Dave Williams	Swift Current Broncos (WCJHL)
Round 3	49	Per Arne Alexandersson	Leksand, Sweden
Round 4	67	Peter Driscoll	Kingston Canadians (OHA)
Round 5	85	Mike Palmateer	Toronto Marlies (OHA)
Round 6	103	Bill Hassard	Wexford Raiders Jr. A
Round 7	121	Kevin Devine	Toronto Marlies (OHA)
Round 8	139	Kevin Kemp	Ottawa 67's (OHA)
Round 9	155	Dave Syvret	St. Catharines Black Hawks (OHA)
Round 10	170	Andy Stoesz	Selkirk Steelers (Manitoba Jr. A)
Round 11	185	Martin Feschuk	Saskatoon Blades (WCJHL)

1975 Montreal, June 3
(6th choice overall)

Round 1	6	Don Ashby	Calgary Centennials (WCJHL)
Round 2	24	Doug Jarvis	Peterborough Petes (OHA)
Round 3	42	Bruce Boudreau	Toronto Marlies (OHA)
Round 4	60	traded to Boston (Rick Adduono)	
Round 5	78	Ted Long	Hamilton Fincups (OHA)
Round 6	96	Kevin Campbell	St. Lawrence University Skating Saints (ECAC)
Round 7	114	Mario Rouillard	Trois Rivières Draveurs (QMJHL)
Round 8	132	Ron Wilson	Providence College Friars (HE)
Round 9	149	Paul Evans	Peterborough Petes (OHA)
Round 10	165	Jean Latendresse	Shawinigan Falls Dynamos (QMJHL)
Round 10a	166	Paul Crowley	Sudbury Wolves (OHA)
Round 10	179	Dan D'Alvise	Royal York Rangers (OHA)
Round 10	180	Jack Laine	Bowling Green State University Falcons (CCHA)
Round 11	188	Ken Holland	Medicine Hat Tigers (WCJHL)
Round 11	189	Bob Barnes	Hamilton Fincups (OHA)
Round 11	191	Gary Burns	University of New Hampshire Wildcats (ECAC)
Round 11	193	Jim Montgomery	Hull Olympics (QMJHL)
Round 12	199	Rick Martin	London Knights (OHA)

a. acquired from Chicago

1976 Montreal, June 1
(12th choice overall)

Round			
Round 1	12	traded to Canadiens (Peter Lee)	
Round 2	30	Randy Carlyle	Sudbury Wolves (OHA)
Round 3	48	Alain Belanger	Sherbrooke Castors (QMJHL)
Round 3a	52	Gary McFayden	Hull Festivals (QMJHL)
Round 4	66	Tim Williams	Victoria Cougars (WCJHL)
Round 5	84	Greg Hotham	Kingston Canadiens (OHA)
Round 6	102	Dan Djakalovic	Kingston Canadiens (OHA)
Round 7	116	Chuck Skjodt	Windsor Spitfires (OHA)

a. acquired from Boston

1977 Montreal, June 14
(11th choice overall)

Round			
Round 1	11	John Anderson	Toronto Marlies (OHA)
Round 1a	12	Trevor Johansen	Toronto Marlies (OHA)
Round 2b	24	Bob Gladney	Oshawa Generals (OHA)
Round 2	29	Rocky Saganiuk	Medicine Hat Tigers (WCJHL)
Round 3	47	traded to Colorado (Randy Pierce) on March 8, 1977 for Tracy Pratt	
Round 4	65	Dan Eastman	London Knights (OHA)
Round 5	83	John Wilson	Windsor Spitfires (OHA)
Round 6	101	Roy Sommer	Calgary Centennials (WCJHL)
Round 7	119	Lynn Jorgenson	Toronto Marlies (OHA)
Round 8	134	Kevin Howe	Sault Ste. Marie Greyhounds (OHA)
Round 9	149	Ray Robertson	St. Lawrence University Skating Saints (ECAC)

a. acquired from Penguins with Blaine Stoughton on September 13, 1974, for Rick Kehoe
b. acquired from Chicago on September 28, 1976, for the rights to Jim Harrison

1978 Montreal, June 15
(12th choice overall)

Round			
Round 1	12	traded to Detroit (Brent Peterson) with Errol Thompson, a 2nd-round draft choice in 1978 (Al Jensen), and a 1st-round draft choice in 1980 (Mike Blaisdell) on March 13, 1978, for Dan Maloney and a 2nd-round draft choice in 1980 (Craig Muni)	
Round 2a	21	Joel Quenneville	Windsor Spitfires (OHA)
Round 2	31	traded to Detroit (Al Jensen) with Errol Thompson, a 1st-round draft choice in 1978 (Brent Peterson), and a 1st-round draft choice in 1980 (Mike Blaisdell) on March 13, 1978, for Dan Maloney and a 2nd-round draft choice in 1980 (Craig Muni)	
Round 3	48	Mark Kirton	Peterborough Petes (OHA)
Round 4	65	Bob Parent	Kitchener Rangers (OHA)
Round 5	81	Jordy Douglas	Flin Flon Bombers (WCJHL)
Round 6b	92	Mel Hewitt	Calgary Centennials (WCJHL)
Round 6	98	Norman Lefebvre	Trois Rivières Draveurs (QMJHL)
Round 7	115	John Scammell	Lethbridge Broncos (WCJHL)
Round 8	132	Kevin Reinhart	Kitchener Rangers (OHA)
Round 9	149	Mike Waghorne	University of New Hampshire Wildcats (HE)
Round 10	166	Laurie Cuvelier	St. Francis-Xavier University (CIAU)

Round 11	181	traded to St. Louis (Jean-Francois Boutin)	
Round 12	197	traded to St. Louis (Paul Stasiuk)	
Round 13	210	traded to St. Louis (Brian Crombeen)	
Round 14	221	traded to St. Louis (Blair Wheeler)	

a. acquired from St. Louis with cash as compensation for the signing of Rod Seiling on September 9, 1976
b. acquired from Penguins

1979 Montreal, August 9
(9th choice overall)

Round 1	9	Laurie Boschman	Brandon Wheat Kings (WCJHL)
Round 2	30	traded to Los Angeles (Mark Hardy) with Brian Glennie, Kurt Walker, and Scott Garland on June 14, 1978, for Dave Hutchison and Lorne Stamler	
Round 3	51	Normand Aubin	Verdun Black Hawks (QMJHL)
Round 4	72	Vincent Tremblay	Quebec Remparts (QMJHL)
Round 5	93	Frank Nigro	London Knights (OHA)
Round 6	114	Bill McCreary	Colgate University Red Raiders (ECAC)

1980 Montreal, June 11
(11th choice overall)

Round 1	11	traded to Detroit (Mike Blaisdell) with Errol Thompson, a 1st-round draft choice in 1978 (Brent Peterson), and a 2nd-round draft choice in 1978 (Al Jensen), on March 13, 1978, for Dan Maloney and a 2nd-round draft choice in 1980 (Craig Muni)	
Round 2a	25	Craig Muni	Kingston Canadians (OHA)
Round 2	32	traded to Calgary (Kevin Lavallee)	
Round 2b	26	Bob McGill	Victoria Cougars (WCJHL)
Round 3c	43	Fred Boimistruck	Cornwall Royals (QMJHL)
Round 3	53	traded to Minnesota (Randy Velischek) on October 5, 197 for Walt McKechnie	
Round 3	55	acquired from Calgary then traded to Washington (Torrie Robertson) with Mike Palmateer on June 11, 1980, for Robert Picard, Tim Coulis, and a 2nd-round draft choice in 1980 (Bob McGill). Originally acquired with Dave Shand on June 10, 1980, for a 2nd-round draft choice in 1980 (Kevin Lavallee)	
Round 4	74	Stewart Gavin	Toronto Marlies (OHA)
Round 5	95	Hugh Larkin	Sault Ste. Marie Greyhounds (OHA)
Round 6	116	Ron Dennis	Princeton University Tigers (ECAC)
Round 7	137	Russ Adam	Kitchener Rangers (OHA)
Round 8	158	Fred Perlini	Toronto Marlies (OHA)
Round 9	179	Darwin McCutcheon	Toronto Marlies (OHA)
Round 10	200	Paul Higgins	Henry Carr High School (Toronto)

a. acquired from Detroit with Dan Maloney on March 13, 1978, for Errol Thompson, a 1st-round draft choice in 1978 (Brent Peterson), a 2nd round draft choice in 1978 (Al Jensen), and a 1st-round draft choice in 1980 (Mike Blaisdell)
b. acquired from Washington with Robert Picard and Tim Coulis on June 11, 1980 for Mike Palmateer and a 3rd-round draft choice in 1980 (Torrie Robertson)
c. acquired from Colorado on March 3, 1980, for Walt McKechnie

1981 Montreal, June 10
(6th choice overall)

Round 1	6	Jim Benning	Portland Winter Hawks (WHL)
Round 2a	24	Gary Yaremchuk	Portland Winter Hawks (WHL)
Round 2	27	traded to Minnesota (Dave Donnelly) on March 10, 1981 for Ron Zanussi and a 3rd-round draft choice in 1981 (Ernie Godden)	
Round 3	48	traded to Colorado (Ulrich Heimer) on January 30, 1981 for René Robert	
Round 3b	55	Ernie Godden	Windsor Spitfires (OHL)
Round 4	69	traded to Minnesota (Terry Tait) on June 14, 1978 for Paul Harrison	
Round 5	90	Normand Lefrancois	Trois Rivières Draveurs (QMJHL)
Round 5c	102	Barry Brigley	Calgary Wranglers (WHL)
Round 6	111	traded to Edmonton (Steve Smith)	
Round 7	132	Andrew Wright	Peterborough Petes (OHL)
Round 8	153	Richard Turmel	Shawinigan Cataracts (QMJHL)
Round 9	174	Greg Barber	Victoria Cougars (WHL)
Round 10	195	Marc Magnan	Lethbridge Broncos (WHL)

a. acquired from Colorado on October 19, 1978, for Jack Valiquette
b. acquired from Minnesota on March 10, 1981, with Ron Zanussi for a 2nd-round draft choice in 1981 (Dave Donnelly)
c. acquired from Los Angeles on March 10, 1981, for Jim Rutherford

1982 Montreal, June 9
(3rd choice overall)

Round 1	3	Gary Nylund	Portland Winter Hawks (WHL)
Round 2	24	Gary Leeman	Regina Pats (WHL)
Round 2a	25	Peter Ihnacak	Czech National Team
Round 3	45	Ken Wregget	Lethbridge Broncos (WHL)
Round 4	66	traded to Detroit (Craig Coxe) with a 5th-round draft choice in 1983 (Joey Kocur) on March 8, 1982 for Jim Korn	
Round 4b	73	Vladimir Ruzicka	C.H.Z. Litvinov (Czechoslovakia)
Round 5	87	Eduard Uvira	Czech National Team
Round 5c	99	Sylvain Charland	Shawinigan Cataracts (QMJHL)
Round 6	108	Ron Dreger	Saskatoon Blades (WHL)
Round 6d	115	Craig Kales	Niagara Falls Flyers (OHL)
Round 7	129	Dom Campedelli	Cohasset High School (Massachusetts)
Round 7e	139	Jeff Triano	Toronto Marlies (OHL)
Round 8	150	traded to Canadiens (Steve Smith) with Robert Picard on March 10, 1981 for Michel Larocque	
Round 9	171	Miroslav Ihnacak	Czechoslovakia
Round 10	192	Leigh Verstraete	Calgary Wranglers (WHL)
Round 11	213	Tim Loven	Red River High School (North Dakota)
Round 12	234	Jim Appleby	Winnipeg Warriors (WHL)

a. acquired from Flyers via Hartford with Rich Costello and future considerations (Ken Strong) on January 20, 1982, for Darryl Sittler
b. acquired from Penguins
c. acquired from the Rangers on October 16, 1981, for Pat Hickey
d. acquired from Penguins on February 3, 1982, for Greg Hotham
e. acquired from Nordiques with Miroslav Frycer on March 9, 1982, for Wilf Paiement

1983 Montreal, June 8
(7th choice overall)

Round 1	7	Russ Courtnall	Victoria Cougars (WHL)
Round 2	28	Jeff Jackson	Brantford Alexanders (OHL)
Round 3	49	Allan Bester	Brantford Alexanders (OHL)
Round 4	70	traded to Los Angeles (later traded to Detroit—David Korol) on October 19, 1982, for Greg Terrion	
Round 5a	85	Dan Hodgson	Prince Albert Raiders (WHL)
Round 5	91	traded to Detroit (Joey Kocur) with a 4th-round draft choice in 1982 (Craig Coxe) on March 8, 1982, for Jim Korn	
Round 6	112	traded to Los Angeles (Kevin Stevens) with Bob Gladney on August 10, 1981, for Don Luce	
Round 7	133	Cam Plante	Brandon Wheat Kings (WHL)
Round 8	154	Paul Bifano	Burnaby, B.C. Tier II
Round 9	175	Cliff Albrecht	Princeton University Tigers (ECAC)
Round 10b	191	Greg Rolston	Power High School (Michigan)
Round 10	196	Brian Ross	Kitchener Rangers (OHL)
Round 11	217	Mike Tomlak	Cornwall Royals (OHL)
Round 12	238	Ron Choules	Trois Rivières Draveurs (QMJHL)

a. acquired from Penguins
b. acquired from Hartford on October 5, 1982, for Paul Marshall

1984 Montreal, June 9
(4th choice overall)

Round 1	4	Al Iafrate	Belleville Bulls (OHL)
Round 2	25	Todd Gill	Windsor Spitfires (OHL)
Round 3	46	traded to Canadiens (later traded to Minnesota—Ken Hodge Jr.) on December 17, 1982, for Dan Daoust	
Round 4	67	Jeff Reese	London Knights (OHL)
Round 5	88	Jack Capuano	Kent High School (Massachusetts)
Round 6	109	Fabian Joseph	Victoria Cougars (WHL)
Round 7	130	Joe MacInnis	Watertown High School (Massachusetts)
Round 8	151	Derek Laxdal	Brandon Wheat Kings (WHL)
Round 9	172	Dan Turner	Medicine Hat Tigers (WHL)
Round 10	192	David Buckley	Trinity-Pawling High School (Massachusetts)
Round 11	213	Mikael Wurst	Ohio State University Buckeyes (CCHA)
Round 12	233	Peter Slanina	Czech National Team

1985 Toronto, June 15
(1st choice overall)

Round 1	1	Wendel Clark	Saskatoon Blades (WHL)
Round 2	22	Ken Spangler	Calgary Wranglers (WHL)
Round 3	43	Dave Tomlinson	Brandon Wheat Kings (WHL)
Round 4	64	Greg Vey	Peterborough Petes (OHL)
Round 5	85	Jeff Serowik	Lawrence Academy (New Hampshire)
Round 6	106	Jiri Latal	Sparta Praha (Czech League)
Round 7	127	Tim Bean	North Bay Centennials (OHL)
Round 8	148	Andy Donahue	Belmont Hill High School (Massachusetts)

Round 9	169	Todd Whittemore	Kent High School (Massachusetts)
Round 10	190	Bob Reynolds	St. Clair Shores (Michigan)
Round 11	211	Tim Armstrong	Toronto Marlies (OHL)
Round 12	232	Mitch Murphy	St. Paul's High School (Minnesota)

1986 Montreal, June 21
(6th choice overall)

Round 1	6	Vincent Damphousse	Laval Titans (QMJHL)
Round 2	27	traded to Canadiens (Benoît Brunet) on December 17, 1982, for Gaston Gingras	
Round 2a	36	Darryl Shannon	Windsor Spitfires (OHL)
Round 3	48	Sean Boland	Toronto Marlies (OHL)
Round 4	69	Kent Hulst	Windsor Spitfires (OHL)
Round 5	90	Scott Taylor	Kitchener Rangers (OHL)
Round 6	111	Stephane Giguere	St. Jean Castors (QMJHL)
Round 7	132	Danny Hie	Ottawa 67's (OHL)
Round 8	153	Steve Brennan	New Prep High School (Massachusetts)
Round 9	174	Brian Bellefeuille	Canterbury High School (Massachusetts)
Round 10	195	Sean Davidson	Toronto Marlies (OHL)
Round 11	216	Mark Holick	Saskatoon Blades (WHL)
Round 12	237	Brian Hoard	Hamilton Steelhawks (OHL)

a. acquired from Canadiens on September 18, 1985, for Dom Campedelli

1987 Detroit, June 13
(7th choice overall)

Round 1	7	Luke Richardson	Peterborough Petes (OHL)
Round 2	28	Daniel Marois	Chicoutimi Sagueneens (QMJHL)
Round 3	49	John McIntyre	Guelph Platers (OHL)
Round 4	70	traded to Calgary (Tim Harris) on May 29, 1985, for Don Edwards	
Round 4a	71	Joe Sacco	Medford High School (Massachusetts)
Round 5	91	Mike Eastwood	Western Michigan University Broncos (CCHA)
Round 6	112	Damian Rhodes	Richfield High School (Minnesota)
Round 7	133	Trevor Jobe	Moose Jaw Warriors (WHL)
Round 8	154	Chris Jensen	Northwood High School (Illinois)
Round 9	175	Brian Blad	Belleville Bulls (OHL)
Round 10	196	Ron Bernacci	Hamilton Steelhawks (OHL)
Round 11	217	Ken Alexander	Hamilton Steelhawks (OHL)
Round 12	238	Alex Weinrich	North Yarmouth Academy (Maine)

a. acquired from Chicago with Jerome Dupont and Ken Yaremchuk on September 6, 1986, as compensation for the Hawks' signing of Gary Nylund

1988 Montreal, June 11
(6th choice overall)

Round 1	6	Scott Pearson	Kingston Canadians (OHL)
Round 2	27	Tie Domi	Peterborough Petes (OHL)
Round 3	48	Peter Ing	Windsor Spitfires (OHL)
Round 4	69	Ted Crowley	Lawrence Academy (New Hampshire)
Round 5a	86	Len Esau	Humboldt Tier II Jr. A (Saskatchewan)

Round 5	90	traded to Calgary (Scott Matusovich) on September 17, 1987, for Dale Degray
Round 6	111	traded to the Islanders (Pavel Gross) on March 8, 1988, for Brian Curran
Round 7	132	Matt Mallgrave	St. Paul's High School (Minnesota)
Round 8	153	Roger Elvenas	Rogle Angelholm (Sweden)
Round 9	174	Mike Delay	Canterbury High School (Massachusetts)
Round 10	195	David Sacco	Medford High School (Massachusetts)
Round 11	216	Mike Gregorio	Cushing Academy High School (Massachusetts)
Round 12	237	Peter Deboer	Windsor Spitfires (OHL)

a. acquired from Vancouver on October 3, 1986, for Brad Maxwell

1989 Minnesota, June 17
(3rd choice overall)

Round 1	3	Scott Thornton	Belleville Bulls (OHL)
Round 1a	12	Rob Pearson	Belleville Bulls (OHL)
Round 1b	21	Steve Bancroft	Belleville Bulls (OHL)
Round 2	24	traded to Calgary (Kent Manderville) on June 16, 1989 for Rob Ramage
Round 3	45	traded to the Rangers (Rob Zamuner) with Jeff Jackson on March 5, 1987, for Mark Osborne
Round 4	66	Matt Martin	Avon Old Farms (Massachusetts)
Round 5	87	traded to Flyers (later traded to Minnesota—Pat McLeod) on December 4, 1987, for Mike Stothers
Round 5c	96	Keith Carney	Mount St. Charles High School (Minnesota)
Round 6	108	David Burke	Cornell University Big Red (ECAC)
Round 6d	125	Michael Doers	Northwood Prep High School (New York)
Round 7	129	Keith Merkler	Portledge High School (New York)
Round 8	150	Derek Langille	North Bay Centennials (OHL)
Round 9	171	Jeffrey St. Laurent	Berwick High School (Maine)
Round 10	192	Justin Tomberlin	Greenway High School (Massachusetts)
Round 11	213	Mike Jackson	Toronto Marlies (OHL)
Round 12	234	Steve Chartrand	Drummondville Voltigeurs (QMJHL)

a. acquired from Flyers via Calgary on March 6, 1989, for Ken Wregget
b. acquired from Flyers via Calgary on March 6, 1989, for Ken Wregget
c. acquired from Flyers on February 7, 1989, for Al Secord
d. acquired from Canadiens with John Kordic on November 7,1988, for Russ Courtnall

1990 Vancouver, June 16
(10th choice overall)

Round 1	10	Drake Berehowsky	Kingston Canadians (OHL)
Round 2	31	Felix Potvin	Chicoutimi Sagueneens (QMJHL)
Round 3	52	traded to Philadelphia (Al Kinisky) on June 16, 1990, for Kevin Maguire and an 8th-round draft choice in 1991 (Dmitri Mironov)
Round 4	73	Darby Hendrickson	Richfield High School (Minnesota)
Round 4a	80	Greg Walters	Ottawa 67's (OHL)
Round 5	94	traded to Washington (Mark Ouimet) on June 29, 1989, for Lou Franceschetti
Round 6	115	Alexander Godynyuk	Sokol Kiev (USSR)

Round 7	136	Eric Lacroix	Governor Dummer (Quebec)
Round 8	157	Dan Stiver	University of Michigan Wolverines (CCHA)
Round 9	178	Robert Horyna	Dukla Jihlava (Czech League)
Round 10	199	Rob Chebator	Arlington High School (Massachusetts)
Round 11	220	Scott Malone	Northfield-Mount Hermon (Massachusetts)
Round 12	241	Nick Vachon	Governor Dummer (Quebec)

a. acquired from Edmonton on December 21, 1989, for Vladimir Ruzicka

1991 Buffalo, June 9
(3rd choice overall)

Round 1	3	traded to New Jersey (Scott Niedermayer) on October 16, 1989, for Tom Kurvers
Round 2	25	traded to Quebec (later traded to Washington—Eric Lavigne) on November 17, 1990, with Scott Pearson and a 2nd-round draft choice in 1992 (Tuomas Gronman) for Aaron Broten, Michel Petit, and Lucien Deblois
Round 3	47	Yanic Perreault	Trois Rivières Draveurs (QMJHL)
Round 4	69	Terry Chitaroni	Sudbury Wolves (OHL)
Round 5	91	traded to Flyers (later traded to Winnipeg—Juha Ylonen) with a 7th-round draft choice in 1991 (Andrei Lomakin) on September 8, 1989, for Mark LaForest
Round 5a	102	Alexei Kudashov	Krylja Sovetov (USSR)
Round 6	113	Jeff Perry	Owen Sound Platers (OHL)
Round 6b	120	Alexander Kuzminsky	Sokol Kiev (USSR)
Round 7	132	traded to Flyers (Andrei Lomakin) with a 5th-round draft choice in 1991 (later traded to Winnipeg—Juha Ylonen) on September 8, 1989, for Mark LaForest
Round 7	135	Martin Prochazka	Poldi Kladvo (Czechoslovakia)
Round 8	157	traded to Quebec Nordiques (Aaron Asp) as compensation for the Leafs' signing of Doug Carpenter as coach on August 16, 1989
Round 8c	160	Dmitri Mironov	Soviet Wings (USSR)
Round 8d	164	Robb McIntyre	Dubuque Jr. A (USHL)
Round 8e	167	Thomas Kucharcik	Dukla Jihlava (Czech League)
Round 9	179	Guy Lehoux	Drummondville Voltigeurs (QMJHL)
Round 10	201	Gary Miller	North Bay Centennials (OHL)
Round 11	223	Johnathan Kelley	Arlington High School (Massachusetts)
Round 12	245	Chris O'Rourke	University of Alaska Fairbanks Nanooks (WCHA)

a. acquired from Washington on January 24, 1991, for Paul Fenton and John Kordic
b. acquired from Detroit on March 5, 1991, for Allan Bester
c. acquired from Flyers with Kevin Maguire on June 16, 1990, for a 3rd-round draft choice in 1990 (Al Kinisky)
d. acquired from Detroit on February 5, 1991, for Brad Marsh
e. acquired from Buffalo with Mike Foligno on December 17, 1990, for Brian Curran and Lou Franceschetti

1992 Montreal, June 20
(5th choice overall)

Round 1	5	traded to the Islanders (Darius Kasparaitis) on June 20, 1992 for a 1st-round draft choice in 1992 (Brandon Convery) and a 2nd-round draft choice in 1992 (later traded to Washington—Jim Carey)

Round 1a	8	Brandon Convery	Sudbury Wolves (OHL)
Round 1b	23	Grant Marshall	Ottawa 67's (OHL)
Round 2	29	traded to Quebec Nordiques (Tuomas Gronman) on November 17, 1990, with Scott Pearson and a 2nd-round draft choice in 1991 (later traded to Washington—Eric Lavigne) for Aaron Broten, Michel Petit, and Lucien Deblois	
Round 2	32	acquired from Islanders on June 20, 1992 with a 1st-round draft choice in 1992 (Brandon Convery) for a 1st-round draft choice in 1992 (Darius Kasparaitis), then traded to Washington (Jim Carey)	
Round 3	53	traded to Washington (Stefan Usdorf)	
Round 4	77	Nikolai Borschevsky	Spartak Moscow (Russia)
Round 4c	95	Mark Raiter	Saskatoon Blades (WHL)
Round 5	101	Janne Gronvall	Lukko Rauma (Finland)
Round 5d	106	Chris Deruiter	Kingston Canadians (OHL)
Round 6	125	Mikael Hakansson	Nacka (Sweden)
Round 7	149	Patrik Augusta	Dukla Jihlava (Czech League)
Round 8	173	Ryan Vandenbussche	Cornwall Royals (OHL)
Round 9	197	Wayne Clarke	Rensselaer Polytechnic Institute Engineers (ECAC)
Round 10	221	Sergei Simonov	Kristall Saratov (Russia)
Round 11	245	Nathan Dempsey	Regina Pats (WHL)

a. acquired from the Islanders on June 20, 1992, with a 2nd-round draft choice in 1992 (later traded to Washington) for a 1st-round draft choice in 1992 (Darius Kasparaitis)
b. acquired from Washington
c. acquired from Washington
d. acquired from Minnesota via Buffalo on March 10, 1992, for Dave Hannan

1993 Quebec City, June 26
(19th choice overall)

Round 1a	12	Kenny Jonsson	Rogle Angelholm (Sweden)
Round 1	19	Landon Wilson	Dubuque Jr. A (USHL)
Round 2	45	traded to Hartford (later traded to San Jose—Vlastimil Kroupa) on November 24, 1992 for John Cullen	
Round 3	71	traded to Flyers (Vaclav Prospal) on July 26, 1991, for Mike Bullard	
Round 4	97	traded to Washington (later traded to Winnipeg, then to Detroit—John Jakopin)	
Round 5	123	Zdenek Nedved	Sudbury Wolves (OHL)
Round 6	149	Paul Vincent	Cushing Academy High School (Massachusetts)
Round 7	175	Jeff Andrews	North Bay Centennials (OHL)
Round 8	201	David Brumby	Tri-City Americans (WHL)
Round 9	227	traded to Ottawa (Paval Demitra) on February 25, 1993, for Brad Miller	
Round 10	253	Kyle Ferguson	Michigan Tech University Huskies (WCHA)
Round 11	279	Mikhail Lapin	Western Michigan University Broncos (CCHA)

a. acquired from Buffalo with Dave Andreychuk and Daren Puppa on February 2, 1993, for Grant Fuhr and a 5th-round draft choice in 1995 (Kevin Popp)

1994 Hartford, June 28–29
(22nd choice overall)

Round 1	10	acquired from Quebec via Flyers and then traded to Washington (Nolan Baumgartner) with Rob Pearson on June 28, 1994, for Mike Ridley and a 1st-round draft choice in 1994 (Eric Fichaud)	

Round 1a	16	Eric Fichaud	Chicoutimi Sagueneens (QMJHL)
Round 1	22	traded to Quebec Nordiques (Jeffrey Kealty) on June 28, 1994, with Wendel Clark, Sylvain Lefebvre, and Landon Wilson for Mats Sundin, Garth Butcher, Todd Warriner, and a 1st-round draft choice in 1994 (traded to Washington later in the day—Nolan Baumgartner—with Rob Pearson for Mike Ridley)	
Round 2	48	Sean Haggerty	Detroit Jr. Red Wings (OHL)
Round 3b	64	Fredrik Modin	Sundsvall (Sweden)
Round 3	74	traded to Canadiens (Martin Belanger) on August 20, 1992, for Sylvain Lefebvre	
Round 4	100	traded to the Rangers (Alexander Korobolin) with Scott Malone on March 21, 1994, for Mike Gartner	
Round 5	126	Mark Deyell	Saskatoon Blades (WHL)
Round 6	135	acquired from Hartford (later traded to the Rangers—Yuri Litvinov) on January 25, 1994, with Mark Greig for Ted Crowley	
Round 6	152	Kam White	Newmarket Royals (OHL)
Round 7	178	Tommi Rajamaki	Assat Pori Jrs. (Finland)
Round 8	204	Rob Butler	Niagara Jr. A
Round 9	230	traded to Hartford (Matt Ball) on March 18,1994, for Ken Belanger	
Round 10	256	Sergei Berezin	Khimik Voskresensk (Russia)
Round 11	282	Doug Nolan	Catholic Memorial High School (Massachusetts)

a. acquired from Washington via St. Louis with Mike Ridley on June 28, 1994, for Rob Pearson and a 1st-round draft choice in 1994 (Nolan Baumgartner)
b. acquired from the Islanders June 28, 1994, for a 2nd-round draft choice in 1995 (D.J. Smith)

1995 Edmonton, July 8
(15th choice overall)

Round 1	15	Jeff Ware	Oshawa Generals (OHL)
Round 2	41	traded to the Islanders (Denis Smith) on June 28, 1994, for a 3rd-round draft choice in 1994 (Fredrik Modin)	
Round 3a	54	Ryan Pepperall	Kitchener Rangers (OHL)
Round 3	67	traded to Winnipeg Jets (Brad Isbister) with Mike Eastwood on April 7, 1995, for Tie Domi	
Round 4	93	traded to Washington (Sebastien Charpentier) on February 10, 1995 for Warren Rychel	
Round 5	119	traded to Buffalo (Kevin Popp) on February 2, 1993, with Grant Fuhr for Dave Andreychuk, Daren Puppa, and a 1st-round draft choice in 1993 (Kenny Jonsson)	
Round 6b	139	Doug Bonner	Seattle Thunderbirds (WHL)
Round 6	145	Yannick Tremblay	Beauport Harfangs (QMJHL)
Round 7	171	Marek Melenovsky	Dukla Jihlava (Czech League)
Round 8	197	Mark Murphy	Stratford Jr. B
Round 9	223	Danlil Markov	Spartak Moscow (Russia)

a. acquired from the Islanders with Benoît Hogue and a 5th-round draft choice in 1996 (Brandon Sudgen) on April 6, 1995, for Eric Fichaud
b. acquired from Hartford

1996 St. Louis, June 22
(15th choice overall)

Round 1	15	traded to Flyers (Dainius Zubrus) with a 2nd-round draft choice in 1997 (Jean-Marc Pelletier) on August 30, 1995, for Dmitry Yushkevich and a 2nd-round draft choice in 1996 (Francis Larivee)	
Round 2a	36	Marek Posmyk	Dukla Jihlava (Czech League)
Round 2	41	traded to Penguins (later sent to New Jersey—Joshua Dewolf) with Dmitri Mironov on July 8, 1995, for Larry Murphy	
Round 2b	50	Francis Larivee	Laval Titans (QMJHL)
Round 3c	66	Mike Lankshear	Guelph Storm (OHL)
Round 3	68	Konstantin Kalmikov	Detroit Falcons (Colonial League)
Round 4	84	acquired from Los Angeles on July 14, 1994, for Yanic Perreault then traded to Flyers with a 1st-round draft choice in 1996 (Dainius Zubrus) and a 2nd-round draft choice in 1997 (Jean-Marc Pelletier) on August 30, 1995, for Dmitry Yushkevich and a 2nd-round draft choice in 1996 (Francis Larivee); Flyers later traded the selection back to Los Angeles (Mikael Simons)	
Round 4d	86	Jason Sessa	Lake Superior State University Lakers (CCHA)
Round 4	92	acquired March 20, 1996, from Anaheim for Ken Baumgartner, then traded to Canadiens (Kim Staal)	
Round 4	96	traded to Los Angeles (Eric Belanger) with Eric Lacroix and Chris Snell on October 3, 1994, for Kelly Fairchild, Dixon Ward, Guy Leveque, and Shayne Toporowski	
Round 4e	103	Vladimir Antipov	Torpedo Yaroslavl (Russia)
Round 5f	110	Peter Cava	Sault Ste. Marie Greyhounds (OHL)
Round 5g	111	Brandon Sudgen	London Knights (OHL)
Round 5	124	traded to Flyers (Per-Ragna Bergovist) on July 8, 1995, for Rob Zettler	
Round 6h	140	Dmitri Yakushin	Pembroke (Tier II)
Round 6i	148	Chris Bogas	Michigan State University Spartans (CCHA)
Round 6	151	Lucio DeMartinis	Shawinigan Cataracts (QMJHL)
Round 7	178	Reggie Berg	University of Minnesota Golden Gophers (WCHA)
Round 8	204	Tomas Kaberle	Poldi Kladno (Czech League)
Round 9	230	Jared Hope	Spokane Chiefs (WHL)

a. acquired from New Jersey with either a 4th-round draft choice in 1998 or a 3rd-round draft choice in 1999 on March 13, 1996, for Dave Andreychuk (Toronto opted for a 3rd-round draft choice in 1999 and later traded the selection back to New Jersey on February 25, 1997, with Doug Gilmour and Dave Ellett for Alyn McCauley, Steve Sullivan, and Jason Smith)

b. acquired from Flyers with Dmitry Yushkevich on August 30, 1995, for a 1st-round draft choice in 1996 (Dainius Zubrus), a 4th-round draft choice in 1996 (later traded to Los Angeles—Mikael Simons), and a 2nd-round draft choice in 1997 (Jean-Marc Pelletier)

c. acquired from Calgary June 22, 1996, for Dave Gagner

d. acquired from Edmonton with Peter White on December 4, 1995, for Kent Manderville

e. acquired from Phoenix on June 22, 1996, for Mike Gartner

f. acquired from San Jose with Jamie Baker on June 14, 1996, for Todd Gill

g. acquired from Islanders with Benoît Hogue and a 3rd-round draft choice in 1995 (Ryan Pepperall) on April 6,1995, for Eric Fichaud

h. acquired from Dallas with Dave Gagner on January 26, 1996, for Benoît Hogue and Randy Wood

i. acquired from Calgary on April 6, 1995, for Nikolai Borschevsky

1997 Pittsburgh, June 24
(4th choice overall)

Round 1	4	traded to Islanders (Roberto Luongo) with Kenny Jonsson, Darby Hendrickson, and Sean Haggerty on March 13, 1996, for Wendel Clark, Mathieu Schneider, and Denis Smith	
Round 2	30	traded to Flyers (Jean-Marc Pelletier) with a 1st-round draft choice in 1996 (Dainius Zubrus) and a 4th-round draft choice in 1996 (later traded to Los Angeles—Mikael Simmons) on August 30, 1995, for Dmitry Yushkevich and a 2nd-round draft choice in 1996 (Francis Larivee)	
Round 3a	57	Jeff Farkas	Boston College Eagles (HE)
Round 4	84	Adam Mair	Owen Sound Platers (OHL)
Round 5	111	Frantisek Mrazek	Ceske-Budejovice (Czech Republic)
Round 6	138	Eric Gooldy	Detroit Jr. Red Wings (OHL)
Round 7	165	Hugo Marchand	Victoriaville Tigers (QMJHL)
Round 8	194	Russ Bartlett	Phillips-Exeter Academy (Massachusetts)
Round 9	221	Jonathan Hedstrom	Skelleftea (Sweden)

a. Leafs held 56th pick, but the NHL awarded the 40th selection overall to St. Louis as compensation for losing Wayne Gretzky to the Rangers as a free agent. Thus, all selections after 40th were moved down one spot.

1998 Buffalo, June 27
(8th choice overall)

Round 1a	10	Nikolai Antropov	Torpedo Ust-Kamenogorsk (Kazakhstan)
Round 2	35	Petr Svoboda	Havlickuv Brod (Czech Division I)
Round 3	67	traded to Tampa Bay (later sent to Edmonton—Alex Henry) for Craig Wolanin on January 31, 1997	
Round 3b	69	Jamie Hodson	Brandon Wheat Kings (WHL)
Round 4c	87	Alexei Ponikarovsky	Dynamo-2 Moscow (Russia 2)
Round 4	94	traded to Chicago (Matthias Trattning)	
Round 4	113	acquired from New Jersey (later sent to Edmonton—Kristian Antila) with a 2nd-round draft choice in 1996 (Marek Posmyk) for Dave Andreychuk on March 13, 1996	
Round 5	123	traded to Islanders (Jiri Dopita) for Darby Hendrickson on October 11, 1996	
Round 5d	126	Morgen Waren	Moncton Wildcats (QMJHL)
Round 6	154	Allan Rourke	Kitchener Rangers (OHL)
Round 7	181	Jonathan Gagnon	Cape Breton Screaming Eagles (QMJHL)
Round 8	208	traded to Carolina (Jaroslav Svoboda) for Kelly Chase on March 18, 1997	
Round 8e	215	Dwight Wolfe	Halifax Mooseheads (QMJHL)
Round 8f	228	Mihail Travnicek	Chemopetrol Litvinov Jr.
Round 9	236	Sergei Rostov	Dynamo-2 Moscow (Russia 2)

a. acquired from Chicago
b. acquired from Chicago
c. acquired from Detroit via Tampa Bay for Jamie Macoun on March 24, 1998
d. acquired from Chicago via Carolina
e. acquired from Ottawa for Per Gustafsson on March 17, 1998
f. acquired from Dallas for Mike Kennedy on March 24, 1998

1999 Boston, June 26
(24th choice overall)

Round 1	24	Luca Cereda	Ambri-Piotta (Swiss League)
Round 2	60	Peter Reynolds	London Knights (OHL)
Round 3	92	traded to Los Angeles (Cory Campbell) with Jason Podollan for Yanic Perreault on March 23, 1999	
Round 3	95	Acquired from New Jersey on March 13, 1996, with a 2nd-round draft choice in 1996 (Marek Posmyk) for Dave Andreychuk and later traded back to New Jersey (Andre Lakos) with Doug Gilmour and Dave Ellett for Jason Smith, Steve Sullivan, and Alyn McCauley on February 25, 1997	
Round 4a	108	Mirko Murovic	Moncton Wildcats (QMJHL)
Round 4b	110	Jonathan Zion	Ottawa 67's (OHL)
Round 4	121	traded to Carolina (later sent to Nashville—Yevgeny Pavlov) for Jeff Brown on January 2, 1998	
Round 5	151	Vaclav Zavoral	Litvinov Jr. (Czech Republic)
Round 6c	161	Jan Sochar	Slavia Praha (Czech Republic)
Round 6	182	traded to Islanders (later sent to Tampa Bay—Fedor Fedorov) with Felix Potvin for Bryan Berard and a 6th-round draft choice in 1999 (Jan Sochar) on January 9, 1999	
Round 7	211	Vladimir Kulkov	CSKA Moscow Jr. (Russia)
Round 8	239	Pierre Hedin	MoDo Ornskoldsvik (Sweden)
Round 9	267	Peter Metcalf	University of Maine Black Bears (HE)

a. acquired from Rangers with Alexander Karpovtsev for Mathieu Schneider on October 14, 1998
b. acquired from Edmonton with a 2nd-round draft choice in 2000 (Kris Vernarsky) for Jason Smith on March 23, 1999
c. acquired from Islanders with Bryan Berard for Felix Potvin and a 6th-round draft choice in 1999 (Jan Sochar) on January 9, 1999

2000 Calgary, June 24
(24th choice overall)

Round 1	24	Brad Boyes	Erie Otters (OHL)
Round 2		traded to Boston on October 21, 1999, for the rights to match arbitration award to Dmitri Khristich of Boston	
Round 2a	51	Kris Vernarsky	Plymouth Whalers (OHL)
Round 3b	70	Mikael Telqvist	Djurgardens (Sweden)
Round 3	90	Jean-François Racine	Drummondville Voltigeurs (QMJHL)
Round 4c	100	Miguel Delisle	Ottawa 67's (OHL)
Round 4	121	Leafs' selection awarded to Anaheim because of tampering charges in their hiring of Thommie Bergman and fined $100,000 (Anaheim later traded selection to Chicago, then to Washington—Ryan Vanbuskirk)	
Round 5		traded to Tampa Bay (Pavel Sedov) with Mike Johnson and a 6th-round draft choice in 2000 (Aaron Gionet) on February 9, 2000, for Darcy Tucker and a 4th-round draft choice in 2000 (Miguel Delisle)	
Round 6		traded to Tampa Bay with Mike Johnson and a 5th-round draft choice in 2000 (Pavel Sedov) on February 9, 2000, for Darcy Tucker and a 4th-round draft choice in 2000 (Miguel Delisle)	
Round 6d	179	Vadim Sozinov	Novokuznetsk (Russia)
Round 7e	209	Markus Seikola	TPS Jr. (Finland)

Round 7	223	Lubos Velebny	Zvolen Jr.
Round 8	254	Alexander Shinkar	Cherepovets (Russia)
Round 9f	265	Jean-Philippe Cote	Cape Breton Screaming Eagles (QMJHL)

a. acquired from Edmonton with a 4th-round draft choice in 1999 (Jonathan Zion) for Jason Smith on March 23, 1999

b. acquired from Tampa Bay on November 29, 1999, for Todd Warriner

c. acquired from Tampa Bay with Darcy Tucker on February 9, 2000, for Mike Johnson, Marek Posmyk, a 5th-round draft choice in 2000 (Pavel Sedov), and and a 6th-round draft choice in 2000 (Aaron Gionet)

d. acquired from Anaheim with a 7th-round draft choice in 2000 (Markus Seikola) for the rights to Jonathan Hedstrom

e. acquired from Anaheim with a 6th-round draft choice in 2000 (Vadim Sozinov) for the rights to Jonathan Hedstrom

f. Toronto and Tampa Bay exchanged 9th-round draft choices after the Lightning hired Jeff Reese, goalie in St. John's, as a goaltender consultant, August 6, 1999 (Toronto selected Cote; Tampa Bay traded their selection to Philadelphia—Milan Kopecky)

2001 Florida, June 23-24
(17th overall)

Round 1	17	Carlo Colaiacovo	Erie Otters (OHL)
Round 2a	39	Karel Pilar	Litvinov (Czech Republic)
Round 2	49	traded to Los Angeles (Mike Cammelleri) on March 13, 2001, with Adam Mair for Aki Berg	
Round 3b	65	Brendan Bell	Ottawa 67's (OHL)
Round 3	82	Jay Harrison	Brampton Battalion (OHL)
Round 3c	88	Nicolas Corbeil	Sherbrooke Castors (QMJHL)
Round 4	115	traded to Chicago (Vladimir Gusev) on October 2, 2000, with Alexander Karpovtsev for Bryan McCabe	
Round 5d	134	Kyle Wellwood	Belleville Bulls (OHL)
Round 5	152	traded to Tampa Bay (Terry Denike) on February 9, 2000, with Mike Johnson, Marek Posmyk, a 5th-round draft choice in 2000 (Pavel Sedov), and a 6th-round draft choice in 2000 (Aaron Gionet) for Darcy Tucker, a 4th-round draft choice in 2000 (Miguel Delisle), and future considerations (a 5th-round draft choice in 2001 (Kyle Wellwood))	
Round 6e	168	Max Kondratiev	Tagliatti Jr. (Russia)
Round 6	183	Jaroslav Sklenar	Brno Jr. (Czech Republic)
Round 7f	198	Ivan Kolozvary	Trencin Jr. (Slovakia)
Round 7	213	Jan Chovan	Belleville Bulls (OHL)
Round 8	246	Tomas Mojzis	Moose Jaw Warriors (WHL)
Round 9	276	Mike Knoepfli	Georgetown (OPGA)

a acquired from Chicago on October 8,1999, for Sylvain Côté

b acquired from Washington (originally owned by Tampa Bay) on December 1, 2000, for Dmitri Khristich

c acquired from Chicago on June 23, 2001, for Igor Korolev

d acquired as future considerations from Tampa Bay on February 9, 2000, with Darcy Tucker and a 4th-round draft choice in 2000 (Miguel Delisle) for Mike Johnson, Marek Posmyk, a 5th-round draft choice in 2000 (Pavel Sedov), a 6th-round draft choice in 2000 (Aaron Gionet), and future considerations (a 5th-round draft choice in 2001 (Terry Denike))
e acquired from Atlanta on July 15, 1999, for Martin Prochazka
f acquired from Tampa Bay on October 1, 1999, with Cory Cross for Fredrik Modin

TORONTO will host the 2002 Entry Draft, June 21-23, at the Air Canada Centre

All-Time Year-by-Year Standings

The column immediately before the total points column indicates the teams' yearly penalty minutes. From 1917 to 1921, when the schedule was divided in two, year-end penalty minutes are listed in the second half of the schedule. The Stanley Cup winner for each season is printed in **bold type**. After playoff scores, goalies who have registered a shutout will appear in square brackets (for example, [Broda] means Turk Broda registered a shutout).

1917–1918

		GP	W	L	GF	GA	PIM	PTS
First Half	Montreal Canadiens	14	10	4	81	47		20
	Toronto Arenas	14	8	6	71	75		16
	Ottawa Senators	14	5	9	67	79		10
	Montreal Wanderers	6	1	5	17	35		2
Second Half	Toronto Arenas	8	5	3	37	34	205	10
	Ottawa Senators	8	4	4	35	35	142	8
	Montreal Canadiens	8	3	5	34	37	167	6

- winner of first half played winner of second half in a two-game total goals series for a place in the Stanley Cup finals against the winner of the Pacific Coast Hockey League and the Western Canada Hockey League. If one team won both halves, it went to the best-of-five finals automatically.
- from 1917 to 1921, games were played until a winner decided
- minor penalties three minutes, majors five minutes, match penalties meant no substitute allowed for the rest of the game
- forward passing permitted in a newly created neutral zone
- Montreal Arena burned down on January 2, 1918, and Wanderers withdrew from the league. Toronto and Montreal each counted a win for defaulted games with the Wanderers.

NHL Finals:	March 11	Toronto 7	Canadiens 3	(at Toronto)
	March 13	Toronto 3	Canadiens 4	(at Montreal)

Toronto won 2-game total goals 10–7

Stanley Cup Finals:	March 20	Toronto 5	Vancouver 3	(at Toronto)
	March 23	Vancouver 6	Toronto 4	(at Toronto)
	March 26	Toronto 6	Vancouver 3	(at Toronto)
	March 28	Vancouver 8	Toronto 1	(at Toronto)
	March 30	Toronto 2	Vancouver 1	(at Toronto)

Toronto won Stanley Cup best-of-five 3–2

- Adams and Crawford not allowed to participate because the NHL and PCHA established a rule whereby all players acquired after February 1, 1918, were ineligible for the playoffs.

1918–1919

		GP	W	L	GF	GA	PIM	PTS
First Half	Montreal Canadiens	10	7	3	57	50		14
	Ottawa Senators	10	5	5	39	39		10
	Toronto Arenas	10	3	7	42	49		6
Second Half	Ottawa Senators	8	7	1	32	14	215	14
	Montreal Canadiens	8	3	5	31	28	257	6
	Toronto Arenas	8	2	6	22	43	239	4

- did not qualify for playoffs
- Spanish influenza epidemic caused the cancellation of the Stanley Cup finals.
- the 1918–19 season was supposed to be, like the ones before and after it, a 24-game schedule. However, when Montreal and Ottawa clinched first place in both halves early, Toronto manager Charlie Querrie refused to play the remaining games, fearing a lack of fan interest. The league almost sued the Arenas, but instead Montreal and Ottawa played a best-of-four series, rather than a two-game total-goals series, to create extra home dates for the clubs.

1919–1920

		GP	W	L	GF	GA	PIM	PTS
First Half	**Ottawa Senators**	12	9	3	59	23		18
	Montreal Canadiens	12	8	4	62	51		16
	Toronto St. Pats	12	5	7	52	62		10
	Quebec Bulldogs	12	2	10	44	81		4
Second Half	Ottawa Senators	12	10	2	62	41	237	20
	Toronto St. Pats	12	7	5	67	44	219	14
	Montreal Canadiens	12	5	7	67	62	221	10
	Quebec Bulldogs	12	2	10	47	96	114	4

- did not qualify for playoffs
- games 4 and 5 of Ottawa–Seattle finals played at Mutual Street Arena, Toronto

1920–1921

		GP	W	L	GF	GA	PIM	PTS
First Half	**Ottawa Senators**	10	8	2	49	23		16
	Toronto St. Pats	10	5	5	39	47		10
	Montreal Canadiens	10	4	6	37	51		8
	Hamilton Tigers	10	3	7	34	38		6

Second Half	Toronto St. Pats	14	10	4	66	53	258	20
	Montreal Canadiens	14	9	5	75	48	285	18
	Ottawa Senators	14	6	8	48	52	177	12
	Hamilton Tigers	14	3	11	58	94	154	6

NHL Finals: March 10   Ottawa 5   Toronto 0   (at Ottawa) [Benedict]
March 15   Ottawa 2   Toronto 0   (at Toronto) [Benedict]
Ottawa won 2-game total goals 7–0

1921–1922

	GP	W	L	T	GF	GA	PIM	PTS
Ottawa Senators	24	14	8	2	106	84	99	30
Toronto St. Pats	24	13	10	1	98	97	114	27
Montreal Canadiens	24	12	11	1	88	94	174	25
Hamilton Tigers	24	7	17	0	88	105	76	14

- overtime limited to 20 minutes (not sudden death); minor penalties reduced from three to two minutes
- top two teams advance to playoffs; winner met the Canadian Hockey Association–Western Canadian Hockey League Champion for the Stanley Cup

NHL Finals: March 11   Toronto 5   Ottawa 4   (at Toronto)
March 13   Toronto 0   Ottawa 0   (at Ottawa)
                                                  [Roach (T)/ Benedict (O)]
Toronto won 2-game total goals 5–4

Stanley Cup Finals: March 17   Vancouver 4 Toronto 3   (at Toronto)
March 21   Toronto 2   Vancouver 1   (at Toronto)
                                                  (Dye 4:50 OT)
March 23   Vancouver 3 Toronto 0   (at Toronto) [Lehman]
March 25   Toronto 6   Vancouver 0   (at Toronto) [Roach]
March 28   Toronto 5   Vancouver 1   (at Toronto)
Toronto won Stanley Cup best-of-five 3–2

1922–1923

	GP	W	L	T	GF	GA	PIM	PTS
Ottawa Senators	24	14	9	1	77	54	188	29
Montreal Canadiens	24	13	9	2	73	61	174	28
Toronto St. Pats	24	13	10	1	82	88	200	27
Hamilton Tigers	24	6	18	0	81	110	182	12

- did not qualify for playoffs

1923–1924

	GP	W	L	T	GF	GA	PIM	PTS
Ottawa Senators	24	16	8	0	74	54	154	32
Montreal Canadiens	24	13	11	0	59	48	146	26
Toronto St. Pats	24	10	14	0	59	85	178	20
Hamilton Tigers	24	9	15	0	63	68	81	18

- did not qualify for playoffs
- a player given a match penalty may be replaced after 20 minutes

1924–1925

	GP	W	L	T	GF	GA	PIM	PTS
Hamilton Tigers	30	19	10	1	90	60	332	39
Toronto St. Pats	30	19	11	0	90	84	253	38
Montreal Canadiens	30	17	11	2	93	56	371	36
Ottawa Senators	30	17	12	1	83	66	331	35
Montreal Maroons	30	9	19	2	45	65	268	20
Boston Bruins	30	6	24	0	49	119	264	12

- the top two teams (Hamilton and Toronto) were supposed to compete for the NHL championship and the right to advance to the Stanley Cup Finals against the WCHL winners. However, the Tigers' players demanded more money for these extra games and the NHL simply disqualified the team. Thus, the St. Pats played the Canadiens.

NHL Semi-finals: March 11   Canadiens 3 Toronto 2   (at Montreal)
March 13   Canadiens 2 Toronto 0   (at Toronto) [Vezina]
Canadiens won 2-games total goals 5–2

Stanley Cup won by **Victoria Cougars** (PCHL)

1925–1926

	GP	W	L	T	GF	GA	PIM	PTS
Ottawa Senators	36	24	8	4	77	42	341	52
Montreal Maroons	36	20	11	5	91	73	554	45
Pittsburgh Pirates	36	19	16	1	82	70	264	39
Boston Bruins	36	17	15	4	92	85	279	38
New York Americans	36	12	20	4	68	89	361	28
Toronto St. Pats	36	12	21	3	92	114	325	27
Montreal Canadiens	36	11	24	1	79	108	458	23

- did not qualify for playoffs

1926–1927

		GP	W	L	T	GF	GA	PIM	PTS
Canadian Division	**Ottawa Senators**	44	30	10	4	86	69	607	64
	Montreal Canadiens	44	28	14	2	99	67	395	58
	Montreal Maroons	44	20	20	4	71	68	716	44
	New York Americans	44	17	25	2	82	91	349	36
	Toronto St. Pats	44	15	24	5	79	94	546	35
American Division	New York Rangers	44	25	13	6	95	72	385	56
	Boston Bruins	44	21	20	3	97	89	521	45
	Chicago Black Hawks	44	19	22	3	115	116	448	41
	Pittsburgh Pirates	44	15	26	3	79	108	230	33
	Detroit Cougars	44	12	28	4	76	105	409	28

- • did not qualify for playoffs
- • on February 14, 1927, the St. Pats changed their name to the Maple Leafs

1927–1928

		GP	W	L	T	GF	GA	PIM	PTS
Canadian Division	Montreal Canadiens	44	26	11	7	116	48	496	59
	Montreal Maroons	44	24	14	6	96	77	549	54
	Ottawa Senators	44	20	14	10	78	57	483	50
	Toronto Maple Leafs	44	18	18	8	89	88	436	44
	New York Americans	44	11	27	6	63	128	563	28
American Division	Boston Bruins	44	20	13	11	77	70	558	51
	New York Rangers	44	19	16	9	94	79	462	47
	Pittsburgh Pirates	44	19	17	8	67	76	395	46
	Detroit Cougars	44	19	19	6	88	79	395	44
	Chicago Black Hawks	44	7	34	3	68	134	375	17

- • did not qualify for playoffs
- • overtime limited to 10 minutes of sudden death; forward passing now allowed in defending zone

1928–1929

		GP	W	L	T	GF	GA	PIM	PTS
Canadian Division	Montreal Canadiens	44	22	7	15	71	43	465	59
	New York Americans	44	19	13	12	53	53	486	50
	Toronto Maple Leafs	44	21	18	5	85	69	541	47
	Ottawa Senators	44	14	17	13	54	67	461	41
	Montreal Maroons	44	15	20	9	67	65	638	39

American Division	Boston Bruins	44	26	13	5	89	52	472	57
	New York Rangers	44	21	13	10	72	65	384	52
	Detroit Cougars	44	19	16	9	72	63	381	47
	Pittsburgh Pirates	44	9	27	8	46	80	324	26
	Chicago Black Hawks	44	7	29	8	33	85	363	22

- overtime set at 10 minutes without sudden death; passing allowed into, but not in, the offensive zone.
- the two division winners played a best-of-five series and the two second-place teams and third-place teams played two-game total goals series. Those two winners then played to see who would play the winner of the two division champions' series.

Quarter-finals:	March 19	Toronto 3	Cougars 1	(at Detroit)
	March 21	Toronto 4	Cougars 1	(at Toronto)
	Toronto won 2-game total goals 7–2			

Semi-finals:	March 24	Rangers 1	Toronto 0	(at New York) [Roach]
	March 26	Rangers 2	Toronto 1	(at Toronto) (F. Boucher 2:03 OT)
	Rangers won best-of-three 2–0			

1929–1930

		GP	W	L	T	GF	GA	PIM	PTS
Canadian Division	Montreal Maroons	44	23	16	5	141	114	651	51
	Montreal Canadiens	44	21	14	9	142	114	600	51
	Ottawa Senators	44	21	15	8	138	118	536	50
	Toronto Maple Leafs	44	17	21	6	116	124	613	40
	New York Americans	44	14	25	5	113	161	372	33
American Division	Boston Bruins	44	38	5	1	179	98	449	77
	Chicago Black Hawks	44	21	18	5	117	111	573	47
	New York Rangers	44	17	17	10	136	143	445	44
	Detroit Falcons	44	14	24	6	117	133	474	34
	Pittsburgh Pirates	44	5	36	3	102	185	384	13

- did not qualify for playoffs
- forward passing allowed in all three zones, producing twice the number of goals

1930–1931

		GP	W	L	T	GF	GA	PIM	PTS
Canadian Division	Montreal Canadiens	44	26	10	8	129	89	602	60
	Toronto Maple Leafs	44	22	13	9	118	99	540	53
	Montreal Maroons	44	20	18	6	105	106	568	46
	New York Americans	44	18	16	10	76	74	495	46
	Ottawa Senators	44	10	30	4	91	142	486	24

American Division		GP	W	L	T	GF	GA	PIM	PTS
	Boston Bruins	44	28	10	6	143	90	403	62
	Chicago Black Hawks	44	24	17	3	108	78	416	51
	New York Rangers	44	19	16	9	106	87	514	47
	Detroit Falcons	44	16	21	7	102	105	429	39
	Philadelphia Quakers	44	4	36	4	76	184	477	12

Quarter-finals: March 24   Toronto 2   Chicago 2   (at Toronto)
March 26   Chicago 2   Toronto 1   (at Chicago)
(S. Adams 19:20 OT)
Chicago won 2-game total goals 4–3

1931–1932

		GP	W	L	T	GF	GA	PIM	PTS
Canadian Division	Montreal Canadiens	48	25	16	7	128	111	450	57
	Toronto Maple Leafs	48	23	18	7	155	127	625	53
	Montreal Maroons	48	19	22	7	142	139	593	45
	New York Americans	48	16	24	8	95	142	596	40
American Division	New York Rangers	48	23	17	8	134	112	511	54
	Chicago Black Hawks	48	18	19	11	86	101	464	47
	Detroit Falcons	48	18	20	10	95	108	415	46
	Boston Bruins	48	15	21	12	122	117	373	42

Quarter-finals: March 27   Chicago 1   Toronto 0   (at Chicago) [Gardiner]
March 29   Toronto 6   Chicago 1   (at Toronto)
Toronto won 2-game total goals 6–2

Semi-finals: March 31   Toronto 1   Maroons 1   (at Montreal)
April 2   Toronto 3   Maroons 2   (at Toronto) (Gracie 17:59 OT)
Toronto won 2-game total goals 4–3

Finals: April 5   Toronto 6   Rangers 4   (at New York)
April 7   Toronto 6   Rangers 2   (at Boston)
April 9   Toronto 6   Rangers 4   (at Toronto)
Toronto won Stanley Cup best-of-five 3–0

- Madison Square Garden unavailable April 7 because of circus
- because of the scores in the finals (6–4, 6–2, 6–4) this series has long been dubbed the "Tennis Series"
- all members of this team were given gold coins by Conn Smythe as lifetime passes to the Gardens

1932–1933

		GP	W	L	T	GF	GA	PIM	PTS
Canadian Division	Toronto Maple Leafs	48	24	18	6	119	111	622	54
	Montreal Maroons	48	22	20	6	135	119	442	50
	Montreal Canadiens	48	18	25	5	92	115	468	41
	New York Americans	48	15	22	11	91	118	460	41
	Ottawa Senators	48	11	27	10	88	131	398	32
American Division	Boston Bruins	48	25	15	8	124	88	517	58
	Detroit Falcons	48	25	15	8	111	93	462	58
	New York Rangers	48	23	17	8	135	107	599	54
	Chicago Black Hawks	48	16	20	12	88	101	401	44

Semi-finals:	March 25	Boston 2	Toronto 1	(at Boston) (Barry 14:14 OT)
	March 28	Toronto 1	Boston 0	(at Boston) [Chabot] (H. Jackson 15:03 OT)
	March 30	Boston 2	Toronto 1	(at Toronto) (Shore 4:23 OT)
	April 1	Toronto 5	Boston 3	(at Toronto)
	April 3	Toronto 1	Boston 0	(at Toronto) [Chabot] (Doraty 104:46 OT)

Toronto won best-of-five 3–2

Finals:	April 4	Rangers 5	Toronto 1	(at New York)
	April 8	Rangers 3	Toronto 1	(at Toronto)
	April 11	Toronto 3	Rangers 2	(at Toronto)
	April 13	Rangers 1	Toronto 0	(at Toronto) [Aitkenhead] (Bill Cook 7:33 OT)

Rangers won Stanley Cup best-of-five 3–1

1933–1934

		GP	W	L	T	GF	GA	PIM	PTS
Canadian Division	Toronto Maple Leafs	48	26	13	9	174	119	529	61
	Montreal Canadiens	48	22	20	6	99	101	308	50
	Montreal Maroons	48	19	18	11	117	122	414	49
	New York Americans	48	15	23	10	104	132	365	40
	Ottawa Senators	48	13	29	6	115	143	344	32
American Division	Detroit Red Wings	48	24	14	10	113	98	368	58
	Chicago Black Hawks	48	20	17	11	88	83	337	51
	New York Rangers	48	21	19	8	120	113	401	50
	Boston Bruins	48	18	25	5	111	130	385	41

Semi-finals:	March 22	Detroit 2	Toronto 1	(at Toronto)
				(H. Lewis 1:33 OT)
	March 24	Detroit 6	Toronto 3	(at Toronto)
	March 26	Toronto 3	Detroit 1	(at Detroit)
	March 28	Toronto 5	Detroit 1	(at Detroit)
	March 30	Detroit 1	Toronto 0	(at Detroit) [Cude]
	Detroit won best-of-five 3–2			

1934–1935

		GP	W	L	T	GF	GA	PIM	PTS
Canadian Division	Toronto Maple Leafs	48	30	14	4	157	111	444	64
	Montreal Maroons	48	24	19	5	123	92	380	53
	Montreal Canadiens	48	19	23	6	110	145	314	44
	New York Americans	48	12	27	9	100	142	250	33
	St. Louis Eagles	48	11	31	6	86	144	385	28
American Division	Boston Bruins	48	26	16	6	129	112	368	58
	Chicago Black Hawks	48	26	17	5	118	88	375	57
	New York Rangers	48	22	20	6	137	139	334	50
	Detroit Red Wings	48	19	22	7	127	114	305	45

Semi-finals:	March 23	Boston 1	Toronto 0	(at Boston) [Thompson]
				(Clapper 33:26 OT)
	March 26	Toronto 2	Boston 0	(at Boston) [Hainsworth]
	March 28	Toronto 3	Boston 0	(at Toronto) [Hainsworth]
	March 30	Toronto 2	Boston 1	(at Toronto)
				(P. Kelly 1:36 OT)
	Toronto won best-of-five 3–1			

Finals:	April 4	Maroons 3	Toronto 2	(at Toronto)
				(D. Trottier 5:28 OT)
	April 6	Maroons 3	Toronto 1	(at Toronto)
	April 9	Maroons 4	Toronto 1	(at Montreal)
	Maroons won Stanley Cup best-of-five 3–0			

1935–1936

		GP	W	L	T	GF	GA	PIM	PTS
Canadian Division	Montreal Maroons	48	22	16	10	114	106	504	54
	Toronto Maple Leafs	48	23	19	6	126	106	579	52
	New York Americans	48	16	25	7	109	122	392	39
	Montreal Canadiens	48	11	26	11	82	123	317	33
American Division	**Detroit Red Wings**	48	24	16	8	124	103	384	56
	Boston Bruins	48	22	20	6	92	83	397	50
	Chicago Black Hawks	48	21	19	8	93	92	411	50
	New York Rangers	48	19	17	12	91	96	381	50

Quarter-finals:	March 24	Boston 3	Toronto 0	(at Boston) [Thompson]
	March 26	Toronto 8	Boston 3	(at Toronto)
	Toronto won 2-game total goals 8–6			

Semi-finals:	March 28	Toronto 3	Americans 1	(at Toronto)
	March 31	Americans 1	Toronto 0	(at New York)[Worters]
	April 2	Toronto 3	Americans 1	(at Toronto)
	Toronto won best-of-three 2–1			

Finals:	April 5	Detroit 3	Toronto 1	(at Detroit)
	April 7	Detroit 9	Toronto 4	(at Detroit)
	April 9	Toronto 4	Detroit 3	(at Toronto) (Boll :31 OT)
	April 11	Detroit 3	Toronto 2	(at Toronto)
	Detroit won Stanley Cup best-of-five 3–1			

1936–1937

		GP	W	L	T	GF	GA	PIM	PTS
Canadian Division	Montreal Canadiens	48	24	18	6	115	111	298	54
	Montreal Maroons	48	22	17	9	126	110	379	53
	Toronto Maple Leafs	48	22	21	5	119	115	371	49
	New York Americans	48	15	29	4	122	161	481	34
American Division	**Detroit Red Wings**	48	25	14	9	128	102	244	59
	Boston Bruins	48	23	18	7	120	110	303	53
	New York Rangers	48	19	20	9	117	106	312	47
	Chicago Black Hawks	48	14	27	7	99	131	291	35

Quarter-finals:	March 23	Rangers 3	Toronto 0	(at Toronto) [Kerr]
	March 25	Rangers 2	Toronto 1	(at New York)
				(Pratt 13:05 OT)
	Rangers won best-of-three 2–0			

1937–1938

		GP	W	L	T	GF	GA	PIM	PTS
Canadian Division	Toronto Maple Leafs	48	24	15	9	151	127	404	57
	New York Americans	48	19	18	11	110	111	327	49
	Montreal Canadiens	48	18	17	13	123	128	340	49
	Montreal Maroons	48	12	30	6	101	149	470	30
American Division	Boston Bruins	48	30	11	7	142	89	284	67
	New York Rangers	48	27	15	6	149	96	435	60
	Chicago Black Hawks	48	14	25	9	97	139	238	37
	Detroit Red Wings	48	12	25	11	99	133	258	35

Semi-finals:	March 24	Toronto 1	Boston 0	(at Toronto) [Broda] (Parsons 21:32 OT)
	March 26	Toronto 2	Boston 1	(at Toronto)
	March 29	Toronto 3	Boston 2	(at Boston) (Drillon 10:04 OT)

Toronto won best-of-five 3–0

Finals:	April 5	Chicago 3	Toronto 1	(at Toronto)*
	April 7	Toronto 5	Chicago 1	(at Toronto)
	April 10	Chicago 2	Toronto 1	(at Chicago)
	April 12	Chicago 4	Toronto 1	(at Chicago)

Chicago won Stanley Cup best-of-five 3–1

* Hawks goalie Alfie Moore pulled out of a local Toronto tavern to play in goal for Chicago.

1938–1939

	GP	W	L	T	GF	GA	PIM	PTS
Boston Bruins	48	36	10	2	156	76	251	74
New York Rangers	48	26	16	6	149	105	393	58
Toronto Maple Leafs	48	19	20	9	114	107	370	47
New York Americans	48	17	21	10	119	157	276	44
Detroit Red Wings	48	18	24	6	107	128	240	42
Montreal Canadiens	48	15	24	9	115	146	294	39
Chicago Black Hawks	48	12	28	8	91	132	367	32

• only the last-place team did not qualify for the playoffs with the new one-division, 7-team format. The first- and second-place teams played a best-of-seven to advance to the finals. The second played third and fourth played fifth in best-of-three series, the two winners playing another best-of-three to advance to the finals

Quarter-finals:	March 21	Toronto 4	Americans 0 (at Toronto) [Broda]
	March 23	Toronto 2	Americans 0 (at New York) [Broda]

Toronto won best-of-three 2–0

Semi-finals:	March 28	Toronto 4	Detroit 1	(at Toronto)
	March 30	Detroit 3	Toronto 1	(at Detroit)
	April 1	Toronto 5	Detroit 4	(at Toronto) (Drillon 5:42 OT)

Toronto won best-of-three 2–1

Finals:	April 6	Boston 2	Toronto 1	(at Boston)
	April 9	Toronto 3	Boston 2	(at Boston) (Romnes 10:38 OT)
	April 11	Boston 3	Toronto 1	(at Toronto)
	April 13	Boston 2	Toronto 0	(at Toronto) [Brimsek]
	April 16	Boston 3	Toronto 1	(at Boston)

Boston won Stanley Cup best-of-seven 4–1

1939–1940

	GP	W	L	T	GF	GA	PIM	PTS
Boston Bruins	48	31	12	5	170	98	345	67
New York Rangers	48	27	11	10	136	77	520	64
Toronto Maple Leafs	48	25	17	6	134	110	485	56
Chicago Black Hawks	48	23	19	6	112	120	340	52
Detroit Red Wings	48	16	26	6	90	126	250	38
New York Americans	48	15	29	4	106	140	232	34
Montreal Canadiens	48	10	33	5	90	167	338	25

Quarter-finals: March 19   Toronto 3   Chicago 2   (at Toronto) (Apps 6:35 OT)
March 21   Toronto 2   Chicago 1   (at Chicago)
Toronto won best-of-three 2–0

Semi-finals: March 26   Toronto 2   Detroit 1   (at Toronto)
March 28   Toronto 3   Detroit 1   (at Detroit)*
Toronto won best-of-three 2–0

Finals: April 2   Rangers 2   Toronto 1   (at New York)
(Pike 15:30 OT)

April 3   Rangers 6   Toronto 2   (at New York)
April 6   Toronto 2   Rangers 1   (at Toronto)
April 9   Toronto 3   Rangers 0   (at Toronto) [Broda]
April 11   Rangers 2   Toronto 1   (at Toronto)
(Patrick 31:43 OT)

April 13   Rangers 3   Toronto 2   (at Toronto)
(B. Hextall 2:07 OT)

Rangers won Stanley Cup best-of-seven 4–2

* huge brawl at 19:30 of the 3rd period resulted in 17 players being fined
• game of April 11 could not be played at Madison Square Garden because it was previously booked for the circus

1940–1941

	GP	W	L	T	GF	GA	PIM	PTS
Boston Bruins	48	27	8	13	168	102	246	67
Toronto Maple Leafs	48	28	14	6	145	99	306	62
Detroit Red Wings	48	21	16	11	112	102	337	53
New York Rangers	48	21	19	8	143	125	356	50
Chicago Black Hawks	48	16	25	7	112	139	335	39
Montreal Canadiens	48	16	26	6	121	147	435	38
New York Americans	48	8	29	11	99	186	231	27

Semi-finals:	March 20	Boston 3	Toronto 0	(at Boston) [Brimsek]
	March 22	Toronto 5	Boston 3	(at Boston)
	March 25	Toronto 7	Boston 2	(at Toronto)
	March 27	Boston 2	Toronto 1	(at Toronto)
	March 29	Toronto 2	Boston 1	(at Boston)
				(Langelle 17:31 OT)
	April 1	Boston 2	Toronto 1	(at Toronto)
	April 3	Boston 2	Toronto 1	(at Boston)

Boston won best-of-seven 4–3

1941–1942

	GP	W	L	T	GF	GA	PIM	PTS
New York Rangers	48	29	17	2	177	143	400	60
Toronto Maple Leafs	48	27	18	3	158	136	341	57
Boston Bruins	48	25	17	6	160	118	349	56
Chicago Black Hawks	48	22	23	3	145	155	365	47
Detroit Red Wings	48	19	25	4	140	147	440	42
Montreal Canadiens	48	18	27	3	134	173	504	39
Brooklyn Americans	48	16	29	3	133	175	425	35

Semi-finals:	March 21	Toronto 3	Rangers 1	(at Toronto)
	March 22	Toronto 4	Rangers 2	(at New York)
	March 24	Rangers 3	Toronto 0	(at New York) [Henry]
	March 28	Toronto 2	Rangers 1	(at Toronto)
	March 29	Rangers 3	Toronto 1	(at New York)
	March 31	Toronto 3	Rangers 2	(at Toronto)*

Toronto won best-of-seven 4–2

* N. Metz scores series-winning goal at 19:54

Finals:	April 4	Detroit 3	Toronto 2	(at Toronto)
	April 7	Detroit 4	Toronto 2	(at Toronto)
	April 9	Detroit 5	Toronto 2	(at Detroit)
	April 12	Toronto 4	Detroit 3	(at Detroit)
	April 14	Toronto 9	Detroit 3	(at Toronto)
	April 16	Toronto 3	Detroit 0	(at Detroit) [Broda]
	April 18	Toronto 3	Detroit 1	(at Toronto)

Toronto won Stanley Cup best-of-seven 4–3

• first and only time in NHL history that a team has trailed 3–0 in the finals and won the Stanley Cup

1942–1943

	GP	W	L	T	GF	GA	PIM	PTS
Detroit Red Wings	50	25	14	11	169	124	371	61
Boston Bruins	50	24	17	9	195	176	364	57
Toronto Maple Leafs	50	22	19	9	198	159	431	53
Montreal Canadiens	50	19	19	12	181	191	318	50
Chicago Black Hawks	50	17	18	15	179	180	361	49
New York Rangers	50	11	31	8	161	253	352	30

- because of wartime restrictions on train schedules, overtime was eliminated as of November 21, 1942
- the top four teams qualified for the playoffs in the six-team league, and both rounds were best-of-seven series

Semi-finals:

March 21	Detroit 4	Toronto 2	(at Detroit)
March 23	Toronto 3	Detroit 2	(at Detroit)
			(McLean 70:18 OT)
March 25	Detroit 4	Toronto 2	(at Toronto)
March 27	Toronto 6	Detroit 3	(at Toronto)
March 28	Detroit 4	Toronto 2	(at Detroit)
March 30	Detroit 3	Toronto 2	(at Toronto)
			(Schriner (T) tied game at
			19:43/A. Brown 9:21 OT)

Detroit won best-of-seven 4–2

1943–1944

	GP	W	L	T	GF	GA	PIM	PTS
Montreal Canadiens	50	38	5	7	234	109	557	83
Detroit Red Wings	50	26	18	6	214	177	374	58
Toronto Maple Leafs	50	23	23	4	214	174	303	50
Chicago Black Hawks	50	22	23	5	178	187	240	49
Boston Bruins	50	19	26	5	223	268	207	43
New York Rangers	50	6	39	5	162	310	253	17

Semi-finals:

March 21	Toronto 3	Canadiens 1	(at Montreal)
March 23	Canadiens 5	Toronto 1	(at Montreal)*
March 25	Canadiens 2	Toronto 1	(at Toronto)
March 28	Canadiens 4	Toronto 1	(at Toronto)
March 30	Canadiens 11	Toronto 0	(at Montreal)[Durnan]

Canadiens won best-of-seven 4–1

* M. Richard scored five goals, the first of which was on a strange play: Bob Davidson was checking Richard, and as play moved along the boards a fan took Davidson's stick! He appealed to referee Chadwick to no avail, and went to get his stick back. The fan threw it on the ice, and at the same time Richard knocked in a rebound to score!

1944–1945

	GP	W	L	T	GF	GA	PIM	PTS
Montreal Canadiens	50	38	8	4	228	121	376	80
Detroit Red Wings	50	31	14	5	218	161	260	67
Toronto Maple Leafs	50	24	22	4	183	161	317	52
Boston Bruins	50	16	30	4	179	219	275	36
Chicago Black Hawks	50	13	30	7	141	194	245	33
New York Rangers	50	11	29	10	154	247	305	32

Semi-finals:

March 20	Toronto 1	Canadiens 0	(at Montreal) [McCool]
March 22	Toronto 3	Canadiens 2	(at Montreal)
March 24	Canadiens 4	Toronto 1	(at Toronto)
March 27	Toronto 4	Canadiens 3	(at Toronto) (Bodnar 12:36 OT)
March 29	Canadiens 10	Toronto 3	(at Montreal)
March 31	Toronto 3	Canadiens 2	(at Toronto)

Toronto won best-of-seven 4–2

Finals:

April 6	Toronto 1	Detroit 0	(at Detroit) [McCool]
April 8	Toronto 2	Detroit 0	(at Detroit) [McCool]
April 12	Toronto 1	Detroit 0	(at Toronto) [McCool]
April 14	Detroit 5	Toronto 3	(at Toronto)
April 19	Detroit 2	Toronto 0	(at Detroit) [Lumley]
April 21	Detroit 1	Toronto 0	(at Toronto) [Lumley] (E. Bruneteau 14:16 OT)
April 22	Toronto 2	Detroit 1	(at Detroit)

Toronto won Stanley Cup best-of-seven 4–3

1945–1946

	GP	W	L	T	GF	GA	PIM	PTS
Montreal Canadiens	50	28	17	5	172	134	337	61
Boston Bruins	50	24	18	8	167	156	273	56
Chicago Black Hawks	50	23	20	7	200	178	339	53
Detroit Red Wings	50	20	20	10	146	159	298	50
Toronto Maple Leafs	50	19	24	7	174	185	247	45
New York Rangers	50	13	28	9	144	191	285	35

• did not qualify for playoffs

1946–1947

	GP	W	L	T	GF	GA	PIM	PTS
Montreal Canadiens	60	34	16	10	189	138	561	78
Toronto Maple Leafs	60	31	19	10	209	172	669	72
Boston Bruins	60	26	23	11	190	175	463	63
Detroit Red Wings	60	22	27	11	190	193	535	55
New York Rangers	60	22	32	6	167	186	426	50
Chicago Black Hawks	60	19	37	4	193	274	467	42

Semi-finals:

March 26	Toronto 3	Detroit 2	(at Toronto) (Meeker 3:05 OT)
March 29	Detroit 9	Toronto 1	(at Toronto)
April 1	Toronto 4	Detroit 1	(at Detroit)
April 3	Toronto 4	Detroit 1	(at Detroit)
April 5	Toronto 6	Detroit 1	(at Toronto)

Toronto won best-of-seven 4–1

Finals:

April 8	Canadiens 6	Toronto 0	(at Montreal) [Durnan]
April 10	Toronto 4	Canadiens 0	(at Montreal) [Broda]*
April 12	Toronto 4	Canadiens 2	(at Toronto)
April 15	Toronto 2	Canadiens 1	(at Toronto) (Apps 16:36 OT)
April 17	Canadiens 3	Toronto 1	(at Montreal)
April 19	Toronto 2	Canadiens 1	(at Toronto)

Toronto won Stanley Cup best-of-seven 4–2

* in frustration, Maurice Richard struck Bill Ezinicki over the head with his stick and was fined $250 and suspended one game

1947–1948

	GP	W	L	T	GF	GA	PIM	PTS
Toronto Maple Leafs	60	32	15	13	182	143	758	77
Detroit Red Wings	60	30	18	12	187	148	593	72
Boston Bruins	60	23	24	13	167	168	515	59
New York Rangers	60	21	26	13	176	201	480	55
Montreal Canadiens	60	20	29	11	147	169	724	51
Chicago Black Hawks	60	20	34	6	195	225	572	46

Semi-finals:

March 24	Toronto 5	Boston 4	(at Toronto) (N. Metz 17:03 OT)
March 27	Toronto 5	Boston 3	(at Toronto)*
March 30	Toronto 5	Boston 1	(at Boston)
April 1	Boston 3	Toronto 2	(at Boston)
April 3	Toronto 3	Boston 2	(at Toronto)

Toronto won best-of-seven 4–1

* Broda (T) and Lumley (B) got into a fight after the final bell and both received 10-minute misconduct penalties

Finals:	April 7	Toronto 5	Detroit 3	(at Toronto)
	April 10	Toronto 4	Detroit 2	(at Toronto)
	April 11	Toronto 2	Detroit 0	(at Detroit) [Broda]
	April 14	Toronto 7	Detroit 2	(at Detroit)

Toronto won Stanley Cup best-of-seven 4–0

1948–1949

	GP	W	L	T	GF	GA	PIM	PTS
Detroit Red Wings	60	34	19	7	195	145	621	75
Boston Bruins	60	29	23	8	178	163	434	66
Montreal Canadiens	60	28	23	9	152	126	782	65
Toronto Maple Leafs	60	22	25	13	147	161	706	57
Chicago Black Hawks	60	21	31	8	173	211	695	50
New York Rangers	60	18	31	11	133	172	413	47

Semi-finals:	March 22	Toronto 3	Boston 0	(at Boston) [Broda]
	March 24	Toronto 3	Boston 2	(at Boston)
	March 26	Boston 5	Toronto 4	(at Toronto)
				(Dumart 16:14 OT)
	March 29	Toronto 3	Boston 1	(at Toronto)
	March 30	Toronto 3	Boston 2	(at Boston)

Toronto won best-of-seven 4–1

Finals:	April 8	Toronto 3	Detroit 2	(at Detroit) (Klukay 17:31 OT)
	April 10	Toronto 3	Detroit 1	(at Detroit)
	April 13	Toronto 3	Detroit 1	(at Toronto)
	April 16	Toronto 3	Detroit 1	(at Toronto)

Toronto won Stanley Cup best-of-seven 4–0

1949–1950

	GP	W	L	T	GF	GA	PIM	PTS
Detroit Red Wings	70	37	19	14	229	164	736	88
Montreal Canadiens	70	29	22	19	172	150	736	77
Toronto Maple Leafs	70	31	27	12	176	173	804	74
New York Rangers	70	28	31	11	170	189	639	67
Boston Bruins	70	22	32	16	198	228	449	60
Chicago Black Hawks	70	22	38	10	203	244	620	54

Semi-finals:	March 28	Toronto 5	Detroit 0	(at Detroit) [Broda]*
	March 30	Detroit 3	Toronto 1	(at Detroit)
	April 1	Toronto 2	Detroit 0	(at Toronto) [Broda]
	April 4	Detroit 2	Toronto 1	(at Toronto) (Reise 20:38 OT)
	April 6	Toronto 2	Detroit 0	(at Detroit) [Broda]
	April 8	Detroit 4	Toronto 0	(at Toronto) [Lumley]
	April 9	Detroit 1	Toronto 0	(at Detroit) [Lumley]
				(Reise 8:39 OT)

Detroit won best-of-seven 4–3

* accounts vary as to whether Ted Kennedy tripped Gordie Howe or simply avoided a Howe check, but at 8:46 of the 3rd, Howe crashed head first into the boards. He suffered a fractured skull, broken nose, and scratched eyeball, and came close to death. He did not play again until the start of the 1950–51 season.
* on April 13 and 15 during the Detroit–Rangers final, two games were played at Maple Leaf Gardens because Madison Square Garden was previously booked

1950–1951

	GP	W	L	T	GF	GA	PIM	PTS
Detroit Red Wings	70	44	13	13	236	139	566	101
Toronto Maple Leafs	70	41	16	13	212	138	823	95
Montreal Canadiens	70	25	30	15	173	184	835	65
Boston Bruins	70	22	30	18	178	197	656	62
New York Rangers	70	20	29	21	169	201	774	61
Chicago Black Hawks	70	13	47	10	171	280	615	36

Semi-finals:

March 28	Boston 2	Toronto 0	(at Toronto) [Gelineau]
March 31	Toronto 1	Boston 1	(at Toronto) (20:00 OT)*
April 1	Toronto 3	Boston 0	(at Boston) [Broda]
April 3	Toronto 3	Boston 1	(at Boston)
April 7	Toronto 4	Boston 1	(at Toronto)
April 8	Toronto 6	Boston 0	(at Boston) [Broda]

Toronto won best-of-seven 4–1

* halted after one period of overtime due to Toronto Curfew Law

Finals:

April 11	Toronto 3	Canadiens 2	(at Toronto) (S. Smith 5:51 OT)
April 14	Canadiens 3	Toronto 2	(at Toronto) (M.Richard 2:55 OT)
April 17	Toronto 2	Canadiens 1	(at Montreal) (Kennedy 4:47 OT)
April 19	Toronto 3	Canadiens 2	(at Montreal) (H. Watson 5:15 OT)
April 21	Toronto 3	Canadiens 2	(at Toronto) (Barilko 2:53 OT)

Toronto won Stanley Cup best-of-seven 4–1

1951–1952

	GP	W	L	T	GF	GA	PIM	PTS
Detroit Red Wings	70	44	14	12	215	133	694	100
Montreal Canadiens	70	34	26	10	195	164	661	78
Toronto Maple Leafs	70	29	25	16	168	157	841	74
Boston Bruins	70	25	29	16	162	176	601	66
New York Rangers	70	23	34	13	192	219	532	59
Chicago Black Hawks	70	17	44	9	158	241	627	43

Semi-finals:

March 25	Detroit 3	Toronto 0	(at Detroit) [Sawchuk]
March 27	Detroit 1	Toronto 0	(at Detroit) [Sawchuk]
March 29	Detroit 6	Toronto 2	(at Toronto)
April 1	Detroit 3	Toronto 1	(at Toronto)

Detroit won best-of-seven 4–0

1952–1953

	GP	W	L	T	GF	GA	PIM	PTS
Detroit Red Wings	70	36	16	18	222	133	645	90
Montreal Canadiens	70	28	23	19	155	148	777	75
Boston Bruins	70	28	29	13	152	172	528	69
Chicago Black Hawks	70	27	28	15	169	175	736	69
Toronto Maple Leafs	70	27	30	13	156	167	812	67
New York Rangers	70	17	37	16	152	211	548	50

• did not qualify for playoffs

1953–1954

	GP	W	L	T	GF	GA	PIM	PTS
Detroit Red Wings	70	37	19	14	191	132	814	88
Montreal Canadiens	70	35	24	11	195	141	1064	81
Toronto Maple Leafs	70	32	24	14	152	131	1022	78
Boston Bruins	70	32	28	10	177	181	685	74
New York Rangers	70	29	31	10	161	182	717	68
Chicago Black Hawks	70	12	51	7	133	242	797	31

Semi-finals:

March 23	Detroit 5	Toronto 0	(at Detroit) [Sawchuk]*
March 25	Toronto 3	Detroit 1	(at Detroit)
March 27	Detroit 3	Toronto 1	(at Toronto)
March 30	Detroit 2	Toronto 1	(at Toronto)
April 1	Detroit 4	Toronto 3	(at Detroit) (Lindsay 21:01 OT)

Detroit won best-of-seven 4–1

* Sloan (T) fined $425 for pushing referee Chadwick in the face

1954–1955

	GP	W	L	T	GF	GA	PIM	PTS
Detroit Red Wings	70	42	17	11	204	134	827	95
Montreal Canadiens	70	41	18	11	228	157	890	93
Toronto Maple Leafs	70	24	24	22	147	135	990	70
Boston Bruins	70	23	26	21	169	188	863	67
New York Rangers	70	17	35	18	150	210	690	52
Chicago Black Hawks	70	13	40	17	161	235	733	43

Semi-finals:	March 22	Detroit 7	Toronto 4	(at Detroit)
	March 24	Detroit 2	Toronto 1	(at Detroit)
	March 26	Detroit 2	Toronto 1	(at Toronto)
	March 29	Detroit 3	Toronto 0	(at Toronto) [Sawchuk]

Detroit won best-of-seven 4–0

1955–1956

	GP	W	L	T	GF	GA	PIM	PTS
Montreal Canadiens	70	45	15	10	222	131	977	100
Detroit Red Wings	70	30	24	16	183	148	794	76
New York Rangers	70	32	28	10	204	203	911	74
Toronto Maple Leafs	70	24	33	13	153	181	1051	61
Boston Bruins	70	23	34	13	147	185	929	59
Chicago Black Hawks	70	19	39	12	155	216	826	50

Semi-finals:	March 20	Detroit 3	Toronto 2	(at Detroit)
	March 22	Detroit 3	Toronto 1	(at Detroit)
	March 24	Detroit 5	Toronto 4	(at Toronto) (Lindsay 4:22 OT)
	March 27	Toronto 2	Detroit 0	(at Toronto) [Lumley]
	March 29	Detroit 3	Toronto 1	(at Detroit)

Detroit won best-of-seven 4–1

1956–1957

	GP	W	L	T	GF	GA	PIM	PTS
Detroit Red Wings	70	38	20	12	198	157	656	88
Montreal Canadiens	70	35	23	12	210	155	870	82
Boston Bruins	70	34	24	12	195	174	978	80
New York Rangers	70	26	30	14	184	227	870	66
Toronto Maple Leafs	70	21	34	15	174	192	829	57
Chicago Black Hawks	70	16	39	15	169	225	809	47

- did not qualify for playoffs
- penalized player allowed to return after a power-play goal had been scored by the opposition

1957–1958

	GP	W	L	T	GF	GA	PIM	PTS
Montreal Canadiens	70	43	17	10	250	158	945	96
New York Rangers	70	32	25	13	195	188	781	77
Detroit Red Wings	70	29	29	12	176	207	758	70
Boston Bruins	70	27	28	15	199	194	849	69
Chicago Black Hawks	70	24	39	7	163	202	906	55
Toronto Maple Leafs	70	21	38	11	192	226	861	53

- did not qualify for playoffs

1958–1959

	GP	W	L	T	GF	GA	PIM	PTS
Montreal Canadiens	70	39	18	13	258	158	760	91
Boston Bruins	70	32	29	9	205	215	838	73
Chicago Black Hawks	70	28	29	13	197	208	921	69
Toronto Maple Leafs	70	27	32	11	189	201	846	65
New York Rangers	70	26	32	12	201	217	860	64
Detroit Red Wings	70	25	37	8	167	218	613	58

Semi-finals:

March 24	Boston 5	Toronto 1	(at Boston)
March 26	Boston 4	Toronto 2	(at Boston)
March 28	Toronto 3	Boston 2	(at Toronto) (Ehman 5:02 OT)
March 31	Toronto 3	Boston 2	(at Toronto)
			(F. Mahovlich 11:21 OT)
April 2	Toronto 4	Boston 1	(at Boston)
April 4	Boston 5	Toronto 4	(at Toronto)
April 7	Toronto 3	Boston 2	(at Boston)

Toronto won best-of-seven 4–3

Finals:

April 9	Canadiens 5	Toronto 3	(at Montreal)
April 11	Canadiens 3	Toronto 1	(at Montreal)
April 14	Toronto 3	Canadiens 2	(at Toronto) (Duff 10:06 OT)
April 16	Canadiens 3	Toronto 2	(at Toronto)
April 18	Canadiens 5	Toronto 3	(at Montreal)

Canadiens won Stanley Cup best-of-seven 4–1

1959–1960

	GP	W	L	T	GF	GA	PIM	PTS
Montreal Canadiens	70	40	18	12	255	178	756	92
Toronto Maple Leafs	70	35	26	9	199	195	859	79
Chicago Black Hawks	70	28	29	13	191	180	970	69
Detroit Red Wings	70	26	29	15	186	197	538	67
Boston Bruins	70	28	34	8	220	241	932	64
New York Rangers	70	17	38	15	187	247	850	49

Semi-finals:

March 23	Detroit 2	Toronto 1	(at Toronto)
March 26	Toronto 4	Detroit 2	(at Toronto)
March 27	Toronto 5	Detroit 4	(at Detroit)
			(F. Mahovlich 43:00 OT)
March 29	Detroit 2	Toronto 1	(at Detroit)
			(Melnyk 1:54 OT)
April 2	Toronto 5	Detroit 4	(at Toronto)
April 3	Toronto 4	Detroit 2	(at Detroit)

Toronto won best-of-seven 4–2

Finals: April 7   Canadiens 4 Toronto 2   (at Montreal)
             April 9   Canadiens 2 Toronto 1   (at Montreal)
             April 12   Canadiens 5 Toronto 2   (at Toronto)
             April 14   Canadiens 4 Toronto 0   (at Toronto) [Plante]
             Canadiens won Stanley Cup best-of-seven 4–0

1960–1961

	GP	W	L	T	GF	GA	PIM	PTS
Montreal Canadiens	70	41	19	10	254	188	811	92
Toronto Maple Leafs	70	39	19	12	234	176	844	90
Chicago Black Hawks	70	29	24	17	198	180	1022	75
Detroit Red Wings	70	25	29	16	195	215	655	66
New York Rangers	70	22	38	10	204	248	591	54
Boston Bruins	70	15	42	13	176	254	810	43

Semi-finals: March 22   Toronto 3   Detroit 2   (at Toronto)
                                                    (Armstrong 24:51 OT)
                March 25   Detroit 4   Toronto 2   (at Toronto)
                March 26   Detroit 2   Toronto 0   (at Detroit) [Sawchuk]
                March 28   Detroit 4   Toronto 1   (at Detroit)
                April 1   Detroit 3   Toronto 2   (at Toronto)
                Detroit won best-of-seven 4–1

1961–1962

	GP	W	L	T	GF	GA	PIM	PTS
Montreal Canadiens	70	42	14	14	259	166	818	98
Toronto Maple Leafs	70	37	22	11	232	180	762	85
Chicago Black Hawks	70	31	26	13	217	186	894	75
New York Rangers	70	26	32	12	195	207	668	64
Detroit Red Wings	70	23	33	14	184	219	684	60
Boston Bruins	70	15	47	8	177	306	712	38

Semi-finals: March 27   Toronto 4   Rangers 2   (at Toronto)
                March 29   Toronto 2   Rangers 1   (at Toronto)
                April 1   Rangers 5   Toronto 4   (at New York)
                April 3   Rangers 4   Toronto 2   (at New York)
                April 5   Toronto 3   Rangers 2   (at Toronto) (Kelly 24:23 OT)
                April 7   Toronto 7   Rangers 1   (at Toronto)
                Toronto won best-of-seven 4–2

Finals: April 10   Toronto 4   Chicago 1   (at Toronto)
             April 12   Toronto 3   Chicago 2   (at Toronto)
             April 15   Chicago 3   Toronto 0   (at Chicago) [Hall]
             April 17   Chicago 4   Toronto 1   (at Chicago)
             April 19   Toronto 8   Chicago 4   (at Toronto)
             April 22   Toronto 2   Chicago 1   (at Chicago)
             Toronto won Stanley Cup best-of-seven 4–2

1962–1963

	GP	W	L	T	GF	GA	PIM	PTS
Toronto Maple Leafs	70	35	23	12	221	180	816	82
Chicago Black Hawks	70	32	21	17	194	178	906	81
Montreal Canadiens	70	28	19	23	225	183	751	79
Detroit Red Wings	70	32	25	13	200	194	964	77
New York Rangers	70	22	36	12	211	233	657	56
Boston Bruins	70	14	39	17	198	281	636	45

Semi-finals:

March 26	Toronto 3	Canadiens 1 (at Toronto)
March 28	Toronto 3	Canadiens 2 (at Toronto)
March 30	Toronto 2	Canadiens 0 (at Montreal) [Bower]
April 2	Canadiens 3	Toronto 1 (at Montreal)
April 4	Toronto 5	Canadiens 0 (at Toronto) [Bower]

Toronto won best-of-seven 4–1

Finals:

April 9	Toronto 4	Detroit 2	(at Toronto)
April 11	Toronto 4	Detroit 2	(at Toronto)
April 14	Detroit 3	Toronto 2	(at Detroit)
April 16	Toronto 4	Detroit 2	(at Detroit)
April 18	Toronto 3	Detroit 1	(at Toronto)

Toronto won Stanley Cup best-of-seven 4–1

1963–1964

	GP	W	L	T	GF	GA	PIM	PTS
Montreal Canadiens	70	36	21	13	209	167	982	85
Chicago Black Hawks	70	36	22	12	218	169	1116	84
Toronto Maple Leafs	70	33	25	12	192	172	928	78
Detroit Red Wings	70	30	29	11	191	204	771	71
New York Rangers	70	22	38	10	186	242	715	54
Boston Bruins	70	18	40	12	170	212	858	48

Semi-finals:

March 26	Canadiens 2	Toronto 0	(at Montreal) [Hodge]
March 28	Toronto 2	Canadiens 1	(at Montreal)
March 31	Canadiens 3	Toronto 2	(at Toronto)
April 2	Toronto 5	Canadiens 3	(at Toronto)
April 4	Canadiens 4	Toronto 2	(at Montreal)
April 7	Toronto 3	Canadiens 0	(at Toronto) [Bower]
April 9	Toronto 3	Canadiens 1	(at Montreal)

Toronto won best-of-seven 4–3

Finals:	April 11	Toronto 3	Detroit 2	(at Toronto)
	April 14	Detroit 4	Toronto 3	(at Toronto) (Jeffrey 7:52 OT)
	April 16	Detroit 4	Toronto 3	(at Detroit)
	April 18	Toronto 4	Detroit 2	(at Detroit)
	April 21	Detroit 2	Toronto 1	(at Toronto)
	April 23	Toronto 4	Detroit 3	(at Detroit) (Baun 1:43 OT)*
	April 25	Toronto 4	Detroit 0	(at Toronto) [Bower]

Toronto won Stanley Cup best-of-seven 4–3

* after blocking a Gordie Howe slapshot in the 3rd, Baun was carried off the ice on a stretcher with a broken bone in his foot. He returned for the overtime to score the winning goal with the foot frozen.

1964–1965

	GP	W	L	T	GF	GA	PIM	PTS
Detroit Red Wings	70	40	23	7	224	175	1121	87
Montreal Canadiens	70	36	23	11	211	185	1033	83
Chicago Black Hawks	70	34	28	8	224	176	1051	76
Toronto Maple Leafs	70	30	26	14	204	173	1068	74
New York Rangers	70	20	38	12	179	246	760	52
Boston Bruins	70	21	43	6	166	253	946	48

Semi-finals:	April 1	Canadiens 3	Toronto 2	(at Montreal)
	April 3	Canadiens 3	Toronto 1	(at Montreal)
	April 6	Toronto 3	Canadiens 2	(at Toronto) (Keon 4:17 OT)
	April 8	Toronto 4	Canadiens 2	(at Toronto)
	April 10	Canadiens 3	Toronto 1	(at Montreal)
	April 13	Canadiens 4	Toronto 3	(at Toronto)
				(C. Provost 16:33 OT)

Canadiens won best-of-seven 4–2

1965–1966

	GP	W	L	T	GF	GA	PIM	PTS
Montreal Canadiens	70	41	21	8	239	173	884	90
Chicago Black Hawks	70	37	25	8	240	187	815	82
Toronto Maple Leafs	70	34	25	11	208	187	811	79
Detroit Red Wings	70	31	27	12	221	194	804	74
Boston Bruins	70	21	43	6	174	275	787	48
New York Rangers	70	18	41	11	195	261	894	47

Semi-finals:	April 7	Canadiens 4	Toronto 3	(at Montreal)
	April 9	Canadiens 2	Toronto 0	(at Montreal) [Worsley]
	April 12	Canadiens 5	Toronto 2	(at Toronto) (Beliveau 19:50 en)
	April 14	Canadiens 4	Toronto 1	(at Toronto)

Canadiens won best-of-seven 4–0

1966–1967

	GP	W	L	T	GF	GA	PIM	PTS
Chicago Black Hawks	70	41	17	12	264	170	757	94
Montreal Canadiens	70	32	25	13	202	188	879	77
Toronto Maple Leafs	70	32	27	11	204	211	736	75
New York Rangers	70	30	28	12	188	189	666	72
Detroit Red Wings	70	27	39	4	212	241	719	58
Boston Bruins	70	17	43	10	182	253	764	44

Semi-finals:

April 6	Chicago 5	Toronto 2	(at Chicago)
April 9	Toronto 3	Chicago 1	(at Chicago)
April 11	Toronto 3	Chicago 1	(at Toronto)
April 13	Chicago 4	Toronto 3	(at Toronto)
April 15	Toronto 4	Chicago 2	(at Chicago)
April 18	Toronto 3	Chicago 1	(at Toronto)

Toronto won best-of-seven 4–2

Finals:

April 20	Canadiens 6	Toronto 2	(at Montreal)
April 22	Toronto 3	Canadiens 0	(at Montreal) [Bower]
April 25	Toronto 3	Canadiens 2	(at Toronto)
			(Pulford 28:26 OT)
April 27	Canadiens 6	Toronto 2	(at Toronto)
April 29	Toronto 4	Canadiens 1	(at Montreal)
May 2	Toronto 3	Canadiens 1	(at Toronto)

Toronto won Stanley Cup best-of-seven 4–2

1967–1968

		GP	W	L	T	GF	GA	PIM	PTS
East Division	**Montreal Canadiens**	74	42	22	10	236	167	700	94
	New York Rangers	74	39	23	12	226	183	673	90
	Boston Bruins	74	37	27	10	259	216	1043	84
	Chicago Black Hawks	74	32	26	16	212	222	606	80
	Toronto Maple Leafs	74	33	31	10	209	176	634	76
	Detroit Red Wings	74	27	35	12	245	257	759	66
West Division	Philadelphia Flyers	74	31	32	11	173	179	987	73
	Los Angeles Kings	74	31	33	10	200	224	810	72
	St. Louis Blues	74	27	31	16	177	191	792	70
	Minnesota North Stars	74	27	32	15	191	226	738	69
	Pittsburgh Penguins	74	27	34	13	195	216	554	67
	Oakland Seals	74	15	42	17	153	219	787	47

- did not qualify for playoffs
- top four teams in each division qualified for the playoffs

1968–1969

		GP	W	L	T	GF	GA	PIM	PTS
East Division	**Montreal Canadiens**	76	46	19	11	271	202	780	103
	Boston Bruins	76	42	18	16	303	221	1297	100
	New York Rangers	76	41	26	9	231	196	806	91
	Toronto Maple Leafs	76	35	26	15	234	217	961	85
	Detroit Red Wings	76	33	31	12	239	221	885	78
	Chicago Black Hawks	76	34	33	9	280	246	842	77
West Division	St. Louis Blues	76	37	25	14	204	157	838	88
	Oakland Seals	76	29	36	11	219	251	811	69
	Philadelphia Flyers	76	20	35	21	174	225	964	61
	Los Angeles Kings	76	24	42	10	185	260	698	58
	Pittsburgh Penguins	76	20	45	11	189	252	677	51
	Minnesota North Stars	76	18	43	15	189	270	862	51

Quarter-finals:	April 2	Boston 10	Toronto 0	(at Boston) [Cheevers]*
	April 3	Boston 7	Toronto 0	(at Boston) [Cheevers]
	April 5	Boston 4	Toronto 3	(at Toronto)
	April 6	Boston 3	Toronto 2	(at Toronto)

Boston won best-of-seven 4–0

* Quinn (T) knocks Bobby Orr out cold; F. Kennedy fined $1,000 and suspended for four games for hitting linesman John Ashley

1969–1970

		GP	W	L	T	GF	GA	PIM	PTS
East Division	Chicago Black Hawks	76	45	22	9	250	170	887	99
	Boston Bruins	76	40	17	19	277	216	1184	99
	Detroit Red Wings	76	40	21	15	246	199	899	95
	New York Rangers	76	38	22	16	246	189	843	92
	Montreal Canadiens	76	38	22	16	244	201	874	92
	Toronto Maple Leafs	76	29	34	13	222	242	886	71
West Division	St. Louis Blues	76	37	27	12	224	179	862	86
	Pittsburgh Penguins	76	26	38	12	182	238	1034	64
	Minnesota North Stars	76	19	35	22	224	257	988	60
	Oakland Seals	76	22	40	14	169	243	835	58
	Philadelphia Flyers	76	17	35	24	197	225	1107	58
	Los Angeles Kings	76	14	52	10	168	290	967	38

* did not qualify for playoffs

1970–1971

		GP	W	L	T	GF	GA	PIM	PTS
East Division	Boston Bruins	78	57	14	7	399	207	1146	121
	New York Rangers	78	49	18	11	259	177	944	109
	Montreal Canadiens	78	42	23	13	291	216	1261	97
	Toronto Maple Leafs	78	37	33	8	248	211	1127	82
	Buffalo Sabres	78	24	39	15	217	291	1178	63
	Vancouver Canucks	78	24	46	8	229	296	1357	56
	Detroit Red Wings	78	22	45	11	209	308	968	55
West Division	Chicago Black Hawks	78	49	20	9	277	184	1268	107
	St. Louis Blues	78	34	25	19	223	208	1068	87
	Philadelphia Flyers	78	28	33	17	207	225	1052	73
	Minnesota North Stars	78	28	34	16	191	223	894	72
	Los Angeles Kings	78	25	40	13	239	303	767	63
	Pittsburgh Penguins	78	21	37	20	221	240	1073	62
	California Golden Seals	78	20	53	5	199	320	931	45

Quarter-finals:	April 7	Rangers 5	Toronto 4	(at New York)
	April 8	Toronto 4	Rangers 1	(at New York)*
	April 10	Toronto 3	Rangers 1	(at Toronto)
	April 11	Rangers 4	Toronto 2	(at Toronto)
	April 13	Rangers 3	Toronto 1	(at New York)
	April 15	Rangers 2	Toronto 1	(at Toronto) (Nevin 9:07 OT)

Rangers won best-of-seven 4–2

* during a melee, the Rangers' Vic Hadfield threw Leafs goalie Jacques Plante's mask into the crowd; it was not recovered, and Bernie Parent was forced to take over in goal for Toronto

1971–1972

		GP	W	L	T	GF	GA	PIM	PTS
East Division	**Boston Bruins**	78	54	13	11	330	204	1106	119
	New York Rangers	78	48	17	13	317	192	1006	109
	Montreal Canadiens	78	46	16	16	307	205	771	108
	Toronto Maple Leafs	78	33	31	14	209	208	877	80
	Detroit Red Wings	78	33	35	10	261	262	846	76
	Buffalo Sabres	78	16	43	19	203	289	817	51
	Vancouver Canucks	78	20	50	8	203	297	1084	48
West Division	Chicago Black Hawks	78	46	17	15	256	166	836	107
	Minnesota North Stars	78	37	29	12	212	191	845	86
	St. Louis Blues	78	28	39	11	208	247	1138	67
	Pittsburgh Penguins	78	26	38	14	220	258	970	66
	Philadelphia Flyers	78	26	38	14	200	236	1219	66
	California Golden Seals	78	21	39	18	216	288	1001	60
	Los Angeles Kings	78	20	49	9	206	305	709	49

Quarter-finals:	April 5	Boston 5	Toronto 0	(at Boston) [Cheevers]
	April 6	Toronto 4	Boston 3	(at Boston) (Harrison 2:58 OT)
	April 8	Boston 2	Toronto 0	(at Toronto) [Cheevers]
	April 9	Boston 5	Toronto 4	(at Toronto)
	April 11	Boston 3	Toronto 2	(at Boston)

Boston won best-of-seven 4–1

1972–1973

		GP	W	L	T	GF	GA	PIM	PTS
East Division	**Montreal Canadiens**	78	52	10	16	329	184	783	120
	Boston Bruins	78	51	22	5	330	235	1097	107
	New York Rangers	78	47	23	8	297	208	765	102
	Buffalo Sabres	78	37	27	14	257	219	940	88
	Detroit Red Wings	78	37	29	12	265	243	893	86
	Toronto Maple Leafs	78	27	41	10	247	279	716	64
	Vancouver Canucks	78	22	47	9	233	339	943	53
	New York Islanders	78	12	60	6	170	347	881	30
West Division	Chicago Black Hawks	78	42	27	9	284	225	864	93
	Philadelphia Flyers	78	37	30	11	296	256	1756	85
	Minnesota North Stars	78	37	30	11	254	230	881	85
	St. Louis Blues	78	32	34	12	233	251	1195	76
	Pittsburgh Penguins	78	32	37	9	257	265	866	73
	Los Angeles Kings	78	31	36	11	232	245	888	73
	Atlanta Flames	78	25	38	15	191	239	852	65
	California Golden Seals	78	16	46	16	213	323	840	48

• did not qualify for playoffs

1973–1974

		GP	W	L	T	GF	GA	PIM	PTS
East Division	Boston Bruins	78	52	17	9	349	221	968	113
	Montreal Canadiens	78	45	24	9	293	240	761	99
	New York Rangers	78	40	24	14	300	251	782	94
	Toronto Maple Leafs	78	35	27	16	274	230	903	86
	Buffalo Sabres	78	32	34	12	242	250	787	76
	Detroit Red Wings	78	29	39	10	255	319	917	68
	Vancouver Canucks	78	24	43	11	224	296	952	59
	New York Islanders	78	19	41	18	182	247	1075	56

West Division	Philadelphia Flyers	78	50	16	12	273	164	1750	112
	Chicago Black Hawks	78	41	14	23	272	164	877	105
	Los Angeles Kings	78	33	33	12	233	231	1055	78
	Atlanta Flames	78	30	34	14	214	238	841	74
	Pittsburgh Penguins	78	28	41	9	242	273	950	65
	St. Louis Blues	78	26	40	12	206	248	1147	64
	Minnesota North Stars	78	23	38	17	235	275	821	63
	California Golden Seals	78	13	55	10	195	342	651	36

Quarter-finals:	April 10	Boston 1	Toronto 0	(at Boston) [Gilbert]
	April 11	Boston 6	Toronto 3	(at Toronto)
	April 13	Boston 6	Toronto 3	(at Toronto)
	April 14	Boston 4	Toronto 3	(at Toronto) (Hodge 1:27 OT)
	Boston won best-of-seven 4–0			

1974–1975
Prince of Wales Conference

		GP	W	L	T	GF	GA	PIM	PTS
Adams Division	Buffalo Sabres	80	49	16	15	354	240	1229	113
	Boston Bruins	80	40	26	14	345	245	1153	94
	Toronto Maple Leafs	80	31	33	16	280	309	1079	78
	California Golden Seals	80	19	48	13	212	316	1101	51
Norris Division	Montreal Canadiens	80	47	14	19	374	225	1155	113
	Los Angeles Kings	80	42	17	21	269	185	1185	105
	Pittsburgh Penguins	80	37	28	15	326	289	1119	89
	Detroit Red Wings	80	23	45	12	259	335	1078	58
	Washington Capitals	80	8	67	5	181	446	1085	21

Clarence Campbell Conference

Patrick Division	Philadelphia Flyers	80	51	18	11	293	181	1969	113
	New York Rangers	80	37	29	14	319	276	1053	88
	New York Islanders	80	33	25	22	264	221	1118	88
	Atlanta Flames	80	34	31	15	243	233	915	83
Smythe Division	Vancouver Canucks	80	38	32	10	271	254	965	86
	St. Louis Blues	80	35	31	14	269	267	1275	84
	Chicago Black Hawks	80	37	35	8	268	241	1112	82
	Minnesota North Stars	80	23	50	7	221	341	1106	53
	Kansas City Scouts	80	15	54	11	184	328	744	41

- the top three teams in each division qualified for the playoffs. The four division champions received byes, and all second- and third-place clubs were ranked 1–8 by points, #1 playing #8, #2 and #7, etc. The first round was best-of-three, the subsequent rounds best-of-seven.

Preliminary Round:	April 8	Los Angeles 3	Toronto 2	(at Los Angeles) (Murphy 8:53 ᴏᴛ)
	April 10	Toronto 3	Los Angeles 2	(at Toronto) (Stoughton 10:19 ᴏᴛ)
	April 11	Toronto 2	Los Angeles 1	(at Los Angeles)
	Toronto won best-of-three 2–1			

Quarter-finals:	April 13	Philadelphia 6	Toronto 3	(at Philadelphia)
	April 15	Philadelphia 3	Toronto 0	(at Philadelphia) [Parent]
	April 17	Philadelphia 2	Toronto 0	(at Toronto) [Parent]
	April 19	Philadelphia 4	Toronto 3	(at Toronto) (Dupont 1:45 ᴏᴛ)
	Philadelphia won best-of-seven 4–0			

1975–1976
Prince of Wales Conference

		GP	W	L	T	GF	GA	PIM	PTS
Adams Division	Boston Bruins	80	48	15	17	313	237	1195	113
	Buffalo Sabres	80	46	21	13	339	240	943	105
	Toronto Maple Leafs	80	34	31	15	294	276	1368	83
	California Golden Seals	80	27	42	11	250	278	1058	65
Norris Division	**Montreal Canadiens**	80	58	11	11	337	174	977	127
	Los Angeles Kings	80	38	33	9	263	265	1022	85
	Pittsburgh Penguins	80	35	33	12	339	303	1004	82
	Detroit Red Wings	80	26	44	10	226	300	1922	62
	Washington Capitals	80	11	59	10	224	394	951	32

Clarence Campbell Conference

		GP	W	L	T	GF	GA	PIM	PTS
Patrick Division	Philadelphia Flyers	80	51	13	16	348	209	1980	118
	New York Islanders	80	42	21	17	297	190	1277	101
	Atlanta Flames	80	35	33	12	262	237	928	82
	New York Rangers	80	29	42	9	262	333	911	67
Smythe Division	Chicago Black Hawks	80	32	30	18	254	261	944	82
	Vancouver Canucks	80	33	32	15	271	272	1122	81
	St. Louis Blues	80	29	37	14	249	290	1274	72
	Minnesota North Stars	80	20	53	7	195	303	1191	47
	Kansas City Scouts	80	12	56	12	190	351	984	36

Preliminary Round:	April 6	Toronto 4	Pittsburgh 1	(at Toronto)
	April 8	Pittsburgh 2	Toronto 0	(at Pittsburgh) [Plasse]
	April 9	Toronto 4	Pittsburgh 0	(at Toronto) [Thomas]
	Toronto won best-of-three 2–1			

Quarter-finals: *	April 12	Philadelphia 4	Toronto 1	(at Philadelphia)
	April 13	Philadelphia 3	Toronto 1	(at Philadelphia)
	April 15	Toronto 5	Philadelphia 4	(at Toronto)
	April 17	Toronto 4	Philadelphia 3	(at Toronto)
	April 20	Philadelphia 7	Toronto 1	(at Philadelphia)
	April 22	Toronto 8	Philadelphia 5	(at Toronto)
	April 25	Philadelphia 7	Toronto 3	(at Philadelphia)

Philadelphia won best-of-seven 4–3

* Leafs coach Red Kelly used "Pyramid Power" to try to inspire the Leafs, placing pyramids in the dressing room, under the players' bench, and anywhere else in an effort to give his team a psychological edge

1976–1977
Prince of Wales Conference

		GP	W	L	T	GF	GA	PIM	PTS
Adams Division	Boston Bruins	80	49	23	8	312	240	1065	106
	Buffalo Sabres	80	48	24	8	301	220	848	104
	Toronto Maple Leafs	80	33	32	15	301	285	1200	81
	Cleveland Barons	80	25	42	13	240	292	1011	63
Norris Division	**Montreal Canadiens**	80	60	8	12	387	171	764	132
	Los Angeles Kings	80	34	31	15	271	241	1186	83
	Pittsburgh Penguins	80	34	33	13	240	252	669	81
	Washington Capitals	80	24	42	14	221	307	1231	62
	Detroit Red Wings	80	16	55	9	183	309	1332	41

Clarence Campbell Conference

		GP	W	L	T	GF	GA	PIM	PTS
Patrick Division	Philadelphia Flyers	80	48	16	16	323	213	1547	112
	New York Islanders	80	47	21	12	288	193	1012	106
	Atlanta Flames	80	34	34	12	264	265	889	80
	New York Rangers	80	29	37	14	272	310	1172	64
Smythe Division	St. Louis Blues	80	32	39	9	239	276	877	73
	Minnesota North Stars	80	23	39	18	240	310	774	64
	Chicago Black Hawks	80	26	43	11	240	298	1104	63
	Vancouver Canucks	80	25	42	13	235	294	1078	63
	Colorado Rockies	80	20	46	14	226	307	978	54

Preliminary Round:	April 5	Toronto 4	Pittsburgh 2	(at Pittsburgh)
	April 7	Pittsburgh 6	Toronto 4	(at Toronto)
	April 9	Toronto 5	Pittsburgh 2	(at Pittsburgh)

Toronto won best-of-three 2–1

Quarter-finals:	April 11	Toronto 3	Philadelphia 2	(at Philadelphia)
	April 13	Toronto 4	Philadelphia 1	(at Philadelphia)
	April 15	Philadelphia 4	Toronto 3	(at Toronto)
				(MacLeish 2:55 OT)
	April 17	Philadelphia 6	Toronto 5	(at Toronto)
				(Leach 19:10 OT)
	April 19	Philadelphia 2	Toronto 0	(at Philadelphia)
				[Stephenson]
	April 21	Philadelphia 4	Toronto 3	(at Toronto)

Philadelphia won best-of-seven 4–2

1977–1978
Prince of Wales Conference

		GP	W	L	T	GF	GA	PIM	PTS
Adams Division	Boston Bruins	80	51	18	11	333	218	1237	113
	Buffalo Sabres	80	44	19	17	288	215	800	105
	Toronto Maple Leafs	80	41	29	10	271	237	1258	92
	Cleveland Barons	80	22	45	13	230	325	1010	57
Norris Division	**Montreal Canadiens**	80	59	10	11	359	183	745	129
	Detroit Red Wings	80	32	34	14	252	266	1534	78
	Los Angeles Kings	80	31	34	15	243	245	903	77
	Pittsburgh Penguins	80	25	37	18	254	321	1300	68
	Washington Capitals	80	17	49	14	195	321	1332	48

Clarence Campbell Conference

		GP	W	L	T	GF	GA	PIM	PTS
Patrick Division	New York Islanders	80	48	17	15	334	210	938	111
	Philadelphia Flyers	80	45	20	15	296	200	1668	105
	Atlanta Flames	80	34	27	19	274	252	984	87
	New York Rangers	80	30	37	13	279	280	1057	73
Smythe Division	Chicago Black Hawks	80	32	29	19	230	220	1308	83
	Colorado Rockies	80	19	40	21	257	305	818	59
	Vancouver Canucks	80	20	43	17	239	320	962	57
	St. Louis Blues	80	20	47	13	195	304	845	53
	Minnesota North Stars	80	18	53	9	218	325	1096	45

• playoff format altered so that all 1st- and 2nd-place teams qualified and the next best four regardless of division

Preliminary Round:	April 11	Toronto 7	Los Angeles 3	(at Toronto)
	April 13	Toronto 4	Los Angeles 0	(at Los Angeles)
				[Palmateer]

Toronto won best-of-three 2–0

Quarter-finals:	April 17	Islanders 4	Toronto 1	(at New York)
	April 19	Islanders 3	Toronto 2	(at New York)
				(Bossy 2:50 OT)
	April 21	Toronto 2	Islanders 0	(at Toronto) [Palmateer]
	April 23	Toronto 3	Islanders 1	(at Toronto)
	April 25	Islanders 2	Toronto 1	(at New York)
				(Nystrom 8:02 OT)
	April 27	Toronto 5	Islanders 2	(at Toronto)
	April 29	Toronto 2	Islanders 1	(at New York)
				(McDonald 4:13 OT)

Toronto won best-of-seven 4–3

Semi-finals:	May 2	Canadiens 5	Toronto 3	(at Montreal)
	May 4	Canadiens 3	Toronto 2	(at Montreal)
	May 6	Canadiens 6	Toronto 1	(at Toronto)
	May 9	Canadiens 2	Toronto 0	(at Toronto) [K.Dryden]

Canadiens won best-of-seven 4–0

1978–1979
Prince of Wales Conference

		GP	W	L	T	GF	GA	PIM	PTS
Adams Division	Boston Bruins	80	43	23	14	316	270	1222	100
	Buffalo Sabres	80	36	28	16	280	263	1026	88
	Toronto Maple Leafs	80	34	33	13	267	252	1440	81
	Minnesota North Stars	80	28	40	12	257	289	1102	68
Norris Division	**Montreal Canadiens**	80	52	17	11	337	204	803	115
	Pittsburgh Penguins	80	36	31	13	281	279	1039	85
	Los Angeles Kings	80	34	34	12	292	286	1134	80
	Washington Capitals	80	24	41	15	273	338	1312	63
	Detroit Red Wings	80	23	41	16	252	295	1359	62

Clarence Campbell Conference

Patrick Division	New York Islanders	80	51	15	14	358	214	1077	116
	Philadelphia Flyers	80	40	25	15	281	248	1548	95
	New York Rangers	80	40	29	11	316	292	1214	91
	Atlanta Flames	80	41	31	8	327	280	1158	90
Smythe Division	Chicago Black Hawks	80	29	36	15	244	277	1254	73
	Vancouver Canucks	80	25	42	13	217	291	1134	63
	St. Louis Blues	80	18	50	12	249	348	1055	48
	Colorado Rockies	80	15	53	12	210	331	838	42

| *Preliminary Round:* | April 10 | Toronto 2 | Atlanta 1 | (at Atlanta) |
| | April 12 | Toronto 7 | Atlanta 4 | (at Toronto) |

Toronto won best-of-three 2–0

Quarter-finals:	April 16	Canadiens 5 Toronto 2	(at Montreal)
	April 18	Canadiens 5 Toronto 1	(at Montreal)
	April 21	Canadiens 4 Toronto 3	(at Toronto) (Connor 25:25 OT)
	April 22	Canadiens 5 Toronto 4	(at Toronto) (Robinson 4:14 OT)
	Canadiens won best-of-seven 4–0		

1979–1980
Prince of Wales Conference

		GP	W	L	T	GF	GA	PIM	PTS
Adams Division	Buffalo Sabres	80	47	17	16	318	201	967	110
	Boston Bruins	80	46	21	13	310	234	1460	105
	Minnesota North Stars	80	36	28	16	311	253	1064	88
	Toronto Maple Leafs	80	35	40	5	304	327	1158	75
	Quebec Nordiques	80	25	44	11	248	313	1062	61
Norris Division	Montreal Canadiens	80	47	20	13	328	240	874	107
	Los Angeles Kings	80	30	36	14	290	313	1124	74
	Pittsburgh Penguins	80	30	37	13	251	303	1038	73
	Hartford Whalers	80	27	34	19	303	312	875	73
	Detroit Red Wings	80	26	43	11	268	306	1114	63

Clarence Campbell Conference

		GP	W	L	T	GF	GA	PIM	PTS
Patrick Division	Philadelphia Flyers	80	48	12	20	327	254	1844	116
	New York Islanders	80	39	28	13	281	247	1298	91
	New York Rangers	80	38	32	10	308	284	1342	86
	Atlanta Flames	80	35	32	13	282	269	1048	83
	Washington Capitals	80	27	40	13	261	293	1198	67
Smythe Division	Chicago Black Hawks	80	34	27	19	241	250	1325	87
	St. Louis Blues	80	34	34	12	266	278	1037	80
	Vancouver Canucks	80	27	37	16	256	281	1808	70
	Edmonton Oilers	80	28	39	13	301	322	1528	69
	Winnipeg Jets	80	20	49	11	214	314	1251	51
	Colorado Rockies	80	19	48	13	234	308	1020	51

• top four teams in each division qualified for the playoffs

Preliminary Round:	April 8	Minnesota 6 Toronto 3	(at Minnesota)*
	April 9	Minnesota 7 Toronto 2	(at Minnesota)
	April 11	Minnesota 4 Toronto 3	(at Toronto)
			(Al MacAdam :32 OT)
	Minnesota won best-of-five 3–0		

* Leafs coach Punch Imlach started five defencemen for the opening faceoff

1980–1981
Prince of Wales Conference

		GP	W	L	T	GF	GA	PIM	PTS
Adams Division	Buffalo Sabres	80	39	20	21	327	250	1194	99
	Boston Bruins	80	37	30	13	316	272	1836	87
	Minnesota North Stars	80	35	28	17	291	263	1624	87
	Quebec Nordiques	80	30	32	18	314	318	1524	78
	Toronto Maple Leafs	80	28	37	15	322	367	1830	71
Norris Division	Montreal Canadiens	80	45	22	13	332	232	1398	103
	Los Angeles Kings	80	43	24	13	337	290	1627	99
	Pittsburgh Penguins	80	30	37	13	302	345	1807	73
	Hartford Whalers	80	21	41	18	292	372	1584	60
	Detroit Red Wings	80	19	43	18	252	339	1687	56

Clarence Campbell Conference

		GP	W	L	T	GF	GA	PIM	PTS
Patrick Division	**New York Islanders**	80	48	18	14	355	260	1442	110
	Philadelphia Flyers	80	41	24	15	313	249	2621	97
	Calgary Flames	80	39	27	14	329	298	1450	92
	New York Rangers	80	30	36	14	312	317	1981	74
	Washington Capitals	80	26	36	18	286	317	1872	70
Smythe Division	St. Louis Blues	80	45	18	17	352	281	1657	107
	Chicago Black Hawks	80	31	33	16	304	315	1660	78
	Vancouver Canucks	80	28	32	20	289	301	1892	76
	Edmonton Oilers	80	29	35	16	328	327	1544	74
	Colorado Rockies	80	22	45	13	258	344	1418	57
	Winnipeg Jets	80	9	57	14	246	400	1191	32

Preliminary Round:	April 8	Islanders 9	Toronto 2	(at New York)
	April 9	Islanders 5	Toronto 1	(at New York)
	April 11	Islanders 6	Toronto 1	(at Toronto)
	Islanders won best-of-five 3–0			

1981–1982
Clarence Campbell Conference

		GP	W	L	T	GF	GA	PIM	PTS
Norris Division	Minnesota North Stars	80	37	23	20	346	288	1358	94
	Winnipeg Jets	80	33	33	14	319	332	1314	80
	St. Louis Blues	80	32	40	8	315	349	1579	72
	Chicago Black Hawks	80	30	38	12	332	363	1775	72
	Toronto Maple Leafs	80	20	44	16	298	380	1888	56
	Detroit Red Wings	80	21	47	12	270	351	1250	54

Smythe Division	Edmonton Oilers	80	48	17	15	417	295	1473	111
	Vancouver Canucks	80	30	33	17	290	286	1840	77
	Calgary Flames	80	29	34	17	334	345	1331	75
	Los Angeles Kings	80	24	41	15	314	369	1730	63
	Colorado Rockies	80	18	49	13	241	362	1138	49

Prince of Wales Conference

Adams Division	Montreal Canadiens	80	46	17	17	360	223	1463	109
	Boston Bruins	80	43	27	10	323	285	1266	96
	Buffalo Sabres	80	39	26	15	307	273	1425	93
	Quebec Nordiques	80	33	31	16	356	345	1757	82
	Hartford Whalers	80	21	41	18	264	351	1493	60

Patrick Division	**New York Islanders**	80	54	16	10	385	250	1328	118
	New York Rangers	80	39	27	14	316	306	1402	92
	Philadelphia Flyers	80	38	31	11	325	313	2493	87
	Pittsburgh Penguins	80	31	36	13	310	337	2212	75
	Washington Capitals	80	26	41	13	319	338	1932	65

• did not qualify for playoffs

1982–1983

Clarence Campbell Conference

		GP	W	L	T	GF	GA	PIM	PTS
Norris Division	Chicago Black Hawks	80	47	23	10	338	268	1185	104
	Minnesota North Stars	80	40	24	16	321	290	1520	96
	Toronto Maple Leafs	80	28	40	12	293	330	1481	68
	St. Louis Blues	80	25	40	15	285	316	1281	65
	Detroit Red Wings	80	21	44	15	263	344	1064	57
Smythe Division	Edmonton Oilers	80	47	21	12	424	315	1771	106
	Calgary Flames	80	32	34	14	321	317	1146	78
	Vancouver Canucks	80	30	35	15	303	309	1639	75
	Winnipeg Jets	80	33	39	8	311	333	1089	74
	Los Angeles Kings	80	27	41	12	308	365	1367	66

Prince of Wales Conference

Adams Division	Boston Bruins	80	50	20	10	327	228	1202	110
	Montreal Canadiens	80	42	24	14	350	286	1116	98
	Buffalo Sabres	80	38	29	13	318	285	1031	89
	Quebec Nordiques	80	34	34	12	343	336	1648	80
	Hartford Whalers	80	19	54	7	261	403	1392	45

Patrick Division	Philadelphia Flyers	80	49	23	8	326	240	1337	106
	New York Islanders	80	42	26	12	302	226	1266	96
	Washington Capitals	80	39	25	16	306	283	1329	94
	New York Rangers	80	35	35	10	306	287	1100	80
	New Jersey Devils	80	17	49	14	230	338	1270	48
	Pittsburgh Penguins	80	18	53	9	257	394	1859	45

Preliminary Round:	April 6	Minnesota 5	Toronto 4	(at Minnesota)
	April 7	Minnesota 5	Toronto 4	(at Minnesota)
				(B. Smith 5:03 OT)
	April 9	Toronto 6	Minnesota 3	(at Toronto)
	April 10	Minnesota 5	Toronto 4	(at Toronto)
				(Ciccarelli 8:05 OT)

Minnesota won best-of-five 3–1

1983–1984
Clarence Campbell Conference

		GP	W	L	T	GF	GA	PIM	PTS
Norris Division	Minnesota North Stars	80	39	31	10	345	344	1696	88
	St. Louis Blues	80	32	41	7	293	316	1614	71
	Detroit Red Wings	80	31	42	7	298	323	1546	69
	Chicago Black Hawks	80	30	42	8	277	311	1358	68
	Toronto Maple Leafs	80	26	45	9	303	387	1682	61
Smythe Division	**Edmonton Oilers**	80	57	18	5	446	314	1577	119
	Calgary Flames	80	34	32	14	311	314	1390	82
	Vancouver Canucks	80	32	39	9	306	328	1474	73
	Winnipeg Jets	80	31	38	11	340	374	1579	73
	Los Angeles Kings	80	23	44	13	309	376	1265	59

Prince of Wales Conference

Adams Division	Boston Bruins	80	49	25	6	336	261	1606	104
	Buffalo Sabres	80	48	25	7	315	257	1190	103
	Quebec Nordiques	80	42	28	10	360	278	1600	94
	Montreal Canadiens	80	35	40	5	286	295	1371	75
	Hartford Whalers	80	28	42	10	288	320	1184	66
Patrick Division	New York Islanders	80	50	26	4	357	269	1157	104
	Washington Capitals	80	48	27	5	308	226	1252	101
	Philadelphia Flyers	80	44	26	10	350	290	1488	98
	New York Rangers	80	42	29	9	314	304	1471	93
	New Jersey Devils	80	17	56	7	231	350	1352	41
	Pittsburgh Penguins	80	16	58	6	254	390	1695	38

- did not qualify for playoffs
- five-minute sudden death overtime introduced

1984–1985
Clarence Campbell Conference

		GP	W	L	T	GF	GA	PIM	PTS
Norris Division	St. Louis Blues	80	37	31	12	299	288	1301	86
	Chicago Black Hawks	80	38	35	7	309	299	1432	83
	Detroit Red Wings	80	27	41	12	313	357	1741	66
	Minnesota North Stars	80	25	43	12	268	321	1735	62
	Toronto Maple Leafs	80	20	52	8	253	358	1627	48
Smythe Division	**Edmonton Oilers**	80	49	20	11	401	298	1567	109
	Winnipeg Jets	80	43	27	10	358	332	1540	96
	Calgary Flames	80	41	27	12	363	302	1400	94
	Los Angeles Kings	80	34	32	14	339	326	1413	82
	Vancouver Canucks	80	25	46	9	284	401	1451	59

Prince of Wales Conference

		GP	W	L	T	GF	GA	PIM	PTS
Adams Division	Montreal Canadiens	80	41	27	12	309	262	1464	94
	Quebec Nordiques	80	41	30	9	323	275	1643	91
	Buffalo Sabres	80	38	28	14	290	237	1221	90
	Boston Bruins	80	36	34	10	303	287	1825	82
	Hartford Whalers	80	30	41	9	268	318	1606	69
Patrick Division	Philadelphia Flyers	80	53	20	7	348	241	1540	113
	Washington Capitals	80	46	25	9	322	240	1161	101
	New York Islanders	80	40	34	6	345	312	1516	86
	New York Rangers	80	26	44	10	295	345	1301	62
	New Jersey Devils	80	22	48	10	264	346	1282	54
	Pittsburgh Penguins	80	24	51	5	276	385	1493	53

• did not qualify for playoffs

1985–1986
Clarence Campbell Conference

		GP	W	L	T	GF	GA	PIM	PTS
Norris Division	Chicago Black Hawks	80	39	33	8	351	349	1537	86
	Minnesota North Stars	80	38	33	9	327	305	1672	85
	St. Louis Blues	80	37	34	9	302	291	1478	83
	Toronto Maple Leafs	80	25	48	7	311	386	1716	57
	Detroit Red Wings	80	17	57	6	266	415	2393	40
Smythe Division	Edmonton Oilers	80	56	17	7	426	310	1928	119
	Calgary Flames	80	40	31	9	354	315	2297	89
	Winnipeg Jets	80	26	47	7	295	372	1774	59
	Vancouver Canucks	80	23	44	13	282	333	1813	59
	Los Angeles Kings	80	23	49	8	284	389	2004	54

Prince of Wales Conference

Adams Division									
Adams Division	Quebec Nordiques	80	43	31	6	330	289	1847	92
	Montreal Canadiens	80	40	33	7	330	280	1372	87
	Boston Bruins	80	37	31	12	311	288	1919	86
	Hartford Whalers	80	40	36	4	332	302	1759	84
	Buffalo Sabres	80	37	37	6	296	291	1608	80
Patrick Division	Philadelphia Flyers	80	53	23	4	335	241	2025	110
	Washington Capitals	80	50	23	7	315	272	1418	107
	New York Islanders	80	39	29	12	327	284	1343	90
	New York Rangers	80	36	38	6	280	276	1496	78
	Pittsburgh Penguins	80	34	38	8	313	305	1538	76
	New Jersey Devils	80	28	49	3	300	374	1424	59

1st Round:	April 9	Toronto 5	Chicago 3	(at Chicago)
	April 10	Toronto 6	Chicago 4	(at Chicago)
	April 12	Toronto 7	Chicago 2	(at Toronto)

Toronto won best-of-five 3–0

Quarter-finals:	April 18	St. Louis 6	Toronto 1	(at St. Louis)
	April 20	Toronto 3	St. Louis 0	(at St. Louis) [Wregget]
	April 22	Toronto 5	St. Louis 2	(at Toronto)
	April 24	St. Louis 7	Toronto 4	(at Toronto)
	April 26	St. Louis 4	Toronto 3	(at St. Louis)
				(Reeds 7:11 OT)
	April 28	Toronto 5	St. Louis 3	(at Toronto)
	April 30	St. Louis 2	Toronto 1	(at St. Louis)

St. Louis won best-of-seven 4–3

1986–1987

Clarence Campbell Conference

		GP	W	L	T	GF	GA	PIM	PTS
Norris Division	St. Louis Blues	80	32	33	15	281	293	1972	79
	Detroit Red Wings	80	34	36	10	260	274	2209	78
	Chicago Blackhawks	80	29	37	14	290	310	1692	72
	Toronto Maple Leafs	80	32	42	6	286	319	1827	70
	Minnesota North Stars	80	30	40	10	296	314	1936	70
Smythe Division	**Edmonton Oilers**	80	50	24	6	372	284	1721	106
	Calgary Flames	80	46	31	3	318	289	2036	95
	Winnipeg Jets	80	40	32	8	279	271	1537	88
	Los Angeles Kings	80	31	41	8	318	341	2038	70
	Vancouver Canucks	80	29	43	8	282	314	1917	66

Prince of Wales Conference

Adams Division									
	Hartford Whalers	80	43	30	7	287	270	1496	93
	Montreal Canadiens	80	41	29	10	277	241	1802	92
	Boston Bruins	80	39	34	7	301	276	1870	85
	Quebec Nordiques	80	31	39	10	267	276	1741	72
	Buffalo Sabres	80	28	44	8	280	308	1810	64

Patrick Division									
	Philadelphia Flyers	80	46	26	8	310	245	2082	100
	Washington Capitals	80	38	32	10	285	278	1720	86
	New York Islanders	80	35	33	12	279	281	1857	82
	New York Rangers	80	34	38	8	307	323	1718	76
	Pittsburgh Penguins	80	30	38	12	297	290	1693	72
	New Jersey Devils	80	29	45	6	293	368	1735	64

1st Round:				
	April 8	St. Louis 3	Toronto 1	(at St. Louis)
	April 9	Toronto 3	St. Louis 2	(at St. Louis) (Lanz 10:17 OT)
	April 11	St. Louis 5	Toronto 3	(at Toronto)
	April 12	Toronto 2	St. Louis 1	(at Toronto)
	April 14	Toronto 2	St. Louis 1	(at St. Louis)
	April 16	Toronto 4	St. Louis 0	(at Toronto) [Wregget]

Toronto won best-of-seven 4–2

Quarter-finals:				
	April 21	Toronto 4	Detroit 2	(at Detroit)
	April 23	Toronto 7	Detroit 2	(at Detroit)
	April 25	Detroit 4	Toronto 2	(at Toronto)
	April 27	Toronto 3	Detroit 2	(at Toronto) (Allison 9:31 OT)
	April 29	Detroit 3	Toronto 0	(at Detroit) [Hanlon]
	May 1	Detroit 4	Toronto 2	(at Toronto)
	May 3	Detroit 3	Toronto 0	(at Detroit) [Hanlon]

Detroit won best-of-seven 4–3

1987–1988
Clarence Campbell Conference

		GP	W	L	T	GF	GA	PIM	PTS
Norris Division	Detroit Red Wings	80	41	28	11	322	269	2391	93
	St. Louis Blues	80	34	38	8	278	294	1919	76
	Chicago Black Hawks	80	30	41	9	284	326	2228	69
	Toronto Maple Leafs	80	21	49	10	273	345	1782	52
	Minnesota North Stars	80	19	48	13	242	349	2313	51
Smythe Division	Calgary Flames	80	48	23	9	397	305	2431	105
	Edmonton Oilers	80	44	25	11	363	288	2173	99
	Winnipeg Jets	80	33	36	11	292	310	2278	77
	Los Angeles Kings	80	30	42	8	318	359	2124	68
	Vancouver Canucks	80	25	46	9	272	320	2196	59

Prince of Wales Conference

Adams Division									
	Montreal Canadiens	80	45	22	13	298	238	1830	103
	Boston Bruins	80	44	30	6	300	251	2443	94
	Buffalo Sabres	80	37	32	11	283	305	2277	85
	Hartford Whalers	80	35	38	7	249	267	2046	77
	Quebec Nordiques	80	32	43	5	271	306	2042	69

Patrick Division									
	New York Islanders	80	39	31	10	308	267	1732	88
	Washington Capitals	80	38	33	9	281	249	1680	85
	Philadelphia Flyers	80	38	33	9	292	282	2194	85
	New Jersey Devils	80	38	36	6	295	296	2315	82
	New York Rangers	80	36	34	10	300	283	1775	82
	Pittsburgh Penguins	80	36	35	9	319	316	2211	81

1st Round:				
	April 6	Toronto 6	Detroit 2	(at Detroit)
	April 7	Detroit 6	Toronto 2	(at Detroit)
	April 9	Detroit 6	Toronto 3	(at Toronto)
	April 10	Detroit 8	Toronto 0	(at Toronto) [Hanlon]
	April 12	Toronto 6	Detroit 5	(at Detroit)
				(Olczyk :34 OT)
	April 14	Detroit 5	Toronto 3	(at Toronto)

Detroit won best-of-seven 4–2

1988–1989
Clarence Campbell Conference

		GP	W	L	T	GF	GA	PIM	PTS
Norris Division	Detroit Red Wings	80	34	34	12	313	316	2245	80
	St. Louis Blues	80	33	35	12	275	285	1675	78
	Minnesota North Stars	80	27	37	16	258	278	1972	70
	Chicago Blackhawks	80	27	41	12	297	335	2496	66
	Toronto Maple Leafs	80	28	46	6	259	342	1740	62
Smythe Division	**Calgary Flames**	80	54	17	9	354	226	2444	117
	Los Angeles Kings	80	42	31	7	376	335	2215	91
	Edmonton Oilers	80	38	34	8	325	306	1931	84
	Vancouver Canucks	80	33	39	8	251	253	1569	74
	Winnipeg Jets	80	26	42	12	300	355	1843	64

Prince of Wales Conference

Adams Division									
	Montreal Canadiens	80	53	18	9	315	218	1537	115
	Boston Bruins	80	37	29	14	289	256	1929	88
	Buffalo Sabres	80	38	35	7	291	299	2034	83
	Hartford Whalers	80	37	38	5	299	290	1672	79
	Quebec Nordiques	80	27	46	7	269	342	2004	61

Patrick Division									
Washington Capitals	80	41	29	10	305	259	1836	92
Pittsburgh Penguins	80	40	33	7	347	349	2670	87
New York Rangers	80	37	35	8	310	307	1891	82
Philadelphia Flyers	80	36	36	8	307	285	2317	80
New Jersey Devils	80	27	41	12	281	325	2499	66
New York Islanders	80	28	47	5	265	325	1822	61

• did not qualify for playoffs

1989–1990
Clarence Campbell Conference

		GP	W	L	T	GF	GA	PIM	PTS
Norris Division	Chicago Blackhawks	80	41	33	6	316	294	2426	88
	St. Louis Blues	80	37	34	9	295	279	1809	83
	Toronto Maple Leafs	80	38	38	4	337	358	2419	80
	Minnesota North Stars	80	36	40	4	284	291	2041	76
	Detroit Red Wings	80	28	38	14	288	323	2140	70
Smythe Division	Calgary Flames	80	42	23	15	348	265	1751	99
	Edmonton Oilers	80	38	28	14	315	283	2046	90
	Winnipeg Jets	80	37	32	11	298	290	1639	85
	Los Angeles Kings	80	34	39	7	338	337	1844	75
	Vancouver Canucks	80	25	41	14	245	306	1644	64

Prince of Wales Conference

Adams Division	Boston Bruins	80	46	25	9	289	232	1458	101
	Buffalo Sabres	80	45	27	8	286	248	1449	98
	Montreal Canadiens	80	41	28	11	288	234	1590	93
	Hartford Whalers	80	38	33	9	275	268	2102	85
	Quebec Nordiques	80	12	61	7	240	407	2104	31
Patrick Division	New York Rangers	80	36	31	13	279	267	2021	85
	New Jersey Devils	80	37	34	9	295	288	1659	83
	Washington Capitals	80	36	38	6	284	275	2204	78
	New York Islanders	80	31	38	11	281	288	1777	73
	Pittsburgh Penguins	80	32	40	8	318	359	2132	72
	Philadelphia Flyers	80	30	39	11	290	297	2067	71

1st Round:				
April 4	St. Louis 4	Toronto 2	(at St. Louis)	
April 6	St. Louis 4	Toronto 2	(at St. Louis)	
April 8	St. Louis 6	Toronto 5	(at Toronto)	
			(Momesso 6:04 OT)	
April 10	Toronto 4	St. Louis 2	(at Toronto)	
April 12	St. Louis 4	Toronto 3	(at St. Louis)	

St. Louis won best-of-seven 4–1

1990–1991
Clarence Campbell Conference

		GP	W	L	T	GF	GA	PIM	PTS
Norris Division	Chicago Blackhawks	80	49	23	8	284	211	2412	106
	St. Louis Blues	80	47	22	11	310	250	1987	105
	Detroit Red Wings	80	34	38	8	273	298	1940	76
	Minnesota North Stars	80	27	39	14	256	266	1964	68
	Toronto Maple Leafs	80	23	46	11	241	318	1962	57
Smythe Division	Los Angeles Kings	80	46	24	10	340	254	2228	102
	Calgary Flames	80	46	26	8	344	263	2201	100
	Edmonton Oilers	80	37	37	6	272	272	1823	80
	Vancouver Canucks	80	28	43	9	243	315	2063	65
	Winnipeg Jets	80	26	43	11	260	288	1675	63

Prince of Wales Conference

		GP	W	L	T	GF	GA	PIM	PTS
Adams Division	Boston Bruins	80	44	24	12	299	264	1694	100
	Montreal Canadiens	80	39	30	11	273	249	1425	89
	Buffalo Sabres	80	31	30	19	292	278	1733	81
	Hartford Whalers	80	31	38	11	238	276	2209	73
	Quebec Nordiques	80	16	50	14	236	354	1741	46
Patrick Division	**Pittsburgh Penguins**	80	41	33	6	342	305	1641	88
	New York Rangers	80	36	31	13	297	265	1893	85
	Washington Capitals	80	37	36	7	258	258	1839	81
	New Jersey Devils	80	32	33	15	272	264	2024	79
	Philadelphia Flyers	80	33	37	10	252	267	1945	76
	New York Islanders	80	25	45	10	223	290	1723	60

• did not qualify for playoffs

1991–1992
Clarence Campbell Conference

		GP	W	L	T	GF	GA	PIM	PTS
Norris Division	Detroit Red Wings	80	43	25	12	320	256	2078	98
	Chicago Blackhawks	80	36	29	15	257	236	2663	87
	St. Louis Blues	80	36	33	11	279	266	2041	83
	Minnesota North Stars	80	32	42	6	246	278	2169	70
	Toronto Maple Leafs	80	30	43	7	234	294	1734	67
Smythe Division	Vancouver Canucks	80	42	26	12	285	250	2075	96
	Los Angeles Kings	80	35	31	14	287	296	2161	84
	Edmonton Oilers	80	36	34	10	295	297	1907	82
	Winnipeg Jets	80	33	32	15	251	244	1907	81
	Calgary Flames	80	31	37	12	296	305	2643	74
	San Jose Sharks	80	17	58	5	219	359	1894	39

Prince of Wales Conference

Adams Division									
	Montreal Canadiens	80	41	28	11	267	207	1556	93
	Boston Bruins	80	36	32	12	270	275	1752	84
	Buffalo Sabres	80	31	37	12	289	299	2713	74
	Hartford Whalers	80	26	41	13	247	283	1793	65
	Quebec Nordiques	80	20	48	12	255	318	2044	52
Patrick Division	New York Rangers	80	50	25	5	321	246	1805	105
	Washington Capitals	80	45	27	8	330	275	1777	98
	Pittsburgh Penguins	80	39	32	9	343	308	1907	87
	New Jersey Devils	80	38	31	11	289	259	1611	87
	New York Islanders	80	34	35	11	291	299	1713	79
	Philadelphia Flyers	80	32	37	11	252	273	1838	75

• did not qualify for playoffs

1992–1993

Clarence Campbell Conference

		GP	W	L	T	GF	GA	PIM	PTS
Norris Division	Chicago Blackhawks	84	47	25	12	279	230	2394	106
	Detroit Red Wings	84	47	28	9	369	280	1832	103
	Toronto Maple Leafs	84	44	29	11	288	241	1815	99
	St. Louis Blues	84	37	36	11	282	278	1889	85
	Minnesota North Stars	84	36	38	10	272	293	1885	82
	Tampa Bay Lightning	84	23	54	7	245	332	1625	53
Smythe Division	Vancouver Canucks	84	46	29	9	346	278	2326	101
	Calgary Flames	84	43	30	11	322	282	1951	97
	Los Angeles Kings	84	39	35	10	338	340	2247	88
	Winnipeg Jets	84	40	37	7	322	320	1851	87
	Edmonton Oilers	84	26	50	8	242	337	2027	60
	San Jose Sharks	84	11	71	2	218	414	2134	24

Prince of Wales Conference

Adams Division									
	Boston Bruins	84	51	26	7	332	268	1552	109
	Quebec Nordiques	84	47	27	10	351	300	1846	104
	Montreal Canadiens	84	48	30	6	326	280	1788	102
	Buffalo Sabres	84	38	36	10	335	297	1873	86
	Hartford Whalers	84	26	52	6	284	369	2354	58
	Ottawa Senators	84	10	70	4	202	395	1716	24
Patrick Division	Pittsburgh Penguins	84	56	21	7	367	268	1776	119
	Washington Capitals	84	43	34	7	325	286	1709	93
	New York Islanders	84	40	37	7	335	297	1701	87
	New Jersey Devils	84	40	37	7	308	299	1815	87
	Philadelphia Flyers	84	36	37	11	319	319	1887	83
	New York Rangers	84	34	39	11	304	308	1657	79

1st Round:	April 19	Detroit 6	Toronto 3	(at Detroit)
	April 21	Detroit 6	Toronto 2	(at Detroit)
	April 23	Toronto 4	Detroit 2	(at Toronto)
	April 25	Toronto 3	Detroit 2	(at Toronto)
	April 27	Toronto 5	Detroit 4	(at Detroit)
				(Foligno 2:05 OT)
	April 29	Detroit 7	Toronto 3	(at Toronto)
	May 1	Toronto 4	Detroit 3	(at Detroit)
				(Borschevsky 2:35 OT)

Toronto won best-of-seven 4–3

Quarter-finals:	May 3	Toronto 2	St. Louis 1	(at Toronto)
				(Gilmour 23:16 OT)
	May 5	St. Louis 2	Toronto 1	(at Toronto)
				(J. Brown 23:03 OT)
	May 7	St. Louis 4	Toronto 3	(at St. Louis)
	May 9	Toronto 4	St. Louis 1	(at St. Louis)
	May 11	Toronto 5	St. Louis 1	(at Toronto)
	May 13	St. Louis 2	Toronto 1	(at St. Louis)
	May 15	Toronto 6	St. Louis 0	(at Toronto) [Potvin]

Toronto won best-of-seven 4–3

Semi-finals:	May 17	Toronto 4	Los Angeles 1	(at Toronto)
	May 19	Los Angeles 3	Toronto 2	(at Toronto)
	May 21	Los Angeles 4	Toronto 2	(at Los Angeles)
	May 23	Toronto 4	Los Angeles 2	(at Los Angeles)
	May 25	Toronto 3	Los Angeles 2	(at Toronto)
				(G. Anderson 19:20 OT)
	May 27	Los Angeles 5	Toronto 4	(at Los Angeles)
				(Gretzky 1:41 OT)*
	May 29	Los Angeles 5	Toronto 4	(at Toronto)

Los Angeles won best-of-seven 4–3

* early in the overtime, Gilmour was cut by a Gretzky high-stick in plain view of referee Kerry Fraser. No penalty was called, and seconds later Gretzky won the game for Los Angeles.

1993–1994
Western Conference

		GP	W	L	T	GF	GA	PIM	PTS
Central Division	Detroit Red Wings	84	46	30	8	356	275	1775	100
	Toronto Maple Leafs	84	43	29	12	280	243	1877	98
	Dallas Stars	84	42	29	13	286	265	1919	97
	St. Louis Blues	84	40	33	11	270	283	1659	91
	Chicago Blackhawks	84	39	36	9	254	240	2125	87
	Winnipeg Jets	84	24	51	9	245	344	2143	57

Pacific Division	Calgary Flames	84	42	29	13	302	256 1847	97
	Vancouver Canucks	84	41	40	3	279	276 1923	85
	San Jose Sharks	84	33	35	16	252	265 1343	82
	Mighty Ducks of Anaheim	84	33	46	5	229	251 1507	71
	Los Angeles Kings	84	27	45	12	294	322 2017	66
	Edmonton Oilers	84	25	45	14	261	305 1858	64

Eastern Conference

Northeast Division	Pittsburgh Penguins	84	44	27	13	299	285 1624	101
	Boston Bruins	84	42	29	13	289	252 1442	97
	Montreal Canadiens	84	41	29	14	283	248 1524	96
	Buffalo Sabres	84	43	32	9	282	218 1760	95
	Quebec Nordiques	84	34	42	8	277	292 1625	76
	Hartford Whalers	84	27	48	9	227	288 1809	63
	Ottawa Senators	84	14	61	9	201	397 1710	37

Atlantic Division	**New York Rangers**	84	52	24	8	299	231 1688	112
	New Jersey Devils	84	47	25	12	306	220 1734	106
	Washington Capitals	84	39	35	10	277	263 2007	88
	New York Islanders	84	36	36	12	282	264 1787	84
	Florida Panthers	84	33	34	17	233	233 1620	83
	Philadelphia Flyers	84	35	39	10	294	314 1697	80
	Tampa Bay Lightning	84	30	43	11	224	251 1579	71

• the top eight teams in each conference qualified for the playoffs

1st Round:	April 18	Toronto 5	Chicago 1	(at Toronto)
	April 20	Toronto 1	Chicago 0	(at Toronto) [Potvin]
				(Gill 2:15 OT)
	April 23	Chicago 5	Toronto 4	(at Chicago)
	April 24	Chicago 4	Toronto 3	(at Chicago)
				(Roenick 1:23 OT)
	April 26	Toronto 1	Chicago 0	(at Toronto) [Potvin]
	April 28	Toronto 1	Chicago 0	(at Chicago) [Potvin]
	Toronto won best-of-seven 4–2			

Quarter-finals:	May 2	San Jose 3	Toronto 2	(at Toronto)
	May 4	Toronto 5	San Jose 1	(at Toronto)
	May 6	San Jose 5	Toronto 2	(at San Jose)
	May 8	Toronto 8	San Jose 3	(at San Jose)
	May 10	San Jose 5	Toronto 2	(at San Jose)
	May 12	Toronto 3	San Jose 2	(at Toronto)
				(Gartner 8:53 OT)
	May 14	Toronto 4	San Jose 2	(at Toronto)
	Toronto won best-of-seven 4–3			

Semi-finals:	May 16	Toronto 3	Vancouver 2	(at Toronto)
				(Zezel 16:55 OT)
	May 18	Vancouver 4	Toronto 3	(at Toronto)
	May 20	Vancouver 4	Toronto 0	(at Vancouver)[McLean]
	May 22	Vancouver 2	Toronto 0	(at Vancouver)[McLean]
	May 24	Vancouver 4	Toronto 3	(at Vancouver)
				(G. Adams 20:14 OT)

Vancouver won best-of-seven 4–1

1994–1995
Western Conference

		GP	W	L	T	GF	GA	PIM	PTS
Central Division	Detroit Red Wings	48	33	11	4	180	117	932	70
	St. Louis Blues	48	28	15	5	178	135	1077	61
	Chicago Blackhawks	48	24	19	5	156	115	1123	53
	Toronto Maple Leafs	48	21	19	8	135	146	744	50
	Dallas Stars	48	17	23	8	136	135	1117	42
	Winnipeg Jets	48	16	25	7	157	177	1141	39
Pacific Division	Calgary Flames	48	24	17	7	163	135	1249	55
	Vancouver Canucks	48	18	18	12	153	148	1093	48
	San Jose Sharks	48	19	25	4	129	161	840	42
	Los Angeles Kings	48	16	23	9	142	174	978	41
	Edmonton Oilers	48	17	27	4	136	183	1183	38
	Mighty Ducks of Anaheim	48	16	27	5	125	164	731	37

Eastern Conference

		GP	W	L	T	GF	GA	PIM	PTS
Northeast Division	Quebec Nordiques	48	30	13	5	185	134	770	65
	Pittsburgh Penguins	48	29	16	3	181	158	1036	61
	Boston Bruins	48	27	18	3	150	127	793	57
	Buffalo Sabres	48	22	19	7	130	119	1022	51
	Hartford Whalers	48	19	24	5	127	141	915	43
	Montreal Canadiens	48	18	23	7	125	148	840	43
	Ottawa Senators	48	9	34	5	116	174	749	23
Atlantic Division	Philadelphia Flyers	48	28	16	4	150	132	741	60
	New Jersey Devils	48	22	18	8	136	121	787	52
	Washington Capitals	48	22	18	8	136	120	1144	52
	New York Rangers	48	22	23	3	139	134	781	47
	Florida Panthers	48	20	22	6	115	127	770	46
	Tampa Bay Lightning	48	17	28	3	120	144	1040	37
	New York Islanders	48	15	28	5	126	158	901	35

1st Round:	May 7	Toronto 5	Chicago 3	(at Chicago)
	May 9	Toronto 3	Chicago 0	(at Chicago) [Potvin]
	May 11	Chicago 3	Toronto 2	(at Toronto)
	May 13	Chicago 3	Toronto 1	(at Toronto)
	May 15	Chicago 4	Toronto 2	(at Chicago)
	May 17	Toronto 5	Chicago 4	(at Toronto)
				(Wood 10:00 OT)
	May 19	Chicago 5	Toronto 2	(at Chicago)

Chicago won best-of-seven 4–3

1995–1996
Western Conference

		GP	W	L	T	GF	GA	PIM	PTS
Central Division	Detroit Red Wings	82	62	13	7	325	181	1551	131
	Chicago Blackhawks	82	40	28	14	273	220	1880	94
	Toronto Maple Leafs	82	34	36	12	247	252	1742	80
	St. Louis Blues	82	32	34	16	219	248	1823	80
	Winnipeg Jets	82	36	40	6	275	291	1622	78
	Dallas Stars	82	26	42	14	227	280	1652	66
Pacific Division	**Colorado Avalanche**	82	47	25	10	326	240	1536	104
	Calgary Flames	82	34	37	11	241	240	1524	79
	Vancouver Canucks	82	32	35	15	278	278	1546	79
	Mighty Ducks of Anaheim	82	35	39	8	234	247	1707	78
	Edmonton Oilers	82	30	44	8	240	304	1709	68
	Los Angeles Kings	82	24	40	18	256	302	1460	66
	San Jose Sharks	82	20	55	7	252	357	1480	47

Eastern Conference

		GP	W	L	T	GF	GA	PIM	PTS
Northeast Division	Pittsburgh Penguins	82	49	29	4	362	284	1623	102
	Boston Bruins	82	40	31	11	282	269	1039	91
	Montreal Canadiens	82	40	32	10	265	248	1847	90
	Hartford Whalers	82	34	39	9	237	259	1834	77
	Buffalo Sabres	82	33	42	7	247	262	2195	73
	Ottawa Senators	82	18	59	5	191	291	1553	41
Atlantic Division	Philadelphia Flyers	82	45	24	13	282	208	1785	103
	New York Rangers	82	41	27	14	272	237	1849	96
	Florida Panthers	82	41	31	10	254	234	1494	92
	Washington Capitals	82	39	32	11	234	204	1553	89
	Tampa Bay Lightning	82	38	32	12	238	248	1628	88
	New Jersey Devils	82	37	33	12	215	202	1486	86
	New York Islanders	82	22	50	10	229	315	1669	54

1st Round:	April 16	St. Louis 3	Toronto 1	(at Toronto)
	April 18	Toronto 5	St. Louis 4	(at Toronto)
				(Sundin 4:02 OT)
	April 21	St. Louis 3	Toronto 2	(at St. Louis)
				(G. Anderson 1:24 OT)
	April 23	St. Louis 5	Toronto 1	(at St. Louis)
	April 25	Toronto 5	St. Louis 4	(at Toronto)
				(Gartner 7:31 OT)
	April 27	St. Louis 2	Toronto 1	(at St. Louis)

St. Louis won best-of-seven 4–2

1996–1997
Western Conference

		GP	W	L	T	GF	GA	PIM	PTS
Central Division	Dallas Stars	82	48	26	8	252	198	1325	104
	Detroit Red Wings	82	38	26	18	253	197	1582	94
	Phoenix Coyotes	82	38	37	7	240	243	1582	83
	St. Louis Blues	82	36	35	11	236	239	1336	83
	Chicago Blackhawks	82	34	35	13	223	210	1763	81
	Toronto Maple Leafs	82	30	44	8	230	273	1331	68
Pacific Division	Colorado Avalanche	82	49	24	9	277	205	1361	107
	Mighty Ducks of Anaheim	82	36	33	13	245	233	1710	85
	Edmonton Oilers	82	36	37	9	252	247	1368	81
	Vancouver Canucks	82	35	40	7	257	273	1607	77
	Calgary Flames	82	32	41	9	214	239	1444	73
	Los Angeles Kings	82	28	43	11	214	268	1638	67
	San Jose Sharks	82	27	47	8	211	278	2085	62

Eastern Conference

		GP	W	L	T	GF	GA	PIM	PTS
Northeast Division	Buffalo Sabres	82	40	30	12	237	208	1840	92
	Pittsburgh Penguins	82	38	36	8	285	280	1498	84
	Ottawa Senators	82	31	36	15	226	234	1087	77
	Montreal Canadiens	82	31	36	15	249	276	1469	77
	Hartford Whalers	82	32	39	11	226	256	1513	75
	Boston Bruins	82	26	47	9	234	300	1369	61
Atlantic Division	New Jersey Devils	82	45	23	14	231	182	1135	104
	Philadelphia Flyers	82	45	24	13	274	217	1699	103
	Florida Panthers	82	35	28	19	221	201	1628	89
	New York Rangers	82	38	34	10	258	231	1481	86
	Washington Capitals	82	33	40	9	214	231	1652	75
	Tampa Bay Lightning	82	32	40	10	217	247	1686	74
	New York Islanders	82	29	41	12	240	250	1640	70

• did not qualify for playoffs

1997–98
Western Conference

		GP	W	L	T	GF	GA	PIM	PTS
Central Division	Dallas Stars	82	49	22	11	242	167	1301	109
	Detroit Red Wings	82	44	23	15	250	196	1346	103
	St. Louis Blues	82	45	29	8	256	204	1414	98
	Phoenix Coyotes	82	35	35	12	224	227	1602	82
	Chicago Blackhawks	82	30	39	13	192	199	1546	73
	Toronto Maple Leafs	82	30	43	9	194	237	1481	69
Pacific Division	Colorado Avalanche	82	39	26	17	231	205	1729	95
	Los Angeles Kings	82	38	33	11	227	225	1763	87
	Edmonton Oilers	82	35	37	10	215	224	1690	80
	San Jose Sharks	82	34	38	10	210	216	1417	78
	Calgary Flames	82	26	41	15	217	252	1859	67
	Mighty Ducks of Anaheim	82	26	43	13	205	261	1843	65
	Vancouver Canucks	82	25	43	14	224	273	2166	64

Eastern Conference

		GP	W	L	T	GF	GA	PIM	PTS
Northeast Division	Pittsburgh Penguins	82	40	24	18	228	188	1225	98
	Boston Bruins	82	39	30	13	221	194	1117	91
	Buffalo Sabres	82	36	29	17	211	187	1768	89
	Montreal Canadiens	82	37	32	13	235	208	1547	87
	Ottawa Senators	82	34	33	15	193	20	1091	83
	Carolina Hurricanes	82	33	41	8	200	219	1455	74
Atlantic Division	New Jersey Devils	82	48	23	11	225	166	1488	107
	Philadelphia Flyers	82	42	29	11	242	193	1766	95
	Washington Capitals	82	40	30	12	219	202	1198	92
	New York Islanders	82	30	41	11	212	225	1646	71
	New York Rangers	82	25	39	18	197	231	1548	68
	Florida Panthers	82	24	43	15	203	256	1676	63
	Tampa Bay Lightning	82	17	55	10	151	269	1823	44

• did not qualify for playoffs

1998–99
Eastern Conference

		GP	W	L	T	GF	GA	PIM	PTS
Northeast Division	Ottawa Senators	82	44	23	15	239	179	892	103
	Toronto Maple Leafs	82	45	30	7	268	231	1095	97
	Boston Bruins	82	39	30	13	214	181	1182	91
	Buffalo Sabres	82	37	28	17	207	175	1561	91
	Montreal Canadiens	82	32	39	11	184	209	1299	75

Atlantic Division	New Jersey Devils	82	47	24	11	248	196	1355	105
	Philadelphia Flyers	82	37	26	19	231	196	1075	93
	Pittsburgh Penguins	82	38	30	14	242	225	977	90
	New York Rangers	82	33	38	11	217	227	1087	77
	New York Islanders	82	24	48	10	194	244	1111	58
Southeast Division	Carolina Hurricanes	82	34	30	18	210	202	1158	86
	Florida Panthers	82	30	34	18	210	228	1522	78
	Washington Capitals	82	31	45	6	200	218	1281	68
	Tampa Bay Lightning	82	19	54	9	179	292	1316	47

Western Conference

Central Division	Detroit Red Wings	82	43	32	7	245	202	1202	93
	St. Louis Blues	82	37	32	13	237	209	1308	87
	Chicago Blackhawks	82	29	41	12	202	248	1807	70
	Nashville Predators	82	28	47	7	190	261	1420	63
Pacific Division	**Dallas Stars**	82	51	19	12	236	168	1108	114
	Phoenix Coyotes	82	39	31	12	205	197	1412	90
	Mighty Ducks of Anaheim	82	35	34	13	215	206	1323	83
	San Jose Sharks	82	31	33	18	196	191	1423	80
	Los Angeles Kings	82	32	45	5	189	222	1383	69
Northwest Division	Colorado Avalanche	82	44	28	10	239	205	1619	98
	Edmonton Oilers	82	33	37	12	230	226	1373	78
	Calgary Flames	82	30	40	12	211	234	1389	72
	Vancouver Canucks	82	23	47	12	192	258	1764	58

1st Round:	April 22	Philadelphia 3	Toronto 0	(at Toronto) [Vanbiesbrouck]
	April 24	Toronto 2	Philadelphia 1	(at Toronto)
	April 26	Toronto 2	Philadelphia 1	(at Philadelphia)
	April 28	Philadelphia 5	Toronto 2	(at Philadelphia)
	April 30	Toronto 2	Philadelphia 1	(at Toronto) (Perreault 11:51 OT)
	May 2	Toronto 1	Philadelphia 0	(at Philadelphia) (Berezin 19:00 3rd) [Joseph]

Toronto won best-of-seven 4–2

Conference Semi-finals:	May 7	Pittsburgh 2	Toronto 0	(at Toronto) [Barrasso]
	May 9	Toronto 4	Pittsburgh 2	(at Toronto)
	May 11	Pittsburgh 4	Toronto 3	(at Pittsburgh)
	May 13	Toronto 3	Pittsburgh 2	(at Pittsburgh) (Berezin 2:18 OT)

May 15	Toronto 4	Pittsburgh 1	(at Toronto)
May 17	Toronto 4	Pittsburgh 3	(at Pittsburgh)
			(Valk 1:57 OT)

Toronto won best-of-seven 4–2

Conference Finals:	May 23	Buffalo 5	Toronto 4	(at Toronto)
	May 25	Toronto 6	Buffalo 3	(at Toronto)
	May 27	Buffalo 4	Toronto 2	(at Buffalo)
	May 29	Buffalo 5	Toronto 2	(at Buffalo)
	May 31	Buffalo 4	Toronto 2	(at Toronto)

Buffalo won best-of-seven 4–1

1999–2000
Eastern Conference

		GP	W	L	T	OTL	GF	GA	PIM	PTS
Northeast Division	Toronto Maple Leafs	82	45	30	7	3	246	222	1103	100
	Ottawa Senators	82	41	30	11	2	244	210	850	95
	Buffalo Sabres	82	35	36	11	4	213	204	1173	85
	Montreal Canadiens	82	35	38	9	4	196	194	1067	83
	Boston Bruins	82	24	39	19	6	210	248	865	73
Atlantic Division	Philadelphia Flyers	82	45	25	12	3	237	179	1233	105
	New Jersey Devils	82	45	29	8	5	251	203	1313	103
	Pittsburgh Penguins	82	37	37	8	6	241	236	1221	88
	New York Rangers	82	29	42	12	3	218	246	916	73
	New York Islanders	82	24	49	9	1	194	275	1376	58
Southeast Division	Washington Capitals	82	44	26	12	2	227	194	994	102
	Florida Panthers	82	43	33	6	6	244	209	1329	98
	Carolina Hurricanes	82	37	35	10	0	217	216	799	84
	Tampa Bay Lightning	82	19	54	9	7	204	309	1733	54
	Atlanta Thrashers	82	14	61	7	4	170	313	1422	39

Western Conference

		GP	W	L	T	OTL	GF	GA	PIM	PTS
Central Division	St. Louis Blues	82	51	20	11	1	248	165	1139	114
	Detroit Red Wings	82	48	24	10	2	278	210	1014	108
	Chicago Blackhawks	82	33	39	10	2	242	245	1444	78
	Nashville Predators	82	28	47	7	7	199	240	946	70
Northwest Division	Colorado Avalanche	82	42	29	11	1	233	201	1118	96
	Edmonton Oilers	82	32	34	16	8	226	212	1344	88
	Vancouver Canucks	82	30	37	15	8	227	237	1047	83
	Calgary Flames	82	31	41	10	5	211	256	1267	77

Pacific Division										
Dallas Stars	82	43	29	10	6	211	184	1029	102
Los Angeles Kings	82	39	31	12	4	245	228	1313	94
Phoenix Coyotes	82	39	35	8	4	232	228	940	90
San Jose Sharks	82	35	37	10	7	225	214	1292	87
Mighty Ducks of Anaheim	82	34	36	12	3	217	227	926	83

- OTL overtime loss (a team losing in overtime is awarded one point)

1st Round:				
April 12	Toronto 2	Ottawa 0	(at Toronto) [Joseph]
April 15	Toronto 5	Ottawa 1	(at Toronto)
April 17	Ottawa 4	Toronto 3	(at Ottawa)
April 19	Ottawa 2	Toronto 1	(at Ottawa)
April 22	Toronto 2	Ottawa 1	(at Toronto)
			(Thomas 14:47 OT)
April 24	Toronto 4	Ottawa 2	(at Ottawa)

Toronto won best-of-seven 4–2

Conference Semi-finals:				
April 27	Toronto 2	New Jersey 1	(at Toronto)
April 29	New Jersey 1	Toronto 0	(at Toronto)
			(White 6:41 1st)
			[Brodeur]
May 1	New Jersey 5	Toronto 1	(at New Jersey)
May 3	Toronto 3	New Jersey 2	(at New Jersey)
May 6	New Jersey 4	Toronto 3	(at Toronto)
May 8	New Jersey 3	Toronto 0	(at New Jersey)
			[Brodeur]

New Jersey won best-of seven 4–2

2000–01
Eastern Conference

		GP	W	L	T	OTL	GF	GA	PIM	PTS
East Division	Ottawa Senators	82	48	21	9	4	274	205	1052	109
	Buffalo Sabres	82	46	30	5	1	218	184	1241	98
	Toronto Maple Leafs	82	37	29	11	5	232	207	1424	90
	Boston Bruins	82	36	30	8	8	227	249	1307	88
	Montreal Canadiens	82	28	40	8	6	206	232	1002	70
Atlantic Division	New Jersey Devils	82	48	19	12	3	295	195	1217	111
	Philadelphia Flyers	82	43	25	11	3	240	207	1175	100
	Pittsburgh Penguins	82	42	28	9	3	281	256	1573	96
	New York Rangers	82	33	43	5	1	250	290	1504	72
	New York Islanders	82	21	51	7	3	185	268	1325	52
Southeast Division	Washington Capitals	82	41	27	10	4	233	211	1131	96
	Carolina Hurricanes	82	38	32	9	3	212	225	1073	88
	Florida Panthers	82	22	38	13	9	200	246	1499	66
	Atlanta Thrashers	82	23	45	12	2	211	289	1494	60
	Tampa Bay Lightning	82	24	47	6	5	201	280	1384	59

Western Conference

Central Division										
Detroit Red Wings	82	49	20	9	4	253	202	1062	111
St. Louis Blues	82	43	22	12	5	249	195	1331	103
Nashville Predators	82	34	36	9	3	186	200	936	80
Chicago Blackhawks	82	29	40	8	5	210	246	977	71
Columbus Blue Jackets	82	28	39	9	6	190	233	1214	71

Northwest Division										
Colorado Avalanche	82	52	16	10	4	270	192	1122	118
Edmonton Oilers	82	39	28	12	3	243	222	1277	93
Vancouver Canucks	82	36	28	11	7	239	238	1091	90
Calgary Flames	82	27	36	15	4	197	236	1362	73
Minnesota Wild	82	25	39	13	5	168	210	1174	68

Pacific Division										
Dallas Stars	82	48	24	8	2	241	187	1031	106
San Jose Sharks	82	40	27	12	3	217	192	1354	95
Los Angeles Kings	82	38	28	13	3	252	228	1176	92
Phoenix Coyotes	82	35	27	17	3	214	212	1325	90
Mighty Ducks of Anaheim	82	25	41	11	5	188	245	1124	66

1st Round:

April 13	Toronto 1	Ottawa 0	(at Ottawa) [Sundin 10:49 OT] [Joseph]
April 14	Toronto 3	Ottawa 0	(at Ottawa) [Joseph]
April 16	Toronto 3	Ottawa 2	(at Toronto) [Cross 2:16 OT]
April 18	Toronto 3	Ottawa 1	(at Toronto)

Toronto won best-of-seven 4–0

Conference Semi-finals:

April 26	Toronto 2	New Jersey 0	(at New Jersey) [Joseph]
April 28	New Jersey 6	Toronto 5	(at New Jersey) [McKay 5:31 OT]
May 1	New Jersey 3	Toronto 2	(at Toronto) [Rafalski 7:00 OT]
May 3	Toronto 3	New Jersey 1	(at Toronto)
May 5	Toronto 3	New Jersey 2	(at New Jersey)
May 7	New Jersey 4	Toronto 2	(at Toronto)
May 9	New Jersey 5	Toronto 1	(at New Jersey)

New Jersey won best-of-seven 4–3

0–0 Games

Toronto has been involved in 33 scoreless games since 1917. (Goalies are listed in brackets under their respective teams; shots are included from 1955–56, when the NHL began to keep such records.)

1.	February 3, 1927	Toronto St. Pats (John Roach)	at	New York Americans (Vernon Forbes)
2.	December 6, 1927	Toronto Maple Leafs (John Roach)	at	Ottawa Senators (Alex Connell)
3.	December 10, 1927	Ottawa Senators (Alex Connell)	at	Toronto Maple Leafs (John Roach)
4.	February 21, 1928	Toronto Maple Leafs (John Roach)	at	Montreal Canadiens (George Hainsworth)
5.	March 3, 1928	Boston Bruins (Hal Winkler)	at	Toronto Maple Leafs (Joe Ironstone)
6.	February 5, 1929	Toronto Maple Leafs (Lorne Chabot)	at	Pittsburgh Pirates (Joe Miller)
7.	November 13, 1930	New York Americans (Roy Worters)	at	Toronto Maple Leafs (Lorne Chabot)
8.	November 20, 1930	Toronto Maple Leafs (Ben Grant)	at	New York Americans (Roy Worters)
9.	January 26, 1935	Detroit Red Wings (John Ross Roach)	at	Toronto Maple Leafs (George Hainsworth)
10.	December 19, 1935	Boston Bruins (Cecil Thompson)	at	Toronto Maple Leafs (George Hainsworth)
11.	March 3, 1936	Toronto Maple Leafs (George Hainsworth)	at	New York Rangers (Dave Kerr)
12.	January 2, 1937	Montreal Maroons (Alex Connell)	at	Toronto Maple Leafs (Turk Broda)
13.	March 1, 1941	Boston Bruins (Frank Brimsek)	at	Toronto Maple Leafs (Turk Broda)
14.	January 27, 1942	Toronto Maple Leafs (Turk Broda)	at	Boston Bruins (Frank Brimsek)
15.	February 20, 1944	Toronto Maple Leafs (Paul Bibeault)	at	Chicago Black Hawks (Mike Karakas)
16.	November 30, 1947	Toronto Maple Leafs (Turk Broda)	at	Boston Bruins (Frank Brimsek)
17.	November 30, 1950	Toronto Maple Leafs (Al Rollins)	at	Montreal Canadiens (Gerry McNeil)
18.	December 2, 1950	Chicago Black Hawks (Harry Lumley)	at	Toronto Maple Leafs (Rollins/Broda)*

* Broda replaced Rollins at 6:50 of 2nd period, after Rollins's nose was broken from a shot.

19.	January 21, 1951	Toronto Maple Leafs (Al Rollins)	at	Detroit Red Wings (Terry Sawchuk)
20.	January 3, 1954	Toronto Maple Leafs (Harry Lumley)	at	Detroit Red Wings (Terry Sawchuk)
21.	February 17, 1954	Detroit Red Wings (Terry Sawchuk)	at	Toronto Maple Leafs (Harry Lumley)

22.	February 25, 1954	Toronto Maple Leafs (Harry Lumley)	at	Montreal Canadiens (Jacques Plante)
23.	January 12, 1955	Toronto Maple Leafs (Harry Lumley)	at	New York Rangers (Gump Worsley)
24.	March 10, 1955	Toronto Maple Leafs (Harry Lumley)	at	Montreal Canadiens (Jacques Plante)
25.	December 8, 1956	New York Rangers (Gump Worsley—38)	at	Toronto Maple Leafs (Ed Chadwick—22)
26.	March 3, 1957	Toronto Maple Leafs (Ed Chadwick—19)	at	Chicago Black Hawks (Al Rollins—20)
27.	December 4, 1957	Montreal Canadiens (Jacques Plante—27)	at	Toronto Maple Leafs (Ed Chadwick—26)
28.	December 27, 1961	Chicago Black Hawks (Glenn Hall—30)	at	Toronto Maple Leafs (Johnny Bower—30)
29.	January 13, 1965	Chicago Black Hawks (Denis DeJordy—20)	at	Toronto Maple Leafs (Johnny Bower—19)
30.	October 27, 1971	Vancouver Canucks (Dunc Wilson—34)	at	Toronto Maple Leafs (Bernie Parent—20)
31.	December 21, 1987	Minnesota North Stars (Kari Takko—33)	at	Toronto Maple Leafs (Allan Bester—28)
32.	November 4, 1997	Toronto Maple Leafs (Healy—16/Cousineau—6)	at	San Jose Sharks (Vernon—19)
33.	November 4, 2000	Toronto Maple Leafs (Joseph—36)	at	St. Louis Blues (Turek—16)

All-Time Records, Game

Most Goals For *(home team in bold)*

March 16, 1957	**Toronto** 14	Rangers 1
January 2, 1971	**Toronto** 13	Detroit 0
January 8, 1944	**Toronto** 12	Boston 3
March 8, 1947	**Toronto** 12	Chicago 4
December 6, 1947	**Toronto** 12	Chicago 5

Most Goals Against

(home team in bold)

January 10, 1920	**Canadiens** 14	Toronto 7
March 19, 1981	**Buffalo** 14	Toronto 4
January 11, 1919	**Canadiens** 13	Toronto 4

Most Goals, Both Teams

21*	January 10, 1920
	Toronto 7 at Canadiens 14
20	January 8, 1986
	Edmonton 9 at Toronto 11
19	December 19, 1917
	Toronto 9 at Wanderers 10

* NHL record (tied with one other)

Greatest Comeback

5 goals	December 30, 1989
	Boston 6 at Toronto 7 (OT)

• Toronto rallied from 6–1 down at 18:55 of 2nd

Worst Blown Lead

5 goals	November 29, 2000
	St. Louis 6 at Toronto 5 (OT)

• St. Louis rallied from 5–0 down at 4:51 of 3rd

	January 26, 1987*
	Calgary 6 at Toronto 5 (OT)

• Calgary rallied from 5–0 down at 6:02 of 3rd

* NHL record

Highest Tie Scores

7–7	—Toronto at California
	March 7, 1976
	—Vancouver at Toronto
	January 4, 1988
	—Detroit at Toronto
	December 27, 1989

Penalty-Free Games, Regular Season

1. February 11, 1922
   Toronto 4 at Ottawa 4
2. March 21, 1927
   Toronto 4 at Americans 1
3. December 14, 1933
   Toronto 0 at Canadiens 2
4. February 23, 1935
   Chicago 1 at Toronto 4
5. November 10, 1938
   Toronto 2 at Canadiens 0
6. February 11, 1939
   Canadiens 3 at Toronto 3
7. January 9, 1941
   Rangers 2 at Toronto 3*
8. January 11, 1941
   Americans 0 at Toronto 9*
9. February 20, 1944
   Toronto 0 at Chicago 0**
10. December 29, 1945
    Boston 4 at Toronto 3
11. March 28, 2001
    Boston 3 at Toronto 0

* Toronto is the only team in the NHL to play two consecutive games without a penalty being called against either team
** Toronto and Chicago are the only teams to play a scoreless, penalty-free game

All-Time Team Records

Most Consecutive Years in Playoffs
15   1930–1945
9   1958–1967

Most Consecutive Years Missing Playoffs
3   1925–1928

Most Wins, Season
45   1999–2000 (82 games)
      1998–99 (82 games)
44   1992–93 (84 games)

Fewest Wins, Season *(since 1946–47)*
20   1984–85 (80 games)
      1981–82 (80 games)

Best Win Percentage, Season
.679   1950–51 (70 games)
.667   1934–35 (48 games)
.646   1940–41 (48 games)

Worst Win Percentage, Season
.278   1918–19 (18 games)
.300   1984–85 (80 games)
.325   1987–88 (80 games)

Fewest Losses, Season *(since 1946–47)*
15   1947–48 (60 games)
16   1950–51 (70 games)

Most Losses, Season
52   1984–85 (80 games)
49   1987–88 (80 games)

Most Ties, Season
22   1954–55 (70 games)

Fewest Ties, Season *(since 1946–47)*
4   1989–90 (80 games)

Most Points, Season
100   1999–2000 (82 games)
99   1992–93 (84 games)
98   1993–94 (84 games)
95   1950–51 (70 games)

Fewest Points, Season *(since 1946–47)*
45   1945–46 (50 games)
48   1984–85 (80 games)

Most Wins Home, Season
25   1961–62 (35 dates)
      1992–93 (42 dates)

Fewest Wins Home, Season
(since 1946–47)
12   1948–49 (30 dates)
      1956–57 (35 dates)
      1957–58 (35 dates)
      1981–82 (40 dates)

Fewest Losses Home, Season
(since 1946–47)
3   1947–48 (30 dates)
5   1961–62 (35 dates)

Most Losses Home, Season
28   1984–85 (40 dates)

Most Ties Home, Season
11   1954–55 (35 dates)

Fewest Ties Home, Season

(since 1946–47)

2	1946–47 (30 dates)
	1984–85 (40 dates)
	1989–90 (40 dates)

Most Wins Road, Season

22	1998–99 (41 dates)
21	1999–2000 (41 dates)

Fewest Wins Road, Season

(since 1946–47)

3	1955–56 (35 dates)
7	1972–73 (39 dates)
	1987–88 (40 dates)

Fewest Losses Road, Season

(since 1946–47)

8	1950–51 (35 dates)

Most Losses Road, Season

29	1972–73 (39 dates)
	1983–84 (40 dates)
	1987–88 (40 dates)

Most Ties Road, Season

11	1954–55 (35 dates)
	1964–65 (35 dates)

Fewest Ties Road, Season

(since 1946–47)

1	1979–80 (40 dates)
	1988–89 (40 dates)

Most Goals For, Season

337	1989–90 (80 games)
322	1980–81 (80 games)

Fewest Goals For, Season

(since 1946–47)

147	1954–55 (70 games)
152	1953–54 (70 games)

Fewest Goals Against, Season

(70-game schedule)

131	1953–54 (70 games)
135	1954–55 (70 games)

Most Goals Against, Season

387	1983–84 (80 games)
386	1985–86 (80 games)

Most Consecutive Wins

10	October 7–October 28, 1993*
9	January 31–February 28, 1925

* NHL record for start of a season

Most Consecutive Wins, Home

9	November 11–December 26, 1953

Most Consecutive Wins, Road

7	November 14–December 15, 1950
	December 4–January 5, 1960–61

Longest Undefeated Streak

11	October 15–November 8, 1950
	January 6–Feb 1, 1994

Longest Undefeated Streak, Home

18	November 28–March 10, 1933–34
	October 31–January 23, 1953–54

Longest Undefeated Streak, Road

9	November 30–January 11, 1947–48

Longest Losing Streak

10	January 15–February 8, 1967
9	February 23–March 13, 1982
	October 16–November 6, 1985

Longest Losing Streak, Home

7	November 10–December 5, 1984
	January 25–February 25, 1985

Longest Losing Streak, Road

11	February 20–April 1, 1988

Longest Winless Streak

15	December 26–January 25, 1987–88
13	October 16–November 14, 1985

Longest Winless Streak, Home

11	December 19–January 25, 1988

Longest Winless Streak, Road

18	October 6–January 5, 1982–83

Most Consecutive Overtime Games

5	December 13–23, 1986

Most Consecutive Ties

3	November 10–17, 1951

Most Consecutive Games Without a Tie

74	January 17, 1923– December 19, 1925
53	March 5–December 26, 1989

Longest Shutout Streak *(minutes)*

331:42	November 13–25, 1930
214:46	November 11–19, 1939

Longest Streak Being Shutout

(minutes)

215:48	December 11–21, 1926
188:56	December 23–30, 1925

Most Consecutive Games Without Being Shutout

130	January 14, 1976– November 11, 1977

Most Consecutive Games Without Recording a Shutout

393	November 18, 1981– October 30, 1986

Most Games on Consecutive Nights

Twice the Leafs have played games on three successive nights:

1955	November 11
	Toronto 0 at Chicago 2
	November 12
	Boston 3 at Toronto 2
	November 13
	Toronto 1 at Rangers 4
1977	February 12
	Washington 0 at Toronto 10
	February 13
	Toronto 3 at Rangers 8
	February 14
	Toronto 2 at Buffalo 7

Most Consecutive Games Against One Opponent

3	vs. Hamilton Tigers, January 3–12, 1921
	vs. Detroit, March 11–14, 1943
	vs. Detroit, December 16–25, 1944

Most Consecutive Road Games Against One Opponent

2	vs. Boston, February 5 and 8, 1950

Longest Home Stand

9 games   February 7–March 3, 1973
8 games   December 23–January 15, 1989–90

Longest Road Trip

7 games   January 28–February 12, 1968
          January 19–February 2, 1969
          January 19–February 1, 1972
          January 11–25, 1976
          January 16–27, 1980
          January 12–28, 1999

Shots on Goal Records

Most Shots, Game, Leafs

61   February 25, 1976
          Detroit 0 at Toronto 8

Fewest Shots, Game, Leafs

9   March 4, 1999
          Toronto 4 at St. Louis 0
11   January 19, 1956
          Toronto 1 at Canadiens 3

Most Shots, Game, Opponent

65   March 15, 1984
          Toronto 3 at Hartford 5

Fewest Shots, Game, Opponent

13   October 12, 1955
          Toronto 2 at Boston 0
          March 9, 1975
          Toronto 4 at Washington 4

Most Shots, Game, Both Teams

109   October 9, 1955
          Toronto 1 at Chicago 3
          (Toronto 58, Chicago 51)

Most Shots, Period, Both Teams

46   December 18, 1976, 3rd period
          Colorado 2 at Toronto 4
          (Colorado 25, Toronto 21)

Most Shots, Period, Leafs

30   February 25, 1976, 1st period
          Detroit 0 at Toronto 8

Most Shots, Period, Opponent

32   March 15, 1984, 2nd period
          Toronto 3 at Hartford 5

Fewest Shots, Period, Leafs

0   April 3, 2000,
          2nd period, vs. Buffalo
          Toronto 2 at Buffalo 3

Fewest Shots, Period, Opponent

1 (five times); most recently: January 11,
1994, 1st period, Toronto 2 at Washington 1

Years the Leafs Led the League, Regular Season

Goals, Individual

1920–21	Babe Dye	35
1922–23	Babe Dye	26
1924–25	Babe Dye	38
1928–29	Ace Bailey	22
1930–31	Charlie Conacher	31
1933–34	Charlie Conacher	32
1934–35	Charlie Conacher	36
1935–36	Charlie Conacher	23
	Bill Thoms	23
1937–38	Gord Drillon	26
1945–46	Gaye Stewart	37

Assists, Individual

1919–20	Corb Dennenay	12
1920–21	Harry Cameron	9*
1922–23	Babe Dye	11
1931–32	Joe Primeau	37
1933–34	Joe Primeau	32
1936–37	Syl Apps	29
1937–38	Syl Apps	29
1950–51	Ted Kennedy	43*
1963–64	Andy Bathgate	58**

* tied with one other
** played part of season with Rangers

Points, Individual

1922–23	Babe Dye	37
1924–25	Babe Dye	44
1928–29	Ace Bailey	32
1931–32	Harvey Jackson	53
1933–34	Charlie Conacher	52
1934–35	Charlie Conacher	57
1937–38	Gord Drillon	52

Penalty Minutes, Individual

1919–20	Cully Wilson	79
1923–24	Bert Corbeau	55
1925–26	Bert Corbeau	121
1932–33	Red Horner	144
1933–34	Red Horner	126*
1934–35	Red Horner	125
1935–36	Red Horner	167
1936–37	Red Horner	124
1937–38	Red Horner	82*
1938–39	Red Horner	85
1939–40	Red Horner	87
1946–47	Gus Mortson	133
1947–48	Bill Barilko	147
1948–49	Bill Ezinicki	145
1949–50	Bill Ezinicki	144
1950–51	Gus Mortson	142
1959–60	Carl Brewer	150
1964–65	Carl Brewer	177
1968–69	Forbes Kennedy	219+
1976–77	Tiger Williams	338
1978–79	Tiger Williams	298

* prior to 1946–47, match penalties were not included in penalty minutes statistics
+ played part of season with Flyers

Goals Scored, Team

1917–18	37 (2nd half)
1919–20	67* (2nd half)
1922–23	82
1925–26	92*
1931–32	155
1933–34	174
1934–35	157
1935–36	126
1937–38	151
1942–43	198
1946–47	209
1998–99	268

* tied with one other

Goals Against, Team

1917–18	34 (second half)
1940–41	199
1947–48	143
1950–51	138
1953–54	131
1960–61	176
1964–65	173

Goals Against Average, Individual

1940–41	Turk Broda	2.00
1947–48	Turk Broda	2.38
1950–51	Al Rollins	1.77
1953–54	Harry Lumley	1.86
1960–61	Johnny Bower	2.50
1963–64	Johnny Bower	2.11
1964–65	Johnny Bower	2.38
1965–66	Johnny Bower	2.25
1970–71	Jacques Plante	1.88
1992–93	Felix Potvin	2.50

Penalty Minutes, Team

1917–18	205
1922–23	200
1923–24	178
1931–32	625
1932–33	622
1933–34	529
1934–35	444
1935–36	579
1942–43	431
1946–47	669
1947–48	758
1949–50	804
1951–52	841
1952–53	812
1954–55	990
1955–56	1051

Leafs All-Time Leaders, Regular Season

Most Seasons

George Armstrong	21
Tim Horton	20
Ron Ellis	16
Borje Salming	16
Dave Keon	15

Most Games, Career

George Armstrong	1187
Tim Horton	1185
Borje Salming	1099
Dave Keon	1062
Ron Ellis	1034

Only five players have played 1,000 games in a Leafs sweater:

1. Tim Horton, November 19, 1967, at Boston
2. George Armstrong, January 7, 1968, at Rangers
3. Dave Keon, November 20, 1974, vs. Pittsburgh
4. Ron Ellis, March 22, 1980, vs. Buffalo
5. Borje Salming, January 4, 1988, vs. Vancouver

By Position

Centre	Dave Keon	1062
	Bob Pulford	947
Left Wing	Frank Mahovlich	720
	Sid Smith	601
Right Wing	George Armstrong	1187
	Ron Ellis	1034
Defence	Tim Horton	1185
	Borje Salming	1099

Most Points, Career

Darryl Sittler	916
Dave Keon	858
Borje Salming	768
George Armstrong	713
Ron Ellis	640
Frank Mahovlich	597

By Position

Centre	Darryl Sittler	916
	Dave Keon	858

Charlie Conacher

Left Wing	Frank Mahovlich	597
	Wendel Clark	418
Right Wing	George Armstrong	713
	Ron Ellis	640
Defence	Borje Salming	768
	Tim Horton	458

1000th Point

Four players have scored their 1,000th career point while playing for the Leafs:

1. Norm Ullman
   (earned an assist in his 1,113th game)
   October 16, 1971, Rangers 5 at Toronto 3
2. Glenn Anderson
   (scored a goal in his 954th game)
   February 22, 1993,
   Toronto 8 at Vancouver 1
3. Doug Gilmour
   (earned an assist in his 935th game)
   December 23, 1995,
   Edmonton 1 at Toronto 6
4. Larry Murphy
   (scored a goal in his 1,228th game)
   March 27, 1996, Toronto 6 at Vancouver 2

Most Goals, Career

Darryl Sittler	389
Dave Keon	365
Ron Ellis	332
Rick Vaive	299
George Armstrong	296
Frank Mahovlich	296

By Position

Centre	Darryl Sittler	389
	Dave Keon	365
Left Wing	Frank Mahovlich	296
	Wendel Clark	246
Right Wing	Ron Ellis	332
	Rick Vaive	299
Defence	Borje Salming	148
	Ian Turnbull	112

Most Assists, Career

Borje Salming	620
Darryl Sittler	527
Dave Keon	493
George Armstrong	417
Tim Horton	349

By Position

Centre	Darryl Sittler	527
	Dave Keon	493
Left Wing	Frank Mahovlich	301
	Vincent Damphousse	211
Right Wing	George Armstrong	417
	Ron Ellis	308
Defence	Borje Salming	620
	Tim Horton	349

Most Penalty Minutes, Career

Tiger Williams	1670
Tie Domi	1620
Wendel Clark	1434
Tim Horton	1389

By Position

Centre	Darryl Sittler	763
	Bob Pulford	691
Left Wing	Tiger Williams	1670
	Wendel Clark	1434
Right Wing	Tie Domi	1620
	Rick Vaive	940
Defence	Tim Horton	1389
	Borje Salming	1292

Most Points, Season

Doug Gilmour (1992–93)	127
Darryl Sittler (1977–78)	117
Doug Gilmour (1993–94)	111
Darryl Sittler (1975–76)	100

100th Point, Season

Only four times has a Leaf scored 100 points or more in a season.

1. Darryl Sittler, April 3, 1976, vs. Boston at Maple Leaf Gardens (assist)
2. Darryl Sittler, March 12, 1978, vs. Pittsburgh at the Civic Arena (assist)
3. Doug Gilmour, March 3, 1993, vs. Minnesota at Maple Leaf Gardens (assist)
4. Doug Gilmour, March 23, 1994, vs. Florida at the Miami Arena (goal)

By Position

Centre	Doug Gilmour	127
	Darryl Sittler	117
Left Wing	Dave Andreychuk	99
	Vincent Damphousse	94
Right Wing	Wilf Paiement	97
	Gary Leeman	95
Defence	Ian Turnbull	79
	Borje Salming	78

Most Point-Scoring Games in a Row

18	Darryl Sittler, January 26–March 8, 1978
	Ed Olczyk, December 2–January 8, 1989–90

Most Goal-Scoring Games in a Row

10	Babe Dye, January 17–February 19, 1921
	John Anderson, March 18–April 7, 1985

Most Games in a Row with an Assist

12	Norm Ullman, December 12–January 6, 1970–71

Most Goals, Season

Rick Vaive (1981–82)	54
Dave Andreychuk (1992–93)	54*
Dave Andreychuk (1993–94)	53
Rick Vaive (1983–84)	52
Rick Vaive (1982–83)	51
Gary Leeman (1989–90)	51

* includes 29 with Buffalo

50th Goal, Season

On six occasions Leafs have scored 50 goals or more in a season:

1. Rick Vaive, March 24, 1982, vs. St. Louis (Mike Liut) at Maple Leaf Gardens
2. Rick Vaive, March 30, 1983, vs. Detroit (Gilles Gilbert) at Joe Louis Arena
3. Rick Vaive, March 14, 1984, vs. Minnesota (Gilles Meloche) at Maple Leaf Gardens
4. Gary Leeman, March 28, 1990, vs. Islanders (Mark Fitzpatrick) at Maple Leaf Gardens
5. Dave Andreychuk, March 23, 1993, vs. Winnipeg (Bob Essensa) at the Arena
6. Dave Andreychuk, March 24, 1994, vs. San Jose (Arturs Irbe) at Maple Leaf Gardens

By Position

Centre	Darryl Sittler	45
	Darryl Sittler	43
Left Wing	Dave Andreychuk	54*
	Dave Andreychuk	53

* includes 29 with Buffalo

Right Wing	Rick Vaive	54
	Rick Vaive	52
Defence	Al Iafrate	22
	Ian Turnbull	22

Most Assists, Season

Doug Gilmour (1992–93)	95
Doug Gilmour (1993–94)	84
Darryl Sittler (1977–78)	72
Borje Salming (1976–77)	66

By Position

Centre	Doug Gilmour	95
	Doug Gilmour	84
Left Wing	Vincent Damphousse	61
	Vincent Damphousse	47
Right Wing	Wilf Paiement	57
	Lanny McDonald	56
Defence	Borje Salming	66
	Borje Salming	61

Most Penalty Minutes, Season

Tiger Williams (1977–78)	351
Tiger Williams (1976–77)	338
Brian Curran (1989–90)	301

By Position

Centre	Laurie Boschman	178
	Laurie Boschman	150
Left Wing	Tiger Williams	351
	Tiger Williams	338
Right Wing	Tie Domi	297
	John Kordic	252
Defence	Brian Curran	301
	Bob McGill	263

All-Time Goalie Records, Regular Season

Most Shutouts, Career

Turk Broda	62
Harry Lumley	34
Lorne Chabot	33
Johnny Bower	33

Most Wins, Career

Turk Broda	302
Johnny Bower	220
Felix Potvin	131
Mike Palmateer	126

Most Losses, Career

Turk Broda	224
Johnny Bower	161
Felix Potvin	114

Best Goals Against Average, Career
(*minumum 100 games*)

Al Rollins	2.05
Lorne Chabot	2.20
Harry Lumley	2.21

Most Games, Career

Turk Broda	629
Johnny Bower	472
Felix Potvin	297
Mike Palmateer	296

Most Games, Season

Felix Potvin (1996–97)	74
Harry Lumley (1952–53)	70
Ed Chadwick (1956–57)	70
Ed Chadwick (1957–58)	70

Most Wins, Season

Curtis Joseph (1999–2000)	36
Curtis Joseph (1998–99)	35
Johnny Bower (1959–60)	34
Mike Palmateer (1977–78)	34
Felix Potvin (1993–94)	34

Most Losses, Season

Ed Chadwick (1957–58)	38
Felix Potvin (1996–97)	36
Ken Wregget (1987–88)	35

Most Shutouts, Season

Harry Lumley (1953–54)	13
Lorne Chabot (1928–29)	12
Harry Lumley (1952–53)	10

Best Goals Against Average, Season

(minimum 40 games or half a season)

Lorne Chabot (1928–29)	1.64
Al Rollins (1950–51)	1.77
Harry Lumley (1953–54)	1.86
Jacques Plante (1970–71)	1.88
Harry Lumley (1954–55)	1.94
John Roach (1927–28)	1.96

Most Consecutive Shutouts, Regular Season

Three Games	Lorne Chabot
	November 13, 15, 18, 1930

Most Assists, Goalie, Career

Mike Palmateer	16
Ken Wregget	10
Curtis Joseph	7

Most Assists, Goalie, Season

Curtis Joseph (1998–99)	5
Mike Palmateer (1978–79)	5
Ken Wregget (1987–88)	5

Most Penalty Minutes, Goalie, Career

Mike Palmateer	95
Ken Wregget	86
Terry Sawchuk	38
Johnny Bower	36
Curtis Joseph	28

Most Penalty Minutes, Goalie, Season

Ken Wregget (1987–88)	40
Mike Palmateer (1983–84)	28

Most Minutes Played, Career

Turk Broda	38,168
Johnny Bower	27,396
Felix Potvin	17,298

Most Minutes Played, Season

Felix Potvin (1996–97)	4,271
Harry Lumley (1952–53)	4,200
Ed Chadwick (1956–57)	4,200
Ed Chadwick (1957–58)	4,200

Goalie Win Records, Most 20+ and 30+ Seasons

Most 20+ Win Seasons

10	Turk Broda

Most Consecutive 20+ Win Seasons

5	Johnny Bower (1959–64)

Most 30+ Win Seasons

3	Turk Broda
	Johnny Bower
	Curtis Joseph

Most Consecutive 30+ Win Seasons

3	Johnny Bower (1959–62)
	Curtis Joseph (1998–2001)

Leafs All-Time Records, Game and Period

Most Points Individual
Game
10*   Darryl Sittler, February 7, 1976
        (6 goals, 4 assists)
        Boston 4 at Toronto 11
7   Darryl Sittler, October 14, 1978
        (3 goals, 4 assists)
        Islanders 7 at Toronto 10

* NHL record

Period
5   Darryl Sittler, 2nd period,
        February 7, 1976
        Boston 4 at Toronto 11

4   Charlie Conacher, 3rd period,
        March 19, 1932
        Chicago 3 at Toronto 11
        Mickey Roach, 2nd period,
        March 6, 1920
        Bulldogs 2 at Toronto 11
        Busher Jackson, 3rd period,
        November 20, 1934
        Toronto 5 at St. Louis 2
        Harry Watson, 2nd period,
        December 6, 1947
        Chicago 5 at Toronto 12
        Wendel Clark, 2nd period,
        November 9, 1996
        Edmonton 3 at Toronto 7

Most Goals Individual, Period
4*   Mickey Roach, 2nd period,
        March 6, 1920
        Bulldogs 2 at Toronto 11

        Busher Jackson, 3rd period,
        November 20, 1934
        Toronto 5 at St. Louis 2
* NHL record (tied with 7 others)

Most Assists Individual
Game
6   Babe Pratt, January 8, 1944
        Boston 3 at Toronto 12
        Doug Gilmour, February 13,
        1993
        Minnesota 1 at Toronto 6

Period
3   Charlie Conacher, 3rd period
        March 19, 1932
        Chicago 3 at Toronto 11
        Pete Langelle, 1st period,
        November 30, 1940
        Americans 1 at Toronto 6
        Babe Pratt, 3rd period,
        December 17, 1942
        Toronto 8 at Canadiens 14
        Mel Hill, 1st period,
        January 9, 1945
        Rangers 5 at Toronto 4
        Brian Cullen, 3rd period
        January 25, 1958
        Rangers 1 at Toronto 7
        Matts Sundin, 1st period,
        November 10, 1995
        Washington 1 at Toronto 6

Most Points, Game, Defenceman
6   Babe Pratt, January 8, 1944
        (6 assists)
        Boston 3 at Toronto 12
5   Hap Day, November 19, 1929
        (4 goals, 1 assist)
        Toronto 5 at Pirates 10
        Ian Turnbull, February 2, 1977
        (5 goals)
        Detroit 1 at Toronto 9

Most Goals, Game, Defenceman

5*   Ian Turnbull, February 2, 1977
      Detroit 1 at Toronto 9
4   Hap Day, November 19, 1929
      Toronto 5 at Pirates 10
      Harry Cameron, December 26,
      1917
      Canadiens 5 at Arenas 7
* NHL record

Most Assists, Game, Defenceman

6*   Babe Pratt, January 8, 1944
      Boston 3 at Toronto 12
* NHL record (tied with 5 others)

Most Goals, Team, Period

7   3rd period, February 13, 1960
      Detroit 1 at Toronto 7

Overtime Records, Regular Season

YEAR	GP	W	L	T					
1917–18	1	0	1	0	1939–40	9	1	2	6
1918–19	2	0	2	0	1940–41	9	3	0	6
1919–20	0	0	0	0	1941–42	8	2	3	3
1920–21	3	2	1	0	**Totals**	**174**	**33**	**33**	**108**
1921–22	1	0	0	1	1983–84	13	1	3	9
1922–23	4	3	0	1	1984–85	15	5	2	8
1923–24	0.	0	0	0	1985–86	17	4	6	7
1924–25	0	0	0	0	1986–87	13	3	4	6
1925–26	5	0	2	3	1987–88	13	1	2	10
1926–27	8	1	2	5	1988–89	11	1	4	6
1927–28	12	1	3	8	1989–90	11	3	4	4
1928–29	8	0	3	5	1990–91	16	3	2	11
1929–30	11	2	3	6	1991–92	11	4	0	7
1930–31	9	0	0	9	1992–93	13	1	1	11
1931–32	14	4	3	7	1993–94	17	4	1	12
1932–33	7	1	0	6	1994–95	8	0	0	8
1933–34	13	2	2	9	1995–96	18	4	2	12
1934–35	8	3	1	4	1996–97	9	0	1	8
1935–36	12	4	2	6	1997–98	10	1	0	9
1936–37	9	2	2	5	1998–99	14	6	1	7
1937–38	10	1	0	9	1999–00	17	7	3	7
1938–39	11	1	1	9	2000–01	19	3	5	11
					Totals	**245**	**51**	**41**	**153**

Most Overtime Goals, Career

Mats Sundin	7
Wendel Clark	6
Charlie Conacher	5
Harvey Jackson	5
Ace Bailey	4
Nick Metz	4
Steve Thomas	4

Most Goals in Overtime, One Game

3*   Ken Doraty, January 16, 1934
     Toronto 7 at Ottawa 4
2   Harold Cotton, December 14, 1929
     Rangers 6 at Toronto 7
* NHL record

Fastest Goal from Start of Overtime Period

6 seconds*	Mats Sundin
	December 30, 1995
9 seconds	Hank Goldup
	February 10, 1940
18 seconds	Wendel Clark
	February 5, 1992

* NHL record

Leafs Rookie Records, Regular Season

Most Points, Season, Rookie

74   Nikolai Borschevsky (1992–93)*
66   Peter Ihnacak (1982–83)
62   Gus Bodnar (1943–44)
* because of his age (27), Borschevsky was not considered a rookie by the NHL. This total, however, represents his first year in the league.

Most Goals, Season, Rookie

34   Wendel Clark (1985–86)
     Nikolai Borschevsky (1992–93)
31   Daniel Marois (1988–89)

Most Assists, Season, Rookie

40   Gus Bodnar (1943–44)
     Nikolai Borschevsky (1992–93)
38   Peter Ihnacak (1982–83)

Most Penalty Minutes, Season, Rookie

253   Bob McGill (1981–82)
227   Wendel Clark (1985–86)

Most Points, Rookie, Game

5   Howie Meeker, January 8, 1947
     Chicago 4 at Toronto 10

Most Goals, Rookie, Game

5*   Howie Meeker, January 8, 1947
     Chicago 4 at Toronto 10
4   Red Heron, March 14, 1940
     Toronto 8 at Canadiens 4
     Hank Goldup, November 30, 1940
     Americans 1 at Toronto 6
* NHL record

Most Assists, Rookie, Game

4   Pat Boutette, February 25, 1976
     Detroit 0 at Toronto 8
     Dan Daoust, January 2, 1983
     Detroit 3 at Toronto 6

Most Successful Leaf Debuts in the NHL

(rookies who have registered a point in their first game as a Leaf)

Gus Bodnar	2 goals, 1 assist*
Gaye Stewart	2 goals, 1 assist
Jack McLean	1 goal, 2 assists
Joe Matte	2 goals
Shep Mayer	2 goals
George Boothman	1 goal, 1 assist
Wally Boyer	1 goal, 1 assist**
Brad Selwood	1 goal, 1 assist
Ron Wilson	1 goal, 1 assist
Lanny McDonald	2 assists
Charlie Sands	2 assists
Gary Aldcorn	1 goal
Claire Alexander	1 goal
Red Armstrong	1 goal+
Andy Blair	1 goal
Garth Boesch	1 goal
Red Carr	1 goal
Charlie Conacher	1 goal
Les Costello	1 goal%
Daryl Evans	1 goal
Bob Gracie	1 goal
Rolly Huard	1 goal++
Miroslav Ihnacak	1 goal
Mark Kirton	1 goal
Les Kozak	1 goal
Daniel Marois	1 goal
Don Metz	1 goal
David Sacco	1 goal
Don Webster	1 goal
Leo Boivin	1 assist
Laurie Boschman	1 assist

Bill Burega	1 assist
Wayne Carleton	1 assist
Murph Chamberlain	1 assist
Jack Church	1 assist
Marty Dallman	1 assist
Vincent Damphousse	1 assist
Frank Dunlap	1 assist
Kelly Fairchild	1 assist
Ernie Godden	1 assist
Ted Hampson	1 assist
Dan Hodgson	1 assist
Greg Hotham	1 assist
Ron Hurst	1 assist
Peter Ihnacak	1 assist
Mike Johnson	1 assist
Rick Kehoe	1 assist
Ted Kennedy	1 assist
Kent Manderville	1 assist
Danny Markov	1 assist
Johnny McCormack	1 assist
Bob McGill	1 assist
Moe Morris	1 assist
Ken Murray	1 assist
Fred Perlini	1 assist
Bud Poile	1 assist
Rod Seiling	1 assist
Harry Taylor	1 assist

* scored his first goal after just 15 seconds, an NHL record
** short-handed goal
\+ scored his first goal after just 25 seconds
\++ scored in his only career NHL game
% playoff game

Power-Play, Short-Handed, and Empty-Net Goal Records

Most Power-Play Goals, Career, Individual

Because penalty times were not accurately and consistently recorded prior to 1932–33, power-play and short-handed goals cannot be calculated before then.

Darryl Sittler	120
Rick Vaive	90
Wendel Clark	75
Dave Keon	65

Most Power-Play Goals, Individual, Season

21	Dave Andreychuk	(1993–94)
	Wendel Clark	(1993–94)
18	Rick Vaive	(1982–83)
17	Darryl Sittler	(1979–80)
	Rick Vaive	(1983–84)
16	Lanny McDonald	(1976–77)
	Lanny McDonald	(1978–79)

Most Short-Handed Goals, Career, Individual

Dave Keon	30
Bob Pulford	27
Gaye Stewart	15
Greg Terrion	13
Dave Reid	13
Russ Courtnall	13

Most Short-Handed Goals, Individual, Season

8	Dave Keon	(1970–71)
	Dave Reid	(1990–91)
6	Dave Keon	(1968–69)
	Russ Courtnall	(1986–87)
	Mats Sundin	(1995–96)

Empty-Net Goals, All-Time Leaders, Regular Season

Dave Keon	9
Bob Pulford	7

Hat Trick Records

Most Hat Tricks, Career

Darryl Sittler	18
Charlie Conacher	14
Babe Dye	12
Rick Vaive	10

Most Hat Tricks, Season

Darryl Sittler (1980–81)	5
Rick Vaive (1983–84)	4
Babe Dye (1922–23)	4

Consecutive Hat Tricks

Only five times has a Leaf scored three goals in two consecutive games:

1. Charlie Conacher, March 19 and 21, 1931, vs. Chicago and Ottawa
2. Lanny McDonald, March 31 and April 1, 1979, vs. Minnesota and Buffalo
3. Darryl Sittler, March 2 and 5, 1980, vs. Detroit and Pittsburgh
4. Darryl Sittler, October 25 and 26, 1980, vs. Los Angeles and Vancouver
5. Wendel Clark, February 28 and March 4, 1994, vs. Ottawa and Detroit

Darryl Sittler	6
Rick Vaive	6
Bill Derlago	6
Mark Osborne	5
Mats Sundin	5

Two Empty-Net Goals in One Game

Bill Derlago is the only Leaf to score two empty-net goals in one game, February 4, 1984, vs. Detroit. He scored at 19:09 and then again at 19:52 of the 3rd period. Final score, Toronto 6 at Detroit 3. On only two other occasions has the team scored two empty-net goals in one game:

1. October 8, 1983
   Toronto 6 at Los Angeles 3
   Greg Terrion   19:10
   Rick Vaive   19:50
2. January 27, 1988
   Los Angeles 2 at Toronto 5
   Mark Osborne   19:04
   Gary Leeman   19:44

Three Hat Tricks in One Game, Team

On only one occasion has Toronto ever had three players score three goals each in the same game:

1. December 22, 1917
   Corb Dennenay, Reg Noble, and Harry Meeking.

Two Hat Tricks in One Game, Team

On eight occasions, two Leafs players have scored three goals in the same game:

1. March 21, 1931
   Ace Bailey (4 goals) and Charlie Conacher
2. January 30, 1937
   Gord Drillon and Harvey Jackson
3. February 19, 1944
   Jack Hamilton and Bud Poile
4. October 29, 1944
   Lorne Carr and Sweeney Schriner
5. March 2, 1946
   Syl Apps (4 goals) and Sweeney Schriner
6. December 6, 1947
   Max Bentley and Harry Watson
7. March 16, 1957
   Brian Cullen and Sid Smith
8. December 18, 1965
   Dave Keon and Bob Pulford

Records and Breakdown of All 20-, 30-, 40-, and 50-Goal Seasons, Individual

(number of games it took each player to reach each milestone)
r = rookie season

Jack Adams

1924–25	27 games to score 20 goals
1925–26	33 games to score 20 goals

Glenn Anderson

1991–92	64 games to score 20 goals
1992–93	63 games to score 20 goals

John Anderson

1979–80	58 games to score 20 goals
1981–82	31 games to score 20 goals
	61 games to score 30 goals
1982–83	57 games to score 20 goals
	78 games to score 30 goals
1983–84	32 games to score 20 goals
	55 games to score 30 goals
1984–85	66 games to score 20 goals
	73 games to score 30 goals

Dave Andreychuk

1992–93	19 games to score 20 goals*
	53 games to score 30 goals**
	63 games to score 40 goals**
	72 games to score 50 goals**
1993–94	27 games to score 20 goals
	37 games to score 30 goals
	51 games to score 40 goals
	74 games to score 50 goals
1994–95	45 games to score 20 goals
1995–96	61 games to score 20 goals

* acquired mid-season (total is for Leaf goals only)
** includes 29 goals in 52 games with Buffalo

Syl Apps

1937–38	41 games to score 20 goals
1940–41	39 games to score 20 goals
1942–43	27 games to score 20 goals
1945–46	33 games to score 20 goals
1946–47	46 games to score 20 goals
1947–48	49 games to score 20 goals

George Armstrong

1958–59	57 games to score 20 goals
1959–60	65 games to score 20 goals
1961–62	61 games to score 20 goals
1963–64	65 games to score 20 goals

Ace Bailey

1928–29	37 games to score 20 goals
1929–30	41 games to score 20 goals
1930–31	40 games to score 20 goals

Max Bentley

1947–48r	37 games to score 20 goals
1949–50	59 games to score 20 goals
1950–51	62 games to score 20 goals
1951–52	51 games to score 20 goals

Sergei Berezin

1996–97r	59 games to score 20 goals
1998–99	46 games to score 20 goals
	69 games to score 30 goals
1999–2000	52 games to score 20 goals
2000–01	64 games to score 20 goals

Gus Bodnar

1943–44r	47 games to score 20 goals

Nikolai Borschevsky

1992–93r	43 games to score 20 goals
	69 games to score 30 goals

Lorne Carr

1942–43	28 games to score 20 goals
1943–44	28 games to score 20 goals
	44 games to score 30 goals
1944–45	42 games to score 20 goals

Bill Carson

1927–28	31 games to score 20 goals

Wendel Clark

1985–86r	42 games to score 20 goals
	54 games to score 30 goals

1986–87	38 games to score 20 goals
	69 games to score 30 goals
1993–94	20 games to score 20 goals
	42 games to score 30 goals
	56 games to score 40 goals
1996–97	44 games to score 20 goals
	65 games to score 30 goals

Charlie Conacher

1929–30r	35 games to score 20 goals
1930–31	29 games to score 20 goals
	37 games to score 30 goals
1931–32	24 games to score 20 goals
	40 games to score 30 goals
1933–34	25 games to score 20 goals
	36 games to score 30 goals
1934–35	35 games to score 20 goals
	44 games to score 30 goals
1935–36	39 games to score 20 goals

Baldy Cotton

| 1929–30 | 38 games to score 20 goals |

Russ Courtnall

1985–86	61 games to score 20 goals
1986–87	57 games to score 20 goals
1987–88	40 games to score 20 goals

Brian Cullen

| 1957–58 | 57 games to score 20 goals |

Vincent Damphousse

1986–87r	76 games to score 20 goals
1988–89	60 games to score 20 goals
1989–90	63 games to score 20 goals
	72 games to score 30 goals
1990–91	64 games to score 20 goals

Corb Dennenay

| 1917–18 | 19 games to score 20 goals |
| 1919–20 | 18 games to score 20 goals |

Gord Drillon

1937–38	41 games to score 20 goals
	48 games to score 30 goals
1939–40	43 games to score 20 goals
1940–41	40 games to score 20 goals
1941–42	36 games to score 20 goals

Dick Duff

1956–57	50 games to score 20 goals
1957–58	53 games to score 20 goals
1958–59	51 games to score 20 goals

Babe Dye

1920–21	13 games to score 20 goals
	19 games to score 30 goals
1921–22	17 games to score 20 goals
	24 games to score 30 goals
1922–23	14 games to score 20 goals
1924–25	15 games to score 20 goals
	23 games to score 30 goals

Ron Ellis

1964–65r	59 games to score 20 goals
1966–67	60 games to score 20 goals
1967–68	61 games to score 20 goals
1968–69	61 games to score 20 goals
1969–70	43 games to score 20 goals
	66 games to score 30 goals
1970–71	50 games to score 20 goals
1971–72	74 games to score 20 goals
1972–73	57 games to score 20 goals
1973–74	58 games to score 20 goals
1974–75	49 games to score 20 goals
	73 games to score 30 goals
1977–78	57 games to score 20 goals

Tom Fergus

1985–86	47 games to score 20 goals
1986–87	44 games to score 20 goals
1988–89	66 games to score 20 goals

Lou Franceschetti

| 1989–90 | 59 games to score 20 goals |

Miroslav Frycer

1982–83	54 games to score 20 goals
1984–85	46 games to score 20 goals
1985–86	48 games to score 20 goals

Cal Gardner

| 1950–51 | 51 games to score 20 goals |

Doug Gilmour

1992–93	54 games to score 20 goals
	74 games to score 30 goals
1993–94	54 games to score 20 goals
1995–96	57 games to score 20 goals
	76 games to score 30 goals

Jack Hamilton

1943–44	39 games to score 20 goals

Inge Hammarstrom

1973–74r	64 games to score 20 goals
1974–75	59 games to score 20 goals
1976–77	58 games to score 20 goals

Billy Harris

1958–59	52 games to score 20 goals

Paul Henderson

1968–69	51 games to score 20 goals
1969–70	62 games to score 20 goals
1970–71	48 games to score 20 goals
1971–72	34 games to score 20 goals
	60 games to score 30 goals
1973–74	51 games to score 20 goals

Pat Hickey

1978–80	42 games to score 20 goals

Jonas Hoglund

1999–2000	42 games to score 20 goals
2000–01	64 games to score 20 goals

Al Iafrate

1987–88	58 games to score 20 goals
1989–90	73 games to score 20 goals

Peter Ihnacak

1982–83r	56 games to score 20 goals
1984–85	48 games to score 20 goals

Harvey Jackson

1931–32	35 games to score 20 goals
1932–33	37 games to score 20 goals
1933–34	38 games to score 20 goals
1934–35	33 games to score 20 goals
1936–37	40 games to score 20 goals

Mike Johnson

1998–99	65 games to score 20 goals

Red Kelly

1960–61	60 games to score 20 goals
1961–62	49 games to score 20 goals
1962–63	65 games to score 20 goals

Ted Kennedy

1943–44	38 games to score 20 goals
1944–45	35 games to score 20 goals
1946–47	40 games to score 20 goals
1947–48	50 games to score 20 goals
1949–50	52 games to score 20 goals

Dave Keon

1960–61r	68 games to score 20 goals
1961–62	45 games to score 20 goals
1962–63	48 games to score 20 goals
1963–64	67 games to score 20 goals
1964–65	61 games to score 20 goals
1965–66	54 games to score 20 goals
1968–69	53 games to score 20 goals
1969–70	40 games to score 20 goals
	60 games to score 30 goals
1970–71	37 games to score 20 goals
	58 games to score 30 goals
1972–73	46 games to score 20 goals
	64 games to score 30 goals
1973–74	58 games to score 20 goals

Derek King

1997–98	76 games to score 20 goals
1998–99	64 games to score 30 goals

Igor Korolev

1999–2000	79 games to score 20 goals

Gary Leeman

1986–87	73 games to score 20 goals
1987–88	48 games to score 20 goals
	80 games to score 30 goals
1988–89	42 games to score 20 goals
	55 games to score 30 goals
1989–90	37 games to score 20 goals
	49 games to score 30 goals
	61 games to score 40 goals
	78 games to score 50 goals

Billy MacMillan

1970–71r   66 games to score 20 goals

Frank Mahovlich

1957–58	53 games to score 20 goals
1958–59	60 games to score 20 goals
1960–61	26 games to score 20 goals
	33 games to score 30 goals
	48 games to score 40 goals
1961–62	38 games to score 20 goals
	58 games to score 30 goals
1962–63	31 games to score 20 goals
	56 games to score 30 goals
1963–64	50 games to score 20 goals
1964–65	50 games to score 20 goals
1965–66	43 games to score 20 goals
	62 games to score 30 goals

Dan Maloney

1980–81   60 games to score 20 goals

Daniel Marois

1988–89r	54 games to score 20 goals
	73 games to score 30 goals
1989–90	34 games to score 20 goals
	54 games to score 30 goals
1990–91	67 games to score 20 goals

Terry Martin

1980–81	65 games to score 20 goals
1981–82	45 games to score 20 goals

Lanny McDonald

1975–76	41 games to score 20 goals
	57 games to score 30 goals
1976–77	26 games to score 20 goals
	49 games to score 30 goals
	70 games to score 40 goals
1977–78	26 games to score 20 goals
	42 games to score 30 goals
	61 games to score 40 goals
1978–79	48 games to score 20 goals
	61 games to score 30 goals
	76 games to score 40 goals

Walt McKechnie

1978–79   55 games to score 20 goals

Howie Meeker

1946–47r   40 games to score 20 goals

Nick Metz

1944–45   43 games to score 20 goals

Kirk Muller

1996–97   63 games to score 20 goals

Bob Nevin

1960–61   67 games to score 20 goals

Reg Noble

1917–18	13 games to score 20 goals
1919–20	19 games to score 20 goals
1920–21	24 games to score 20 goals

Ed Olczyk

1987–88	44 games to score 20 goals
	60 games to score 30 goals
	78 games to score 40 goals
1988–89	38 games to score 20 goals
	65 games to score 30 goals
1989–90	43 games to score 20 goals
	70 games to score 30 goals

Mark Osborne

1987–88	64 games to score 20 goals
1989–90	62 games to score 20 goals

Wilf Paiement

1979–80	37 games to score 20 goals*
	71 games to score 30 goals**
1980–81	45 games to score 20 goals
	59 games to score 30 goals
	80 games to score 40 goals

* acquired mid-season (total is for Leafs goals only)

** includes 10 goals in 34 games with Rockies

Jim Pappin

1966–67   63 games to score 20 goals

Yanic Perreault

2000–01   60 games to score 20 goals

Rob Pearson

1992–93   69 games to score 20 goals

Walt Poddubny

1982–83	44 games to score 20 goals

Bob Pulford

1958–59	61 games to score 20 goals
1959–60	54 games to score 20 goals
1965–66	40 games to score 20 goals
1967–68	74 games to score 20 goals

Gary Roberts

2000–01	55 games to score 20 goals

Rocky Saganiuk

1979–80	66 games to score 20 goals

Sweeney Schriner

1940–41	36 games to score 20 goals
1941–42	47 games to score 20 goals
1944–45	24 games to score 20 goals

Eddie Shack

1965–66	42 games to score 20 goals

Darryl Sittler

1972–73	59 games to score 20 goals
1973–74	42 games to score 20 goals
	57 games to score 30 goals
1974–75	40 games to score 20 goals
	61 games to score 30 goals
1975–76	44 games to score 20 goals
	60 games to score 30 goals
	75 games to score 40 goals
1976–77	47 games to score 20 goals
	61 games to score 30 goals
1977–78	36 games to score 20 goals
	55 games to score 30 goals
	64 games to score 40 goals
1978–79	41 games to score 20 goals
	56 games to score 30 goals
1979–80	44 games to score 20 goals
	57 games to score 30 goals
	67 games to score 40 goals
1980–81	35 games to score 20 goals
	48 games to score 30 goals
	70 games to score 40 goals

Tod Sloan

1950–51	46 games to score 20 goals
	69 games to score 30 goals

1951–52	58 games to score 20 goals
1955–56	39 games to score 20 goals
	52 games to score 30 goals

Sid Smith

1949–50	61 games to score 20 goals
1950–51	48 games to score 20 goals
	70 games to score 30 goals
1951–52	61 games to score 20 goals
1952–53	70 games to score 20 goals
1953–54	62 games to score 20 goals
1954–55	40 games to score 20 goals
	63 games to score 30 goals

Marian Stastny

1985–86	49 games to score 20 goals

Gaye Stewart

1942–43r	25 games to score 20 goals
1945–46	29 games to score 20 goals
	40 games to score 30 goals

Ron Stewart

1958–59	64 games to score 20 goals

Blaine Stoughton

1974–75	66 games to score 20 goals

Steve Sullivan

1998–99	62 games to score 20 goals

Mats Sundin

1994–95	37 games to score 20 goals
1995–96	41 games to score 20 goals
	67 games to score 30 goals
1996–97	35 games to score 20 goals
	54 games to score 30 goals
	79 games to score 40 goals
1997–98	44 games to score 20 goals
	76 games to score 30 goals
1998–99	56 games to score 20 goals
	80 games to score 30 goals
1999–2000	35 games to score 20 goals
	62 games to score 30 goals
2000–01	60 games to score 20 goals

Billy Taylor

1945–46	47 games to score 20 goals

Steve Thomas

1985–86	63 games to score 20 goals
1986–87	44 games to score 20 goals
	68 games to score 30 goals
1998–99	50 games to score 20 goals
1999–2000	68 games to score 20 goals

Errol Thompson

1974–75	54 games to score 20 goals
1975–76	44 games to score 20 goals
	57 games to score 30 goals
	69 games to score 40 goals
1976–77	33 games to score 20 goals

Bill Thoms

1935–36	43 games to score 20 goals

Ian Turnbull

1975–76	71 games to score 20 goals
1976–77	61 games to score 20 goals

Norm Ullman

1968–69	35 games to score 20 goals
	63 games to score 30 goals
1970–71	35 games to score 20 goals
	67 games to score 30 goals
1971–72	64 games to score 20 goals
1972–73	65 games to score 20 goals
1973–74	62 games to score 20 goals

Rick Vaive

1980–81	39 games to score 20 goals
	72 games to score 30 goals
1981–82	30 games to score 20 goals
	43 games to score 30 goals
	61 games to score 40 goals
	72 games to score 50 goals

1982–83	34 games to score 20 goals
	44 games to score 30 goals
	56 games to score 40 goals
	76 games to score 50 goals
1983–84	27 games to score 20 goals
	36 games to score 30 goals
	49 games to score 40 goals
	69 games to score 50 goals
1984–85	41 games to score 20 goals
	64 games to score 30 goals
1985–86	40 games to score 20 goals
	54 games to score 30 goals
1986–87	55 games to score 20 goals
	64 games to score 30 goals

Mike Walton

1967–68	36 games to score 20 goals
	71 games to score 30 goals
1968–69	59 games to score 20 goals
1969–70	54 games to score 20 goals

Harry Watson

1947–48	56 games to score 20 goals
1948–49	49 games to score 20 goals
1951–52	55 games to score 20 goals
1953–54	59 games to score 20 goals

Tiger Williams

1975–76	75 games to score 20 goals
1979–80	47 games to score 20 goals

Cully Wilson

1919–20	23 games to score 20 goals

Fastest to Reach 20 Goals

13 games	Reg Noble (1917–18)
	Babe Dye (1920–21)
14 games	Babe Dye (1922–23)
15 games	Babe Dye (1924–25)
17 games	Babe Dye (1921–22)
18 games	Corb Dennenay (1917–18)
19 games	Corb Dennenay (1919–20)
	Reg Noble (1919–20)
	Dave Andreychuk (1992–93)*
20 games	Wendel Clark (1993–94)

* Leaf goals only (acquired mid-season)

Fastest to Reach 30 Goals

19 games	Babe Dye (1920–21)
23 games	Babe Dye (1924–25)
24 games	Babe Dye (1921–22)
33 games	Frank Mahovlich (1960–61)
36 games	Rick Vaive (1983–84)

Fastest to Reach 40 Goals

48 games	Frank Mahovlich (1960–61)
49 games	Rick Vaive (1983–84)

Fastest to Reach 50 Goals

69 games	Rick Vaive (1983–84)
72 games	Rick Vaive (1981–82)
	Dave Andreychuk (1992–93)*

* includes 29 goals in 52 games with Buffalo

Most 20+ Goal Seasons

11	Ron Ellis
	Dave Keon
9	Darryl Sittler

Most Consecutive 20+ Goal Seasons

9	Ron Ellis (1966–75)
	Darryl Sittler (1972–81)
7	Rick Vaive (1980–87)
	Mats Sundin (1994–2001)

Most 30+ Goal Seasons

8	Darryl Sittler
7	Rick Vaive

Most Consecutive 30+ Goal Seasons

8	Darryl Sittler (1973–81)
7	Rick Vaive (1980–87)

Most 40+ Goal Seasons

4	Lanny McDonald
3	Darryl Sittler
	Rick Vaive

Most Consecutive 40+ Goal Seasons

3	Lanny McDonald (1976–79)
	Rick Vaive (1981–84)

Most 50+ Goal Seasons

3	Rick Vaive
2	Dave Andreychuk
1	Gary Leeman

Most Consecutive 50+ Goal Seasons

3	Rick Vaive (1981–84)
2	Dave Andreychuk (1992–94)

Wendel Clark

Penalty Shot Records

Scoring Summary

G=Goals; M=Misses; Sh=Shots

	G	M	Sh
Greg Terrion	2	0	2
Lanny McDonald	2	1	3
Syl Apps	1	0	1
Bill Barilko	1	0	1
King Clancy	1	0	1
Wendel Clark	1	0	1
Bob Goldham	1	0	1
Jack Hamilton	1	0	1
Red Kelly	1	0	1
Derek King	1	0	1
Frank Mahovlich	1	0	1
Bud Poile	1	0	1
Sweeney Schriner	1	0	1
Billy Taylor	1	0	1
Rick Vaive	1	0	1
Dave Keon	1	1	2
Mats Sundin	1	1	2
Mike Walton	1	1	2
Charlie Conacher	1	3	4
Kevyn Adams	0	1	1
Dave Andreychuk	0	1	1
Max Bentley	0	1	1
Dan Daoust	0	1	1
Gord Drillon	0	1	1
Paul Henderson	0	2	2
Joe Klukay	0	1	1
Tom Kurvers	0	1	1
Gary Leeman	0	1	1
Dan Maloney	0	1	1
Terry Martin	0	1	1
Don McKenney	0	1	1
Wayne Presley	0	1	1
Bob Pulford	0	1	1
Tod Sloan	0	1	1
Pete Stemkowski	0	1	1
Ron Stewart	0	1	1
Steve Sullivan	0	1	1
Norm Ullman	0	1	1
Peter Zezel	0	1	1

Leaf Goalies' Record, Penalty Shots

Sa=Saves; GA=Goals Allowed; Sh=Shots faced

	Sa	GA	Sh
George Hainsworth	7	2	9
Allan Bester	5	0	5
Mike Palmateer	3	1	4
Felix Potvin	2	0	2
Jeff Reese	2	0	2
Damian Rhodes	2	0	2
Turk Broda	2	1	3
Curtis Joseph	2	1	3
Johnny Bower	2	2	4
Bernie Parent	2	1	3
Ken Wregget	2	1	3
Don Edwards	1	0	1
Peter Ing	1	0	1
Bunny Larocque	1	0	1
Harry Lumley	1	0	1
Frank McCool	1	0	1
Rick St. Croix	1	0	1
Grant Fuhr	1	1	2
Tim Bernhardt	0	1	1
Paul Harrison	0	1	1
Don Simmons	0	1	1
Rick Wamsley	0	1	1
Dunc Wilson	0	1	1
Gord McRae	0	2	2
Terry Sawchuk	0	2	2

Only once have the Leafs played in a game in which two penalty shots were called, October 15, 1983 at the Gardens (one for, one against), one of only ten games in history with two penalty shots called. Mike Walton was the first player to take penalty shots in two consecutive games, on March 9 and 10, 1968. Greg Terrion is one of only five players to score two penalty shot goals in one season.

Speed Records, Regular Season

Fastest Goal From Start of Game

7 seconds   Charlie Conacher,
February 6, 1932,
Boston 0 at Toronto 6

8 seconds   Ted Kennedy, October 24, 1953,
Boston 3 at Toronto 2

Fastest Goal From Start of Period

7 seconds   Charlie Conacher,
February 6, 1932, 1st period,
Boston 0 at Toronto 6
Al Iafrate,
March 22, 1986, 3rd period,
New Jersey 6 at Toronto 3

Fastest Two Goals, Team

4 seconds*   Ed Olczyk (5:24) and Gary
Leeman (5:28), 3rd period,
December 29, 1988,
Toronto 6 at Quebec 5

8 seconds   Syl Apps (13:15) and Harvey
Jackson (13:23), January 23,
1937, 3rd period,
Rangers 0 at Toronto 4

* NHL record (tied with two others)

Fastest Two Goals, Individual

7 seconds   Harvey Jackson (12:50 and
12:57), February 18, 1932,
2nd period,
Rangers 3 at Toronto 5

Fastest Two Goals, Both Teams

7 seconds   March 15, 1964,
3rd period vs. Rangers
Jim Neilson (1:27 Rangers) and
Tim Horton (1:34 Toronto),
Toronto 3 at Rangers 1
October 11, 1970,
3rd period vs. Vancouver
Andre Boudrias
(9:00 Vancouver) and Norm
Ullman (9:07 Toronto),
Toronto 3 at Vancouver 5
February 25, 1992,
3rd period vs. New Jersey
Randy McKay (9:06 New Jersey)
and Peter Zezel (9:13 Toronto),
New Jersey 5 at Toronto 5

Fastest Three Goals, Team

39 seconds   January 20, 1940,
1st period vs. Americans
Sweeney Schriner (3:25), Harry
Taylor (3:52), Pep Kelly (4:04),
Americans 1 at Toronto 5

Fastest Three Goals, Individual

2:54   Lanny McDonald (8:24, 9:25,
11:18), October 16, 1976, 1st
period vs. Flyers at Maple
Leaf Gardens

3:20   Bud Poile, February 19, 1944,
3rd period vs. Boston at Maple
Leaf Gardens

Fastest Four Goals, Both Teams

53 seconds*   October 15, 1983, 2nd period
vs. Chicago Gaston Gingras
(16:49 Toronto), Denis Savard
(17:12 Chicago), Steve Larmer
(17:27 Chicago), Denis Savard
(17:42 Chicago), Chicago 8 at
Toronto 10

* NHL record

Fastest Five Goals, Both Teams

1:24*   October 15, 1983,
             2nd period vs. Chicago
             Gaston Gingras (16:49 Toronto),
             Denis Savard (17:12 Chicago),
             Steve Larmer (17:27 Chicago),
             Denis Savard (17:42 Chicago),
             John Anderson (18:13 Toronto),
             Chicago 8 at Toronto 10

* NHL record

Fastest Six Goals, Team

7:16   January 12, 1946,
             1st period vs. Detroit
             Gus Bodnar (3:17), Billy Taylor
             (5:48), Gaye Stewart (7:13),
             Syl Apps (7:46), Jack Hamilton
             (9:22), Billy Taylor (10:33),
             Detroit 3 at Toronto 9

Fastest Six Goals, Both Teams

3:15*   January 4, 1944,
             1st period vs. Canadiens
             Maurice Richard (14:10
             Canadiens), Don Webster (15:13
             Toronto), Fern Majeau (15:41
             Canadiens), Bugsy Watson
             (15:52 Canadiens), Lorne Carr
             (16:55 Toronto), Emile Bouchard
             (17:25 Canadiens), Toronto 3 at
             Canadiens 6

* NHL record

Fastest Eight Goals, Both Teams

4:51   March 19, 1938,
             3rd period vs. Americans
             Murph Chamberlain (10:47
             Toronto), Bob Davidson
             (11:22 Toronto), Nels Stewart
             (11:58 Americans), Hooley Smith
             (12:55 Americans), Murph
             Chamberlain (13:07 Toronto),
             John Sorrell (14:12 Americans),
             Buzz Boll (14:45 Toronto),
             Harvey Jackson (15:38 Toronto),
             Americans 5 at Toronto 8

Power-Play and Short-Handed Goal Records, Regular Season

Fastest Two Power-Play Goals, Team

9 seconds Baldy Cotton (2:25) and Hap Day (2:34), 3rd period, January 19, 1933. Boston 0 at Toronto 3

Fastest Two Power-Play Goals, Individual

6 seconds Howie Meeker (10:14 and 10:20), 2nd period, February 9, 1952, Canadiens 2 at Toronto 3

8 seconds Harvey Jackson (17:08 and 17:16), 3rd period, February 3, 1934, Toronto 8 at Ottawa 4

Fastest Three Power-Play Goals, Team

1:16 Howie Meeker (10:14), Howie Meeker (10:20), George Armstrong (11:30), February 9, 1952, 2nd period, Canadiens 2 at Toronto 3

Most Power-Play Goals, Team, Game

5 Tod Sloan 12:24 (1st), Ted Kennedy 10:44 (2nd), Sid Smith 13:43 (2nd), Fleming Mackell 16:54 (3rd), Bob Solinger 17:09 (3rd), December 1, 1951, Rangers 2 at Toronto 8

Most Power-Play Goals, Individual, Game

3* Ted Kennedy, February 5, 1944 Americans 1 at Toronto 3

* NHL record (tied with many others)

Most Short-Handed Goals, Team, Game

3 November 16, 1988 Dan Daoust 12:37 (1st), Ed Olczyk 5:03 (2nd), Al Iafrate 13:21 (2nd), Pittsburgh 5 at Toronto 8

Most Short-Handed Goals, Individual, Game

2 Pep Kelly, January 16, 1938, Toronto 7 at Chicago 2
Gord Drillon, January 29, 1938, Detroit 1 at Toronto 4
Gord Drillon, March 11, 1939, Detroit 1 at Toronto 5
Rudy Migay, November 6, 1954, Chicago 2 at Toronto 5
Larry Regan, October 16, 1960, Toronto 7 at Rangers 2
Bob Pulford, February 7, 1959, Detroit 1 at Toronto 4

Goal With Two Men Short

Darryl Sittler is the only Leaf ever to score while his team was two men short.

March 19, 1980
Pat Hickey penalized at 15:07 (1st), Ian Turnbull penalized at 16:20 (1st), Sittler scored at 16:59 (1st)
Winnipeg 1 at Toronto 9

Penalty Records, Regular Season

Most Penalty Minutes, Team, Game
154   November 15, 1986,
          Detroit 0 at Toronto 6

Most Penalties, Team, Game
33   November 15, 1986,
          Detroit 0 at Toronto 6

**Most Penalty Minutes,
Opponent, Game**
160   January 13, 1986,
          Detroit 4 at Toronto 7

Most Penalties, Opponent, Game
33   January 13, 1986,
          Detroit 4 at Toronto 7

**Most Penalty Minutes,
Both Teams, Game**
300   November 15, 1986,
          Detroit 0 at Toronto 6
          (Toronto 154, Detroit 146)

Most Penalties, Both Teams, Game
66   March 2, 1990
          (Toronto 36, Detroit 30)

Most Penalty Minutes, Team, Period
108   3rd period, January 13, 1986,
          Detroit 4 at Toronto 7

Most Penalties, Team, Period
18   3rd period, January 13, 1986,
          Detroit 4 at Toronto 7

**Most Penalty Minutes,
Both Teams, Period**
242   3rd period, January 13, 1986
          (Detroit 134, Toronto 108)

Most Penalties, Both Teams, Period
41   3rd period, January 13, 1986
          (Detroit 23, Toronto 18)

**Most Penalty Minutes,
Individual, Game**
48   Jim Dorey, October 16, 1968,
          Pittsburgh 2 at Toronto 2
Dorey received two minors in the first period. In the second, he received a minor (at 12:38), then another minor, two majors, two misconducts, and a game misconduct (at 18:47).

Most Penalties, Individual, Game
9   Jim Dorey, October 16, 1968

**Most Penalty Minutes,
Individual, Period**
44   Jim Dorey, October 16, 1968

Most Penalties, Individual, Period
7   Jim Dorey, October 16, 1968

Famous Lines

- THE BACON LINE: Sweeney Schriner, Gus Bodnar, Lorne Carr
- BAY STREET BULLIES: (so called for their aggressive play) Shayne Corson, Gary Roberts, Darcy Tucker
- BRAT LINE: (so called because of their abrasive play) Tiger Williams, Jack Valiquette, Pat Boutette
- CLOTHES LINE (jokingly called the PUKE LINE) (so called because of their mucking and checking qualities, just the opposite of Boston's high-scoring UKE line): Gerry James, Duke Edmundson, Johnny Wilson
- CYCLONE LINE: Bob Davidson, Art Jackson, Nick Metz
- DAD LINE: Gord Drillon, Syl Apps, Bob Davidson
- DYNAMITE LINE (so called for their explosive offense): Gord Drillon, Syl Apps, Harvey Jackson
- FLYIN' FORTS LINE ("Double F" line as called by Conn Smythe) (so called because all three were born in Fort William): Bud Poile, Gus Bodnar, Gaye Stewart
- GEM LINE: Gary Leeman, Ed Olczyk, Mark Osborne
- HEM LINE: Billy Harris, Gerry Ehman, Frank Mahovlich
- HOUND LINE (so called because all three played midget hockey for the Notre Dame Hounds in Wilcox, Saskatchewan): Wendel Clark, Gary Leeman, Russ Courtnall
- HUSKY LINE: Harry Watson, Billy Taylor, Cal Gardner
- INFANT LINE (sometimes BABY LINE) (so called because of their youth): Nick Metz, Pep Kelly, Art Jackson
- JUVENILE LINE (so called because of their youth): Dave Downie, Bob Gracie, Bill Thoms
- KID LINE (so called because of their youth; many succeeding lines were named similarly in the hope of proving to be as successful as this, the most famous of all Leaf lines): Joe Primeau, Charlie Conacher, Harvey Jackson
- (Second) KID LINE: Ted Kennedy, Howie Meeker, Vic Lynn
- KID LINE: Pete Stemkowski, Ron Ellis, Brit Selby
- KID LINE: Pete Stemkowski, Jim Pappin, Bob Pulford
- KID LINE (later called the LEFTOVER LINE): Darryl Sittler, Denis Dupere, Rick Kehoe
- KID LINE: Rocky Saganiuk, John Anderson, Laurie Boschman
- KLM LINE: Ted Kennedy, Vic Lynn, Howie Meeker
- KSS LINE: Ted Kennedy, Sid Smith, Tod Sloan
- LIFE LINE: George Armstrong, Jim Morrison, Jim Thomson George Armstrong, Tod Sloan, Dick Duff
- MAD LINE: Nick Metz, Syl Apps, Gord Drillon
- PEPPER LINE: Andy Blair, Bob Gracie, Frank Finnigan (1931–32); Andy Blair, Bob Gracie, Ken Doraty (1932–33)
- PPS LINE: Jim Pappin, Bob Pulford, Pete Stemkowski
- THE ROCKS or THE YANNIGANS (also called the CLOTHES LINE): Duke Edmundson, Gerry James, Johnny Wilson
- SAW LINE: Tod Sloan, George Armstrong, Harry Watson
- SLOAN LINE: Tod Sloan, Dick Duff, George Armstrong
- THIN LINE (so called because of their stature): Max Bentley, Joe Klukay, Ray Timgren
- THREE ACES LINE (so called because of their goal scoring): Tod Sloan, Dick Duff, George Armstrong
- THREE FEATHERS LINE (so called by Conn Smythe because all three were light-weights but tigers): Ray Timgren, Joe Klukay, Max Bentley
- WING LINE (so called because all were acquired from Detroit in the Frank Mahovlich trade): Norm Ullman, Floyd Smith, Paul Henderson
- THE WOOLWORTH LINE (so called because Metz wore #5, Kelly #15, and Jackson #20, popular prices for products on sale at Woolworth stores): Nick Metz, Pep Kelly, Art Jackson

Youngest and Oldest Leafs

Youngest to Play for the Leafs

Eric Prentice	17, 2 months, 8 days
Ted Kennedy	17, 2 months, 23 days
Ross Johnstone	17, 6 months, 23 days
Chris Speyer	17, 8 months

Oldest to Play for the Leafs

Johnny Bower	45, 1 month, 2 days
Allan Stanley	42, 30 days
Carl Brewer	41, 5 months, 4 days
George Armstrong	40, 8 months, 29 days
Don Marshall	40, 10 days

Brothers, Fathers, and Sons with the Leafs

(b)=brother (f)=father (s)=son

Blair	Chuck (b)/Dusty (b)
Clancy	King (f)/Terry (s)
Conacher	Charlie (f)/Pete (s)
Cullen	Barry (b-f)/Brian (b)/John (s)
Gardner	Cal (f)/Paul (s)
Hannigan	Gord (b)/Pat (b)/Ray (b)
Ihnacak	Miroslav (b)/Peter (b)
Imlach	Punch*(f)/Brent (s)
Jackson	Art (b)/Harvey (b)
Johnson	Bill (f)/Johansen, Trevor (s)
McRae	Basil (b)/Chris (b)
Metz	Don (b)/Nick (b)
Pratt	Babe (f)/Tracy (s)
Sabourin	Bob (b)/Gary (b)
Sacco	David (b)/Joe (b)
Yaremchuk	Gary (b)/Ken (b)

*coached but did not play

Leafs Who Became NHL Officials

R= Referee; L= Linesman

Harry Cameron (R)	Kevin Maguire (R)
King Clancy (R)	Bert McCaffery (L)
Bert Corbeau (R)	Reg Noble (R)
Hap Day (L)	Eddie Powers (R)
Art Duncan (R)	Joe Primeau (L)
Babe Dye (R)	Jesse Spring (R)
Red Horner (L)	Gaye Stewart (R)
Butch Keeling (R)	Carl Voss (R)

Toronto Players (Arenas, St. Pats, and Leafs) Who Enlisted in World War I or II

Lloyd Andrews (WWI)
Syl Apps (WWII)
Amos Arbour (WWI)
Murray Armstrong (WWII)
Doug Baldwin (WWII)
Andy Barbe (WWII)
Baz Bastien (WWII)
Gordie Bell (WWII)
Max Bentley (WWII)
Paul Bibeault (WWII)
Garth Boesch (WWII)
Turk Broda (WWII)
Arthur Brooks (WWI)
George Carey (WWI)
Lex Chisholm (WWII)
Jack Church (WWII)
Bobby Copp (WWII)
Chuck Corrigan (WWII)
Ernie Dickens (WWII)
Gord Drillon (WWII)
Art Duncan (WWI)
Frank Dunlap (WWII)
Jack Forsey (WWII)
Cal Gardner (WWII)
Bob Goldham (WWII)
Hank Goldup (WWII)
Jack Hamilton (WWII)
Sammy Hebert (WWI)
Red Heron (WWII)
Punch Imlach (WWII)
Johnny Ingoldsby (WWII)
Dick Irvin (WWI)

Stan Jackson (WWI and WWII)
James Jarvis (WWII)
Buck Jones (WWII)
Bill Juzda (WWII)
Bingo Kampman (WWII)
Bill Kendall (WWII)
Hec Kilrea (WWII)
Joe Klukay (WWII)
Pete Langelle (WWII)
Howie Lockhart (WWI)
Norm Mann (WWII)
Jean Marois (WWII)
Frank Mathers (WWII)
Shep Mayer (WWII)
Frank McCool (WWII)
John McCreedy (WWII)
Howie Meeker (WWII)
Don Metz (WWII)
Nick Metz (WWII)
Ivan Mitchell (WWI)
Gus Mortson (WWII)
Bud Poile (WWII)
Goldie Prodgers (WWI)
Sweeney Schriner (WWII)
Glenn Smith (WWI)
Conn Smythe (WWII)
Wally Stanowski (WWII)
Gaye Stewart (WWII)
Billy Taylor (WWII)
Rhys Thompson (WWII)
Harry Watson (WWII)

Leafs All-Star Game Facts

Maple Leaf Gardens has hosted eight All-Star Games and the Air Canada Centre has hosted one. The first ever played in the NHL was a benefit game for Ace Bailey, after a hit by Eddie Shore on December 12, 1933, ended Bailey's career. The game was held at the Gardens on February 9, 1934, and raised $23,000. There were two subsequent benefit games, in 1937 for Howie Morenz, and in 1939 for Babe Siebert. In 1947, the game became an annual event and the format was standardized so that the Stanley Cup champions of the previous year played the best of the rest of the league in the champions' rink (with the exception of 1948, when Chicago, in appreciation for its effort in organizing the first game, was awarded the glitter game). The last time this format was used was in 1968, the last time Toronto hosted the Game.

1.	February 14, 1934	MLG	Toronto 7	All-Stars 3
2.	October 13, 1947	MLG	All-Stars 4	Toronto 3
3.	October 10, 1949	MLG	All-Stars 3	Toronto 1
4.	October 9, 1951	MLG	1st Team 2	2nd Team 2
5.	October 6, 1962	MLG	Toronto 4	All-Stars 1
6.	October 5, 1963	MLG	Toronto 3	All-Stars 3
7.	October 10, 1964	MLG	All-Stars 3	Toronto 2
8.	January 16, 1968	MLG	Toronto 4	All-Stars 3
9.	February 6, 2000	ACC	World 9	North America 4

Most Valuable Player (began in 1962)

1962	Eddie Shack
1963	Frank Mahovlich
1968	Bruce Gamble
1991	Vincent Damphousse

Most All-Star Team Selections

6	Tim Horton (3 1st, 3 2nd)		3	Turk Broda (2 1st, 1 2nd)
	Frank Mahovlich (2 1st, 4 2nd)			Gord Drillon (2 1st, 1 2nd)
	Borje Salming (1 1st, 5 2nd)			Johnny Bower (1 1st, 2 2nd)
5	Harvey Jackson (4 1st, 1 2nd)			Sid Smith (1 1st, 2 2nd)
	Charlie Conacher (3 1st, 2 2nd)			Ted Kennedy (3 2nd)
	Syl Apps (2 1st, 3 2nd)			Allan Stanley (3 2nd)
4	King Clancy (2 1st, 2 2nd)			
	Dick Irvin, coach (4 2nd)			

All-Time Leaf Statistics for All-Star Games

Coaches

	G	W	L	T
Punch Imlach	4	2	1	1
Dick Irvin	1	1	0	0
King Clancy	1	0	0	1
Joe Primeau	1	0	0	1
Pat Quinn	1	0	1	0
Hap Day	3	0	3	0

Goalies *(ranked by average)* *(sweater numbers precede name)*

		GP	MINS	GA	W–L–T	GAA
1	Johnny Bower	4	159:43	4	2–0–0	1.50
1	George Hainsworth	1	60:00	3	1–0–0	3.00
30	Bruce Gamble	1	40:00	2	1–0–0	3.00
24	Don Simmons	1	20:00	1	0–0–1	3.00
1	Al Smith	1	20:00	1	0–0–0	3.00
9/1	Harry Lumley	2	63:09	4	0–1–0	3.75
23	Terry Sawchuk	1	30:17	3	0–1–0	5.81
1	Turk Broda	4	208:48	14	0–3–0	4.02
1	Wayne Thomas	1	30:26	4	0–0–0	7.74
29	Felix Potvin	2	40:00	4	0–0–0	6.00
31	Curtis Joseph	1	20:00	3	0–0–0	9.00

Players *(alphabetical)*

		GP	G	A	P	PIM
14	Dave Andreychuk	1	1	1	2	0
10	Syl Apps	2	2	4	6	0
2	Bob Armstrong	1	0	0	0	0
24/17/10	George Armstrong	7	0	2	2	0
19/21	Bill Barilko	3	1	0	1	0
9	Andy Bathgate	1	0	1	1	2
2/21	Bobby Baun	4	0	2	2	8
7	Max Bentley	3	1	1	2	0
5	Andy Blair	1	1	2	3	0
5	Garth Boesch	2	0	0	0	2
17	Buzz Boll	1	0	0	0	0
5	Hugh Bolton	1	0	0	0	0
2/5	Carl Brewer	3	0	0	0	4
24	Dave Burrows	1	0	0	0	0
25	Wayne Carleton	1	0	2	2	0
7	King Clancy	1	0	0	0	0
15	Wendel Clark	1	0	0	0	0
22	Brian Conacher	1	0	0	0	0
8/9	Charlie Conacher	2	1	1	2	0
15	Les Costello	1	0	1	1	0
8	Baldy Cotton	1	1	0	1	0
10	Vincent Damphousse	1	4	0	4	0

23	Bob Dawes	1	0	0	0	0
4	Hap Day	1	1	0	1	0
15	Ken Doraty	1	1	1	2	0
19	Kent Douglas	3	1	1	2	4
12	Gord Drillon	1	0	0	0	0
9/16/8/6	Dick Duff	5	1	0	1	4
8	Gerry Ehman	1	0	1	1	0
4	Dave Ellett	1	0	1	1	0
12/8/11	Ron Ellis	4	1	0	1	2
12	Bill Ezinicki	2	1	1	2	6
12	Fern Flaman	1	0	0	0	0
14	Miroslav Frycer	1	1	0	1	0
17	Cal Gardner	2	0	1	1	0
11	Mike Gartner	1	0	0	0	0
93	Doug Gilmour	2	1	1	2	0
2	Bob Goldham	1	0	0	0	0
15	Billy Harris	4	0	1	1	0
21/17	Paul Henderson	2	1	0	1	0
2/22	Larry Hillman	4	0	2	2	0
5/2	Red Horner	2	0	0	0	2
7/18	Tim Horton	7	0	0	0	10
33	Al Iafrate	2	0	0	0	2
9/11	Busher Jackson	2	2	1	3	0
18	Bill Juzda	2	0	0	0	2
4	Red Kelly	3	0	2	2	2
8/12/9	Ted Kennedy	6	0	1	1	0
14	Dave Keon	8	0	2	2	0
12	Hec Kilrea	1	1	1	2	0
8/17	Joe Klukay	3	0	0	0	0
10	Gary Leeman	1	1	1	2	0
3	Alex Levinsky	1	0	0	0	0
25	Ed Litzenberger	2	1	1	2	0
14	Vic Lynn	3	0	0	0	2
16/22	Fleming MacKell	3	0	0	0	0
8/24	John MacMillan	2	0	0	0	0
22/27/8/ 19/15	Frank Mahovlich	9	4	4	8	6
2	Bob Manno	1	0	0	0	0
20	Frank Mathers	1	0	0	0	0
9	Lanny McDonald	2	2	0	2	2
17	Don McKenney	1	0	0	0	0
18	Jim McKenny	1	0	0	0	0
11/15	Howie Meeker	3	0	0	0	2
5	Don Metz	1	0	0	0	0
16	Rudy Migay	1	0	1	1	2
3/10	Jim Morrison	3	0	1	1	2
3/19	Gus Mortson	5	0	2	2	9*
55	Larry Murphy	1	0	0	0	0
11	Bob Nevin	2	0	0	0	2

11	Murray Oliver	1	1	0	1	0
16	Bert Olmstead	1	0	0	0	0
18	Jim Pappin	2	1	0	1	0
4	Robert Picard	1	0	0	0	0
7	Bud Poile	1	0	0	0	0
10	Joe Primeau	1	0	1	1	0
3	Marcel Pronovost	1	0	0	0	0
20	Bob Pulford	5	1	0	1	0
4	Duane Rupp	1	0	1	1	0
21	Borje Salming	3	0	1	1	4
16	Charlie Sands	1	0	0	0	0
23	Eddie Shack	3	1	0	1	4
27	Darryl Sittler	3	2	2	4	0
12/16/15	Tod Sloan	3	1	1	2	2
8/24	Sid Smith	7	1	1	2	4
2/26/18	Allan Stanley	5	1	1	2	4
3	Wally Stanowski	1	0	0	0	0
12	Pete Stemkowski	1	1	1	2	2
16	Gaye Stewart	1	0	0	0	0
12/17	Ron Stewart	4	0	1	1	4
13	Mats Sundin	6	3	8	11	0
14	Bill Thoms	1	0	1	1	0
4/2/20	Jim Thomson	7	0	0	0	10
22	Ray Timgren	1	0	0	0	0
2	Ian Turnbull	1	0	0	0	0
9/14	Norm Ullman	2	0	3	3	0
22	Rick Vaive	3	2	3	5	0
16	Mike Walton	1	0	0	0	2
24/4	Harry Watson	6	1	4	5	0
36	Dmitry Yushkevich	1	1	1	2	0

* includes a five-minute fighting major with Gordie Howe in 1948

Leafs All-Star Game Records

Most Games Played

9	Frank Mahovlich
8	Dave Keon
7	George Armstrong
	Tim Horton
	Sid Smith
	Jim Thomson

Most Goals

4	Vincent Damphousse
	Frank Mahovlich
3	Mats Sundin

Most Assists

8	Mats Sundin

Most Points

11	Mats Sundin
8	Frank Mahovlich

Most Penalty Minutes

10	Tim Horton
	Jim Thomson
9	Gus Mortson

King Clancy is the only man to play in (1934), referee (1939 and 1947), and coach (1954) an All-Star Game. Only seven players have both played in and coached an All-Star Game. Three of them were Leafs: Happy Day, Joe Primeau, and King Clancy.

Leafs Iron Man Records

Most Complete Seasons Played

Tim Horton	10
Turk Broda	8
Bob Pulford	8
Ron Ellis	7

Leafs Iron Man

Tim Horton played in 486 consecutive games for the Leafs, from February 11, 1961, to February 4, 1968.

Leafs Iron Man Goalie

Turk Broda played 215 consecutive games in goal for Toronto, from February 6, 1946, to November 27, 1949. The beginning and end of the streak are interesting: it began when he returned home from war, playing for the first time in almost three years, and ended with the famous benching by Conn Smythe, who accused Turkey Face of being too fat.

All-Time Leafs Coaching Register, Regular Season

JACK ADAMS
b. Fort William, June 14, 1895
d. Detroit, Michigan, May 1, 1968

1922–23	18	10	7	1

- replaced Querrie on January 6, 1923
- Hockey Hall of Fame 1959 (as a Player)
- replaced by Powers to start 1923–24

GEORGE ARMSTRONG ("the Chief")
b. Borlands Bay, July 6, 1930

1988–89	47	17	26	4

- hired December 19, 1988
- fired August 15, 1989
- Hockey Hall of Fame 1975 (as a Player)

NICK BEVERLEY
b. Toronto, April 21, 1947

1995–96	17	9	6	2

- hired March 5, 1996
- resigned April 27, 1996

JOHN BROPHY ("The Grey Ghost")
b. Halifax, Nova Scotia, January 20, 1933

1986–87	80	32	42	6
1987–88	80	21	49	10
1988–89	33	11	20	2
Totals	193	64	111	18

- hired July 2, 1986
- fired December 19, 1988

PAT BURNS ("Burnsie")
b. St. Henri, Quebec, April 4, 1952

1992–93	84	44	29	11
1993–94	84	43	29	12
1994–95	48	21	19	8
1995–96	65	25	30	10
Totals	281	133	107	41

- hired May 29, 1992
- fired March 4, 1996

DOUG CARPENTER
b. Cornwall, July 1, 1942

1989–90	80	38	38	4
1990–91	11	1	9	1
Totals	91	39	47	5

- hired August 24, 1989
- fired October 26, 1990

DICK CARROLL
b. Guelph, 1886 *d.* Guelph, January 20, 1952

1917–18	22	13	9	0
1918–19	18	5	13	0
1920–21	24	15	9	0
Totals	64	33	31	0

- became Arenas' first coach in NHL
- replaced by Powers for 1921–22

FRANCIS "KING" CLANCY
b. Ottawa, February 25, 1903
d. Toronto, November 8, 1986

1953–54	70	32	24	14
1954–55	70	24	24	22
1955–56	70	24	33	13
1966–67	10	7	1	2
1971–72	15	9	3	3
Totals	235	96	85	54

- hired March 24, 1953
- reassigned to position of assistant general manager April 2, 1956
- coached February 23, 1961, vs. Canadiens, though decision credited to Imlach's record
- coached game of April 9, 1966, when Imlach had the flu, but Clancy was not given official credit for the loss
- coached February 18–March 11, 1967, when Punch Imlach was suffering from exhaustion

- coached February 23–March 22 and March 25–April 2, 1972, when John McLellan was ill with ulcer problems
- Hockey Hall of Fame 1958 (as a Player)

JOE CROZIER ("Crow")

b. Winnipeg, Manitoba, February 19, 1929

1980–81	40	13	22	5

- took over behind the bench March 19, 1980, although did not officially become coach until start of 1980–81
- fired January 8, 1981

CLARENCE "HAPPY"/"HAP" DAY

b. Owen Sound, June 1, 1901
d. St. Thomas, February 17, 1990

1940–41	48	28	14	6
1941–42	48	27	18	3
1942–43	50	22	19	9
1943–44	50	23	23	4
1944–45	50	24	22	4
1945–46	50	19	24	7
1946–47	60	31	19	10
1947–48	60	32	15	13
1948–49	60	22	25	13
1949–50	70	31	27	12
Totals	546	259	206	81

- hired as coach April 17, 1940
- resigned to become assistant general manager; replaced by Primeau
- Hockey Hall of Fame 1961 (as a Player)

DICK DUFF

b. Kirkland Lake, February 18, 1936

1979–80	2	0	2	0

- coached two games (March 15 and 17) after Floyd Smith injured in car crash

ART DUNCAN ("Dunc")

b. Unknown d. Unknown

1930–31	44	22	13	9
1931–32	5	0	3	2
Totals	49	22	16	11

- hired October 13, 1930
- fired November 27, 1931

FRANK HEFFERNAN ("Moose")

b. Peterborough d. New York, New York, December 21, 1938

1919–20	12	5	7	0

- coached first half of season; resigned February 4, 1920, to concentrate on playing, and replaced by team secretary Harry Sproule

GEORGE "PUNCH" IMLACH

b. Toronto, March 15, 1918
d. Toronto, December 1, 1987

1958–59	50	22	20	8
1959–60	70	35	26	9
1960–61	70	39	19	12
1961–62	70	37	22	11
1962–63	70	35	23	12
1963–64	70	33	25	12
1964–65	70	30	26	14
1965–66	70	34	25	11
1966–67	60	25	26	9
1967–68	74	33	31	10
1968–69	76	35	26	15
1979–80	10	5	5	0
Totals	760	363	274	123

- hired July 10, 1958, as assistant general manager
- took over as coach November 28, 1958.
- King Clancy coached for Imlach on April 9, 1966, although Imlach got official credit for the loss
- King Clancy coached February 18–March 11, 1967, for Imlach during illness
- fired April 6, 1969

- while officially coach in 1979–80, Imlach had Joe Crozier behind the bench for the final ten games of the season; Crozier was later made coach for 1980–81
- Hockey Hall of Fame 1984 (as a Builder)

DICK IRVIN

b. Limestone Ridge, July 19, 1892
d. Montreal, Quebec, May 16, 1957

1931–32	43	23	15	5
1932–33	48	24	18	6
1933–34	48	26	13	9
1934–35	48	30	14	4
1935–36	48	23	19	6
1936–37	48	22	21	5
1937–38	48	24	15	9
1938–39	48	19	20	9
1939–40	48	25	17	6
Totals	427	216	152	59

- hired November 28, 1931
- resigned April 16, 1940
- Hockey Hall of Fame 1958 (as a Player)

LEONARD "RED" KELLY

b. Simcoe, July 9, 1927

1973–74	78	35	27	16
1974–75	80	31	33	16
1975–76	80	34	31	15
1976–77	80	33	32	15
Totals	318	133	123	62

- hired August 20, 1973
- fired June 17, 1977
- Hockey Hall of Fame 1969 (as a Player)

DAN MALONEY ("Harley")

b. Barrie, September 24, 1950

1984–85	80	20	52	8
1985–86	80	25	48	7
Totals	160	45	100	15

- hired May 26, 1984
- resigned June 18, 1986

JOHN McLELLAN

b. South Porcupine, August 6, 1928
d. Toronto, October 27, 1979

1969–70	76	29	34	13
1970–71	78	37	33	8
1971–72	63	24	28	11
1972–73	78	27	41	10
Totals	295	117	136	42

- hired April 6, 1969
- missed February 23–March 22 and March 25–April 2, 1972 (15 games), due to ulcers; replaced by King Clancy
- resigned April 17, 1973, for health reasons

HOWIE MEEKER

b. Kitchener, November 4, 1924

1956–57	70	21	34	15

- hired April 11, 1956
- promoted to general manager May 13, 1957, and replaced behind the bench by Reay

MIKE MURPHY ("Murph")

b. Toronto, September 12, 1950

1996–97	82	30	44	8
1997–98	82	30	43	9
Totals	164	60	87	17

- hired July 3, 1996
- fired June 25, 1998

ROGER NEILSON ("Captain Video")

b. Toronto, June 16, 1934

1977–78	80	41	29	10
1978–79	80	34	33	13
Totals	160	75	62	23

- hired July 25, 1977
- fired March 1, 1979
- rehired March 3, 1979
- fired permanently April 22, 1979

MIKE NYKOLUK
b. Toronto, December 11, 1934

1980–81	40	15	15	10
1981–82	80	20	44	16
1982–83	80	28	40	12
1983–84	80	26	45	9
Totals	280	89	144	47

- hired January 10, 1981
- fired April 2, 1984

EDDIE POWERS
b. Elora d. Stouffville, March 11, 1943

1921–22	24	13	10	1
1923–24	24	10	14	0
1924–25	30	19	11	0
1925–26	36	12	21	3
Totals	114	54	56	4

- replaced Carroll to start 1921–22
- replaced by Charlie Querrie to start 1922–23
- replaced Adams, who resigned to continue his playing career in the West
- replaced by Conn Smythe to start 1926–27

JOE PRIMEAU ("Gentleman Joe")
b. Lindsay, January 24, 1906
d. Toronto, May 15, 1989

1950–51	70	41	16	13
1951–52	70	29	25	16
1952–53	70	27	30	13
Totals	210	97	71	42

- hired May 26, 1950
- resigned March 24, 1953
- Hockey Hall of Fame 1963 (as a Player)

CHARLIE QUERRIE ("the Indian Chief")
b. Markham, 1879 d. Toronto, April 5, 1950

| 1922–23 | 6 | 3 | 3 | 0 |

- coached the first six games of 1922–23, replaced January 6, 1923 by Jack Adams

PAT QUINN
b. Hamilton, January 29, 1943

1998–99	82	45	30	7
1999–2000	82	45	30	7
2000–01	82	37	34	11
Totals	246	127	94	25

- hired June 26, 1998
- current Leafs coach and general manager.
- named as head coach for Canada's entry at 2002 Olympics in Salt Lake City, Utah

BILLY REAY
b. Winnipeg, Manitoba, August 21, 1918

1957–58	70	21	38	11
1958–59	20	5	12	3
Totals	90	26	50	14

- hired May 13, 1957
- fired November 28, 1958

FLOYD SMITH ("Smitty")
b. Perth, May 16, 1935

| 1979–80 | 68 | 33 | 30 | 5 |

- hired July 20, 1979
- injured in car crash March 14, 1980; replaced by Duff, then Imlach (Crozier), and never coached again

CONN SMYTHE ("the Hollerin' Major")
b. Toronto, February 1, 1895
d. Toronto, November 18, 1980

1926–27	44	15	24	5
1927–28	44	18	18	8
1928–29	44	21	18	5
1929–30	44	17	21	6
Totals	176	71	81	24

- became coach just prior to buying the team.
- resigned October 13, 1930, and hired Art Duncan as his replacement
- coached University of Toronto Grads team that won gold medal at 1928 Olympics

HARRY SPROULE

  b. Unknown *d.* Unknown

1919–20	12	7	5	0

- replaced Heffernan as coach February 4, 1920
- replaced by Carroll for 1920–21

TOM WATT

  b. Toronto, June 17, 1935

1990–91	69	22	37	10
1991–92	80	30	43	7
Totals	149	52	80	17

- hired October 27, 1990
- reassigned to position of director of professional development May 29, 1992

All-Time Coaching Records, Regular Season

Most Seasons

Hap Day	10
Punch Imlach	10
Dick Irvin	9

Most Games

Punch Imlach	760
Hap Day	546
Dick Irvin	427

Most Wins

Punch Imlach	363
Hap Day	259
Dick Irvin	216

Most Losses

Punch Imlach	274
Hap Day	206
Dick Irvin	152

All-Time Coaching Records by Season
(*includes one tie)

Toronto Arenas

YEAR	COACH	GP	W	L	T	GP	W	L	SERIES
			Regular Season				**Playoffs**		
1917–18	Dick Carroll	22	13	9	0	7	4	3	2–0
1918–19	Dick Carroll	18	5	13	0		DNQ		

Toronto St. Pats

YEAR	COACH	GP	W	L	T	GP	W	L	SERIES
			Regular Season				**Playoffs**		
1919–20	Frank Heffernan	12	5	7	0				
	Harry Sproule	12	7	5	0		DNQ		
		24	12	12	0				
1920–21	Dick Carroll	24	15	9	0	2	0	2	0–1
1921–22	Eddie Powers	24	13	10	1	7*	4	2	2–0
1922–23	Charlie Querrie	6	3	3	0				
	Jack Adams	18	10	7	1		DNQ		
		24	13	10	1				
1923–24	Eddie Powers	24	10	14	0		DNQ		
1924–25	Eddie Powers	30	19	11	0	2	0	2	0–1
1925–26	Eddie Powers	36	12	21	3		DNQ		

Toronto Maple Leafs

YEAR	COACH	GP	W	L	T	GP	W	L	SERIES
			Regular Season				**Playoffs**		
1917–18	Dick Carroll	22	13	9	0	7	4	3	2–0
1926–27	Conn Smythe	44	15	24	5		DNQ		
1927–28	Conn Smythe	44	18	18	8		DNQ		
1928–29	Conn Smythe	44	21	18	5	4	2	2	1–1
1929–30	Conn Smythe	44	17	21	6		DNQ		
1930–31	Art Duncan	44	22	13	9	2*	0	1	0–1
1931–32	Art Duncan	5	0	3	2				
	Dick Irvin	43	23	15	5	7*	5	1	3–0
		48	23	18	7				
1932–33	Dick Irvin	48	24	18	6	9	4	5	1–1
1933–34	Dick Irvin	48	26	13	9	5	2	3	0–1
1934–35	Dick Irvin	48	30	14	4	7	3	4	1–1
1935–36	Dick Irvin	48	23	19	6	9	4	5	2–1
1936–37	Dick Irvin	48	22	21	5	2	0	2	0–1
1937–38	Dick Irvin	48	24	15	9	7	4	3	1–1
1938–39	Dick Irvin	48	19	20	9	10	5	5	2–1
1939–40	Dick Irvin	48	25	17	6	10	6	4	2–1
1940–41	Happy Day	48	28	14	6	7	3	4	0–1
1941–42	Happy Day	48	27	18	3	13	8	5	2–0
1942–43	Happy Day	50	22	19	9	6	2	4	0–1
1943–44	Happy Day	50	23	23	4	5	1	4	0–1
1944–45	Happy Day	50	24	22	4	13	8	5	2–0
1945–46	Happy Day	50	19	24	7		DNQ		
1946–47	Happy Day	60	31	19	10	11	8	3	2–0
1947–48	Happy Day	60	32	15	13	9	8	1	2–0

Season	Coach	GP	W	L	T				
1948–49	Happy Day	60	22	25	13	9	8	1	2–0
1949–50	Happy Day	70	31	27	12	7	3	4	0–1
1950–51	Joe Primeau	70	41	16	13	11*	8	2	2–0
1951–52	Joe Primeau	70	29	25	16	4	0	4	0–1
1952–53	Joe Primeau	70	27	30	13	DNQ			
1953–54	King Clancy	70	32	24	14	5	12	4	0–1
1954–55	King Clancy	70	24	24	22	4	0	4	0–1
1955–56	King Clancy	70	24	33	13	5	1	4	0–1
1956–57	Howie Meeker	70	21	34	15	DNQ			
1957–58	Billy Reay	70	21	38	11	DNQ			
1958–59	Billy Reay	20	5	12	3				
	Punch Imlach	50	22	20	8	12	8	4	1–1
		70	27	32	11				
1959–60	Punch Imlach	70	35	26	9	10	4	6	1–1
1960–61	Punch Imlach	70	39	19	12	5	1	4	0–1
1961–62	Punch Imlach	70	37	22	11	12	8	4	2–0
1962–63	Punch Imlach	70	35	23	12	10	8	2	2–0
1963–64	Punch Imlach	70	33	25	12	14	8	6	2–0
1964–65	Punch Imlach	70	30	26	14	6	2	4	0–1
1965–66	Punch Imlach	70	34	25	11	4	0	4	0–1
1966–67	Punch Imlach	60	25	26	9	12	8	4	2–0
	King Clancy	10	7	1	2				
		70	32	27	11				
1967–68	Punch Imlach	74	33	31	10	DNQ			
1968–69	Punch Imlach	76	35	26	15	4	0	4	0–1
1969–70	John McLellan	76	29	34	13	DNQ			
1970–71	John McLellan	78	37	33	8	6	2	4	0–1
1971–72	John McLellan	63	24	28	11	5	1	4	0–1
	King Clancy	15	9	3	3				
		78	33	31	14				
1972–73	John McLellan	78	27	41	10	DNQ			
1973–74	Red Kelly	78	35	27	16	4	0	4	0–1
1974–75	Red Kelly	80	31	33	16	7	2	5	1–1
1975–76	Red Kelly	80	34	31	15	10	5	5	1–1
1976–77	Red Kelly	80	33	32	15	10	5	5	1–1
1977–78	Roger Neilson	80	41	29	10	13	6	7	2–1
1978–79	Roger Neilson	80	34	33	13	6	2	4	1–1
1979–80	Floyd Smith	68	30	33	5				
	Dick Duff	2	0	2	0				
	Punch Imlach	10	5	5	0	3	0	3	0–1
		80	35	40	5				
1980–81	Joe Crozier	40	13	22	5				
	Mike Nykoluk	40	15	15	10	3	0	3	0–1
		80	28	37	15				
1981–82	Mike Nykoluk	80	20	44	16	DNQ			
1982–83	Mike Nykoluk	80	28	40	12	4	1	3	0–1
1983–84	Mike Nykoluk	80	26	45	9	DNQ			

Season	Coach	GP	W	L	T	GP	W	L	Series
1984–85	Dan Maloney	80	20	52	8			DNQ	
1985–86	Dan Maloney	80	25	48	7	10	6	4	1–1
1986–87	John Brophy	80	32	42	6	13	7	6	1–1
1987–88	John Brophy	80	21	49	10	6	2	4	0–1
1988–89	John Brophy	33	11	20	2				
	G. Armstrong	47	17	26	4			DNQ	
		80	28	46	6				
1989–90	Doug Carpenter	80	38	38	4	5	1	4	0–1
1990–91	Doug Carpenter	11	1	9	1				
	Tom Watt	69	22	37	10			DNQ	
		80	23	46	11				
1991–92	Tom Watt	80	30	43	7			DNQ	
1992–93	Pat Burns	84	44	29	11	21	11	10	2–1
1993–94	Pat Burns	84	43	29	12	18	9	9	2–1
1994–95	Pat Burns	48	21	19	8	7	3	4	0–1
1995–96	Pat Burns	65	25	30	10				
	Nick Beverley	17	9	6	2	6	2	4	0–1
		82	34	36	12				
1996–97	Mike Murphy	82	30	44	8			DNQ	
1997–98	Mike Murphy	82	30	43	9			DNQ	
1998–99	Pat Quinn	82	45	30	7	17	9	8	2–1
1999–2000	Pat Quinn	82	45	30	7	12	6	6	1–1
2000–01	Pat Quinn	82	37	34	11	11	7	4	1–1

Leafs All-Time Player Register

The players' place of birth is assumed to be Ontario unless otherwise noted. References to the years 1917–19 indicate Toronto Arenas; 1919–26 indicate Toronto St. Pats.

For players' records during the 1917–18 season, dashes appear in the assist column because assists weren't awarded that year.

An "R" after the season indicates that the player was a rookie and played his first NHL game in a Leafs uniform; all rookies' first game dates are also listed. An "L" after the year indicates the player's last year in the NHL; all last career game dates are also listed. The L or R that appears after a player's weight indicates which way a skater shoots or with which hand a goalie catches.

From 1917 to 1921, ties were not allowed in the NHL. Thus, for goalies' records during those years, only wins and losses are listed. Also, for goalies, a new feature appears here for the first time anywhere. After the games played, two numbers appear in parentheses. The first number indicates the number of times during a season in which a goalie was pulled from a game; the second indicates the number of times he was inserted into a game to replace another goalie. In the case of a goalie being pulled and then reinserted, one appearance in each column appears. Information on goalies, then, is listed in the following order: games played (pulled/inserted); won–lost–tied; minutes played; goals against; shutouts; goals against average.

DOUG ACOMB

#22 centre   5'10" 165–L
b. Toronto, May 15, 1949

1969–70R/L	2	0	1	1	0

- rights acquired from Portland (WHL) during 1968–69 season
- first and only Leaf games March 7, 11, 1970

RUSS ADAM

#16 centre   5'10" 185–L
b. Windsor, May 5, 1961

1982–83R/L	8	1	2	3	11

- selected 137th overall at 1980 Entry Draft
- first and only Leaf games October 6, 7, 9, 13, 14, 16, 30 and November 3, 1982

JACK ADAMS

#5–9 centre   5'9" 175–R
b. Fort William, June 14, 1895
d. Detroit, Michigan, May 1, 1968

1917–18	8	0	–	0	15
1918–19	17	3	3	6	17
1922–23	23	19	9	28	42
1923–24	22	13	3	16	49
1924–25	27	21	8	29	66
1925–26	36	21	5	26	52
Totals	133	77	28	105	241

- signed February 7, 1918, with the Arenas for the start of the second half of the 1917–18 season, arriving from Sarnia (Senior OHA) after the team folded
- first Arenas game February 11, 1918
- signed in December 1919 as a free agent by Vancouver Millionaires
- acquired December 1922 from Vancouver Millionaires for Corb Dennenay
- missed games of February 23, 27, 1924, with broken ribs
- missed game of February 25, 1925, with the flu
- sold to Ottawa Senators before the 1926–27 season
- became coach and general manager of Detroit, staying with the club until his death
- Hockey Hall of Fame 1959

KEVYN ADAMS ("Ads")
#42 centre   6'1" 195–R
b. Washington, D.C., October 8, 1974

1997–98R	5	0	0	0	7
1998–99	1	0	0	0	0
1999–2000	52	5	8	13	39
Totals	58	5	8	13	46

- signed as a free agent August 7, 1997
- lost to Columbus on June 23, 2000, in Expansion Draft
- played for USA at 1994 WJC (sixth place)
- currently with Columbus Blue Jackets

STEWART ADAMS
#12–17 left wing   5'10" 165–L
b. Calgary, Alberta, October 16, 1904
d. Calgary, Alberta, May 18, 1978

1932–33L	9	0	2	2	0

- bought from Chicago during summer 1932.
- first Leaf game December 29, 1932
- replaced injured Charlie Conacher for games of December 29, January 1, 3, 5, 7, 10, 14, 17 and February 16, 1932–33

GARY ALDCORN
#21–22–26 forward   5'11" 180–L
b. Shaunavon, Saskatchewan, March 7, 1935

1956–57R	22	5	1	6	4
1957–58	59	10	14	24	12
1958–59	5	0	3	3	2
Totals	86	15	18	33	18

- drafted June 4, 1956, from Hornets
- first Leaf game October 11, 1956
- played November 9, 12, 15 and March 4, 5, 1958–59
- claimed by Detroit at the June 1959 Intra-League Draft
- played for Canada at 1965 WC (fourth place)

- became a sculptor of hockey players and teams, commemorating Original Six hockey in particular

CLAIRE ALEXANDER ("The Milkman")
#20 defence   6'1" 175–R
b. Collingwood, June 16, 1945

1974–75R	42	7	11	18	12
1975–76	33	2	6	8	6
1976–77	48	1	12	13	12
Totals	123	10	29	39	30

- had a five-game tryout with Tulsa during 1972–73; won Allan Cup with Orillia Terriers in 1972–73
- signed as a free agent
- first Leaf game November 30, 1974.
- sold January 29, 1978, to Vancouver Canucks
- works as a glazier on contruction sites; daughter, Buffy, won bronze at Sydney Olympics in women's eight

MIKE ALLISON ("Red")
#8 left wing   6' 200–R
b. Fort Frances, March 28, 1961

1986–87	71	7	16	23	66
1987–88	15	0	3	3	10
Totals	86	7	19	26	76

- acquired August 18, 1986, from Rangers for Walt Poddubny
- traded December 14, 1987, to Los Angeles Kings for Sean McKenna

GLENN ANDERSON ("Andy")
#10–9 right wing   5'11" 175–L
b. Vancouver, British Columbia, October 2, 1960

1991–92	72	24	33	57	100
1992–93	76	22	43	65	117
1993–94	73	17	18	35	50
Totals	221	63	94	157	267

- acquired September 19, 1991, with Grant Fuhr and Craig Berube from Edmonton for Vincent Damphousse, Peter Ing, Scott Thornton, and Luke Richardson
- traded March 21, 1994, with Scott Malone and a 4th-round draft choice in 1994 (Alexander Korobolin) to the Rangers for Mike Gartner
- played for Canada at 1980 Olympics (sixth place); won silver medal at 1989 WC and played at 1992 WC (eighth place)

JOHN ANDERSON
#10–28 right wing   5'11" 190–R
b. Toronto, March 28, 1957

1977–78R	17	1	2	3	2
1978–79	71	15	11	26	10
1979–80	74	25	28	53	22
1980–81	75	17	26	43	31
1981–82	69	31	26	57	30
1982–83	80	31	49	80	24
1983–84	73	37	31	68	22
1984–85	75	32	31	63	27
Totals	534	189	204	393	168

- selected 11th overall at 1977 Amateur Draft
- first Leaf game December 4, 1977
- traded August 21, 1985 to Quebec Nordiques for Brad Maxwell
- won silver medal with Canada at 1977 WJC and bronze medals at 1983 and 1985 WC
- has coached in Southern Hockey League and Colonial League

LLOYD "ANDY" ANDREWS ("Shrimp")
#9 forward
b. Tillsonburg, November 4, 1894
d. Unknown

1921–22R	11	0	0	0	0
1922–23	23	5	4	9	10
1923–24	12	2	1	3	0
1924–25L	7	1	0	1	0
Totals	53	8	5	13	10

- signed January 23, 1922, from Niagara Falls (OHA Intermediate)
- first St. Pats game January 25, 1922

DAVE ANDREYCHUK ("Chuckie")
#14 left wing   6'3" 195–R
b. Hamilton, September 29, 1963

1992–93	31	25	13	38	8
1993–94	83	53	46	99	98
1994–95	48	22	16	38	34
1995–96	61	20	24	44	54
Totals	223	120	99	219	194

- acquired February 2, 1993, with Daren Puppa and a 1st-round draft choice in 1993 (Kenny Jonsson) from Sabres for Grant Fuhr and a 5th-round draft choice in 1995 (Kevin Popp)
- traded March 13, 1996, to New Jersey for a 2nd-round draft choice in 1996 (Marek Posmyk) and a 3rd-round draft choice in 1999. (Later traded back to New Jersey on February 25, 1997, with Doug Gilmour and Dave Ellett for Steve Sullivan, Jason Smith, and Alyn McCauley)
- won bronze medal with Canada at 1983 WJC and bronze at 1986 WC

GREG ANDRUSAK
#25 defence   6'1" 195–R
b. Cranbrook, British Columbia, November 14, 1969

1999–2000	9	0	1	1	4

- signed as a free agent on July 19, 1999

- signed as a free agent by San Jose on August 14, 2000
- won bronze medal with Canada at 1995 WC

NIKOLAI ("NIK") ANTROPOV

#9 centre   6'5" 203–L

b. Vost, USSR, February 18, 1980

1999–2000R	66	12	18	30	41
2000–01	52	6	11	17	30
Totals	118	18	29	47	71

- selected 10th overall at 1998 Entry Draft
- played for Kazakhstan at 1999 WJC
- currently with Leafs

SYL APPS ("Slippery Syl")

#10–16 centre   6' 173–R

b. Paris, January 18, 1915

d. Kingston, December 24, 1998

1936–37R	48	16	29	45	10
1937–38	47	21	29	50	9
1938–39	44	15	25	40	4
1939–40	27	13	17	30	5
1940–41	41	20	24	44	6
1941–42	38	18	23	41	0
1942–43	29	23	17	40	2
1945–46	40	24	16	40	2
1946–47	54	25	24	49	6
1947–48L	55	26	27	53	12
Totals	423	201	231	432	56

- signed by Leafs on September 2, 1936
- first Leaf game November 5, 1936
- missed 21 games in 1939–40 with fractured collar bone
- missed last seven games of regular season after injuring knee February 25, 1940
- missed most of December 1941 with ankle injury
- missed most of 1943 after breaking his leg January 30, 1943
- missed 1943–45—in Canadian army.
- missed part of 1945–46 with dislocated rib
- missed part of 1947–48 with skate cut to thigh
- last Leaf game March 21, 1948.
- later became commissioner for athletics in Ontario
- Hockey Hall of Fame 1961

ALGER "AL" ARBOUR ("Radar")

#3–18 defence   6'1" 180–L

b. Sudbury, November 1, 1932

1961–62	52	1	5	6	68
1962–63	4	1	0	1	4
1963–64	6	0	1	1	0
1965–66	4	0	1	1	2
Totals	66	2	7	9	74

- claimed from Chicago at June 1961 Intra-League Draft
- played December 15, 16, 23, 26, 1962
- played October 30 and November 2, 7, 9, 13, 16, 1963, then sent to minors
- played December 11, 12 and March 24, 26, 1965–66
- claimed June 6, 1967, by St. Louis at Expansion Draft
- coached Islanders to four Stanley Cups in 1980s
- Hockey Hall of Fame 1996 (Builder)

AMOS ARBOUR ("Butch")

#7 forward   5'8" 160–L

b. Victoria Harbour

d. Orillia, November 2, 1943

1923–24L	20	1	2	3	4

- acquired from Hamilton Tigers (NHL) in 1923 with Bert Corbeau for Corb Dennenay and Ken Randall
- last St. Pats game March 5, 1924

JACK ARBOUR

#2 forward   5'8" 170–L

b. Wabushene, March 7, 1899

d. Unknown

1928–29L	10	1	0	1	10

- acquired April 9, 1928, with $12,500 from Detroit for Jim Herberts
- only Leaf games November 15, 17, 20, 22, 24, 27 and December 1, 4, 8, 11, 1928
- sold outright in December 1928 to London Panthers

Happy Day, Syl Apps, Conn Smythe

GEORGE ARMSTRONG ("The Chief"/"Chief Shoot-the-Puck"/"Army")
#10-15-20 right wing 6'1" 194-R
b. Borlands Bay, July 6, 1930

1949–50R	2	0	0	0	0
1951–52	20	3	3	6	30
1952–53	52	14	11	25	54
1953–54	63	17	15	32	60
1954–55	66	10	18	28	80
1955–56	67	16	32	48	97
1956–57	54	18	26	44	37
1957–58	59	17	25	42	93
1958–59	59	20	16	36	37
1959–60	70	23	28	51	60
1960–61	47	14	19	33	21
1961–62	70	21	32	53	27
1962–63	70	19	24	43	27
1963–64	66	20	17	37	14
1964–65	59	15	22	37	14
1965–66	70	16	35	51	12
1966–67	70	9	24	33	26
1967–68	62	13	21	34	4
1968–69	53	11	16	27	10
1969–70	49	13	15	28	12
1970–71L	59	7	18	25	6
Totals	1187	296	417	713	721

- Marlie graduate; first Leaf games December 3, 24, 1949
- recalled February 9, 1952, from Hornets
- missed first month of 1952–53 season after separating shoulder in training camp
- missed November 28–December 25, 1957, with torn knee ligaments
- missed part of 1958–59 with groin injury
- missed March 13–end of season, 1968, with knee injury
- missed March 22–end of season, 1970, with knee injury
- retired after 1969–70, but returned November 21, 1970
- last Leaf game April 4, 1971
- coached Toronto Marlies and Leafs and continues to scout for the team
- Hockey Hall of Fame 1975

MURRAY ARMSTRONG
#17 centre   5'10" 170–L
b. Manor, Saskatchewan, January 1, 1916

1937–38R	9	0	0	0	0
1938–39	3	0	1	1	0
Totals	12	0	1	1	0

- drafted May 8, 1936, by Leafs from Philadelphia Ramblers
- first Leaf game December 26, 1937
- traded May 18, 1939, to New York Americans with Harvey Jackson, Buzz Boll, and Doc Romnes for Sweeney Schriner
- later coached at University of Denver for 21 years and five NCAA titles

NORM "RED" ARMSTRONG
#18 defence   5'11" 205–L
b. Owen Sound, October 17, 1938
d. Sault Ste. Marie, July 23, 1974

1962–63R/L	7	1	1	2	2

- first and only Leaf games December 15, 16, 23, 25 and January 1, 5, 17, 1962–63
- career minor-leaguer with Rochester, 1963–71
- traded February 20, 1971, from Rochester to Springfield for Don Eastbrook
- killed in an industrial accident

TIM ARMSTRONG
#8 centre   5'11" 170–R
b. Toronto, May 12, 1967

1988–89R/L	11	1	0	1	6

- selected 211th overall at 1985 Entry Draft
- first and only Leaf games December 29, 31 and January 1, 6, 7, 9, 11, 21, 25, 28, 30, 1988–89

JOHN ARUNDEL
#25 defence   5'11" 181–L
b. Winnipeg, Manitoba, November 4, 1927

1949–50R/L	3	0	0	0	9

- first and only Leaf games December 31 and January 1, 4, 1949–50

DON ASHBY ("Ash")

#9–20–8 centre   6'1" 185–L
b. Kamloops, British Columbia,
March 8, 1955
d. Summerland, British Columbia,
May 30, 1981

1975–76R	50	6	15	21	10
1976–77	76	19	23	42	24
1977–78	12	1	2	3	0
1978–79	3	0	0	0	0
Totals	141	26	40	66	34

- selected 6th overall at 1975 Amateur Draft
- first Leaf game October 11, 1975
- traded March 13, 1979, with Trevor Johansen to Colorado Rockies for Paul Gardner
- killed in a car accident

NORM AUBIN

#24–35 centre   6' 185–L
b. St. Léonard, Quebec, July 26, 1960

1981–82R	43	14	12	26	22
1982–83L	26	4	1	5	8
Totals	69	18	13	31	30

- selected 51st overall at 1979 Entry Draft
- first Leaf game December 31, 1981
- last Leaf game December 11, 1982
- signed as a free agent December 1984 by Edmonton

PATRIK AUGUSTA

#24 right wing   5'10" 180–L
b. Jihlava, Czechoslovakia,
November 13, 1969

1993–94R	2	0	0	0	0

- selected 149th overall at 1992 Entry Draft
- first Leaf games January 1, 2, 1994
- released June 27, 1995
- won bronze medals with Czechoslovakia at 1992 Olympics and 1992 WC

PETE BACKOR

#14 defence   6' 185–L
b. Fort William, April 29, 1919
d. Thunder Bay

1944–45R/L	36	4	5	9	6

- first Leaf game October 28, 1944
- sent to Hornets for 1945–46 season; never played in the NHL again
- last Leaf game February 18, 1945

BOB BAILEY ("Bashin' Bob")

#17–18–20–21–23 right wing   6' 197–R
b. Kenora, May 29, 1931

1953–54R	48	2	7	9	70
1954–55	32	4	2	6	52
1955–56	6	0	0	0	6
Totals	86	6	9	15	128

- acquired May 20, 1953, with Gerry Foley from Cleveland (AHL) for Chuck Blair and $30,000
- first Leaf game October 10, 1953
- sold May 28, 1956, with Bob Sabourin to Springfield for $22,000

IRVINE "ACE" BAILEY

#6–12–8 right wing   5'11 160–L
b. Bracebridge, July 3, 1903
d. Toronto, April 7, 1992

1926–27R	42	15	13	28	82
1927–28	43	9	3	12	72
1928–29	44	22	10	32	78
1929–30	43	22	21	43	69
1930–31	40	23	19	42	46
1931–32	41	8	5	13	62
1932–33	47	10	8	18	52
1933–34L	13	2	3	5	11
Totals	313	111	82	193	472

- signed by St. Pats after graduating from Peterborough (OHA)
- first Leaf game November 17, 1926
- missed only two games (April 19, 23) after breaking jaw during 1926–27 season
- career ended by an Eddie Shore hit on December 12, 1933
- worked in penalty box at Maple Leaf Gardens virtually up to his death
- Hockey Hall of Fame 1975

REID BAILEY
#4–33 defence   6'2" 200–L
b. Toronto, May 28, 1956

1982–83	1	0	0	0	2

- acquired January 15, 1983, from Edmonton for Serge Boisvert
- signed December 9, 1983, as a free agent by Hartford

JAMIE BAKER ("Bakes")
#16 centre   6' 190–L
b. Ottawa, August 31, 1966

1996–97	58	8	8	16	28
1997–98	13	0	5	5	10
Totals	71	8	13	21	38

- acquired June 14, 1996, with a 5th-round draft choice in 1996 (Peter Cava) from San Jose for Todd Gill
- signed as a free agent by San Jose on September 29, 1998

DOUG BALDWIN
#19 defence   6' 175–L
b. Winnipeg, Manitoba, November 2, 1922

1945–46R	15	0	1	1	6

- first Leaf game January 19, 1946 (replacing Babe Pratt)
- after 15 games with Leafs, underwent appendectomy; finished season with Hornets

- traded September 21, 1946, with Billy Taylor and Ray Powell to Detroit for Harry Watson and Gerry Brown

EARL BALFOUR ("Spider")
#16–22–24–25–23 left wing   6'1" 180–L
b. Toronto, January 4, 1933

1951–52R	3	0	0	0	2
1953–54	17	0	1	1	6
1955–56	59	14	5	19	40
1957–58	1	0	0	0	0
Totals	80	14	6	20	48

- Marlie graduate; first Leaf game March 5, 1952
- recalled November 19, 1953, from Hornets
- recalled January 21, 1958, from Rochester; played January 22, 1958
- claimed June 4, 1958, by Chicago at Intra-League Draft

ANDY BARBE
#14 right wing   6' 175–R
b. Coniston, July 27, 1923

1950–51R/L	1	0	0	0	2

- recalled January 17, 1951, from Hornets
- first and only Leaf game January 18, 1951

BILL BARILKO
("Bashing Bill"/"Billy The Kid")
#5–19–21 defence   5'11" 184–L
b. Timmins, March 25, 1927
d. Cochrane, August 26, 1951

1946–47R	18	3	7	10	33
1947–48	57	5	9	14	147
1948–49	60	5	4	9	95
1949–50	59	7	10	17	85
1950–51L	58	6	6	12	96
Totals	252	26	36	62	456

- signed by Leafs in 1946
- recalled February 2, 1947, from Hollywood
- first Leaf game February 6, 1947

- last Leaf game March 25, 1951
- killed in a plane crash 50 miles north of Cochrane on August 26, 1951; wreck found June 6, 1962

ALDEGE "BAZ" BASTIEN

#1 goalie 5'7" 160–L
b. Timmins, August 29, 1920
d. Pittsburgh, Pennsylvania, March 15, 1983

1945–46R/L
5 (0/0)   0–4–1   300   20   0   4.00

- signed October 30, 1940, by Leafs
- missed 1942–45—Canadian army
- first Leaf game October 27, 1945
- played first five games of 1945–46 (0–4–1) when regular Frank McCool held out in contract dispute
- last Leaf game November 7, 1945
- sold outright December 26, 1945, to Hornets
- played mostly with Hornets 1945–49
- forced to retire when struck in the eye by a puck at training camp on September 19, 1949
- became manager for Pittsburgh Hornets and assistant GM in Detroit and later Pittsburgh

ANDY BATHGATE

("Handy Andy"/"Tubby")
#9 right wing 6' 180–R
b. Winnipeg, Manitoba, August 28, 1932

1963–64	15	3	15	18	8
1964–65	55	16	29	45	34
Totals	70	19	44	63	42

- acquired February 22, 1964, with Don McKenney from Rangers for Arnie Brown, Bill Collins, Dick Duff, Bob Nevin, and Rod Seiling
- traded May 20, 1965, with Billy Harris and Gary Jarrett to Detroit for Marcel Pronovost, Lowell MacDonald, Ed Joyal, Larry Jeffrey, and Aut Erickson

- ran a driving range just west of Toronto
- Hockey Hall of Fame 1978

KEN BAUMGARTNER ("Bomber")

#8–22 forward 6'1" 200–L
b. Flin Flon, Manitoba, March 11, 1966

1991–92	11	0	0	0	23
1992–93	63	1	0	1	155
1993–94	64	4	4	8	185
1994–95	2	0	0	0	5
1995–96	60	2	3	5	152
Totals	200	7	7	14	520

- acquired March 10, 1992, with Dave McLlwain from Islanders for Daniel Marois and Claude Loiselle
- missed most of 1994–95 with separated shoulder
- traded March 20, 1996, to Anaheim for a 4th-round draft choice in 1996 (later traded to Canadiens—Kim Staal)
- later admitted to Harvard School of Business

BOB BAUN ("Boomer")

#21–26 defence 5'9" 182–R
b. Lanigan, Saskatchewan, September 9, 1936

1956–57R	20	0	5	5	37
1957–58	67	1	9	10	91
1958–59	51	1	8	9	87
1959–60	61	8	9	17	59
1960–61	70	1	14	15	70
1961–62	65	4	11	15	94
1962–63	48	4	8	12	65
1963–64	52	4	14	18	113
1964–65	70	0	18	18	160
1965–66	44	0	6	6	68
1966–67	54	2	8	10	83
1970–71	58	1	17	18	123
1971–72	74	2	12	14	101
1972–73	5	1	1	2	4
Totals	739	29	140	169	1155

- Marlie graduate; first Leaf game November 29, 1956

- missed January 22–March 1, 1964, with injury
- injured December 11–February 16, 1965–66
- missed part of 1966–67 with broken thumb
- claimed June 6, 1967, by Oakland in Expansion Draft
- acquired November 13, 1970, from St. Louis for Brit Selby
- retired December 1972 (last game October 21, 1972)
- owned Tim Horton's doughnut franchises and a golf course in Southern Ontario

DON BEAUPRE
#33 goalie   5'10" 172–L
b. Waterloo, September 19, 1961

1995–96					
8 (2/2)	0–5–0	336	26	0	4.64
1996–97					
3 (1/1)	0–3–0	110	10	0	5.45
Totals					
11 (3/3)	0–8–0	446	36	0	4.84

- acquired January 23, 1996, from Ottawa with Kirk Muller from Islanders; Leafs sent Damian Rhodes to Ottawa and Ken Belanger to the Islanders; Ottawa sent Bryan Berard and Martin Straka to New York; Islanders sent Wade Redden to the Senators
- demoted November 19, 1996, to St. John's

WADE BELAK
#2 defence   6'5" 222–R
b. Saskatoon, Saskatchewan, July 3, 1976

2000–01	39	1	1	2	110

- claimed off waivers from Calgary on February 22, 2001

ALAIN "BAM BAM" BELANGER
#18 right wing   6'1" 190–R
b. St. Janvier, Quebec, January 18, 1956

1977–78R/L	9	0	1	1	6

- selected 48th overall at 1976 Amateur Draft
- only NHL games February 1, 4, 5, 8, 11, 13, 15, 22, 25, 1978, with Leafs

KEN BELANGER
#43 left wing   6'4" 225–L
b. Sault Ste. Marie, May 14, 1974

1994–95R	3	0	0	0	9

- acquired March 18, 1994, from Hartford for a 9th-round draft choice in 1994 (Matt Ball)
- first Leaf games March 4, 31 and April 3, 1995
- traded January 23, 1996, to the Islanders with Damian Rhodes to Ottawa; Leafs received Kirk Muller from Islanders and Don Beaupre from Ottawa; Ottawa sent Bryan Berard and Martin Straka to New York; Islanders sent Wade Redden to Ottawa

GORDIE BELL
#1–24 goalie   5'10" 164–L
b. Portage La Prairie, Manitoba, March 13, 1925
d. Belleville, November 3, 1980

1945–46R					
8 (0/0)	3–5–0	480	31	0	3.87

- acquired November 25, 1943, with Dudley Garrett and first post-war call on Charlie Rayner from Rangers for Bucko McDonald
- missed 1943–45—Canadian armed forces
- first Leaf game November 8, 1945
- played eight games at start of 1945–46, when regular Frank McCool held out in contract dispute
- traded April 26, 1948, to Springfield with Armand Lemieux, Leo Curik, and Rod Roy for Eldred Kobussen
- later won gold medal with Belleville McFarlands at 1959 WC

PETE BELLEFEUILLE

("Fleeting French-man"/"French Pete")
#10 right wing   5'8" 155–R
b. Trois-Rivières, Quebec, October 19, 1901
d. Unknown

1925–26R	36	14	2	16	22
1926–27	13	0	0	0	12

Totals	49	14	2	16	34

- signed in 1925 after playing with Quebec and Iroquois Falls
- first St. Pats game November 28, 1925
- sent December 27, 1926, to London Tecumsehs for Butch Keeling
- traded outright on January 10, 1927, to Detroit for Slim Halderson

JIM BENNING ("Benji")

#3–15 defence   6' 183–L
b. Edmonton, Alberta, April 29, 1963

1981–82R	74	7	24	31	46
1982–83	74	5	17	22	47
1983–84	79	12	39	51	66
1984–85	80	9	35	44	55
1985–86	52	4	21	25	71
1986–87	5	0	0	0	4

Totals	364	37	136	173	289

- selected 6th overall at 1981 Entry Draft
- first Leaf game October 6, 1981
- traded December 2, 1986, with Dan Hodgson to Vancouver Canucks for Rick Lanz

MAX "THE HAT" BENTLEY

("The Dipsy-doodle Dandy from Deslisle"/"Muscles")
#7 centre   5'8" 158–L
b. Delisle, Saskatchewan, March 1, 1920
d. Saskatoon, Saskatchewan, January 19, 1984

1947–48	53	23	25	48	14
1948–49	60	19	22	41	18
1949–50	69	23	18	41	14
1950–51	67	21	41	62	34
1951–52	69	24	17	41	40
1952–53	36	12	11	23	16

Totals	354	122	134	256	136

- acquired November 2, 1947, with Cy Thomas from Chicago for Gus Bodnar, Ernie Dickens, Bob Goldham, Bud Poile, and Gaye Stewart
- left the team November 28–January 17, 1952–53, because he felt his performance was weak
- sold August 11, 1953 to the Rangers
- Hockey Hall of Fame 1966

BRYAN BERARD ("Bee")

#34 defence   6'1" 190–L
b. Woonsocket, Rhode Island, March 5, 1977

1998–99	38	5	14	19	22
1999–2000	64	3	27	30	42

Totals	102	8	41	49	64

- acquired from the Islanders on January 9, 1999, with a 6th-round draft choice in 1999 (Jan Socher) for Felix Potvin and a 6th-round draft choice in 1999 (later traded to Tampa Bay—Fedor Fedorov)
- suffered career-ending eye injury on March 11, 2000, vs. Ottawa when hit by Marian Hossa's stick
- played for USA at 1995 (fifth place) and 1996 (fifth) WJC, 1997 WC (sixth), and 1998 Olympics (fifth)

DRAKE BEREHOWSKY ("Bear")

#29–24–55 defence   6'1" 210–R
b. Toronto, January 3, 1972

1990–91R	8	0	1	1	25
1991–92	1	0	0	0	0
1992–93	41	4	15	19	61
1993–94	49	2	8	10	63
1994–95	25	0	2	2	15

Totals	124	6	26	32	164

- selected 10th overall at 1990 Entry Draft
- first Leaf game October 4, 1990

- traded April 7, 1995, to Penguins for Grant Jennings
- currently with Vancouver Canucks

SERGEI BEREZIN

#94 forward   5'10" 172–R
b. Voskresensk, Russia, November 5, 1971

1996–97R	73	25	16	41	2
1997–98	68	16	15	31	10
1998–99	76	37	22	59	12
1999–2000	61	26	13	39	2
2000–01	79	22	28	50	8
Totals	357	126	94	220	34

- selected 256th overall at 1994 Entry Draft
- first Leaf game October 5, 1996
- won silver medal at 1991 WJC; played for Russia at 1994 Olympics (fourth place); played at 1994 (fifth), 1995 (fifth), 1996 (fourth), and 1998 (fifth) WC
- currently with Leafs

AKI BERG ("Bergie")

#8 defence   6'3" 215–L
b. Turku, Finland, July 28, 1977

2000–01	11	0	2	2	4

- acquired from Los Angeles on March 13, 2001 for Adam Mair and a 2nd-round draft choice in 2001 (Mike Cammelleri)

BILL BERG

#10 centre   6'1" 190–L
b. St. Catharines, October 21, 1967

1992–93	58	7	8	15	54
1993–94	83	8	11	19	93
1994–95	32	5	1	6	26
1995–96	23	1	1	2	33
Totals	196	21	21	42	206

- claimed on waivers December 3, 1992, from Islanders
- missed 16 games in 1994–95 with strained knee muscles

- missed 30 games in 1995–96 with broken leg
- traded February 29, 1996, to Rangers with Sergio Momesso for Nick Kypreos and Wayne Presley

TIM BERNHARDT ("Timber")

#1 goalie   5'9" 160–L
b. Sarnia, January 17, 1958

1984–85					
37 (2/1)	13–19–4	2182	136	0	3.74
1985–86					
23 (2/2)	4–12–3	1266	107	0	5.07
1986–87L					
1 (0/1)	0–0–0	20	3	0	9.00
Totals					
61 (4/4)	17–31–7	3468	246	0	4.26

- signed December 5, 1984 as a free agent
- last Leaf game October 22, 1986
- won bronze medal with Canada at 1978 WJC

CRAIG BERUBE

#16 left wing   6'2" 205–L
b. Calihoo, Alberta, December 17, 1965

1991–92	40	5	7	12	109

- acquired September 19, 1991, with Grant Fuhr and Glenn Anderson from Edmonton for Vincent Damphousse, Peter Ing, Scott Thornton, and Luke Richardson
- traded January 2, 1992, with Gary Leeman, Michel Petit, Jeff Reese, and Alexander Godynyuk to Calgary for Doug Gilmour, Jamie Macoun, Ric Nattress, Rick Wamsley, and Kent Manderville

ALLAN BESTER ("Ernie"/"Beast"/"Worm")
#31–30 goalie   5'7" 150–L
b. Hamilton, March 26, 1964

1983–84R					
32 (3/1)	11–16–4	1848	134	0	4.35
1984–85					
15 (2/1)	3–9–1	767	54	1	4.22
1985–86					
1 (0/1)	0–0–0	20	2	0	6.00
1986–87					
36 (5/7)	10–14–3	1808	110	2	3.65
1987–88					
30 (3/6)	8–12–5	1607	102	2	3.81
1988–89					
43 (3/1)	17–20–3	2460	156	2	3.80
1989–90					
42 (8/4)	20–16–0	2206	165	0	4.49
1990–91					
6 (2/1)	0–4–0	247	18	0	4.37

Totals
205 (26/22) 69–91–16 10963   741   7   4.06

- selected 49th overall at 1983 Entry Draft
- first Leaf game January 8, 1984
- traded March 5, 1991, to Detroit for a 6th-round draft choice in 1991 (Alexander Kuzminsky)
- played at 1984 WJC (fourth place)

FRANK BIALOWAS ("The Animal")
#36 left wing   5'11" 225–L
b. Winnipeg, Manitoba,
September 25, 1970

1993–94R	3	0	0	0	12

- signed March 20, 1994, as a free agent
- first Leaf games March 26, 28, April 10, 1994
- released June 28, 1995

PAUL BIBEAULT
#1 goalie   5'9" 160–L
b. Montreal, Quebec, April 13, 1919
d. Rigaud, Quebec, August 2, 1970

1943–44					
29 (0/0)	13–14–2	1740	87	5	3.00

- signed January 24, 1944, for $3,000 after being discharged from army with permission from Canadiens and with condition the Habs could reclaim him for one dollar at year's end
- reclaimed by Habs on September 13, 1944
- married Frank Selke's daughter, Evelyn, and later managed the Pointe Claire Arena in Quebec

JACK BIONDA
#22 defence   6' 175–L
b. Huntsville, September 18, 1933
d. London, November 3, 1999

1955–56R	13	0	1	1	18

- first Leaf game October 16, 1955
- sold April 23, 1956, to Boston for $30,000
- member of Canadian Sports Hall of Fame as one of Canada's greatest lacrosse players

ANDY BLAIR
#5–12–11 centre/defence   6'2" 176–L
b. Winnipeg, Manitoba, February 27, 1908
d. Seattle, Washington, December 27, 1977

1928–29R	44	12	15	27	41
1929–30	42	11	10	21	27
1930–31	44	11	8	19	32
1931–32	48	9	14	23	35
1932–33	43	6	9	15	38
1933–34	47	14	9	23	35
1934–35	45	6	14	20	22
1935–36	45	5	4	9	60
Totals	358	74	83	157	290

- won Allan Cup with University of Manitoba in 1928
- signed by Leafs October 28, 1928
- first Leaf game November 15, 1928
- missed games in 1932–33 after being badly cut on the arm in a game January 31, 1933
- sold May 8, 1936, to Chicago for $7,500
- worked in the pipe business until he retired

CHUCK BLAIR

#22 right wing   5'10" 175–R
b. Edinburgh, Scotland, July 23, 1928

1948–49R	1	0	0	0

- Marlie graduate; first and only Leaf game December 4, 1948
- traded summer 1953 to Cleveland (AHL) with $30,000 for Bob Bailey and Jerry Foley

GEORGE "DUSTY" BLAIR

#14 centre   5'8" 160–R
b. South Porcupine, September 15, 1929

1950–51R/L	2	0	0	0

- acquired from Detroit in 1949 for Johnny Wilson
- only Leaf games December 30 and January 6, 1950–51
- traded to Bisons with Frank Sullivan and Jackie LeClair in April 1954 for Brian Cullen

MIKE BLAISDELL ("Blazer")

#22 right wing   6'1" 195–R
b. Moose Jaw, Saskatchewan, January 18, 1960

1987–88	18	3	2	5	2
1988–89L	9	1	0	1	4
Totals	27	4	2	6	6

- signed July 10, 1987, as a free agent from Penguins
- last Leaf games December 17, 19, 23, 26 and January 9, 11, 14, 27, 28, 1988–89
- joined Canadian National Team in 1989
- later played and coached in England

FRANK "MICKEY" BLAKE

#3–20 defence   5'10" 186–L
b. Barriefield, October 31, 1912

1935–36L	8	0	0	0	2

- drafted October 15, 1935, by Leafs from NHL for $1,000 after St. Louis Eagles folded
- first and only Leaf games February 8, 13, 15, 20, 22, 23, 25, 29, 1936
- traded summer 1936 to Cleveland (AHL) for Bill Cunningham

AUGUST "GUS" BODNAR

#8–21 centre   5'10" 160–R
b. Fort William, August 24, 1925

1943–44R	50	22	40	62	18
1944–45	49	8	36	44	18
1945–46	49	14	23	37	14
1946–47	39	4	6	10	10
Totals	187	48	105	153	60

- graduated from Fort William Juniors; signed October 29, 1943
- first Leaf game October 30, 1943
- traded November 2, 1947, with Ernie Dickens, Bob Goldham, Bud Poile, and Gaye Stewart to Chicago for Max Bentley and Cy Thomas
- later coached in OHL and was one of three coaches for Canada's WJC team in 1978 featuring Wayne Gretzky (bronze)

GARTH BOESCH

#5–18 defence   6' 180–R
b. Milestone, Saskatchewan, October 7, 1920
d. California, May 14, 1998

1946–47R	35	4	5	9	47
1947–48	45	2	7	9	52
1948–49	59	1	10	11	43
1949–50L	58	2	6	8	63
Totals	197	9	28	37	205

- signed in 1945 from Saskatoon Seniors (RCAF)
- first Leaf game October 16, 1946
- last Leaf game March 26, 1950
- only moustachioed player of his era

LONNY BOHONOS ("Bo")
#16 right wing   5'11" 190–R
b. Winnipeg, Manitoba, May 20, 1973

1997–98	6	3	3	6	4
1998–99	7	3	0	3	4
Totals	13	6	3	9	8

- acquired from Vancouver on March 7, 1998, for Brandon Convery
- currently plays minor pro

FRED BOIMISTRUCK
#11 defence   5'11" 191–R
b. Sudbury, November 4, 1962

1981–82R	57	2	11	13	32
1982–83L	26	2	3	5	13
Totals	83	4	14	18	45

- selected 43rd overall at 1980 Entry Draft
- first Leaf game October 6, 1981
- last Leaf game December 11, 1982
- released summer 1983
- played at 1981 WJC (seventh place)

SERGE BOISVERT
#12 right wing   5'9" 172–R
b. Drummondville, Quebec, June 1, 1959

1982–83R	17	0	2	2	4

- signed October 9, 1980, as a free agent
- played 1981–82 with Yukijirushi (Japan)
- first Leaf game October 6, 1982
- traded January 15, 1983, to Edmonton for Reid Bailey
- played for Canada at 1988 Olympics (fourth place)

LEO BOIVIN ("Billy")
#16–18–19–21 defence   5'7" 190–L
b. Prescott, August 2, 1932

1951–52R	2	0	1	1	0
1952–53	70	2	13	15	97
1953–54	58	1	6	7	81
1954–55	7	0	0	0	8
Totals	137	3	20	23	186

- acquired November 15, 1950, with Fern Flaman, Phil Maloney, and Ken Smith from Boston for Bill Ezinicki and Vic Lynn
- first Leaf game March 8, 1952
- traded November 9, 1954, to Boston for Joe Klukay
- became a coach with St. Louis and scout after retiring as a player
- Hockey Hall of Fame 1986

FRANK "BUZZ" BOLL
#8–17 left wing   5'10" 166–L
b. Filmore, Saskatchewan, March 6, 1911

1933–34R	42	12	8	20	21
1934–35	47	14	4	18	4
1935–36	44	15	13	28	14
1936–37	25	6	3	9	12
1937–38	44	14	11	25	18
1938–39	11	0	0	0	0
Totals	213	61	39	100	69

- Marlie graduate; first Leaf game November 9, 1933
- missed much of 1936–37 with a broken arm
- missed much of 1938–39 with injured knee; hurt opening night, reinjured March 14, 1939
- traded May 18, 1939, with Murray Armstrong, Busher Jackson, and Doc Romnes to New York Americans for Sweeney Schriner
- retired to his farm in Filmore where he worked until retiring

HUGH BOLTON ("Yug")
#4–19–23–20 defence 6'3" 190–R
b. Toronto, April 15, 1929
d. Toronto, October 17, 1999

1949–50R	2	0	0	0	2
1950–51	13	1	3	4	4
1951–52	60	3	13	16	73
1952–53	9	0	0	0	10
1953–54	9	0	0	0	10
1954–55	69	2	19	21	55
1955–56	67	4	16	20	65
1956–57L	6	0	0	0	2
Totals	235	10	51	61	221

- Marlie graduate; first Leaf games December 1 and 3, 1949
- missed many games in 1952–53 with mononucleosis
- recalled December 8, 1953, from Ottawa when Thomson injured
- recalled February 22, 1954
- missed many games in 1953–54 with a broken jaw
- broke his leg October 25, 1956 vs. Canadiens ending his career
- taught physics in Toronto high schools for 30 years

GEORGE BOOTHMAN ("Pruneface")
#14–16 defence 6'2" 175–R
b. Calgary, Alberta, September 25, 1916

1942–43R	9	1	1	2	4
1943–44L	49	16	18	34	14
Totals	58	17	19	36	18

- signed October 23, 1942, by Leafs
- first Leaf game December 17, 1942
- traded February 2, 1943, for the rest of the season only with Bucko McDonald and Jack Forsey to Providence for Ab DeMarco and Buck Jones
- traded October 13, 1944, with Don Webster to Buffalo (IHL) for Bill Ezinicki
- last Leaf game March 18, 1944

NIKOLAI BORSCHEVSKY
("Nick the Stick")
#16 right wing 5'9" 170–L
b. Tomsk, USSR, January 12, 1965

1992–93	78	34	40	74	28
1993–94	45	14	20	34	10
1994–95	19	0	5	5	0
Totals	142	48	65	113	38

- selected 77th overall at 1992 Entry Draft
- traded April 6, 1995, to Calgary for a 6th-round draft choice in 1996 (Chris Bogas)
- won gold medals with Soviet Union at 1984 WJC and with Unified Team at 1992 Olympics and played with Russia at 1992 WC (fifth place)
- later ran popular hockey schools in Toronto and Southern Ontario

LAURIE BOSCHMAN ("Bosch")
#12 centre 6' 185–L
b. Major, Saskatchewan, June 4, 1960

1979–80R	80	16	32	48	78
1980–81	53	14	19	33	178
1981–82	54	9	19	28	150
Totals	187	39	70	109	406

- selected 9th overall at 1979 Entry Draft
- first Leaf game October 10, 1979
- traded March 8, 1982, to Edmonton for Walt Poddubny and Phil Drouilliard
- a born-again Christian, he later became Ottawa and Eastern Ontario director for Hockey Ministries International, combining belief and hockey programs

BRUCE BOUDREAU ("Gabby")

#12–19–35–11–17–28 centre   5'9" 175–L
b. Toronto, January 9, 1955

1976–77	15	2	5	7	4
1977–78	40	11	18	29	12
1978–79	26	4	3	7	2
1979–80	2	0	0	0	2
1980–81	39	10	14	24	18
1981–82	12	0	2	2	6
Totals	134	27	42	69	44

- selected 42nd overall at 1975 Amateur Draft
- signed October 10, 1985, as a free agent by Chicago
- later coached minor pro

LEO BOURGEAULT

#8–16 defence   5'6" 165–L
b. Sturgeon Falls, January 17, 1903
d. Unknown

1926–27R	22	0	0	0	44

- purchased from Saskatoon in 1926 with Corb Dennenay and Laurie Scott
- sent to the Rangers during 1926–27 season

PAT BOUTETTE ("Booter")

#15 right wing   5'8" 175–L
b. Windsor, March 1, 1952

1975–76R	77	10	22	32	140
1976–77	80	18	18	36	107
1977–78	80	17	19	36	120
1978–79	80	14	19	33	136
1979–80	32	0	4	4	17
Totals	349	59	82	141	520

- selected 139th overall at 1972 Amateur Draft
- first Leaf game October 11, 1975
- traded December 24, 1979, to Hartford for Bob Stephenson
- played for Canada at 1981 WC (fourth place)

JOHNNY BOWER ("China Wall")

#1 goalie   5'11" 182–L
b. Prince Albert, Saskatchewan, November 8, 1924

1958–59						
39 (0/0)	15–17–7	2340	107	3	2.74	
1959–60						
66 (0/0)	34–24–8	3960	180	5	2.73	
1960–61						
58 (0/0)	33–15–10	3480	145	2	2.50	
1961–62						
59 (0/0)	32–17–10	3540	152	2	2.58	
1962–63						
42 (0/0)	20–15–7	2520	110	1	2.62	
1963–64						
51 (2/0)	24–16–11	3009	106	5	2.11	
1964–65						
34 (0/0)	13–13–8	2040	81	3	2.38	
1965–66						
35 (1/1)	18–12–5	1998	75	3	2.25	
1966–67						
24 (2/5)	12–9–3	1431	63	3	2.64	
1967–68						
43 (8/3)	14–18–7	2239	84	4	2.25	
1968–69						
20 (6/7)	5–4–3	779	37	2	2.85	
1969–70L						
1 (0/0)	0–1–0	60	5	0	5.00	

Totals
472(19/16)220–161–79 27396 1145 33 2.51
- claimed June 3, 1958, from Rangers at Intra-League Draft
- last Leaf game December 10, 1969
- retired to become Leafs' goalie coach, a position he held well into the 1980s
- Hockey Hall of Fame 1976

WALLY BOYER

#15 centre   5'8" 165–L
b. Cowan, Manitoba, September 27, 1937

1965–66R	46	4	17	21	23

- Marlie graduate; first Leaf game December 11, 1965
- claimed June 15, 1966, by Canadiens at Intra-League Draft
- later operated a tavern in Midland

BRIAN BRADLEY

#44 centre   5'9" 160–R
b. Kitchener, January 21, 1965

1990–91	26	0	11	11	20
1991–92	59	10	21	31	48
Totals	85	10	32	42	68

- acquired January 12, 1991, from Vancouver Canucks for Tom Kurvers
- claimed June 18, 1992, by Tampa Bay at Expansion Draft
- won gold medal with Canada at 1985 WJC and played at 1988 Olympics (fourth place)
- forced to retire while with Tampa Bay because of post-concussion syndrome

JOHN BRENNEMAN

#24 left wing   5'10" 175–L
b. Fort Erie, January 5, 1943

1966–67	41	6	4	10	4

- claimed June 15, 1966, from the Rangers at Intra-League Draft
- started 1966–67 with Leafs; sent to minors February 22, 1967
- claimed June 6, 1967, by St. Louis at Expansion Draft
- worked for a beer company after leaving hockey

CARL BREWER

#2–18–28 defence   5'10" 180–L
b. Toronto, October 21, 1938

1957–58R	2	0	0	0	0
1958–59	69	3	21	24	125
1959–60	67	4	19	23	150
1960–61	51	1	14	15	92
1961–62	67	1	22	23	89
1962–63	70	2	23	25	168
1963–64	57	4	9	13	114
1964–65	70	4	23	27	177
1979–80L	20	0	5	5	2
Totals	473	19	136	155	917

- Marlie graduate; first Leaf games February 16 and 22, 1958
- missed many games in 1960–61 with torn knee ligaments
- missed first ten games of 1963–64 with broken arm
- retired at training camp in September 1965 after the All-Star game as the result of a dispute with coach Punch Imlach
- reinstated as an amateur through the efforts of his agent, Alan Eagleson
- traded March 3, 1968, with Frank Mahovlich, Pete Stemkowski, and Garry Unger to Detroit for Paul Henderson, Norm Ullman, and Floyd Smith
- signed as a free agent January 2, 1980
- retired after 1979–80 season; last Leaf game March 25, 1980
- won bronze medal with Canada at 1967 WC
- instigated legal action against Alan Eagleson that resulted in Eagleson's expulsion from the game, the Hall of Fame, and acknowledgement of guilt of charges of fraud

DOUG BRINDLEY

#17 centre   6'1" 175–L
b. Walkerton, June 8, 1949

1970–71R/L	3	0	0	0	0

- selected 20th overall at 1969 Amateur Draft
- only Leaf games December 6, 8, 9, 1970
- traded fall 1971 to Vancouver Canucks (WHL) for André Hinse

GREG BRITZ

#16–32 right wing   6' 190–R
b. Buffalo, New York, January 3, 1961

1983–84R	6	0	0	0	2
1984–85	1	0	0	0	2
Totals	7	0	0	0	4

- signed as a free agent November 2, 1983
- first Leaf games November 2, 4, 5, 9, 11, 12, 1983

- played March 18, 1985, with Leafs
- signed October 1986 by Hartford

WALTER "TURK" BRODA

("The Fabulous Fat Man"/"Turkey Face")
#1–19–23 goalie   5′9″ 180–L
b. Brandon, Manitoba, May 15, 1914
d. Toronto, October 17, 1972

1936–37R						
45 (0/0)	22–19–4	2770	106	3	2.30
1937–38						
48 (0/0)	24–15–9	2980	127	6	2.56
1938–39						
48 (0/0)	19–20–9	2990	107	8	2.15
1939–40						
47 (0/0)	25–17–5	2900	108	4	2.23
1940–41						
48 (0/0)	28–14–6	2970	99	5	2.00
1941–42						
48 (0/0)	27–18–3	2960	136	6	2.76
1942–43						
50 (0/0)	22–19–9	3000	159	1	3.18
1945–46						
15 (0/0)	6–6–3	900	53	0	3.53
1946–47						
60 (0/0)	31–19–10	3600	172	4	2.87
1947–48						
60 (0/0)	32–15–13	3600	143	5	2.38
1948–49						
60 (0/0)	22–25–13	3600	161	5	2.68
1949–50						
68 (1/0)	30–25–12	4040	167	9	2.48
1950–51						
31 (0/1)	14–11–5	1827	68	6	2.24
1951–52L						
1 (1/0)	0–1–0	31	3	0	5.81

Totals
629 (2/1) 302–224–101 38168 1609 62 2.53

- bought May 8, 1936, from Windsor Bulldogs (Detroit's IHL affiliate) for $7,500
- first Leaf game November 5, 1936
- missed 1943–45—Canadian army
- played half of the last game of 1951–52 season March 23, 1952, then retired
- later coached Marlies
- Hockey Hall of Fame 1967

ARTHUR BROOKS

#1 goalie
b. Guelph, 1892   d. Unknown

1917–18L						
4 (0/1)	2–1	220	23	0	5.75

- first Arenas game December 19, 1917
- last Arenas game December 29, 1917
- released January 6, 1918, after Holmes signed

WILLIE BROSSART

#25 defence   6′ 190–L
b. Allan, Saskatchewan, May 29, 1949

1973–74	17	0	1	1	20
1974–75	4	0	0	0	2
Totals	21	0	1	1	22

- bought May 23, 1973, from Flyers
- traded November 2, 1974, with Tim Ecclestone to Washington for Rod Seiling

AARON BROTEN

#21 left wing   5′10″ 175–L
b. Roseau, Minnesota, November 14, 1960

1990–91	27	6	4	10	32

- acquired November 17, 1990, with Michel Petit and Lucien Deblois from Quebec Nordiques for Scott Pearson and a 2nd-round draft choice in 1991 (later traded to Washington—Eric Lavigne) and 1992 (Tuomas Gronman)
- signed as a free agent January 21, 1992, by Winnipeg Jets

ARNIE BROWN ("Brownie")

#16–22 defence   5′11″ 185–L
b. Apsley, January 28, 1942

1961–62R	2	0	0	0	0
1963–64	4	0	0	0	6
Totals	6	0	0	0	6

- St. Mike's graduate; first Leaf games October 28 and November 1, 1961

Turk Broda

- played January 18, 19, 22, 1964, with Leafs (sent to minors January 29)
- traded February 22, 1964, with Bill Collins, Dick Duff, Bob Nevin, and Rod Seiling to the Rangers for Andy Bathgate and Don McKenney
- became a sales manager for Monsanto Corporation (plastics division)

JEFF BROWN

#33 defence   6'1" 204–R
b. Ottawa, April 30, 1966

1997–98	19	1	8	9	10

- acquired January 2, 1998, from Carolina for future considerations
- traded to Washington on March 24, 1998, for Sylvain Côté

JEFF BRUBAKER ("Bru")

#23 left wing   6'2" 210–L
b. Hagerstown, Maryland, February 24, 1958

1984–85	68	8	4	12	209
1985–86	21	0	0	0	67
Totals	89	8	4	12	276

- claimed October 9, 1984 from Edmonton in Waiver Draft
- claimed on waivers December 5, 1985, by Edmonton

BILL BRYDGE

#3 defence   5'9" 180–R
b. Renfrew, October 22, 1898
d. Kirkland Lake, November 3, 1949

1926–27R	41	6	3	9	76

- signed in 1926 after winning Allan Cup with Port Arthur Bearcats
- first St. Pats game November 17, 1926
- traded to Detroit Cougars in 1927 for Art Duncan
- later coached Lakeshore Blue Devils to Canadian Senior amateur title

GORD BRYDSON

#14 forward   5'7" 150–R
b. Toronto, January 3, 1907
d. Mississauga, February 4, 2001

1929–30R/L	9	2	0	2	8

- acquired November 14, 1929, from Buffalo Bisons for future considerations (Wes King)
- played November 14, 16, 19, 21, 23, 26, 30 and December 3, 5, 1929, with Leafs
- sold December 6, 1929, to London after Toronto signed Harvey Jackson
- became a golf pro in Mississauga

AL BUCHANAN

#24–25 left wing   5'8" 160–L
b. Winnipeg, Manitoba, May 17, 1927

1948–49R	3	0	1	1	2
1949–50L	1	0	0	0	0
Totals	4	0	1	1	2

- first Leaf games January 2, 5, 8, 1949
- last Leaf game January 14, 1950

MIKE BULLARD

#22 centre   5'10" 185–L
b. Ottawa, March 10, 1961

1991–92L	65	14	14	28	42

- acquired July 29, 1991, from Flyers for a 3rd-round draft choice in 1993 (Vaclav Prospal)
- last Leaf game March 25, 1992
- released summer 1992 and signed with Rapperswil (Swiss League)
- won bronze medal with Canada at 1986 WC

BILL BUREGA ("Boogie")

#20 defence   6'1" 200–L
b. Winnipeg, Manitoba, March 13, 1932

1955–56R/L	4	0	1	1	4

- played January 14, 15, 18, 19, 1956, with Leafs

DAVE BURROWS ("Bone Rack")
#26 defence   6'1" 190–L
b. Toronto, January 11, 1949

1978–79	65	2	11	13	28
1979–80	80	3	16	19	42
1980–81	6	0	0	0	2
Totals	151	5	27	32	72

- acquired June 14, 1978, from Penguins for Randy Carlyle and George Ferguson
- traded November 18, 1980, with Paul Gardner to Penguins for Kim Davis and Paul Marshall
- became director of hockey operations for Teen Ranch, a Christian sports camp in Caledon, Ontario

GARTH BUTCHER
#2 defence   6' 194–R
b. Regina, Saskatchewan, January 8, 1963

1994–95L	45	1	7	8	59

- acquired June 28, 1994, with Mats Sundin, Todd Warriner, and a 1st-round draft choice in 1994 (traded to Washington— Nolan Baumgartner with Rob Pearson for Mike Ridley and a 1st-round draft choice in 1994—Eric Fichaud) from Quebec Nordiques for Wendel Clark, Sylvain Lefebvre, Landon Wilson, and a 1st-round draft choice in 1994 (Jeffrey Kealty)
- last Leaf game May 3, 1995
- released outright October 16, 1995
- won gold medal with Canada at 1982 WJC and played at 1992 WC (eighth place)
- opened a restaurant called The Pump near Toronto after retiring

JERRY BUTLER ("Bugsy")
#17 right wing   6' 180–R
b. Sarnia, February 27, 1951

1977–78	73	9	7	16	49
1978–79	76	8	7	15	52
1979–80	55	7	8	15	29
Totals	204	24	22	46	130

- acquired November 1, 1977, from St. Louis for Inge Hammarstrom
- traded February 18, 1980, with Tiger Williams to Vancouver Canucks for Bill Derlago and Rick Vaive

MIKE BYERS
#24 right wing   5'10" 185–R
b. Toronto, September 11, 1946

1967–68R	10	2	2	4	0
1968–69	5	0	0	0	2
Totals	15	2	2	4	2

- Marlie graduate; first Leaf game December 30, 1967; sent to minors January 3, 1968
- traded March 2, 1969, with Gerry Meehan and Bill Sutherland to Flyers for Brit Selby and Forbes Kennedy
- became senior vice-president for a bank in Los Angeles

JACK CAFFERY
#25 centre   6' 175–R
b. Kingston, June 30, 1934
d. Toronto, December 2, 1992

1954–55R	3	0	0	0	0

- St. Mike's graduate; recalled December 9, 1954, from Hornets
- played December 11, 12, 15, 1954
- sold May 7, 1956, to Boston for cash

LARRY CAHAN ("Hank")
#20 defence   6' 195–R
b. Fort William, December 25, 1933
d. June 25, 1992

1954–55R	58	0	6	6	64
1955–56	21	0	2	2	46
Totals	79	0	8	8	110

- signed in 1953 and assigned to Hornets
- first Leaf game October 7, 1954
- sold June 6, 1956, to Rangers for $15,000

JIM "DUTCH" CAIN

#9 defence   5'11" 180–L
b. Newmarket, December 24, 1912
d. Unknown

1925–26L	23	0	0	0	8

- acquired January 11, 1926, from Maroons for Toots Holway
- last St. Pats game March 17, 1926
- later worked for a scrap metal firm in Newmarket

HARRY CAMERON ("Cammie")

#10–2 defence   5'10" 154–R
b. Pembroke, February 6, 1890
d. Vancouver, British Columbia, October 20, 1953

1917–18	20	17	–	17	17
1918–19	7	7	2	9	23
1919–20	7	3	1	4	0
1920–21	24	18	9	27	35
1921–22	24	19	8	27	18
1922–23L	22	9	6	15	21
Totals	104	73	26	99	114

- signed by the Arenas from the Blueshirts when the NHL was formed
- missed game of February 2, 1918, after breaking training rules (also fined $100)
- suspended January 13, 1919, with Noble for breaking training rules
- loaned January 18 to Ottawa for the balance of the season
- traded January 14, 1920 (after the game), to Canadiens for Goldie Prodgers
- returned from Canadiens for 1921–22 season
- claimed on waivers by Saskatoon in summer of 1923
- last St. Pats game March 5, 1923
- later coached in Saskatchewan
- Hockey Hall of Fame 1962

JACK CAPUANO

#26 defence   6'2" 210–L
b. Cranston, Rhode Island, July 7, 1966

1989–90R	1	0	0	0	0

- selected 88th overall at 1984 Entry Draft
- first Leaf game October 11, 1989
- traded December 20, 1989, with Paul Gagne and Derek Laxdal to the Islanders for Gilles Thibaudeau and Mike Stevens

GEORGE CAREY

#6 right wing   5'6" 140–R
b. Unknown   d. Unknown

1923–24L	4	0	0	0	0

- signed in 1923 from Hamilton Tigers (NHL)
- first and only St. Pats games December 15, 19, 22, 26, 1923

WAYNE CARLETON ("Swoop")

#25–12 left wing   6'2" 215–L
b. Sudbury, August 4, 1946

1965–66R	2	0	1	1	0
1966–67	5	1	0	1	14
1967–68	65	8	11	19	34
1968–69	12	1	3	4	6
1969–70	7	0	1	1	6
Totals	91	10	16	26	60

- first Leaf games January 1 and 2, 1966
- played October 22, 23, 26, 29 and November 2, 1966
- missed March 16–end of season, 1968, with broken wrist
- spent most of time in minors because of injuries and poor relations with Punch Imlach
- traded December 10, 1969, to Boston for Jim Harrison
- became a car salesman in Collingwood

RANDY CARLYLE
#23–28 defence   5'10" 200–L
b. Sudbury, April 19, 1956

1976–77R	45	0	5	5	51
1977–78	49	2	11	13	31
Totals	94	2	16	18	82

- selected 30th overall at 1976 Amateur Draft
- first Leaf game October 5, 1976
- traded June 14, 1978, with George Ferguson to Penguins for Dave Burrows
- won silver medal with Canada at 1989 WC

AL "RED" CARR
#14 left wing   5'8" 178–L
b. Winnipeg, Manitoba, December 29, 1916

1943–44R/L	5	0	1	1	4

- first and only Leaf games October 30, 31 and November 4, 7, 21, 1943

LORNE CARR
#9 right wing   5'8" 161–R
b. Stoughton, Saskatchewan, July 2, 1910

1941–42	47	16	17	33	4
1942–43	50	27	33	60	15
1943–44	50	36	38	74	9
1944–45	47	21	25	46	7
1945–46L	42	5	8	13	2
Totals	236	105	121	226	37

- acquired October 30, 1941, from New York Americans for Red Heron, Nick Knott, Gus Marker, and Peanuts O'Flaherty on a one year lease, all subject to recall
- officially became Leaf property February 2, 1942, when Leafs sent Jack Church and cash to Americans
- began 1945–46 as a coach in Schumacher as part of a Toronto program to provide Ontario North with vocational instructors; rejoined Leafs on November 22, 1945
- last Leaf game March 17, 1946
- later ran a hotel in Calgary

LARRY CARRIÈRE
#3 defence   6'1" 190–L
b. Montreal, Quebec, January 30, 1952

1979–80L	2	0	1	1	0

- signed August 5, 1979, as a free agent
- played April 2 and 6, 1980, with Leafs

DR. BILL CARSON ("Doc")
#15–5 centre   5'8" 158–L
b. Bracebridge, November 25, 1900
d. Parry Sound, May 29, 1967

1926–27R	40	16	6	22	41
1927–28	32	20	6	26	36
1928–29	24	7	6	13	45
Totals	96	43	18	61	122

- signed January 13, 1924, from Grimsby (OHA Intermediate) but then changed his mind and refused to come to Toronto, even though the St. Pats had bought him a pair of skates as a "signing bonus"
- signed April 17, 1926, by St. Pats after graduating from University of Toronto
- first St. Pats game November 17, 1926
- sold January 24, 1928, to Boston for $20,000
- graduated from dentistry program at University of Toronto and practised after retiring from hockey

RAY CERESINO
#16 right wing   5'8" 160–R
b. Port Arthur, April 24, 1929

1948–49R/L	12	1	1	2	2

- Marlie graduate; signed September 15, 1948, by Leafs
- recalled November 30, 1948, from Hornets.
- first Leaf game December 1, 1948
- last Leaf game January 2, 1949
- traded summer 1949 with Tod Sloan and Harry Taylor to Cleveland (AHL) for Bob Solinger

LORNE CHABOT

("Chabotsky"/"Sad Eyes"/"Old Bulwarks")
#1 goalie 6'1" 185–L
b. Montreal, Quebec, October 5, 1900
d. Montreal, Quebec, October 10, 1946

1928–29						
43 (3/0)	20–18–5	2458	67	12	1.64	
1929–30						
42 (0/0)	16–20–6	2620	113	6	2.59	
1930–31						
37 (0/0)	21–8–8	2300	80	6	2.09	
1931–32						
44 (0/0)	22–16–6	2698	106	4	2.36	
1932–33						
48 (0/0)	24–18–6	2948	111	5	2.26	

Totals
214 (3/0) 103–80–31 13024 477 33 2.20

- acquired October 17, 1928, with Alex Gray from Rangers for Butch Keeling and John Ross Roach
- traded summer 1933 to Canadiens for George Hainsworth, but retired, thus nullifying the deal. Chabot agreed to join the Habs on October 1, 1933, thus finalizing the trade
- worked as a salesman in Montreal until his untimely death

ED CHADWICK ("Chad")

#1–20 goalie 5'11" 184–L
b. Fergus, May 8, 1933

1955–56R						
5 (0/0)	2–0–3	300	3	2	0.60	
1956–57						
70 (0/0)	21–34–15	4200	192	5	2.74	
1957–58						
70 (0/0)	21–38–11	4200	226	4	3.23	
1958–59						
31 (0/0)	12–15–4	1860	93	3	3.10	
1959–60						
4 (0/0)	1–2–1	240	15	0	3.75	

Totals
180 (0/0) 57–89–34 10740 529 14 2.96

- recalled February 6, 1956, from Winnipeg Warriors

- first Leaf games February 8, 9, 11, 12, 15, 1956
- recalled December 18, 1959, from Rochester
- traded January 31, 1961, to Boston for Don Simmons
- long-time scout for Cup-winning Edmonton Oilers

ERWIN "MURPH" CHAMBERLAIN

("Old Hardrock")
#8–14 centre 5'11" 172–L
b. Shawville, Quebec, February 14, 1915
d. Beachville, May 8, 1986

1937–38R	43	4	12	16	51
1938–39	48	10	16	26	32
1939–40	40	5	17	22	63

| Totals | 131 | 19 | 45 | 64 | 146 |

- signed September 28, 1937, after winning the Allan Cup with Sudbury Frood Mines
- first Leaf game November 4, 1937
- sold May 11, 1940, to the Canadiens for $7,500
- ran a catalogue distribution centre in Ontario and Manitoba

ANDRÉ CHAMPAGNE

#18 left wing 6' 190–L
b. Eastview, September 19, 1943

1962–63R/L	2	0	0	0	0

- St. Mike's graduate; first and only Leaf games February 23 and 27, 1963

KELLY CHASE ("Chaser")

#39 right wing 5'11" 193–R
b. Porcupine Plain, Saskatchewan, October 25, 1967

1996–97	2	0	0	0	27

- acquired March 18, 1997, from Hartford for an 8th-round draft choice in 1998 (Jaroslav Svoboda)
- traded to St. Louis for future considerations on September 30, 1997

GERRY CHEEVERS ("Cheesey")
#1 goalie   5'11" 175–L
b. St. Catharines, December 7, 1940

1961–62R					
2 (0/0)	1–1–0	120	7	0	3.50

- St. Mike's graduate; signed July 3, 1961, with Leafs
- first Leaf games December 2 and 3, 1961
- claimed June 9, 1965, by Boston at Intra-League Draft
- later worked at Rockingham Park racetrack in Salem, New Hampshire, while managing his own stable of horses
- Hockey Hall of Fame 1985

LEX CHISHOLM
#9–22 centre   5'11" 175–R
b. Galt, April 1, 1915   d. August 6, 1981

1939–40R	28	6	8	14	22
1940–41L	26	4	0	4	8
Totals	54	10	8	18	30

- signed March 15, 1939, with Leafs
- first Leaf game November 18, 1939
- missed end of 1939–40 season when he broke his arm in practice March 6, 1940
- last Leaf game March 16, 1941
- retired September 12, 1941

JACK CHURCH
#16–19–20 defence 5'11" 180–R
b. Kamsack, Saskatchewan, May 24, 1915
d. Toronto, January 5, 1996

1938–39R	3	0	2	2	2
1939–40	31	1	4	5	62
1940–41	11	0	1	1	22
1941–42	27	0	4	4	28
Totals	72	1	11	12	114

- first Leaf game December 10, 1938
- recalled March 27, 1939, from Syracuse for playoffs
- demoted to minors January 27, 1942, and replaced by Bob Goldham

- missed 29 games in 1940–41 with knee injury
- sent, with cash, February 3, 1942, to Brooklyn Americans to complete acquisition of Lorne Carr, who came to the Leafs on loan but was now Toronto property
- worked for Labatt Breweries in Toronto

ROB CIMETTA
#34–14 left wing   6' 190–L
b. Toronto, February 15, 1970

1990–91	25	2	4	6	21
1991–92L	24	4	3	7	12
Totals	49	6	7	13	33

- acquired November 9, 1990, from Boston for Steve Bancroft
- last Leaf game January 25, 1992
- signed as a free agent September 8, 1993, by Chicago
- played for Canada at 1989 WJC (fourth place)

FRANCIS "KING" CLANCY
#7–5 defence   5'9 184–L
b. Ottawa, February 25, 1903
d. Toronto, November 8, 1986

1930–31	44	7	14	21	63
1931–32	48	10	9	19	61
1932–33	48	13	12	25	79
1933–34	46	11	17	28	62
1934–35	47	5	16	21	53
1935–36	47	5	10	15	61
1936–37L	6	1	0	1	4
Totals	286	52	78	130	383

- acquired October 11, 1930, from Ottawa Senators for Art Smith, Eric Pettinger, and $35,000
- retired November 23, 1936, after first six games of year
- played all six positions in one playoff game when with Ottawa Senators
- coached the Leafs, refereed in the NHL, employed by Toronto until his death

KING CLANCY
goalie

1931–32

1 (1/1)	0–0–0	1	1	0	60.00

- allowed a goal with Horner and Levinsky March 15, 1932, while Chabot was serving a penalty

TERRY CLANCY ("Whip")
#7–21 right wing   6'1" 195–L
b. Ottawa, April 2, 1943

1968–69	2	0	0	0	0
1969–70	52	6	5	11	31
1972–73L	32	0	1	1	6
Totals	86	6	6	12	37

- signed as a free agent
- played December 26, 28, 1968
- claimed June 6, 1967, by Oakland at Expansion Draft
- bought May 14, 1968, from Oakland
- sold December 23, 1970, to Canadiens
- bought August 30, 1971, from Canadiens
- rejoined Leafs for 1972–73
- last Leaf game April 1, 1973
- sold October 17, 1973, to Detroit
- played for Canada at 1964 Olympics (fourth place)
- became a commercial insurance broker in Toronto

WENDEL CLARK
#17 left wing   5'11" 194–L
b. Kelvington, Saskatchewan, October 25, 1966

1985–86	66	34	11	45	227
1986–87	80	37	23	60	271
1987–88	28	12	11	23	80
1988–89	15	7	4	11	66
1989–90	38	18	8	26	116
1990–91	63	18	16	34	152
1991–92	43	19	21	40	123
1992–93	66	17	22	39	193
1993–94	64	46	30	76	115
1995–96	13	8	7	15	16

1996–97	65	30	19	49	75
1997–98	47	12	7	19	80
1999–2000L	20	2	2	4	21
Totals	608	260	181	441	1535

- selected 1st overall at 1985 Entry Draft
- missed much of 1987–90 with recurring back injury
- traded June 28, 1994, with Sylvain Lefebvre, Landon Wilson, and a 1st-round draft choice in 1994 (Jeffrey Kealty) to Quebec for Mats Sundin, Garth Butcher, Todd Warriner, and a 1st-round draft choice in 1994 (later traded to Washington—Nolan Baumgartner—with Rob Pearson for Mike Ridley and a 1st-round draft choice in 1994—Eric Fichaud)
- acquired March 13, 1996, with Mathieu Schneider and Denis Smith from Islanders for Kenny Jonsson, Darby Hendrickson, Sean Haggerty, and a 1st-round draft choice in 1997 (Roberto Luongo)
- broke thumb December 10, 1996; returned January 22, 1997
- signed as a free agent January 14, 2000
- retired June 29, 2000, and accepted a job in public relations with the Leafs
- won gold medal with Canada at 1985 WJC

SPRAGUE CLEGHORN ("Peg")
defence   5'10" 190–L
b. Montreal, Quebec, March 11, 1890
d. Montreal, Quebec, July 11, 1956

1920–21	13	3	4	7	26

- sent from Ottawa Senators to Toronto on January 24, 1921, after first half of 1920–21 season
- first St. Pats game January 26, 1921
- released March 13, 1921, by St. Pats between the first and second games of the playoffs vs. Ottawa
- rejoined Ottawa after the Senators eliminated the St. Pats from the 1921 playoffs
- died after being hit by a car while walking to work
- Hockey Hall of Fame 1958

RANLEIGH "GARY" COLLINS
#24 centre   5'11" 190–L
b. Toronto, September 27, 1935

- Marlie graduate
- acquired May 30, 1955, from Chicago in exchange for allowing the Hawks to buy Hank Ciesla from the Canadiens (the Leafs owned Ciesla's rights, even though he played in the minors with the Habs). The Leafs then transferred Bob Duncan from the Marlies to the Jr. Canadiens
- appeared in the NHL only in the 1959 play-offs with the Leafs
- sold November 19, 1959, to Quebec for $12,500

BRIAN CONACHER
#17–22–18 left wing   6'3" 197–L
b. Toronto, August 31, 1941

1961–62R	1	0	0	0	0
1965–66	2	0	0	0	2
1966–67	66	14	13	27	47
1967–68	64	11	14	25	31
Totals	133	25	27	52	80

- Marlie graduate; first Leaf game December 31, 1961
- played 1962–63 for University of Western Ontario
- played 1963–65 with Canadian National Team
- drafted October 5, 1965; played November 27, 28, 1965, with Leafs, then sent to Rochester for the year
- claimed June 12, 1968, by Detroit at Intra-League Draft
- acquired May 22, 1970, with Terry O'Malley from Minnesota for Murray Oliver
- rights sold August 1978 to Detroit
- played at 1964 Olympics (fourth place) and 1965 WC (fourth)
- wrote a book on the state of the game called *Hockey in Canada: The Way It Is*
- became vice-president of building operations for Maple Leaf Gardens during the 1990s

CHARLES "PETE" CONACHER
#16 left wing   5'10" 165–L
b. Toronto, July 29, 1932

1957–58L	5	0	1	1	5

- claimed June 4, 1957, from Rangers at Intra-League Draft
- played November 2, 9, 10, 13, 16, 1957, with Leafs
- won gold medal with Belleville McFarlands at 1959 WC
- worked on the trading floor of the Toronto Stock Exchange until the day he retired

CHARLIE CONACHER ("The Bomber")
#9–6 right wing   6'1" 195–R
b. Toronto, December 20, 1910
d. Toronto, December 30, 1967

1929–30R	38	20	9	29	48
1930–31	37	31	12	43	78
1931–32	44	34	14	48	66
1932–33	40	14	19	33	64
1933–34	42	32	20	52	38
1934–35	47	36	21	57	24
1935–36	44	23	15	38	74
1936–37	15	3	5	8	13
1937–38	19	7	9	16	6
Totals	326	200	124	324	411

- Marlie graduate 1929; first Leaf game November 14, 1929
- missed some games at end of 1929–30 with infected hand
- broke left wrist December 2, 1930, vs. Boston (Jenkins recalled to fill in)
- missed part of 1931–32 with broken hand
- missed one month in 1931–33 with broken collarbone
- missed four games in 1935–36 with torn ligaments in his left shoulder
- missed most of 1936–37 with wrist injury
- missed part of 1937–38 with dislocated shoulder suffered November 18
- retired January 19, 1938, for health reasons
- sold October 11, 1938, to Detroit for $16,000

- later coached in junior and the NHL before going into private business
- Hockey Hall of Fame 1961

CHARLIE CONACHER
goalie

1932–33					
2 (2/2)	0-0-0	4	0	0	0.00
1934–35					
1 (1/1)	0-0-0	3	0	0	0.00
Totals					
3 (3/3)	0-0-0	7	0	0	0.00

- played November 20, 1932, when Chabot penalized
- played March 16, 1933, when Chabot penalized
- played March 16, 1935, when Hainsworth badly cut

BRANDON CONVERY
#12 centre   6'1" 182–R
b. Kingston, February 4, 1974

1995–96R	11	5	2	7	4
1996–97	39	2	8	10	20
Totals	50	7	10	17	24

- selected 8th overall at 1992 Entry Draft
- missed one month of 1995–96 with fractured wrist
- traded to Vancouver on March 7, 1998, for Lonny Bohonos
- won gold medal with Canada at 1994 WJC and bronze at 1995 WC

DAVID COOPER ("Coops")
#42–33 defence   6'2" 204–L
b. Ottawa, November 2, 1973

1996–97R	19	3	3	6	16
1997–98	9	0	4	4	8
2000–01	2	0	0	0	0
Totals	30	3	7	10	24

- signed as a free agent September 18, 1996

- traded July 2, 1998, to Calgary for Ladislav Kohn
- re-signed as a free agent on October 5, 2001
- currently in Leafs system

DR. BOBBY COPP
#2–14 defence   5'11" 180–L
b. Port Elgin, New Brunswick, November 15, 1918

1942–43R	38	3	9	12	24
1950–51L	2	0	0	0	2
Totals	40	3	9	12	26

- first Leaf game October 31, 1942
- retired March 8, 1942, after a fight with Happy Day just before going off to war
- while practising dentistry and playing for Ottawa in the QSHL, Copp was called off the voluntary retired list to replace injured defencemen Bolton and Barilko. He played two weekend games, then retired to return to Ottawa to continue his career as a dentist
- last Leaf games October 21 and 22, 1950

BERT "CON" CORBEAU
("Husky"/"Pig Iron")
#2 defence   5'11" 196–L
b. Penetanguishene, February 9, 1894
d. Georgian Bay, September 22, 1942

1923–24	24	8	6	14	55
1924–25	30	4	3	7	67
1925–26	36	5	5	10	121
1926–27L	41	1	2	3	88
Totals	131	18	16	34	331

- acquired 1923 with Amos Arbour from Hamilton Tigers (NHL) for Corb Dennenay and Ken Randall
- last Leaf game March 26, 1927
- drowned with 20 other men when his power boat capsized

CHUCK CORRIGAN
#19 right wing   6'1" 192–R
b. Moosomin, Saskatchewan, May 22, 1916

1937–38R	3	0	0	0	0

- St. Mike's graduate
- first and only Leaf games November 20, 21, 23, 1937
- sold January 21, 1938, to Springfield for cash

SHAYNE CORSON
#27 centre   6'1" 202–L
b. Barrie, August 13, 1966

2000–01	77	8	18	26	189

- signed as a free agent on July 4, 2000
- won gold medal with Canada at 1985 WJC and silver at 1986 WJC
- currently with Leafs

FATHER LES COSTELLO ("Costie")
#15 left wing   5'8" 158–L
b. South Porcupine, February 16, 1928

1948–49R/L	15	2	3	5	11

- St. Mike's graduate
- recalled March 20, 1948, for playoffs
- first regular season Leaf game October 16, 1948
- last Leaf game December 18, 1948
- retired in 1950 to attend Seminary School and later played for the Flying Fathers, a hockey team made up of priests travelling the world and playing for charity

RICH COSTELLO
#8–16 centre   6' 175–R
b. Farmington, Massachusetts, June 27, 1963

1983–84R	10	2	1	3	2
1985–86L	2	0	1	1	0
Totals	12	2	2	4	2

- acquired January 20, 1982, with 2nd-round draft choice in 1982 (Peter Ihnacak) and future considerations (Ken Strong) from Flyers for Darryl Sittler
- played January 12–February 15, 1984, with Leafs
- played December 28 and January 1, 1985–86, with Leafs
- contract bought out July 1987

SYLVAIN CÔTÉ ("Co-Co")
#3 defence   6' 190–R
b. Quebec City, Quebec, January 19, 1966

1997–98	12	3	6	9	6
1998–99	79	5	24	29	28
1999–2000	3	0	1	1	0
Totals	94	8	31	39	34

- acquired from Washington on March 24, 1998, for Jeff Brown
- traded to Chicago on October 8, 1999, for a 2nd-round draft choice in 2001 (Karel Pilar)
- currently with Dallas Stars
- played with Canada at 1984 WJC (fourth place) and won silver medal at 1986 WJC

HAROLD "BALDY" COTTON ("Lucky")
#8–11–14 left wing 5'10" 159–L
b. Nanticoke, November 5, 1902
d. Campbellford, September 9, 1984

1928–29	12	1	2	3	8
1929–30	41	21	17	38	47
1930–31	43	12	17	29	45
1931–32	47	5	13	18	41
1932–33	48	10	11	21	29
1933–34	47	8	14	22	46
1934–35	47	11	14	25	36
Totals	285	68	88	156	252

- acquired February 12, 1929, from Pirates for Gerald Lowrey and $10,000
- sold October 9, 1935, to Americans for cash
- became long-time scout for the Bruins

JACK "JERRY" COUGHLIN

#8 forward   5'10" 170–R
b. Peterborough, June 6, 1892
d. Unknown

1917–18	6	2	–	2	0

- only Arenas games December 19, 22, 26, 29 and January 2, 5, 1917–18
- released January 6, 1918

RUSS COURTNALL ("Rusty")

#9–16–26 centre   5'11" 183–R
b. Duncan, British Columbia, June 2, 1965

1983–84R	14	3	9	12	6
1984–85	69	12	10	22	44
1985–86	73	22	38	60	52
1986–87	79	29	44	73	90
1987–88	65	23	26	49	47
1988–89	9	1	1	2	4
Totals	309	90	128	218	243

- selected 7th overall at 1983 Entry Draft
- first Leaf game February 26, 1984
- traded November 7, 1988, to Canadiens for John Kordic
- played for Canada at 1984 WJC (fourth place) and then 1984 Olympics (fourth place); won silver at 1991 WC

MARCEL COUSINEAU ("Couz")

#31 goalie   5'9" 171–L
b. Delson, Quebec, April 30, 1973

1996–97R						
13 (2/5)	3–5–1	566	31	1	3.29
1997–98						
2 (1/2)	0–0–0	17	0	0	0.00
Totals						
15 (3/7)	3–5–1	583	31	1	3.19

- signed as a free agent November 13, 1993
- first Leaf game November 21, 1996
- signed as a free agent by Islanders July 29, 1998

DANNY COX ("Silent Danny")

#6–7 left wing   5'11" 176–L
b. Little Current, October 12, 1903
d. August 8, 1982

1926–27R	14	0	1	1	4
1927–28	41	9	6	15	27
1928–29	42	12	7	19	14
1929–30	19	1	5	6	18
Totals	116	22	19	41	63

- signed summer 1926, after winning Allan Cup with Port Arthur
- loaned January 12, 1927, to Hamilton
- missed end of 1927–28 after breaking his leg March 13, 1928, vs. Senators
- taken to hospital November 25, 1929, with serious case of bronchitis
- traded January 6, 1930, until season's end only, to Ottawa Senators for Frank Nighbor, with an option to buy Cox's contract after season; May 4, 1930, Ottawa exercises the option, giving the Leafs cash to complete deal

MIKE CRAIG

#9 right wing   6'1" 185–R
b. St. Marys, June 6, 1971

1994–95	37	5	5	10	12
1995–96	70	8	12	20	42
1996–97	65	7	13	20	62
Totals	172	20	30	50	116

- signed July 29, 1994, as a free agent from Dallas Stars; Leafs lost Peter Zezel and Grant Marshall as compensation
- placed on waivers July 28, 1997
- won gold medals with Canada at 1990 and 1991 WJC

JOHN CRAIGHEAD

#44 forward   6' 195–R
b. Vancouver, British Columbia, November 23, 1971

1996–97R	5	0	0	0	10

- signed as a free agent July 6, 1996

- first Leaf game November 21, 1996
- demoted December 7, 1996, to St. John's
- later played in Europe

RUSSELL "RUSTY" CRAWFORD
#8 left wing   5'11" 165–L
b. Cardinal, November 7, 1885
d. Spruce Home, Saskatchewan,
December 19, 1971

1917–18	7	2	–	2	24
1918–19L	18	7	3	10	51
Totals	25	9	3	12	75

- purchased February 6, 1918, from Ottawa Senators after Senators signed Frank Nighbor
- first Arenas game February 9, 1918
- last Arenas game February 20, 1919
- retired after 1918–19 season, though later played on the West Coast
- Hockey Hall of Fame 1962

DAVE CREIGHTON
#11–22–23 centre   6'1" 181–L
b. Port Arthur, June 24, 1930

1954–55	14	2	1	3	8
1958–59	34	3	9	12	4
1959–60L	14	1	5	6	4
Totals	62	6	15	21	16

- acquired July 20, 1954, from Boston for Fern Flaman and cash
- sold November 16, 1954, to Chicago
- claimed June 1958 at Intra-League Draft
- last Leaf game February 21, 1960
- traded June 1961 to Bisons for Dick Gamble
- became owner and manager of numerous golf courses throughout North America

JIRI CRHA ("George")
#31 goalie   5'11" 170–L
b. Pardubice, Czechoslovakia, April 13, 1950

1979–80R					
15 (1/2)	8–7–0	830	50	0	3.61
1980–81L					
54 (3/4)	20–20–11	3112	211	0	4.07
Totals					
69 (4/6)	28–27–11	3942	261	0	3.97

- signed as a free agent in summer 1979 after defecting from Czechoslovakia
- first Leaf game February 16, 1980
- last Leaf game April 5, 1981
- contract bought out December 3, 1982
- won bronze, silver, silver, and silver medals with Czechoslovakia at 1973, 1974, 1975, and 1978 wc; won silver at 1976 Olympics
- became a player agent for NHLers

CORY CROSS ("Red"/"Crosser")
#4 defence   6'5" 220–L
b. Lloydminster, Alberta, January 3, 1971

1999–2000	71	4	11	15	64
2000–01	41	3	5	8	50
Totals	112	7	16	23	114

- acquired from Tampa Bay on October 1, 1999, with a 7th-round draft choice in 2001 (Ivan Kolozvary) for Fredrik Modin
- won gold medal with Canada at 1997 wc and played at 1998 wc (sixth place)
- currently with Leafs

JOE CROZIER ("Crow")
#23 defence   6' 180–R
b. Winnipeg, Manitoba, February 19, 1929

1959–60R/L	5	0	3	3	2

- first and only Leaf games March 12, 13, 17, 19, 20, 1960
- retired to general manager and coach the Charlotte Checkers
- later became coach for Leafs

BARRY CULLEN

#19 right wing   6' 175–R
b. Ottawa, June 16, 1935

1955–56R	3	0	0	0	4
1956–57	51	6	10	16	30
1957–58	70	16	25	41	37
1958–59	40	6	8	14	17
Totals	164	28	43	71	88

- signed to a contract in 1955
- recalled November 7, 1955, from Winnipeg Warriors to replace injured Nesterenko
- first games with the Leafs November 11, 12, 13, 1955
- missed first month of 1958–59 with torn knee ligaments
- traded June 9, 1959, to Detroit for Frank Roggeveen and Johnny Wilson
- with brother Brian has operated successful car dealerships in Guelph and Grimsby

BRIAN CULLEN

#14–18–22–27–16 centre   5'10" 164–L
b. Ottawa, November 11, 1933

1954–55R	27	3	5	8	6
1955–56	21	2	6	8	8
1956–57	46	8	12	20	27
1957–58	67	20	23	43	29
1958–59	59	4	14	18	10
Totals	220	37	60	97	80

- acquired May 4, 1954, from Bisons for Dusty Blair, Frank Sullivan, and Jackie LeClair
- first Leaf game October 7, 1954
- claimed by the Rangers at 1959 Intra-League Draft
- runs successful car dealership with his brother since 1969 and owns a stable of horses

JOHN CULLEN

#19 centre   5'10" 185–R
b. Puslinch, August 2, 1964

1992–93	47	13	28	41	53
1993–94	53	13	17	30	67
Totals	100	26	45	71	120

- acquired November 24, 1992, from Hartford for a 2nd-round draft choice in 1993 (traded to San Jose—Vlastimil Kroupa)
- signed as a free agent August 3, 1994, by Penguins
- battled back from cancer to resume career with Tampa Bay
- played for Canada at 1990 WC (fourth place)
- currently runs a car dealership in Atlanta

BRIAN CURRAN

#28 defence   6'5" 215–L
b. Toronto, November 5, 1963

1987–88	7	0	1	1	19
1988–89	47	1	4	5	185
1989–90	72	2	9	11	301
1990–91	4	0	0	0	7
Totals	130	3	14	17	512

- acquired March 8, 1988, from Islanders for 6th-round draft choice in 1988 (Pavel Gross)
- traded December 17, 1990, with Lou Franceschetti to Sabres for Mike Foligno and an 8th-round draft choice in 1991 (Tomas Kucharcik)

KEVIN DAHL

#4 defence   5'11" 190–R
b. Regina, Saskatchewn, December 30, 1968

1998–99	3	0	0	0	2

- claimed from St. Louis on October 5, 1998, in Waiver Draft
- signed August 12, 1999, by Islanders as a free agent

- won silver medal with Canada at 1992 Olympics

MARTY DALLMAN
#35–15 centre   5'10" 180–R
b. Niagara Falls, February 15, 1963

1987–88R	2	0	1	1	0
1988–89L	4	0	0	0	0
Totals	6	0	1	1	0

- signed as a free agent in 1986
- first Leaf games March 9, 26, 1988
- last Leaf games November 16, 18, 19, 21, 1988
- played for Austria at 1993 WC (ninth place) and 1994 Olympics (twelfth place)

VINCENT DAMPHOUSSE ("Vinny")
#10 left wing   6'1" 190–L
b. Montreal, Quebec, December 17, 1967

1986–87R	80	21	25	46	26
1987–88	75	12	36	48	40
1988–89	80	26	42	68	75
1989–90	80	33	61	94	56
1990–91	79	26	47	73	65
Totals	394	118	211	329	262

- selected 6th overall at 1986 Entry Draft
- first Leaf game October 9, 1986
- traded September 19, 1991, with Peter Ing, Scott Thornton, and Luke Richardson to Edmonton for Grant Fuhr, Glenn Anderson, and Craig Berube
- currently with San Jose Sharks

DAN DAOUST ("Dangerous Dan"/"Doo")
#24 centre   5'11" 170–L
b. Montreal, Quebec, February 29, 1960

1982–83	48	18	33	51	31
1983–84	78	18	56	74	88
1984–85	79	17	37	54	98
1985–86	80	7	13	20	88
1986–87	33	4	3	7	35
1987–88	67	9	8	17	57

1988–89	68	7	5	12	54
1989–90L	65	7	11	18	89
Totals	518	87	166	253	540

- acquired December 17, 1982, from Canadiens for a 3rd-round draft choice in 1984 (Ken Hodge Jr.)
- missed much of 1986–87 with broken leg
- last Leaf game March 31, 1990
- signed by Ajoie (Swiss League) as a free agent for 1990–91
- later coached Tier II juniors in Markham

HARRY DARRAGH ("Howl")
#16 forward   5'1" 145–R
b. Ottawa, September 13, 1902
d. Ottawa, October 28, 1993

1931–32	48	5	10	15	6
1932–33L	19	1	2	3	0
Totals	67	6	12	18	6

- claimed on waivers in April 1931 for $5,000 from Boston

BOB DAVIDSON ("Rugged")
#4–5–17–18 forward   5'11" 185–L
b. Toronto, February 10, 1912
d. Toronto, September 26, 1996

1934–35R	5	0	0	0	6
1935–36	35	4	4	8	32
1936–37	46	8	7	15	43
1937–38	48	3	17	20	52
1938–39	47	4	10	14	29
1939–40	48	8	18	26	56
1940–41	37	3	6	9	39
1941–42	37	6	20	26	39
1942–43	50	13	23	36	20
1943–44	47	19	28	47	21
1944–45	50	17	18	35	49
1945–46L	41	9	9	18	12
Totals	491	94	160	254	398

- Marlie graduate; signed October 29, 1934
- first Leaf game January 1, 1935
- missed two games December 1936 with back injury

- missed first month of 1940–41 with knee injury
- missed a month in 1941–42 with a bad cut to his foot
- last Leaf game February 27, 1946
- retired after 1945–46 and became a scout for the team for 40 years
- the most recent recipient of the Bickell Cup

KIM DAVIS

#18 centre   5'11" 170–L
b. Flin Flon, Manitoba, October 31, 1957

1980–81L	2	0	0	0	4

- acquired November 18, 1980, with Paul Marshall from Penguins for Dave Burrows and Paul Gardner
- first and only Leaf games November 23, 29, 1980

BOB DAWES

#21–23–25 defence   6'1" 170–L
b. Saskatoon, Saskatchewan, November 29, 1924

1946–47R	1	0	0	0	0
1948–49	5	1	0	1	0
1949–50	11	1	2	3	2
Totals	17	2	2	4	2

- first Leaf game March 23, 1947
- traded during 1949–50 with $40,000 to Cleveland (AHL) for Al Rollins
- worked for Saskatoon Foundation for Crippled Children

CLARENCE "HAP"/"HAPPY" DAY

#4–3 left wing/defence   5'11 175–L
b. Owen Sound, June 14, 1901
d. St. Thomas, February 17, 1990

1924–25R	26	10	12	22	33
1925–26	36	14	2	16	26
1926–27	44	11	5	16	50
1927–28	22	9	8	17	48
1928–29	44	6	6	12	85
1929–30	43	7	14	21	77
1930–31	44	1	13	14	56
1931–32	47	7	8	15	33
1932–33	47	6	14	20	46
1933–34	48	9	10	19	35
1934–35	45	2	4	6	38
1935–36	44	1	13	14	41
1936–37	48	3	4	7	20
Totals	548	86	113	199	588

- signed December 10, 1924, by St. Pats while at University of Toronto
- first St. Pats game December 13, 1924
- played left wing 1924–25 and half of 1925–26
- missed much of 1927–28 with severe Achilles tendon cut sustained February 2, 1928, vs. Canadiens
- traded September 24, 1937, to New York Americans for Wally Stanowski
- became coach of the team in 1940 for ten years, then general manager until 1957
- retired to St. Marys, Ontario, where he became a leading maker of wood axe handles
- Hockey Hall of Fame 1961

LUCIEN DEBLOIS

#27 left wing   5'11" 200–R
b. Joliette, Quebec, June 21, 1957

1990–91	38	10	12	22	30
1991–92	54	8	11	19	39
Totals	92	18	23	41	69

- acquired November 17, 1990, with Michel Petit and Aaron Broten from Quebec Nordiques for Scott Pearson, a 2nd-round draft choice in 1991 (later traded to Washington—Eric Lavigne), and a 2nd-round choice in 1992 (Tuomas Gronman)
- traded March 10, 1992, to Winnipeg Jets for Mark Osborne
- played for Canada at 1981 WC (fourth place)

DALE DEGRAY ("Digger")

#3 defence   6' 200–R

b. Oshawa, September 1, 1963

1987–88	56	6	18	24	63

- acquired October 1987 from Calgary for 5th-round draft choice in 1988 (Scott Matusovich)
- claimed October 3, 1988, in Waiver Draft by Los Angeles Kings
- won bronze medal with Canada at 1995 WC

ALBERT "AB" DEMARCO

#17 centre   6' 168–R

b. North Bay, May 10, 1916

d. North Bay, May 25, 1989

1942–43	4	0	1	1	0

- first and only Leaf games February 4, 6, 7, 21, 1943
- acquired February 2, 1943, with Buck Jones from Providence for Bucko McDonald, George Boothman, and Jack Forsey. Injured shoulder after just four games and demoted
- sold by Providence near end of 1942–43 season to Boston with Norm Calline and Oscar Aubuchon of Providence for $25,000
- became involved in advertising sales in North Bay

NATHAN DEMPSEY ("Greyhound")

#43 forward   6' 184–R

b. Spruce Grove, Alberta, July 14, 1974

1996–97R	14	1	1	2	2
1999–2000	6	0	2	2	2
2000–01	25	1	9	10	4
Totals	45	2	12	14	8

- selected 245th overall at 1992 Entry Draft
- first Leaf game January 31, 1997
- currently in Leaf organization

CORB "FLASH" DENNENAY

(also "Denneny")

#5 left wing   5'8" 142–L

b. Cornwall, January 25, 1894

d. Toronto, January 16, 1963

1917–18	21	20	–	20	8
1918–19	16	7	3	10	15
1919–20	23	23	12	35	18
1920–21	20	17	6	23	27
1921–22	24	19	7	26	28
1922–23	1	1	0	1	0
1926–27	29	7	1	8	24
Totals	134	94	29	123	120

- joined Arenas in 1916, after Toronto Shamrocks folded
- played only December 16, 1922, during 1922–23 season, then traded to Vancouver Millionaires for Jack Adams
- returned to Toronto the following year
- traded to Hamilton Tigers (NHL) in 1923 with Ken Randall for Bert Corbeau and Amos Arbour
- purchased in 1926 from Saskatoon with Leo Bourgeault and Laurie Scott. Legal problems with contract forced him back to Saskatoon during 1926–27 season
- became head masseur at central YMCA in Toronto

GERRY DENOIRD

#10 forward   5'10" 170–R

b. Toronto, August 4, 1902

d. Unknown

1922–23R/L	15	0	0	0	0

- signed from Aura Lee Juniors
- first St. Pats game December 16, 1922
- last St. Pats game March 5, 1923
- reinstated as an amateur in summer 1925

BILL DERLAGO ("Billy D")
#19 centre   5'10" 195–R
b. Birtle, Manitoba, August 25, 1958

1979–80	23	5	12	17	13
1980–81	80	35	39	74	26
1981–82	75	34	50	84	42
1982–83	58	13	24	37	27
1983–84	79	40	20	60	50
1984–85	62	31	31	62	21
1985–86	1	0	0	0	0
Totals	378	158	176	334	179

- acquired February 18, 1980, with Rick Vaive from Vancouver Canucks for Tiger Williams and Jerry Butler
- traded October 11, 1985, to Boston for Tom Fergus
- became a car salesman with Brad Selwood at Al Palladini Motors in Toronto

ERNIE DICKENS
#16–23 defence   6' 175–L
b. Winnipeg, Manitoba, June 25, 1921

1941–42R	10	2	2	4	6
1945–46	15	1	3	4	6
Totals	25	3	5	8	12

- Marlie graduate; signed May 11, 1941, by Leafs
- first Leaf game February 7, 1942
- missed 1942–45—Royal Canadian Air Force
- recalled from Hornets on November 16, 1945
- traded November 2, 1947, with Bud Poile, Gaye Stewart, Bob Goldham, and Gus Bodnar to Chicago for Max Bentley and Cy Thomas

GERALD DIDUCK ("Dids")
#2 defence   6'1" 215–R
b. Edmonton, Alberta, April 6, 1965

1999–2000	26	0	3	3	33

- signed as a free agent February 3, 2000

- played for Canada at 1984 WJC (fourth place)
- traded October 29, 2000, to Dallas for future considerations

PAUL DIPIETRO ("Rocky")
#25 centre   5'9" 189–R
b. Sault Ste. Marie, September 8, 1970

1994–95	12	1	1	2	6
1995–96	20	4	4	8	4
Totals	32	5	5	10	10

- acquired April 6, 1995, from Canadiens for a 4th-round draft choice in 1996 (Kim Staal)
- demoted October 15, 1995, to St. John's, then Houston (IHL) February 13, 1996
- signed as a free agent July 23, 1996, by Los Angeles

TAHIR "TIE" DOMI
("The Albanian Assassin"/"Tugger")
#40–28–8 right wing   5'10" 200–R
b. Windsor, November 1, 1969

1989–90R	2	0	0	0	42
1994–95	9	0	1	1	31
1995–96	72	7	6	13	297
1996–97	80	11	17	28	275
1997–98	80	4	10	14	365
1998–99	72	8	14	22	198
1999–2000	70	5	9	14	198
2000–01	82	13	7	20	214
Totals	467	48	64	112	1620

- selected 27th overall at 1988 Entry Draft
- first Leaf games March 2, 3, 1990
- traded June 29, 1990, with Mark LaForest to the Rangers for Greg Johnston
- acquired April 7, 1995, from Winnipeg Jets for Mike Eastwood and a 3rd-round draft choice in 1995 (Brad Isbister)

KEN DORATY ("Cagey")
#15 forward   5'7" 128–R
b. Stittsville, June 23, 1906
d. Moose Jaw, Saskatchewan, May 4, 1981

1932–33	38	5	11	16	16
1933–34	34	9	10	19	6
1934–35	11	1	4	5	0
Totals	83	15	25	40	22

- recalled from Syracuse on December 1932 to replace injured Bailey
- loaned December 4, 1933, to Bisons
- lightest player ever in the NHL
- sold December 1, 1935, to Cleveland (AHL) for $2,000
- ran a pool hall in Moose Jaw, Saskatchewan, until his death

JIM DOREY ("Flipper")
#8 defence   6'1" 190–L
b. Kingston, August 17, 1947

1968–69R	61	8	22	30	200
1969–70	46	6	11	17	99
1970–71	74	7	22	29	198
1971–72	50	4	19	23	56
Totals	231	25	74	99	553

- selected 23rd overall at 1964 Amateur Draft
- first Leaf game October 13, 1968
- missed January 7–February 22, 1970, with knee injury
- traded February 20, 1972, to the Rangers for Pierre Jarry
- has worked at an insurance company in Kingston for 20 years since retiring

KENT DOUGLAS
#19 defence   5'10" 189–L
b. Cobalt, February 6, 1936

1962–63R	70	7	15	22	105
1963–64	43	0	1	1	29
1964–65	67	5	23	28	129
1965–66	64	6	14	20	97
1966–67	39	2	12	14	48
Totals	283	20	65	85	408

- acquired June 7, 1962, from Springfield for Roger Côté, Bill White, Jim Wilcox, Wally Boyer, and Dick Mattiussi
- first Leaf game October 10, 1962
- claimed June 6, 1967, by Oakland in Expansion Draft
- enjoyed careers in both real estate and as golf pro in the Baltimore area after retiring

BRUCE DOWIE
#1 goalie   5'10" 170–L
b. Oakville, December 9, 1962

1983–84R/L					
2 (0/1)	0–1–0	72	4	0	3.33

- signed as a free agent May 6, 1983
- first and only Leaf games March 17 and April 1, 1984

DAVE DOWNIE
#17 centre   5'7" 168–R
b. Burke's Falls, March 11, 1909

1932–33R/L	11	0	1	1	2

- signed February 12, 1933, from Syracuse
- first and only Leaf games February 14, 16, 18, 23, 25, 28 and March 2, 4, 5, 7, 11, 1933

BRUCE DRAPER
#17 forward   5'10" 157–R
b. Toronto, October 2, 1940
d. Ottawa, January 26, 1968

1962–63R/L	1	0	0	0	0

- St. Mike's graduate 1961 (won Memorial Cup)
- first and only Leaf game March 3, 1963
- career minor-leaguer: played 1961–62 with Rochester and most of 1962–63 with Rochester and Sudbury Wolves, 1963–64 with Denver (WHL), 1964–67 with Hershey
- retired because of illness (leukemia) and passed away a short time later

GORD DRILLON ("Lefty")

#12–21 left wing   6'2" 178–L
b. Moncton, New Brunswick, October 23, 1914
d. Saint John, New Brunswick, September 23, 1986

1936–37R	41	16	17	33	2
1937–38	48	26	26	52	4
1938–39	40	18	16	34	15
1939–40	43	21	19	40	13
1940–41	42	23	21	44	2
1941–42	48	23	18	41	6
Totals	262	127	117	244	42

- signed April 13, 1936
- first Leaf game November 26, 1936
- missed part of 1940–41 with shoulder injury
- sold to Canadiens on October 4, 1942, for cash
- worked in youth programming in Moncton
- Hockey Hall of Fame 1975

DICK DUFF

#9–17 left wing   5'9" 166–L
b. Kirkland Lake, February 18, 1936

1954–55R	3	0	0	0	2
1955–56	69	18	19	37	74
1956–57	70	26	14	40	50
1957–58	65	26	23	49	79
1958–59	69	29	24	53	73
1959–60	67	19	22	41	51
1960–61	67	16	17	33	54
1961–62	51	17	20	37	37

1962–63	69	16	19	35	56
1963–64	52	7	7	14	59
Totals	582	174	165	339	535

- St. Mike's graduate; signed September 23, 1955, with Leafs
- first Leaf game March 10, 1955
- traded February 22, 1964, with Arnie Brown, Bill Collins, Bob Nevin, and Rod Seiling to the Rangers for Andy Bathgate and Don McKenney

ART DUNCAN ("Dunc")

#4–11–3 defence   5'11" 180–R
b. Sault Ste. Marie, July 4, 1894
d. Aurora, April 13, 1975

1927–28	43	7	5	12	97
1928–29	39	4	4	8	53
1929–30	38	4	5	9	49
1930–31L	4	0	0	0	0
Totals	124	15	14	29	199

- acquired from Detroit Cougars in 1927 for Bill Brydge
- last Leaf game February 7, 1931
- an airman in World War I, downed 12 planes and awarded Military Cross

ROCKY DUNDAS

#34 right wing   6' 195–R
b. Regina, Saskatchewan, January 30, 1967

1989–90R/L	5	0	0	0	14

- signed October 4, 1989, as a free agent
- first and only Leaf games October 5, 7, 12, 14, 17, 1989

JUDGE FRANK DUNLAP

#20 forward   6' 185–L
b. Ottawa, August 10, 1924
d. Ottawa, September 26, 1993

1943–44R/L	5	0	1	1	2

- St. Mike's graduate; signed November 5, 1943, by Leafs

- first and only Leaf games November 6, 11, 13, 18, 20, 1943
- played only home games while attending law school
- retired after 1943–44 season (only year in pro hockey) to finish law school
- also played in CFL

DAVE DUNN

#4 defence   6'2" 200–L
b. Wapella, Saskatchewan, August 19, 1948

1974–75	72	3	11	14	142
1975–76L	43	0	8	8	84
Totals	115	3	19	22	226

- acquired October 16, 1974, from Vancouver Canucks for John Grisdale and Gary Monahan
- last Leaf game April 25, 1976
- signed as a free agent June 1, 1976, by Winnipeg Jets
- became assistant coach with Vancouver Canucks

DENIS DUPERE

#17–15 left wing   6'1" 200–L
b. Jonquière, Quebec, June 21, 1948

1970–71R	20	1	2	3	4
1971–72	77	7	10	17	4
1972–73	61	13	23	36	10
1973–74	34	8	9	17	8
Totals	192	29	44	73	26

- acquired May 3, 1970, with Jacques Plante and Guy Trottier from the Rangers for Tim Horton
- first Leaf game February 10, 1971
- claimed June 12, 1974, by Washington at Expansion Draft
- works for wholesale sporting goods company based in Kitchener

JEROME DUPONT ("Jerry"/"J.D.")

#2 defence   6'3" 190–L
b. Ottawa, February 21, 1962

1986–87L	13	0	0	0	23

- acquired September 6, 1986, with Ken Yaremchuk and a 4th-round draft choice in 1987 (Joe Sacco) from Chicago as compensation for Hawks signing Gary Nylund
- last Leaf game February 8, 1987

VITEZSLAV "SLAVA" DURIS

#23–24 defence   6'1" 185–L
b. Pizen, Czechoslovakia, January 5, 1954

1980–81R	57	1	12	13	50
1982–83L	32	2	8	10	12
Totals	89	3	20	23	62

- signed as a free agent September 25, 1980
- first Leaf game October 11, 1980
- last Leaf game December 23, 1982
- career ended after 1982–83 due to chronic back injury

CECIL "BABE" DYE

#6–14–10–2 right wing   5'8" 180–R
b. Hamilton, May 13, 1898
d. Chicago, Illinois, January 2, 1962

1919–20R	21	12	3	15	10
1920–21	23	33	2	35	32
1921–22	24	30	7	37	18
1922–23	22	26	11	37	19
1923–24	19	17	2	19	23
1924–25	29	38	6	44	41
1925–26	31	18	5	23	26
1930–31L	8	0	0	0	0
Totals	177	174	36	210	169

- played with Junior Toronto St. Pats and signed with NHL St. Pats December 15, 1919
- first St. Pats game December 23, 1919
- loaned to Hamilton (NHL) for 1920–21, but when Dennenay broke his hand in the St. Pats' first game of the year, Dye was

recalled and remained in Toronto for the season

- missed game of January 31, 1923, with a high fever
- rejoined St. Pats on January 1, 1924
- sold to Chicago after the 1925–26 season for $14,000
- came out of retirement to play eight games in 1930–31 (November 18, 20, 22, 25, 29 and December 2, 6, 9), before retiring permanently
- became superintendent at Seneca Petroleum Co. in Chicago
- Hockey Hall of Fame 1970

DALLAS EAKINS ("Dally")
#2 defence   6'2" 195–L
b. Dade City, Florida, February 27, 1967

1998–99	18	0	2	2	24

- signed as a free agent July 28, 1998
- signed as a free agent by the Islanders August 12, 1999

MIKE EASTWOOD ("Easty")
#21–32 centre   6'3" 205–R
b. Ottawa, July 1, 1967

1991–92R	9	0	2	2	4
1992–93	12	1	6	7	21
1993–94	54	8	10	18	28
1994–95	36	5	5	10	32
Totals	111	14	23	37	85

- selected 91st overall at 1987 Entry Draft
- first Leaf game November 16, 1991
- traded April 7, 1995, to Winnipeg Jets with a 3rd-round draft choice in 1995 (Brad Isbister) for Tie Domi

TIM ECCLESTONE
#16 right wing   5'10" 195–R
b. Toronto, September 24, 1947

1973–74	46	9	14	23	32
1974–75	5	1	1	2	0
Totals	51	10	15	25	32

- acquired November 29, 1973, from Detroit for Pierre Jarry
- traded November 2, 1974, with Willie Brossart to Washington for Rod Seiling
- runs a restaurant in St. Louis called "TJ's"

GARRY "DUKE" EDMUNDSON
#25 left wing   6' 173–L
b. Sexsmith, Alberta, May 6, 1932

1959–60	39	4	6	10	47
1960–61L	3	0	0	0	0
Totals	42	4	6	10	47

- acquired summer 1959 from Springfield for Frank Roggeveen
- last Leaf games October 6, 12 and December 15, 1960

DON EDWARDS ("Dart")
#30 goalie   5'9" 160–L
b. Hamilton, September 28, 1955

1985–86L
38 (6/6)	12–23–0	2009	160	0	4.78

- acquired May 29, 1985. from Calgary for 4th-round draft choice in 1987 (Tim Harris)
- last Leaf game April 6, 1986
- released August 11, 1987
- both his parents were murdered in Hamilton, and he became active in seeking harsher punishment for killers

MARV EDWARDS

#31 goalie   5'8" 155–L
b. St. Catharines, August 15, 1935

1969–70

25 (2/0)	10–9–4	1420	77	1	3.25

- claimed from Penguins at June 1969 Intra-League Draft
- claimed June 1972 by Salt Lake (for California) in Reverse Draft
- won gold medal with Canada at 1959 WC

GERRY EHMAN ("Tex")

#8–17 right wing   6' 190–R
b. Cudworth, Saskatchewan, November 3, 1932

1958–59	36	12	13	25	12
1959–60	69	12	16	28	26
1960–61	14	1	1	2	2
1963–64	4	1	1	2	0
Totals	123	26	31	57	40

- claimed on waivers December 1959 from Detroit
- played October 30 and November 2, 7, 9, 1963, then sent to minors for the year
- traded October 3, 1967, to Oakland for Bryan Hextall and J.P. Parise
- became director of scouting for the Islanders

DAVE ELLETT ("Roy")

#4 defence   6'1" 200–L
b. Cleveland, Ohio, March 30, 1964

1990–91	60	8	30	38	69
1991–92	79	18	33	51	95
1992–93	70	6	34	40	46
1993–94	68	7	36	43	42
1994–95	33	5	10	15	26
1995–96	80	3	19	22	59
1996–97	56	4	10	14	34
Totals	446	51	172	223	371

- acquired November 10, 1990, with Paul Fenton from Winnipeg Jets for Ed Olczyk and Mark Osborne

- traded February 25, 1997, with Doug Gilmour and a 3rd-round draft choice in 1999 (previously acquired from Devils in Andreychuk trade—Andre Lakos) to New Jersey for Steve Sullivan, Jason Smith, and Alyn McCauley
- played for Canada at 1989 WC (silver)

RON ELLIS

#6–8–11 right wing   5'9" 195–R
b. Lindsay, January 8, 1945

1963–64R	1	0	0	0	0
1964–65	62	23	16	39	14
1965–66	70	19	23	42	24
1966–67	67	22	23	45	14
1967–68	74	28	20	48	8
1968–69	72	25	21	46	12
1969–70	76	35	19	54	14
1970–71	78	24	29	53	10
1971–72	78	23	24	47	17
1972–73	78	22	29	51	22
1973–74	70	23	25	48	12
1974–75	79	32	29	61	25
1977–78	80	26	24	50	17
1978–79	63	16	12	28	10
1979–80	59	12	11	23	6
1980–81L	27	2	3	5	2
Totals	1034	332	308	640	207

- Marlie graduate
- first Leaf game March 11, 1964
- won 1964 Allan Cup with Marlies
- retired just before 1975–76 season; returned September 1977
- retired 1981; last Leaf game January 14, 1981
- played for Canada at 1977 WC (fourth place)
- currently works for Hockey Hall of Fame as director, public relations, and assistant to the president

AUT ERICKSON

#24 defence   6' 188–L

b. Lethbridge, Alberta, January 25, 1938

- acquired May 20, 1965, with Larry Jeffrey, Ed Joyal, Lowell MacDonald, and Marcel Pronovost from Detroit for Andy Bathgate, Billy Harris, and Gary Jarrett
- appeared as a Leaf only in the 1967 playoffs
- claimed June 6, 1967, by Oakland at Expansion Draft
- became assistant general manager with Islanders, then became cargo manager with an airline based in Los Angeles

LEN ESAU

#36 defence   6'3" 190–R

b. Meadow Lake, Saskatchewan, June 3, 1968

1991–92R/L	2	0	0	0	0

- selected 86th overall at 1988 Entry Draft
- first and only Leaf games November 17 and January 3, 1991–92
- traded July 21, 1992, to Quebec Nordiques for Ken McRae
- won bronze medal with Canada at 1995 WC

CHRIS EVANS

#26 defence   5'9" 180–L

b. Toronto, September 14, 1946

1969–70R	2	0	0	0	0

- first and only Leaf games December 10, 11, 1969
- claimed June 9, 1970, by St. Louis at Intra-League Draft

DARYL EVANS

#3 left wing   5'8" 185–L

b. Toronto, January 12, 1961

1986–87L	2	1	0	1	0

- signed by Leafs summer 1986

- first and only Leaf games January 31 and February 2, 1987

PAUL EVANS

#17–28–29 centre   5'11" 175–L

b. Peterborough, February 24, 1955

1976–77R	7	1	1	2	19
1977–78L	4	0	0	0	2
Totals	11	1	1	2	21

- selected 149th overall in 1975 Amateur Draft
- first Leaf games March 5, 7, 9, 12, 13, 15, 16, 1977
- last Leaf games March 8, 9, 11, 12, 1978

BILL EZINICKI

("Wild Bill"/"Ezzie"/"Sweet William")

#12–16–17 right wing 5'10" 170–R

b. Winnipeg, Manitoba, March 11, 1924

1944–45R	8	1	4	5	17
1945–46	24	4	8	12	29
1946–47	60	17	20	37	93
1947–48	60	11	20	31	97
1948–49	52	13	15	28	145
1949–50	67	10	12	22	144
Totals	271	56	79	135	525

- acquired October 13, 1944, from Buffalo (IHL) for Don Webster and George Boothman
- first Leaf game October 28, 1944
- traded November 15, 1950, with Vic Lynn to Boston for Leo Boivin, Fern Flaman, Phil Maloney, and Ken Smith
- bought January 28, 1952, from Boston
- sold December 21, 1954, with Phil Maloney and Hugh Barlow for $10,000 to Vancouver (WHL)
- a scratch golfer, he played semi-pro and after retiring became club pro at a course just outside Boston, where he still lives and plays

KELLY FAIRCHILD

#40–7 centre   5'11" 180–L

b. Hibbing, Minnesota, April 9, 1973

1995–96R	1	0	1	1	2
1996–97	22	0	2	2	2
Totals	23	0	3	3	4

- acquired October 3, 1994, with Dixon Ward, Guy Leveque, and Shayne Toporowski from Los Angeles for Eric Lacroix, Chris Snell, and a 4th-round draft choice in 1996 (Eric Belanger)
- first Leaf game March 20, 1996
- loaned February 10, 1997, to Orlando (IHL); contract turned over to Solar Bears on November 18, 1997

JEFF FARKAS

#39–19 centre   6' 185–L

b. Amherst, Massachusetts, January 24, 1978

2000–01R	2	0	0	0	2

- selected 57th overall at 1997 Entry Draft
- played for USA at 1996 (fifth place), 1997 (silver medal), and 1998 (fifth) WJC
- first regular season Leafs game February 17, 2001

DAVE FARRISH

#23–28 defence   6'1" 195–L

b. Wingham, August 1, 1956

1979–80	20	1	8	9	30
1980–81	74	2	18	20	90
1982–83	56	4	24	28	38
1983–84L	59	4	19	23	57
Totals	209	11	69	80	215

- acquired December 13, 1979, with Terry Martin from Quebec Nordiques for Reg Thomas
- last Leaf game April 1, 1984
- signed as a free agent October 7, 1985, by Flyers

ALEX FAULKNER

#8 centre   5'8" 165–L

b. Bishop's Falls, Newfoundland, May 21, 1936

1961–62R	1	0	0	0	0

- signed December 1960 as a free agent from Conception Bay Cee Bees, Newfoundland (first Newfoundlander to play in the NHL)
- first and only Leaf game December 7, 1961
- claimed by Detroit at June 1962 Intra-League Draft
- operated a senior citizens' home in Newfoundland

TED FAUSS

#2–34 defence   6'2" 205–L

b. Clark Mills, New York, June 30, 1961

1986–87R	15	0	1	1	11
1987–88L	13	0	1	1	4
Totals	28	0	2	2	15

- signed July 21, 1986, as a free agent
- first Leaf game January 15, 1987
- last Leaf game March 3, 1988
- signed December 2, 1988, as free agent by Hartford

DOUG FAVELL

#33 goalie   5'10" 172–L

b. St. Catharines, April 5, 1945

1973–74						
32 (3/2)	14–7–9	1752	79	0	2.71	
1974–75						
39 (5/3)	12–17–6	2149	145	1	4.05	
1975–76						
3 (0/1)	0–2–1	160	15	0	5.63	
Totals						
74 (8/6)	26–26–16	4061	239	1	3.53	

- acquired July 27, 1973, with a 1st-round draft choice in 1973 (Bob Neely) from Flyers for the rights to Bernie Parent and a 2nd-round draft choice in 1973 (Larry Goodenough)

- sold September 15, 1976, to Colorado Rockies
- became manager of a car wholesale and importing business based in St. Catharines

PAUL FENTON
#16 left wing   5'11" 180–L
b. Springfield, Massachusetts, December 22, 1959

1990–91	30	5	10	15	0

- acquired November 10, 1990, with Dave Ellett from Winnipeg Jets for Ed Olczyk and Mark Osborne
- traded January 24, 1991, with John Kordic to Washington for a 5th-round draft choice in 1991 (Alexei Kudashov)
- played for USA at 1985 (fourth place) and 1989 wc (sixth)

TOM FERGUS ("Fergie")
#19 centre   6'3" 210–L
b. Chicago, Illinois, June 16, 1962

1985–86	78	31	42	73	64
1986–87	57	21	28	49	57
1987–88	63	19	31	50	81
1988–89	80	22	45	67	48
1989–90	54	19	26	45	62
1990–91	14	5	4	9	8
1991–92	11	1	3	4	4
Totals	357	118	179	297	324

- acquired October 11, 1985, from Boston for Bill Derlago
- sold December 18, 1991, to Vancouver Canucks for cash
- played for USA at 1985 wc (fourth place)
- runs his own promotional sportswear company in Oakville

GEORGE FERGUSON ("Chief")
#10 centre   6' 195–R
b. Trenton, August 22, 1952

1972–73R	72	10	13	23	34
1973–74	16	0	4	4	4

1974–75	69	19	30	49	61
1975–76	79	12	32	44	76
1976–77	50	9	15	24	24
1977–78	73	7	16	23	37
Totals	359	57	110	167	236

- selected 11th overall at 1972 Amateur Draft
- first Leaf game October 7, 1972
- traded June 4, 1978, with Randy Carlyle to Penguins for Dave Burrows
- became regional sales manager in Pittsburgh of a medical equipment manufacturer

FRANK FINNIGAN ("Finny"/"Fearless Frank"/"The Shawville Express")
#12 right wing   5'8" 178–R
b. Shawville, Quebec, July 9, 1901
d. Shawville, Quebec, December 25, 1991

1931–32	47	8	13	21	45
1934–35	11	2	0	2	2
1935–36	48	2	6	8	10
1936–37L	48	2	7	9	4
Totals	154	14	26	40	61

- loaned to Leafs from Ottawa for 1931–32, when Senators did not field a team Returned to Ottawa for 1932–33
- bought February 13, 1935, from St. Louis Eagles for $8,000
- last Leaf game March 20, 1937
- retired March 28, 1937
- number 8 retired by Ottawa Senators when franchise revived in 1992

ALVIN FISHER
#11 forward   6' 170–R
b. Sault Ste. Marie   d. Unknown

1924–25R/L	9	1	0	1	4

- first and only St. Pats games December 5, 10, 13, 17, 22, 29, 31 and January 3, 10, 1924–25

FERDINAND "FERN" FLAMAN
#3–12 defence   5'10" 190–R
b. Dysart, Saskatchewan, January 25, 1927

1950–51	39	2	6	8	64
1951–52	61	0	7	7	110
1952–53	66	2	6	8	110
1953–54	62	0	8	8	84
Totals	228	4	27	31	368

- acquired November 15, 1950, with Leo Boivin, Phil Maloney, and Ken Smith from Boston for Bill Ezinicki and Vic Lynn
- traded July 20, 1954, to Boston for Dave Creighton and cash
- coached Northeastern University's hockey team for 20 years
- Hockey Hall of Fame 1990

BILL "COWBOY" FLETT
#19 right wing   6'1" 205–R
b. Vermillion, Alberta, July 21, 1943
d. July 12, 1999

1974–75	77	15	25	40	38

- signed during 1962–63 while with Melville Millionaires
- claimed June 6, 1967, by Los Angeles Kings in Expansion Draft
- acquired May 27, 1974, from Flyers for Dave Fortier and Randy Osburn
- claimed May 20, 1975, on waivers by Atlanta
- died of Mickey Mantle disease as a result of sustained alcohol abuse

GERRY FOLEY
#11 right wing   6' 172–R
b. Ware, Massachusetts, September 22, 1932

1954–55R	4	0	0	0	8

- acquired summer 1953 with Bob Bailey from Cleveland (AHL) for Chuck Blair and $30,000
- first and only Leaf games February 26 and March 2, 5, 6, 1955

- claimed June 5, 1956, with Parker MacDonald by Rangers at Intra-League Draft for $30,000
- became deputy mayor in Garson, Ontario, and ran a nursing home

MIKE FOLIGNO
#15–71 right wing   6'2" 195–R
b. Sudbury, January 29, 1959

1990–91	37	8	7	15	65
1991–92	33	6	8	14	50
1992–93	55	13	5	18	84
1993–94	4	0	0	0	4
Totals	129	27	20	47	203

- acquired December 17, 1990, with Sabres 8th-round draft choice in 1991 (Tomas Kucharcik) from Sabres for Lou Franceschetti and Brian Curran
- missed much of 1991–92 with a broken leg
- sold November 5, 1993, to Florida for cash
- played for Canada at 1981 (fourth place), 1986 (bronze medal), and 1987 (fourth) WC
- became assistant coach in the NHL before assuming head coaching job in AHL

VERNER "JAKE" FORBES
("Jumping Jakie")
goalie   5'6" 140–L
b. Toronto, July 4, 1897
d. Burlington

1919–20R						
5 (0/0)	1–4–0	300	21	0	4.20	
1920–21						
20 (0/0)	13–7–0	1221	78	0	3.83	
Totals						
25 (0/0)	14–11–0	1521	99	0	3.91	

- signed February 28, 1920, just before game time
- first Arenas games February 28 and March 3, 6, 10, 13, 1920

- sat out first four games of 1920–21 in contract dispute; signed January 5, 1921
- released after 1920–21 season

JACK FORSEY

#17 forward   5'11" 175–R
b. Swift Current, Saskatchewan, November 7, 1914
d. Unknown

1942–43R/L	19	7	9	16	10

- began 1942–43 in Providence; recalled December 21, 1942
- first Leaf game December 22, 1942
- traded February 2, 1943, with Bucko McDonald and George Boothman to Providence for Ab Demarco and Buck Jones
- last Leaf game March 14, 1943

DAVE FORTIER

#22 defence   5'11" 190–L
b. Sudbury, June 17, 1951

1972–73R	23	1	4	5	63

- selected 23rd overall at 1971 Amateur Draft
- first Leaf game February 14, 1973
- traded May 27, 1974, with Randy Osburn to Flyers for Bill Flett

JIMMY FOWLER ("The Blonde Bouncer")

#3 defence   5'11" 168–L
b. Toronto, April 6, 1915
d. Toronto, October 17, 1985

1936–37R	48	7	11	18	22
1937–38	48	10	12	22	8
1938–39L	39	1	6	7	9
Totals	135	18	29	47	39

- signed October 22, 1935
- first Leaf game November 5, 1936
- loaned May 18, 1939, to New York Americans for 1939–40 with Americans' option to buy his contract for $7,500 after that season. Fowler, however, retired, so

Conn Smythe sent Murray Armstrong, Chuck Shannon, and Bummer Doran to the Americans on the same terms
- last Leaf game March 19, 1939

LOU FRANCESCHETTI

#15 left wing   6' 190–L
b. Toronto, March 28, 1958

1989–90	80	21	15	36	127
1990–91	16	1	1	2	30
Totals	96	22	16	38	157

- acquired June 29, 1989, from Washington for 5th-round draft choice in 1990 (Mark Ouimet)
- traded December 17, 1990, with Brian Curran to Sabres for Mike Foligno and an 8th-round draft choice in 1991 (Tomas Kucharcik)

MIROSLAV FRYCER ("Mirko")

#14 right wing   6' 200–R
b. Ostrava, Czechoslovakia, September 27, 1959

1981–82	10	4	6	10	31
1982–83	67	25	30	55	90
1983–84	47	10	16	26	55
1984–85	65	25	30	55	55
1985–86	73	32	43	75	74
1986–87	29	7	8	15	28
1987–88	38	12	20	32	41
Totals	329	115	153	268	374

- acquired March 9, 1982, with a 7th-round draft choice in 1982 (Jeff Triano) from Quebec Nordiques for Wilf Paiement
- traded June 10, 1988, to Detroit for Darren Veitch
- played for Czechoslovakia at 1978 (fourth place) and 1979 (bronze medal) WJC; won silvers at 1979 and 1981 WC; played in 1980 Olympics (fifth)

GRANT FUHR ("Fuhrsie")
#31 goalie   5'10" 186–R
b. Spruce Grove, Alberta,
September 28, 1962

1991–92					
66 (5/2)	25–33–5	3774	230	2	3.66
1992–93					
29 (3/1)	13–9–4	1665	87	1	3.14
Totals					
95 (8/3)	38–42–9	5439	317	3	3.50

- acquired September 19, 1991, with Glenn
  Anderson and Craig Berube from
  Edmonton for Vincent Damphousse, Peter
  Ing, Scott Thornton, and Luke Richardson
- traded February 2, 1993, with a 5th-round
  draft choice in 1995 (Kevin Popp) to
  Sabres for Dave Andreychuk, Daren
  Puppa, and a 1st-round choice in 1993
  (Kenny Jonsson)
- won silver medal with Canada at 1989 WC
- just retired, Fuhr hopes to become a
  pro golfer

PAUL GAGNE
#18–41 left wing   5'10" 180–L
b. Iroquois Falls, February 6, 1962

1988–89	16	3	2	5	6

- signed as a free agent July 28, 1988
- traded December 20, 1989, with Jack
  Capuano and Derek Laxdal to the
  Islanders for Gilles Thibaudeau and
  Mike Stevens

DAVE GAGNER
#15 centre   5'10" 180–L
b. Chatham, December 11, 1964

1995–96	28	7	15	22	59

- acquired January 28, 1996, with a 6th-
  round draft choice in 1996 (Dmitri
  Yakushin) from Dallas for Benoît Hogue
  and Randy Wood
- traded June 22, 1996, to Calgary for a
  3rd-round draft choice in 1996 (Mike
  Lankshear)

- played for Canada at 1984 WJC (fourth
  place), 1984 Olympics (fourth place), and
  1993 WC (fourth)
- later entered a business venture with an
  artificial ice company

BRUCE GAMBLE
("Paladin"/"Smiley Bates"/"Smiley")
#1–30 goalie   5'9" 200–L
b. Port Arthur, May 24, 1938
d. Niagara Falls, December 30, 1982

1965–66					
10 (2/1)[+]	5–2–2	501	21	4	2.51
1966–67					
23 (2/3)	5–10–4	1185	67	0	3.39
1967–68					
41 (3/8)	19–13–3	2201	85	5	2.32
1968–69					
61 (8/6)	28–20–11	3446	161	3	2.80
1969–70					
52 (2/2)	19–24–9	3057	156	5	3.06
1970–71					
23 (1/3)	6–14–1	1286	83	2	3.87
Totals					
210 (18/23)	82–83–30	11676	573	19	2.94

+ not included is the game of April 2, 1966,
  when Punch Imlach changed his goalies—
  Gamble and Sawchuk—every five minutes
  or so all game long
- acquired September 1965 from Springfield
  for Larry Johnston and Bill Smith
- traded February 1, 1971, with Mike Walton
  and the Leafs' 1st-round choice in 1971
  (Pierre Plante) to Flyers for Bernie Parent
  and the Flyers' 2nd-round choice in 1971
  (Rick Kehoe)
- died of a heart attack during an old-
  timers' game

DICK GAMBLE

#9 left wing   6' 178–L
b. Moncton, New Brunswick,
November 16, 1928

1965–66	2	1	0	1	0
1966–67L	1	0	0	0	0
Totals	3	1	0	1	0

- acquired June 1961 from Bisons for Dave Creighton
- first Leaf games March 5 and 6, 1966, then sent to Rochester
- brought up February 1, 1967, to replace injured Mahovlich
- played most of 1961–69 with Rochester, becoming player/coach in 1968–69; retired as a player next year
- sells campers near Rochester, New York

CAL GARDNER

("Ginger"/"Red"/"Torchy"/"Pearly")
#17 centre   6'1" 175–L
b. Transcona, Manitoba, October 30, 1924

1948–49	53	13	22	35	35
1949–50	30	7	19	26	12
1950–51	66	23	28	51	42
1951–52	70	15	26	41	40
Totals	219	58	95	153	129

- acquired April 26, 1948, with Bill Juzda, René Trudell, Frankie Mathers, and the rights to Ray McMurray from the Rangers for Wally Stanowski, Moe Morris, and the rights to Orville Lavell
- traded September 11, 1952, with Roy Hannigan, Gus Mortson, and Al Rollins to Chicago for Harry Lumley
- worked in radio in Toronto, first as an analyst, then as an ad salesman

PAUL GARDNER

#18 centre   6' 195–L
b. Fort Erie, March 5, 1956

1978–79	11	7	2	9	0
1979–80	45	11	13	24	10
Totals	56	18	15	33	10

- acquired March 13, 1979, from Colorado Rockies for Don Ashby and Trevor Johansen
- traded November 18, 1980, with Dave Burrows to Penguins for Kim Davis and Paul Marshall

RAY GARIEPY ("Rockabye Ray")

#2 defence   5'8" 180–L
b. Toronto, September 4, 1928

1955–56L	1	0	0	0	4

- acquired September 28, 1954, from Boston for Syracuse goalie John Henderson
- first and only Leaf game January 29, 1956
- bought June 7, 1956, by Hershey with Gil Mayer, Jack Price, Willie Marshall, Bob Hassard, and Bob Solinger when Hornets folded

SCOTT GARLAND

#25 centre   6'1" 185–R
b. Regina, Saskatchewan, May 16, 1952
d. Montreal, Quebec, June 9, 1979

1975–76R	16	4	3	7	8
1976–77	69	9	20	29	83
Totals	85	13	23	36	91

- signed in autumn 1973 as a free agent
- first Leaf game January 11, 1976
- traded June 14, 1978, with Brian Glennie, Kurt Walker, and the Leafs' 2nd-round choice in 1979 (Mark Hardy) to Los Angeles Kings for Dave Hutchison and Lorne Stamler

MIKE GARTNER ("Garts")

#11 right wing   6' 190–R
b. Ottawa, October 29, 1959

1993–94	10	6	6	12	4
1994–95	38	12	8	20	6
1995–96	82	35	19	54	52
Totals	130	53	33	86	62

- acquired March 21, 1994, from the Rangers for Glenn Anderson, Scott Malone, and a

4th-round draft choice in 1994 (Alexander Korobolin)
- traded June 22, 1996, to Phoenix for a 4th-round draft choice in 1996 (Vladimir Antipov)
- won bronze medal with Canada at 1978 WJC; played at 1981 (fourth), 1982 (bronze), 1983 (bronze), and 1993 (fourth) WC
- currently active in the NHLPA with programs aimed at helping kids around the world receive hockey equipment

STEWART "STU" GAVIN
#9–17 forward   6' 190–L
b. Ottawa, March 15, 1960

1980–81R	14	1	2	3	13
1981–82	38	5	6	11	29
1982–83	63	6	5	11	44
1983–84	80	10	22	32	90
1984–85	73	12	13	25	38
Totals	268	34	48	82	214

- drafted 74th overall in 1980 Entry Draft
- first Leaf game October 11, 1980
- traded October 7, 1985, to Hartford for Chris Kotsopoulos
- worked for a financial services company in Toronto

EDDIE GERARD
forward   5'9" 168–L
b. Ottawa, February 22, 1890
d. Ottawa, August 7, 1937

- appeared for St. Pats only in the 1922 playoffs
- played NHL finals with Ottawa, then joined St. Pats after elimination, playing March 25, 1922, vs. Vancouver Millionaires to replace injured Cameron
- became Chief Clerk for the Department of Geodetic Survey in Ottawa
- Hockey Hall of Fame 1945

JOHN GIBSON
#23 defence   6'3" 210–L
b. St. Catharines, June 2, 1959

1981–82	27	0	2	2	67

- acquired November 11, 1981, with Billy Harris from Los Angeles Kings for Ian Turnbull
- signed as a free agent September 19, 1983, by Winnipeg Jets

TODD GILL ("Giller")
#23–29–11–3 defence   6' 185–L
b. Brockville, November 9, 1965

1984–85R	10	1	0	1	13
1985–86	15	1	2	3	28
1986–87	61	4	27	31	92
1987–88	65	8	17	25	131
1988–89	59	11	14	25	72
1989–90	48	1	14	15	92
1990–91	72	2	22	24	113
1991–92	74	2	15	17	91
1992–93	69	11	32	43	66
1993–94	45	4	24	28	44
1994–95	47	7	25	32	64
1995–96	74	7	18	25	116
Totals	639	59	210	269	922

- selected 25th overall at 1984 Entry Draft
- first Leaf game February 9, 1985
- played left wing for 39 games in 1988–89
- traded June 14, 1996, to San Jose for Jamie Baker and a 5th-round draft choice in 1996 (Peter Cava)
- played for Canada at 1992 WC (eighth place)

DOUG GILMOUR ("Killer")

#93 centre   5'11" 170–L
b. Kingston, June 25, 1963

1991–92	40	15	34	49	32
1992–93	83	32	95	127	100
1993–94	83	27	84	111	105
1994–95	44	10	23	33	26
1995–96	81	32	40	72	77
1996–97	61	15	45	60	46
Totals	392	131	321	452	386

- acquired January 2, 1992, with Jamie Macoun, Ric Nattress, Rick Wamsley, and Kent Manderville from Calgary for Gary Leeman, Michel Petit, Jeff Reese, Craig Berube, and Alexander Godynyuk
- traded February 25, 1997, with Dave Ellett and a 3rd-round draft choice in 1999 (previously acquired from New Jersey in Andreychuk trade—Andre Lakos) to New Jersey for Steve Sullivan, Jason Smith, and Alyn McCauley
- played for Canada at 1981 wjc (seventh place) and 1990 wc (fourth place)
- currently a Leafs season ticket holder

GASTON GINGRAS

#11 defence   6' 190–L
b. Temiscamingue, Quebec, February 13, 1959

1982–83	45	10	18	28	10
1983–84	59	7	20	27	16
1984–85	5	0	2	2	0
Totals	109	17	40	57	26

- acquired December 17, 1982, from Canadiens for 2nd-round draft choice in 1985 or 1986 (Canadiens chose 1986—Benôit Brûnet)
- traded February 14, 1985, to Canadiens for Larry Landon

KENNY GIRARD

#27 right wing   6' 184–R
b. Toronto, December 8, 1936

1956–57R	3	0	1	1	2
1957–58	3	0	0	0	0
1959–60L	1	0	0	0	0
Totals	7	0	1	1	2

- Marlie graduate
- first Leaf games November 29 and December 1, 2, 1956
- last Leaf game January 14, 1960

BRIAN GLENNIE ("Blunt")

#24 defence   6'1" 200–L
b. Toronto, August 29, 1946

1969–70R	52	1	14	15	50
1970–71	54	0	8	8	31
1971–72	61	2	8	10	44
1972–73	44	1	10	11	54
1973–74	65	4	18	22	100
1974–75	63	1	7	8	110
1975–76	69	0	8	8	75
1976–77	69	1	10	11	73
1977–78	77	2	15	17	62
Totals	554	12	98	110	599

- Marlie graduate 1967
- first Leaf game October 11, 1969
- played 1967–68 with Canadian National Team (1968 Olympics)
- missed December 10–January 31 (21 games) in 1969–70 with torn knee ligaments
- traded June 14, 1978, with Scott Garland, Kurt Walker, and the Leafs' 2nd-round choice in 1979 (Mark Hardy) to Los Angeles Kings for Dave Hutchison and Lorne Stamler
- won bronze medal with Canada at 1968 Olympics

ERNIE GODDEN

#18 centre   5'7" 154–L
b. Keswick, March 13, 1961

1981–82R/L	5	1	1	2	6

- selected 55th overall at 1981 Entry Draft
- first and only Leaf games November 28, 29 and December 2, 5, 12, 1981

ALEXANDER GODYNYUK

#93 defence   6' 207–L
b. Kiev, USSR, January 27, 1970

1990–91R	18	0	3	3	16
1991–92	39	3	6	9	59
Totals	57	3	9	12	75

- selected 115th overall at 1990 Entry Draft
- first Leaf game February 6, 1991
- began 1990–91 with Sokol Kiev; also played part of year with Newmarket
- traded January 2, 1992, with Gary Leeman, Michel Petit, Jeff Reese, and Craig Berube to Calgary for Doug Gilmour, Jamie Macoun, Ric Nattress, Rick Wamsley, and Kent Manderville
- won gold medal with Soviet Union in 1989 and silver in 1990 at WJC; played for Ukraine at 1999 WC (fourteenth place)

BOB GOLDHAM ("Golden Boy")

#2–14–17 defence   6'1" 195–R
b. Georgetown, May 12, 1922
d. Toronto, September 6, 1991

1941–42R	19	4	7	11	25
1945–46	49	7	14	21	44
1946–47	11	1	1	2	10
Totals	79	12	22	34	79

- Marlie graduate
- first Leaf game January 27, 1942
- missed 1942–45—Royal Canadian Navy
- missed part of 1946–47 with torn knee ligaments
- missed most of 1946–47 with broken arm
- traded November 2, 1947, with Bud Poile, Gaye Stewart, Gus Bodnar, and Ernie

Dickens to Chicago for Max Bentley and Cy Thomas

- became popular intermission analyst with *Hockey Night in Canada* throughout the 1970s

HANK GOLDUP

#20–23 left wing   5'11" 175–L
b. Kingston, October 29, 1918

1940–41R	26	10	5	15	9
1941–42	44	12	18	30	13
1942–43	8	1	7	8	4
Totals	78	23	30	53	26

- played 1938–39 with Toronto Goodyears; signed April 20, 1939, by Leafs
- played in 1940 playoffs
- first regular season Leaf game November 2, 1940
- missed much of 1940–41 with broken hip
- traded November 27, 1942, with Dudley Garrett to the Rangers for Babe Pratt
- later worked with Molson's, Jordan Wines, and Victoriaville stick manufacturers

ED GORMAN

#3 defence   6' 180–L
b. Buckingham, Quebec, September 25, 1892
d. Ottawa, March 10, 1963

1927–28L	19	0	1	1	30

- bought from Ottawa Senators on October 25, 1927
- first Leaf game November 15, 1927
- last Leaf game January 12, 1928
- demoted to Ravinas, but refused to go; suspended, then signed with Kitchener (Can Pro) on February 13, 1928

CHRIS GOVEDARIS

#8 left wing   6' 200–L
b. Toronto, February 2, 1970

1993–94	12	2	2	4	14

- signed as a free agent September 7, 1993, from Hartford
- traded February 17, 1995, to Detroit for Gord Kruppke
- won bronze medal with Canada at 1995 WC

BOB GRACIE
#14 left wing 5′8″ 155–L
b. North Bay, November 8, 1910
d. Houston, Texas, August 3, 1963

1930–31R	7	4	2	6	4
1931–32	48	13	8	21	29
1932–33	48	9	13	22	27
Totals	103	26	23	49	60

- Marlie graduate; signed with the Leafs March 2, 1931
- first Leaf game March 3, 1931
- traded March 14, 1933, to Ottawa with $12,000 for Hec Kilrea
- later operated a nightclub in California

PAT GRAHAM
#23 left wing 6′1″ 190–L
b. Toronto, May 25, 1961

1983–84L	41	4	4	8	65

- acquired August 15, 1983, with Nick Ricci from Penguins for Rocky Saganiuk and Vincent Tremblay
- last Leaf game March 28, 1984
- played 1984–85 in West Germany, then signed as a free agent by Adirondack
- currently a chiropractor

BENNY GRANT
#1–15–17–16 goalie 5′11″ 160–L
b. Owen Sound, July 14, 1908
d. Unknown

1928–29R						
3 (0/3)	1–0–0	110	4	0	2.18	
1929–30						
2 (0/0)	1–1–0	130	11	0	5.08	
1930–31						
7 (0/0)	1–5–1	430	19	2	2.65	
1931–32						
5 (0/0)	1–2–1	320	18	1	3.38	
1943–44						
20 (0/0)	9–9–2	1200	83	0	4.15	
Totals						
36 (0/3)	13–17–4	2190	135	3	3.70	

- bought November 2, 1928, from London Panthers
- first Leaf game January 10, 1929
- loaned December 27, 1930, to Boston Tigers for the year, subject to instant recall
- loaned December 19, 1929, for one game to New York Americans
- loaned January 24, 1930, to Minneapolis Millers for rest of season
- recalled February 12, 1932, from Syracuse because of Chabot suspension
- loaned December 6, 1933, to Americans for rest of season while Roy Worters recovered from injury
- signed October 7, 1943, as free agent
- worked as a stock clerk for Imperial Oil in Owen Sound

ALEX GRAY
#9 right wing 5′10″ 170–R
b. Glasgow, Scotland, June 21, 1899
d. April 10, 1986

1928–29L	6	0	0	0	2

- acquired October 17, 1928, with Lorne Chabot from the Rangers for Butch Keeling and John Ross Roach
- only Leaf games November 15, 17, 20, 22, 24, 27, 1928
- sold November 28, 1928, to Toronto Millionaires

MARK GREIG
#11 right wing 5′11″ 190–R
b. High River, Alberta, January 25, 1970

1993–94	13	2	2	4	10

- acquired January 25, 1994, with a 6th-round draft choice in 1994 (later traded to Rangers—Yuri Litvinov) from Hartford for Ted Crowley
- signed August 9, 1994, as a free agent by Calgary

JOHN GRISDALE ("Gris")
#3 defence   6' 195–R
b. Geraldton, August 23, 1948

1972–73R	49	1	7	8	76
1974–75	2	0	0	0	4
Totals	51	1	7	8	80

- played four games with Tulsa in 1970–71 as a tryout
- signed by Leafs at 1971 training camp
- first Leaf game October 21, 1972
- traded October 16, 1974, with Gary Monahan to Vancouver Canucks for Dave Dunn

LLOYD GROSS
#11 left wing   5'8" 175–L
b. Kitchener, October 15, 1907

1926–27R	16	1	1	2	0

- signed March 7, 1927, after playing with Kitchener (OHA) in 1925–26
- first Leaf game March 10, 1927
- didn't play in NHL again until 1933–34 with New York Americans

PER GUSTAFSSON ("Gus")
#24 defence   6'2" 190–L
b. Osterham, Sweden, June 6, 1970

1997–98	22	1	4	5	10

- acquired from Florida on June 13, 1997, for Mike Lankshear
- traded to Ottawa on March 17, 1998, for an 8th-round draft choice in 1998 (Dwight Wolfe)
- played for Sweden at 1996 WC (sixth place) and 1997 WC (silver medal)

SEAN HAGGERTY
#52 left wing   6'1" 186–L
b. Rye, New York, February 11, 1976

1995–96R	1	0	0	0	0

- selected 48th overall at 1994 Entry Draft
- first and only Leaf game February 22, 1996
- traded March 13, 1996, with Kenny Jonsson, Darby Hendrickson, and a 1st-round draft choice in 1997 (Roberto Luongo) to the Islanders for Wendel Clark, Mathieu Schneider, and D.J. Smith
- played for USA at 1995 WJC (fifth place) and 2000 WC

GEORGE HAINSWORTH
#1 goalie   5'6" 150–L
b. Toronto, June 26, 1895
d. Gravenhurst, October 9, 1950

1933–34					
48 (0/0)	26–13–9	3010	119	3	2.37
1934–35					
48 (0/0)	30–14–4	2957	111	8	2.25
1935–36					
48 (0/0)	23–19–6	3000	106	8	2.12
1936–37					
3 (0/0)	0–2–1	190	9	0	2.84
Totals					
147 (0/0)	79–48–20	9157	345	19	2.26

- acquired summer 1933 from Canadiens for Lorne Chabot, but Chabot retired, nullifying the deal. On October 1, 1933, Chabot agreed to join the Habs, so the deal was finalized
- released November 24, 1936, after three games
- killed in a car crash
- Hockey Hall of Fame 1961

HAROLD "SLIM" HALDERSON
#14 defence   6'3" 200–R
b. Winnipeg, Manitoba, January 6, 1900
d. August 1, 1965

1926–27L	26	1	2	3	36

- acquired January 7, 1927, from Detroit for Pete Bellefeuille
- last Leaf game March 26, 1927
- won gold medal with Canada at 1920 Olympics

BOB HALKIDIS ("Hawk")

#33 defence   5'11" 200–L
b. Toronto, March 5, 1966

1991–92L	46	3	3	6	145

- signed as a free agent July 24, 1991
- last Leaf game March 9, 1992
- signed September 2, 1983, as free agent by Detroit

HERB "HAP" HAMEL

#14 forward   5'11" 155–R
b. New Hamburg, June 8, 1904
d. Unknown

1930–31R/L	4	0	0	0	4

- first and only Leaf games December 9, 13, 18, 20, 1930

PIERRE HAMEL

#31–32 goalie   5'9" 170–L
b. Montreal, Quebec, September 16, 1952

1974–75R					
4 (0/1)	1–2–0	195	18	0	5.54
1978–79					
1 (0/1)	0–0–0	1	0	0	0.00
Totals					
5 (0/2)	1–2–0	196	18	0	5.51

- signed as a free agent at 1974 training camp
- first Leaf games November 15, 16, 20 and February 15, 1974–75
- claimed June 13, 1979, at Expansion Draft by Winnipeg Jets

JACK HAMILTON ("Gabby")

#15–19–22–17 centre   5'7 170–L
b. Trenton, June 2, 1925
d. Unknown

1942–43R	13	1	6	7	4
1943–44	49	20	17	37	4
1945–46L	40	7	9	16	12
Totals	102	28	32	60	20

- first Leaf game October 31, 1942
- missed 1944–45—Canadian armed forces
- last Leaf game March 17, 1946
- traded September 10, 1948, with cash to Providence for Dan Lewicki (originally acquired August 12, 1948)

REG HAMILTON

#3–5–20–22 defence   5'11" 180–L
b. Toronto, April 29, 1914
d. June 12, 1991

1935–36R	7	0	0	0	0
1936–37	39	3	7	10	32
1937–38	45	1	4	5	43
1938–39	48	0	7	7	54
1939–40	23	2	2	4	23
1940–41	45	3	12	15	59
1941–42	22	0	4	4	27
1942–43	48	4	17	21	68
1943–44	39	4	12	16	32
1944–45	50	3	12	15	41
Totals	366	20	77	97	379

- graduate St. Mike's in 1934
- first Leaf games December 10, 14, 17, 19, 21, 26, 28, 1935
- missed much of 1941–42 with serious knee injury
- sold to Chicago on July 9, 1945
- worked in the purchasing department of Carlton Cards in Toronto

INGE HAMMARSTROM
#11 left wing   6' 180–L
b. Sundsvall, Sweden, January 20, 1948

1973–74R	66	20	23	43	14
1974–75	69	21	20	41	23
1975–76	76	19	21	40	21
1976–77	78	24	17	41	16
1977–78	3	1	1	2	6
Totals	292	85	82	167	80

- signed as free agent May 12, 1973
- first Leaf game October 10, 1973
- traded November 1, 1977, to St. Louis for Jerry Butler
- won bronze medals with Sweden at 1971 and 1972 WC, silver at 1973 WC, bronze at 1979 WC; played at 1981 WC (fourth) and 1972 Olympics (fourth)

KEN HAMMOND
#29 defence   6'1" 190–L
b. Port Credit, August 22, 1963

1988–89	14	0	2	2	12

- acquired January 30, 1989, from Denver Rangers (IHL) for loan of Chris McRae to Denver
- sold August 20, 1990, to Boston for cash

EDWARD "TED" HAMPSON
#14 centre   5'8" 173–L
b. Togo, Saskatchewan, December 11, 1936

1959–60R	41	2	8	10	17

- claimed on waivers September 18, 1959, from Rangers for $20,000
- first Leaf game October 10, 1959
- claimed June 7, 1960, at Intra-League Draft by Rangers
- became director of scouting for St. Louis Blues

DAVE HANNAN
#9 centre   5'10" 185–L
b. Sudbury, November 26, 1961

1989–90	39	6	9	15	55
1990–91	74	11	23	34	82
1991–92	35	2	2	4	16
Totals	148	19	34	53	153

- claimed October 2, 1989, from Penguins in waiver draft
- traded March 10, 1992, to Sabres for a 5th-round draft choice in 1992 (Chris Deruiter)
- won silver medal with Canada at 1992 Olympics

GORD HANNIGAN ("Hopalong")
#17–22–23 centre   5'7" 163–L
b. Schumacher, January 19, 1929
d. Edmonton, Alberta, November 16, 1966

1952–53R	65	17	18	35	51
1953–54	35	4	4	8	18
1954–55	13	0	2	2	8
1955–56L	48	8	7	15	40
Totals	161	29	31	60	117

- St. Mike's graduate
- first Leaf game October 11, 1952
- last Leaf game March 18, 1956
- acquired by Edmonton (WHL) for 1957–58

PAT HANNIGAN
#23 right wing   5'10" 190–R
b. Timmins, March 5, 1936

1959–60R	1	0	0	0	0

- St. Mike's graduate
- recalled December 15, 1959, from Rochester
- first and only Leaf game December 17, 1959
- traded November 7, 1960, with Johnny Wilson to the Rangers for Eddie Shack
- later became popular broadcaster of Buffalo Sabres games

RAY HANNIGAN

#16 forward   5'8" 155–R
b. Schumacher, July 14, 1927

1948–49R/L	3	0	0	0	2

- St. Mike's graduate
- first and only Leaf games February 26 and March 2, 13, 1949
- traded September 11, 1952, with Cal Gardner, Gus Mortson, and Al Rollins to Chicago for Harry Lumley

DAVID HARLOCK

#28–38 defence   6'2" 205–L
b. Toronto, March 16, 1971

1993–94R	6	0	0	0	0
1994–95	1	0	0	0	0
1995–96	1	0	0	0	0
Totals	8	0	0	0	0

- signed as a free agent August 20, 1993
- first Leaf games March 9, 10 and April 5, 8, 12, 14, 1994
- played April 5, 1995 with Leafs
- played February 12, 1996
- won gold medal with Canada at 1991 WJC and silver at 1992 Olympics
- signed as a free agent by Washington on August 20, 1997

BILLY HARRIS ("Hinky")

#15 centre   6' 165–L
b. Toronto, July 29, 1935

1955–56R	70	9	13	22	8
1956–57	23	4	6	10	6
1957–58	68	16	28	44	32
1958–59	70	22	30	52	29
1959–60	70	13	25	38	29
1960–61	66	12	27	39	30
1961–62	67	15	10	25	14
1962–63	65	8	24	32	22
1963–64	63	6	12	18	17
1964–65	48	1	6	7	0
Totals	610	106	181	287	187

- Marlie graduate 1955 (Memorial Cup winner)
- signed May 10, 1955, with Leafs
- first Leaf game October 6, 1955
- traded May 20, 1965, with Andy Bathgate and Gary Jarrett to Detroit for Marcel Pronovost, Lowell MacDonald, Aut Erickson, Larry Jeffrey, and Ed Joyal
- an avid photographer, he wrote a book on the Leafs of the 1960s illustrated with his own pictures
- became heavily involved in Leaf alumni relations

BILLY HARRIS

#16 right wing   6'2" 195–L
b. Toronto, January 29, 1952

1981–82	20	2	0	2	4
1982–83	76	11	19	30	26
1983–84	50	7	10	17	14
Totals	146	20	29	49	44

- acquired November 11, 1981, with John Gibson from Los Angeles Kings for Ian Turnbull
- rights sold February 15, 1984, to Los Angeles Kings
- worked for a marina, first in Toronto, then Georgian Bay

GEORGE "DUKE" HARRIS ("The Duker")

#17 right wing   6' 204–R
b. Sarnia, February 25, 1942

1967–68L	4	0	0	0	0

- bought December 23, 1967, from Minnesota
- first and only Leaf games February 7, 11, 12, 14, 1968
- signed in summer 1972 with Houston Aeros (WHA)

JIM HARRISON ("Max")
#7–12 centre   5'11" 185–R
b. Bonnyville, Alberta, July 9, 1947

1969–70	31	7	10	17	36
1970–71	78	13	20	33	108
1971–72	66	19	17	36	104
Totals	175	39	47	86	248

- acquired December 10, 1969, from Boston for Wayne Carleton
- missed March 7–end of season, 1970 with broken finger
- signed June 21, 1972, with Alberta Oilers (WHA)
- NHL rights traded September 28, 1976, to Chicago for a 2nd-round draft choice in 1977 (Bob Gladney)
- debilitating back injury ended his playing days and prevented him from holding a steady job

PAUL HARRISON
#30 goalie   6'1" 175–L
b. Timmins, February 11, 1955

1978–79						
25 (3/2)	8–12–3	1403	82	1	3.51	
1979–80						
30 (9/6)	9–17–2	1492	110	0	4.42	
Totals						
55 (12/8)	17–29–5	2895	192	1	3.98	

- acquired June 14, 1978, from Minnesota for a 4th-round draft choice in 1981 (Terry Tait)
- traded September 11, 1981, to Penguins for future considerations

BOB HASSARD
#17–20–25 centre   6' 165–R
b. Lloydminster, Saskatchewan, March 26, 1929

1949–50R	1	0	0	0	0
1950–51	12	0	1	1	0
1952–53	70	8	23	31	14
1953–54	26	1	4	5	4
Totals	109	9	28	37	18

- Marlie graduate 1951
- first Leaf game November 19, 1949
- sold April 4, 1954, to Chicago for $20,000
- long-time insurance agent in Stouffville

TODD HAWKINS
#8 forward   6'1" 195–R
b. Kingston, August 2, 1966

1991–92	2	0	0	0	0

- acquired January 22, 1991, from Vancouver Canucks for Brian Blad
- signed as a free agent August 20, 1993, by Penguins

GLENN HEALY ("Heals")
#30 goalie   5'10" 185–L
b. Pickering, August 23, 1962

1997–98					
21 (2/4)	4–10–2	1068	53	0	2.98
1998–99					
9 (0/0)	6–3–0	546	27	0	2.97
1999–2000					
20 (0/1)	9–10–0	1164	59	2	3.04
2000–01					
15 (0/1)	4–7–3	871	38	0	2.62
Totals					
65 (2/6)	23–30–5	3649	177	2	2.91

- signed as a free agent August 8, 1997
- NHL's finest bagpiper

SAMMY HEBERT
#9 goalie   5'10" 145–R
b. Ottawa, March 31, 1894
d. July 23, 1965

1917–18					
2 (1/0)	1–1	80	10	0	7.50

- first and only Arenas games December 19 and January 2, 1917–18
- loaned February 17, 1918, to Ottawa

FRANK HEFFERNAN ("Moose")

#6 forward   6' 200–L

b. Peterborough

d. New York, New York, December 21, 1938

1919–20R/L	17	0	0	0	0

- signed in 1919 from Hamilton (OHA Senior)
- first St. Pats game December 23, 1919
- last St. Pats game March 6, 1920

PAUL HENDERSON

#19 left wing   5'11" 180–R

b. Kincardine, January 28, 1943

1967–68	13	5	6	11	8
1968–69	74	27	32	59	16
1969–70	67	20	22	42	18
1970–71	72	30	30	60	34
1971–72	73	38	19	57	32
1972–73	40	18	16	34	18
1973–74	69	24	31	55	40
Totals	408	162	156	318	166

- acquired March 3, 1968, with Norm Ullman and Floyd Smith from Detroit for Frank Mahovlich, Pete Stemkowski, Garry Unger, and the rights to Carl Brewer
- scored winning goal in games 6,7, and 8 of Summit Series, culminating September 28, 1972
- signed July 1974 with Toronto Toros (WHA)

DARBY HENDRICKSON

#37–16–14 centre   6' 185–L

b. Richfield, Minnesota, August 28, 1972

1994–95R	8	0	1	1	4
1995–96	46	6	6	12	47
1996–97	64	11	6	17	47
1997–98	80	8	4	12	67
1998–99	35	2	3	5	30
Totals	233	27	20	47	195

- selected 73rd overall at 1990 Entry Draft
- first regular season Leaf game February 10, 1995

- traded March 13, 1996, with Kenny Jonsson, Sean Haggerty, and a 1st-round draft choice in 1997 (Roberto Luongo) to the Islanders for Wendel Clark, Mathieu Schneider, and Denis Smith
- reacquired October 11, 1996, from Islanders for a 5th-round draft choice in 1998 (Jiri Dopita); sent immediately to St. John's for conditioning
- traded to Vancouver for Chris McAllister on February 16, 1999
- played for USA at 1994 Olympics (eighth place); won bronze medal at 1996 WC and played in 1997 WC (sixth), 1999 WC (sixth), and 2000 WC (fifth)
- currently with Minnesota Wild

JIMMY HERBERTS ("Sailor")

#7 forward   5'10" 185–R

b. Collingwood, October 31, 1897

d. Buffalo, New York, December 5, 1968

1927–28	43	15	4	19	64

- acquired December 22, 1927, from Boston for $17,500 and the rights to Eric Pettinger
- traded April 9, 1928, to Detroit Cougars for Jack Arbour and $12,500

BOB "RED" HERON

#16–17–18 centre   5'11" 170–L

b. Toronto, December 31, 1917

1938–39R	6	0	0	0	0
1939–40	42	11	12	23	12
1940–41	35	9	5	14	12
Totals	83	20	17	37	24

- joined Syracuse in March 1938
- first Leaf games December 24, 31 and January 1, 3, 7, 21, 1938–39
- recalled March 27, 1939, from Syracuse for playoffs
- traded October 30, 1941, to New York Americans with Nick Knott, Gus Marker, and Peanuts O'Flaherty on a one-year lease, all subject to recall, for Lorne Carr

JAMIE HEWARD
#36–26 defence   6'2" 207–R
b. Regina, Saskatchewan, March 30, 1971

1995–96R	5	0	0	0	0
1996–97	20	1	4	5	6
Totals	25	1	4	5	6

- signed as a free agent May 4, 1995; began 1995–96 in St. John's
- first and only Leaf games February 3, 5, 7, 8, 10, 1996
- signed as a free agent July 10, 1997, by Flyers

PAT HICKEY ("Hitch")
#15–16 left wing   6'1" 190–L
b. Brantford, May 15, 1953

1979–80	45	22	16	38	16
1980–81	72	16	33	49	49
1981–82	1	0	0	0	0
Totals	118	38	49	87	65

- acquired December 29, 1979, with Wilf Paiement from Colorado Rockies for Lanny McDonald and Joel Quenneville
- traded October 16, 1981, to the Rangers for a 5th-round draft choice in 1982 (Sylvain Charland)
- won bronze medal with Canada at 1978 WC
- became general manager in the AHL, though previously and since involved in private business

PAUL HIGGINS
#17–29 right wing   6'1" 195–R
b. Saint John, New Brunswick, January 13, 1962

1981–82R	3	0	0	0	17
1982–83L	23	0	0	0	135
Totals	26	0	0	0	152

- selected 200th overall at 1980 Entry Draft
- first player ever drafted into NHL directly from high school

- first Leaf games February 23 and March 4, 6, 1982
- last Leaf game March 30, 1983
- released September 1983

MEL HILL ("Sudden Death")
#8 right wing   5'10" 175–R
b. Glenboro, Manitoba, February 15, 1914
d. Fort Qu'Appelle, Saskatchewan, April 11, 1996

1942–43	49	17	27	44	47
1943–44	17	9	10	19	16
1944–45	45	18	17	35	14
1945–46L	35	5	7	12	10
Totals	146	49	61	110	87

- purchased October 5, 1942, when Brooklyn Americans folded
- missed most of 1943–44 with broken ankle
- last Leaf game February 6, 1946
- went into the soft drink business in Regina, Saskatchewan

LARRY HILLMAN
#2–16–22 defence   6' 181–R
b. Kirkland Lake, February 5, 1937

1960–61	62	3	10	13	59
1961–62	5	0	0	0	4
1962–63	5	0	0	0	2
1963–64	33	0	4	4	31
1964–65	2	0	0	0	2
1965–66	48	3	25	28	34
1966–67	55	4	19	23	40
1967–68	55	3	17	20	13
Totals	265	13	75	88	185

- claimed from Boston on June 7, 1960, Intra-League Draft
- missed most of 1961–62 with serious shoulder injury; played part of year with Rochester
- played December 4–18, 1963, with Leafs
- played October 15 and November 18, 1964

- claimed by Minnesota via Rangers on June 12, 1968, at Intra-League Draft
- ran a tourist camp in Englehart, Ontario, and sells real estate
- ran a hunting and fishing camp near Kirkland Lake

ANDRÉ HINSE
#23 left wing   5'9" 172-L
b. Trois Rivières, Quebec, April 19, 1945

1967–68R/L	4	0	0	0	0

- signed as a free agent at training camp 1966
- first and only Leaf games February 7, 11, 12, 14, 1968
- sent to Phoenix summer 1969
- acquired fall 1971 from Vancouver Canucks for Doug Brindley
- signed by Houston Aeros in summer 1973

DAN HODGSON
#16 centre   5'10" 165-R
b. Fort Vermillion, Alberta, August 29, 1965

1985–86R	40	13	12	25	12

- selected 85th overall at 1983 Entry Draft
- first Leaf game October 16, 1985
- traded December 2, 1986, with Jim Benning to Vancouver Canucks for Rick Lanz

JONAS HOGLUND ("Hogie")
#14 right wing   6'3" 215-R
b. Hamaro, Sweden, August 29, 1972

1999–2000	82	29	27	56	10
2000–01	82	23	26	49	14
Totals	164	52	53	105	24

- signed as a free agent July 13, 1999
- won silver medal with Sweden at 1992 WJC and 1997 WC

BENOÎT HOGUE ("Benny")
#28–32–33 centre   5'10" 190-L
b. Repentigny, Quebec, October 28, 1966

1994–95	12	3	3	6	0
1995–96	44	12	25	37	68
Totals	56	15	28	43	68

- acquired April 6, 1995, with a 3rd-round draft choice in 1995 (Ryan Pepperall) and a 5th-round draft choice in 1996 (Brandon Sudgen) from the Islanders for Eric Fichaud
- traded January 28, 1996, with Randy Wood to Dallas for Dave Gagner and a 6th-round draft choice in 1996 (Dmitri Yakushin)

WILLIAM "FLASH" HOLLETT
("Headline")
#15–3 defence   6' 184-L
b. North Sydney, Nova Scotia, April 13, 1912
d. Mississauga, April 20, 1999

1933–34R	5	0	0	0	4
1934–35	48	10	16	26	38
1935–36	11	1	4	5	8
Totals	64	11	20	31	50

- signed from the Toronto Maple Leaf lacrosse team in 1933
- recalled December 20, 1933, from Bisons to replace suspended Horner (re: Bailey incident)
- first Leaf games December 23, 26, 28, 30 and January 1, 1933–34
- loaned January 2, 1934, to Ottawa Senators for rest of season
- sold January 15, 1936, to Boston for $16,500
- became a partner in a flourishing business until he retired

HARRY HOLMES ("Hap"/"Happy")
#1 goalie   5'10" 170–L
b. Aurora, April 15, 1889
d. Ft. Lauderdale, Florida, June 28, 1941

1917–18
16 (0/0)   10–6–0   965   76   0   4.73
1918–19
2 (0/0)   0–2–0   120   9   0   4.50

Totals
18 (0/0)   10–8–0   1085   85   0   4.70

- signed by Wanderers in December 1917 from Seattle (PCHA), but when the Wanderers' arena burned down he became Arenas property in the dispersal of players on January 5, 1918
- first Arenas game January 9, 1918
- signed from Seattle (PCHA) in fall 1918 under an agreement whereby he could be reclaimed at any time
- played December 23 and 26, 1918, then recalled by Seattle
- owned a fruit farm in Florida
- Hockey Hall of Fame 1972

ALBERT "TOOTS" HOLWAY
(sometimes "Holloway")
#3 defence   6'1" 190–L
b. Toronto, September 24, 1902
d. Belleville, November 20, 1968

1923–24R	6	1	0	1	0
1924–25	25	2	2	4	20
1925–26	12	0	0	0	0
Totals	43	3	2	5	20

- signed February 13, 1924 from Belleville and Brockville
- first St. Pats game February 16, 1924
- missed game of December 5, 1924, with a bad knee; missed many other games in 1924–25 with a bad cut on his ankle
- traded January 11, 1926, to Maroons for Dutch Cain

LARRY HOPKINS
#12 left wing   6'1" 215–L
b. Oshawa, March 17, 1954

1977–78R	2	0	0	0	0

- played two games with Leafs as a free agent, March 8, 9, 1978
- signed by Winnipeg Jets as a free agent August 15, 1979

GEORGE "SHORTY" HORNE
#8 forward   5'6" 170–R
b. Sudbury, June 27, 1904
d. Lake Gogama, August 1, 1929

1928–29L	39	9	3	12	32

- acquired April 16, 1928, from Stratford Nationals for Freddy Elliott and $2,500
- last Leaf game March 16, 1929
- drowned at his cottage

REG "RED" HORNER
#2–15–11 defence   6' 190–R
b. Lynden, May 28, 1909

1928–29R	22	0	0	0	30
1929–30	33	2	7	9	96
1930–31	42	1	11	12	71
1931–32	42	7	9	16	97
1932–33	48	3	8	11	144
1933–34	40	11	10	21	146
1934–35	46	4	8	12	125
1935–36	43	2	9	11	167
1936–37	48	3	9	12	124
1937–38	47	4	20	24	92
1938–39	48	4	10	14	85
1939–40L	31	1	9	10	87
Totals	490	42	110	152	1264

- turned pro December 22, 1928, while still with Marlies
- first Leaf game December 22, 1928
- missed much of 1928–29 with broken hand
- missed part of 1931–32 with broken collarbone
- suspended six games in 1933–34 for attack on Eddie Shore in Bailey incident

- missed five games in 1935–36 with concussion
- last Leaf game March 17, 1940
- retired April 18, 1940
- later became a linesman
- Hockey Hall of Fame 1965 (oldest living Hall of Famer)

RED HORNER
goalie

1928–29					
1 (1/1)	0–0	2	0	0	0.00
1931–32					
1 (1/1)	0–0	1	1	0	60.00
Totals					
2 (2/2)	0–0	3	1	0	20.00

- played January 29, 1929, when Chabot penalized
- allowed a goal, along with Alex Levinsky and King Clancy, March 15, 1932, while Chabot serving a penalty

MILES "TIM" HORTON ("Superman")
#7–16–20 defence   5'10" 180–R
b. Cochrane, January 12, 1930
d. St. Catharines, February 21, 1974

1949–50R	1	0	0	0	2
1951–52	4	0	0	0	8
1952–53	70	2	14	16	85
1953–54	70	7	24	31	94
1954–55	67	5	9	14	84
1955–56	35	0	5	5	36
1956–57	66	6	19	25	72
1957–58	53	6	20	26	39
1958–59	70	5	21	26	76
1959–60	70	3	29	32	69
1960–61	57	6	15	21	75
1961–62	70	10	28	38	88
1962–63	70	6	19	25	69
1963–64	70	9	20	29	71
1964–65	70	12	16	28	95
1965–66	70	6	22	28	76
1966–67	70	8	17	25	70
1967–68	69	4	23	27	82
1968–69	74	11	29	40	107
1969–70	59	3	19	22	91
Totals	1185	109	349	458	1389

- St. Mike's graduate
- first Leaf game March 26, 1950
- missed much of 1955–56 with a broken leg and jaw after a check by Bill Gadsby on March 12, 1955 (the previous season!)
- missed 13 games in 1960–61 with torn abdominal muscles
- played part of 1964–65 on right wing
- opened first Tim Horton's doughnut stores in 1960s while with the Leafs
- traded March 3, 1970, to the Rangers for Jacques Plante, Denis Dupere, and Guy Trottier
- died in single-car accident driving home to Buffalo after a game against Toronto

JOSEPH "BRONCO" HORVATH
#17 centre   5'10" 185–L
b. Port Colborne, March 12, 1930

1962–63	9	0	4	4	12

- claimed January 1963 from Rangers on waivers
- claimed June 6, 1967, by Minnesota at Expansion Draft
- ran cleaning service business in Massachusetts

GREG HOTHAM
#4–2–8 defence   5'11" 185–R
b. London, March 7, 1956

1979–80R	46	3	10	13	10
1980–81	11	1	1	2	11
1981–82	3	0	0	0	0
Totals	60	4	11	15	21

- selected 84th overall at 1976 Amateur Draft
- first Leaf game October 10, 1979
- traded February 3, 1982, to Penguins for a 6th-round draft choice in 1982 (Craig Kales)

Tim Horton

FRANK HOWARD

#17–21 defence   6' 170–L
b. London, October 15, 1915

1936–37R/L	2	0	0	0	0

- signed October 22, 1935
- first and only Leaf and NHL games November 26, 28, 1936

SYD HOWE

#15 centre   5'9" 165–L
b. Ottawa, September 18, 1911
d. Ottawa, May 26, 1976

1931–32	3	0	0	0	0

- loaned to Leafs for 1931–32 when Ottawa Senators didn't field a team, but played most of the season in Syracuse (demoted November 19, 1931)
- first Leaf game November 12, 1931
- returned to Ottawa in 1932
- worked for civil service in Ottawa
- Hockey Hall of Fame 1965

ROLLY HUARD

#9 forward   5'10" 170–L
b. Ottawa, September 6, 1902
d. Unknown

1930–31R/L	1	1	0	1	0

- acquired by Buffalo from Windsor Hornets for Mike Neville
- scored a goal December 13, 1930, in his only NHL game, one of only two players to do so

GREG HUBICK

#19 defence   5'11" 183–L
b. Strasbourg, Saskatchewan, November 12, 1951

1975–76R	72	6	8	14	10

- acquired June 26, 1975, from Canadiens for Doug Jarvis
- first Leaf game October 11, 1975

- signed September 7, 1979, by Vancouver Canucks as a free agent

MIKE HUDSON ("Huddy")

#15 forward   6'1" 205–L
b. Guelph, February 6, 1967

1995–96	28	2	0	2	29

- signed as a free agent August 28, 1995
- claimed on waivers January 4, 1996, by St. Louis

RON HURST

#21–22 right wing   5'9" 175–R
b. Toronto, May 18, 1931

1955–56R	50	7	5	12	62
1956–57L	14	2	2	4	8
Totals	64	9	7	16	70

- signed in 1955
- first Leaf game November 13, 1955
- last Leaf game January 5, 1957
- traded summer 1958 with Wally Boyer and Mike Nykoluk to Hershey for Willie Marshall
- later became a stockbroker in Toronto

DAVE HUTCHISON

#23–33 defence   6'3" 205–R
b. London, May 2, 1952

1978–79	79	4	15	19	235
1979–80	31	1	6	7	28
1983–84L	47	0	3	3	137
Totals	157	5	24	29	400

- acquired June 14, 1978, with Lorne Stamler from Los Angeles Kings for Brian Glennie, Scott Garland, Kurt Walker, and a 2nd-round draft choice in 1979 (Mark Hardy)
- traded January 10, 1980, to Chicago for Pat Ribble
- signed as a free agent November 15, 1983
- last Leaf game April 1, 1984

AL IAFRATE ("Skis")
#33 defence   6'3" 220–L
b. Dearborn, Michigan, March 21, 1966

1984–85R	68	5	16	21	51
1985–86	65	8	25	33	40
1986–87	80	9	21	30	55
1987–88	77	22	30	52	80
1988–89	65	13	20	33	72
1989–90	75	21	42	63	135
1990–91	42	3	15	18	113
Totals	472	81	169	250	546

- selected 4th overall in 1984 Entry Draft
- first Leaf game October 11, 1984
- traded January 16, 1991, to Washington for Peter Zezel and Bob Rouse
- self-proclaimed "Human Highlight Film" retired because of recurring injuries
- played for USA at 1984 Olympics (seventh place) and 1998 WC (twelfth)

MIROSLAV IHNACAK
#27 left wing   5'11" 175–L
b. Poprad, Czechoslovakia, November 19, 1962

1985–86R	21	2	4	6	27
1986–87	34	6	5	11	12
Totals	55	8	9	17	39

- selected 171st in 1982 Entry Draft
- first Leaf game January 10, 1986
- signed November 18, 1988, as a free agent by Detroit

PETER IHNACAK
#18–15 centre   5'11" 180–R
b. Poprad, Czechoslovakia, May 3, 1957

1982–83R	80	28	38	66	44
1983–84	47	10	13	23	24
1984–85	70	22	22	44	24
1985–86	63	18	27	45	16
1986–87	58	12	27	39	16
1987–88	68	10	20	30	41
1988–89	26	2	16	18	10
1989–90L	5	0	2	2	0
Totals	417	102	165	267	175

- selected 25th overall at 1982 Entry Draft
- first Leaf game October 6, 1982
- last Leaf games January 15 and March 14, 16, 17, 19, 1990
- signed by Freiburg (Germany) for 1990–91 season
- won bronze medals with Czechoslovakia at 1977 WJC and 1982 WC
- coached extensively after retiring, primarily in Nuremberg

BRENT IMLACH
#9–24 forward   5'9" 165–R
b. Toronto, November 16, 1946

1965–66R	2	0	0	0	0
1966–67L	1	0	0	0	0
Totals	3	0	0	0	0

- first Leaf games January 16 and March 3, 1966
- played December 25, 1966
- sold August 31, 1970, to Sabres with Floyd Smith
- became vice-president and general manager of Vancouver Canadians baseball team

PETER ING
#31–1 goalie   6'2" 165–L
b. Toronto, April 28, 1969

1989–90R					
3 (1/1)	0–2–1	182	18	0	5.93
1990–91					
56 (10/7)	16–29–8	3162	200	1	3.80
Totals					
59 (11/8)	16–31–9	3344	218	1	3.91

- selected 48th overall at 1988 Entry Draft
- first Leaf games November 16 and December 6, 27, 1989
- traded September 19, 1991, with Vincent Damphousse, Luke Richardson, and Scott Thornton to Edmonton for Grant Fuhr, Glenn Anderson, and Craig Berube

JOHNNY INGOLDSBY ("Ding")

#11–20 right wing   6'2" 210–R
b. Toronto, June 21, 1924
d. August 10, 1982

1942–43R	8	0	1	1	0
1943–44L	21	5	0	5	15
Totals	29	5	1	6	15

- signed November 17, 1942, while still with the Marlies
- first Leaf game November 26, 1942
- last Leaf game January 29, 1944
- left February 7, 1944, to join the Canadian army

RALPH INTRANUOVO

#20 centre   5'8" 185–L
b. East York, Ontario, December 11, 1973

1996–97	3	0	1	1	0

- claimed in Waiver Draft on September 30, 1996, from Edmonton for $60,000
- only Leaf games October 5, 8, 12, 1996
- lost on waivers October 25, 1996, to Edmonton
- won gold medal with Canada at 1993 WJC and bronze at 1995 WC

JOE IRONSTONE ("Kelly")

#1 goalie   5'6" 180–R
b. Sudbury, June 28, 1898
d. Sudbury, December 12, 1972

1927–28L						
1 (0/0)	0–0–1	70	0	1	0.00

- recorded shutout in only appearance in a Leaf uniform, March 3, 1928 (0–0 overtime tie with Boston at Arena Gardens)
- replaced Roach, who had kidney stones
- also played with Brantford Falcons in Can Pro League and with Toronto Ravinas (1927–28)
- later ran a clothing store in Sudbury with his brother

ART JACKSON

#16–17–18–20–15 centre 5'8" 155–L
b. Toronto, December 15, 1915
d. St. Catharines, May 14, 1971

1934–35R	20	1	3	4	4
1935–36	48	5	15	20	14
1936–37	14	2	0	2	2
1944–45L	31	9	13	22	6
Totals	113	17	31	48	26

- St. Mike's graduate 1934
- first Leaf game November 8, 1934
- sold September 24, 1937, to Boston for cash
- bought December 23, 1944, from Boston for $7,500
- last Leaf game March 18, 1945
- became a personnel manager for the Port Weller Dry Docks Ltd. in St. Catharines

HARVEY "BUSHER" JACKSON

#11–9 forward   5'11" 195–L
b. Toronto, January 19, 1911
d. Toronto, June 25, 1966

1929–30R	32	12	6	18	29
1930–31	43	18	13	31	81
1931–32	48	28	25	53	63
1932–33	48	27	17	44	43
1933–34	38	20	18	38	38
1934–35	42	22	22	44	27
1935–36	47	11	11	22	19
1936–37	46	21	19	40	12
1937–38	48	17	17	34	18
1938–39	42	10	17	27	12
Totals	434	186	165	351	342

- Marlie graduate in 1928; signed with Toronto December 6, 1929
- first Leaf game December 7, 1929
- missed part of 1933–34 with shoulder injury
- missed games in 1934–35 with broken ribs
- missed first game of 1935–36 in contract dispute

- traded May 18, 1939, with Murray Armstrong, Buzz Boll, and Doc Romnes to the New York Americans for Sweeney Schriner
- later suffered from alcoholism; Conn Smythe objected so strenuously to Jackson's induction into the Hockey Hall of Fame because of Busher's off-ice transgressions that he blocked the induction for many years. When it finally passed, in 1971, Smythe resigned in protest

JEFF JACKSON ("Jax"/"Jesse")
#12–25 left wing   6'1" 195–L
b. Dresden, April 24, 1965

1984–85R	17	0	1	1	24
1985–86	5	1	2	3	2
1986–87	55	8	7	15	64
Totals	77	9	10	19	90

- selected 28th overall at 1983 Entry Draft
- first Leaf game October 11, 1984
- traded March 5, 1987, with 3rd-round draft choice in 1989 (Rob Zamuner) to the Rangers for Mark Osborne
- won gold medal with Canada at 1985 WJC

STANTON "STAN" JACKSON
#10 left wing   6' 180–L
b. Amherst, Nova Scotia, 1898
d. Ridgeway, November 28, 1955

1921–22R	1	0	0	0	0
1923–24	21	1	1	2	6
1924–25	4	0	0	0	0
Totals	26	1	1	2	6

- signed by St. Pats in 1921 from Maritime Independent League (Imparoyal)
- first St. Pats game December 24, 1921
- released December 15, 1924; signed with Boston
- worked as an immigration officer on Peace Bridge in Fort Erie

PAUL JACOBS
#12 forward   5'8" 160–L
b. Unknown   d. Unknown

1918–19R/L	5	0	0	0	0

- first and only Arenas games January 7, 14, 21, 31 and February 4, 1919
- a Native Indian who played lacrosse with the Leasides in 1917–18

EDWIN "GERRY" JAMES
#11–16–19 right wing   5'11" 191–R
b. Regina, Saskatchewan, October 22, 1934

1954–55R	1	0	0	0	0
1955–56	46	3	3	6	50
1956–57	53	4	12	16	90
1957–58	15	3	2	5	61
1959–60L	34	4	9	13	56
Totals	149	14	26	40	257

- Marlie graduate 1955
- first Leaf game February 24, 1955
- signed November 22, 1955, with Leafs
- missed one month in 1956–57 with torn shoulder ligaments
- missed all of 1958–59 with injury (broken left leg)
- played for Winnipeg Blue Bombers (CFL) 1952–63
- last Leaf game March 20, 1960
- released in 1960
- managed a motel and coached Yorkton Terriers

VALMORE "VAL" JAMES
#28 left wing   6'2" 205–L
b. Ocala, Florida, February 14, 1957

1986–87L	4	0	0	0	14

- signed October 3, 1985, as a free agent from Sabres
- first and only Leaf games November 24, 26, 28, 29, 1986

GARY JARRETT
#24 left wing   5'8" 170–L
b. Toronto, September 3, 1942

1960–61R	1	0	0	0	0

- first and only Leaf game November 26, 1960
- traded May 20, 1965, with Andy Bathgate and Billy Harris to Detroit for Marcel Pronovost, Aut Erickson, Larry Jeffrey, Ed Joyal, and Lowell MacDonald
- ran a real estate company in Denver

PIERRE JARRY ("Pete")
#8 left wing   5'11" 182–R
b. Montreal, Quebec, March 30, 1949

1971–72	18	3	4	7	13
1972–73	74	19	18	37	42
1973–74	12	2	8	10	10
Totals	104	24	30	54	65

- acquired February 20, 1972, from the Rangers for Jim Dorey
- traded November 29, 1973, to Detroit for Tim Ecclestone

JIM "BUD" JARVIS
#17 left wing   5'6" 165–L
b. Fort William, December 7, 1907

1936–37L	24	1	0	1	0

- acquired December 18, 1936, from Buffalo when team folded
- sold November 7, 1937, by Syracuse to Providence for cash
- last Leaf game February 21, 1937

WES JARVIS
#12–11–32 centre   5'11" 185–L
b. Toronto, May 30, 1958

1984–85	26	0	1	1	2
1985–86	2	1	0	1	2
1987–88L	1	0	0	0	0
Totals	29	1	1	2	4

- signed October 2, 1984, as a free agent
- last Leaf game March 26, 1988
- played all of 1986–87 and most of 1987–90 with Newmarket
- later ran mini-hockey rink in Newmarket designed for children and 3-on-3 adult play

LARRY JEFFREY
#15–22 left wing   5'11" 189–L
b. Zurich, October 12, 1940

1965–66	20	1	1	2	22
1966–67	56	11	17	28	27
Totals	76	12	18	30	49

- acquired May 20, 1965, with Marcel Pronovost, Lowell MacDonald, Ed Joyal, and Aut Erickson from Detroit for Andy Bathgate, Billy Harris, and Gary Jarrett
- played first 20 games of 1965–66 with Leafs
- claimed June 6, 1967, by Penguins in Expansion Draft
- settled in Goderich and runs sporting goods store, ad agency, and farming business

ROGER "BROADWAY" JENKINS
#12 defence   5'11" 173–R
b. Appleton, Wisconsin, November 18, 1911

1930–31R	21	0	0	0	12

- acquired December 4, 1930, on loan from Chicago via London because of Conacher injury
- first Leaf game December 6, 1930
- recalled February 4, 1931, by Chicago

GRANT JENNINGS
#3 defence   6'3" 210–L
b. Hudson Bay, Saskatchewan, May 5, 1965

1994–95	10	0	2	2	7

- acquired April 7, 1995, from Penguins for Drake Berehowsky
- released June 27, 1995

TREVOR JOHANSEN
#2–4 defence   5'9" 200–R
b. Thunder Bay, March 30, 1957

1977–78R	79	2	14	16	82
1978–79	40	1	4	5	48
1981–82L	13	1	3	4	4
Totals	132	4	21	25	134

- selected 12th overall at 1977 Amateur Draft
- first Leaf game October 13, 1977
- traded March 13, 1979, with Don Ashby to Colorado Rockies for Paul Gardner
- claimed on waivers February 19, 1982, from Los Angeles Kings
- last Leaf game March 24, 1982
- won silver medal with Canada at 1977 WJC and played at 1979 WC (fourth place)

BILL "RED" JOHNSON
#21 centre   6' 163–R
b. Port Arthur, July 27, 1928

1949–50R/L	1	0	0	0	0

- played only one game in NHL, November 26, 1949
- sold December 21, 1954, to Reds (AHL)
- changed name from Johansen to sound more Canadian (son Trevor later played for Leafs with family spelling)

DANNY JOHNSON
#22 centre   5'11" 170–L
b. Winnipegosis, Manitoba, October 1, 1944
d. March 6, 1993

1969–70R	1	0	0	0	0

- first and only Leaf game March 5, 1970
- claimed June 10, 1970, by Vancouver Canucks at Expansion Draft

MIKE JOHNSON
#20 right wing   6'2" 190–R
b. Scarborough, October 3, 1974

1996–97R	13	2	2	4	4
1997–98	82	15	32	47	24
1998–99	79	20	24	44	35
1999–2000	52	11	14	25	23
Totals	226	48	72	120	86

- signed as a free agent March 15, 1997
- first Leaf game March 16, 1997
- traded to Tampa Bay on February 9, 2000, with Marek Posmyk, a 5th-round draft choice in 2000 (Pavel Sedov), a 6th-round draft choice in 2000 (Aaron Gionet), and future considerations for Darcy Tucker, a 4th-round draft choice in 2000 (Miguel Delisle), and future considerations
- played for Canada at 2000 WC

TERRY JOHNSON
#20 defence   6'3" 210–L
b. Calgary, Alberta, November 28, 1958

1986–87L	48	0	1	1	104

- acquired October 3, 1986, from Calgary for Jim Korn
- last Leaf game February 8, 1987

EDDIE JOHNSTON ("E.J.")
#1 goalie   6' 190–L
b. Montreal, Quebec, November 23, 1935

1973–74					
26 (1/1)	12–9–4	1516	78	1	3.09

- acquired May 22, 1973, with a 1st-round draft choice in 1973 (Ian Turnbull) from Boston for Jacques Plante and a 3rd-round draft choice in 1973 (Doug Gibson)
- traded May 27, 1974, to St. Louis for Gary Sabourin

GREG JOHNSTON

#16 right wing   6'1" 205–R
b. Barrie, January 14, 1965

1990–91	1	0	0	0	0
1991–92L	3	0	1	1	5
Totals	4	0	1	1	5

- acquired June 29, 1990, from the Rangers for Tie Domi and Mark LaForest
- last Leaf games February 3, 8, 15, 1992

ROSS JOHNSTONE ("Blondie")

#12 defence   6' 185–L
b. Montreal, Quebec, April 7, 1926

1943–44R	18	2	0	2	6
1944–45L	24	3	4	7	8
Totals	42	5	4	9	14

- signed October 24, 1943, after graduating from the Oshawa Generals
- first Leaf game October 30, 1943
- last Leaf game February 27, 1945
- suspended at 1946 training camp after refusing to go to Tulsa (reinstated January 1, 1947, and sent on loan to Springfield)
- later started his own general contracting business in Toronto

ALVIN "BUCK" JONES

#14 defence   6' 180–R
b. Owen Sound, August 17, 1918

1942–43L	16	0	0	0	22

- acquired February 2, 1943, with Ab DeMarco for the season from Providence (AHL) for Bucko McDonald, George Boothman, and Jack Forsey
- acquired summer 1942 from Detroit
- missed 1943–46—Royal Canadian Electrical and Mechanical Engineers
- last Leaf game March 14, 1943
- sold May 14, 1947, to Tulsa
- worked for Maas Brothers in Tampa

JIMMY JONES

#16 centre   5'9" 177–R
b. Woodbridge, January 2, 1953

1977–78	78	4	9	13	23
1978–79	69	9	9	18	45
1979–80L	1	0	0	0	0
Totals	148	13	18	31	68

- signed October 25, 1977, as free agent
- last Leaf game October 14, 1979
- released unconditionally prior to 1980–81 season

KENNY JONSSON

#19 defence   6'3" 195–L
b. Angelholm, Sweden, October 6, 1974

1994–95R	39	2	7	9	16
1995–96	50	4	22	26	22
Totals	89	6	29	35	38

- selected 12th overall at 1993 Entry Draft
- first Leaf game January 20, 1995
- traded March 13, 1996, with Darby Hendrickson, Sean Haggerty, and a 1st-round draft choice in 1997 (Roberto Luongo) to the Islanders for Wendel Clark, Mathieu Schneider, and Denis Smith
- won silver medals with Sweden at 1993 and 1994 WJC, gold at 1994 Olympics, bronze at 1994 WC and played at 1996 WC (sixth place)
- currently plays for New York Islanders

CURTIS JOSEPH ("CUJO")

#31 goalie   5'11" 190–L
b. Keswick, April 29, 1967

1998–99					
67 (1/0)	35–24–7	4001	171	3	2.56
1999–2000					
63 (1/0)	36–20–7	3801	158	4	2.49
2000–01					
68 (1/0)	33–27–8	4100	163	6	2.39
Totals					
198 (3/0)	104–71–22	11902	492	13	2.48

Curtis Joseph

- signed as a free agent on July 15, 1998
- won silver medal with Canada at 1996 WC
- currently with Leafs

EDDIE JOYAL
#24 centre   6' 180–L
b. Edmonton, Alberta, May 8, 1940

| 1965–66 | 14 | 0 | 2 | 2 | 2 |

- acquired May 20, 1965, with Marcel Pronovost, Lowell MacDonald, Aut Erickson, and Larry Jeffrey from Detroit for Andy Bathgate, Billy Harris, and Gary Jarrett
- recalled October 5, 1965, from Rochester, then demoted November 24 and played the rest of the season with Tulsa and Rochester
- claimed June 6, 1967, by Los Angeles Kings at Expansion Draft
- established a real estate business with his wife in San Diego

BILL JUZDA ("Fireman"/"Beast")
#18 defence   5'8" 203–R
b. Winnipeg, Manitoba, October 29, 1920

1948–49	38	1	2	3	23
1949–50	62	1	14	15	68
1950–51	65	0	9	9	64
1951–52L	46	1	4	5	65
Totals	211	3	29	32	220

- acquired April 26, 1948, with Cal Gardner, René Trudel, Frankie Mathers, and the rights to Ray McMurray from the Rangers for Wally Stanowski, Moe Morris, and the rights to Orville Lavell
- last Leaf game March 19, 1952
- released outright September 2, 1952
- moved from his summer job to a full-time job after retiring, becoming an engineer for CPR in Manitoba

TOMAS KABERLE ("Kaba"/"Kabby")

#15 defence   6'2" 200–L
b. Rakovnik, Czechoslovakia,
March 2, 1978

1998–99R	57	4	18	22	12
1999–2000	82	7	33	40	24
2000–01	82	6	39	45	24
Totals	221	17	90	107	60

- selected 204th overall at 1996 Entry Draft
- played for Czech Republic at 1998 WJC (fourth place)

RUDOLPH "BINGO" KAMPMAN ("Samson")

#7–17–20 defence   5'9" 187–R
b. Kitchener, March 12, 1914
d. Kitchener, December 23, 1987

1937–38R	32	1	2	3	56
1938–39	41	2	8	10	52
1939–40	39	6	9	15	59
1940–41	39	1	4	5	53
1941–42L	38	4	7	11	67
Totals	189	14	30	44	287

- won Allan Cup with Sudbury Tigers 1936–37
- first Leaf game December 25, 1937
- began 1937–38 with Syracuse before joining the Leafs full-time November 17, 1937
- joined the Canadian Armed Services after 1941–42 (last game April 18, 1942, in playoffs)
- sent October 28, 1945, to Boston to complete deal that sent Art Jackson to Toronto
- last regular season game February 22, 1942
- became sales rep in Kitchener for Labatt's and Carling

ALEXANDER KARPOVTSEV ("Potsie")

#52 defence   6'1" 205–R
b. Moscow, USSR, April 7, 1970

1998–99	56	2	25	27	52
1999–2000	69	3	14	17	54
Totals	125	5	39	44	106

- acquired from Rangers on October 14, 1998, with a 4th-round draft choice in 1999 (Mirko Murovic) for Mathieu Schneider
- won silver medal with Soviet Union at 1990 WJC and gold with Russia at 1993 WC
- traded to Chicago with a 4th-round draft choice in 2001 (Vladimir Gusev) on October 2, 2000, for Bryan McCabe

MIKE KASZYCKI

#14–16–20 centre   5'9" 190–L
b. Milton, February 27, 1956

1979–80	25	4	4	8	10
1980–81	6	0	2	2	2
1982–83L	22	1	13	14	10
Totals	53	5	19	24	22

- acquired February 16, 1980, from Washington for Pat Ribble
- last Leaf game January 12, 1983
- joined Ambri-Piotta (Swiss League) for 1985–86

MEL "BUTCH" KEELING

#10–18 left wing   6' 180–L
b. Owen Sound, August 10, 1905
d. Toronto, November 13, 1984

1926–27R	30	11	2	13	29
1927–28	43	10	6	16	52
Totals	73	21	8	29	81

- acquired December 27, 1926, from London Tecumsehs for Pete Bellefeuille
- traded October 17, 1928, with John Ross Roach to the Rangers for Lorne Chabot and Alex Gray
- later coached in AHA

LARRY KEENAN

#8 left wing   5'10" 177–L
b. North Bay, October 1, 1940

1961–62R	2	0	0	0	0

- St. Mike's graduate; signed June 21, 1961, by Leafs

- first and only Leaf games February 18, 21, 1962
- claimed June 6, 1967, by St. Louis at Expansion Draft
- established a successful coffee-supply business in North Bay

RICK KEHOE
#16–17 right wing   5'11" 180–R
b. Windsor, July 15, 1951

1971–72R	38	8	8	16	4
1972–73	77	33	42	75	20
1973–74	69	18	22	40	8
Totals	184	59	72	131	32

- selected 22nd overall at 1971 Amateur Draft
- first Leaf game January 1, 1972
- traded September 13, 1974, to Penguins for Blaine Stoughton and a 1st-round draft choice in 1977 (Trevor Johansen)
- stayed in Pittsburgh as assistant coach, winning Cups in 1991 and 1992

LEONARD "RED" KELLY
#4 centre   6' 195–L
b. Simcoe, July 9, 1927

1959–60	18	6	5	11	8
1960–61	64	20	50	70	12
1961–62	58	22	27	49	6
1962–63	66	20	40	60	8
1963–64	70	11	34	45	16
1964–65	70	18	28	46	8
1965–66	63	8	24	32	12
1966–67L	61	14	24	38	4
Totals	470	119	232	351	74

- on February 5, 1960, Kelly and Detroit teammate Billy McNeill were traded to the Rangers for Bill Gadsby and Eddie Shack. However, both Kelly and McNeill refused to go! On February 10, 1960, general manager Jack Adams traded Kelly to Toronto for Marc Reaume
- last Leaf game March 26, 1967
- traded June 8, 1967, to Los Angeles Kings for Ken Block and immediately named Kings' first head coach

- acted as MP for York West while playing
- Hockey Hall of Fame 1969 (five-year waiting period waived)
- ran international aircraft maintenance company

REGIS "PEP" KELLY ("Pepper")
#9–15–16–5 forward   5'6" 152–R
b. North Bay, January 9, 1914 d. 1990

1934–35R	47	11	8	19	14
1935–36	42	11	8	19	24
1936–37	16	2	0	2	8
1937–38	43	9	10	19	25
1938–39	48	11	11	22	12
1939–40	34	11	9	20	15
Totals	230	55	46	101	98

- St. Mike's graduate in 1934; signed October 3, 1934
- first Leaf game November 8, 1934
- traded December 29, 1936, to Chicago for Bill Kendall, but only for the balance of the season
- sold May 10, 1940, to Chicago for cash
- worked for CPR until he retired

STANLEY KEMP
#16 defence   5'9" 165–R
b. Hamilton, March 2, 1924

1948–49R/L	1	0	0	0	2

- acquired by Hornets from Providence in 1946 for $7,000
- first and only Leaf and NHL game January 23, 1949

BILL "COWBOY" KENDALL
#24 forward   5'8" 168–R
b. Winnipeg, Manitoba, April 1, 1910

1936–37	15	2	4	6	4

- acquired December 29, 1936, from Chicago for Pep Kelly, but only for the balance of the season

FORBES KENNEDY ("Spud")

#22 centre   5'8" 185–L
b. Dorchester, New Brunswick,
August 18, 1935

1968–69L	13	0	3	3	24

- acquired March 2, 1969, with Brit Selby from Flyers for Mike Byers, Bill Sutherland, and Gerry Meehan
- first and only Leaf games March 5, 6, 8, 12, 13, 15, 16, 19, 22, 23, 26, 29, 30, 1969
- sold May 30, 1969, to Penguins
- coached in minors and minor pros almost from the day he retired to the present

MIKE KENNEDY

#39 centre   6'1" 195–R
b. Vancouver, British Columbia,
April 13, 1972

1997–98	13	0	1	1	14

- signed as a free agent on July 2, 1997
- traded to Dallas on March 24, 1998, for an 8th-round draft choice in 1998 (Mikhail Travnicek)

TED "TEEDER" KENNEDY

#9–10–12–20 centre   5'11" 180–R
b. Humberstone, December 12, 1925

1942–43R	2	0	1	1	0
1943–44	49	26	23	49	2
1944–45	49	29	25	54	14
1945–46	21	3	2	5	4
1946–47	60	28	32	60	27
1947–48	60	25	21	46	32
1948–49	59	18	21	39	25
1949–50	43	20	24	44	34
1950–51	63	18	43	61	32
1951–52	70	19	33	52	33
1952–53	43	14	23	37	42
1953–54	67	15	23	38	78
1954–55	70	10	42	52	74
1956–57L	30	6	16	22	35
Totals	686	231	329	560	432

- acquired February 28, 1943, from Canadiens for post-war rights to Frankie Eddolls (who had been signed June 3, 1940 by Leafs)
- first Leaf game March 7, 1943
- missed end of 1952–53 with broken collarbone suffered January 1, 1953, in fight with Milt Schmidt
- retired April 4, 1954; un-retired July 20, 1954
- returned January 6, 1957, to help team until season's end
- last Leaf game March 17, 1957
- considered one of the greatest faceoff men of all time
- later ran a racetrack in Southern Ontario
- Hockey Hall of Fame 1966

DAVE KEON

#14 centre   5'9" 167–L
b. Noranda, Quebec, March 22, 1940

1960–61R	70	20	25	45	6
1961–62	64	26	35	61	2
1962–63	68	28	28	56	2
1963–64	70	23	37	60	6
1964–65	65	21	29	50	10
1965–66	69	24	30	54	4
1966–67	66	19	33	52	2
1967–68	67	11	37	48	4
1968–69	75	27	34	61	12
1969–70	72	32	30	62	6
1970–71	76	38	38	76	4
1971–72	72	18	30	48	4
1972–73	76	37	36	73	2
1973–74	74	25	28	53	7
1974–75	78	16	43	59	4
Totals	1062	365	493	858	75

- St. Mike's graduate 1960
- first Leaf game October 6, 1960
- signed after 1974–75 season with Minnesota Fighting Saints (WHA) as a free agent
- moved to Florida to sell real estate in Palm Beach Gardens
- Hockey Hall of Fame 1986

DMITRI KHRISTICH ("Deem")
#8 left wing   6'2" 195–R
b. Kiev, USSR, July 23, 1969

1999–2000	53	12	18	30	24
2000–01	27	3	6	9	8
Totals	80	15	24	39	32

- acquired from Boston on October 20, 1999, for a 2nd-round draft choice in 2000 (Ivan Huml)
- won gold medal with Soviet Union at 1989 WJC and 1990 WC
- traded December 1, 2000, to Washington for a 3rd-round draft choice in 2001 (Brendan Bell)

HEC KILREA ("Hurricane Hec")
#12 left wing   5'7 175–L
b. Blackburn, June 11, 1907
d. Detroit, Michigan, December 6, 1969

1933–34	43	10	13	23	15
1934–35	46	11	13	24	16
Totals	89	21	26	47	31

- acquired March 14, 1933, from Ottawa for Bob Gracie and $12,500
- traded in September 1935 to Detroit for Knucker Irvine and $7,500
- worked for Ford Motor Co. in Detroit after World War II

DEREK KING ("Yoda"/"Kinger")
#7 left wing   6' 212–L
b. Hamilton, February 11, 1967

1997–98	77	21	25	46	43
1998–99	81	24	28	52	20
1999–2000	3	0	0	0	2
Totals	161	45	53	98	65

- signed as a free agent on July 4, 1997
- traded to St. Louis on October 20, 1999, with a conditional draft choice in 2001 for Tyler Harlton and a conditional draft choice in 2001
- played with Canada at 1992 WC (eighth place)

KRIS KING ("Kinger")
#12 left wing   5'11" 208–L
b. Bracebridge, February 18, 1966

1997–98	82	3	3	6	199
1998–99	67	2	2	4	105
1999–2000	39	2	4	6	55
Totals	188	7	9	16	359

- signed as a free agent on July 23, 1997
- released summer 2000

MARK KIRTON ("Kirt")
#20 centre   5'10" 170–L
b. Regina, Saskatchewan, February 3, 1958

1979–80R	2	1	0	1	2
1980–81	11	0	0	0	0
Totals	13	1	0	1	2

- selected 48th overall at 1987 Entry Draft
- first Leaf game October 10, 1979
- traded December 4, 1980, to Detroit for Jim Rutherford

BILL KITCHEN
#26 defence   6'1" 200–L
b. Schomburg, October 2, 1960

1984–85L	29	1	4	5	27

- signed August 16, 1984 as a free agent
- last Leaf game February 21, 1985

JOE KLUKAY ("Duke of Paducah"/"Kluke")
#8–17–19 left wing   6' 175–L
b. Sault Ste. Marie, November 6, 1922

1946–47R	55	9	20	29	12
1947–48	59	15	15	30	28
1948–49	45	11	10	21	11
1949–50	70	15	16	31	19
1950–51	70	14	16	30	16
1951–52	43	4	8	12	6
1954–55	56	8	8	16	44
1955–56L	18	0	1	1	2
Totals	416	76	94	170	138

- signed March 15, 1943, by Leafs

- played one game in 1943 playoffs (March 28)
- missed 1943–45—Royal Canadian Navy
- first Leaf regular season game October 16, 1946
- missed November–December 1948 with fractured foot
- sold September 16, 1952, to Boston for Dave Creighton
- acquired November 9, 1954, from Boston for Leo Boivin
- last Leaf game November 20, 1955
- operated a machine at a tool and die company for 45 years

PAUL "BILL" KNOX
#11 right wing   5′10″ 160–R
b. Toronto, November 23, 1933

1954–55R/L	1	0	0	0	0

- St. Mike's graduate
- recalled March 11, 1955, from University of Toronto Blues
- first and only Leaf game March 12, 1955
- won bronze medal with Canada at 1956 Olympics

LADISLAV KOHN
#39 right wing   5′11″ 194–L
b. Uherske Hradiste, Czechoslovakia, March 4, 1975

1998–99	16	1	3	4	4

- acquired from Calgary on July 2, 1998, for David Cooper
- claimed by Atlanta in Waiver Draft on September 27, 1999
- played with Czech Republic at 1995 WJC (sixth place)

MARK KOLESAR
#37 left wing   6′1″ 188–R
b. Neepawa, Manitoba, January 23, 1973

1995–96R	21	2	2	4	14
1996–97	7	0	0	0	0
Totals	28	2	2	4	14

- signed as free agent May 24, 1994
- played in Europe since 1998

JOHN KORDIC
#27 right wing   6′2″ 210–R
b. Edmonton, Alberta, March 22, 1965
d. L'ancienne Lorette, Quebec, August 8, 1992

1988–89	46	1	2	3	185
1989–90	55	9	4	13	252
1990–91	3	0	0	0	9
Totals	104	10	6	16	446

- acquired November 7, 1988, with a 6th-round draft choice in 1989 (Michael Doers) from Canadiens for Russ Courtnall
- traded January 24, 1991, with Paul Fenton to Washington for a 5th-round draft choice in 1991 (Alexei Kudashov)
- died in a struggle with police after a drug-induced rampage

JIM KORN
#20 forward   6′3″ 210–L
b. Hopkins, Minnesota, July 28, 1957

1981–82	11	1	3	4	44
1982–83	80	8	21	29	236
1983–84	65	12	14	26	257
1984–85	41	5	5	10	171
Totals	197	26	43	69	708

- acquired March 8, 1982, from Detroit for a 4th-round draft choice in 1982 (Craig Coxe) and a 5th-round draft choice in 1983 (Joey Kocur)
- traded October 3, 1986, to Calgary for Terry Johnson

IGOR KOROLEV ("Iggy")
#22 right wing   6′1″ 187–L
b. Moscow, USSR, September 6, 1970

1997–98	78	17	22	39	22
1998–99	66	13	34	47	46
1999–2000	80	20	26	46	22
2000–01	73	10	19	29	28
Totals	297	60	101	161	118

- signed as a free agent on September 29, 1997
- traded to Chicago on June 23, 2001, for a 3rd-round draft choice in 2001 (Nicolas Corbeil)

CHRIS KOTSOPOULOS ("Kotsy")
#26 defence   6'3" 215–R
b. Toronto, November 27, 1958

1985–86	61	6	11	17	83
1986–87	43	2	10	12	75
1987–88	21	2	2	4	19
1988–89	57	1	14	15	44
Totals	182	11	37	48	221

- acquired October 7, 1985, from Hartford for Stewart Gavin
- signed June 23, 1989 as a free agent by Detroit

LES KOZAK
#8 forward   6' 185–L
b. Yorkton, Saskatchewan, October 28, 1940

1961–62R/L	12	1	0	1	2

- St. Mike's graduate; signed June 28, 1961, by Leafs
- first Leaf game January 13, 1962
- first and only Leaf games January 13, 14, 17, 20, 21, 24, 27, 28 and February 1, 3, 4, 7, 1962
- career ended during 1962–63 season when he suffered a fractured skull
- earned a PhD in a biochemistry and became a staff scientist at a prominent laboratory

STEVE KRAFTCHECK
#4 defence   5'10" 185–R
b. Tinturn, March 3, 1929
d. Providence, Rhode Island, August 10, 1997

1958–59L	8	1	0	1	0

- signed August 21, 1958, after being acquired from Cleveland (AHL) for cash and the rights to Ian Anderson

- only games with the Leafs October 11, 12, 16, 18, 19, 25, 26, 29, 1958
- demoted to Rochester on October 31, 1958, to become player/coach

MIKE KRUSHELNYSKI ("Kruiser")
#26 centre   6'2" 200–L
b. Montreal, Quebec, April 27, 1960

1990–91	59	17	22	39	48
1991–92	72	9	15	24	72
1992–93	84	19	20	39	62
1993–94	54	5	6	11	28
Totals	269	50	63	113	210

- acquired November 9, 1990, from Los Angeles Kings for John McIntyre
- signed August 1, 1994, as a free agent by Detroit

ALEXEI KUDASHOV
#20 centre   6' 190–R
b. Moscow, USSR, July 21, 1971

1993–94R	25	1	0	1	4

- selected 102nd overall at 1991 Entry Draft
- first Leaf game October 15, 1993
- released June 27, 1995
- won silver medals with Soviet Union at 1990 and 1991 WJC; played for Russia at 1998 WC (fifth), 1999 WC (fifth), and 2000 WC

ORLAND KURTENBACH
#25 centre   6'2" 195–L
b. Cudworth, Saskatchewan, September 7,1936

1965–66	70	9	6	15	54

- acquired June 8, 1965, with Pat Stapleton and Andy Hebenton from Boston for Ron Stewart
- claimed June 15, 1966, by Rangers at Intra-League Draft
- became an insurance broker in British Columbia after retiring

TOM KURVERS

#25 defence   6'2" 195–L
b. Minneapolis, Minnesota,
September 14, 1962

1989–90	70	15	37	52	29
1990–91	19	0	3	3	8
Totals	89	15	40	55	37

- acquired October 16, 1989, from New Jersey for a 1st-round draft choice in 1991 (Scott Niedermeyer)
- traded January 12, 1991, to Vancouver Canucks for Brian Bradley
- played for USA at 1982 WJC (sixth place), 1987 WC (seventh), and 1989 WC (fifth)

NICK KYPREOS ("Kipper")

#32 left wing   6' 205–L
b. Toronto, June 4, 1966

1995–96	19	1	1	2	30
1996–97R	35	3	2	5	62
Totals	54	4	3	7	92

- acquired February 29, 1996, with Wayne Presley from Rangers for Sergio Momesso and Bill Berg
- missed much of 1996–97 with a broken ankle suffered in a fight November 19, 1996
- suffered a career-ending concussion in exhibition game at Madison Square Garden fighting Ryan VandenBussche on September 15, 1997
- became hockey analyst for Toronto television station

ERIC LACROIX

#41 left wing   6'1" 205–L
b. Montreal, Quebec, July 15, 1971

1993–94R	3	0	0	0	2

- selected 136th overall at 1990 Entry Draft
- first Leaf games November 17, 18, 27, 1993
- traded October 3, 1994, with Chris Snell and a 4th-round draft choice in 1996 (Eric

Belanger) to Los Angeles Kings for Dixon Ward, Guy Leveque, Shayne Toporowski, and Kelly Fairchild

MARK LAFOREST ("Trees")

#1 goalie   5'11" 190–L
b. Welland, July 10, 1962

1989–90L						
27 (4/7)	9–14–0	1343	87	0	3.89

- acquired September 8, 1989, from Flyers for a 5th-round draft choice in 1991 (later traded to Winnipeg—Juha Ylonen) and a 7th-round draft choice in 1991 (Andrei Lomakin)
- last Leaf game March 28, 1990
- traded June 29, 1990 with Tie Domi to the Rangers for Greg Johnston

LARRY LANDON

#11 right wing   6' 191–R
b. Niagara Falls, May 4, 1958

1984–85L	7	0	0	0	2

- acquired February 14, 1985, from Canadiens for Gaston Gingras
- released after 1984–85
- last Leaf game March 24, 1985

PETE LANGELLE ("Snake Hips")

#8–21 centre   5'10" 170–L
b. Winnipeg, Manitoba, November 4, 1917

1938–39R	2	1	0	1	0
1939–40	39	7	14	21	2
1940–41	48	4	15	19	0
1941–42L	48	10	22	32	9
Totals	137	22	51	73	11

- Winnipeg Monarchs graduate; signed October 27, 1937
- recalled March 15, 1939, from Syracuse
- first Leaf games March 18 and 19, 1939
- last Leaf game March 19, 1942
- joined air force 1942–46
- worked for Labatt's in Manitoba for 30 years

RICK LANZ ("Rico"/"Lanzer")
#4 defence   6'2" 203–R
b. Karlouy Vary, Czechoslovakia,
September 16, 1961

1986–87	44	2	19	21	32
1987–88	75	6	22	28	65
1988–89	32	1	9	10	18
Totals	151	9	50	59	115

• acquired December 2, 1986, from
  Vancouver Canucks for Jim Benning and
  Dan Hodgson
• signed August 13, 1990, as a free agent
  by Chicago
• played for Canada at 1980 WJC (fifth
  place) and won bronze medal at 1983 WC

MICHEL "BUNNY" LAROCQUE
#1 goalie   5'10" 185–L
b. Hull, Quebec, April 16, 1952
d. Hull, Quebec, July 29, 1992

1980–81					
8 (1/0)	3–3–2	460	40	0	5.22
1981–82					
50 (6/7)	10–24–8	2647	207	0	4.69
1982–83					
16 (1/3)	3–8–3	845	68	0	4.89
Totals					
74 (8/10)	16–35–13	3952	315	0	4.79

• acquired March 10, 1981, from Canadiens
  for Robert Picard and an 8th-round draft
  choice in 1982 (Steve Smith)
• traded January 11, 1983, to Flyers for Rick
  St. Croix

GUY LAROSE ("Rosie")
#11 centre   5'9" 175–L
b. Hull, Quebec, August 31, 1967

1991–92	34	9	5	14	27
1992–93	9	0	0	0	8
1993–94L	10	1	2	3	10
Totals	53	10	7	17	45

• acquired December 26, 1991, from the
  Rangers for Mike Stevens

• last Leaf game December 29, 1993
• claimed on waivers January 1, 1994,
  by Calgary

CRAIG LAUGHLIN
#14–18 right wing   6' 190–R
b. Toronto, September 19, 1957

1988–89L	66	10	13	23	41

• signed June 10, 1988, as a free agent from
  Los Angeles Kings
• last Leaf game March 14, 1989
• released after 1988–89 season

PAUL LAWLESS
#20 left wing   5'11" 185–L
b. Toronto, July 2, 1964

1988–89	7	0	0	0	0
1989–90L	6	0	1	1	0
Totals	13	0	1	1	0

• acquired February 25, 1989, from
  Vancouver Canucks for Peter Deboer
• last Leaf games October 5, 7, 11, 12, 14,
  17, 1989
• played 1990–91 with Lausanne (Swiss
  League)

DEREK LAXDAL
#34–28–35–15 right wing   6'1" 175–R
b. St. Boniface, Manitoba, February 21, 1966

1984–85R	3	0	0	0	6
1986–87	2	0	0	0	7
1987–88	5	0	0	0	6
1988–89	41	9	6	15	65
Totals	51	9	6	15	84

• selected 151st overall at 1984 Entry Draft
• first Leaf games April 3, 6, 7, 1985
• traded December 20, 1989, with Paul
  Gagne and Jack Capuano to the Islanders
  for Gilles Thibaudeau and Mike Stevens
• won silver medal with Canada at 1986 WJC

GARY LEEMAN

#4–11 right wing   5'11" 175–R
b. Toronto, February 19, 1964

1983–84R	52	4	8	12	31
1984–85	53	5	26	31	72
1985–86	53	9	23	32	20
1986–87	80	21	31	52	66
1987–88	80	30	31	61	62
1988–89	61	32	43	75	66
1989–90	80	51	44	95	63
1990–91	52	17	12	29	39
1991–92	34	7	13	20	44
Totals	545	176	231	407	463

- selected 24th overall at 1982 Entry Draft
- first Leaf game October 8, 1983
- traded January 2, 1992, with Michel Petit, Craig Berube, Alexander Godynyuk, and Jeff Reese to Calgary for Doug Gilmour, Jamie Macoun, Ric Nattress, Rick Wamsley, and Kent Manderville
- won bronze medal with Canada at 1983 WJC and played in 1984 WJC (fourth place)

SYLVAIN LEFEBVRE

#2 defence   6'2" 204–L
b. Richmond, Quebec, October 14, 1967

1992–93	81	2	12	14	90
1993–94	84	2	9	11	79
Totals	165	4	21	25	169

- acquired August 20, 1992, from Canadiens for a 3rd-round draft choice in 1994 (Martin Belanger)
- traded June 28, 1994, with Wendel Clark, Landon Wilson, and a 1st-round draft choice in 1994 (Jeffrey Kealty) to Quebec Nordiques for Mats Sundin, Garth Butcher, Todd Warriner, and a 1st-round draft choice in 1994 (traded to Washington—Nolan Baumgartner—with Rob Pearson for Mike Ridley and a 1st-round draft choice—Eric Fichaud)
- currently with New York Rangers

ALEX LEVINSKY ("Mine Boy")

#3–16 defence   5'10" 184–R
b. Syracuse, New York, February 2, 1910
d. Toronto, 1990

1930–31R	7	0	1	1	2
1931–32	47	5	5	10	29
1932–33	48	1	4	5	61
1933–34	47	5	11	16	38
Totals	149	11	21	32	130

- Marlie graduate 1930; signed March 2, 1931
- first Leaf game March 3, 1931
- sold April 12, 1934, to the Rangers for $10,000
- ran bowling alley and car dealership in Toronto

ALEX LEVINSKY

goalie

1931–32					
1 (1/1)	0–0–0	1	1	0	60.00

- allowed a goal, along with Horner and Clancy, March 15, 1932, while Chabot serving a penalty

DANNY LEWICKI ("Dashin' Danny")

#21–23 left wing   5'9" 152–L
b. Fort William, March 12, 1931

1950–51R	61	16	18	34	26
1951–52	51	4	9	13	26
1952–53	4	1	3	4	2
1953–54	7	0	1	1	12
Totals	123	21	31	52	66

- acquired August 12, 1948, from Providence for cash and a player to be named later (Jack Hamilton—September 10, 1948)
- first Leaf game October 14, 1950
- missed November 25–December 13, 1951, with knee injury
- played February 1, 5, 7, 8, 1953, after being recalled due to injuries to Bentley and Migay

- sold July 20, 1954, to Rangers
- later worked for CHUM radio in Toronto

RICK LEY

#2–26 defence   5'9" 185–L
b. Orillia, November 2, 1948

1968–69R	38	1	11	12	39
1969–70	48	2	13	15	102
1970–71	76	4	16	20	151
1971–72	67	1	14	15	124
Totals	229	8	54	62	416

- selected 16th overall at 1966 Amateur Draft
- first Leaf game October 13, 1968
- missed November 8–January 7, 1969–70, with injured knee
- signed July 1972 with New England Whalers
- selected by Leafs in WHA Reclamation Draft June 9, 1979
- claimed June 13, 1979, by Hartford at Expansion Draft
- currently Leafs' assistant coach

BOB LIDDINGTON

#26 left wing   6' 175–L
b. Calgary, Alberta, September 15, 1948

1970–71R/L	11	0	1	1	2

- played all of 1969–70 and most of 1970–71 with Tulsa
- first and only Leaf games October 11, 14, 17, 18, 21, 24, 31 and November 1, 4, 6, 7, 1970

BERT LINDSAY

#1 goalie   5'7" 160–R
b. Guelph, July 23, 1881
d. Sarnia, November 11, 1960

1918–19L					
16 (0/0)	5–11–0	979	83	0	5.09

- replaced Holmes in goal after Holmes was recalled by Seattle on December 26, 1918

- first Arenas game December 28, 1918
- last Arenas game February 20, 1919
- father of Ted Lindsay
- ran car dealership in Renfrew

KEN LINSEMAN ("The Rat")

#13 centre   5'11" 180–L
b. Kingston, August 11, 1958

1991–92L	2	0	0	0	2

- bought on October 7, 1991, from Edmonton for cash
- only Leaf games October 12, 21, 1991
- released outright near start of 1991–92; signed with Asiago (Italian League)

ED LITZENBERGER ("Litz")

#25 right wing   6'3" 194–R
b. Neudorf, Saskatchewan, July 15, 1932

1961–62	37	10	10	20	14
1962–63	58	5	13	18	10
1963–64L	19	2	0	2	0
Totals	114	17	23	40	24

- claimed December 29, 1961, on waivers from Detroit
- played first 19 games of 1963–64, then sent to Rochester on December 4 for the season
- last Leaf game December 1, 1963
- involved in NHL alumni activities in the Toronto area

HOWIE LOCKHART ("Holes")

#1 goalie   5'8" 180–L
b. North Bay, 1895   d. Unknown

1919–20R					
5 (1/3)	4–1–0	268	20	0	4.48
1923–24					
1 (0/0)	0–1–0	60	5	0	5.00
Totals					
6 (1/3)	4–2–0	328	25	0	3.67

- signed from 228th Battalion

- first Arenas games January 31 and February 16, 18, 21, 25, 1920
- played March 6, 1920, with Quebec Bulldogs
- played December 19, 1923, when Roach had a finger injury

CLAUDE LOISELLE
#15 centre   5'11" 195–L
b. Ottawa, May 29, 1963

1990–91	7	1	1	2	2
1991–92	64	6	9	15	102
Totals	71	7	10	17	104

- claimed March 5, 1991, on waivers from Quebec Nordiques
- traded March 10, 1992, with Daniel Marois to the Islanders for Ken Baumgartner and Dave McLlwain

WILF LOUGHLIN
#8 forward   6'2" 200–L
b. Carroll, Manitoba, February 28, 1896
d. June 25, 1966

1923–24R/L	14	0	0	0	2

- bought from Victoria Cougars in 1923
- first St. Pats game December 15, 1923
- last St. Pats game February 13, 1924

RON LOW ("Lowtide")
#30 goalie   6'1" 205–L
b. Birtle, Manitoba, June 21, 1950

1972–73L					
42 (3/5)	12–24–4	2343	152	1	3.89

- selected 103rd overall at 1970 Amateur Draft
- last Leaf game April 1, 1973
- claimed June 12, 1974, by Washington at Expansion Draft
- later became only former goalie to coach two teams (Edmonton, Rangers) and also became the winningest former-goalie coach in NHL history

GERRY LOWREY
#9–14 left wing   5'8" 150–L
b. Ottawa, February 14, 1906
d. Ottawa, October 20, 1979

1927–28R	25	6	5	11	29
1928–29	28	3	9	12	24
Totals	53	9	14	23	53

- drafted from Ravinas on January 11, 1928
- first Leaf game January 12, 1928
- traded February 12, 1929, with $10,000 to Pirates for Baldy Cotton

DON LUCE
#20 centre   6'2" 185–L
b. London, October 2, 1948

1981–82L	39	4	4	8	32

- acquired August 10, 1981, from Los Angeles Kings for Bob Gladney and a 6th-round draft choice in 1983 (Kevin Stevens)
- last Leaf game February 18, 1982

HARRY LUMLEY ("Apple Cheeks")
#1 goalie   6' 195–L
b. Owen Sound, November 11, 1926
d. Owen Sound, September 13, 1998

1952–53					
70 (0/0)	27–30–13	4200	167	10	2.39
1953–54					
69 (0/0)	32–24–13	4140	128	13	1.86
1954–55					
69 (0/0)	24–23–22	4140	134	8	1.94
1955–56					
59 (1/0)	21–28–10	3520	159	3	2.71
Totals					
267 (1/0)	104–105–58	16000	588	34	2.21

- acquired September 11, 1952, from Chicago for Cal Gardner, Ray Hannigan, Gus Mortson, and Al Rollins
- sold May 21, 1956, with Eric Nesterenko for $40,000 to Chicago
- ran a car dealership in Owen Sound
- Hockey Hall of Fame 1980

JOE LUNDRIGAN

#2 defence   5'11" 180–L
b. Corner Brook, Newfoundland,
September 12, 1948

1972–73R	49	2	8	10	20

- signed in 1971
- first Leaf game October 29, 1972
- claimed June 12, 1974, by Washington at Expansion Draft

VIC LYNN

#14 defence   5'9" 185–L
b. Saskatoon, Saskatchewan,
January 26, 1925

1946–47	31	6	14	20	44
1947–48	60	12	22	34	53
1948–49	52	7	9	16	36
1949–50	70	7	13	20	39
Totals	213	32	58	90	172

- acquired September 21, 1946, from Bisons (AHL) for Gerry Brown
- missed games in 1946–47 after stick-swinging incident with Red Hamill
- missed November 20–March 5, 1946–47, after tearing shoulder muscles
- missed games in 1948–49 after Red Hamill attacked him February 20, 1949, with his stick
- traded November 15, 1950, with Bill Ezinicki to Boston for Leo Boivin, Fern Flaman, Phil Maloney, and Ken Smith
- ran a hotel in Saskatchewan until retiring

PARKER MacDONALD

#21 left wing   5'11" 184–L
b. Sydney, Nova Scotia, June 14, 1933

1952–53R	1	0	0	0	0
1954–55	62	8	3	11	36
Totals	63	8	3	11	36

- Marlie graduate 1952
- first Leaf game February 28, 1953

- claimed June 5, 1956, with Jerry Foley by the Rangers at the Intra-League Draft for $30,000
- later coached in CHL and NHL

BLAIR MacKASEY

#16 defence   6'2" 200–R
b. Hamilton, December 13, 1955

1976–77R/L	1	0	0	0	2

- rights acquired September 27, 1976, from Washington for Grant Cole
- first and only Leaf and NHL game October 5, 1976

FLEMING MacKELL

("Mac"/"Sukey"/"Flame")
#16–22 centre   5'7" 167–L
b. Montreal, Quebec, April 30, 1929

1947–48R	3	0	0	0	2
1948–49	11	1	1	2	6
1949–50	36	7	13	20	24
1950–51	70	12	13	25	40
1951–52	32	2	8	10	16
Totals	152	22	35	57	88

- St. Mike's graduate 1947; signed September 25, 1947, by Leafs
- first Leaf games October 18, 19, 25, 1947
- traded January 9, 1952, to Boston for Jim Morrison
- became a car salesman in Montreal for 27 years after retiring

DON MacLEAN ("Mac")

#37 centre   6'2" 199–L
b. Sydney, Nova Scotia, January 14, 1977

2000–01	3	0	1	1	2

- acquired from Los Angeles for Craig Charron on February 23, 2000
- currently in the Leafs' system

BILLY MacMILLAN ("Yakky")
#12–23 right wing   5'10" 180–L
b. Charlottetown, Prince Edward Island, March 7, 1943

1970–71R	76	22	19	41	42
1971–72	61	10	7	17	39
Totals	137	32	26	58	81

- first Leaf game October 11, 1970
- claimed June 6, 1972, by Atlanta in Expansion Draft
- won bronze medal with Canada at 1966 WC and 1968 Olympics
- stayed in the NHL as coach and general manager after retiring

JOHN MacMILLAN
#8–24–25 right wing   5'9" 185–L
b. Milk River, Alberta, October 25, 1935

1960–61R	31	3	5	8	8
1961–62	31	1	0	1	8
1962–63	6	1	1	2	6
1963–64	13	0	0	0	10
Totals	81	5	6	11	32

- Denver University graduate 1960; signed with Leafs in October 1960
- first Leaf game December 3, 1960
- claimed on waivers December 3, 1963, by Detroit for $20,000

AL MacNEIL
#11–22–24 defence   5'10" 180–L
b. Sydney, Nova Scotia, September 27, 1935

1955–56R	1	0	0	0	2
1956–57	53	4	8	12	84
1957–58	13	0	0	0	9
1959–60	4	0	0	0	2
Totals	71	4	8	12	97

- called up January 27, 1956, from Marlies
- first Leaf game January 28, 1956
- traded June 7, 1960, to Canadiens for Stan Smrke
- later coached Canadiens to Stanley Cup

JAMIE MACOUN ("Cooner")
#34 defence   6'2" 197–L
b. Newmarket, August 17, 1961

1991–92	39	3	13	16	18
1992–93	77	4	15	19	55
1993–94	82	3	27	30	115
1994–95	46	2	8	10	75
1995–96	82	0	8	8	87
1996–97	73	1	10	11	93
1997–98	67	0	7	7	63
Totals	466	13	88	101	506

- acquired January 2, 1992, with Doug Gilmour, Ric Nattress, Rick Wamsley, and Kent Manderville from Calgary for Gary Leeman, Michel Petit, Craig Berube, Jeff Reese, and Alexander Godynyuk
- traded to Detroit on March 24, 1998, for a 4th-round draft choice in 1998 (previously acquired from Tampa Bay—Alexei Ponikarovsky)
- one of only a few undrafted players to play 1,000 NHL games
- played at 1985 WC (silver medal), 1990 WC (fourth place), and 1991 WC (silver)

DARYL MAGGS
#24 defence   6'2" 195–R
b. Victoria, British Columbia, April 6, 1949

1979–80L	5	0	0	0	0

- signed as a free agent December 1979 after returning from German League
- played December 17, 19, 27, 29 and January 5, 1979–80 with Leafs

MARC MAGNAN
#35 left wing   5'11" 195–L
b. Beaumont, Alberta, February 17, 1962

1982–83R/L	4	0	1	1	5

- selected 195th overall at 1981 Entry Draft
- first and only Leaf games December 14, 15, 18, 29, 1982

KEVIN MAGUIRE

#28–18 right wing   6'2" 200–R

b. Toronto, January 5, 1963

1986–87R	17	0	0	0	74
1990–91	63	9	5	14	180
1991–92L	8	1	0	1	4
Totals	88	10	5	15	258

- signed October 10, 1984, as a free agent
- first Leaf game December 26, 1986
- claimed October 5, 1987, by Sabres in Waiver Draft
- acquired June 16, 1990, with an 8th-round draft choice in 1991 (Dmitri Mironov) from Flyers for a 3rd-round draft choice in 1990 (Al Kinisky)
- last Leaf games December 11, 12, 20, 23, 26, 28 and January 3, 4, 1991–92
- retired after 1991–92 and became a referee; today working in the NHL

FRANK MAHOVLICH

("The Big M"/"Gutch")

#22–27 left wing   6' 205–L

b. Timmins, January 10, 1938

1956–57R	3	1	0	1	2
1957–58	67	20	16	36	67
1958–59	63	22	27	49	94
1959–60	70	18	21	39	61
1960–61	70	48	36	84	131
1961–62	70	33	38	71	87
1962–63	67	36	37	73	56
1963–64	70	26	29	55	66
1964–65	59	23	28	51	76
1965–66	68	32	24	56	68
1966–67	63	18	28	46	44
1967–68	50	19	17	36	30
Totals	720	296	301	597	782

- St. Mike's graduate; signed May 13, 1957, with Leafs
- first Leaf game March 20, 1957
- missed November 14–December 5, 1964, suffering from depression
- missed first two games of 1966–67 in contract dispute
- missed November 2–25, 1967, suffering from depression
- traded March 3, 1968, with Pete Stemkowski, Garry Unger, and the rights to Carl Brewer to Detroit for Paul Henderson, Norm Ullman, and Floyd Smith
- ran successful travel agency after retiring
- named to Canada's Senate by Prime Minister Jean Chrétien
- Hockey Hall of Fame 1981

ADAM MAIR ("Bomber")

#21 centre   6'2" 195–R

b. Hamilton, February 15, 1979

1999–2000R	8	1	0	1	6
2000–01	16	0	2	2	14
Totals	24	1	2	3	20

- selected 84th overall at 1997 Entry Draft
- won silver medal at WJC in 1999
- traded March 13, 2001, with a 2nd-round draft choice in 2001 (Mike Cammelleri) to Los Angeles for Aki Berg

DAN MALONEY ("Harley"/"Satch")

#9 left wing   6'2" 195–L

b. Barrie, September 24, 1950

1977–78	13	3	4	7	25
1978–79	77	17	36	53	157
1979–80	71	17	16	33	102
1980–81	65	20	21	41	183
1981–82L	44	8	7	15	71
Totals	270	65	84	149	538

- acquired March 13, 1978, with a 2nd-round draft choice in 1980 (Craig Muni) from Detroit for Errol Thompson, a 1st-round draft choice in 1977 (Brent Peterson), a 2nd-round draft choice in 1978 (Al Jensen), and a 1st-round draft choice in 1980 (Mike Blaisdell)
- last Leaf game March 30, 1982
- retired after 1981–82 to become Leafs' assistant coach, later becoming head coach
- later became a realtor in Barrie

PHIL MALONEY
#25–23 centre   5'9" 170–L
b. Ottawa, October 6, 1927

1950–51	1	1	0	1	0
1952–53	29	2	6	8	2
Totals	30	3	6	9	2

- acquired November 15, 1950, with Leo Boivin, Fern Flaman, and Ken Smith from Boston for Vic Lynn and Bill Ezinicki
- sold December 21, 1954, with Bill Ezinicki and Hugh Barlow for $10,000 to Vancouver (WHL)

KENT MANDERVILLE ("Mandy")
#18 left wing   6'3" 207–L
b. Edmonton, Alberta, April 12, 1971

1991–92R	15	0	4	4	0
1992–93	18	1	1	2	17
1993–94	67	7	9	16	63
1994–95	36	0	1	1	22
Totals	136	8	15	23	102

- acquired January 2, 1992, with Doug Gilmour, Jamie Macoun, Ric Nattress, and Rick Wamsley from Calgary for Gary Leeman, Michel Petit, Jeff Reese, Craig Berube and Alexander Godynyuk
- first Leaf game March 4, 1992
- traded December 4, 1995, to Edmonton for Peter White and a 4th-round draft choice in 1996 (Jason Sessa)
- won gold medals with Canada at 1990 and 1991 WJC and silver at 1992 Olympics

CESARE MANIAGO ("Hail Caesar")
#1 goalie   6'3" 195–L
b. Trail, British Columbia, January 13, 1939

1960–61R						
7 (0/0)	4–2–1	420	18	0	2.57	

- St. Mike's graduate
- first and only Leaf games February 25, 26 and March 1, 4, 5, 16, 18, 1961

- claimed June 13, 1961, by Canadiens at Intra-League draft
- has run a sporting goods business since leaving hockey

NORM MANN
#8–21–19 right wing   5'10" 155–R
b. Bradford, England, March 3, 1914
d. Mattawa, February 9, 1994

1938–39	16	0	0	0	2
1940–41L	15	0	3	3	2
Totals	31	0	3	3	4

- signed October 7, 1935
- lost May 10, 1937, to Rangers at Intra-League Draft
- bought November 7, 1938, by the Leafs from the Rangers for $4,000; kept with Leafs on four-game trial to replace injured Drillon
- first Leaf game November 10, 1938
- sold October 30, 1941, outright to Providence
- joined Navy in 1941—never played in NHL again
- last Leaf game March 11, 1941

BOB MANNO
#3–18 defence   6' 185–L
b. Niagara Falls, October 31, 1956

1981–82	72	9	41	50	67

- signed September 30, 1981, as a free agent
- played in Merano (Italian League) 1982–83
- signed August 2, 1983, as a free agent by Detroit

DAVE MANSON ("Charlie")
#3 defence   6'2" 200–L
b. Prince Albert, Saskatchewan, January 27, 1967

2000–01	74	4	7	11	93

- signed as a free agent on August 16, 2000

MILAN MARCETTA ("Millie")

#25 centre　　　　　6'1" 195–L
b. Cadomin, Alberta, September 19, 1936

- acquired August 8, 1963, from defunct Calgary team (WHL)
- appeared as a Leaf only in the 1967 playoffs
- sold December 27, 1967, to Minnesota
- manages a condominium building in Coquitlam, B.C.

BRIAN MARCHINKO

#22 centre　　　　　6' 180–R
b. Weyburn, Saskatchewan, August 2, 1948

1970–71R	2	0	0	0	0
1971–72	3	0	0	0	0
Totals	5	0	0	0	0

- graduated from Flin Flon (WHL) in 1969
- first Leaf games October 11, 14, 1970
- played October 16, 17, 20, 1971, with Leafs
- claimed June 6, 1972, by the Islanders at Expansion Draft

GUS MARKER ("Senator")

#14–18 forward　　　　5'9" 162–R
b. Wetaskewin, Saskatchewan, August 1, 1907
d. Kingston, October 7, 1997

1938–39	43	9	6	15	11
1939–40	42	10	9	19	15
1940–41	27	4	5	9	10
Totals	112	23	20	43	36

- bought November 3, 1938, from the Maroons
- traded October 30, 1941, to New York Americans with Red Heron, Nick Knott, and Peanuts O'Flaherty on a one-year lease, all subject to recall, for Lorne Carr

JACK MARKLE

#21 forward　　　　　5'9" 155–R
b. Thessalon, May 15, 1907
d. June 25, 1956

1935–36R/L	8	0	1	1	0

- recalled January 19, 1936, from Syracuse to replace injured Conacher
- first and only Leaf games January 23, 25, 30 and February 1, 2, 4, 6, 8, 1936

DANIIL "DANNY" MARKOV

("Elvis"/"Sputnik")

#55 defence　　　　　6'1" 196–L
b. Moscow, USSR, July 11, 1976

1997–98R	25	2	5	7	28
1998–99	57	4	8	12	47
1999–2000	59	0	10	10	28
2000–01	59	3	13	16	34
Totals	200	9	36	45	137

- selected 223rd overall at 1995 Entry Draft
- played for Russia at 1998 WC (fifth place)
- traded June 12, 2001, to Phoenix for Robert Reichel, Travis Green, and Craig Mills

JACK MARKS

right wing　　　　　6' 180–L
b. Brantford, June 11, 1885
d. Toronto, August 19, 1945

1917–18	5	0	–	0	0

- signed as a free agent after Wanderers' building burned down and players released January 5, 1918

DANIEL MAROIS

#32 right wing　　　　6' 190–R
b. Montreal, Quebec, October 3, 1968

1988–89R	76	31	23	54	76
1989–90	68	39	37	76	82
1990–91	78	21	9	30	112
1991–92	63	15	11	26	76
Totals	285	106	80	186	346

- selected 28th overall at 1987 Entry Draft
- first regular season Leaf game October 6, 1988
- traded March 10, 1992, with Claude Loiselle to the Islanders for Ken Baumgartner and Dave McLlwain
- signed as a free agent August 20, 1996

JEAN MAROIS
#1 goalie   5'8" 155–L
b. Quebec City, Quebec, May 11, 1924
d. Quebec City, Quebec, 1996

1943–44R						
1 (0/0)	1–0–0	60	4	0	4.00	

- played December 18, 1943, as an 18-year-old St. Mike's student
- played only two other games in NHL, with Chicago in 1953–54

BRAD MARSH
#3 defence   6'3" 220–L
b. London, March 31, 1958

1988–89	80	1	15	16	79
1989–90	79	1	13	14	95
1990–91	20	0	0	0	15
Totals	179	2	28	30	189

- claimed October 3, 1988, at Waiver Draft
- traded February 5, 1991, to Detroit for an 8th-round draft choice in 1991 (Robb McIntyre)
- bought June 10, 1992, from Detroit
- traded July 20, 1992, to Ottawa Senators for future considerations
- won silver medal with Canada at 1977 WJC, bronze at 1978 WJC, and played at 1979 WC (fourth place)
- currently runs a bar in Corel Centre, Ottawa

GARY MARSH
#18 left wing   5'9" 172–L
b. Toronto, March 9, 1946

1968–69L	1	0	0	0	0

- put on reserve list June 12, 1968, from Detroit
- first and only Leaf game October 27, 1968

DON MARSHALL
#22 left wing   5'10" 166–L
b. Verdun, Quebec, March 23, 1932

1971–72L	50	2	14	16	0

- claimed June 8, 1971, from Sabres at Intra-League Draft
- retired after 1971–72 season; last Leaf game April 2, 1972
- became a sales rep for a mechanical products company in Montreal

PAUL MARSHALL
#28–15 left wing   6'2" 180–L
b. Toronto, September 7, 1960

1980–81	13	0	2	2	2
1981–82	10	2	2	4	2
Totals	23	2	4	6	4

- acquired November 18, 1980, with Kim Davis from Penguins for Dave Burrows and Paul Gardner
- traded October 5, 1982, to Hartford for a 10th-round draft choice in 1983 (Greg Rolston)

WILLIE MARSHALL ("The Whip")
#8–21–24 centre   5'10" 160–L
b. Kirkland Lake, December 1, 1931

1952–53R	2	0	0	0	0
1954–55	16	1	4	5	0
1955–56	6	0	0	0	0
1958–59L	9	0	1	1	2
Totals	33	1	5	6	2

- St. Mike's graduate 1950
- first Leaf games February 28 and March 1, 1953
- traded in June 1956 to Hershey for Gerry Ehman

- acquired April 29, 1958, from Hershey for Ron Hurst, Mike Nykoluk, and Wally Boyer (on a two-year loan)
- last Leaf games October 11, 12, 16, 18, 19, 29 and December 18, 20, 21, 1958
- played next 20 years in minors
- became president of a mining company in Western Canada

JACK MARTIN

#24 forward   5'11" 184–L
b. St. Catharines, November 29, 1940

1960–61R/L	1	0	0	0	0

- St. Mike's graduate
- first and only Leaf game November 27, 1960

MATT MARTIN ("Marty")

#33–3 defence   6'3" 205–L
b. New Haven, Connecticut, April 30, 1971

1993–94R	12	0	1	1	6
1994–95	15	0	0	0	13
1995–96	13	0	0	0	14
1996–97	36	0	4	4	38
Totals	76	0	5	5	71

- selected 66th overall at 1989 Entry Draft
- first Leaf game October 19, 1993
- missed much of 1995–96 with a broken ankle
- signed as a free agent by Dallas on July 24, 1998
- played for USA at 1994 Olympics (eighth place) and 1997 WC (sixth)

TERRY MARTIN

#25 left wing   5'11" 195–L
b. Barrie, October 25, 1955

1979–80	37	6	15	21	2
1980–81	69	23	14	37	32
1981–82	72	25	24	49	39
1982–83	76	14	13	27	28
1983–84	63	15	10	25	51
Totals	317	83	76	159	152

- acquired December 13, 1979, with Dave Farrish from Quebec Nordiques for Reg Thomas
- claimed October 9, 1984, by Edmonton at Waiver Draft
- has stayed in hockey as a coach in junior, assistant in the NHL, and scout with Buffalo

TOM MARTIN

#17 right wing   5'9" 170–R
b. Toronto, October 16, 1947

1967–68R/L	3	1	0	1	0

- selected 5th overall at 1964 Amateur Draft
- first and only Leaf games December 27 and March 30, 31, 1967–68
- claimed June 9, 1970, by Detroit at Intra-League Draft
- coached the Marlies and minor pros for years

PAUL MASNICK

#8 centre   5'9" 165–R
b. Regina, Saskatchewan, April 14, 1931

1957–58L	41	2	9	11	14

- bought September 30, 1957, from Canadiens
- first Leaf game December 7, 1957
- last Leaf game March 23, 1958

FRANK MATHERS

#20 defence   6' 182–L
b. Winnipeg, Manitoba, March 29, 1924

1948–49R	15	1	2	3	2
1949–50	6	0	1	1	2
1951–52L	2	0	0	0	0
Totals	23	1	3	4	4

- acquired April 26, 1948, from the Rangers with Cal Gardner, Bill Juzda, René Trudell, and the rights to Ray McMurray for Wally Stanowski, Moe Morris, and the rights to Orville Lavell
- first Leaf game October 16, 1948

- last Leaf games December 16, 20, 1951
- retired September 16, 1952, then accepted demotion to Pittsburgh on October 24, 1952
- contract purchased in summer 1956 by Hershey when Hornets folded
- coached and managed in AHL the rest of his career

JOE MATTE

defence 5'11" 180–R
b. Bourget, March 6, 1893
d. June 13, 1961

1919–20R	16	8	2	10	12

- signed January 15, 1920, on loan from Canadiens for the year
- first St. Pats game January 17, 1920
- loaned to the Hamilton Tigers (NHL) for the 1920–21 season

BRAD MAXWELL

#4 defence 6'2" 195–R
b. Brandon, Manitoba, July 8, 1957

1985–86	52	8	18	26	108

- acquired August 21, 1985, from Quebec Nordiques for John Anderson
- traded October 3, 1986, to Vancouver Canucks for a 5th-round draft choice in 1988 (Len Esau)
- played at 1978 WC (bronze medal), 1979 WC (fourth place), and 1982 WC (bronze)

WALLY MAXWELL

#26 forward 5'10" 155–L
b. Ottawa, August 24, 1933

1952–53R/L	2	0	0	0	0

- first and only games January 10 and 14, 1953

GIL MAYER ("The Needle")

#25–21–22–1–20 goalie 5'6" 135–L
b. Ottawa, August 24, 1930

1949–50R						
1 (0/0)	0–1–0	60	2	0	2.00
1953–54						
1 (0/0)	0–0–1	60	3	0	3.00
1954–55						
1 (0/0)	0–1–0	60	1	0	1.00
1955–56L						
6 (0/0)	1–5–0	360	19	0	3.17
Totals						
9 (0/0)	1–7–1	540	25	0	2.78

- bought in 1949 from Bisons for cash
- played December 1, 1949, when Turk Broda benched for being too fat
- played March 4, 1954
- played October 21, 1954
- played January 25, 28, 29 and February 1, 4, 5, 1956, when Lumley injured
- bought by Hershey in June 1956 when Hornets folded
- worked for Rhode Island Building Department

SHEP MAYER

#18–22 forward 5'8" 180–R
b. Sturgeon Falls, September 11, 1923

1942–43R/L	2	1	2	3	4

- first and only Leaf games October 31 and November 7, 1942, then joined the Canadian military
- re-signed August 24, 1945, though never played in the NHL again

GARY McADAM

#12 left wing 5'11" 175–L
b. Smiths Falls, December 31, 1955

1985–86L	15	1	6	7	0

- signed July 31, 1985, as a free agent
- suffered eye injury November 26, 1985, vs. Penguins and never played again

CHRIS McALLISTER ("Cally")
#33 defence   6'7" 235–L
b. Saskatoon, Saskatchewan, June 16, 1985

1998–99	20	0	2	2	39
1999–2000	36	0	3	3	68
Totals	56	0	5	5	107

- acquired from Vancouver on February 16, 1999, for Darby Hendrickson
- traded September 26, 2000, to Flyers for Regan Kelly

CLIFF McBRIDE
#12 defence   5'11" 187–R
b. Toronto, January 10, 1909
d. Unknown

1929–30L	1	0	0	0	0

- acquired December 7, 1928, from Maroons as future considerations in deal of November 28, 1928, that sent Dave Trottier and $15,000 to the Maroons
- sent November 13, 1929, to London (Can Pro)
- recalled for one game only, November 26, 1929

BRYAN McCABE
#24 defence   6'1" 210–L
b. St. Catharines, June 8, 1975

2000–01	82	5	24	29	123

- acquired October 2, 2000, from Chicago for Alexander Karpovtsev and a 4th-round draft choice in 2001 (Vladimir Gusev)
- currently with Leafs
- won gold medals with Canada at 1994 and 1995 WJC; played at 1997 WC (gold), 1998 WC (sixth), and 1999 WC (fourth)

BERT McCAFFREY ("Mac")
#7 forward   5'10" 180–R
b. Listowel, 1895   d. April 15, 1955

1924–25R	30	9	6	15	12
1925–26	36	14	7	21	42
1926–27	43	5	5	10	43
1927–28	8	1	1	2	9
Totals	117	29	19	48	106

- signed in 1924 after winning 1923–24 Allan Cup and 1924 Olympic gold with Toronto Granites
- first St. Pats game November 29, 1924
- traded December 12, 1927, with cash to Pirates; Ty Arbour traded from Pirates to Chicago; Eddie Rodden from Chicago to Toronto

ALYN McCAULEY ("Shooter"/"Mac")
#18 centre   5'11" 185–L
b. Brockville, May 29, 1977

1997–98	60	6	10	16	6
1998–99	39	9	15	24	2
1999–2000	45	5	5	10	10
2000–01	14	1	0	1	0
Totals	158	21	30	51	18

- acquired from New Jersey on February 25, 1997, with Jason Smith and Steve Sullivan for Doug Gilmour, Dave Ellett, and a 3rd-round draft choice in 1999 (previously acquired from New Jersey in Andreychuck trade—Andre Lakos)
- suffered season-ending concussion March 3, 1999
- currently with Leafs
- won gold medals with Canada at 1996 and 1997 WJC

KEVIN McCLELLAND
#20 right wing   6'2" 205–R
b. Oshawa, July 4, 1962

1991–92	18	0	1	1	33

- signed September 2, 1991, as a free agent
- traded August 12, 1993, to Winnipeg Jets for cash

FRANK McCOOL ("Ulcers")

#1 goalie	6' 170–L
b. Calgary, Alberta, October 27, 1918	
d. Calgary, Alberta, May 20, 1973	

1944–45R						
50 (0/0)	24–22–4	3000	161	4	3.22
1945–46L						
22 (0/0)	10–9–3	1320	81	0	3.68
Totals						
72 (0/0)	34–31–7	4320	242	4	3.36

- signed after being discharged from Canadian army
- missed start of 1945–46 in contract dispute: Baz Bastien played the first five games (0–4–1), then Gordie Bell (3–5)
- first Leaf game October 28, 1944
- when Turk Broda was discharged from army later in the season, McCool retired
- last Leaf game February 3, 1946
- worked for *Calgary Albertan* newspaper for the rest of his life

JOHN McCORMACK ("Goose")

#20 centre	6' 185–L
b. Edmonton, Alberta, August 2, 1925	

1947–48R	3	0	1	1	0
1948–49	1	0	0	0	0
1949–50	34	6	5	11	0
1950–51	46	6	7	13	2
Totals	84	12	13	25	2

- Marlie graduate 1948
- brought up in 1947–48 to replace injured Syl Apps
- first Leaf game January 31, 1948
- played with Leafs January 19, 1949
- demoted by Conn Smythe to Hornets during 1950–51 season because he got married during the season
- sold September 21, 1951, to the Canadiens
- later ran his own steel company in Whitby

DALE McCOURT

#12 centre	5'10" 180–R
b. Falconbridge, January 26, 1957	

1983–84L	72	19	24	43	10

- signed October 22, 1983, as a free agent
- last Leaf and NHL game April 1, 1984
- later challenged NHL's compensation ruling, refusing to go to Los Angeles after Detroit signed Rogie Vachon (he won his case, but was later traded)
- won silver medal with Canada at 1977 WJC; played at 1979 WC (fourth) and 1981 WC (fourth)

BILL McCREARY

#28 right wing	6' 190–R
b. Springfield, Massachusetts, April 15, 1960	

1980–81R/L	12	1	0	1	4

- selected 114th overall at 1979 Entry Draft
- first Leaf game December 30, 1980
- last Leaf and NHL game January 30, 1981

JOHNNY McCREEDY

#14–20 right wing	5'8" 160–R
b. Winnipeg, Manitoba, March 23, 1911	
d. Toronto, December 7, 1979	

1941–42R	47	15	8	23	14
1944–45L	17	2	4	6	11
Totals	64	17	12	29	25

- Winnipeg Monarchs graduate; signed July 15, 1941, with Leafs
- first Leaf game November 8, 1941
- replaced injured Don Metz in 1941–42
- missed 1942–44—Royal Canadian Air Force
- returned to university after 1944–45
- last Leaf and NHL game March 18, 1945
- won gold medal with Canada at 1939 WC
- became chairman and CEO of Inco Metals Co.

DARWIN McCUTCHEON
#2 defence   6'4" 190–L
b. Listowel, April 19, 1962

1981–82R/L	1	0	0	0	2

- selected 179th overall at 1980 Entry Draft
- first and only Leaf and NHL game December 31, 1981

JACK McDONALD
left wing
b. Quebec City, Quebec, February 28, 1888
d. January 24, 1958

1920–21	8	0	1	1	0

- started 1920–21 with Canadiens

LANNY McDONALD
#7 right wing   6' 194–R
b. Hanna, Alberta, February 16, 1953

1973–74R	70	14	16	30	43
1974–75	64	17	27	44	86
1975–76	75	37	56	93	70
1976–77	80	46	44	90	77
1977–78	74	47	40	87	54
1978–79	79	43	42	85	32
1979–80	35	15	15	30	10
Totals	477	219	240	459	372

- selected 4th overall at 1973 Amateur Draft
- first Leaf game October 10, 1973
- traded December 29, 1979, with Joel Quenneville to Colorado Rockies for Pat Hickey and Wilf Paiement
- played for Canada at 1981 WC (fourth place)
- joined Calgary Flames front office for more than a decade
- Hockey Hall of Fame 1992

WILFRED "BUCKO" McDONALD
#3–19 defence   5'9" 205–L
b. Fergus, October 31, 1911
d. Burks Falls, July 19, 1991

1938–39	33	3	3	6	20
1939–40	34	2	5	7	13
1940–41	31	6	11	17	12
1941–42	48	2	19	21	24
1942–43	40	2	11	13	39
1943–44	9	2	4	6	8
Totals	195	17	53	70	116

- bought December 19, 1938, from Detroit for Bill Thomson and $10,000
- loaned February 2, 1943, to Providence for the rest of the season with George Boothman and Jack Forsey for Ab DeMarco and Buck Jones
- traded November 25, 1943, to Rangers for Gordie Bell, Dudley Garrett, and first post-war call to Charlie Rayner
- later entered politics and became a member of Parliament

BOB "BIG DADDY" McGILL
#4–15–8–26 defence   6'1" 193–R
b. Edmonton, Alberta, April 27, 1962

1981–82R	68	1	10	11	263
1982–83	30	0	0	0	146
1983–84	11	0	2	2	51
1984–85	72	0	5	5	250
1985–86	61	1	4	5	141
1986–87	56	1	4	5	103
1992–93	19	1	0	1	34
Totals	317	4	25	29	988

- selected 26th overall at 1980 Entry Draft
- first Leaf game October 6, 1981
- traded September 4, 1987, with Rick Vaive and Steve Thomas to Chicago for Ed Olczyk and Al Secord
- claimed on waivers September 9, 1992, from Tampa Bay
- signed September 7, 1993, as a free agent by the Islanders

JOHN McINTYRE ("Mac")
#44 centre   6'1" 180–L
b. Ravenswood, April 29, 1969

1989–90R	59	5	12	17	117
1990–91	13	0	3	3	25
Totals	72	5	15	20	142

- selected 49th overall at 1987 Entry Draft
- first Leaf game October 25, 1989
- traded November 9, 1990, to Los Angeles Kings for Mike Krushelnyski
- played for Canada at 1989 WJC (fourth place)

LARRY McINTYRE

#25 defence   6'1" 190–L
b. Moose Jaw, Saskatchewan, July 13, 1949

1969–70R	1	0	0	0	0
1972–73L	40	0	3	3	26
Totals	41	0	3	3	26

- selected 31st overall at 1969 Amateur Draft
- first Leaf game January 7, 1970
- last game April 1, 1973
- traded May 29, 1973, with Murray Heatley to Vancouver Canucks for Dunc Wilson

WALT McKECHNIE

#11 centre   6'2" 200–L
b. London, June 19, 1947

1978–79	79	25	36	61	18
1979–80	54	7	36	43	4
Totals	133	32	72	104	22

- acquired October 5, 1978, from Minnesota for a 3rd-round draft choice in 1980 (Randy Velischek)
- traded March 3, 1980, to Colorado Rockies for a 3rd-round draft choice in 1980 (Fred Boimistruck)
- played for Canada at 1977 WC (fourth place)
- later opened a restaurant in Southern Ontario cottage country

SEAN McKENNA

#8–21 right wing   6' 190–R
b. Asbestos, Quebec, March 7, 1962

1987–88	40	5	5	10	12
1988–89	3	0	1	1	0
1989–90L	5	0	0	0	20
Totals	48	5	6	11	32

- acquired December 14, 1987, from Los Angeles Kings for Mike Allison
- first and only Leaf games October 25, 27, 28 and November 15, 16, 1989

DON McKENNEY ("Slip")

#17 centre   6' 175–L
b. Smiths Falls, April 30, 1934

1963–64	15	9	17	26	2
1964–65	52	6	13	19	6
Totals	67	15	30	45	8

- acquired February 22, 1964, with Andy Bathgate from the Rangers for Dick Duff, Bob Nevin, Rod Seiling, Bill Collins, and Arnie Brown
- played in minors January 20–February 28, 1965
- claimed on waivers June 8, 1965, by Detroit
- assisted Fern Flaman at Northeastern University for 19 years as coach and scout

JIM McKENNY ("Howie")

#18–25 defence   6' 185–R
b. Ottawa, December 1, 1946

1965–66R	2	0	0	0	2
1966–67	6	1	0	1	0
1967–68	5	1	0	1	0
1968–69	7	0	0	0	2
1969–70	73	11	33	44	34
1970–71	68	4	26	30	42
1971–72	76	5	31	36	27
1972–73	77	11	41	52	55
1973–74	77	14	28	42	36
1974–75	66	8	35	43	31
1975–76	46	10	19	29	19
1976–77	76	14	31	45	36
1977–78	15	2	2	4	8
1978–79	10	1	1	2	2
Totals	604	82	247	329	294

- selected 17th overall at 1963 Amateur Draft
- first Leaf games February 26 and 27, 1966, then sent back to juniors

- played February 18, 22, 23, 25, 26 and March 1, 1967; the rest of the year in Rochester
- played February 17, 21, 24, 25, 28, 1968; the rest of the year in Rochester
- missed most of 1967–68 with leg injury
- missed start of season to November 4, 1970, with dislocated elbow
- sold May 10, 1978, to Minnesota for future considerations (Owen Lloyd)
- longtime sports reporter for City-TV in Toronto

MURRAY McLACHLAN
#31 goalie   6′ 195–L
b. London, October 20, 1948

1970–71R/L						
2 (1/1)	0–1–0	25	4	0	9.60	

- signed after graduating from University of Minnesota
- first and only Leaf and NHL games November 18 and 19, 1970

JACK McLEAN
#7–18 centre   5′8″ 165–R
b. Winnipeg, Manitoba, January 31, 1923

1942–43R	27	9	8	17	33
1943–44	32	3	15	18	30
1944–45L	8	2	1	3	13
Totals	67	14	24	38	76

- signed November 10, 1942, by Leafs
- first Leaf game November 12, 1942
- played only home games in 1944–45 while attending university
- missed part of 1944–45 with broken ankle; retired after season
- last Leaf game December 16, 1944
- later became an engineer in Ottawa

JOHN McLELLAN
#14 centre   5′11″ 150–L
b. South Porcupine, August 6, 1928
d. Toronto, October 27, 1979

1951–52R/L	2	0	0	0	0

- Marlie graduate
- only Leaf games December 29, 30, 1951
- traded September 16, 1954, with cash to Cleveland (AHL) for Hugh Barlow
- won gold medal with Belleville McFarlands at 1959 WC
- later became Leaf coach

DAVE McLLWAIN
#7 forward   6′ 190–L
b. Seaforth, January 9, 1967

1991–92	11	1	2	3	4
1992–93	66	14	4	18	30
Totals	77	15	6	21	34

- acquired March 10, 1992, with Ken Baumgartner from the Islanders for Daniel Marois and Claude Loiselle
- claimed October 3, 1993, by Ottawa Senators at Waiver Draft
- played for Canada at 1987 WJC (disqualified)

GERRY McNAMARA
#1 goalie   6′2″ 190–L
b. Sturgeon Falls, September 22, 1934

1960–61R					
5 (0/0)	2–2–1	300	13	0	2.60
1969–70L					
2 (0/2)	0–0–0	23	2	0	5.22
Totals					
7 (0/2)	2–2–1	323	15	0	2.79

- St. Mike's graduate
- recalled from Sudbury Wolves in February 1961 to replace injured Johnny Bower; played February 15, 18, 19, 23 and March 19, 1961

- played January 14 and 23, 1970
- later became unpopular Leaf general manager during worst years of franchise

BASIL McRAE
#26 left wing   6'2" 205–L
b. Beaverton, January 5, 1961

1983–84	3	0	0	0	19
1984–85	1	0	0	0	0
Totals	4	0	0	0	19

- acquired August 12, 1983, from Quebec Nordiques for Richard Turmel
- signed July 17, 1985, as a free agent by Detroit

CHRIS McRAE
#32–29 left wing   6' 200–L
b. Beaverton, August 26, 1965

1987–88R	11	0	0	0	65
1988–89	3	0	0	0	12
Totals	14	0	0	0	77

- signed October 16, 1985, as a free agent
- first Leaf game December 18, 1987
- traded February 21, 1989, to the Rangers for Ken Hammond

GORD McRAE ("The Bird")
#1–31 goalie   6' 180–L
b. Sherbrooke, Quebec, April 12, 1948

1972–73R						
11 (0/1)	7–3–0	620	39	0	3.77	
1974–75						
20 (2/1)	10–3–6	1063	57	0	3.22	
1975–76						
20 (2/6)	6–5–2	956	59	0	3.70	
1976–77						
2 (0/0)	0–1–1	120	9	0	4.50	
1977–78L						
18 (1/0)	7–10–1	1040	57	1	3.29	
Totals						
71 (5/8)	30–22–10	3799	221	1	3.49	

- signed as a free agent on December 18, 1971
- first Leaf game January 31, 1973
- last Leaf game April 9, 1978

KEN McRAE
#36–40 centre   6'1" 195–R
b. Winchester, April 23, 1968

1992–93	2	0	0	0	2
1993–94	9	1	1	2	36
Totals	11	1	1	2	38

- acquired July 21, 1992, from Quebec Nordiques for Len Esau
- signed September 9, 1994, as a free agent by Edmonton

GERRY MEEHAN
#26–27 centre   6'2" 200–L
b. Toronto, September 3, 1946

1968–69R	25	0	2	2	2

- selected 21st overall at 1963 Amateur Draft
- first Leaf game December 1, 1968
- traded March 2, 1969, with Mike Byers and Bill Sutherland to Flyers for Forbes Kennedy and Brit Selby
- later became player agent

HOWIE MEEKER ("Hurricane Howie")
#11–15 right wing   5'8" 165–R
b. Kitchener, November 4, 1924

1946–47R	55	27	18	45	76
1947–48	58	14	20	34	62
1948–49	30	7	7	14	56
1949–50	70	18	22	40	35
1950–51	49	6	14	20	24
1951–52	54	9	14	23	50
1952–53	25	1	7	8	26
1953–54L	5	1	0	1	0
Totals	346	83	102	185	329

- signed April 12, 1946, from Stratford Seniors
- first Leaf game October 16, 1946

- fractured collarbone December 26, 1948, in practice; missed most of the rest of the year
- missed much of 1952–53 with back injury that forced him to retire at Leafs 1953 training camp. He was allowed to coach Stratford Indians (OHA Senior A) subject to immediate recall
- recalled November 20, 1953, when both Armstrong and Bailey injured
- last Leaf games November 21, 22, 26, 28, 29, 1953
- later became coach and then general manager of the Leafs
- worked as game analyst for *Hockey Night in Canada* for many years, espousing skills for young players

HARRY MEEKING ("Meek")
#7 left wing   5'7" 160–R
b. Kitchener, November 4, 1894
d. February 2, 1972

1917–18	20	10	–	10	19
1918–19	14	7	3	10	22
Totals	34	17	3	20	41

- signed from Glace Bay (Maritime Independent League)
- suspended February 12, 1919, by the Arenas for the rest of the season. Manager Querrie wrote: "Under paragraph No. 2 in your contract you are suspended. Your playing in the last three games has not been satisfactory to the club and we feel you didn't give your best services to us or try at all in the last Ottawa fixture"
- released outright February 18, 1919, and left to play for Glace Bay

BARRY MELROSE
#26 defence   6' 205–R
b. Kelvington, Saskatchewan, July 15, 1956

1980–81	57	2	5	7	166
1981–82	64	1	5	6	186
1982–83	52	2	5	7	68
Totals	173	5	15	20	420

- claimed on waivers November 30, 1980, from Minnesota
- signed September 6, 1983, as a free agent by Detroit
- later became coach of L.A. Kings and then colour commentator for that team

DON METZ
#11–15–18 right wing   5'9" 165–R
b. Wilcox, Saskatchewan, January 10, 1916

1939–40R	10	1	1	2	4
1940–41	31	4	10	14	6
1941–42	25	2	3	5	8
1945–46	7	1	0	1	0
1946–47	40	4	9	13	10
1947–48	26	4	6	10	2
1948–49L	33	4	6	10	12
Totals	172	20	35	55	42

- joined Leafs late in 1938–39 after three years with Toronto Goodyears
- first Leaf game November 19, 1939
- missed part of 1940–41 with knee injury
- missed much of 1941–42 with broken ankle
- missed 1942–45—Royal Canadian Air Force
- demoted January 2, 1948, to Hornets for two weeks to help undermanned team
- recalled December 26, 1948, from Hornets to replace injured Meeker
- last Leaf game March 20, 1949
- retired April 19, 1949, and returned to farming in Saskatchewan with his brother

NICK METZ ("Handy Andy"/"Red"/"Pop")
#5-15-19-17-10 left wing 5'11" 160-L
b. Wilcox, Saskatchewan, February 16, 1914
d. Regina, Saskatchewan, August 25, 1990

1934–35R	18	2	2	4	4
1935–36	38	14	6	20	14
1936–37	48	9	11	20	19
1937–38	48	15	7	22	12
1938–39	47	11	10	21	15
1939–40	31	6	5	11	2
1940–41	47	14	21	35	10
1941–42	30	11	9	20	20
1944–45	50	22	13	35	26
1945–46	41	11	11	22	4
1946–47	60	12	16	28	15
1947–48L	60	4	8	12	8
Totals	518	131	119	250	149

- St. Mike's graduate 1934
- first Leaf game November 8, 1934
- missed ten games in 1935–36 with leg injury
- missed many games December–January 1939–40 with concussion
- missed 1942–44—Royal Canadian Engineers; returned to the Leafs on October 19, 1944
- last Leaf game March 21, 1948
- retired April 22, 1948, and returned to Saskatchewan to the family farm

LARRY MICKEY
#12 right wing 5'11" 180-R
b. Lacombe, Alberta, October 21, 1943
d. Amherst, New York, July 23, 1982

1968–69	55	8	19	27	43

- claimed June 12, 1968, from Rangers at Intra-League Draft
- claimed June 11, 1969, by Canadiens at Intra-League Draft
- coached minor hockey after retiring in 1975, primarily in Northeastern Hockey League
- committed suicide by carbon monoxide poisoning

RUDY MIGAY ("Toy Terrier")
#11-14-22-21 centre 5'10" 175-L
b. Fort William, November 18, 1928

1949–50R	18	1	5	6	8
1951–52	19	2	1	3	12
1952–53	40	5	4	9	22
1953–54	70	8	15	23	60
1954–55	67	8	16	24	66
1955–56	70	12	16	28	52
1956–57	66	15	20	35	51
1957–58	48	7	14	21	18
1958–59	19	1	1	2	4
1959–60L	1	0	0	0	0
Totals	418	59	92	151	293

- St. Mike's graduate; signed September 15, 1948
- first Leaf game December 1, 1949
- missed much of 1951–52 after suffering torn knee ligaments November 8, 1951
- last Leaf game October 10, 1959
- became Buffalo Sabres scout based in Thunder Bay

JOHN "JIM" MIKOL
#16 defence 6' 175-R
b. Kitchener, June 11, 1938

1962–63R	4	0	1	1	2

- acquired summer 1962 from Cleveland (AHL)
- first and only Leaf games October 14, 18, 20, 21, 1962
- sold outright August 26, 1963, to Cleveland (AHL)

MIKE MILLAR
#36 right wing 5'10" 170-L
b. St. Catharines, April 28, 1965

1990–91L	7	2	2	4	2

- signed July 19, 1990, as a free agent
- first Leaf game December 12, 1990
- played most of 1990–91 with Newmarket, then retired
- only Leaf games December 12, 15, 19, 22, 23, 27, 29, 1990

EARL MILLER

#15 forward   5'11" 185-L
b. Regina, Saskatchewan, September 12, 1905
d. Regina, Saskatchewan, June 20, 1936

1931–32L	15	3	3	6	10

- bought February 7, 1932, from Chicago
- last Leaf game March 22, 1932

DMITRI MIRONOV ("Tree")

#15 defence   6'2" 191-R
b. Moscow, USSR, December 25, 1965

1991–92R	7	1	0	1	0
1992–93	59	7	24	31	40
1993–94	76	9	27	36	78
1994–95	33	5	12	17	28
Totals	175	22	63	85	146

- selected 160th overall at 1991 Entry Draft
- first Leaf game March 17, 1992
- traded July 8, 1995, with a 2nd-round draft choice in 1996 (later sent to New Jersey—Joshua Dewolf) to Penguins for Larry Murphy
- won bronze medal with Soviet Union at 1991 WC, gold with Russia at 1992 Olympics, placed fifth at 1992 WC; won silver at 1998 Olympics, and played at 2000 WC

IVAN "MIKE" MITCHELL

goalie
b. Unknown   d. Unknown

1919–20R 15 (3/1)	7–7–0	872	65	0	4.47
1920–21 4 (0/0)	2–2–0	240	22	0	5.50
1921–22L 2 (0/0)	2–0–0	120	6	0	3.00
Totals 21 (3/1)	11–9–0	1232	93	0	4.53

- signed in 1919 from PCHA
- first Arenas game December 23, 1919

- loaned from Hamilton when Roach injured in practice prior to season opener of 1921–22
- played first two games of 1921–22; missed rest of season with food poisoning

FREDRIK "FREDDY" MODIN

#19 forward   6'3" 202-L
b. Sundsvall, Sweden, October 8, 1974

1996–97R	76	6	7	13	24
1997–98	74	16	16	32	32
1998–99	67	16	15	31	35
Totals	217	38	38	76	91

- selected 64th overall at 1994 Entry Draft
- played 1995–96 with Brynas Gavle (Sweden)
- first Leaf game October 5, 1996
- traded to Tampa Bay on October 1, 1999, for Cory Cross and a 7th-round draft choice in 2001 (Ivan Kolozvary)

LYLE MOFFAT

#26 left wing   5'10" 180-L
b. Calgary, Alberta, March 19, 1948

1972–73R	1	0	0	0	0
1974–75	22	2	7	9	13
Totals	23	2	7	9	13

- signed at training camp 1971
- first Leaf game March 4, 1973
- signed in July 1975 by Cleveland Crusaders (WHA) as free agent

SERGIO MOMESSO ("Mo")

#7 left wing   6'3" 215-L
b. Montreal, Quebec, September 4, 1965

1995–96	54	7	8	15	112

- acquired July 8, 1995, from Vancouver Canucks for Mike Ridley
- traded February 29, 1996, to Rangers with Bill Berg for Nick Kypreos and Wayne Presley

GARRY MONAHAN ("Mondo")
#14–20 left wing   6' 185–L
b. Barrie, October 20, 1946

1970–71	78	15	22	37	79
1971–72	78	14	17	31	47
1972–73	78	13	18	31	53
1973–74	78	9	16	25	70
1974–75	1	0	0	0	0
1978–79L	62	4	7	11	25
Totals	375	55	80	135	274

- acquired September 3, 1970, with Brian Murphy from Los Angeles Kings for Bob Pulford
- traded October 16, 1974, with John Grisdale to Vancouver Canucks for Dave Dunn
- bought September 13, 1978, from Vancouver Canucks
- last Leaf game April 7, 1979
- played 1979–80 with Seibu, Tokyo
- became a broadcaster, stockbroker, and later real estate agent in Vancouver after retiring

DICKIE MOORE ("Digging Dicker")
#16 right wing   5'10" 185–R
b. Montreal, Quebec, January 6, 1931

1964–65	38	2	4	6	68

- claimed June 10, 1964, from Canadiens at Intra-League Draft
- retired due to chronic back injury at end of 1964–65 season
- runs rental businesses in Montreal
- Hockey Hall of Fame 1974

ELWYN "MOE" MORRIS
#5 defence   5'7" 185–L
b. Toronto, January 3, 1921
d. Toronto, February 6, 2000

1943–44R	50	12	21	33	22
1944–45	29	0	2	2	18
1945–46	38	1	5	6	10
Totals	117	13	28	41	50

- Marlie graduate; signed June 15, 1943, by Leafs
- first Leaf game October 30, 1943
- sent November 26, 1945, to Hornets
- acquired April 26, 1948, by the Rangers with Wally Stanowski, and the rights to Orville Lavell for Cal Gardner, René Trudell, Bill Juzda, and the rights to Ray McMurray
- also played for the Toronto Argonauts (CFL) in 1940 and 1941, despite having full sight in just one eye
- became a car salesman in Stratford

JIM MORRISON ("Moe")
#3–14–21–22–24 defence   5'10" 183–L
b. Montreal, Quebec, October 11, 1931

1951–52	17	0	1	1	4
1952–53	56	1	8	9	36
1953–54	60	9	11	20	51
1954–55	70	5	12	17	84
1955–56	63	2	17	19	77
1956–57	63	3	17	20	44
1957–58	70	3	21	24	62
Totals	399	23	87	110	358

- acquired January 9, 1952, from Boston for Fleming Mackell
- traded October 3, 1958, to Boston for Allan Stanley
- became junior and minor pro coach, then Bruins scout centred in Toronto

GERALD "GUS" MORTSON
("Old Hardrock"/"The Nugget"/"The Gold Dust Twins" with Jim Thomson)
#3–19 defence   5'11" 190–L
b. New Liskeard, January 24, 1925

1946–47R	60	5	13	18	133
1947–48	58	7	11	18	118
1948–49	60	2	13	15	85
1949–50	68	3	14	17	125
1950–51	60	3	10	13	142
1951–52	65	1	10	11	106
Totals	371	21	71	92	709

- St. Mike's graduate
- first Leaf game October 16, 1946
- released from Canadian navy in 1945
- traded September 11, 1952, with Al Rollins, Cal Gardner, and Ray Hannigan to Chicago for Harry Lumley
- managed a pizza plant in Toronto and later sold mining equipment

RICHARD MULHERN

#8 defence   6'1" 188–L
b. Edmonton, Alberta, March 1, 1955

1979–80	26	0	10	10	11

- claimed on waivers February 10, 1980, from Los Angeles Kings
- sold December 2, 1980, to Winnipeg Jets

KIRK MULLER

#21 left wing   6' 205–L
b. Kingston, February 8, 1966

1995–96	36	9	16	25	42
1996–97	66	20	17	37	85
Totals	102	29	33	62	127

- acquired January 23, 1996, from Islanders with Don Beaupre from Ottawa; Leafs sent Damian Rhodes to Ottawa and Ken Belanger to the Islanders; Ottawa sent Bryan Berard and Martin Straka to New York; Islanders sent Wade Redden to the Senators
- traded March 18, 1997, to Florida for Jason Podollan
- played for Canada at 1984 WJC (fourth place) and 1984 Olympics (fourth place); played at 1985 WC (silver), 1986 WC (bronze), 1987 WC (fourth), and 1989 WC (silver)

HARRY MUMMERY ("Mumm")

#2–10 defence   6' 245–L
b. Chicago, Illinois, August 25, 1889
d. Brandon, Manitoba, December 9, 1945

1917–18	18	3	–	3	24
1918–19	13	2	0	2	27
Totals	31	5	0	5	51

- acquired December 1917 in the dispersal of players from Quebec (NHA)
- missed first three games of 1917–18 in contract dispute
- signed by Quebec Bulldogs (NHL) in summer 1919

CRAIG MUNI

#32–33–29–26–34 defence 6'3" 200–L
b. Toronto, July 19, 1962

1981–82R	3	0	0	0	2
1982–83	2	0	1	1	0
1984–85	8	0	0	0	0
1985–86	6	0	1	1	4
Totals	19	0	2	2	6

- selected 25th overall at 1980 Entry Draft
- first Leaf games December 31, March 30 and April 3, 1981–82
- signed August 18, 1986 as a free agent by Edmonton

GERRY MUNRO

#9 defence   5'10" 175–L
b. Sault Ste. Marie, November 20, 1897
d. Unknown

1925–26L	7	0	0	0	8

- purchased from Maroons in summer 1925
- only St. Pats games November 28, December 5, 9, 12, 19, 26 and January 1, 1925–26

LARRY MURPHY

#55 defence   6'2" 210–R
b. Scarborough, March 8, 1961

1995–96	82	12	49	61	34
1996–97	69	7	32	39	20
Totals	151	19	81	100	54

- acquired July 8, 1995, from Penguins for Dmitri Mironov and a 2nd-round draft choice in 1996 (later sent to New Jersey— Joshua Dewolf)
- traded March 18, 1997, to Detroit for future considerations
- surpassed Tim Horton for most games played all-time by a defenceman and is second all-time only to Gordie Howe
- played for Canada at 1980 WJC (fifth place); played at 1985 WC (silver), 1987 WC (fourth), and 2000 WC (fourth)

KEN MURRAY

#3–7 defence   6' 180–R
b. Toronto, January 22, 1948

1969–70R	1	0	1	1	2
1970–71	4	0	0	0	0
Totals	5	0	1	1	2

- first Leaf game April 5, 1970
- claimed June 8, 1971, by Sabres at Intra-League Draft

RANDY MURRAY

#26–3 defence   6'1" 195–R
b. Chatham, August 24, 1945

1969–70R/L	4	0	0	0	2

- first and only Leaf games November 9, 12, 15 and April 5, 1969–70

RIC NATTRESS

#2 defence   6'2" 210–R
b. Hamilton, May 25, 1962

1991–92	36	2	14	16	32

- acquired January 2, 1992, with Doug Gilmour, Jamie Macoun, Rick Wamsley, and Kent Manderville from Calgary for Gary Leeman, Michel Petit, Craig Berube, Alexander Godynyuk, and Jeff Reese
- signed August 21, 1992, as a free agent by Flyers
- won silver medal with Canada at 1991 WC

ZDENEK NEDVED ("Zed")

#45–20–10 right wing   6' 185–L
b. Pzkladno, Czechoslovakia, March 3, 1975

1994–95R	1	0	0	0	2
1995–96	7	1	1	2	6
1996–97	23	3	5	8	6
Totals	31	4	6	10	14

- selected 123rd overall in 1993 Entry Draft
- first Leaf game February 8, 1995
- played all of 1993–94 and most of 1994–95 with Sudbury Wolves
- missed half of 1995–96 with shoulder injury
- recalled from St. John's on January 6, 1997; demoted March 19, 1997
- later played in Europe

BOB NEELY ("Waldo")

#3 left wing   6'1" 210 L
b. Sarnia, November 9, 1953

1973–74R	54	5	7	12	98
1974–75	57	5	16	21	61
1975–76	69	9	13	22	89
1976–77	70	17	16	33	16
1977–78	11	0	1	1	0
Totals	261	36	53	89	264

- selected 10th overall at 1973 Amateur Draft
- first Leaf game October 10, 1973
- sold May 30, 1978, to Colorado Rockies

GORDIE NELSON

#27 defence   5'7" 180–L
b. Kinistino, Saskatchewan, May 10, 1947

1969–70R/L	3	0	0	0	11

- first and only Leaf games December 10, 11, 13, 1969
- acquired summer 1971 by Phoenix (WHL)

ERIC NESTERENKO ("Elbows"/"Nester")

#16–19–25 right wing 6'2" 197–R
b. Flin Flon, Manitoba, October 31, 1933

1951–52R	1	0	0	0	0
1952–53	35	10	6	16	27
1953–54	68	14	9	23	70
1954–55	62	15	15	30	99
1955–56	40	4	6	10	65
Totals	206	43	36	79	261

- first Leaf game March 5, 1952
- sold May 21, 1956, with Harry Lumley to Chicago for $40,000
- became part-time actor and ski patrol officer in Colorado

MIKE NEVILLE

#8 forward   5'9" 170–R
b. Grand Mère, Quebec, October 11, 1896
d. Unknown

1917–18	1	1	–	1	0
1924–25	12	1	0	1	4
1925–26	33	3	3	6	8
Totals	46	5	3	8	12

- acquired from London for 1924–25
- signed with Hamilton Tigers (OHA) prior to 1926–27

BOB NEVIN ("Nevvy")

#11 right wing   6' 190–R
b. South Porcupine, March 18, 1938

1957–58R	4	0	0	0	0
1958–59	2	0	0	0	2
1960–61	68	21	37	58	13
1961–62	69	15	30	45	10
1962–63	58	12	21	33	4
1963–64	49	7	12	19	26
Totals	250	55	100	155	55

- Marlie graduate; signed June 11, 1958, with Leafs
- first Leaf games December 8, January 25 and February 16, 22, 1957–58
- traded February 22, 1964, with Dick Duff, Rod Seiling, Arnie Brown, and Bill Collins to the Rangers for Andy Bathgate and Don McKenney
- became a man of leisure after leaving hockey

FRANK "DUTCH" NIGHBOR

("The Pembroke Peach"/"The Pembroke Pippin"/"The Flying Dutchman")
#7 centre   5'9" 160–L
b. Pembroke, January 26, 1893
d. Pembroke, April 13, 1966

1929–30L	22	2	0	2	2

- acquired January 6, 1930, from Ottawa Senators for Danny Cox until season's end only with an option to buy Cox's contract after. On May 4, 1930, Ottawa exercises the option, giving the Leafs cash to complete the deal
- last Leaf game March 18, 1930
- established an insurance company with his son in Pembroke
- Hockey Hall of Fame 1947

FRANK NIGRO

#32–16 centre   5'9" 180–R
b. Richmond Hill, February 11, 1960

1982–83R	51	6	15	21	23
1983–84L	17	2	3	5	16
Totals	68	8	18	26	39

- selected 93rd overall at 1979 Entry Draft
- first Leaf game October 23, 1982
- last Leaf game March 28, 1984
- signed with Merano (Italian League) summer 1984

- played with Italy (B pool) at 1989 wc (silver medal), 1990 wc (silver), 1991 wc (gold), and 1992 Olympics (twelfth place)

REG NOBLE

#8–4 left wing   5'8" 180–L
b. Collingwood, June 23, 1895
d. Alliston, January 19, 1962

1917–18	20	28	–	28	23
1918–19	17	11	3	14	35
1919–20	24	24	7	31	51
1920–21	24	20	6	26	54
1921–22	24	17	8	25	10
1922–23	24	12	10	22	41
1923–24	23	12	3	15	23
1924–25	3	1	0	1	4
Totals	159	125	37	162	241

- joined Arenas after NHA disbanded
- suspended for game of February 2, 1918, and fined $100 for breaking training rules
- suspended with Cameron on January 13, 1919, for breaking training rules; reinstated January 18
- sold December 9, 1924, to Maroons for $6,000
- Hockey Hall of Fame 1962

PAT NOLAN

forward   5'8" 170–L
b. Charlottetown, Prince Edward Island, December 1, 1897
d. April 12, 1957

1921–22R/L	2	0	0	0	0

- played most of 1921–22 in the Maritime Independent League (New Glasgow)
- first St. Pats game December 24, 1921

MIKE NYKOLUK

#24–27 right wing   5'11" 212–R
b. Toronto, December 11, 1934

1956–57R/L	32	3	1	4	20

- Marlie graduate

- recalled October 29, 1956, from Rochester to replace injured Brian Cullan
- recalled December 2, 1956, from Rochester when Billy Harris demoted
- first Leaf game October 31, 1956
- last Leaf game February 10, 1957
- traded summer 1958 with Ron Hurst and Wally Boyer to Hershey for Willie Marshall
- later became cigar-chomping coach for the Leafs

GARY NYLUND ("Beaker")

#2 defence   6'4" 210–L
b. Surrey, British Columbia, October 28, 1963

1982–83R	16	0	3	3	16
1983–84	47	2	14	16	103
1984–85	76	3	17	20	99
1985–86	79	2	16	18	180
Totals	218	7	50	57	398

- selected 3rd overall at 1982 Entry Draft
- first Leaf game February 6, 1982
- signed August 27, 1986, as a free agent by Chicago
- won gold medal with Canada at 1982 WJC

GERRY O'FLAHERTY

#16 left wing   5'10" 182–L
b. Pittsburgh, Pennsylvania, August 31, 1950

1971–72R	2	0	0	0	0

- selected 36th overall at 1970 Amateur Draft
- first and only Leaf games December 25, 26, 1971
- claimed June 5, 1972, by Vancouver Canucks at Intra-League Draft

ED OLCZYK ("Eddie O")

#16 centre   6'1" 200–L
b. Chicago, Illinois, August 16, 1966

1987–88	80	42	33	75	55
1988–89	80	38	52	90	75

1989–90	79	32	56	88	78
1990–91	18	4	10	14	13
Totals	257	116	151	267	221

- acquired September 4, 1987, with Al Secord from Chicago for Rick Vaive, Steve Thomas, and Bob McGill
- traded November 10, 1990, with Mark Osborne to Winnipeg Jets for Dave Ellett and Paul Fenton
- played for USA at 1984 Olympics (seventh place), 1985 WC (fourth), 1986 WC (sixth), 1987 WC (seventh), 1989 WC (sixth), and 1993 WC (sixth)

MURRAY OLIVER
#11 centre   5'9" 170–L
b. Hamilton, November 14, 1937

1967–68	74	16	21	37	18
1968–69	76	14	36	50	16
1969–70	76	14	33	47	16
Totals	226	44	90	134	50

- acquired May 15, 1967, with cash from Boston for Eddie Shack
- traded May 22, 1970, to Minnesota for Brian Conacher and Terry O'Malley
- later became a pro scout for Minnesota and then Vancouver

BERT OLMSTEAD
#16 left wing   6'2" 183–L
b. Scepter, Saskatchewan, September 4, 1926

1958–59	70	10	31	41	74
1959–60	53	15	21	36	63
1960–61	67	18	34	52	84
1961–62L	56	13	23	36	10
Totals	246	56	109	165	231

- claimed June 4, 1958, from the Canadiens at Intra-League draft
- last Leaf game March 11, 1962
- coached in WHL and NHL
- Hockey Hall of Fame 1985

TOM "WINDY" O'NEILL
#18 right wing   5'10" 155–R
b. Deseronto, September 28, 1923
d. Toronto, February 13, 1973

1943–44R	33	8	7	15	29
1944–45L	33	2	5	7	24
Totals	66	10	12	22	53

- St. Mike's graduate 1942
- first Leaf game November 27, 1942
- last Leaf game March 10, 1945
- best piano-playing hockeyist of his era
- became Toronto-area lawyer

MARK OSBORNE ("Ozzie")
#12–21 left wing   6'2" 205–L
b. Toronto, August 13, 1961

1986–87	16	5	10	15	12
1987–88	79	23	37	60	102
1988–89	75	16	30	46	112
1989–90	78	23	50	73	91
1990–91	18	3	3	6	4
1991–92	11	3	1	4	8
1992–93	76	12	14	26	89
1993–94	73	9	15	24	145
Totals	426	94	160	254	563

- acquired March 5, 1987, from the Rangers for Jeff Jackson and a 3rd-round draft choice in 1989 (Rob Zamuner)
- traded November 10, 1990, with Ed Olczyk to Winnipeg Jets for Dave Ellett and Paul Fenton
- acquired March 10, 1992, from Winnipeg Jets for Lucien Deblois
- signed August 26, 1994, as a free agent by the Rangers

RANDY OSBURN
#16 left wing   6' 190–L
b. Collingwood, November 26, 1952

1972–73R	26	0	2	2	0

- selected 27th overall in 1972 Amateur Draft

- first Leaf game October 7, 1972
- traded May 27, 1974, with Dave Fortier to Flyers for Bill Flett

WILF PAIEMENT
#99 right wing   6'1" 210–R
b. Earlton, October 16, 1955

1979–80	41	20	28	48	72
1980–81	77	40	57	97	145
1981–82	69	18	40	58	203
Totals	187	78	125	203	420

- acquired December 29, 1979, with Pat Hickey from Colorado Rockies for Lanny McDonald and Joel Quenneville
- traded March 9, 1982, to Quebec Nordiques for Miroslav Frycer and a 7th-round draft choice in 1982 (Jeff Triano)
- played for Canada at 1977 wc (fourth place), 1978 wc (bronze medal), and 1979 wc (fourth)

MIKE PALMATEER
("The Popcorn Kid"/"Palmy")
#29 goalie   5'9" 170–R
b. Toronto, January 13, 1954

1976–77R						
50 (4/1)	23–18–8	2877	154	4	3.21	
1977–78						
63 (0/1)	34–19–9	3760	172	5	2.74	
1978–79						
58 (2/2)	26–21–10	3396	167	4	2.95	
1979–80						
38 (5/4)	16–14–3	2039	125	2	3.68	
1982–83						
53 (6/0)	21–23–7	2955	197	0	3.99	
1983–84L						
34 (3/4)	9–17–4	1831	149	0	4.88	
Totals						
296 (20/12)	129–112–41	16858	964	15	3.43	

- selected 85th overall in 1974 Amateur Draft
- first Leaf game October 28, 1976

- traded June 11, 1980, with a 3rd-round draft choice in 1980 (Torrie Robertson) to Washington for Robert Picard, Tim Coulis, and a 2nd-round draft choice in 1980 (Bob McGill)
- bought September 9, 1982, from Washington
- last Leaf game February 5, 1984
- later ran a hamburger fast-food restaurant just north of Toronto and is now goalie coach with New York Islanders

JIM PAPPIN ("Pappy")
#17–18 right wing   6'1" 190–R
b. Copper Cliff, September 10, 1939

1963–64R	50	11	8	19	33
1964–65	44	9	9	18	33
1965–66	7	0	3	3	8
1966–67	64	21	11	32	89
1967–68	58	13	15	28	37
Totals	223	54	46	100	200

- Marlie graduate 1960
- first Leaf game November 23, 1963
- started 1964–65 with Leafs, sent to Rochester on February 4 for the rest of the season
- played first seven games of 1965–66, then demoted to Rochester on November 7 for the rest of the season
- played in Rochester from January 19–29 during 1966–67
- started 1967–68 with the Leafs, then demoted to Rochester on February 11 for the rest of the year
- traded March 23, 1968, to Chicago for Pierre Pilote
- became a scout for the St. Louis Blues

BERNIE PARENT

#30 goalie   5'10" 180–R

b. Montreal, Quebec, April 3, 1945

1970–71

18 (0/1)   7–7–3   1040   46   0   2.65

1971–72

47 (0/3)   17–18–9   2715   116   3   2.56

Totals

65 (0/4)   24–25–12   3755   162   3   2.59

- acquired February 1, 1971, with a 2nd-round draft choice in 1971 (Rick Kehoe) from Flyers for Bruce Gamble, Mike Walton, and a 1st-round draft choice in 1971 (Pierre Plante)
- rights traded July 27, 1973, with a 2nd-round draft choice in 1973 (Larry Goodenough) to Flyers for Doug Favell and a 1st-round draft choice in 1973 (Bob Neely)
- Hockey Hall of Fame 1984

BOB PARENT

#31 goalie   5'9" 175–R

b. Windsor, February 19, 1958

1981–82R

2 (0/0)   0–2–0   120   13   0   6.50

1982–83L

1 (0/1)   0–0–0   40   2   0   3.00

Totals

3 (0/1)   0–2–0   160   15   0   5.63

- selected 65th overall at 1978 Amateur Draft
- first Leaf games March 6, 10, 1982
- played with Leafs on February 26, 1983

JEAN-PAUL "J.P." PARISE

#17 left wing   5'9" 175–L

b. Smooth Rock Falls, December 11, 1941

1967–68   1   0   1   1   0

- acquired October 3, 1967, with Bryan Hextall from Oakland for Gerry Ehman
- first and only Leaf game November 15, 1967, then sent to Rochester for the year

- sold December 27, 1967, to Minnesota
- became involved in insurance for many years until he accepted an offer to run a hockey program at a prep school in Minnesota

GEORGE PARSONS

("Bubs"/"Cannonball")

#16–18–25–22 left wing   5'11" 174–L

b. Toronto, June 28, 1914

d. Toronto, June 30, 1998

1936–37R	5	0	0	0	0
1937–38	30	5	6	11	6
1938–39L	29	7	7	14	14
Totals	64	12	13	25	20

- signed October 22, 1935
- first Leaf game November 28, 1936
- struck in the eye by Earl Robinson's stick in a game March 4, 1939, vs. Chicago—forced to retire
- later worked for CCM and the NHL, designing the gauge used by officials to determine the legality of a stick's curve

GEORGE "PADDY" PATTERSON

#6 right wing   6'1" 176–r

b. Kingston, May 22, 1906

d. Kingston, January 22, 1977

1926–27R	17	4	2	6	17
1927–28	12	1	0	1	17
Totals	29	5	2	7	34

- bought February 6, 1927, from Hamilton Tigers (OHL)
- first St. Pats game February 8, 1927
- scored first Maple Leaf franchise goal February 17, 1927
- sent to Ravinas (Can Pro) on December 26, 1927
- traded February 8, 1928, to Canadiens for Gerry Carson

ROB PEARSON

#12 right wing   6'1" 185–R
b. Oshawa, August 3, 1971

1991–92R	47	14	10	24	58
1992–93	78	23	14	37	211
1993–94	67	12	18	30	189
Totals	192	49	42	91	458

- selected 12th overall at 1989 Entry Draft
- first Leaf game October 3, 1991
- traded June 28, 1994, with a 1st-round draft choice in 1994 (Nolan Baumgartner) to Washington for Mike Ridley and a 1st-round draft choice in 1994 (Eric Fichaud)

SCOTT PEARSON

#18–22 left wing   6'1" 205–L
b. Cornwall, December 19, 1969

1988–89R	9	0	1	1	2
1989–90	41	5	10	15	90
1990–91	12	0	0	0	20
1996–97	1	0	0	0	2
Totals	63	5	11	16	114

- selected 6th overall at 1988 Entry Draft
- first Leaf game October 6, 1988
- traded November 7, 1990, with a 2nd-round draft choice in 1991 (later traded to Washington—Eric Lavigne) and a 2nd-round draft choice in 1992 (Tuomas Gronman) to Quebec Nordiques for Michel Petit, Lucien Deblois, and Aaron Broten
- signed as a free agent July 8, 1996

TOM PEDERSON

#24 defence   5'9" 175–R
b. Bloomington, Minnesota, January 14, 1970

1996–97	15	1	2	3	9

- signed as a free agent December 13, 1996
- started 1996–97 in Japan, playing for Seibu Tetsudo Bears
- played for USA at 1989 WJC (fifth place), 1991 WC (fourth), and 1996 WC (sixth)

MIKE PELYK ("Mike Mikita"/"Kita")

#4–21–28 defence   6'1" 188–L
b. Toronto, September 29, 1947

1967–68R	24	0	3	3	55
1968–69	65	3	9	12	146
1969–70	36	1	3	4	37
1970–71	73	5	21	26	54
1971–72	46	1	4	5	44
1972–73	72	3	16	19	118
1973–74	71	12	19	31	94
1976–77	13	0	2	2	4
1977–78L	41	1	11	12	14
Totals	441	26	88	114	566

- selected 17th overall at 1964 Amateur Draft
- first Leaf game February 7, 1968
- missed November 19–January 4, 1969–70, with a broken collarbone
- signed July 1974 by Cincinnati Stingers (WHA) but loaned to Vancouver Blazers for the 1974–75 season
- signed September 1976 from Cincinnati (WHA) in exchange for Leafs keeping the rights to Randy Carlyle, who had agreed, but not signed, to play with Cincinnati
- last Leaf game April 9, 1978
- signed August 22, 1979, as free agent by Sabres
- became involved in many business opportunities after retiring, including commercial real estate, a development company, and a business consultant operation

FRED PERLINI

#8–28–29–32–34 centre 6'2" 175–L
b. Sault Ste. Marie, April 12, 1962

1981–82R	7	2	3	5	0
1983–84L	1	0	0	0	0
Totals	8	2	3	5	0

- selected 158th overall at 1980 Entry Draft
- first Leaf game December 30, 1981
- on Saturday, February 20, 1982, played afternoon game with Marlies, night game with Leafs
- last Leaf game April 1, 1984

YANIC PERREAULT ("Yan")
#44 centre 5'11" 182–L
b. Sherbrooke, Quebec, April 4, 1971

1993–94R	13	3	3	6	0
1998–99	12	7	8	15	12
1999–2000	58	18	27	45	22
2000–01	76	24	28	52	52
Totals	159	52	66	118	86

- selected 47th overall at 1991 Entry Draft
- first Leaf game November 6, 1993
- traded June 14, 1994, to Los Angeles for a 4th-round draft choice in 1996 (later traded to Flyers with a 1st-round draft choice in 1996 (Dainius Zubrus) and a 2nd-round draft choice in 1997 for Dmitri Yushkevich and a 2nd-round draft choice in 1996 (Francis Larivee); Flyers later traded pick back to Los Angeles (Mikael Simmons)
- reacquired from Los Angeles on March 23, 1999, for Jason Podollan and a 3rd-round draft choice in 1999 (Cory Campbell)
- won silver medal with Canada at 1996 WC

MICHEL PETIT
#22–24 defence 6'1" 205–R
b. St. Malo, Quebec, February 12, 1964

1990–91	54	9	19	28	132
1991–92	34	1	13	14	85
Totals	88	10	32	42	217

- acquired November 17, 1990, with Lucien Deblois and Aaron Broten from Quebec Nordiques for Scott Pearson, a 2nd-round draft choice in 1991 (later traded to Washington—Eric Lavigne), and a 2nd-round draft choice in 1992 (Tuomas Gronman)
- traded January 2, 1992, with Gary Leeman, Craig Berube, Jeff Reese, and Alexander Godynyuk to Calgary for Doug Gilmour, Jamie Macoun, Ric Nattress, Rick Wamsley, and Kent Manderville
- played with Canada at 1990 WC (fourth place)

- holds NHL record for playing with most teams (10)
- retired because of concussions

ERIC "COWBOY" PETTINGER ("Gosh")
#10 left wing 6' 175–L
b. North Bierley, England, December 14, 1904
d. December 24, 1968

1928–29	25	3	3	6	24
1929–30	43	4	9	13	40
Totals	68	7	12	19	64

- acquired January 8, 1929, with the rights to Hugh Plaxton from Boston in return for the rights to George Owen
- traded October 11, 1930, with Art Smith and $35,000 to Ottawa Senators for King Clancy

ROBERT PICARD
#4 defence 6'2" 207–L
b. Montreal, Quebec, May 25, 1957

1980–81	59	6	19	25	68

- acquired June 11, 1980, with Tim Coulis and a 2nd-round draft choice in 1980 (Bob McGill) from Washington for Mike Palmateer and a 3rd-round draft choice in 1980 (Torrie Robertson)
- traded March 10, 1981, with an 8th-round draft choice in 1982 (Steve Smith) to Canadiens for Michel Larocque
- played with Canada at 1978 WC (bronze medal) and 1979 WC (fourth place)

PIERRE PILOTE ("Pete")
#2 defence 5'10" 178–L
b. Kenogami, Quebec, December 11, 1931

1968–69L	69	3	18	21	46

- acquired May 23, 1968, from Chicago for Jim Pappin
- last Leaf game March 30, 1969
- claimed June 12, 1969, by Sabres in Reverse Draft

- owned a car dealership and small chain of laundromats, and became a hobby farmer after his playing days
- Hockey Hall of Fame 1975

CAM PLANTE

#11 defence   6′1″ 195–L
b. Brandon, Manitoba, March 12, 1964

1984–85R/L	2	0	0	0	0

- selected 133rd overall at 1983 Entry Draft
- first and only Leaf games March 16, 18, 1985

JACQUES PLANTE ("Jake the Snake")

#1 goalie   6′ 175–L
b. Mont Carmel, Quebec, January 17, 1929
d. Geneva, Switzerland, February 26, 1986

1970–71					
40 (3/0)	24–11–4	2329	73	4	1.88
1971–72					
34 (3/0)	16–13–5	1965	86	2	2.63
1972–73					
32 (5/2)	8–14–6	1717	87	1	3.04

Totals
106 (11/2)   48–38–15   6011   246   7   2.46

- acquired May 3, 1970, with Denis Dupere and Guy Trottier from the Rangers for Tim Horton
- traded March 3, 1973, with a 3rd-round draft choice in 1973 (Doug Gibson) to Boston for a 1st-round draft choice in 1973 (Ian Turnbull) and future considerations (Ed Johnston)
- wrote the first book on goaltending, coached goalies in the WHA, and died of stomach cancer
- Hockey Hall of Fame 1978

WALT PODDUBNY ("Sarge")

#8–12 left wing   6′1″ 210–L
b. Thunder Bay, February 14, 1960

1981–82	11	3	4	7	8
1982–83	72	28	31	59	71
1983–84	38	11	14	25	48
1984–85	32	5	15	20	26
1985–86	33	12	22	34	25

Totals   186   59   86   145   178

- acquired March 8, 1982, with Phil Drouilliard from Edmonton for Laurie Boschman
- traded August 18, 1986, to the Rangers for Mike Allison

JASON PODOLLAN ("Pods")

#7–37 right wing   6′1″ 192–R
b. Vernon, British Columbia, February 18, 1976

1996–97	10	0	3	3	6
1998–99	4	0	0	0	0

Totals   14   0   3   3   6

- acquired March 18, 1997, from Florida for Kirk Muller
- traded to Los Angeles with a 3rd-round draft choice in 1999 (Cory Campbell) for Yanic Perreault on March 23, 1999
- won gold medal with Canada at 1996 WJC

NORMAN "BUD" POILE

#7–11–16–25 centre   6′ 185–R
b. Fort William, February 10, 1924

1942–43R	48	16	19	35	24
1943–44	11	6	8	14	9
1945–46	9	1	8	9	0
1946–47	59	19	17	36	19
1947–48	4	2	0	2	0

Totals   131   44   52   96   52

- first Leaf game October 31, 1942
- missed 1944–45 with Canadian armed forces; returned February 27, 1946
- traded November 2, 1947, with Gus Bodnar, Gaye Stewart, Bob Goldham, and

Ernie Dickens to Chicago for Max Bentley and Cy Thomas
- became general manager in Vancouver and Philadelphia after expansion, and later commissioner of IHL for many years
- Hockey Hall of Fame 1990 (Builder)

ALEXEI PONIKAROVSKY
#39 right wing   6'4" 196–L
b. Kiev, USSR, April 9, 1980

2000–01R	22	1	3	4	14

- selected 87th overall at 1998 Entry Draft
- first Leafs game January 10, 2001

FELIX POTVIN ("The Cat")
#29 goalie   6' 180–L
b. Montreal, Quebec, June 23, 1971

1991–92R						
4 (0/1)	0–2–1	210	8	0	2.29	
1992–93						
48 (1/2)	25–15–7	2781	116	2	2.50	
1993–94						
66 (4/0)	34–22–9	3883	187	3	2.89	
1994–95						
36 (1/0)	15–13–7	2144	104	0	2.91	
1995–96						
69 (3/3)	30–26–11	4009	192	2	2.87	
1996–97						
74 (6/3)	27–36–7	4271	224	0	3.15	
1997–98						
67 (5/2)	26–33–7	3864	176	5	2.73	
1998–99						
5 (0/0)	3–2–0	299	19	0	3.81	

Totals
369 (20/11) 160–149–49 21461 1026 12 2.87

- selected 31st overall at 1990 Entry Draft
- first Leaf game November 14, 1991
- traded to the Islanders on January 9, 1999, with a 6th-round draft choice in 1999 (later traded to Tampa Bay—Fedor Fedorov) for Bryan Berard and a 6th-round draft choice in 1999 (Jan Sochar)
- won gold medal with Canada at 1991 WJC and played at 1998 WC (sixth place)
- currently with Los Angeles Kings

TRACY PRATT
#4 defence   6'2" 195–L
b. New York, New York, March 8, 1943

1976–77L	11	0	1	1	8

- acquired March 8, 1977, from Colorado Rockies for a 3rd-round draft choice in 1977 (Randy Pierce)
- only Leaf games March 9, 12, 13, 15, 16, 19, 21, 26, 27, 30 and April 2, 1977
- later ran a nightclub in British Columbia

WALTER "BABE" PRATT
("The Honest Brakeman"/"The Big Pussycat")
#4–2–12 defence   6'3" 210–L
b. Stony Mountain, Manitoba, January 7, 1916
d. Vancouver, British Columbia, December 16, 1988

1942–43	40	12	25	37	34
1943–44	50	17	40	57	30
1944–45	50	18	23	41	39
1945–46	41	5	20	25	36
Totals	181	52	108	160	139

- acquired November 27, 1942, from the Rangers for Hank Goldup and Dudley Garrett
- missed one month of 1942–43 with separated shoulder
- sold June 23, 1946, to Boston for cash and the rights to Eric Pogue
- became a spokesman for the Vancouver Canucks
- Hockey Hall of Fame 1966

ERIC PRENTICE ("Doc")
#17 defence   5'11" 150–L
b. Schumacher, August 22, 1926

1943–44R/L	5	0	0	0	4

- signed October 29, 1943
- first and only Leaf games October 30, 31 and November 4, 7, 18, 1943
- traded October 11, 1945, to Detroit for George Mara

WAYNE PRESLEY
#18 right wing   5'11" 180–R
b. Dearborn, Michigan, March 23, 1965

1995–96	19	2	2	4	14

- acquired February 29, 1996, with Nick Kypreos from Rangers for Sergio Momesso and Bill Berg
- bought out mid-October 1996

NOEL PRICE
#23 defence   6' 185–L
b. Brockville, December 9, 1935

1957–58R	1	0	0	0	5
1958–59	28	0	0	0	4
Totals	29	0	0	0	9

- St. Mike's graduate
- first Leaf game October 23, 1957
- traded October 25, 1959, to the Rangers for Hank Ciesla, Earl Johnson, and rights to Bill Kennedy
- taught hockey to kids in Ontario's North

JOE PRIMEAU ("Little Joe"/"Gentleman Joe")
#10–7–15 centre   5'11" 153–L
b. Lindsay, January 29, 1906
d. Toronto, May 15, 1989

1927–28R	2	0	0	0	0
1928–29	6	0	1	1	2
1929–30	43	5	21	26	22
1930–31	38	9	32	41	18
1931–32	46	13	37	50	25
1932–33	48	11	21	32	4
1933–34	45	14	32	46	8
1934–35	37	10	20	30	16
1935–36L	45	4	13	17	10
Totals	310	66	177	243	105

- St. Mike's graduate
- first Leaf game November 22, 1927
- loaned November 28, 1928, to London, subject to immediate recall
- retired August 21, 1936
- last Leaf game March 21, 1936
- later coached Leafs
- Hockey Hall of Fame 1963

MARTIN PROCHAZKA
#21 right wing   5'11" 180–R
b. Slany, Czechoslovakia, March 3, 1972

1997–98R	29	2	4	6	8

- selected 135th overall at 1991 Entry Draft
- traded to Atlanta for a 6th-round draft choice in 2001 (Max Kondratiev)
- played for Czechoslovakia at 1990 WJC (bronze medal), 1991 WJC (bronze), and 1992 WJC (fifth place); played for Cezch Republic at 1995 WC (fourth), 1996 WC (gold), 1997 WC (bronze), 1998 Olympics (gold), 1998 WC (bronze), 1999 WC (gold), 2000 WC (gold), and 2001 WC (gold)

GEORGE "GOLDIE" PRODGERS
(sometimes "Prodger")
forward   5'10" 180–R
b. London, October 18, 1891
d. London, October 25, 1935

1919–20R	16	8	6	14	2

- acquired January 14, 1920, from Canadiens for Harry Cameron (after that night's game)
- loaned by Toronto to Hamilton Tigers (NHL) during season to coach team
- later coached amateur teams in Southern Ontario

MARCEL PRONOVOST
#3 defence   6' 190–L
b. Lac la Tortue, Quebec, June 15, 1930

1965–66	54	2	8	10	34
1966–67	58	2	12	14	28
1967–68	70	3	17	20	48
1968–69	34	1	2	3	20
1969–70L	7	0	1	1	4
Totals	223	8	40	48	134

- acquired May 20, 1965, with Lowell MacDonald, Larry Jeffrey, Ed Joyal, and Aut Erickson from Detroit for Andy Bathgate, Billy Harris, and Gary Jarrett

- played most of 1969–70 and part of 1970–71 with Tulsa as a player/coach before retiring as a player to continue as coach
- last Leaf game December 27, 1969
- part of Detroit front office for Stanley Cups in 1997 and 1998
- Hockey Hall of Fame 1978

AL PUDAS

#14 left wing   5'10" 160–L
b. Siikajoki, Finland, February 17, 1899
d. Thunder Bay, October 28, 1976

1926–27R/L	4	0	0	0	0

- signed in fall 1926 and assigned to Port Arthur
- recalled December 28, 1926, from Windsor
- first and only St. Pats games December 30 and January 1, 4, 8, 1926–27
- sent to Windsor Hornets January 10, 1927; never made it back to the NHL
- coached Canada's 1936 Olympic team (silver medal)

BOB PULFORD ("Pully")

#20 left wing   5'11" 188–L
b. Newton Robinson, March 31, 1936

1956–57R	65	11	11	22	32
1957–58	70	14	17	31	48
1958–59	70	23	14	37	53
1959–60	70	24	28	52	81
1960–61	40	11	18	29	41
1961–62	70	18	21	39	98
1962–63	70	19	25	44	49
1963–64	70	18	30	48	73
1964–65	65	19	20	39	46
1965–66	70	28	28	56	51
1966–67	67	17	28	45	28
1967–68	74	20	30	50	40
1968–69	72	11	23	34	20
1969–70	74	18	19	37	31
Totals	947	251	312	563	691

- Marlie graduate (won Allan Cup 1954–55 and 1955–56)
- first Leaf game October 25, 1956

- traded September 3, 1970, to Los Angeles Kings for Garry Monahan and Brian Murphy
- has been general manager or coach with Chicago since 1977
- Hockey Hall of Fame 1991

DAREN PUPPA ("Poops")

#1 goalie   6'3" 205–R
b. Kirkland Lake, March 23, 1963

1992–93					
8 (0/0)	6–2–0	479	18	2	2.25

- acquired February 2, 1993, with Dave Andreychuk and a 1st-round draft choice in 1993 (Kenny Jonsson) from Sabres for Grant Fuhr and a 5th-round draft choice in 1995 (Kevin Popp)
- claimed June 24, 1993, by Florida in Expansion Draft

JOEL QUENNEVILLE ("Herbie")

#3 defence   6'1" 200–L
b. Windsor, September 15, 1958

1978–79R	61	2	9	11	60
1979–80	32	1	4	5	24
Totals	93	3	13	16	84

- selected 21st overall at 1978 Amateur Draft
- first Leaf game October 22, 1978
- traded December 29, 1979, with Lanny McDonald to Colorado Rockies for Pat Hickey and Wilf Paiement
- currently coach of St. Louis Blues

PAT QUINN

#23 defence   6'3" 215–L
b. Hamilton, January 19, 1943

1968–69R	40	2	7	9	95
1969–70	59	0	5	5	88
Totals	99	2	12	14	183

- bought March 25, 1968, from St. Louis
- first Leaf game November 27, 1968

- played October 16–November 24, 1968, in Tulsa
- missed December 7–27, 1969, with a torn shoulder muscle; sent to Tulsa February 28–March 5, 1970
- claimed June 10, 1970, by Vancouver Canucks at Expansion Draft
- current coach and general manager of the Leafs

ROB RAMAGE ("Rammer")
#8 defence   6'2" 200–L
b. Byron, January 11, 1959

1989–90	80	8	41	49	202
1990–91	80	10	25	35	173
Totals	160	18	66	84	375

- acquired June 16, 1989, from Calgary for a 2nd-round draft choice in 1989 (Kent Manderville)
- claimed May 30, 1991, by Minnesota at Expansion Draft
- won silver medal with Canada at 1977 WJC and bronze at 1978 WJC; played at 1981 WC (fourth place)
- worked for a brokerage firm in St. Louis

BEATTIE RAMSAY
#2 defence   5'7" 143–L
b. Lumsden, Saskatchewan, December 12, 1895
d. Regina, Saskatchewan, October 1, 1952

1927–28R/L	43	0	2	2	10

- signed for the 1927–28 season on March 16, 1927, while still coach of hockey at Princeton University
- member of University of Toronto Grads gold medal team at 1928 Olympics
- first Leaf game November 15, 1927
- last Leaf game March 24, 1928

KEN RANDALL
#3 right wing   5'10" 180–R
b. Kingston, December 14, 1888
d. Toronto, June 17, 1947

1917–18	20	12	–	12	55
1918–19	14	7	6	13	27
1919–20	21	10	7	17	43
1920–21	21	6	1	7	58
1921–22	24	10	6	16	20
1922–23	24	3	5	8	51
Totals	124	48	25	73	254

- missed last game of 1918–19 to play in Glace Bay
- missed first three games of 1920–21 in contract dispute
- traded December 1923 with Corb Denneny to Hamilton Tigers (NHL) for Bert Corbeau and Amos Arbour
- coached after retiring in 1928

MARC REAUME
#2–25 defence   6'1" 185–L
b. Lasalle, Quebec, February 7, 1934

1954–55R	1	0	0	0	4
1955–56	48	0	12	12	50
1956–57	63	6	14	20	81
1957–58	68	1	7	8	49
1958–59	51	1	5	6	67
1959–60	36	0	1	1	6
Totals	267	8	39	47	257

- St. Mike's graduate 1952
- first Leaf game March 20, 1955
- traded February 10, 1960, to Detroit for Red Kelly
- career ended by injuries suffered in a car crash in 1971

JEFF REESE ("Reeser")
#1–35 goalie   5'9" 170–L
b. Brantford, March 24, 1966

1987–88R						
5 (1/1)	1–2–1	249	17	0	4.10	
1988–89						
10 (2/3)	2–6–1	486	40	0	4.94	

1989–90
21 (2/3)   9–6–3   1101   81   0   4.42
1990–91
30 (7/11)   6–13–3   1430   92   1   3.86
1991–92
8 (1/3)   1–5–1   413   20   1   2.91
1998–99
2 (0/1)   1–1–0   106   8   0   4.53

Totals
76 (13/22) 20-33-9 3785 258 2 4.13

- selected 67th overall at 1984 Entry Draft
- first Leaf games January 10, 13, 15, 27 and February 14, 1988
- traded January 2, 1992, with Gary Leeman, Michel Petit, Craig Berube, and Alexander Godynyuk to Calgary for Doug Gilmour, Jamie Macoun, Ric Nattress, Rick Wamsley, and Kent Manderville
- while with Calgary set a record for goalies by recording three assists in one game
- signed as a free agent on January 5, 1999
- traded to Tampa Bay on August 6, 1999, with a 9th-round draft choice in 2000 (later traded to Philadelphia—Milan Kopecky) for a 9th-round draft choice in 2000 (Jean-Phillipe Côté)

LARRY REGAN
#8 right wing   5'9" 178–R
b. North Bay, August 9, 1930

1958–59	32	4	21	25	2
1959–60	47	4	16	20	6
1960–61L	37	3	5	8	2

Totals   116   11   42   53   10

- claimed on waivers January 7, 1959, from Boston
- last Leaf game March 19, 1961
- became playing coach of Hornets on June 14, 1961
- later coached in Austria

DAVE REID
#18–25 forward   6'2" 180–L
b. Toronto, January 11, 1934
d. 1978

1952–53R	2	0	0	0	0
1954–55	1	0	0	0	0
1955–56L	4	0	0	0	0

Totals   7   0   0   0   0

- first Leaf games December 10 and 13, 1952
- played March 20, 1955
- played November 3, 11, 16, 19, 1955

DAVID REID
#34–14 left wing   6'1" 205–L
b. Toronto, May 15, 1964

1988–89	77	9	21	30	22
1989–90	70	9	19	28	9
1990–91	69	15	13	28	18

Totals   216   33   53   86   49

- signed June 23, 1988, as free agent
- signed December 1, 1991, as free agent by Boston
- won Stanley Cup with Colorado in 2000–01

REG "RUSTY" REID
#12 forward   5'8" 138–L
b. Seaforth, February 17, 1899
d. Stratford, mid-1980s

1924–25R	28	2	0	2	2
1925–26L	12	0	0	0	2

Totals   40   2   0   2   4

- signed November 12, 1924, from Seaforth (OHA Intermediate)
- first St. Pats game November 29, 1924
- last St. Pats game January 9, 1926
- moved to Stratford and became a salesman after retiring

BOBBY REYNOLDS

#20 left wing   5'11" 175–L
b. Flint, Michigan, July 14, 1967

1989–90R/L	7	1	1	2	0

- selected 190th overall at 1985 Entry Draft
- first and only Leaf games March 14, 16, 17, 19, 21, 24, 28, 1990
- traded March 5, 1991, to Washington for Robert Mendel

DAMIAN RHODES ("Dusty")

#31–1 goalie   6' 165–L
b. St. Paul, Minnesota, May 28, 1969

1990–91R						
1 (0/0)	1–0–0	60	1	0	1.00
1993–94						
22 (0/4)	9–7–3	1213	53	0	2.62
1994–95						
13 (0/1)	6–6–1	760	34	0	2.68
1995–96						
11 (1/1)	4–5–1	624	29	0	2.79
Totals						
47 (1/6)	20–18–5	2657	117	0	2.64

- selected 112th overall at 1987 Entry Draft
- first Leaf game March 22, 1991
- traded January 23, 1996, to Ottawa with Ken Belanger to the Islanders; Leafs received Kirk Muller from New York and Don Beaupre from Ottawa; Ottawa sent Bryan Berard and Martin Straka to Islanders; New York sent Wade Redden to Senators
- played for USA at 1988 WJC (sixth place) and at 2000 WC (fifth)
- currently with Atlanta Thrashers

PAT RIBBLE

#3 defence   6'4" 210–L
b. Leamington, April 26, 1954

1979–80	13	0	2	2	2

- acquired January 10, 1980, from Chicago for Dave Hutchison

- traded February 16, 1980, to Washington for Mike Kaszycki
- won bronze medal with Canada at 1978 WC

LUKE RICHARDSON

#2 defence   6'3" 215–L
b. Ottawa, March 26, 1969

1987–88R	78	4	6	10	90
1988–89	55	2	7	9	106
1989–90	67	4	14	18	122
1990–91	78	1	9	10	238
Totals	278	11	36	47	556

- selected 7th overall in 1987 Entry Draft
- first Leaf game October 8, 1987
- traded September 19, 1991, with Vincent Damphousse, Peter Ing, and Scott Thornton to Edmonton for Grant Fuhr, Glenn Anderson, and Craig Berube
- played for Canada at 1987 WJC (disqualified); won gold medal at 1994 WC and silver at 1996 WC

CURT RIDLEY

#1–33–35 goalie   6' 190–L
b. Minnedosa, Manitoba, October 24, 1951

1979–80						
3 (1/1)	0–1–0	110	8	0	4.36
1980–81L						
3 (1/1)	1–1–0	124	12	0	5.81
Totals						
6 (2/2)	1–2–0	234	20	0	5.13

- bought February 10, 1980, from Vancouver Canucks
- last Leaf games November 9, 19, 28, 1980

MIKE RIDLEY

#7 centre   6' 195–L
b. Winnipeg, Manitoba, July 8, 1963

1994–95	48	10	27	37	14

- acquired June 28, 1994, with a 1st-round draft choice in 1994 (Eric Fichaud) from

Washington for Rob Pearson and a 1st-round draft choice in 1994 (Nolan Baumgartner)

- traded July 9, 1995, to Vancouver Canucks for Sergio Momesso

DAVE RITCHIE
#11 forward   5'8" 180–R
b. Montreal, January 12, 1892
d. Unknown

1918–19	5	0	0	0	9

- first and only Arenas games January 21, 28 and February 4, 6, 11, 1919
- signed with Quebec Bulldogs (NHL) for the 1919–20 season

JOHN ROSS ROACH
("The Port Perry Woodpecker"/"Rossie")
#1 goalie   5'5" 130–L
b. Port Perry, June 23, 1900
d. Windsor, July 9, 1973

1921–22R						
22 (0/0)	11–10–1	1340	91	0	4.07
1922–23					
24 (0/0)	13–10–1	1469	88	1	3.59
1923–24					
23 (0/0)	10–13–0	1380	80	1	3.48
1924–25					
30 (0/0)	19–11–0	1800	84	1	2.80
1925–26					
36 (0/0)	12–21–3	2210	114	2	3.10
1926–27					
44 (0/0)	15–24–5	2764	94	4	2.04
1927–28					
43 (0/0)	18–18–7	2690	88	4	1.96

Totals
222 (0/0) 98–107–17 13653 639 13 2.81

- signed December 5, 1921, after graduating from Toronto Granites
- traded October 17, 1928, with Butch Keeling to the Rangers for Lorne Chabot, Alex Gray, and $20,000

MICHAEL "MICKEY" ROACH ("Port")
#8 centre   5'7" 160–L
b. Boston, Massachusetts, May 1, 1895
d. Whitby, April 1, 1977

1919–20R	20	10	2	12	4
1920–21	8	1	0	1	2
Totals	28	11	2	13	6

- signed from Hamilton (OHA Senior) on December 16, 1919
- first St. Pats game December 23, 1919
- sent to Hamilton Tigers (NHL) in January 1921

RENÉ ROBERT
#14 right wing   5'10" 184–R
b. Trois-Rivières, Quebec, December 31, 1948

1970–71R	5	0	0	0	0
1980–81	14	6	7	13	8
1981–82L	55	13	24	37	37
Totals	74	19	31	50	45

- first games March 13, 14, 18, 20, 21, 1971
- claimed June 8, 1971, by Penguins at Intra-League Draft
- acquired January 30, 1981, from Colorado Rockies for a 3rd-round draft choice in 1981 (Ulrich Heimer)
- released during 1981–82 season
- last Leaf game March 3, 1982
- current president of NHL Alumni Association

GARY ROBERTS
#7 left wing   6'1" 190–L
b. North York, May 23, 1966

2000–01	82	29	24	53	109

- signed as a free agent on July 4, 2000
- currently with Leafs
- won silver medal with Canada at 1986 WJC

FRED ROBERTSON

#18–17 defence   5'10" 198–L
b. Carlisle, England, October 22, 1911

1931–32R	11	0	0	0	23

- Marlie graduate 1931; signed as a free agent February 24, 1932
- first and only Leaf games February 25, 27 and March 1, 5, 10, 12, 15, 17, 19, 20, 22, 1932
- sold to Detroit on November 13, 1933, for $6,500

EDDIE RODDEN

#12 forward   5'7" 150–R
b. Toronto, March 22, 1901
d. Toronto, September 10, 1986

1927–28	25	3	6	9	36

- acquired December 12, 1927, from Chicago; Leafs sent Bert McCaffery and cash to Pirates; Pirates sent Ty Arbour to Chicago
- sold to Boston for cash on June 20, 1928

ELWIN "AL" ROLLINS ("Ally")

#23 goalie   6'2" 175–L
b. Vanguard, Saskatchewan, October 9, 1926
d. Calgary, Alberta, July 27, 1996

1949–50R							
2 (0/1)	1–1–0	100	4	1	2.40		
1950–51							
40 (1/0)	27–5–8	2373	70	5	1.77		
1951–52							
70 (0/1)	29–24–16	4170	154	5	2.22		

Totals
112 (1/2)   57–30–24   6643   228   11   2.06

- bought November 30, 1949, from Cleveland (AHL) for Bob Dawes, future considerations and $40,000
- first Leaf games December 24 and March 25, 1949–50

- traded September 11, 1952, with Gus Mortson, Cal Gardner, and Ray Hannigan to Chicago for Harry Lumley
- remained in hockey all his life as a coach, player agent, and team manager

ELWIN "DOC" ROMNES

#7 forward   5'11" 156–L
b. White Bear, Minnesota, January 1, 1907
d. Colorado Springs, Colorado, July 21, 1984

1938–39	36	7	16	23	0

- acquired December 7, 1938, from Chicago for Bill Thoms
- traded May 18, 1939, with Busher Jackson, Buzz Boll, and Murray Armstrong to New York Americans for Sweeney Schriner

BILL ROOT ("Rooter")

#25–28–34 defence   6'2" 210–R
b. Toronto, September 6, 1959

1984–85	35	1	1	2	23
1985–86	27	0	1	1	29
1986–87	34	3	3	6	37
Totals	96	4	5	9	89

- acquired August 21, 1984, with a 2nd-round draft choice in 1986 (Darryl Shannon) from Canadiens for Dom Campedelli
- traded September 9, 1987, to Hartford for Dave Semenko
- acquired June 21, 1988, from Flyers for Mike Stothers

BOB ROUSE

#28–3 defence   6'1" 210–R
b. Surrey, British Columbia, June 18, 1964

1990–91	13	2	4	6	10
1991–92	79	3	19	22	97
1992–93	82	3	11	14	130
1993–94	63	5	11	16	101
Totals	237	13	45	58	338

- acquired January 16, 1991, with Peter Zezel from Washington for Al Iafrate
- signed August 5, 1994, as a free agent by Detroit
- played for Canada at 1987 WC (fourth place)

DUANE RUPP
#3–4–17 defence   6'1" 185–L
b. MacNutt, Saskatchewan, March 29, 1938

1964–65	2	0	0	0	0
1965–66	2	0	1	1	0
1966–67	3	0	0	0	0
1967–68	71	1	8	9	42
Totals	78	1	9	10	42

- acquired June 25, 1964, with Ed Ehrenverth from the Rangers for Lou Angotti and Ed Lawson
- played February 21, 24, 1965
- played February 9, 13, 1966
- played February 15 and March 11, 12, 1967
- claimed June 12, 1968, by Minnesota at Intra-League Draft
- coached in AHL for years before becoming manager of an arena in Pittsburgh

JIM RUTHERFORD
#1 goalie   5'8" 168–L
b. Beeton, February 17, 1949

1980–81					
18 (1/2)	4–10–2	961	82	0	5.12

- acquired December 4, 1980, from Detroit for Mark Kirton
- traded March 10, 1981, to Los Angeles Kings for a 5th-round draft choice in 1981 (Barry Brigley)
- played for Canada at 1977 WC (fourth place) and 1979 WC (fourth)
- currently general manager of Carolina Hurricanes

WARREN RYCHEL
#21 left wing   6' 190–L
b. Tecumseh, May 12, 1967

1994–95	26	1	6	7	101

- acquired February 10, 1995, from Washington for a 4th-round draft choice in 1995 (Sebastien Charpentier)
- traded October 2, 1995, to Colorado Avalanche for future considerations (cash)

BOB SABOURIN
#16 right wing   5'9" 205–L
b. Sudbury, March 17, 1933

1951–52R/L	1	0	0	0	2

- first and only Leaf game March 13, 1952, while attending St. Mike's
- sold May 28, 1956, to Springfield with Bob Bailey for $22,000

GARY SABOURIN
#15 right wing   5'11" 180–R
b. Parry Sound, December 4, 1943

1974–75	55	5	18	23	26

- acquired May 27, 1974, from St. Louis for Ed Johnston
- traded June 20, 1975, to California for Stan Weir
- has run a food franchise in Chatham, Ontario, since retiring because of knee injuries

DAVID SACCO
#7 forward   6' 180–R
b. Malden, Massachusetts, July 31, 1970

1993–94R	4	1	1	2	4

- selected 195th overall at 1988 Entry Draft
- first and only Leaf games March 4, 5, 7, 9, 1994
- traded September 28, 1994, to Anaheim for Terry Yake
- played for USA at 1993 WC (sixth place) and 1994 Olympics (eighth)

JOE SACCO

#20–24 left wing   6'1" 180–R
b. Medford, Massachusetts,
February 4, 1969

1990–91R	20	0	5	5	2
1991–92	17	7	4	11	6
1992–93	23	4	4	8	8
Totals	60	11	13	24	16

- selected 71st overall at 1987 Entry Draft
- first Leaf game November 10, 1990
- claimed June 24, 1993, by Anaheim in the Expansion Draft
- played for USA at 1989 WJC (fifth place), 1990 WC (fifth), 1994 WC (fourth), and 1996 WC (bronze medal)

ROCKY SAGANIUK

#7–8 forward   5'8" 185–R
b. Myrnam, Alberta, October 15, 1957

1978–79R	16	3	5	8	9
1979–80	75	24	23	47	52
1980–81	71	12	18	30	52
1981–82	65	17	16	33	49
1982–83	3	0	0	0	2
Totals	230	56	62	118	164

- selected 29th overall at 1977 Amateur Draft
- first Leaf game December 13, 1978
- traded August 15, 1983, with Vincent Tremblay to Penguins for Pat Graham and Nick Ricci
- went into business in St. Catharines

RICK ST. CROIX

#1 goalie   5'10" 160–L
b. Kenora, January 3, 1955

1982–83						
16 (0/2)	4–9–2	920	57	0	3.80
1983–84						
20 (9/5)	5–10–0	939	80	0	5.11
1984–85L						
11 (1/0)	2–9–0	628	54	0	5.16
Totals						
47 (10/7)	11–28–2	2487	191	0	4.61

- acquired January 11, 1983, from Flyers for Michel Larocque
- released after 1984–85

BORJE SALMING ("King"/"B.J.")

#21 defence   6'1" 193–L
b. Kiruna, Sweden, April 17, 1951

1973–74R	76	5	34	39	48
1974–75	60	12	25	37	34
1975–76	78	16	41	57	70
1976–77	76	12	66	78	46
1977–78	80	16	60	76	70
1978–79	78	17	56	73	76
1979–80	74	19	52	71	94
1980–81	72	5	61	66	154
1981–82	69	12	44	56	170
1982–83	69	7	38	45	104
1983–84	68	5	38	43	92
1984–85	73	6	33	39	76
1985–86	41	7	15	22	48
1986–87	56	4	16	20	42
1987–88	66	2	24	26	82
1988–89	63	3	17	20	86
Totals	1099	148	620	768	1292

- signed May 12, 1973, as free agent
- first Leaf game October 10, 1973
- signed June 12, 1989, as a free agent by Detroit
- played for Sweden at 1972 WC (bronze medal), 1973 WC (silver), 1989 WC (fourth), and 1992 Olympics (fifth)
- Hockey Hall of Fame 1996; IIHF Hall of Fame 1998

PHIL SAMIS

#23 defence   5'10" 180–R
b. Edmonton, Alberta, December 28, 1927

1949–50R/L	2	0	0	0	0

- signed September 25, 1947, by Leafs
- called up for 1948 playoffs
- first and only regular season Leaf games November 20, 23, 1949
- sent to Cleveland (AHL) summer 1950

CHARLIE SANDS

#3–16–17 centre   5'9" 160–R
b. Fort William, March 23, 1911
d. Hollywood, California, April 16, 1953

1932–33R	3	0	3	3	0
1933–34	45	8	8	16	2
Totals	48	8	11	19	2

- signed as free agent March 27, 1932
- first Leaf games March 18, 21, 23, 1933
- recalled March 17, 1933, to replace injured Bailey
- sold to Boston at the start of the 1934–35 season
- later played in Pasadena league, and after retiring from hockey worked at the Hollywood Bowl

TERRY SAWCHUK ("Ukey"/"Saw")

#30–24 goalie   6' 195–L
b. Winnipeg, Manitoba, December 28, 1929
d. Long Beach, New York, May 31, 1970

1964–65					
36 (0/0)	17–13–6	2160	92	1	2.56
1965–66					
27 (1/2)[+]	10–11–4	1521	80	1	3.16
1966–67					
28 (7/1)	15–5–4	1409	66	2	2.81
Totals					
91 (8/3)	42–29–14	5090	238	4	2.81

- + game of April 2, 1966, he and Gamble alternated every five minutes as an experiment of coach Punch Imlach
- claimed June 10, 1964, from Detroit in Intra-League Draft
- last regular season Leaf game April 2, 1967
- claimed June 6, 1967, by Los Angeles Kings at Expansion Draft
- died in a bar while wrestling with good friend Ron Stewart

MATHIEU SCHNEIDER

#72 defence   5'11" 189–L
b. New York, New York, June 12, 1969

1995–96	13	2	5	7	10
1996–97	26	5	7	12	20
1997–98	76	11	26	37	44
Totals	115	18	38	56	74

- acquired March 13, 1996, with Wendel Clark and Denis Smith from the Islanders for Kenny Jonsson, Darby Hendrickson, Sean Haggerty, and a 1st-round draft choice in 1997 (Roberto Luongo)
- missed 56 games in 1996–97 with groin injury
- traded to Rangers on October 14, 1998, for Alexander Karpovtsev and a 4th-round draft choice in 1999 (Mirko Murovic)
- member of USA World Cup 1996 winning team
- currently with Los Angeles Kings

DAVE "SWEENEY" SCHRINER

#11 left wing   6' 185–L
b. Saratov, Russia, November 30, 1911
d. Montreal, Quebec, July 5, 1990

1939–40	39	11	15	26	10
1940–41	48	24	14	38	6
1941–42	47	20	16	36	21
1942–43	37	19	17	36	13
1944–45	26	22	15	37	10
1945–46L	47	13	6	19	15
Totals	244	109	83	192	75

- acquired May 18, 1939, from New York Americans for Busher Jackson, Doc Romnes, Buzz Boll, and Murray Armstrong
- missed part of 1942–43 with torn knee ligaments
- missed 1943–44—Canadian army
- missed November 18, 1944–January 10, 1945, with injured leg
- last game March 17, 1946
- worked in oil and gas industry in Calgary
- Hockey Hall of Fame 1962

ROD SCHUTT

#25 left wing   5'10" 185–L
b. Bancroft, October 13, 1956

1985–86L	6	0	0	0

* signed October 3, 1985, as a free agent
* only Leaf games December 10, 11, 14, 15, 18, 20, 1985

GANTON SCOTT

#11–12–7 right wing   5'9" 165–R
b. Preston, March 23, 1903
d. Unknown

1922–23R	17	0	0	0	0
1923–24	4	0	0	0	0
1926–27L	1	0	0	0	0
Totals	22	0	0	0	0

* signed from Aura Lee Juniors
* first St. Pats game December 16, 1922
* sent to Hamilton Tigers (NHL) during 1923–24
* purchased from Saskatoon in 1926

AL SECORD

#20 left wing   6'1" 205–L
b. Sudbury, March 3, 1958

1987–88	74	15	27	42	221
1988–89	40	5	10	15	71
Totals	114	20	37	57	292

* acquired September 4, 1987, with Ed Olczyk from Chicago for Rick Vaive, Steve Thomas, and Bob McGill
* traded February 7, 1989, to Flyers for a 5th-round draft choice in 1989 (Keith Carney)
* won silver medal with Canada at 1977 WJC and played at 1987 WC (fourth place)

RON SEDLBAUER

#18 left wing   6'3" 200–L
b. Burlington, October 22, 1954

1980–81L	21	10	4	14	14

* bought February 18, 1981, from Chicago
* last Leaf game April 5, 1981

ROD SEILING

#16–17 defence   6' 195–L
b. Elmira, November 14, 1944

1962–63R	1	0	1	1	0
1974–75	60	5	12	17	40
1975–76	77	3	16	19	46
Totals	138	8	29	37	86

* Marlie graduate
* first Leaf game March 2, 1963
* traded February 22, 1964, with Dick Duff, Bob Nevin, Bill Collins, and Arnie Brown to the Rangers for Andy Bathgate and Don McKenney
* acquired November 2, 1974, from Washington for Tim Ecclestone and Willie Brossart
* signed September 9, 1976, as a free agent by St. Louis; as compensation, Leafs received a 2nd-round draft choice in 1978 (Joel Quenneville) and cash
* played for Canada at 1964 Olympics (fourth place)
* worked for Canadian Race Horsing Hall of Fame

BRITON "BRIT" SELBY

("Panda"—Junior A nickname)
#8–11–15 left wing   5'10" 175–L
b. Kingston, March 27, 1945

1964–65R	3	2	0	2	2
1965–66	61	14	13	27	26
1966–67	6	1	1	2	0
1968–69	14	2	2	4	19
1969–70	74	10	13	23	40
1970–71	11	0	1	1	6
Totals	169	29	30	59	93

* Marlie graduate
* first Leaf games January 2, 3, 6, 1965
* played October 22, 23, 26, 29 and November 3, 6, 1966

- claimed June 6, 1967, by Flyers at Expansion Draft
- acquired March 2, 1969, with Forbes Kennedy from Flyers for Mike Byers, Gerry Meehan, and Bill Sutherland
- traded November 13, 1970, to St. Louis for Bob Baun
- teaches high school history and economics in Toronto

BRAD SELWOOD

#3 defence 6'1" 200–L
b. Leamington, March 18, 1948

1970–71R	28	2	10	12	13
1971–72	72	4	17	21	58
Totals	100	6	27	33	71

- selected 10th overall at 1968 Amateur Draft.
- first Leaf game October 11, 1970
- missed November 21–January 16, 1970–71, with back injury; sent to Tulsa but recalled March 3
- claimed June 5, 1972, by Canadiens at Intra-League Draft

DAVE SEMENKO ("Sammy")

#27 left wing 6'3" 200–L
b. Winnipeg, Manitoba, July 12, 1957

1987–88L	70	2	3	5	107

- acquired September 9, 1987, from Hartford for Bill Root
- quit team March 22, 1988

JEFF SEROWIK

#34 defence 6' 190–R
b. Manchester, New Hampshire, October 1, 1967

1990–91R/L	1	0	0	0	0

- selected 85th overall at 1985 Entry Draft
- first and only Leaf game October 6, 1990
- signed July 20, 1993, as a free agent by Florida

EDDIE SHACK ("The Entertainer"/ "Clown Prince of Hockey")

#23 right wing 6'1" 200–L
b. Sudbury, February 11, 1937

1960–61	55	14	14	28	90
1961–62	44	7	14	21	62
1962–63	63	16	9	25	97
1963–64	64	11	10	21	128
1964–65	67	5	9	14	68
1965–66	63	26	17	43	88
1966–67	63	11	14	25	58
1973–74	59	7	8	15	74
1974–75L	26	2	1	3	11
Totals	504	99	96	195	676

- acquired November 7, 1960, from Rangers for Pat Hannigan and Johnny Wilson
- missed many games in 1961–62 with torn knee ligaments
- traded May 15, 1967, to Boston for Murray Oliver and cash
- bought July 3, 1973, from Penguins
- released after 1974–75 season: last Leaf game February 23, 1975
- became popular in Toronto for his sale of Christmas trees every December

DAVE SHAND

#3–4 defence 6'2" 200–R
b. Cold Lake, Alberta, August 11, 1956

1980–81	47	0	4	4	60
1982–83	1	0	1	1	2
Totals	48	0	5	5	62

- acquired June 10, 1980, with a 3rd-round draft choice in 1980 (later traded to Washington for a 2nd-round draft choice in 1980 [Kevin Lavallee])
- traded October 6, 1983, to Washington for Lee Norwood
- later graduated from Michigan Law School; practises employment law in Michigan and has become a player-agent for a handful of minor pros

DARRYL SHANNON

#34–29–28–4 defence 6'2" 195–L
b. Barrie, June 21, 1968

1988–89R	14	1	3	4	6
1989–90	10	0	1	1	12
1990–91	10	0	1	1	0
1991–92	48	2	8	10	23
1992–93L	16	0	0	0	11
Totals	98	3	13	16	52

- selected 36th overall at 1986 Entry Draft
- first Leaf game March 1, 1989
- signed June 30, 1993, as free agent by Winnipeg Jets

NORMAN SHAY

#3 forward 5'9" 155–L
b. Huntsville, February 3, 1899
d. Unknown

1925–26L	22	3	1	4	18

- acquired January 13, 1926, from Boston for cash
- retired after season

DOUG SHEDDEN

#37–12 centre 6' 185–R
b. Wallaceburg, April 29, 1961

1988–89	1	0	0	0	2
1990–91L	23	8	10	18	10
Totals	24	8	10	18	12

- signed August 4, 1988, as a free agent
- played most of 1988–91 with Newmarket
- last Leaf game January 12, 1991
- later coached in ECHL

JACK SHILL ("Porky")

#7–19–20–18 defence 5'11" 181–L
b. Toronto, January 12, 1913
d. October 25, 1976

1933–34R	7	0	1	1	0
1935–36	3	0	1	1	0
1936–37	32	4	4	8	26
Totals	42	4	6	10	26

- Marlie graduate; signed March 1, 1934
- first Leaf game March 3, 1934
- traded to Boston summer 1934
- began 1935–36 to replace Harvey Jackson, who sat out first game in contract dispute
- re-signed by Toronto in 1935
- sold September 24, 1937, to New York Americans for cash

DON SIMMONS ("Dippy")

#1–24 goalie 5'10" 150–R
b. Port Colborne, September 13, 1931

1961–62					
9 (0/0)	4–4–1	540	21	1	2.33
1962–63					
28 (0/0)	15–8–5	1680	70	1	2.50
1963–64					
21 (0/2)	9–9–1	1191	63	3	3.17
Totals					
58 (0/2)	28–21–7	3411	154	5	2.71

- acquired January 31, 1961, from Boston for Ed Chadwick
- claimed June 8, 1965, by Rangers at Intra-League Draft
- began tradition of going to bench on delayed penalties
- later ran a sporting goods store in Fort Erie

DARRYL SITTLER ("Sit")

#27 centre 6' 190–L
b. Kitchener, September 18, 1950

1970–71R	49	10	8	18	37
1971–72	74	15	17	32	44
1972–73	78	29	48	77	69
1973–74	78	38	46	84	55
1974–75	72	36	44	80	47
1975–76	79	41	59	100	90
1976–77	73	38	52	90	89
1977–78	80	45	72	117	100
1978–79	70	36	51	87	69
1979–80	73	40	57	97	62
1980–81	80	43	53	96	77
1981–82	38	18	20	38	24
Totals	844	389	527	916	763

Darryl Sittler

- selected 8th overall at 1970 Amateur Draft
- first Leaf game October 11, 1970
- missed 28 games in 1970–71 (January 17–March 21) with a broken wrist
- in 1976 he scored ten points in one game, five goals in a playoff game, and scored the winner in overtime in the Canada Cup finals
- traded January 20, 1982, to Flyers for Rich Costello, a 2nd-round draft choice in 1982 (Peter Ihnacak) and future considerations (Ken Strong)
- won bronze medals at 1982 and 1983 WC
- currently performs public relations work for the Leafs

ALFRED "ALFIE" SKINNER

#6 right wing   5'10" 180–R
b. Toronto, January 26, 1896
d. Toronto, April 23, 1961

1917–18	19	13	–	13	20
1918–19	17	12	3	15	26
Totals	36	25	3	28	46

- joined Arenas in 1916 after Toronto Shamrocks folded
- left to play for Vancouver Millionaires after 1918–19 season
- worked for City of Toronto and active in politics

ALOYSIUS "TOD" SLOAN

("Trigger"/"Slinker")
 #11–15–20–22 centre 5'10" 175–R
 b. Vinton, Quebec, November 30, 1927

1947–48R	1	0	0	0	0
1948–49	29	3	4	7	0
1950–51	70	31	25	56	105
1951–52	68	25	23	48	89
1952–53	70	15	10	25	76
1953–54	67	11	32	43	100
1954–55	63	13	15	28	89
1955–56	70	37	29	66	100
1956–57	52	14	21	35	33
1957–58	59	13	25	38	58
Totals	549	162	184	346	650

- St. Mike's graduate; signed April 30, 1946
- first Leaf game December 25, 1947
- recalled from Pittsburgh on December 26, 1948, to replace injured Meeker
- traded to the Cleveland (AHL) in 1949 with Harry Taylor and Ray Ceresino for Bob Solinger
- purchased from Cleveland (AHL) during training camp 1950
- suffered fractured shoulder at end of 1955–56; missed most of 1956 playoffs
- sold June 4, 1958, to Chicago
- ran a resort on Jackson's Point until he retired

DARRYL SLY

#21 defence   5'10" 185–R
b. Collingwood, April 3, 1939

1965–66R	2	0	0	0	0
1967–68	17	0	0	0	4
Totals	19	0	0	0	4

- St. Mike's graduate 1961
- first Leaf games December 15, 16, 1965, then sent to Rochester for the rest of the year
- won silver medal with Canada at 1960 Olympics and gold at 1961 WC

DALE SMEDSMO

#23 left wing   6'1" 195–L
b. Roseau, Minnesota, April 23, 1951

1972–73R/L	4	0	0	0	0

- selected 93rd overall at 1971 Amateur Draft
- first and only Leaf games February 14, 17, 21, 24, 1973
- signed June 6, 1976, by Cincinnati Stingers (WHA)

AL SMITH ("Fat Albert"/"The Bear")
#1–30–31 goalie   6'1" 200–L
b. Toronto, November 10, 1945

1965–66R					
2 (0/2)	2–0–0	62	2	0	1.94
1966–67					
1 (0/0)	0–1–0	60	5	0	5.00
1968–69					
7 (1/2)	2–2–1	335	16	0	2.87
Totals					
10 (1/4)	4–3–1	457	23	0	3.02

- Marlie graduate
- first Leaf games February 20, 23, 1966
- played December 31, 1966
- claimed June 11, 1969, by Penguins at Intra-League Draft
- cab driver and playwright in Toronto

ART SMITH
#2–3–12 forward   5'10" 190–R
b. Toronto, November 29, 1906
d. Toronto, May 15, 1962

1927–28R	15	5	3	8	22
1928–29	43	5	0	5	91
1929–30	43	3	3	6	75
Totals	101	13	6	19	188

- played most of 1927–28 with Toronto Ravinas
- first Leaf game February 11, 1928
- traded October 11, 1930, with Eric Pettinger and $35,000 to Ottawa Senators for King Clancy
- played for Toronto Argonauts (CFL) after hockey, and was president of Art Smith Construction Supply Ltd. at time of death

BRAD SMITH ("Motor City Smitty")
#29 right wing   6'1" 195–R
b. Windsor, April 13, 1958

1985–86	42	5	17	22	84
1986–87L	47	5	7	12	172
Totals	89	10	24	34	256

- signed July 2, 1985, as free agent from Detroit
- last Leaf game April 4, 1987
- retired after 1986–87 due to chronic back condition
- scouts for Colorado

D.J. SMITH
#4 defence   6'1" 200–L
b. Windsor, May 13, 1977

1996–97R	8	0	1	1	7
1999–2000	3	0	0	0	5
Totals	11	0	1	1	12

- signed December 19, 1996, with Leafs
- first Leaf game March 26, 1997
- in the Leafs' system

FLOYD SMITH ("Smitty")
#17 right wing   5'10" 180–R
b. Perth, May 16, 1935

1967–68	6	6	1	7	0
1968–69	64	15	19	34	22
1969–70	61	4	14	18	13
Totals	131	25	34	59	35

- acquired March 3, 1968, with Paul Henderson and Norm Ullman from Detroit for Frank Mahovlich, Garry Unger, Pete Stemkowski, and the rights to Carl Brewer
- sold August 31, 1970, with Brent Imlach to Sabres
- later became coach of the Leafs and then a scout for the team

GARY SMITH ("Suitcase")
#1 goalie   6'4" 215–L
b. Ottawa, February 4, 1944

1965–66R						
3 (2/0)	0–2–0	118	7	0	3.56	
1966–67						
2 (0/1)	0–2–0	115	7	0	3.65	
Totals						
5 (2/1)	0–4–0	233	14	0	3.61	

- Marlie graduate
- first Leaf games February 19, 20, 23, 1966
- claimed June 6, 1967, by Oakland at Expansion Draft
- serves court papers to citizens in Vancouver

GLENN SMITH
forward   5'8" 180–L
b. Moosomin, Saskatchewan, May 27, 1873
d. Unknown

1921–22R/L	9	0	0	0	0

- first St. Pats game December 21, 1921

JASON SMITH
#25 defence   6'3" 205–R
b. Calgary, Alberta, November 2, 1973

1996–97	21	0	5	5	16
1997–98	81	3	13	16	100
1998–99	60	2	11	13	8
Totals	162	5	29	34	124

- acquired February 25, 1997, with Steve Sullivan and Alyn McCauley from New Jersey for Doug Gilmour, Dave Ellett, and a 3rd-round draft choice in 1999 (previously acquired from Devils for Andreychuk trade—Andre Lakos)
- traded to Edmonton for a 4th-round draft choice in 1999 (Jonathan Zion) and a 2nd-round draft choice in 2000 (Kris Vernarsky) on March 23, 1999
- won gold medal with Canada at 1993 WJC
- currently with Edmonton Oilers

SID SMITH ("Muff")
#8–16–22–24 left wing 5'10 177–L
b. Toronto, July 11, 1925

1946–47R	14	2	1	3	0
1947–48	31	7	10	17	10
1948–49	1	0	0	0	0
1949–50	68	22	23	45	6
1950–51	70	30	21	51	10
1951–52	70	27	30	57	6
1952–53	70	20	19	39	6
1953–54	70	22	16	38	28
1954–55	70	33	21	54	14
1955–56	55	4	17	21	8
1956–57	70	17	24	41	4
1957–58L	12	2	1	3	2
Totals	601	186	183	369	94

- signed December 8, 1946, by Leafs
- first Leaf game February 6, 1947
- played half of 1947–48 and most of 1948–49 with Hornets by way of recuperation after sustaining a serious knee injury March 27, 1947, vs. Boston
- last Leaf games October 8, 12, 17, 19, 20, 23, 26, 30, 31 and November 6, 7, 10, 1957
- placed on waivers November 11, 1957; became playing coach of Whitby Dunlops same day
- reinstated as an amateur; won gold medal with Canada at 1958 WC
- sold fine paper stock for a printing company for 25 years

DR. ROD SMYLIE
#9–11 left wing   5'10" 170–L
b. Toronto, September 28, 1895
d. Toronto, March 3, 1985

1920–21R	23	2	0	2	2
1921–22	21	0	0	0	2
1922–23	2	0	0	0	0
1924–25	11	0	0	0	0
1925–26L	6	0	0	0	0
Totals	63	2	0	2	4

- played with Dentals (OHA) 1917–20
- first St. Pats game December 22, 1920

- played 1920–22 while studying medicine and interning at St. Michael's Hospital
- played December 30 and January 1, 5, 9, 12, 15, 1926
- sent to Ottawa Senators prior to 1923–24 season
- reacquired summer 1924
- retired to run private practice in Toronto

GREG SMYTH

#28–25 defence 6'3" 212–R
b. Oakville, April 23, 1966

1993–94	11	0	1	1	38
1996–97	2	0	0	0	0
Totals	13	0	1	1	38

- acquired December 7, 1993, from Florida for cash
- first Leaf game December 11, 1993
- claimed on waivers January 8, 1994, by Chicago
- signed as free agent August 13, 1996

CHRIS SNELL

#38 defence 5'10" 190–L
b. Regina, Saskatchewan, May 12, 1971

1993–94R	2	0	0	0	2

- signed August 3, 1993, as free agent
- first and only Leaf games February 26, 28, 1994
- traded October 5, 1994, with Eric Lacroix and a 4th-round draft choice in 1996 (Eric Belanger) to Los Angeles Kings for Dixon Ward, Guy Leveque, Kelly Fairchild, and Shayne Toporowski

BOB SOLINGER ("Solly")

#11–21–23–25 left wing 5'10" 190–L
b. Star City, Saskatchewan, December 23, 1925

1951–52R	24	5	3	8	4
1952–53	18	1	1	2	2
1953–54	39	3	2	5	2
1954–55	17	1	5	6	11
Totals	98	10	11	21	19

- acquired summer 1949 from Cleveland (AHL) for Tod Sloan, Harry Taylor, and Ray Ceresino
- first Leaf game November 1, 1951
- called up from Hornets on December 27, 1954, to replace injured Ron Stewart
- bought June 7, 1956, by Hershey when Hornets folded

BRIAN SPENCER ("Spinner")

#15–22 left wing 5'11" 185–L
b. Fort St. James, British Columbia, September 3, 1949
d. Riviera Beach, Florida, June 3, 1988

1969–70R	9	0	0	0	12
1970–71	50	9	15	24	115
1971–72	36	1	5	6	65
Totals	95	10	20	30	192

- selected 55th overall at 1969 Amateur Draft
- first Leaf game March 14, 1970
- missed much of 1971–72 with broken kneecap
- claimed June 6, 1972, by Islanders at Expansion Draft
- acquitted of murder charges in 1987, but was himself murdered by gunshot a few months later; his life story became a TV movie directed by Atom Egoyan

CHRIS SPEYER

#11 defence 5'10" 170–L
b. Toronto, February 6, 1907
d. Unknown

1923–24R	4	0	0	0	0
1924–25	2	0	0	0	0
Totals	6	0	0	0	0

- signed in 1924 from Aura Lee Juniors
- first St. Pats games February 23, 27 and March 1, 5, 1924
- released outright December 15, 1924

JESSE SPRING ("Jess")

#14 defence   6' 185–L
b. Alba, Pennsylvania, January 18, 1901
d. Toronto, March 25, 1942

1926–27	5	0	0	0	0

- first and only Leaf games November 20, 25, 30 and December 9, 18, 1926
- played with Pirates 1925–26 and New York Americans 1928–29
- one-time middleweight boxing champion

TED STACKHOUSE

defence   6'1" 200–R
b. New Glasgow, Nova Scotia, November 2, 1894
d. Mount Holley, New Jersey, November 24, 1975

1921–22R/L	12	0	0	0	2

- played part of 1921–22 in Maritime Independent League (New Glasgow)
- first St. Pats game December 24, 1921

LORNE STAMLER

#12 left wing   6' 190–L
b. Winnipeg, Manitoba, August 9, 1951

1978–79	45	4	3	7	2

- acquired June 14, 1978, with Dave Hutchison from Los Angeles Kings for Brian Glennie, Kurt Walker, Scott Garland and a 2nd-round draft choice in 1979 (Mark Hardy)
- claimed June 13, 1979, by Winnipeg Jets in Expansion Draft
- currently runs his own chemical business in Florida

ALLAN STANLEY ("Sam"/"Snowshoes")

#26 defence   6'2" 191–L
b. Timmins, March 1, 1926

1958–59	70	1	22	23	47
1959–60	64	10	23	33	22
1960–61	68	9	25	34	42
1961–62	60	9	26	35	24
1962–63	61	4	15	19	22
1963–64	70	6	21	27	60
1964–65	64	2	15	17	30
1965–66	59	4	14	18	35
1966–67	53	1	12	13	20
1967–68	64	1	13	14	16
Totals	633	47	186	233	318

- acquired October 3, 1958, from Boston for Jim Morrison
- last Leaf game March 31, 1968
- drafted June 13, 1968, by Quebec (AHL) in Reverse Draft
- operated a resort in Bobcaygeon until he retired
- Hockey Hall of Fame 1981

WALLY STANOWSKI

("Whirling Dervish"/"The Hat")
#2–3–20–16 defence   5'11" 180–L
b. Winnipeg, Manitoba, April 28, 1919

1939–40R	27	2	7	9	11
1940–41	47	7	14	21	35
1941–42	24	1	7	8	10
1944–45	34	2	9	11	16
1945–46	45	3	10	13	10
1946–47	51	3	16	19	12
1947–48	54	2	11	13	12
Totals	282	20	74	94	106

- acquired in 1937 from New York Americans for Hap Day
- first Leaf game November 4, 1939
- missed 1942–44—Canadian armed forces; discharged November 23, 1944
- missed many games after injuring knee March 5, 1947
- traded April 26, 1948, to the Rangers with Moe Morris and the rights to Orville Lavell for Cal Gardner, Bill Juzda, René Trudell, Frank Mathers, and rights to Ray McMurray
- sold construction equipment for 20 years after retiring

MARIAN STASTNY

#10 right wing   5'10" 195–L
b. Bratislava, Czechoslovakia,
January 8, 1953

1985–86L	70	23	30	53	21

- signed August 12, 1985, as free agent
- last game April 6, 1986

PHIL STEIN ("The Happy Dutchman")

#1 goalie   5'10" 160–L
b. Toronto, September 13, 1913

1939–40R/L

1 (0/0)	0–0–1	70	2	0	1.71

- signed October 30, 1934, and sent to Syracuse
- recalled January 15, 1940, from Omaha to replace injured Broda
- first and only Leaf game January 18, 1940
- sold October 21, 1940, to New Haven
- managed Leaside Memorial Gardens in Toronto

PETE STEMKOWSKI ("Stemmer")

#12–25 centre   6'1" 210–L
b. Winnipeg, Manitoba, August 25, 1943

1963–64R	1	0	0	0	2
1964–65	36	5	15	20	33
1965–66	56	4	12	16	55
1966–67	68	13	22	35	75
1967–68	60	7	15	22	82
Totals	221	29	64	93	247

- first Leaf game January 18, 1964
- traded March 3, 1968, with Frank Mahovlich, Garry Unger, and the rights to Carl Brewer to Detroit for Norm Ullman, Paul Henderson, and Floyd Smith
- currently scout for San Jose Sharks

BOB STEPHENSON

#15 defence   6'1" 187–R
b. Saskatoon, Saskatchewan,
February 1, 1954

1979–80L	14	2	2	4	4

- acquired December 24, 1979, from Hartford for Pat Boutette
- last Leaf game January 9, 1980

MIKE STEVENS

#26 left wing   5'11" 195–L
b. Kitchener, December 30, 1965

1989–90L	1	0	0	0	0

- acquired December 20, 1989, with Gilles Thibaudeau from the Islanders for Paul Gagne, Derek Laxdal, and Jack Capuano
- only Leaf game January 27, 1990
- traded December 26, 1991, to the Rangers for Guy Larose

BILL STEWART

#17 defence   6'2" 180–R
b. Toronto, October 6, 1957

1983–84	56	2	17	19	116
1984–85	27	0	2	2	32
Totals	83	2	19	21	148

- signed September 10, 1983, as a free agent
- signed September 15, 1985, by Minnesota as a free agent
- played for Italy at 1992 Olympics (twelfth place), 1992 WC (ninth), 1993 WC (eighth), and 1994 Olympics (ninth)
- later coached briefly in NHL, then OHL (suspended in 1999–2000 for smuggling a player over Canada-US border)

JAMES "GAYE" STEWART

("The Gaye One"/"Swish")
#15–16 left wing   5'11" 175–L
b. Fort William, June 28, 1923

1942–43R	48	24	23	47	20
1945–46	50	37	15	52	8
1946–47	60	19	14	33	15
1947–48	7	1	0	1	9
Totals	165	81	52	133	52

- Marlie graduate 1942; signed March 5, 1942, with Leafs

- first regular season game October 31, 1942
- missed 1943–45—Canadian army
- traded November 2, 1947, with Gus Bodnar, Bud Poile, Bob Goldham, and Ernie Dickens to Chicago for Max Bentley and Cy Thomas
- later became a sales representative for a beer company in Southern Ontario for 28 years

RON STEWART ("Stew")
#12–19–24 right wing 6'1" 197–R
b. Calgary, Alberta, July 11, 1932

1952–53R	70	13	22	35	29
1953–54	70	14	11	25	72
1954–55	53	14	5	19	20
1955–56	69	13	14	27	35
1956–57	65	15	20	35	28
1957–58	70	15	24	39	51
1958–59	70	21	13	34	23
1959–60	67	14	20	34	28
1960–61	51	13	12	25	8
1961–62	60	8	9	17	14
1962–63	63	16	16	32	26
1963–64	65	14	5	19	46
1964–65	65	16	11	27	33
Totals	838	186	182	368	413

- won Memorial Cup in 1951–52 with Guelph Biltmores
- signed October 6, 1952, with Leafs
- joined Leafs 1952–53—never played a game in the minors
- first Leaf game October 11, 1952
- broke jaw December 27, 1954, in Detroit
- missed many games in 1960–61 with broken ankle
- traded June 8, 1965, to Boston for Pat Stapleton, Andy Hebenton, and Orland Kurtenbach
- play-fighting with Terry Sawchuk led to the goalie's accidental death

MIKE STOTHERS
#25 defence 6'4" 212–L
b. Toronto, February 22, 1962

1987–88L	18	0	1	1	42

- acquired December 4, 1987, from Flyers for a 5th-round draft choice in 1989 (later traded to Minnesota—Pat MacLeod)
- last Leaf game February 22, 1988
- traded June 21, 1988, to Flyers for Bill Root

BLAINE STOUGHTON ("Stash")
#17 right wing 5'11" 185–R
b. Gilbert Plains, Manitoba, March 13, 1953

1974–75	78	23	14	37	24
1975–76	43	6	11	17	8
Totals	121	29	25	54	32

- acquired September 13, 1974, with a 1st-round draft choice in 1977 (Trevor Johansen) from Penguins for Rick Kehoe
- claimed June 13, 1979, by Hartford at Expansion Draft

KEN STRONG
#23–32 left wing 5'11" 185–L
b. Toronto, May 9, 1963

1982–83R	2	0	0	0	0
1983–84	2	0	2	2	2
1984–85L	11	2	0	2	4
Totals	15	2	2	4	6

- acquired January 20, 1982, from Flyers to complete Darryl Sittler trade
- first Leaf games April 2, 3, 1983
- last Leaf game February 14, 1985
- played for Austria (B pool) at 1992 WC (gold medal), 1994 Olympics (twelfth place), 1994 WC (eighth), and 1995 WC (eleventh)

BILLY "RED" STUART ("Ginger")
#3 defence 5'11" 175–L
b. Sackville, New Brunswick, February 1, 1900
d. March 7, 1978

1920–21R	18	2	1	3	4
1921–22	24	3	6	9	16
1922–23	23	7	3	10	16
1923–24	24	4	3	7	16

1924–25	5	0	0	0	0
Totals	94	16	13	29	52

- joined St. Pats from Maritime Independent League January 4, 1921
- first St. Pats game January 12, 1921
- sold December 14, 1924, to Boston

FRANK "SULLY" SULLIVAN
#25 defence   5′11″ 178–R
b. Toronto, June 16, 1929

1949–50R	1	0	0	0	0
1952–53	5	0	0	0	2
Totals	6	0	0	0	2

- first Leaf game March 11, 1950
- recalled November 10, 1952
- traded April 1954 with Dusty Blair and Jackie LeClair to Bisons for Brian Cullen
- won gold medal with Edmonton Mercurys team at 1952 Olympics

STEVE SULLIVAN ("Sully")
#11 right wing   5′9″ 155–R
b. Timmins, July 6, 1974

1996–97	21	5	11	16	23
1997–98	63	10	18	28	40
1998–99	63	20	20	40	28
1999–2000	7	0	1	1	4
Totals	154	35	50	85	95

- acquired February 25, 1997, with Jason Smith and Alyn McCauley from New Jersey for Doug Gilmour, Dave Ellett, and a 3rd-round draft choice in 1999 (previously acquired in Andreychuk trade—Andre Lakos)
- claimed on waivers by Chicago on October 23, 1999
- played for Canada at 2000 WC (fourth)
- currently with Chicago Blackhawks

MATS SUNDIN ("Weed")
#13 centre   6′4″ 215–R
b. Bromma, Sweden, February 13, 1971

1994–95	47	23	24	47	14
1995–96	76	33	50	83	46
1996–97	82	41	53	94	59
1997–98	82	33	41	74	49
1998–99	82	31	52	83	58
1999–2000	73	32	41	73	46
2000–01	82	28	46	74	46
Totals	524	221	307	528	348

- acquired June 28, 1994, with Garth Butcher, Todd Warriner, and a 1st-round draft choice in 1994 (later traded to Washington—Nolan Baumgartner—with Rob Pearson for Mike Ridley and a 1st-round draft choice in 1994—Eric Fichaud) from Quebec Nordiques for Wendel Clark, Sylvain Lefebvre, Landon Wilson, and a 1st-round draft choice in 1994 (Jeffrey Kealty)
- became first non-Canadian captain of Leafs
- played for Sweden at 1990 WJC (fifth place), 1990 WC (silver medal), 1991 WC (gold), 1992 WC (gold), 1994 WC (bronze), 1998 Olympics (fifth), 1998 WC (gold), and 2001 WC (bronze)
- currently with Leafs

BILL SUTHERLAND
#15 centre   5′10″ 176–L
b. Regina, Saskatchewan, November 10, 1934

1968–69	44	7	5	12	14

- claimed June 1968 from Minnesota at Intra-League Draft
- traded March 2, 1969, with Gerry Meehan and Mike Byers for Brit Selby and Forbes Kennedy

RICH SUTTER

#20 right wing   5'11" 188–R
b. Viking, Alberta, December 2, 1963

1994–95	18	0	3	3	10

- acquired March 13, 1995, from Tampa Bay for future considerations (cash)
- released June 27, 1995

PETR SVOBODA

#23 defence   6'3" 200–R
b. Jihlava, Czechoslovakia, June 20, 1980

2000–01	18	1	2	3	10

- selected 35th overall at 1998 Entry Draft
- first Leaf game October 7, 2000

BOB SYKES

#25 left wing   6' 200–L
b. Sudbury, September 26, 1951

1974–75R/L	2	0	0	0	0

- selected 65th overall at 1971 Amateur Draft
- first and only Leaf games February 12, 15, 1974

BILLY TAYLOR ("Billy the Kid")

#19–21–7 centre   5'9" 150–R
b. Winnipeg, Manitoba, May 3, 1919
d. Whitby, June 12, 1990

1939–40R	29	4	6	10	9
1940–41	47	9	26	35	15
1941–42	48	12	26	38	20
1942–43	50	18	42	60	2
1945–46	48	23	18	41	14
Totals	222	66	118	184	60

- Leafs' mascot when 1931–32 team won the Cup
- signed May 1, 1939, by Leafs
- first Leaf game November 4, 1939
- missed 1943–45—Canadian army; re-signed August 24, 1945

- traded September 21, 1946, with Doug Baldwin and Ray Powell to Detroit for Harry Watson and Gerry Brown
- later expelled from the league for gambling; the ban was lifted in 1970 and he scouted for the Pittsburgh Penguins

HARRY TAYLOR

#17–21 centre   5'8" 165–R
b. St. James, Manitoba, March 28, 1926

1946–47R	9	0	2	2	0
1948–49	42	4	7	11	30
Totals	51	4	9	13	30

- first Leaf game November 17, 1946
- loaned to Providence for 1947–48
- started 1948–49 with Hornets; called up November 14, 1948, and stayed the year
- traded on September 6, 1949, with Tod Sloan and Ray Ceresino to Cleveland (AHL) for Bob Solinger

GREG TERRION ("Tubby")

#7 left wing   5'11" 190–L
b. Marmora, May 2, 1960

1982–83	74	16	16	32	59
1983–84	79	15	24	39	36
1984–85	72	14	17	31	20
1985–86	76	10	22	32	31
1986–87	67	7	8	15	6
1987–88L	59	4	16	20	65
Totals	427	66	103	169	217

- acquired October 19, 1982, from Los Angeles Kings for a 4th-round draft choice in 1983 (later transferred to Detroit—David Korol)
- last Leaf game April 2, 1988
- operates a gas station in Marmora, Ontario

GILLES THIBAUDEAU ("T-Bone"/"Bud")
#7 centre   5'10" 165–L
b. Montreal, Quebec, March 4, 1963

1989–90	21	7	11	18	13
1990–91L	20	2	7	9	4
Totals	41	9	18	27	17

- acquired December 20, 1989, with Mike Stevens from the Islanders for Paul Gagne, Derek Laxdal, and Jack Capuano
- last Leaf game November 19, 1990
- left to join Lugano (Swiss League) for 1991–92

CY THOMAS
#22 forward   5'10" 185–L
b. Dowlais, Wales, August 5, 1926

1947–48L	8	1	2	3	4

- acquired November 2, 1947, with Max Bentley from Chicago for Gus Bodnar, Bob Goldham, Bud Poile, Gaye Stewart, and Ernie Dickens
- first and only Leaf games November 6, 8, 12, 15 and December 3, 14, 21, 25, 1947
- broke wrist during 1947–48

STEVE THOMAS ("Stumpy")
#12–32–25 left wing   5'11" 185–R
b. Stockport, England, July 15, 1963

1984–85R	18	1	1	2	2
1985–86	65	20	37	57	36
1986–87	78	35	27	62	114
1998–99	78	28	45	73	26
1999–2000	81	26	37	63	68
2000–01	57	8	26	34	46
Totals	377	118	173	291	292

- signed May 12, 1984, as a free agent
- first Leaf game November 7, 1984
- traded September 4, 1987, with Rick Vaive and Bob McGill to Chicago for Ed Olczyk and Al Secord
- signed as a free agent on July 30, 1998

- played for Canada at 1991 WC (silver medal), 1992 WC (eighth place), 1994 WC (gold), and 1996 WC (silver)

WAYNE THOMAS
#30–33 goalie   6'2" 195–L
b. Ottawa, October 9, 1947

1975–76					
64 (6/1)	28–24–12	3684	196	2	3.19
1976–77					
33 (1/4)	10–13–6	1803	116	1	3.86
Totals					
97 (7/5)	38–37–18	5487	312	3	3.41

- acquired June 17, 1975, from Canadiens for a 1st-round draft choice in 1976 (Peter Lee)
- claimed October 10, 1977, by the Rangers at Waiver Draft

ERROL THOMPSON ("Spud")
#12–22 left wing   5'8" 180–L
b. Summerside, Prince Edward Island, May 28, 1950

1970–71R	1	0	0	0	0
1972–73	68	13	19	32	8
1973–74	56	7	8	15	6
1974–75	65	25	17	42	12
1975–76	75	43	37	80	26
1976–77	41	21	16	37	8
1977–78	59	17	22	39	10
Totals	365	126	119	245	70

- selected 22nd overall at 1970 Amateur Draft
- first Leaf game March 28, 1971
- traded March 13, 1978, with a 1st-round draft choice in 1978 (Brent Peterson), a 2nd-round draft choice in 1978 (Al Jensen), and a 1st-round draft choice in 1980 (Mike Blaisdell) to Detroit for Dan Maloney and a 2nd-round draft choice in 1980 (Craig Muni)
- later worked in PEI as a sales rep for a beer company

BILL THOMS

#7–14–16–29 centre   5'9" 170–L
b. Newmarket, March 5, 1910
d. Toronto, December 26, 1964

1932–33R	29	3	9	12	15
1933–34	47	8	18	26	24
1934–35	47	9	13	22	15
1935–36	48	23	15	38	29
1936–37	48	10	9	19	14
1937–38	48	14	24	38	14
1938–39	12	1	4	5	4
Totals	279	68	92	160	115

- Marlie graduate
- first Leaf game January 3, 1933
- traded December 7, 1938, to Chicago for Doc Romnes
- retired from hockey in 1945 after serious illness
- later worked for *Toronto Telegram* until his death

JIM THOMSON ("Jeems"/"The Gold Dust Twins" with Gus Mortson)

#2–20 defence   6' 190–R
b. Winnipeg, Manitoba, February 23, 1927
d. Toronto, May 18, 1991

1945–46R	5	0	1	1	4
1946–47	60	2	14	16	97
1947–48	59	0	29	29	82
1948–49	60	4	16	20	56
1949–50	70	0	13	13	76
1950–51	69	3	33	36	76
1951–52	70	0	25	25	86
1952–53	69	0	22	22	73
1953–54	61	2	24	26	86
1954–55	70	4	12	16	63
1955–56	62	0	7	7	96
1956–57	62	0	12	12	50
Totals	717	15	208	223	846

- St. Mike's graduate; signed October 16, 1945, with Leafs
- first Leaf game November 10, 1945
- missed much of December 1953 with injured knee
- contract sold August 5, 1957, to Chicago for one year for $15,000
- contract returned to Toronto after 1957–58, but Thomson retired August 17, 1958
- heavily involved with Ted Lindsay of Detroit in trying to form a players' association

RHYS THOMSON

#17 defence   6'1" 195–L
b. Toronto, August 9, 1918
d. Unknown

1942–43L	18	0	2	2	22

- bought November 6, 1942, from Buffalo for cash
- first Leaf game November 12, 1942
- last Leaf game December 20, 1942, then released

SCOTT THORNTON

#24 centre   6'2" 200–L
b. London, January 9, 1971

1990–91R	33	1	3	4	30

- selected 3rd overall at 1989 Entry Draft
- first Leaf game October 4, 1990
- traded September 19, 1991, with Vincent Damphousse, Luke Richardson, and Peter Ing to Edmonton for Grant Fuhr, Glenn Anderson, and Craig Berube
- won gold medal with Canada at 1991 WJC and played at 1999 WC (fourth place)

RAY TIMGREN ("Golden Boy, Mark II")

#22 left wing   5'9" 161–L
b. Windsor, September 29, 1928
d. Lindsay, November 25, 1999

1948–49R	36	3	12	15	9
1949–50	68	7	18	25	22
1950–51	70	1	9	10	20
1951–52	50	2	4	6	11
1952–53	12	0	0	0	4
1954–55L	1	0	0	0	2
Totals	237	13	43	56	68

- Marlie graduate
- first Leaf game December 18, 1948
- traded October 4, 1954, to Chicago for Jack Price
- loaned from Chicago on November 16, 1954
- last Leaf game March 19, 1955
- later became a school teacher in Toronto

DAVE TOMLINSON
#14–37 centre   5'11" 177–L
b. North Vancouver, British Columbia, May 8, 1969

1991–92R	3	0	0	0	2
1992–93	3	0	0	0	2
Totals	6	0	0	0	4

- selected 43rd overall at 1985 Entry Draft
- first Leaf games December 12, 14, 18, 1991
- played January 8, 9, 11, 1993
- sold August 3, 1993, to Florida

SHAYNE TOPOROWSKI ("Topper")
#41 forward   6'2" 222–R
b. Paddockwood, Saskatchewan, August 6, 1975

1996–97R	3	0	0	0	7

- acquired October 3, 1994, with Dixon Ward, Guy Leveque, and Kelly Fairchild for Eric Lacroix, Chris Snell, and a 4th-round draft choice in 1996 (Eric Belanger)
- first Leaf game January 7, 1997
- signed as free agent by St. Louis on September 9, 1997

VINCENT TREMBLAY
#1–30–29 goalie   5'11" 185–L
b. Quebec City, Quebec, October 21, 1959

1979–80R						
10 (2/5)	2–1–0	329	28	0	5.11	
1980–81						
3 (1/0)	0–3–0	143	16	0	6.71	
1981–82						
40 (7/6)	10–18–8	2033	153	1	4.52	
1982–83						
1 (0/1)	0–0–0	40	2	0	3.00	
Totals						
54 (10/12)	12–22–8	2545	199	1	4.69	

- selected 72nd overall at 1979 Entry Draft
- first Leaf game January 7, 1980
- traded August 15, 1983, with Rocky Saganiuk to Penguins for Pat Graham and Nick Ricci

YANNICK TREMBLAY
#38 defence   6'2" 178–R
b. Montreal, Quebec, November 15, 1975

1996–97R	5	0	0	0	0
1997–98	38	2	4	6	6
1998–99	35	2	7	9	16
Totals	78	4	11	15	22

- selected 145th overall at 1995 Entry Draft
- first Leaf game March 27, 1997
- claimed by Atlanta in Expansion Draft on June 25, 1999
- played for Canada at 2000 WC (fourth)

GUY TROTTIER ("The Mouse")
#11 right wing   5'8" 165–R
b. Hull, Quebec, April 1, 1941

1970–71	61	19	5	24	21
1971–72L	52	9	12	21	16
Totals	113	28	17	45	37

- acquired March 3, 1970, with Jacques Plante and Denis Dupere from the Rangers for Tim Horton
- last Leaf game April 9, 1972
- signed with Ottawa (WHA) for 1972–73

DARCY TUCKER
#16 centre   5'11" 185–L
b. Castor, Alberta, March 15, 1975

1999–2000	27	7	10	17	55
2000–01	82	16	21	37	141
Totals	109	23	31	54	196

- acquired from Tampa Bay on February 9, 2000, with a 4th-round draft choice in 2000 (Miguel Delisle) and future considerations for Mike Johnson, Marek Posmyk, a 5th-round draft choice in 2000 (Pavel Sedov), a 6th-round draft choice in 2000 (Aaron Gionet), and future considerations
- married to Shayne Corson's sister, Shannon
- won gold medal with Canada at 1995 WJC
- currently with Leafs

IAN TURNBULL ("Bull"/"Hawk")
#2 defence 6' 200–L
b. Montreal, Quebec, December 22, 1953

1973–74R	78	8	27	35	74
1974–75	22	6	7	13	44
1975–76	76	20	36	56	90
1976–77	80	22	57	79	84
1977–78	77	14	47	61	77
1978–79	80	12	51	63	80
1979–80	75	11	28	39	90
1980–81	80	19	47	66	104
1981–82	12	0	2	2	8
Totals	580	112	302	414	651

- selected 15th overall at 1973 Amateur Draft
- first Leaf game October 10, 1973
- traded November 11, 1981, to Los Angeles Kings for John Gibson and Billy Harris
- started selling real estate in California, which in turn led to starting company that funds mortgages for companies there

NORM ULLMAN
#9 centre 5'10" 185–L
b. Provost, Alberta, December 26, 1935

1967–68	13	5	12	17	2
1968–69	75	35	42	77	41
1969–70	74	18	42	60	37
1970–71	73	34	51	85	24
1971–72	77	23	50	73	26
1972–73	65	20	35	55	10
1973–74	78	22	47	69	12
1974–75L	80	9	26	35	8
Totals	535	166	305	471	160

- acquired March 3, 1968, with Paul Henderson and Floyd Smith from Detroit for Frank Mahovlich, Pete Stemkowski, Garry Unger, and the rights to Carl Brewer
- released after 1974–75 (last Leaf game April 6, 1975)
- became a sales rep for a typewritter ribbon company in Toronto
- Hockey Hall of Fame 1982

GARRY UNGER ("Iron Man")
#15 centre 6' 185–L
b. Edmonton, Alberta, December 7, 1947

1967–68R	15	1	1	2	4

- signed in fall of 1966
- first Leaf game November 4, 1967
- traded March 3, 1968, with Frank Mahovlich, Pete Stemkowski, and the rights to Carl Brewer to Detroit for Norm Ullman, Paul Henderson, and Floyd Smith
- went on to establish NHL Iron Man record
- played for Canada at 1978 WC (bronze medal) and 1979 WC (fourth place)

RICK VAIVE ("Squid")
#22–20 right wing 6' 200–R
b. Ottawa, May 14, 1959

1979–80	22	9	7	16	77
1980–81	75	33	29	62	229
1981–82	77	54	35	89	157
1982–83	78	51	28	79	105
1983–84	76	52	41	93	114
1984–85	72	35	33	68	112
1985–86	61	33	31	64	85
1986–87	73	32	34	66	61
Totals	534	299	238	537	940

- acquired February 18, 1980, with Bill Derlago from Vancouver Canucks for Tiger Williams and Jerry Butler

Rick Vaive

- traded September 4, 1987, with Steve Thomas and Bob McGill to Chicago for Ed Olczyk and Al Secord
- won bronze medal with Canada at 1978 WJC, bronze at 1982 WC, and silver at 1985 WC
- turned to coaching after retiring, most recently with Mississauga Ice Dogs (OHL)

JACK VALIQUETTE

#8 centre   6'2" 195–L
b. St. Thomas, March 18, 1956

1974–75R	1	0	0	0	0
1975–76	45	10	23	33	30
1976–77	66	15	30	45	7
1977–78	60	8	13	21	15
Totals	172	33	66	99	52

- selected 13th overall at 1974 Amateur Draft
- first Leaf game November 22, 1974
- traded October 19, 1978, to Colorado Rockies for a 2nd-round draft choice in 1981 (Gary Yaremchuk)
- operated a sporting goods store in Orillia

GARRY VALK

#10 left wing   6'1" 205–L
b. Edmonton, Alberta, November 27, 1967

1998–99	77	8	21	29	53
1999–2000	73	10	14	24	44
2000–01	74	8	18	26	46
Totals	224	26	53	79	143

- signed as free agent on October 8, 1998

DARREN VEITCH

#25–26 defence   5'11" 195–R
b. Saskatoon, Saskatchewan, April 24, 1960

1988–89	37	3	7	10	16
1990–91L	2	0	1	1	0
Totals	39	3	8	11	16

- acquired June 10, 1988, from Detroit for Miroslav Frycer

- traded March 5, 1991, to St. Louis for Keith Osborne
- last Leaf games October 24, 25, 1990

LEIGH VERSTRAETE

#34–28–25 right wing   5'11" 185–R
b. Pincher Creek, Alberta, January 6, 1962

1982–83R	3	0	0	0	5
1984–85	2	0	0	0	2
1987–88L	3	0	1	1	9
Totals	8	0	1	1	16

- selected 192nd overall in 1982 Entry Draft
- first Leaf games December 14, 15, 18, 1982
- played January 9, 22, 1985
- played October 17, 21, 24, 1987

CARL VOSS

#6 centre   5'8" 168–L
b. Chelsea, Massachusetts, January 6, 1907
d. Lake Park, Florida, September 13, 1994

1926–27R	12	0	0	0	0
1928–29	2	0	0	0	0
Totals	14	0	0	0	0

- first player to sign with Conn Smythe as a Maple Leaf, February 16, 1927
- first Leaf game February 17, 1927
- played December 29 and January 1, 1928–29, on loan from London when injuries to Duncan and Horner left the Leafs with just two defencemen
- loaned to Bisons for 1929–30 as part of the deal that brought Gord Brydson to the Leafs
- sold to Bisons outright October 21, 1930
- became NHL referee-in-chief

KURT WALKER

#26 defence   6'3" 200–R
b. Weymouth, Massachusetts, June 10, 1954

1975–76R	5	0	0	0	49
1976–77	26	2	3	5	34
1977–78L	40	2	2	4	69
Totals	71	4	5	9	152

- signed as free agent in autumn 1975
- first Leaf game March 20, 1976
- last Leaf game March 27, 1978
- traded June 14, 1978, with Brian Glennie, Scott Garland, and a 2nd-round draft choice in 1979 (Mark Hardy) to Los Angeles Kings for Dave Hutchison and Lorne Stamler

MIKE WALTON ("Shaky")

#15–16 centre   5'10" 175–R
b. Kirkland Lake, January 3, 1945

1965–66R	6	1	3	4	0
1966–67	31	7	10	17	13
1967–68	73	30	29	59	48
1968–69	66	22	21	43	34
1969–70	58	21	34	55	68
1970–71	23	3	10	13	21
Totals	257	84	107	191	184

- won Memorial Cup with Marlies in 1963–64
- first Leaf games November 20, 21, 24, 27, 28 and December 1, 1965, then sent to Rochester
- traded February 1, 1971, with Bruce Gamble and a 1st-round draft choice in 1971 (Pierre Plante) to Flyers for Bernie Parent and a 2nd-round draft choice in 1971 (Rick Kehoe)
- runs restaurant in Toronto called Shaky's

RICK WAMSLEY ("Wammer"/"Gump")

#30 goalie   5'11" 185–L
b. Simcoe, May 25, 1959

1991–92					
8 (1/1)	4–3–0	428	27	0	3.79
1992–93L					
3 (0/1)	0–3–0	160	15	0	5.63
Totals					
11 (1/2)	4–6–0	588	42	0	4.29

- acquired January 2, 1992, with Doug Gilmour, Jamie Macoun, Ric Nattress, and Kent Manderville from Calgary for Gary Leeman, Michel Petit, Craig Berube, Alexander Godynyuk, and Jeff Reese
- last Leaf games December 6, 11 and January 17, 1992–93
- retired during 1992–93 to become Leafs' goaltending consultant
- won bronze medals with Canada at 1983 WC and 1985 WC

DIXON WARD

#12 right wing   6' 200–R
b. Leduc, Alberta, September 23, 1968

1994–95	22	0	3	3	31

- acquired October 3, 1994, with Guy Leveque, Kelly Fairchild and Shayne Toporowski from Los Angeles Kings for Eric Lacroix, Chris Snell and a 4th-round draft choice in 1996 (Eric Belanger)
- released June 28, 1995

RON WARD

#25 centre   5'10" 180–R
b. Cornwall, September 12, 1944

1969–70	18	0	1	1	2

- turned pro with Tulsa in 1965
- first Leaf game October 11, 1969
- claimed June 10, 1970, by Vancouver Canucks at Expansion Draft

JEFF WARE

#23 defence   6'4" 220–L
b. Toronto, May 19, 1977

1996–97R	13	0	0	0	6
1997–98	2	0	0	0	0
Totals	15	0	0	0	6

- selected 15th overall at 1995 Entry Draft
- first Leaf game October 5, 1996
- traded to Florida for David Nemirovsky on February 17, 1999
- won gold medal with Canada at 1997 WJC

BOB WARNER

#16 defence   5'11" 180–L
b. Grimsby, December 13, 1950

1976–77R/L	10	1	1	2	4

- signed September 3, 1975, as a free agent
- only Leaf games February 25, 26, March 2, 7, 9, 12, 13, 15, 16 and April 2, 1977

TODD WARRINER

#8 left wing   6'1" 188–L
b. Blenheim, January 3, 1974

1994–95R	5	0	0	0	0
1995–96	57	7	8	15	26
1996–97	75	12	21	33	41
1997–98	45	5	8	13	20
1998–99	53	9	10	19	28
1999–2000	18	3	1	4	2
Totals	253	36	40	84	117

- acquired June 28, 1994, with Mats Sundin, Garth Butcher, and 1st-round draft choice in 1994 (later traded to Washington—Nolan Baumgartner—with Rob Pearson for Mike Ridley and a 1st-round draft choice—Eric Fichaud) from Quebec Nordiques for Wendel Clark, Sylvain Lefebvre, Landon Wilson, and a 1st-round draft choice in 1994 (Jeffrey Kealty)
- won silver medal with Canada at 1994 Olympics
- traded to Tampa Bay on November 29, 1999, for a 3rd-round draft choice in 2000 (Mikael Telqvist)

HARRY WATSON ("Whipper")

#4 left wing   6'1" 203–L
b. Saskatoon, Saskatchewan, May 6, 1923

1946–47	44	19	15	34	10
1947–48	57	21	20	41	16
1948–49	60	26	19	45	0
1949–50	60	19	16	35	11
1950–51	68	18	19	37	18
1951–52	70	22	17	39	18
1952–53	63	16	8	24	8
1953–54	70	21	7	28	30
1954–55	8	1	1	2	0
Totals	500	163	122	285	111

- acquired September 21, 1946, with Gerry Brown from Detroit for Doug Baldwin, Billy Taylor, and Ray Powell
- missed first part of 1954–55 with torn knee ligaments suffered October 31, 1954, vs. Rangers
- sold December 10, 1954, to Chicago
- after coaching for years, worked for a small business that supplies pricing machines to retail shops in Markham
- Hockey Hall of Fame 1994

DON WEBSTER

#19 left wing   5'7" 180–L
b. Toronto, July 3, 1924
d. Unknown

1943–44R/L	27	7	6	13	28

- signed October 24, 1942, and sent to Providence
- first Leaf game November 11, 1943
- traded October 13, 1944, with George Boothman to Buffalo (IHL) for Bill Ezinicki
- last Leaf game March 18, 1944

STAN WEIR

#14 centre   6'1" 180–L

b. Ponoka, Alberta, March 17, 1952

1975–76	64	19	32	51	22
1976–77	65	11	19	30	14
1977–78	30	12	5	17	4
Totals	159	42	56	98	40

- acquired June 20, 1975, from California for Gary Sabourin
- claimed on waivers July 4, 1979, by Edmonton

TREVOR "BLAKE" WESLEY

#28 defence   6'1" 200–L

b. Red Deer, Alberta, July 10, 1959

1985–86L	27	0	1	1	21

- signed July 31, 1985, as free agent
- last Leaf game January 19, 1986
- signed August 1987, as free agent by Boston

PETER WHITE

#18 centre   5'11" 200–L

b. Montreal, Quebec, March 15, 1969

1995–96	1	0	0	0	0

- acquired December 4, 1995, with a 4th-round draft choice in 1996 (Jason Sessa) from Oilers for Kent Manderville
- first and only Leaf game December 5, 1995
- demoted December 7, 1995, to St. John's; loaned January 23, 1996 to Atlanta (IHC) for balance of season
- signed as free agent August 19, 1996, by Flyers

ROD WILLARD

#28 left wing   6' 190–L

b. New Liskeard, May 1, 1960

1982–83R/L	1	0	0	0	0

- signed September 14, 1982, as a free agent

- first and only Leaf game November 17, 1982
- traded January 23, 1983, to Chicago for Dave Snopek

DAVE "TIGER" WILLIAMS

#22 left wing   5'11" 190–L

b. Weyburn, Saskatchewan, February 3, 1954

1974–75R	42	10	19	29	187
1975–76	78	21	19	40	299
1976–77	77	18	25	43	338
1977–78	78	19	31	50	351
1978–79	77	19	20	39	298
1979–80	55	22	18	40	197
Totals	407	109	132	241	1670

- selected 31st overall at 1974 Amateur Draft
- first Leaf game January 7, 1975
- traded February 18, 1980, with Jerry Butler to Vancouver Canucks for Rick Vaive and Bill Derlago
- later played professional roller hockey

CAROL "CULLY" WILSON

#7 right wing   5'8" 180–L

b. Winnipeg, Manitoba, 1893

d. Unknown

1919–20R	23	21	5	26	79
1920–21	8	2	1	3	16
Totals	31	23	6	29	95

- signed December 9, 1919
- first Arenas game December 23, 1919
- signed December 21, 1920, for 1920–21; played second half of season with Canadiens

DUNC WILSON

#1–30 goalie   5'11" 175–L
b. Toronto, March 22, 1948

1973–74
24 (1/2)   9–11–3   1412   68   1   2.89
1974–75
25 (1/3)   8–11–4   1393   86   0   3.70

Totals
49 (2/5)   17–22–7   2805   154   1   3.29

- acquired May 29, 1973, from Vancouver Canucks for Murray Heatley and Larry McIntyre
- claimed on waivers February 15, 1975, by Rangers

JOHNNY WILSON ("Iron Man")

#19 left wing   5'10" 175–L
b. Kincardine, June 14, 1929

1959–60	70	15	16	31	8
1960–61	3	0	1	1	0
Totals	73	15	17	32	8

- traded to Detroit in 1949 for Dusty Blair
- acquired June 9, 1959, with Frank Roggeveen from Detroit for Barry Cullen
- traded November 7, 1960, with Pat Hannigan to Rangers for Eddie Shack
- later coached in NHL (his nephew is Ron Wilson)

ROSS "LEFTY" WILSON

#1 goalie   5'11" 178–L
b. Toronto, October 15, 1919

1955–56
1 (0/1)   0–0–0   13   0   0   0.00

- replaced injured Harry Lumley during third period of game, January 22, 1956
- Detroit trainer for decades

RON WILSON

#11–14 defence   5'10" 170–R
b. Windsor, May 28, 1955

1977–78R	13	2	1	3	0
1978–79	46	5	12	17	4
1979–80	5	0	2	2	2
Totals	64	7	15	22	6

- selected 132nd overall at 1975 Amateur Draft
- first Leaf game March 4, 1978
- played with Kloten and Davos (Swiss League) 1980–85
- signed March 7, 1986, as free agent by Minnesota
- played for USA at 1975 WC (sixth place), 1981 WC (fifth), and 1987 WC (seventh)
- later coached in the NHL and internationally for USA, notably that country's win in the 1996 World Cup of Hockey

CRAIG WOLANIN ("Wooly")

#26 defence   6'4" 215–L
b. Grosse Pointe, Michigan, July 27, 1967

1997–98   10   0   0   0   6

- acquired January 31, 1997, from Tampa Bay for a 3rd-round draft choice in 1998 (traded to Edmonton—Alex Henry)
- missed most of 1997–99 with serious knee injury
- signed as a free agent by Detroit (IHL) on January 31, 1999

RANDY WOOD

#24 left wing   6' 195–L
b. Princeton, New Jersey, October 12, 1963

1994–95	48	13	11	24	34
1995–96	46	7	9	16	36
Totals	94	20	20	40	70

- claimed on waivers January 18, 1995, from Sabres

- traded January 28, 1996, with Benoît Hogue to Dallas for Dave Gagner and a 6th-round draft choice in 1996(Dmitri Yakushin)
- played for USA at 1986 WC (sixth place) and 1989 WC (sixth)

KEN WREGGET

#31–30 goalie 6'1" 195–L
b. Brandon, Manitoba, March 25, 1964

1983–84R					
3 (1/0)	1–1–1	165	14	0	5.09
1984–85					
23 (1/4)	2–15–3	1278	103	0	4.84
1985–86					
30 (4/3)	9–13–4	1566	113	0	4.33
1986–87					
56 (8/5)	22–28–3	3026	200	0	3.97
1987–88					
56 (7/4)	12–35–4	3000	222	2	4.44
1988–89					
32 (0/1)	9–20–2	1888	139	0	4.42

Totals
200 (21/17) 55–112–17 10923 791 2 4.34

- selected 45th overall in the 1982 Amateur Draft
- traded March 6, 1989, to Flyers for two 1st-round draft choices in 1989 (Rob Pearson and Steve Bancroft)
- played for Canada at 1984 WJC (fourth place) and 1990 WC (fourth place)

TERRY YAKE ("Yaker")

#25 right wing 5'11" 190–R
b. New Westminster, British Columbia, October 22, 1968

1994–95	19	3	2	5	2

- acquired September 28, 1994, from Anaheim for David Sacco
- released June 27, 1995

DMITRI YAKUSHIN

#49 defence 6' 200–L
b. Kharkov, USSR, January 21, 1978

1999–2000R	2	0	0	0	2

- selected 140th overall at 1996 Entry Draft
- currently in Leafs' organization

GARY YAREMCHUK ("Weasel")

#8–25–28–32 centre 6' 185–L
b. Edmonton, Alberta, August 15, 1961

1981–82R	18	0	3	3	10
1982–83	3	0	0	0	2
1983–84	1	0	0	0	0
1984–85L	12	1	1	2	16
Totals	34	1	4	5	28

- selected 24th overall at 1981 Entry Draft
- first Leaf game October 6, 1981
- signed August 13, 1985, as free agent by Detroit
- last Leaf game April 7, 1985

KEN YAREMCHUK ("Yammer")

#16–15–34 centre 5'11" 185–R
b. Edmonton, Alberta, January 1, 1964

1986–87	20	3	8	11	16
1987–88	16	2	5	7	10
1988–89L	11	1	0	1	2
Totals	47	6	13	19	28

- acquired September 6, 1986, with Jerome Dupont and a 4th-round draft choice in 1987 (Joe Sacco) from Chicago as compensation for signing Gary Nylund
- last Leaf games November 21, 23, 25, 26, December 1, 9, 10, 12, 15 and February 17, 18, 1988–89
- played for Canada at 1988 Olympics (fourth place)
- later played in Europe

DMITRI YUSHKEVICH (later DMITRY)
("Tree"/"Yushkie")
#25–36 defence   5'11" 208–R
b. Yaroslavl, USSR, November 19, 1971

1995–96	69	1	10	11	54
1996–97	74	4	10	14	56
1997–98	72	0	12	12	78
1998–99	78	6	22	28	88
1999–2000	77	3	24	27	55
2000–01	81	5	19	24	52
Totals	451	19	97	116	383

- acquired August 30, 1995, with a 2nd-round draft choice in 1996 (Francis Larivee) from Flyers for a 1st-round draft choice in 1996 (Dainius Zubrus), a 4th-round draft choice in 1996 (later traded to Los Angeles—Mikael Simmons), and a 2nd-round draft choice in 1997 (Jean-Marc Pelletier)
- played with Soviet Union at 1989 WJC (gold medal), 1990 WJC (silver), and 1991 WJC (silver); won gold medal with Russia at 1992 Olympics; played at 1992 WC (fifth place), 1993 WC (gold), 1994 WC (fifth), and 1998 Olympics (silver)

RON ZANUSSI
#39–32 right wing   5'11" 180–R
b. Toronto, August 31, 1956

1980–81	12	3	0	3	6
1981–82L	43	0	8	8	14
Totals	55	3	8	11	20

- acquired March 10, 1981, with a 3rd-round draft choice in 1981 (Ernie Godden) from Minnesota for a 2nd-round draft choice in 1981 (Dave Donnelly)
- last Leaf game February 10, 1982

ROB ZETTLER ("Zets")
#3–2 defence   6'3" 195–L
b. Sept-Iles, Quebec, March 8, 1968

1995–96	29	0	1	1	48
1996–97	48	2	12	14	51
1997–98	59	0	7	7	108
Totals	136	2	20	22	207

- acquired July 8, 1995, from Flyers for a 5th-round draft choice in 1996 (Per-Ragna Bergovist)
- claimed by Nashville in Expansion Draft on June 26, 1998

PETER ZEZEL
#25 centre   5'11" 200–L
b. Toronto, April 22, 1965

1990–91	32	14	14	28	4
1991–92	64	16	33	49	26
1992–93	70	12	23	35	24
1993–94	41	8	8	16	19
Totals	207	50	78	128	73

- acquired January 16, 1991, with Bob Rouse from Washington for Al Iafrate
- lost August 10, 1994, with Grant Marshall to Dallas Stars as equal compensation for Leafs signing Mike Craig

Coaching Register, Playoffs

YEAR	GP	W	L	T	SERIES

NICK BEVERLEY

YEAR	GP	W	L	T	SERIES
1996	6	2	4	0	0-1

JOHN BROPHY

YEAR	GP	W	L	T	SERIES
1987	13	7	6	0	1-1
1988	6	2	4	0	0-1
Totals	19	9	10	0	1-2

PAT BURNS

YEAR	GP	W	L	T	SERIES
1993	21	11	10	0	2-1
1994	18	9	9	0	2-1
1995	7	3	4	0	0-1
Totals	46	23	23	0	4-3

DOUG CARPENTER

YEAR	GP	W	L	T	SERIES
1990	5	1	4	0	0-1

DICK CARROLL

YEAR	GP	W	L	T	SERIES
1918	7	4	3	0	2-0
1921	2	0	2	0	0-1
Totals	9	4	5	0	1-1

KING CLANCY

YEAR	GP	W	L	T	SERIES
1954	5	1	4	0	0-1
1955	4	0	4	0	0-1
1956	5	1	4	0	0-1
Totals	14	2	12	0	0-3

HAPPY DAY

YEAR	GP	W	L	T	SERIES
1941	7	3	4	0	0-1
1942	13	8	5	0	2-0
1943	6	2	4	0	0-1
1944	5	1	4	0	0-1
1945	13	8	5	0	2-0
1947	11	8	3	0	2-0
1948	9	8	1	0	2-0
1949	9	8	1	0	2-0
1950	7	3	4	0	0-1
Totals	80	49	31	0	10-4

ART DUNCAN

YEAR	GP	W	L	T	SERIES
1931	2	0	1	1	0-1

PUNCH IMLACH

YEAR	GP	W	L	T	SERIES
1959	12	8	4	0	1-1
1960	10	4	6	0	1-1
1961	5	1	4	0	0-1
1962	12	8	4	0	2-0
1963	10	8	2	0	2-0
1964	14	8	6	0	2-0
1965	6	2	4	0	0-1
1966	4	0	4	0	0-1
1967	12	8	4	0	2-0
1969	4	0	4	0	0-1
1980	3	0	3	0	0-1
Total	92	47	45	0	10-7

DICK IRVIN

YEAR	GP	W	L	T	SERIES
1932	7	5	1	1	3-0
1933	9	4	5	0	1-1
1934	5	2	3	0	0-1
1935	7	3	4	0	1-1
1936	9	4	5	0	2-1
1937	2	0	2	0	0-1
1938	7	4	3	0	1-1
1939	10	5	5	0	2-1
1940	10	6	4	0	2-1
Totals	66	33	32	1	12-8

RED KELLY

1974	4	0	4	0	0–1
1975	7	2	5	0	1–1
1976	10	5	5	0	1–1
1977	10	5	5	0	1–1
Totals	31	12	19	0	3–4

DAN MALONEY

1986	10	6	4	0	1–1

JOHN McLELLAN

1971	6	2	4	0	0–1
1972	5	1	4	0	0–1
Totals	11	3	8	0	0–2

ROGER NEILSON

1978	13	6	7	0	2–1
1979	6	2	4	0	1–1
Totals	19	8	11	0	3–2

MIKE NYKOLUK

1981	3	0	3	0	0–1
1983	4	1	3	0	0–1
Totals	7	1	6	0	0–2

EDDIE POWERS

1922	7	4	2	1	2–0
1925	2	0	2	0	0–1
Totals	9	4	4	1	2–1

JOE PRIMEAU

1951	11	8	2	1	2–0
1952	4	0	4	0	0–1
Totals	15	8	6	1	2–1

PAT QUINN

1999	17	9	8	0	2–1
2000	12	6	6	0	1–1
2001	11	7	4	0	1–1
Totals	40	22	18	0	4–3

CONN SMYTHE

1929	4	2	2	0	1–1

All-Time Coaching Records, Playoffs

Stanley Cups

Happy Day	5
Punch Imlach	4
Dick Irvin	1
Joe Primeau	1
Dick Carroll	1 (Arenas)
Eddie Powers	1 (St. Pats)

Most Seasons in Playoffs

Dick Irvin	9
Happy Day	9
Punch Imlach	9
Red Kelly	4

Most Games in Playoffs

Punch Imlach	92
Happy Day	80
Dick Irvin	66
Pat Quinn	40

Most Wins in Playoffs

Happy Day	49
Punch Imlach	44
Dick Irvin	33
Pat Quinn	22

Most Losses in Playoffs

Punch Imlach	49
Dick Irvin	32
Happy Day	31

Winning Percentage, All Coaches, Playoffs

.643	Eddie Powers
.613	Happy Day
.600	Dan Maloney
.567	Joe Primeau
.550	Pat Quinn
.508	Dick Irvin
.500	Pat Burns
.500	Conn Smythe
.474	John Brophy
.473	Punch Imlach
.421	Roger Neilson
.367	Red Kelly
.364	Dick Carroll
.333	Nick Beverley
.273	John McLellan
.250	Mike Nykoluk
.250	Art Duncan
.200	Doug Carpenter
.143	King Clancy
.000	Floyd Smith
.000	Joe Crozier

Leafs All-Time Playoff Register

r = indicates a player's rookie season

JACK ADAMS

1918r	2	2	0	2	3
1925	2	1	0	1	7
Totals	4	3	0	3	10

KEVYN ADAMS

1999	7	0	2	2	14
2000	12	1	0	1	7
Totals	19	1	2	3	21

CLAIRE ALEXANDER

1975 r	7	0	0	0	0
1976	9	2	4	6	4
Totals	16	2	4	4	4

MIKE ALLISON

1987	13	3	5	8	15

GLENN ANDERSON

1993	21	7	11	18	31

JOHN ANDERSON

1978r	2	0	0	0	0
1979	6	0	2	2	0
1980	3	1	1	2	0
1981	2	0	0	0	0
1983	4	2	4	6	0
Totals	17	3	7	10	0

LLOYD ANDREWS

1922r	7	2	0	2	5

DAVE ANDREYCHUK

1993	21	12	7	19	35
1994	18	5	5	10	16
1995	7	3	2	5	25
Totals	46	20	14	34	76

GREG ANDRUSAK

2000	3	0	0	0	2

NIKOLAI ANTROPOV

2000	3	0	0	0	4
2001	9	2	1	3	12
Totals	12	2	1	3	16

SYL APPS

1937r	2	0	1	1	0
1938	7	1	4	5	0
1939	10	2	6	8	2
1940	10	5	2	7	2
1941	7	3	2	5	2
1942	13	5	9	14	2
1947	11	5	1	6	0
1948	9	4	4	8	0
Totals	69	25	29	54	8

AL ARBOUR

1962r	8	0	0	0	6
1964	1	0	0	0	0
1965	1	0	0	0	2
Totals	9	0	0	0	8

GEORGE ARMSTRONG

1952r	4	0	0	0	2
1954	5	1	0	1	2
1955	4	1	0	1	4
1956	5	4	2	6	0
1959	12	0	4	4	10
1960	10	1	4	5	4
1961	5	1	1	2	0
1962	12	7	5	12	2
1963	10	3	6	9	4
1964	14	5	8	13	10
1965	6	1	0	1	4
1966	4	0	1	1	4
1967	9	2	1	3	6
1969	4	0	0	0	0
1971	6	0	2	2	0
Totals	110	26	34	60	52

MURRAY ARMSTRONG

1938r	3	0	0	0	0

DON ASHBY

1977	9	1	0	1	4

NORMAND AUBIN

1983	1	0	0	0	0

ACE BAILEY

1929	4	1	2	3	4
1931	2	1	1	2	0
1932	7	1	0	1	4
1933	8	0	1	1	4
Totals	21	3	4	7	12

BOB BAILEY

1954r	5	0	2	2	4
1955	1	0	0	0	0
Totals	6	0	2	2	4

REID BAILEY

1983	2	0	0	0	2

EARL BALFOUR

1952r	1	0	0	0	0
1956	3	0	1	1	2
Totals	4	0	1	1	2

BILL BARILKO

1947r	11	0	3	3	18
1948	9	1	0	1	17
1949	9	0	1	1	20
1950	7	1	1	2	18
1951	11	3	2	5	31
Totals	47	5	7	12	104

ANDY BATHGATE

1964	14	5	4	9	25
1965	6	1	0	1	6
Totals	20	6	4	10	31

KEN BAUMGARTNER

1993	7	1	0	1	0
1994	10	0	0	0	18
Totals	17	1	0	1	18

BOB BAUN

1959	12	0	0	0	24
1960	10	1	0	1	17
1961	3	0	0	0	8
1962	12	0	3	3	19
1963	10	0	3	3	6
1964	14	2	3	5	42
1965	6	0	1	1	14
1966	4	0	1	1	8
1967	10	0	0	0	4
1971	6	0	1	1	19
1972	5	0	0	0	4
Totals	92	3	12	15	165

DON BEAUPRE

1996r					
2 (0/2)	0–0	20	2	0	6.00

JIM BENNING

1983	4	1	1	2	2

BRYAN BERARD

1999	17	1	8	9	8

MAX BENTLEY

1948	9	4	7	11	0
1949	9	4	3	7	2
1950	7	3	3	6	0
1951	11	2	11	13	4
1952	4	1	0	1	2
Totals	40	14	24	38	8

SERGEI BEREZIN

1999	17	6	6	12	4
2000	12	4	4	8	0
2001	11	2	5	7	2
Totals	40	12	15	27	6

AKI BERG

2001	11	0	2	2	4

BILL BERG

1993	21	1	1	2	18
1994	18	1	2	3	10
1995	7	0	1	1	4
Totals	46	2	4	6	32

ALLAN BESTER

1987					
1 (0/1)	0–0	39	1	0	1.54
1988					
5 (1/0)	2–3	253	21	0	4.98
1990					
4 (0/1)	0–3	196	14	0	4.29
Totals					
10 (1/2)	2–6	488	36	0	4.43

PAUL BIBEAULT

1944r					
5 (0/0)	1–4	300	23	0	4.60

ANDY BLAIR

1929r	4	3	0	3	2
1931	2	1	0	1	0
1932	7	2	2	4	6
1933	9	0	2	2	4
1934	5	0	2	2	16
1935	2	0	0	0	2
1936	9	0	0	0	2
Totals	38	6	6	12	32

MIKE BLAISDELL

1988	6	1	2	3	10

GUS BODNAR

1944r	5	0	0	0	0
1945	13	3	1	4	4
1947	1	0	0	0	0
Totals	19	3	1	4	4

GARTH BOESCH

1947r	11	0	2	2	6
1948	8	2	1	3	2
1949	9	0	2	2	6
1950	6	0	0	0	4
Totals	34	2	5	7	18

LONNY BOHONOS

1999	9	3	6	9	2

LEO BOIVIN

1954	5	0	0	0	2

BUZZ BOLL

1933r	1	0	0	0	0
1934	5	0	0	0	9
1935	5	0	0	0	0
1936	9	7	3	10	2
1937	2	0	0	0	0
1938	7	0	0	0	2
Totals	29	7	3	10	13

HUGH BOLTON

1952r	3	0	0	0	4
1954	5	0	1	1	4
1955	4	0	3	3	6
1956	5	0	1	1	0
Totals	17	0	5	5	14

GEORGE BOOTHMAN

1944r	5	2	1	3	2

NIKOLAI BORSCHEVSKY

1993r	16	2	7	9	0
1994	15	2	2	4	4
Totals	31	4	9	13	4

LAURIE BOSCHMAN

1980r	3	1	1	2	18
1981	3	0	0	0	7
Totals	6	1	1	2	25

BRUCE BOUDREAU

1977	3	0	0	0	0
1981	2	1	0	1	0
1983	4	1	0	1	4
Totals	9	2	0	2	4

PAT BOUTETTE

1976r	10	1	4	5	16
1977	9	0	4	4	17
1978	13	3	3	6	40
1979	6	2	2	4	22
Totals	38	6	13	19	95

JOHNNY BOWER

1959

12 (0/0) 5–7 749 39 0 3.12

1960

10 (0/0) 4–6 645 31 0 2.88

1961

3 (0/0) 0–3 180 9 0 3.00

1962

10 (1/0) 5–4 579 22 0 2.28

1963*

10 (0/0) 8–2 600 16 2 1.60

1964

14 (0/0) 8–6 850 30 2 2.12

1965

5 (0/0) 2–3 317 13 0 2.46

1966

2 (0/0) 0–2 120 8 0 4.00

1967

4 (1/1) 2–0 155 5 1 1.94

1969

4 (0/3) 0–2 154 11 0 4.29

Totals

74 (2/4) 34–35 4349 184 5 2.58

* one assist

WALLY BOYER

| 1966r | 4 | 0 | 1 | 1 | 0 |

CARL BREWER

1959r	12	0	6	6	40
1960	10	2	3	5	16
1961	5	0	0	0	4
1962	8	0	2	2	22
1963	10	0	1	1	12
1964	12	0	1	1	30
1965	6	1	2	3	12
Totals	63	3	15	18	136

TURK BRODA

1937

2 (0/0) 0–2 134 5 0 2.24

1938

7 (0/0) 3–4 453 13 1 1.72

1939

10 (0/0) 5–5 617 20 2 1.94

1940

10 (0/0) 6–4 658 19 1 1.46

1941

7 (0/0) 3–4 438 15 0 2.05

1942

13 (0/0) 8–5 780 31 1 2.38

1943

6 (0/0) 2–4 441 20 0 2.72

1947

11 (0/0) 8–3 681 27 1 2.38

1948

9 (0/0) 8–1 558 20 1 2.15

1949

9 (0/0) 8–1 575 15 1 1.57

1950

7 (0/0) 3–4 450 10 3 1.33

1951

8 (0/1) 5–1* 493 9 2 1.10

1952

2 (0/0) 0–2 120 7 0 3.50

Totals

101 (0/1) 59–40–1 6398 211 13 1.97

* one tie

WILLIE BROSSART

| 1974 | 1 | 0 | 0 | 0 | 0 |

DAVE BURROWS

1979	6	0	1	1	7
1980	3	0	1	1	2
Totals	9	0	2	2	9

GARTH BUTCHER

| 1995 7 | 0 | 0 | 0 | 8 | |

JERRY BUTLER

1978	13	1	1	2	18
1979	6	0	0	0	4
Totals	19	1	1	2	22

LARRY CAHAN

1955r	4	0	0	0	0

HARRY CAMERON

1918	7	3	2	5	0
1921	2	0	0	0	2
1922	7	0	1	1	27
Totals	16	3	3	6	29

RANDY CARLYLE

1977r	9	0	1	1	20
1978	7	0	1	1	8
Totals	16	0	2	2	28

LORNE CARR

1942	13	3	2	5	6
1943	6	1	2	3	0
1944	5	0	1	1	0
1945	13	2	2	4	5
Totals	37	6	7	13	11

LARRY CARRIÈRE

1980	2	0	0	0	0

LORNE CHABOT

1929					
4 (0/0)	2–2	243	5	0	1.23
1931					
2 (0/0)	0–2	140	4	0	1.71
1932					
7 (0/0)	5–1*	438	15	0	2.05
1933					
9 (0/0)	4–5	688	18	2	1.57
Totals					
22 (0/0)	11–10	1509	42	2	1.57

* one tie

MURPH CHAMBERLAIN

1938r	5	0	0	0	2
1939	10	2	5	7	4
1940	3	0	0	0	0
Totals	18	2	5	7	6

LEX CHISHOLM

1941	3	1	0	1	0

JACK CHURCH

1939r	1	0	0	0	0
1940	10	1	1	2	6
1941	5	0	0	0	8
Totals	16	1	1	2	14

KING CLANCY

1931	2	1	0	1	0
1932	7	2	1	3	14
1933	9	0	3	3	14
1934	3	0	0	0	8
1935	7	1	0	1	8
1936	9	2	2	4	10
Totals	37	6	6	12	54

WENDEL CLARK

1986r	10	5	1	6	47
1987	13	6	5	11	38
1990	5	1	1	2	19
1993	21	10	10	20	51
1994	18	9	7	16	24
1996	6	2	2	4	2
2000	6	1	1	2	4
Totals	79	34	27	61	185

SPRAGUE CLEGHORN

1921	2	0	0	0	0

GARY COLLINS

1959r	2	0	0	0	0

BRIAN CONACHER

1967r	12	3	2	5	21

CHARLIE CONACHER

1931	2	0	1	1	0
1932	7	6	2	8	6
1933	9	1	1	2	10
1934	5	3	2	5	0
1935	7	1	4	5	6
1936	9	3	2	5	12
1937	2	0	0	0	5
Totals	41	14	12	26	39

BRANDON CONVERY

1996	5	0	0	0	2

BERT CORBEAU

1925	2	0	0	0	10

SHAYNE CORSON

2001	11	1	1	2	14

LES COSTELLO

1948r	5	2	2	4	2
1950	1	0	0	0	0
Totals	6	2	2	4	2

SYLVAIN CÔTÉ

1999	17	2	1	3	10

BALDY COTTON

1929	4	0	0	0	2
1931	2	0	0	0	2
1932	7	2	2	4	8
1933	9	0	3	3	6
1934	5	0	2	2	0
1935	7	0	0	0	17
Totals	34	2	7	9	35

RUSS COURTNALL

1986	10	3	6	9	8
1987	13	3	4	7	11
1988	6	2	1	3	0
Totals	29	8	11	19	19

DANNY COX

1929	4	0	1	1	4

MIKE CRAIG

1995	2	0	1	1	2
1996	6	0	0	0	18
Totals	8	0	1	1	20

RUSTY CRAWFORD

1918	2	2	1	3	0

DAVE CREIGHTON

1959	5	0	1	1	0

JIRI CRHA

1980					
2 (0/0)	0–2	121	10	0	4.96
1981					
3 (2/1)	0–2	65	11	0	10.15
Totals					
5 (2/1)	0–4	186	21	0	6.77

CORY CROSS

2000	12	0	2	2	2
2001	11	2	1	3	10
Totals	23	2	3	5	12

BARRY CULLEN

1959	2	0	0	0	0

BRIAN CULLEN

1955r	4	1	0	1	0
1956	5	1	0	1	2
1959	10	1	0	1	0
Totals	19	3	0	3	2

JOHN CULLEN

1993	12	2	3	5	0
1994	3	0	0	0	0
Totals	15	2	3	5	0

BRIAN CURRAN

1988	6	0	0	0	41
1990	5	0	1	1	19
Totals	11	0	1	1	60

VINCENT DAMPHOUSSE

1987r	12	1	5	6	8
1988	6	0	1	1	10
1990	5	0	2	2	2
Totals	23	1	8	9	20

DAN DAOUST

1986	10	2	2	4	19
1987	13	5	2	7	42
1988	4	0	0	0	2
1990	5	0	1	1	20
Totals	32	7	5	12	83

HAROLD DARRAGH

1932	7	0	1	1	2

BOB DAVIDSON

1936r	9	1	3	4	2
1937	2	0	0	0	5
1938	7	0	2	2	10
1939	10	1	1	2	6
1940	10	0	3	3	16
1941	7	0	2	2	7
1942	13	1	2	3	20
1943	6	1	2	3	7
1944	5	0	0	0	4
1945	13	1	2	3	2
Totals	82	5	17	22	79

BOB DAWES

1949r	9	0	0	0	2

HAPPY DAY

1925	2	0	0	0	0
1929	4	1	0	1	4
1931	2	0	3	3	7
1932	7	3	3	6	6
1933	9	0	1	1	21
1934	5	0	0	0	6
1935	7	0	0	0	4
1936	9	0	0	0	8
1937	2	0	0	0	0
Totals	47	4	7	11	56

DALE DEGRAY

1988	5	0	1	1	16

CORB DENNENAY

1918	7	3	2	5	3
1921	2	0	0	0	0
1922	7	4	2	6	2
Totals	16	7	4	11	5

BILL DERLAGO

1980	3	0	0	0	4
1981	3	1	0	1	2
1983	4	3	0	3	2
Totals	10	4	0	4	8

ERNIE DICKENS

1942r	13	0	0	0	4

GERALD DIDUCK

2000	10	0	1	1	14

PAUL DIPIETRO

1995	7	1	1	2	0

TIE DOMI

1995	7	1	0	1	0
1996	6	0	2	2	4
1999	14	0	2	2	24
2000	12	0	1	1	20
2001	8	0	1	1	20
Totals	47	1	6	7	68

KEN DORATY

1933	9	5	0	5	4
1934	5	2	2	4	0
1935	1	0	0	0	0
Totals	15	7	2	9	4

JIM DOREY

1969r	4	0	1	1	21
1971	6	0	1	1	19
Totals	10	0	2	2	40

KENT DOUGLAS

1963r	10	1	1	2	2
1965	5	0	1	1	19
1966	4	0	1	1	12
Totals	19	1	3	4	33

GORD DRILLON

1937r	2	0	0	0	0
1938	7	7	1	8	2
1939	10	7	6	13	4
1940	10	3	1	4	0
1941	7	3	2	5	2
1942	9	2	3	5	2
Totals	45	22	13	35	10

DICK DUFF

1956r	5	1	4	5	2
1959	12	4	3	7	8
1960	10	2	4	6	6
1961	5	0	1	1	2
1962	12	3	10	13	20
1963	10	4	1	5	2
Totals	54	14	23	37	40

ART DUNCAN

1929	4	0	0	0	4
1931	1	0	0	0	0
Totals	5	0	0	0	4

DAVE DUNN

1975	7	1	1	2	24
1976	3	0	0	0	17
Totals	10	1	1	2	41

DENIS DUPERE

1971r	6	0	0	0	0
1972	5	0	0	0	0
1974	3	0	0	0	0
Totals	14	0	0	0	0

SLAVA DURIS

1981r	3	0	1	1	2

BABE DYE

1921	2	0	0	0	9
1922	7	11	2	13	5
1925	2	0	0	0	0
Totals	11	11	2	13	14

DALLAS EAKINS

1999	1	0	0	0	0

MIKE EASTWOOD

1993r	10	1	2	3	8
1994	18	3	2	5	12
Totals	28	4	4	8	20

TIM ECCLESTONE

1974	4	0	1	1	0

GARRY EDMUNDSON

1960	9	0	1	1	4

GERRY EHMAN

1959	12	6	7	13	8
1960	9	0	0	0	0
1964	9	1	0	1	4
Totals	30	7	7	14	12

DAVE ELLETT

1993	21	4	8	12	8
1994	18	3	15	18	31
1995	7	0	2	2	0
1996	6	0	0	0	4
Totals	52	7	25	32	43

RON ELLIS

1965r	6	3	0	3	2
1966	4	0	0	0	2
1967	12	2	1	3	4
1969	4	2	1	3	2
1971	6	1	1	2	2
1972	5	1	1	2	4
1974	4	2	1	3	0
1975	7	3	0	3	2
1978	13	3	2	5	0
1979	6	1	1	2	2
1980	3	0	0	0	0
Totals	70	18	8	26	20

AUT ERICKSON

1967	1	0	0	0	2

DARYL EVANS

1987r	1	0	0	0	0

PAUL EVANS

1977r	2	0	0	0	0

BILL EZINICKI

1947	11	0	2	2	30
1948	9	3	1	4	6
1949	9	1	4	5	20
1950	5	0	0	0	13
Totals	34	4	7	11	69

JEFF FARKAS

2000r	3	1	0	1	0

DAVE FARRISH

1980	3	0	0	0	10
1981	1	0	0	0	0
Totals	4	0	0	0	10

DOUG FAVELL

1974r					
3 (0/0)	0–3	182	10	0	3.30

TOM FERGUS

1986	10	5	7	12	6
1987	2	0	1	1	2
1988	6	2	3	5	2
1990	5	2	1	3	4
Totals	23	9	12	21	14

GEORGE FERGUSON

1974	3	0	1	1	2
1975	7	1	0	1	7
1976	10	2	4	6	2
1977	9	0	3	3	7
1978	13	5	1	6	7
Totals	42	8	9	17	25

FRANK FINNIGAN

1932	7	2	3	5	8
1935	7	1	2	3	2
1936	9	0	3	3	0
1937	2	0	0	0	0
Totals	25	3	8	11	10

FERN FLAMAN

1951	9	1	0	1	8
1952	4	0	2	2	18
1954	2	0	0	0	0
Totals	15	1	2	3	26

BILL FLETT

1975	5	0	0	0	2

MIKE FOLIGNO

1993	18	2	6	8	42

JAKE FORBES

1921r					
2 (0/0)	0–2	120	7	0	3.50

JACK FORSEY

1943r	3	0	1	1	0

JIM FOWLER

1937r	2	0	0	0	0
1938	7	0	2	2	0
1939	9	0	1	1	2
Totals	18	0	3	3	2

LOU FRANCESCHETTI

1990	5	0	1	1	26

MIROSLAV FRYCER

1983	4	2	5	7	0
1986	10	1	3	4	10
1988	3	0	0	0	6
Totals	17	3	8	11	16

DAVE GAGNER

1996	6	0	2	2	6

BRUCE GAMBLE

1969r					
3 (3/0)	0–2	86	13	0	9.07

CAL GARDNER

1949	9	2	5	7	0
1950	7	1	0	1	4
1951	11	1	1	2	4
1952	3	0	0	0	2
Totals	30	4	6	10	10

PAUL GARDNER

1979	6	0	1	1	4

SCOTT GARLAND

1976r	7	1	2	3	35

MIKE GARTNER

1994	18	5	6	11	14
1995	5	2	2	4	2
1996	6	4	1	5	4
Totals	29	11	9	20	20

STEWART GAVIN

1983	4	0	0	0	0

EDDIE GERARD

1922	1	0	0	0	0

TODD GILL

1986r	1	0	0	0	0
1987	13	2	2	4	42
1988	6	1	3	4	20
1990	5	0	3	3	16
1993	21	1	10	11	26
1994	18	1	5	6	37
1995	7	0	3	3	6
1996	6	0	0	0	24
Totals	77	5	26	31	171

DOUG GILMOUR

1993	21	10	25	35	30
1994	18	6	22	28	42
1995	7	0	6	6	6
1996	6	1	7	8	12
Totals	52	17	60	77	90

GASTON GINGRAS

1983	3	1	2	3	2

BRIAN GLENNIE

1971	3	0	0	0	0
1972	5	0	0	0	25
1974	3	0	0	0	10
1976	6	0	1	1	15
1977	2	0	0	0	0
1978	13	0	0	0	16
Totals	32	0	1	1	66

BOB GOLDHAM

1942r	13	2	2	4	31

HANK GOLDUP

1940r	10	5	1	6	4
1941	7	0	0	0	0
1942	9	0	0	0	2
Totals	26	5	1	6	6

CHRIS GOVEDARIS

1994	2	0	0	0	0

BOB GRACIE

1931r	2	0	0	0	0
1932	7	3	1	4	0
1933	9	0	1	1	0
Totals	18	3	2	5	0

GEORGE HAINSWORTH

1934					
5 (0/0)	2–3	302	11	0	2.19
1935					
7 (0/0)	3–4	460	12	2	1.57

1936

9 (0/0)	3–6	541	27	0	2.99

Totals					
21 (0/0)	8–13	1303	50	2	2.30

JACK HAMILTON

1943r	6	1	1	2	0
1944	5	1	0	1	0
Totals	11	2	1	3	0

REG HAMILTON

1937r	2	0	1	1	2
1938	7	0	1	1	2
1939	10	0	2	2	4
1940	10	0	0	0	0
1941	7	1	2	3	13
1943	6	1	1	2	9
1944	5	1	0	1	8
1945	13	0	0	0	6
Totals	60	3	7	10	44

INGE HAMMARSTROM

1974r	4	1	0	1	0
1975	7	1	3	4	4
1977	2	0	0	0	0
Totals	13	2	3	5	4

DAVE HANNAN

1990	3	1	0	1	4

GORD HANNIGAN

1954	5	2	0	2	4
1956	4	0	0	0	4
Totals	9	2	0	2	8

BILLY HARRIS

1956r	5	1	0	1	4

BILLY HARRIS

1983	4	0	1	1	2

JIM HARRISON

1971	6	0	1	1	33
1972	5	1	0	1	10
Totals	11	1	1	2	43

PAUL HARRISON

1979

2 (0/1)	0–1	91	7	0	4.62

1981

1 (0/1)	0–0	40	1	0	1.50

Totals					
3 (0/2)	0–1	131	8	0	3.66

GLENN HEALY

1999

1 (0/1)	0–0	20	0	0	0.00

PAUL HENDERSON

1969	4	0	1	1	0
1971	6	5	1	6	4
1972	5	1	2	3	6
1974	4	0	2	2	2
Totals	19	6	6	12	12

DARBY HENDRICKSON

1994r	2	0	0	0	0

1959–1964 (top right table)

1959	12	3	4	7	16
1960	9	0	3	3	4
1961	5	1	0	1	0
1962	12	2	1	3	2
1963	10	0	1	1	0
1964	9	1	1	2	4
Totals	62	8	10	18	30

RED HERON

1939r	2	0	0	0	4
1940	9	2	0	2	2
1941	7	0	2	2	0
Totals	18	2	2	4	6

PAT HICKEY

1980	3	0	0	0	2
1981	2	0	0	0	0
Totals	5	0	0	0	2

PAUL HIGGINS

1983r	1	0	0	0	0

MEL HILL

1943	6	3	0	3	0
1945	13	2	3	5	6
Totals	19	5	3	8	6

LARRY HILLMAN

1961	5	0	0	0	0
1964	11	0	0	0	2
1966	4	1	1	2	6
1967	12	1	2	3	0
Totals	32	2	3	5	8

JONAS HOGLUND

2000	12	2	4	6	2
2001	10	0	0	0	4
Totals	22	2	4	6	6

BENOÎT HOGUE

1995	7	0	0	0	6

FLASH HOLLETT

1935r	7	0	0	0	6

HARRY HOLMES

1918r					
7 (0/0)	4–3	420	26	0	3.71

TOOTS HOLWAY

1925	2	0	0	0	0

GEORGE HORNE

1929	4	0	0	0	4

RED HORNER

1929r	4	1	0	1	2
1931	2	0	0	0	4
1932	7	2	2	4	20
1933	9	1	0	1	10
1934	5	1	0	1	6
1935	7	0	1	1	4
1936	9	1	2	3	22
1937	2	0	0	0	7
1938	7	0	1	1	14
1939	10	1	2	3	26
1940	9	0	2	2	55
Totals	71	7	10	17	170

TIM HORTON

1950r	1	0	0	0	2
1954	5	1	1	2	4
1956	2	0	0	0	4
1959	12	0	3	3	16
1960	10	0	1	1	6
1961	5	0	0	0	0
1962	12	3	13	16	16
1963	10	1	3	4	10
1964	14	0	4	4	20
1965	6	0	2	2	13

1966	4	1	0	1	12
1967	12	3	5	8	25
1969	4	0	0	0	7
Totals	97	9	32	41	135

RON HURST

1956r	3	0	2	2	4

DAVE HUTCHISON

1979	6	0	3	3	23

AL IAFRATE

1986	10	0	3	3	4
1987	13	1	3	4	11
1988	6	3	4	7	6
Totals	29	4	10	14	21

MIROSLAV IHNACAK

1987	1	0	0	0	0

PETER IHNACAK

1986	10	2	3	5	12
1987	13	2	4	6	9
1988	5	0	3	3	4
Totals	28	4	10	14	25

ART JACKSON

1935	7	0	0	0	2
1936	8	0	3	3	2
1937	2	0	0	0	0
1945	8	0	0	0	0
Totals	25	0	3	3	4

HARVEY JACKSON

1931	2	0	0	0	2
1932	7	5	2	7	13
1933	9	3	1	4	2
1934	5	1	0	1	8
1935	7	3	2	5	2
1936	9	3	2	5	4
1937	2	1	0	1	2
1938	6	1	0	1	8
1939	7	0	1	1	2
Totals	54	17	8	25	43

GERRY JAMES

1956r	5	1	0	1	8
1960	10	0	0	0	0
Totals	15	1	0	1	8

PIERRE JARRY

1972	5	0	1	1	0

WES JARVIS

1987	2	0	0	0	2

LARRY JEFFREY

1967	6	0	1	1	4

GRANT JENNINGS

1995	4	0	0	0	0

TREVOR JOHANSEN

1978r	13	0	3	3	21

MIKE JOHNSON

1999	17	3	2	5	4

TERRY JOHNSON

1987	2	0	0	0	0
1988	3	0	0	0	10
Totals	5	0	0	0	10

EDDIE JOHNSTON

1974r					
1 (0/0)	0–1	60	6	0	6.00

ROSS JOHNSTONE

1944r	3	0	0	0	0

BUCK JONES

1943	6	0	0	0	8

JIMMY JONES

1978	13	1	5	6	7
1979	6	0	0	0	4
Totals	19	1	5	6	11

KENNY JONSSON

1995r	4	0	0	0	0

CURTIS JOSEPH

1999					
17 (1/0)	9–8–0	1011	41	1	2.43
2000					
12 (0/0)	6–6–0	729	25	1	2.06
2001					
11 (0/0)	7–4–0	685	24	3	2.10
Totals					
40 (1/0)	22-18-0	2425	90	5	2.23

BILL JUZDA

1949	9	0	2	2	8
1950	7	0	0	0	16
1951	11	0	0	0	7
1952	3	0	0	0	2
Totals	30	0	2	2	33

TOMAS KABERLE

1999	14	0	3	3	2
2000	12	1	4	5	0
2001	11	1	3	4	0
Totals	37	2	10	12	2

BINGO KAMPMAN

1938r	7	0	1	1	6
1939	10	1	1	2	20
1940	10	0	0	0	0
1941	7	0	0	0	0
1942	13	0	2	2	12
Totals	47	1	4	5	38

ALEXANDER KARPOVTSEV

2000	11	0	3	3	4

MIKE KASZYCKI

1980	2	0	0	0	2

RICK KEHOE

1972r	2	0	0	0	2

RED KELLY

1960	10	3	8	11	2
1961	2	1	0	1	0
1962	12	4	6	10	0
1963	10	2	6	8	6
1964	14	4	9	13	4
1965	6	3	2	5	2
1966	4	0	2	2	0
1967	12	0	5	5	2
Totals	70	17	38	55	16

PEP KELLY

1935r	7	2	0	2	4
1936	9	2	3	5	4
1938	7	2	2	4	2
1939	10	1	0	1	0
1940	6	0	1	1	0
Totals	39	7	6	13	10

FORBES KENNEDY

1969	1	0	0	0	38

TED KENNEDY

1944	5	1	1	2	4
1945	13	7	2	9	2
1947	11	4	5	9	4
1948	9	8	6	14	0
1949	9	2	6	8	2
1950	7	1	2	3	8
1951	11	4	5	9	6
1952	4	0	0	0	4
1954	5	1	1	2	2
1955	4	1	3	4	0
Totals	78	29	31	60	32

DAVE KEON

1961r	5	1	1	2	0
1962	12	5	3	8	0
1963	10	7	5	12	0
1964	14	7	2	9	2
1965	6	2	2	4	2
1966	4	0	2	2	0
1967	12	3	5	8	0
1969	4	1	3	4	2
1971	6	3	2	5	0
1972	5	2	3	5	0
1974	4	1	2	3	0
1975	7	0	5	5	0
Totals	89	32	35	67	6

DMITRI KHRISTICH

2000	12	1	2	3	0

HEC KILREA

1934	5	2	0	2	2
1935	6	0	0	0	4
Totals	11	2	0	2	6

DEREK KING

1999	16	1	3	4	4

KRIS KING

1999	17	1	1	2	25
2000	1	0	0	0	2
Totals	18	1	1	2	27

JOE KLUKAY

1943r	1	0	0	0	0
1947	11	1	0	1	0
1948	9	1	1	2	2
1949	9	2	3	5	4
1950	7	3	0	3	4
1951	11	4	3	7	0
1952	4	1	1	2	0
1955	4	0	0	0	4
Totals	56	12	8	20	14

LADISLAV KOHN

1999	2	0	0	0	5

MARK KOLESAR

1996	3	1	0	1	2

JOHN KORDIC

1990	5	0	1	1	33

JIM KORN

1983	3	0	0	0	26

IGOR KOROLEV

1999	1	0	0	0	0
2000	12	0	4	4	6
2001	11	0	0	0	0
Totals	24	0	4	4	6

CHRIS KOTSOPOULOS

1986	10	1	0	1	14
1987	7	0	0	0	14
Totals	17	1	0	1	28

MIKE KRUSHELNYSKI

1993	16	3	7	10	8
1994	6	0	0	0	0
Totals	22	3	7	10	8

ORLAND KURTENBACH

1966	4	0	0	0	20

TOM KURVERS

1990	5	0	3	3	4

NICK KYPREOS

1996	5	0	0	0	4

ERIC LACROIX

1994r	2	0	0	0	0

PETE LANGELLE

1939r	11	1	2	3	2
1940	10	0	3	3	0
1941	7	1	1	2	0
1942	13	3	3	6	2
Totals	41	5	9	14	4

RICK LANZ

1987	13	1	3	4	27
1988	1	0	0	0	2
Totals	14	1	3	4	29

MICHEL LAROCQUE

1981r					
2 (1/1)	0–1	75	8	0	6.40

GARY LEEMAN

1983r	2	0	0	0	2
1986	10	2	10	12	2
1987	5	0	1	1	14
1988	2	2	0	2	2
1990	5	3	3	6	16
Totals	24	7	14	21	36

SYLVAIN LEFEBVRE

1993	21	3	3	6	20
1994	18	0	3	3	16
Totals	39	3	6	9	36

ALEX LEVINSKY

1931r	2	0	0	0	0
1932	7	0	0	0	6
1933	9	1	0	1	14
1934	5	0	0	0	6
Totals	23	1	0	1	26

DANNY LEWICKI

1951r	9	0	0	0	0

RICK LEY

1969r	3	0	0	0	9
1971	6	0	2	2	4
1972	5	0	0	0	7
Totals	14	0	2	2	20

ED LITZENBERGER

1962	10	0	2	2	4
1963	9	1	2	3	6
1964	1	0	0	0	10
Totals	20	1	4	5	20

HARRY LUMLEY

1954					
5 (0/0)	1–4	322	15	0	2.80
1955					
4 (0/0)	0–4	240	14	0	3.50
1956					
5 (0/0)	1–4	305	14	1	2.75
Totals					
14 (0/0)	2–12	867	43	1	2.98

VIC LYNN

1947	11	4	1	5	16
1948	9	2	5	7	20
1949	8	0	1	1	2
1950	7	0	2	2	2
Totals	35	6	9	15	40

PARKER MacDONALD

1955r	4	0	0	0	4

FLEMING MACKELL

1949r	9	2	4	6	4
1950	7	1	1	2	11
1951	11	2	3	5	9
Totals	27	5	8	13	24

BILLY MacMILLAN

1971r	6	0	3	3	2
1972	5	0	0	0	0
Totals	11	0	3	3	2

JOHN MacMILLAN

1961r	4	0	0	0	0
1962	3	0	0	0	0
1963	1	0	0	0	0
Totals	8	0	0	0	0

JAMIE MACOUN

1993	21	0	6	6	36
1994	18	1	1	2	12
1995	7	1	2	3	8
1996	6	0	2	2	8
Totals	52	2	11	13	64

KEVIN MAGUIRE

1987r	1	0	0	0	0

FRANK MAHOVLICH

1959	12	6	5	11	18
1960	10	3	1	4	27
1961	5	1	1	2	6
1962	12	6	6	12	29
1963	9	0	2	2	8
1964	14	4	11	15	20
1965	6	0	3	3	9
1966	4	1	0	1	10
1967	12	3	7	10	8
Totals	84	24	36	60	135

ADAM MAIR

1999r	5	1	0	1	14
2000	5	0	0	0	8
Totals	10	1	0	1	22

DAN MALONEY

1978	13	1	3	4	17
1979	6	3	3	6	2
1981	3	0	0	0	4
Totals	22	4	6	10	23

Frank Mahovlich

KENT MANDERVILLE

1993r	18	1	0	1	8
1994	12	1	0	1	4
1995	7	0	0	0	6
Totals	37	2	0	2	18

CESARE MANIAGO

1961r					
2 (0/)	1–1	145	6	0	2.48

NORM MANN

1936r	1	0	0	0	0

DAVE MANSON

2001	2	0	0	0	2

MILAN MARCETTA

1967	3	0	0	0	0

GUS MARKER

1939	10	2	2	4	0
1940	10	1	3	4	23
1941	7	0	0	0	5
Totals	27	3	5	8	28

DANNY MARKOV

1999r	17	0	6	6	18
2000	12	0	3	3	10
2001	11	1	1	2	12
Totals	40	1	10	11	40

DANIEL MAROIS

1988r	3	1	0	1	0
1990	5	2	2	4	12
Totals	8	3	2	5	12

BRAD MARSH

1990	5	1	0	1	2

DON MARSHALL

1972	1	0	0	0	0

TERRY MARTIN

1980	3	2	0	2	7
1981	3	0	0	0	0
1983	4	0	0	0	9
Totals	10	2	0	2	16

BRAD MAXWELL

1986	3	0	1	1	12

CHRIS McALLISTER

1999	6	0	1	1	4

BRIAN McCABE

2001	11	2	3	5	16

ALYN McCAULEY

2000	5	0	0	0	6
2001	10	0	0	0	2
Totals	15	0	0	0	8

FRANK McCOOL

1945r					
13 (0/0)	8–5	808	30	4	2.23

JOHN McCORMACK

1950r	6	1	0	1	0

JOHN McCREEDY

1942r	13	4	3	7	6
1945	8	0	0	0	0
Totals	21	4	3	7	6

BUCKO McDONALD

1939	10	0	0	0	4
1940	10	0	0	0	0
1941	7	2	0	2	2
1942	13	0	1	1	2
1943	6	1	0	1	4
Totals	46	3	1	4	12

LANNY McDONALD

1975	7	0	0	0	2
1976	10	4	4	8	4
1977	9	10	7	17	6
1978	13	3	4	7	10
1979	6	3	2	5	0
Totals	45	20	17	37	22

BOB McGILL

1986	9	0	0	0	35
1987	3	0	0	0	0
Totals	12	0	0	0	35

JOHN McINTYRE

1990r	2	0	0	0	2

WALT McKECHNIE

1979	6	4	3	7	9

SEAN McKENNA

1988	2	0	0	0	0

DON McKENNEY

1964	12	4	8	12	0
1965	6	0	0	0	0
Totals	18	4	8	12	0

JIM McKENNY

1971	6	2	1	3	2
1972	5	3	0	3	2
1974	4	0	2	2	0
1975	7	0	1	1	2
1976	6	2	3	5	2
1977	9	0	2	2	2
Totals	37	7	9	16	10

JACK McLEAN

1943r	6	2	2	4	2
1944	3	0	0	0	6
1945 ·	4	0	0	0	0
Totals	13	2	2	4	8

DAVE McLLWAIN

1993	4	0	0	0	0

GORD McRAE

1975					
7 (0/0)	2–5	442	21	0	2.85
1976					
1 (0/1)	0–0	13	1	0	4.62
Totals					
8 (0/1)	2–5	455	22	0	2.90

KEN McRAE

1994	6	0	0	0	4

HOWIE MEEKER

1947r	11	3	3	6	6
1948	9	2	4	6	15
1950	7	0	1	1	4
1951	11	1	1	2	14
1952	4	0	0	0	11
Totals	42	6	9	15	50

HARRY MEEKING

1918	7	4	2	6	0

BARRY MELROSE

1981	3	0	1	1	15
1983	4	0	1	1	23
Totals	7	0	2	2	38

DON METZ

1940r	2	0	0	0	0
1941	5	1	1	2	2
1942	13	4	3	7	0
1945	11	0	1	1	4
1947	11	2	3	5	4
1948	2	0	0	0	0
1949	3	0	0	0	0
Totals	47	7	8	15	10

NICK METZ

1935r	6	1	1	2	0
1937	2	0	0	0	0
1938	7	0	2	2	0
1939	10	3	3	6	6
1940	9	1	3	4	9
1941	7	3	4	7	0
1942	13	4	4	8	12
1945	7	1	1	2	2

1947	6	4	2	6	0
1948	9	2	0	2	2
Totals	76	19	20	39	31

LARRY MICKEY

1969	3	0	0	0	5

RUDY MIGAY

1954	5	1	0	1	4
1955	3	0	0	0	10
1956	5	0	0	0	6
1959	2	0	0	0	0
Totals	15	1	0	1	20

EARL MILLER

1932	7	0	0	0	0

DMITRI MIRONOV

1993	14	1	2	3	2
1994	18	6	9	15	6
1995	6	2	1	3	2
Totals	38	9	12	21	10

FREDRIK MODIN

1999	8	0	0	0	6

GARRY MONAHAN

1971	6	2	0	2	2
1972	5	0	0	0	0
1974	4	0	1	1	7
Totals	15	2	1	3	9

DICKIE MOORE

1965	5	1	1	2	6

ELWYN MORRIS

1944r	5	1	2	3	2
1945	13	3	0	3	14
Totals	18	4	2	6	16

JIM MORRISON

1952	2	0	0	0	0
1954	5	0	0	0	4
1955	4	0	1	1	4
1956	5	0	0	0	4
Totals	16	0	1	1	12

GUS MORTSON

1947r	11	1	3	4	22
1948	5	1	2	3	2
1949	9	2	1	3	8
1950	7	0	0	0	18
1951	11	0	1	1	4
1952	4	0	0	0	8
Totals	47	4	7	11	62

RICHARD MULHERN

1980	1	0	0	0	0

KIRK MULLER

1996	6	3	2	5	0

HARRY MUMMERY

1918	7	1	4	5	0

LARRY MURPHY

1996	6	0	2	2	4

BOB NEELY

1974r	4	1	3	4	0
1975	3	0	0	0	2
1976	10	3	1	4	7
1977	9	1	3	4	6
Totals	26	5	7	12	15

ERIC NESTERENKO

1954	5	0	1	1	9
1955	4	0	1	1	6
Totals	9	0	2	2	15

MIKE NEVILLE

1925	2	0	0	0	0

BOB NEVIN

1961r	5	1	0	1	2
1962	12	2	4	6	6
1963	10	3	0	3	2
Totals	27	6	4	10	10

FRANK NIGRO

1983r	3	0	0	0	2

REG NOBLE

1918	7	3	2	5	3
1921	2	0	0	0	0
1922	7	0	2	2	20
Totals	16	3	4	7	23

GARY NYLUND

1986	10	0	2	2	25

ED OLCZYK

1988	6	5	4	9	2
1990	5	1	2	3	14
Totals	11	6	6	12	16

MURRAY OLIVER

1969	4	1	2	3	0

BERT OLMSTEAD

1959	12	4	2	6	13
1960	10	3	4	7	0
1961	3	1	2	3	10
1962	4	0	1	1	0
Totals	29	8	9	17	23

WINDY O'NEILL

1944r	4	0	0	0	6

MARK OSBORNE

1987	9	1	3	4	6
1988	6	1	3	4	16
1990	5	2	3	5	12
1993	19	1	1	2	16
1994	18	4	2	6	52
Totals	57	9	12	21	102

WILF PAIEMENT

1980	3	0	2	2	17
1981	3	0	0	0	2
Totals	6	0	2	2	19

MIKE PALMATEER

1977r					
6 (1/0)	3–3	360	16	0	2.67
1978					
13 (0/0)	6–7	795	32	2	2.42
1979					
5 (1/0)	2–3	298	17	0	3.42
1980					
1 (0/0)	0–1	60	7	0	7.00
1983					
4 (1/1)	1–3	252	17	0	4.05
Totals					
29 (3/1)	12–17	1765	89	2	2.99

JIM PAPPIN

1964r	11	0	0	0	0
1967	12	7	8	15	12
Totals	23	7	8	15	12

BERNIE PARENT

1971					
4 (1/0)	2–2	235	9	0	2.30
1972					
4 (0/0)	1–3	243	13	0	3.21
Totals					
8 (1/0)	3–5	478	22	0	2.76

GEORGE PARSONS

1938r	7	3	2	5	11

ROB PEARSON

1993	14	2	2	4	31
1994	14	1	0	1	32
Totals	28	3	2	5	63

SCOTT PEARSON

1990r	2	2	0	2	10

MIKE PELYK

1969	4	0	0	0	8
1971	6	0	0	0	10
1972	5	0	0	0	8
1974	4	0	0	0	4
1977	9	0	2	2	4
1978	12	0	1	1	7
Totals	40	0	3	3	41

YANIC PERREAULT

1999	17	3	6	9	6
2000	1	0	1	1	0
2001	11	2	3	5	4
Totals	29	5	10	15	10

ERIC PETTINGER

1929	4	1	0	1	8

PIERRE PILOTE

1969	4	0	1	1	4

JACQUES PLANTE

1971						
3 (0/1)	0–2	134	7		0	3.13
1972						
1 (0/0)	0–1	60	5		0	5.00
Totals						
4 (0/1)	0–3	194	12		0	3.71

WALT PODDUBNY

1983	4	3	1	4	0
1986	9	4	1	5	4
Totals	13	7	2	9	4

BUD POILE

1943r	6	2	4	6	4
1947	7	2	0	2	2
Totals	13	4	4	8	6

FELIX POTVIN

1993r					
21 (1/0)	11–10	1308	62	1	2.84
1994					
18 (1/0)	9–9	1124	46	3	2.46
1995					
7 (0/0)	3–4	424	20	1	2.83
1996					
6 (0/0)	2–4	350	19	0	3.26
Totals					
52 (2/0)	25–27	3206	147	5	2.75

TRACY PRATT

1977	4	0	0	0	0

"BABE" PRATT

1943	6	1	2	3	8
1944	5	0	3	3	4
1945	13	2	4	6	8
Totals	24	3	9	12	20

WAYNE PRESLEY

1996	5	0	0	0	2

NOEL PRICE

1959r	5	0	0	0	2

JOE PRIMEAU

1931	2	0	0	0	0
1932	7	0	6	6	2
1933	8	0	1	1	4
1934	5	2	4	6	6
1935	7	0	3	3	0
1936	9	3	4	7	0
Totals	38	5	18	23	12

MARCEL PRONOVOST

1966	4	0	0	0	6
1967	12	1	0	1	8
Totals	16	1	0	1	14

BOB PULFORD

1959	12	4	4	8	8
1960	10	4	1	5	10
1961	5	0	0	0	8
1962	12	7	1	8	24
1963	10	2	5	7	14
1964	14	5	3	8	20
1965	6	1	1	2	16
1966	4	1	1	2	12
1967	12	1	10	11	12
1969	4	0	0	0	2
Totals	89	25	26	51	126

DAREN PUPPA

1993r

1 (0/1)	0–0	20	1	0	3.00

JOEL QUENNEVILLE

1979r	6	0	1	1	4

PAT QUINN

1969r	4	0	0	0	13

ROB RAMAGE

1990	5	1	2	3	20

KEN RANDALL

1918	7	2	1	3	0
1921	2	0	0	0	6
1922	5	2	0	2	13
Totals	14	4	1	5	19

MARC REAUME

1955r	4	0	0	0	2
1956	5	0	2	2	6
1959	10	0	0	0	0
Totals	19	0	2	2	8

JEFF REESE

1990r

2 (1/0)	1–1	108	6	0	3.33

LARRY REGAN

1959	8	1	1	2	2
1960	10	3	3	6	0
1961	4	0	0	0	0
Totals	22	4	4	8	2

DAVE REID

1990	3	0	0	0	0

REG REID

1925r	2	0	0	0	0

DAMIAN RHODES

1994r

1 (1/1)	0–0	1	1	0	0.00

LUKE RICHARDSON

1988r	2	0	0	0	0
1990	5	0	0	0	22
Totals	7	0	0	0	22

MIKE RIDLEY

1995	7	3	1	4	2

JOHN ROSS ROACH

1922					
7 (0/0)	4–2*	425	13	2	1.84
1925					
2 (0/0)	0–2	120	5	0	2.50
Totals					
9 (0/0)	4–4–1	545	18	2	1.98

* one tie

RENÉ ROBERT

1981	3	0	2	2	2

GARY ROBERTS

2001	11	2	9	11	0

FRED ROBERTSON

1932r	7	0	0	0	0

AL ROLLINS

1951					
4 (1/0)	3–1	211	6	0	1.71
1952					
2 (0/0)	0–2	120	6	0	3.00
Totals					
6 (1/0)	3–3	331	12	0	2.18

DOC ROMNES

1939	10	1	4	5	0

BILL ROOT

1986	7	0	2	2	13
1987	13	1	0	1	12
Totals	20	1	2	3	25

BOB ROUSE

1993	21	3	8	11	29
1994	18	0	3	3	29
Totals	39	3	11	14	58

WARREN RYCHEL

1995	3	0	0	0	0

ROCKY SAGANIUK

1979r	3	1	0	1	5
1980	3	0	0	0	10
Totals	6	1	0	1	15

RICK ST. CROIX

1983r					
1 (1/1)	0–0	1	1	0	60.00

BORJE SALMING

1974r	4	0	1	1	4
1975	7	0	4	4	6
1976	10	3	4	7	9
1977	9	3	6	9	6
1978	6	2	2	4	6
1979	6	0	1	1	8
1980	3	1	1	2	2
1981	3	0	2	2	4
1983	4	1	4	5	10
1986	10	1	6	7	14

1987	13	0	3	3	14
1988	6	1	3	4	8
Totals	81	12	37	49	91

PHIL SAMIS

1948r	5	0	1	1	2

CHARLIE SANDS

1933r	9	2	2	4	2
1934	4	1	0	1	0
Totals	13	3	2	5	2

TERRY SAWCHUK

1965					
1 (0/0)	0–1	60	3	0	3.00
1966					
2 (0/0)	0–2	120	6	0	3.00
1967					
10 (1/1)	6–4	568	25	0	2.64
Totals					
13 (1/1)	6–7	748	34	0	2.73

MATHIEU SCHNEIDER

1996	6	0	4	4	8

"SWEENEY" SCHRINER

1940	10	1	3	4	4
1941	7	2	1	3	4
1942	13	6	3	9	10
1943	4	2	2	4	0
1945	13	3	1	4	4
Totals	47	14	10	24	22

AL SECORD

1988	6	1	0	1	16

RON SEDLBAUER

1981	2	0	1	1	2

ROD SEILING

1975	7	0	0	0	0
1976	10	0	1	1	6
Totals	17	0	1	1	6

BRIT SELBY

1966r	4	0	0	0	0
1969	4	0	0	0	4
Totals	8	0	0	0	4

BRAD SELWOOD

1972	5	0	0	0	4

EDDIE SHACK

1961	4	0	0	0	2
1962	9	0	0	0	18
1963	10	2	1	3	11
1964	13	0	1	1	25
1965	5	1	0	1	8
1966	4	2	1	3	33
1967	8	0	0	0	8
1974	4	1	0	1	2
Totals	57	6	3	9	107

DAVE SHAND

1981	3	0	0	0	0
1983	4	1	0	1	13
Totals	7	1	0	1	13

JACK SHILL

1934r	1	0	0	0	0
1936	9	0	3	3	8
1937	2	0	0	0	0
Totals	12	0	3	3	8

DON SIMMONS

1962r					
3 (0/1)	2–0	165	8	0	2.91

DARRYL SITTLER

1971r	6	2	1	3	31
1972	3	0	0	0	2
1974	4	2	1	3	6
1975	7	2	1	3	15
1976	10	5	7	12	19
1977	9	5	16	21	4
1978	13	3	8	11	12
1979	6	5	4	9	17
1980	3	1	2	3	10
1981	3	0	0	0	4
Totals	64	25	40	65	120

ALF SKINNER

1918	5	8	1	9	0

TOD SLOAN

1951	11	4	5	9	18
1952	4	0	0	0	10
1954	5	1	1	2	24
1955	4	0	0	0	2
1956	2	0	0	0	5
Totals	26	5	6	11	59

ART SMITH

1929	4	1	1	2	8

BRAD SMITH

1986	6	2	1	3	20
1987	11	1	1	2	24
Totals	17	3	2	5	44

FLOYD SMITH

1969	4	0	0	0	0

SID SMITH

1948r	2	0	0	0	0
1949	6	5	2	7	0
1950	7	0	3	3	2
1951	11	7	3	10	0
1952	4	0	0	0	0
1954	5	1	1	2	0
1955	4	3	1	4	0
1956	5	1	0	1	0
Totals	44	17	10	27	2

ROD SMYLIE

1921	2	0	0	0	0
1922	6	1	2	3	2
1925	2	0	0	0	0
Totals	10	1	2	3	2

BRIAN SPENCER

1971r	6	0	1	1	17

TED STACKHOUSE

1922r	5	0	0	0	0

ALLAN STANLEY

1959	12	0	3	3	2
1960	10	2	3	5	2
1961	5	0	3	3	0
1962	12	0	3	3	6
1963	10	1	6	7	8
1964	14	1	6	7	20
1965	6	0	1	1	12
1966	1	0	0	0	0
1967	12	0	2	2	10
Totals	82	4	27	31	60

WALLY STANOWSKI

1940r	10	1	0	1	2
1941	7	0	3	3	2
1942	13	2	8	10	2
1945	13	0	1	1	5
1947	8	0	0	0	0
1948	9	0	2	2	2
Totals	60	3	14	17	13

MARIAN STASTNY

1986	3	0	0	0	0

PETE STEMKOWSKI

1965r	6	0	3	3	7
1966	4	0	0	0	26
1967	12	5	7	12	20
Totals	22	5	10	15	53

GAYE STEWART

1942r	3	0	0	0	0
1943	4	0	2	2	4
1947	11	2	5	7	8
Totals	18	2	7	9	12

RON STEWART

1954	5	0	1	1	10
1955	4	0	0	0	2
1956	5	1	1	2	2
1959	12	3	3	6	6
1960	10	0	2	2	2
1961	5	1	0	1	2
1962	11	1	6	7	4
1963	10	4	0	4	2
1964	14	0	4	4	24
1965	6	0	1	1	2
Totals	82	10	18	28	56

BLAINE STOUGHTON

1975	7	4	2	6	2

RED STUART

1921	2	0	0	0	0
1922	7	1	0	1	6
Totals	9	1	0	1	6

STEVE SULLIVAN

1999	13	3	3	6	14

MATS SUNDIN

1995	7	5	4	9	4
1996	6	3	1	4	4
1999	17	8	8	16	16
2000	12	3	5	8	10
2001	11	6	7	13	14
Totals	53	25	25	50	48

RICH SUTTER

1995	4	0	0	0	2

BILLY TAYLOR

1940r	2	1	0	1	0
1941	7	0	3	3	5
1942	13	2	8	10	4
1943	6	2	2	4	0
Totals	28	5	13	18	9

HARRY TAYLOR

1949r	1	0	0	0	0

GREG TERRION

1983	4	1	2	3	2
1986	10	0	3	3	17
1987	13	0	2	2	14
1988	5	0	2	2	4
Totals	32	1	9	10	37

STEVE THOMAS

1986r	10	6	8	14	9
1987	13	2	3	5	13
1999	17	6	3	9	12
2000	12	6	3	9	10
2001	11	6	3	9	4
Totals	63	26	20	46	48

WAYNE THOMAS

1976						
10 (1/0)	5–5	587	34	1	3.48	
1977						
4 (0/1)	1–2	202	12	0	3.56	
Totals						
14 (1/1)	6–7	789	46	1	3.50	

ERROL THOMPSON

1974	2	0	1	1	0
1975	6	0	0	0	9
1976	10	3	3	6	0
1977	9	2	0	2	0
Totals	27	5	4	9	9

BILL THOMS

1933r	9	1	1	2	4
1934	5	0	2	2	0
1935	7	2	0	2	0
1936	9	3	5	8	0
1937	2	0	0	0	0
1938	7	0	1	1	0
Totals	39	6	9	15	4

JIM THOMSON

1947r	11	0	1	1	22
1948	9	1	1	2	9
1949	9	1	5	6	10
1950	7	0	2	2	7
1951	11	0	1	1	34
1952	4	0	0	0	25
1954	3	0	0	0	2
1955	4	0	0	0	16
1956	5	0	3	3	10
Totals	63	2	13	15	135

RAY TIMGREN

1949r	9	3	3	6	2
1950	6	0	4	4	2
1951	11	0	1	1	2
1952	4	0	1	1	0
Totals	30	3	9	12	6

GUY TROTTIER

1971	5	0	0	0	0
1972	4	1	0	1	16
Totals	9	1	0	1	16

DARCY TUCKER

2000	12	4	2	6	15
2001	11	0	2	2	6
Totals	23	4	4	8	21

IAN TURNBULL

1974r	4	0	0	0	8
1975	7	0	2	2	4
1976	10	2	9	11	29
1977	9	4	4	8	10
1978	13	6	10	16	10
1979	6	0	4	4	27
1980	3	0	3	3	2
1981	3	1	0	1	4
Totals	55	13	32	45	94

NORM ULLMAN

1969	4	1	0	1	0
1971	6	0	2	2	2
1972	5	1	3	4	2
1974	4	1	1	2	0
1975	7	0	0	0	2
Totals	26	3	6	9	6

RICK VAIVE

1980	3	1	0	1	11
1981	3	1	0	1	4
1983	4	2	5	7	6
1986	9	6	2	8	9
1987	13	4	2	6	23
Totals	32	14	9	23	53

JACK VALIQUETTE

1976r	10	2	3	5	2
1978	13	1	3	4	2
Totals	23	3	6	9	4

GARRY VALK

1999	17	3	4	7	22
2000	12	1	2	3	14
2001	5	1	0	1	2
Totals	34	5	6	11	38

KURT WALKER

1976r	6	0	0	0	24
1978	10	0	0	0	10
Totals	16	0	0	0	34

MIKE WALTON

1967r	12	4	3	7	2
1969	4	0	0	0	4
Totals	16	4	3	7	6

BOB WARNER

1976r	2	0	0	0	0
1977	2	0	0	0	0
Totals	4	0	0	0	0

TODD WARRINER

1996	6	1	1	2	2
1999	9	0	0	0	2
Totals	15	1	1	2	4

HARRY WATSON

1947	11	3	2	5	6
1948	9	5	2	7	9
1949	9	4	2	6	2
1950	7	0	0	0	2
1951	5	1	2	3	4
1952	4	1	0	1	2
1954	5	0	1	1	2
Totals	50	14	9	23	27

DON WEBSTER

1944r	5	0	0	0	12

STAN WEIR

1976	9	1	3	4	0
1977	7	2	1	3	0
1978	13	3	1	4	0
Totals	29	6	5	11	0

TIGER WILLIAMS

1975r	7	1	3	4	25
1976	10	0	0	0	75
1977	9	3	6	9	29
1978	12	1	2	3	63
1979	6	0	0	0	48
Totals	44	5	11	16	240

JOHNNY WILSON

1960	10	1	2	3	2

RON WILSON

1979r	3	0	1	1	0
1980	3	1	2	3	2
Totals	6	1	3	4	2

RANDY WOOD

1995	7	2	0	2	6

KEN WREGGET

1986						
10 (0/0)	6–4	607	32	1	3.16	
*1987**						
13 (1/0)	7–6	761	29	1	2.29	
1988						
2 (0/1)	0–1	108	11	0	6.11	
Totals						
25 (1/1)	13–11	1476	72	2	2.93	

* one assist

KEN YAREMCHUK

1987	6	0	0	0	0
1988	6	0	2	2	10
Totals	12	0	2	2	10

DMITRY YUSHKEVICH

1996	4	0	0	0	0
1999	17	1	5	6	22
2000	12	1	1	2	4
2001	11	0	4	4	12
Totals	44	2	10	12	38

RON ZANUSSI

1981	3	0	0	0	0

ROB ZETTLER

1996	2	0	0	0	0

PETER ZEZEL

1993	20	2	1	3	6
1994	18	2	4	6	8
Totals	38	4	5	9	14

0–0 Games, Playoffs

March 13, 1922   Toronto St. Pats
                (John Roach)
                at Ottawa Senators
                (Clint Benedict)

Playoff Scoring Records, Game

(*home team in* **bold**)

Most Goals For

April 14, 1942	**Toronto** 9	Detroit 3
March 26, 1936	**Toronto** 8	Boston 3
April 19, 1962	**Toronto** 8	Chicago 4
April 22, 1976	**Toronto** 8	Flyers 5
May 8, 1994	Toronto 8	**San Jose** 3

Most Goals, Both Teams

13	April 7, 1936	**Detroit** 9
		Toronto 4
	March 29, 1945	**Canadiens** 10
		Toronto 3
	April 22, 1976	**Toronto** 8
		Flyers 5

Most Goals Against

March 30, 1944	**Canadiens** 11	Toronto 0
March 29, 1945	**Canadiens** 10	Toronto 3
April 2, 1969	**Boston** 10	Toronto 0

Penalty-Free Games, Playoffs

April 16, 1942   Toronto 3 at Detroit 0
April 8, 1951   Toronto 6 at Boston 0

Team Playoff Records, Series Scoring

Most Goals, 7-Game Series

26	1994 vs. San Jose
25	1942 vs. Detroit

Most Goals, Both Teams, 7-Game Series

56	1976 vs. Philadelphia
54	1993 vs. Detroit

Fewest Goals, 7-Game Series

9*	1945 vs. Detroit
11	1950 vs. Detroit

* NHL record

Fewest Goals, Both Teams, 7-Game Series

18*	1945 vs. Detroit
21	1950 vs. Detroit

* NHL record

Most Goals Allowed, 7-Game Series

33	1976 vs. Philadelphia
30	1993 vs. Detroit

Most Goals, 6-Game Series

22	1962 vs. Rangers
20	1960 vs. Detroit
	1988 vs. Detroit

Fewest Goals Allowed, 7-Game Series

9	1945 vs. Detroit
10	1950 vs. Detroit

Fewest Goals, 6-Game Series

9	1999 vs. Philadelphia
	2000 vs. New Jersey
11	1940 vs. Rangers

Most Goals Allowed, 6-Game Series

32	1988 vs. Detroit
21	1945 vs. Canadiens

Fewest Goals Allowed, 6-Game Series

5	1951 vs. Boston*
9	1994 vs. Chicago
	2000 vs. Ottawa

* one tie

Most Goals, Both Teams, 6-Game Series

52	1988 vs. Detroit

Fewest Goals, Both Teams, 6-Game Series

20*	1999 vs. Philadelphia
22	1951 vs. Boston

* NHL record

Most Goals, 5-Game Series

20	1948 vs. Boston
18	1918 vs. Vancouver
	1947 vs. Detroit

Fewest Goals, 5-Game Series

6	1939 vs. Boston
	1944 vs. Canadiens
8	1954 vs. Detroit
	1961 vs. Detroit

Most Goals Allowed, 5-Game Series

21	1944 vs. Canadiens
21	1918 vs. Vancouver
	1999 vs. Buffalo

Fewest Goals Allowed, 5-Game Series

6	1963 vs. Canadiens
7	1933 vs. Boston

Most Goals, Both Teams, 5-Game Series

39	1918 vs. Vancouver Millionaires
37	1999 vs. Buffalo

Fewest Goals, Both Teams, 5-Game Series

16	1930 vs. Boston
18	1939 vs. Boston

Most Goals, 4-Game Series

17	1948 vs. Detroit
	1983 vs. Minnesota

Fewest Goals, 4-Game Series

3	1952 vs. Detroit
5	1960 vs. Canadiens
	1969 vs. Boston

Most Goals Allowed, 4-Game Series

21	1969 vs. Boston
17	1979 vs. Canadiens

Fewest Goals Allowed, 4-Game Series

2	1935 vs. Boston
3	2001 vs. Ottawa

Most Goals, Both Teams, 4-Game Series

36*	1983 vs. Minnesota
29	1936 vs. Detroit
	1969 vs. Boston
	1979 vs. Canadiens

* NHL record

Fewest Goals, Both Teams, 4-Game Series

9*   1935 vs. Boston

13   2001 vs. Ottawa

* NHL record

Most Goals, 3-Game Series

17   1932 vs. Rangers

       1986 vs. Chicago

10   1977 vs. Pittsburgh

Fewest Goals, 3-Game Series

4   1935 vs. Maroons

     1981 vs. Islanders

Most Goals Allowed, 3-Game Series

17   1981 vs. Islanders

17   1980 vs. Minnesota

Fewest Goals Allowed, 3-Game Series

3   1936 vs. Americans

     1938 vs. Boston

     1976 vs. Pittsburgh

Most Goals, Both Teams, 3-Game Series

28   1932 vs. Rangers

27   1980 vs. Minnesota

      1986 vs. Chicago

Fewest Goals, Both Teams, 3-Game Series

9   1936 vs. Americans

    1938 vs. Boston

Most Goals, 2-Game Series

11*   1978 vs. Los Angeles

10   1918 vs. Canadiens

* NHL record

Fewest Goals, 2-Game Series

0   1921 vs. Ottawa

1   1929 vs. Rangers

    1937 vs. Rangers

Most Goals Allowed, 2-Game Series

7   1918 vs. Canadiens

    1921 vs. Ottawa

Fewest Goals Allowed, 2-Game Series

0   1939 vs. Americans

Most Goals, Both Teams, 2-Game Series

17*   1918 vs. Canadiens

* NHL record

Fewest Goals, Both Teams, 2-Game Series

4   1929 vs. Rangers

Years the Leafs Led the League, Playoffs

Team Records
Most Goals
1918	28
1922	21
1932	28
1936	25
1947	31
1948	38
1949	28
1951	30
1962	40
1967	35

Most Penalty Minutes
1932	95
1934	67
1935	61
1936	76
1945	62
1951	143
1959	173
1960	104
1964	262
1967	146

Individual Records
Most Points
1918	Alf Skinner (Arenas)	9
1922	Babe Dye (St. Pats)	13
1929	Andy Blair & Ace Bailey	3*
1935	Harvey Jackson	5**
1936	Buzz Boll	10
1948	Ted Kennedy	14
1951	Max Bentley	13*
1967	Jim Pappin	15

* tied with one other
** tied with two others

Most Goals
1932	Charlie Conacher	6*
1936	Buzz Boll	7
1938	Gord Drillon	7
1940	Syl Apps & Hank Goldup	5
1945	Ted Kennedy	7
1948	Ted Kennedy	8
1967	Jim Pappin	7

* tied with one other

Most Assists
1932	Joe Primeau	6*
1935	Charlie Conacher	4
1936	Bill Thoms	5
1939	Gord Drillon	7
1942	Syl Apps	9
1948	Max Bentley	7*
1949	Ted Kennedy	6*
1951	Max Bentley	11
1964	Frank Mahovlich	11
1993	Doug Gilmour	25*

* tied with one other

Most Penalty Minutes
1933	Hap Day	21
1934	Andy Blair	16
1936	Red Horner	22
1939	Red Horner	26
1940	Red Horner	55
1945	Moe Morris	14
1948	Vic Lynn	20
1951	Jim Thomson	34
1959	Carl Brewer	40
1960	Frank Mahovlich	27
1964	Bobby Baun	42
1978	Tiger Williams	63

Best Goals Against Average

1938	Turk Broda	1.85
1948	Turk Broda	2.22
1949	Turk Broda	1.67
1950	Turk Broda	1.43
1951	Turk Broda/Al Rollins	1.26
1962	Johnny Bower/Don Simmons/Gerry Cheevers	2.57
1963	Johnny Bower	1.60
1964	Johnny Bower	2.21
1967	Johnny Bower/ Terry Sawchuk	2.50

Most Shutouts

1933	Lorne Chabot	2*
1935	George Hainsworth	2*
1939	Turk Broda	2
1942	Turk Broda	1**
1945	Frank McCool	4***
1948	Turk Broda	1
1949	Turk Broda	1
1950	Turk Broda	3*
1951	Turk Broda	2*
1963	Johnny Bower	2
1964	Johnny Bower	2
1967	Johnny Bower	1
1978	Mike Palmateer	2*

* tied with one other
** tied with three others
*** NHL record (tied with 8 others)

Consecutive Shutouts, Playoffs

For (individual)
Three Games
April 6 & 8 & 12, 1945 (McCool)

Two Games
March 26 & 28, 1935 (Hainsworth)
March 21 & 23, 1939 (Broda)
April 26 & 28, 1994 (Potvin)
April 13 & 14, 2001 (Joseph)

Against (team)
Two Games
March 10 & 15, 1921 (Ottawa)
April 19 & 21, 1945 (Detroit)
April 8 & 9, 1950 (Detroit)
March 25 & 27, 1952 (Detroit)
April 2 & 3, 1969 (Boston)
April 15 & 17, 1975 (Flyers)
May 20 & 22, 1994 (Vancouver)

Career Playoff Records, Individual

Most Seasons
George Armstrong	15
Turk Broda	13
Tim Horton	13

Most Games
George Armstrong	110
Turk Broda	101
Tim Horton	97
Bob Baun	92

By Position
Centre
Dave Keon	89
Bob Pulford	89

Left Wing
Frank Mahovlich	84
Nick Metz	76

Right Wing
George Armstrong	110
Bob Davidson	82
Ron Stewart	82

Defence
Tim Horton	97
Bob Baun	92

Most Goals

Wendel Clark	33
Dave Keon	32
Ted Kennedy	29

By Position

Centre

Dave Keon	32
Ted Kennedy	29

Left Wing

Wendel Clark	33
Frank Mahovlich	24

Right Wing

George Armstrong	26
Lanny McDonald	20

Defence

Ian Turnbull	13
Borje Salming	12

Most Assists

Doug Gilmour	60
Darryl Sittler	40
Red Kelly	38
Borje Salming	37

By Position

Centre

Doug Gilmour	60
Darryl Sittler	40

Left Wing

Frank Mahovlich	36
Wendel Clark	26

Right Wing

George Armstrong	34
Ron Stewart	18

Defence

Borje Salming	37
Tim Horton	32
Ian Turnbull	32

Most Points

Doug Gilmour	77
Dave Keon	67
Darryl Sittler	65
George Armstrong	60
Ted Kennedy	60
Frank Mahovlich	60
Wendel Clark	59

By Position

Centre

Doug Gilmour	77
Dave Keon	67

Left Wing

Frank Mahovlich	60
Wendel Clark	59

Right Wing

George Armstrong	60
Lanny McDonald	37

Defence

Borje Salming	49
Ian Turnbull	45

Most Penalty Minutes

Tiger Williams	240
Wendel Clark	181
Todd Gill	171

By Position

Centre

Bob Pulford	126
Darryl Sittler	120

Left Wing

Tiger Williams	240
Wendel Clark	181

Right Wing

Eddie Shack	107
Pat Boutette	95

Defence

Todd Gill	171
Red Horner	166

Playoff Records, Season

Most Goals

Dave Andreychuk ('93)	12
Doug Gilmour ('93)	10
Wendel Clark ('93)	10
Lanny McDonald ('77)	10

By Position
Centre

Doug Gilmour ('93)	10
Ted Kennedy ('48)	8

Left Wing

Dave Andreychuk ('93)	12
Wendel Clark ('93)	10

Right Wing

Lanny McDonald ('77)	10
George Armstrong ('62)	7
Jim Pappin ('67)	7
Glenn Anderson ('93)	7

Defence

Ian Turnbull ('78)	6
Dmitri Mironov ('94)	6

Most Assists

Doug Gilmour ('93)	25
Doug Gilmour ('94)	22
Darryl Sittler ('77)	16
Dave Ellett ('94)	15

By Position
Centre

Doug Gilmour ('93)	25
Doug Gilmour ('94)	22

Left Wing

Frank Mahovlich ('64)	11
Dick Duff ('62)	10
Wendel Clark ('93)	10

Right Wing

Glenn Anderson ('93)	11
Gary Leeman ('86)	10

Defence

Dave Ellett ('94)	15
Tim Horton ('62)	13

Most Points

Doug Gilmour ('93)	35
Doug Gilmour ('94)	28

By Position
Centre

Doug Gilmour ('93)	35
Doug Gilmour ('94)	28

Left Wing

Wendel Clark ('93)	20
Dave Andreychuk ('93)	19

Right Wing

Glenn Anderson ('93)	18
Lanny McDonald ('77)	17

Defence

Dave Ellett ('94)	18
Tim Horton ('62)	16
Ian Turnbull ('78)	16

Most Penalty Minutes

Tiger Williams ('76)	75
Tiger Williams ('78)	63
Red Horner ('40)	55

By Position
Centre

Dan Daoust ('87)	42
Doug Gilmour ('94)	42

Left Wing

Tiger Williams ('76)	75
Tiger Williams ('78)	63

Right Wing

Mike Foligno ('93)	42
George Armstrong ('55)	40
Pat Boutette ('78)	40

Defence

Red Horner ('40)	55
Bob Baun ('64)	42
Todd Gill ('87)	42

All-Time Goalie Records, Playoffs

Most Seasons
Turk Broda	13
Johnny Bower	10

Most Games, Career
Turk Broda	101
Johnny Bower	74
Felix Potvin	52
Curtis Joseph	40

Most Minutes Played, Career
Turk Broda	6414
Johnny Bower	4349
Felix Potvin	3206
Curtis Joseph	2425

Most Wins, Career
Turk Broda	58
Johnny Bower	34
Felix Potvin	25
Curtis Joseph	22

Most Losses, Career
Turk Broda	42
Johnny Bower	35
Felix Potvin	27
Curtis Joseph	18

Best Goals Against Average
(*minimum 10 games*)
Lorne Chabot	1.57
Turk Broda	1.97
Curtis Joseph	2.23
Frank McCool	2.23

Most Shutouts, Career
Since 1918, Toronto goalies have recorded 43 shutouts in the playoffs:
Turk Broda	13
Johnny Bower	5
Curtis Joseph	5
Frank McCool	4
Felix Potvin	4
John Ross Roach	2
Lorne Chabot	2

George Hainsworth	2
Mike Palmateer	2
Ken Wregget	2
Harry Lumley	1
Wayne Thomas	1

Most Consecutive Shutouts
3 *   Frank McCool vs. Detroit
     in the 1945 Finals
* NHL record (tied with one other)

Longest Shutout Streak, Minutes
188:35 *   Frank McCool
        April 6–14, 1945,
        vs. Detroit
187:40   Curtis Joseph
        April 13–16, 2001
        vs. Ottawa
154:05   Turk Broda
        March 21–28, 1939,
        vs. Americans and Detroit
135:45   George Hainsworth
        March 26–30, 1935,
        vs. Boston
* NHL record

All Penalty Minutes, Goalies
Mike Palmateer	17*
Curtis Joseph	16
Turk Broda	12
Felix Potvin	12
Ken Wregget	10
Johnny Bower	4
Harry Lumley	2
Daren Puppa	2

*   including five-minute fighting major
    April 23, 1978 vs. Islanders

All Assists, Goalies
Only two Leaf goalies have ever registered an assist in the playoffs:
1.   Johnny Bower
      March 26, 1963, vs. Canadiens
2.   Ken Wregget
      April 21, 1987, vs. Detroit

Playoff Game Records, Individual

Most Points, Game

6   Darryl Sittler (5 goals, 1 assist)
       April 22, 1976, vs. Flyers

5   Syl Apps (2 goals, 3 assists)
       April 14, 1942, vs. Detroit
    Don Metz (3 goals, 2 assists)
       April 14, 1942, vs. Detroit
    Frank Mahovlich (2 goals, 3 assists)
       April 2, 1964, vs. Canadiens
    Lanny McDonald (3 goals, 2 assists)
       April 9, 1977, vs. Penguins
    Lanny McDonald (4 goals, 1 assist)
       April 17, 1977, vs. Flyers
    Doug Gilmour (1 goal, 4 assists)
       May 8, 1994, vs. San Jose

Most Points, Period

No Leaf has ever scored 4 points in one play-off period. In addition to those players listed below (3 goals or 3 assists in one period), these Leafs have registered 3 points in one period in the playoffs:

3   Reg Noble (2 goals, 1 assist),
       1st period, March 20, 1918,
       vs. Millionaires
    Charlie Conacher (2 goals, 1 assist),
       2nd period, March 26, 1936,
       vs. Boston
    Don Metz (2 goals, 1 assist),
       2nd period, April 14, 1942,
       vs. Detroit
    Frank Mahovlich (1 goal, 2 assists),
       2nd period, April 19, 1962,
       vs. Chicago
    Frank Mahovlich (2 goals, 1 assist),
       2nd period, April 2, 1964,
       vs. Canadiens
    Lanny McDonald (2 goals, 1 assist),
       2nd period, April 17, 1977,
       vs. Flyers
    Ed Olczyk (1 goal, 2 assists),
       3rd period, April 6, 1988,
       vs. Detroit
    Doug Gilmour (1 goal, 2 assists),
       3rd period, May 17, 1993,
       vs. Los Angeles

Doug Gilmour (1 goal, 2 assists),
    2nd period, May 8, 1994,
    vs. San Jose

Most Goals, Game

5*   Darryl Sittler
      April 22, 1976
* NHL record (tied with four others)

4   Babe Dye, March 28, 1922,
      vs. Millionaires
    Ted Kennedy, March 27, 1948,
      vs. Boston
    Lanny McDonald, April 17, 1977,
      vs. Philadelphia

Most Goals, Period

3*   Harvey Jackson,
      2nd period, April 5, 1932,
      vs. Rangers
    Darryl Sittler,
      2nd period, April 22, 1976,
      vs. Flyers
    George Ferguson,
      3rd period, April 11, 1978,
      vs. Los Angeles
* NHL record (tied with many others)

Most Assists, Game

4   Ian Turnbull,
      April 22, 1976, vs. Flyers
    Darryl Sittler,
      April 9, 1977, vs. Penguins
    Doug Gilmour,
      May 8, 1994, vs. San Jose

Most Assists, Period

3*   Joe Primeau,
      3rd period, April 7, 1932,
      vs. Rangers
    Nick Metz,
      2nd period, March 25, 1941,
      vs. Boston
* NHL record (tied with six others)

Most Penalty Minutes, Game

38 Forbes Kennedy,
April 2, 1969, vs. Boston
Kennedy received a double minor (slashing and roughing) at 10:57 of the 2nd period. At 5:23 of the 3rd, he received a cross-checking minor, and then at 16:14 was assessed a slashing minor, a double major for fighting, a 10-minute misconduct, and a game misconduct.

Most Penalty Minutes, Period

34 Forbes Kennedy,
3rd period, April 2, 1969,
vs. Boston

27 Darryl Sittler,
3rd period, April 8, 1971,
vs. Rangers
Tiger Williams,
3rd period, April 22, 1976,
vs. Flyers

Hat Tricks

1918	March 11	Harry Meeking (Arenas)
1918	March 23	Alf Skinner (Arenas) vs. Millionaires
1932	April 5	Harvey Jackson vs. Rangers
1936	March 26	Charlie Conacher vs. Boston
1941	March 25	Syl Apps vs. Boston
1942	April 14	Don Metz vs. Detroit
1945	April 14	Ted Kennedy vs. Detroit
1949	April 10	Sid Smith vs. Detroit
1962	April 19	Bob Pulford vs. Chicago
1964	April 9	Dave Keon vs. Canadiens
1977	April 9	Lanny McDonald vs. Pittsburgh
1978	April 11	George Ferguson vs. Los Angeles
1988	April 12	Ed Olczyk vs. Detroit
1993	May 27	Wendel Clark vs. Los Angeles
1996	April 25	Mike Gartner vs. St. Louis

Power-Play and Short-Handed Goal Records, Playoffs

Most Power-Play Goals, Team, Game

5 April 15, 1976,
Flyers 4 at Toronto 5

Most Power-Play Goals, Team, Period

4* 2nd period, March 26, 1936,
Boston 3 at Toronto 8
* NHL record

Most Power-Play Goals, Individual, Career

Darryl Sittler	13
Dave Andreychuk	9
Doug Gilmour	9
Wendel Clark	9

Most Power-Play Goals, Individual, Season

| Dmitri Mironov ('94) | 6 |
| Doug Gilmour ('94) | 5 |

Most Power-Play Goals, Individual, Game

3* Sid Smith, April 10, 1949,
Toronto 3 at Detroit 1
* NHL record (tied with 8 others)

Most Power-Play Goals, Individual, Period

2 Charlie Conacher,
  2nd period, March 26, 1936,
  Boston 3 at Toronto 8
 Sid Smith,
  1st period, April 10, 1949,
  Toronto 3 at Detroit 1
 Dmitri Mironov,
  2nd period, May 18, 1994,
  Vancouver 4 at Toronto 3

Most Short-Handed Goals, Team, Game

3* May 8, 1994,
  Toronto 8 at San Jose 3
* NHL record (tied with two others)

Most Short-Handed Goals, Team, Period

2* April 5, 1947, 1st period,
  Detroit 1 at Toronto 6
 April 13, 1965, 1st period,
  Canadiens 4 at Toronto 3
 May 8, 1994, 3rd period,
  Toronto 8 at San Jose 3
* NHL record (tied with 17 others)

Most Short-Handed Goals, Both Teams, Game

4* May 8, 1994,
  Toronto 8 at San Jose 3
* NHL record (tied with two others)

Most Short-Handed Goals, Individual, Career

| Dave Keon | 9 |
| Bob Pulford | 4 |

Most Short-Handed Goals, Individual, Season

Dave Keon ('63)	2
Bob Pulford ('64)	2
Dave Keon ('67)	2
Mark Osborne ('94)	2

Most Short-Handed Goals, Individual, Game

2* Dave Keon,
  April 8, 1963,
  Detroit 1 at Toronto 3
* NHL record (tied with six others)

Most Short-Handed Goals on One Opponents' Power Play, Team

2 April 13, 1965,
  Canadiens 4 at Toronto 3
Keon scored at 2:10 and Kelly at 3:11 of the 1st period during the same penalty

Speed Records, Playoffs

Fastest Goal from Start of Game
15 seconds	Sid Smith, April 11, 1951, Canadiens 2 at Toronto 3
17 seconds	Sid Smith, March 24, 1955, Toronto 1 at Detroit 2

Fastest Goal from Start of Period
10 seconds	Joe Klukay, March 28, 1950, 2nd period, Toronto 5 at Detroit 0

Fastest Two Goals from Start of Game, Individual
1:08*	Dick Duff, April 9, 1963 (1st goal at 49 seconds, 2nd at 1:08), Detroit 2 at Toronto 4

* NHL record

Fastest Two Goals from Start of Game, Team
1:36	Ted Kennedy (1:12) and Vic Lynn (1:36), April 10, 1947, Toronto 4 at Canadiens 0

Fastest Two Goals, Team
11 seconds	Darryl Sittler (4:16) and Ron Ellis (4:27), April 12, 1979, 1st period, Atlanta 4 at Toronto 7

Fastest Two Goals, Individual
12 seconds	Darryl Sittler, April 12, 1979, 1st period (4:04, 4:16), Atlanta 4 at Toronto 7

Fastest Two Goals, Both Teams
10 seconds	April 5, 1936, 1st period vs. Detroit: Wally Kilrea (12:05 Detroit), Buzz Boll (12:15 Toronto), Toronto 1 at Detroit 3

April 12, 1947, 2nd period vs. Canadiens: Vic Lynn (12:23 Toronto), Leo Gravelle (12:33 Canadiens) Canadiens 2 at Toronto 4

Fastest Two Power-Play Goals, Individual
27 seconds	Nick Metz, March 22, 1941 (15:00 & 15:27, 2nd period) Toronto 5 at Boston 3

Fastest Three Goals, Team
23 seconds*	Darryl Sittler (4:04 and 4:16) and Ron Ellis (4:27), April 12, 1979, 1st period, Atlanta 4 at Toronto 7

* NHL record

Fastest Four Goals, Both Teams
1:33*	April 20, 1976, 2nd period vs. Philadelphia: Don Saleski (10:04 Philadelphia), Bob Neely (10:42 Toronto), Gary Dornhoefer (11:24 Philadelphia), Don Saleski (11:37 Philadelphia), Toronto 1 at Philadelphia 7

* NHL record

Fastest Five Goals, Both Teams
4:19	April 9, 1932, 3rd period vs. Rangers: Ace Bailey (15:07 Toronto), Fred Cook (16:32 Rangers), Bob Gracie (17:36 Toronto), Frank Boucher (18:26 Rangers), Frank Boucher (19:26 Rangers), Rangers 4 at Toronto 6

Penalty Shots in the Playoffs

For

April 22, 1999
  Mats Sundin stopped by John
  Vanbiesbrouck (Philadelphia) in
  3–0 Flyers win at the Air Canada Centre
May 29, 1999
  Mats Sundin beat Dominik Hasek
  (Buffalo) in 5–2 Sabres win at Marine
  Midland Arena
Note: Sundin is one of only two players (the
other is Petr Klima) to have taken two career
penalty shots in the playoffs, and the only
man ever to take two in the same playoff year.

Against

April 9, 1988
  Petr Klima (Detroit) beat Allan Bester in
  a 6–3 Red Wings win at Maple Leaf
  Gardens
May 9, 1995
  Patrick Poulin (Chicago) stopped by Felix
  Potvin in a 3–0 Toronto win at the
  United Centre

Leafs Whose First NHL Game Was a Playoff Game

Norm Mann,
  April 2, 1936, vs. Americans
Hank Goldup,
  March 19, 1940, vs. Chicago
Gaye Stewart,
  April 14, 1942, vs. Detroit
Joe Klukay,
  March 28, 1943, vs. Detroit
Phil Samis,
  March 27, 1948, vs. Boston
Les Costello,
  April 3, 1948, vs. Boston
Gary Collins,
  March 24, 1959, vs. Boston

Bob Warner,
  April 17, 1976, vs. Flyers
Gary Leeman,
  April 9, 1983, vs. North Stars
Daniel Marois,
  April 10, 1988, vs. Detroit
Darby Hendrickson,
  April 28, 1994, vs. Chicago
Adam Mair,
  May 11, 1999, vs. Pittsburgh
Jeff Farkas,
  May 3, 2000, vs. New Jersey
The only two Leafs ever to score in their NHL
debut as a playoff game were Les Costello
and Adam Mair.

Shots Records, Playoffs

Most Shots, Game

64	May 3, 1993, vs. St. Louis

Most Shots, Game, Opponent

64	March 27, 1960, vs. Detroit
62	April 25, 1967, vs. Canadiens

Fewest Shots, Game

6	May 8, 2000, vs. New Jersey
13	April 15, 1975, vs. Flyers

Fewest Shots, Game, Opponent

15	April 17, 2000, vs. Ottawa
17	April 26, 1994, vs. Chicago

Most Shots, Period

27 April 15, 1976, 2nd period, vs. Flyers
24 April 13, 1974, 3rd period, vs. Boston

Fewest Shots, Period

1   May 8, 2000, 3rd period,
    vs. New Jersey
2   May 1, 2000, 3rd period,
    vs. New Jersey
    May 8, 2000, 2nd period,
    vs. New Jersey

Most Shots, Period, Opponent

30 April 8, 1980, 2nd period
    vs. North Stars
27 April 9, 1983, 2nd period,
    vs. North Stars

Fewest Shots, Period, Opponent

1   May 7, 1993, 3rd period,
    vs. Los Angeles
1   April 12, 1987, 2nd period,
    vs. St. Louis

Most Shots, Game, Both Teams

118 March 27, 1960
    (Detroit 66, Toronto 52)
116 April 25, 1967
    (Canadiens 62, Toronto 54)

Fewest Shots, Game, Both Teams

33 May 8, 2000
    (New Jersey 27, Toronto 6)
40 April 13, 1978
    (Los Angeles 21, Toronto 19)

Most Shots, Period, Both Teams

38 April 9, 1983
    (North Stars 27, Toronto 11)
37 April 15, 1967
    (Chicago 22, Toronto 15)

Fewest Shots, Period, Both Teams

7   April 28, 1994, 3rd period
    (Toronto 4, Chicago 3)
10 April 11, 1975, 3rd period
    (Toronto 6, Los Angeles 4)
    April 6, 1988, 1st period
    (Detroit 5, Toronto 5)

Stanley Cup Finals, 1917–2001

Appearances

Toronto has appeared in the Stanley Cup
finals 21 times (13-8).
(h) indicates the Cup was presented at Maple
Leaf Gardens, (a) in the opponent's rink;
name after win indicates Cup-winning goal
for Toronto

Won

1918 vs. Vancouver Millionaires
      3–2 (h)—Corb Denneny
1922 vs. Vancouver Millionaires
      3–2 (h)—Babe Dye
1932 vs. Rangers
      3–2 (h)—Ace Bailey

1942 vs. Detroit
      4–3 (h)—Pete Langelle
1945 vs. Detroit
      4–3 (a)—Babe Pratt
1947 vs. Canadiens
      4–2 (h)—Ted Kennedy
1948 vs. Detroit
      4–0 (a)—Harry Watson
1949 vs. Detroit
      4–0 (h)—Cal Gardner
1951 vs. Canadiens
      4–1 (h)—Bill Barilko (OT)
1962 vs. Chicago
      4–2 (a)—Dick Duff
1963 vs. Detroit
      4–1 (h)—Eddie Shack

1964 vs. Detroit
      4–3 (h)—Andy Bathgate
1967 vs. Canadiens
      4–2 (h)—Jim Pappin

Lost

1933 vs. Rangers 1–3 (h)
1935 vs. Maroons 0–3 (a)
1936 vs. Detroit 1–3 (h)
1938 vs. Chicago 1–3 (a)
1939 vs. Boston 1–4 (a)
1940 vs. Rangers 2–4 (h)
1959 vs. Canadiens 1–4 (a)
1960 vs. Canadiens 0–4 (h)

NHL Stanley Cup Finals Records

Team Records Held by the Leafs
Most Overtime Games, Finals
5   Toronto and Canadiens, 1951
    (Toronto won series 4–1)

Most Overtime Games, One Series
5   Toronto and Canadiens, 1951
    (Toronto won series 4–1)

Most Overtime Wins, One Team, One Series
4   Toronto, 1951, vs. Canadiens

Most Goals, One Team, One Period
5   (tied with one other) Toronto,
    April 14, 1942, 2nd period,
    Game 5 vs. Detroit.
    Toronto won game 9–3 and series 4–3.

Most Road Victories, Both Teams, One Series
5   (tied with one other)
    Toronto 3, Detroit 2 in 1945.
    Toronto won series 4–3.

Most Road Victories, One Team, One Series
3   (tied with three others) Toronto, 1945.
    Toronto won games 1, 2, 7 in Detroit
    and won series 4–3.

Most Shutouts, Both Teams, One Series
5   Toronto 3, Detroit 2, 1945.
    Toronto won series 4–3.

Most Shutouts, One Team, One Series
3   (tied with one other) Toronto, 1945.
    Toronto won series 4–3.

Fewest Penalties, Both Teams, One Series
19 Toronto 9, Detroit 10 in 1945.
    Toronto won series 4–3.

Fewest Penalties, One Team, One Series
9   Toronto, 1945, vs. Detroit.
    Toronto won series 4–3.

Fewest Penalty Minutes, Both Teams, One Series
41 Toronto 25, Detroit 16 in 1945.
    Toronto won series 4–3.

Fewest Penalties and Penalty Minutes, Both Teams, One Game
0   Toronto at Detroit, April 16, 1942,
    game 6. Toronto won game 1–0.

Fewest Penalties and Penalty Minutes, One Team, One Game
0   (tied with four others)
    April 16, 1942, vs. Detroit
    April 12, 1945, vs. Detroit

Fastest Two Goals, Both Teams

10 seconds   Toronto at Detroit, Game 1,
             April 5, 1936. Wally Kilrea
             (Detroit) scored at 12:05
             and Buzz Boll (Toronto)
             scored at 12:15,
             1st period.
             Canadiens at Toronto,
             Game 3, April 12, 1947.
             Vic Lynn (Toronto) scored
             at 12:23 and Leo Gravelle
             (Canadiens) scored at
             12:33, 2nd period.

Individual Records Held by Leafs

Most Years in Finals

12   (tied with three others) Red Kelly
     (Detroit 7, Toronto 5)

Most Games Played in Finals

65   (tied with one other)
     Red Kelly (Detroit 37, Toronto 28)

Most Goals in One Final, Individual

9   Babe Dye, Toronto St. Pats, 1922,
    in five games, vs. Vancouver Millionaires

**Most Career Short-Handed
Goals in Finals**

2   (tied with seven others)
    Dave Keon
    Bob Pulford

**Most Short-Handed
Goals, One Finals Series**

2   (tied with three others)
    Dave Keon, 1963, vs. Detroit
    Bob Pulford, 1964, vs. Detroit

Most Career Shutouts in Finals

4   (tied with one other) Turk Broda
    (one in 1940, 1942, 1947, 1948)

**Most Shutouts, Goalie,
One Final Series**

3   Frank McCool, 1945, vs. Detroit
    (seven games)

Overtime Records

Overall Overtime Record: 53–45–1

Home: 34–27–1
Away: 19–18

Most Overtime Games

Turk Broda	22
Red Horner	21
Todd Gill	19

Overtime Records by Team

vs.		
	Detroit	12–9
	Boston	11–5–1
	Canadiens	9–4
	St. Louis	4–4
	Chicago	3–2
	Pittsburgh	2–0
	Los Angeles	2–2
	Millionaires	1–0
	Ottawa	3–0
	San Jose	1–0
	Vancouver	1–1
	Maroons	1–1
	Islanders	1–2
	Rangers	1–7
	Flyers	1–3
	North Stars	0–3
	New Jersey	0–2

Most Overtime Goals

Syl Apps	2
Gord Drillon	2
Frank Mahovlich	2
Mike Gartner	2
Mats Sundin	2

Most Overtime Assists
Doug Gilmour	5
Bob Rouse	3
Wendel Clark	3

Most Overtime Points
Doug Gilmour	6
Frank Mahovlich	4

Most Overtime Penalty Minutes
Bill Barilko	9
Frank Mahovlich	5

Goalie Records in Overtime
(*most minutes played*)
Turk Broda	342:38
Lorne Chabot	185:22
Johnny Bower	154:37

Won-Loss Record for All Goalies
Turk Broda	12–9–1
Felix Potvin	10–5
Johnny Bower	8–3
Curtis Joseph	6–2
Al Rollins	3–0
Lorne Chabot	3–5
Ken Wregget	2–1
George Hainsworth	2–3
John Ross Roach	1–0
Cesare Maniago	1–0
Bernie Parent	1–0
Frank McCool	1–1
Allan Bester	1–1
Gord McRae	1–2
Mike Palmateer	1–8
Jacques Plante	0–1
Doug Favell	0–1
Jiri Crha	0–1
Harry Lumley	0–2

Trophy Winners

O'Brien Trophy
1918	Toronto Arenas
1922	Toronto St. Pats
1933	Toronto Maple Leafs
1934	Toronto Maple Leafs
1935	Toronto Maple Leafs
1938	Toronto Maple Leafs
1941	Toronto Maple Leafs
1942	Toronto Maple Leafs
1947	Toronto Maple Leafs
1947	Toronto Maple Leafs

Calder Memorial Trophy
1937	Syl Apps
1943	Gaye Stewart
1944	Gus Bodnar
1945	Frank McCool
1947	Howie Meeker
1958	Frank Mahovlich
1961	Dave Keon
1963	Kent Douglas
1966	Brit Selby

Hart Memorial Trophy
1944	Babe Pratt
1955	Ted Kennedy

Conn Smythe Trophy
1967	Dave Keon

Frank J. Selke Trophy
1993	Doug Gilmour

King Clancy Trophy
2000	Curtis Joseph

Prince of Wales Trophy
1948	Toronto Maple Leafs
1963	Toronto Maple Leafs

Art Ross Trophy
1923	Babe Dye (St. Pats)
1925	Babe Dye (St. Pats)

1929	Ace Bailey
1932	Harvey Jackson
1934	Charlie Conacher
1935	Charlie Conacher
1938	Gord Drillon

Vezina Trophy

1941	Turk Broda
1948	Turk Broda
1951	Al Rollins
1954	Harry Lumley
1961	Johnny Bower
1965	Johnny Bower & Terry Sawchuk

Jack Adams Award

1993	Pat Burns

Lady Byng Memorial Trophy

1932	Joe Primeau
1938	Gord Drillon
1942	Syl Apps
1952	Sid Smith
1955	Sid Smith
1961	Red Kelly
1962	Dave Keon
1963	Dave Keon

Totem Trophy

"Presented by the Gyro Club of Vancouver, B.C. in commemoration of the city's Golden Jubilee of 1936. This trophy is for annual competition representing the supremacy in hockey on the Pacific Coast and was first competed for by the Toronto Maple Leafs and Chicago Black Hawks April 25–May 1, 1936."

Results

April 25, 1936	Toronto 6	Chicago 3
(exhibition)		

3-game total goals series:

April 27	Chicago 5	Toronto 3
April 29	Toronto 7	Chicago 2
May 1	Toronto 3	Chicago 2

Charlie Conacher Team Trophy

Established after the death of Charlie Conacher in 1968 and given to either Toronto or Montreal, whichever has a better record in games versus each other over the course of the regular season. The trophy was retired in 1971.

1971	Toronto Maple Leafs

Toronto Maple Leafs Team Trophies

J.P. Bickell Memorial Cup

"Presented by Maple Leaf Gardens Limited in respectful memory of J.P. Bickell, esq., and in appreciation of his invaluable services as president from the year of its inauguration in 1931 until 1932, chairman of the board for 11 succeeding years and a director until his decease in 1951. To be awarded to a player of the Maple Leaf hockey team at such times and for such merit as may be designated and determined by the Board of Directors." Awarded at the discretion of the Board of Directors to a Leaf for a tremendous feat, one season of spectacular play, or remarkable service over a number of years.

1953	Ted Kennedy
1954	Harry Lumley
1955	Ted Kennedy
1956	Tod Sloan
1959	George Armstrong & Bob Pulford
1960	Johnny Bower
1961	Red Kelly
1962	Dave Keon
1963	Dave Keon
1964	Johnny Bower
1965	Johnny Bower
1966	Allan Stanley
1967	Terry Sawchuk
1969	Tim Horton
1971	Bob Baun
1972	King Clancy
1979	Mike Palmateer
1993	Doug Gilmour
1995	Bob Davidson

Molson Cup

1974	Borje Salming
1975	Darryl Sittler
1976	Darryl Sittler
1977	Borje Salming
1978	Borje Salming
1979	Darryl Sittler
1980	Borje Salming
1981	Darryl Sittler & Wilf Paiement
1982	Michel Larocque
1983	Rick Vaive
1984	Rick Vaive
1985	Bill Derlago
1986	Ken Wregget
1987	Rick Vaive
1988	Ken Wregget
1989	Gary Leeman

1990	Gary Leeman
1991	Peter Ing
1992	Grant Fuhr
1993	Doug Gilmour
1994	Doug Gilmour
1995	Mats Sundin
1996	Felix Potvin
1997	Felix Potvin
1998	Felix Potvin
1999	Curtis Joseph
2000	Curtis Joseph
2001	Curtis Joseph

Tim Horton Trophy

1996	Larry Murphy

General Managers

1917–24	Charlie Querrie (replaced Jimmy Murphy on December 6, 1917)
1924–27	Eddie Powers
1927–54	Conn Smythe (became manager officially on February 17, 1927 when St. Pats became Maple Leafs; resigned October 1954)
1954–57	Happy Day (hired October 1954; resigned March 25, 1957)
1957	Howie Meeker (hired May 13, 1957; fired October 4, 1957)
1957–58	Run by a committee of seven: Stafford Smythe, John Bassett, George Mara, George Gardiner, Jack Amell, Bill Hatch, Ian Johnston
1958–69	Punch Imlach (hired June 1958; fired April 6, 1969)
1969–79	Jim Gregory (hired April 6, 1969; fired May 1979)

1979–81	Punch Imlach (hired July 4, 1979; suffered a heart attack September 1981 and replaced)
1981–88	Gerry McNamara (hired September 1981; fired February 7, 1988)
1988–89	Gord Stellick (hired April 28, 1988; resigned August 11, 1989)
1989–91	Floyd Smith (hired August 15, 1989; replaced July 2, 1991)
1991–97	Cliff Fletcher (hired July 2, 1991; bought out May 24, 1997)
1997–99	Ken Dryden (hired August 20, 1997; hired Pat Quinn as his replacement on July 14, 1999)
1999–present	Pat Quinn (officially assumed duties as general manager on July 14, 1999)

Captains

1917–18	Ken Randall
1920–24	Reg Noble
1924–25	John Ross Roach
1925–26	Babe Dye (sold as captain)
1926–27	Bert Corbeau (retired as captain)
1927–37	Happy Day (traded as captain)
1937–38	Charlie Conacher/Red Horner (Horner became captain when Conacher retired January 19, 1938
1938–40	Red Horner (retired as captain)
1940–43	Syl Apps (joined Canadian Army)
1943–45	Bob Davidson (captaincy resumed by Apps upon his return from war)
1945–48	Syl Apps (retired as captain)
1948–55	Ted Kennedy (retired as captain)
1955–56	Sid Smith (replaced as captain)
1956–57	Jim Thomson (from start of season until January 12, 1957

	when Ted Kennedy came out of retirement for the rest of the year and resumed his captaincy)
1957–69	George Armstrong (retired as captain, though subsequently returned to play not as captain)
1969–75	Dave Keon (replaced as captain)
1975–81	Darryl Sittler (resigned as captain December 29, 1979; resumed captaincy for start of 1980–81 season; traded as captain)
1981–86	Rick Vaive (removed as captain February 23, 1986)
1986–89	no captain
1989–91	Rob Ramage (lost in expansion draft as captain)
1991–94	Wendel Clark (traded as captain)
1994–97	Doug Gilmour (traded as captain)
1997– present	Mats Sundin (named captain September 30, 1997)

Hockey Hall of Fame Honoured Members

(list is alphabetical; first year indicates year of induction; years in brackets indicate service as a Leaf unless otherwise noted)

Players

1959	Jack Adams (1917–19 Arenas; 1922–26 St. Pats)
1961	Syl Apps (1936–43, 1945–48)
1996	Al Arbour (inducted as a Builder; played with Leafs 1961–64, 1965–66)
1975	George Armstrong (1949–71)
1975	Ace Bailey (1926–34)
1978	Andy Bathgate (1963–65)
1966	Max Bentley (1947–53)
1986	Leo Boivin (1951–54)
1975	Johnny Bower (1958–70)

1966	Turk Broda (1936–43, 1945–52)
1962	Harry Cameron (1919–23 St. Pats)
1985	Gerry Cheevers (1961–62)
1958	King Clancy (1930–37)
1958	Sprague Cleghorn (1920–21 St. Pats)
1961	Charlie Conacher (1929–38)
1962	Rusty Crawford (1917–19 Arenas)
1961	Happy Day (1924–37)
1975	Gord Drillon (1936–42)
1970	Babe Dye (1919–26 St. Pats; 1930–31)
1990	Fern Flaman (1950–54)
2001	Mike Gartner (1993–96)
1945	Eddie Gerard (1921–22 St. Pats)

King Clancy

1961	George Hainsworth (1933–37)
1972	Harry Holmes (1917–19 Arenas)
1965	Red Horner (1928–40)
1977	Tim Horton (1949–70)
1965	Syd Howe (1931–32)
1958	Dick Irvin Sr. (inducted as a Player; coached Leafs 1930–40)
1971	Harvey Jackson (1929–39)
1969	Red Kelly (1960–67) [five-year waiting period waived]
1966	Ted Kennedy (1942–57)
1985	Dave Keon (1960–75)
1980	Harry Lumley (1952–56)
1981	Frank Mahovlich (1956–68)
1992	Frank Mathers (1948–50, 1951–52)
1992	Lanny McDonald (1973–79)
1974	Dickie Moore (1964–65)
1947	Frank Nighbor (1929–30)
1962	Reg Noble (1917–19 Arenas; 1919–25 St. Pats)
1985	Bert Olmstead (1958–62)
1984	Bernie Parent (1970–72)
1975	Pierre Pilote (1968–69)
1978	Jacques Plante (1970–73)
1990	Bud Poile (1942–47)
1966	Babe Pratt (1942–46)
1963	Joe Primeau (1927–36)
1978	Marcel Pronovost (1965–70)
1991	Bob Pulford (1956–70)
1996	Borje Salming (1973–89) (also a member of IIHF Hall of Fame)
1971	Terry Sawchuk (1964–67) [three-year waiting period waived]
1962	Sweeney Schriner (1939–43, 1944–46)
1989	Darryl Sittler (1970–82)
1981	Allan Stanley (1958–68)
1982	Norm Ullman (1968–75)

| 1973 | Carl Voss (1926–27 St. Pats; 1928–29) |
| 1994 | Harry Watson (1946–55) |

Builders

1975	H.E. Ballard (1961–91)
1978	J.P. Bickell (1927–51)
1965	Foster Hewitt (1923–81)
1947	William A. Hewitt
1984	Punch Imlach (1958–69, 1979–81)
1985	Rudy Pilous (1983–85)
1960	Frank J. Selke (1927–46)
1958	Conn Smythe (1927–61)

Leafs' Retired Numbers

| 5 | Bill Barilko (1946–51) |
| 6 | Ace Bailey (1927–34)* |

* Bailey approved Ron Ellis's wearing of number 6 beginning with the 1968–69 season until Ellis retired in February 1981. During Ellis's first retirement, 1975–77, no one wore number 6.

Leafs' Honoured Numbers

Sweater stays in use but is honoured by a banner in the rafters and a special shoulder patch on the current sweater.

1	Turk Broda (ceremony March 11, 1995)
1	Johnny Bower (ceremony March 11, 1995)
7	King Clancy (ceremony November 21, 1995)
7	Tim Horton (ceremony November 21, 1995)
9	Charlie Conacher (ceremony February 28, 1998)
9	Ted Kennedy (ceremony October 3, 1993)
10	George Armstrong (ceremony February 28, 1998)
10	Syl Apps (ceremony October 3, 1993)

All Scores and Dates for All Regular Season Games, 1917–2001

- all shutouts are noted with the goalie's name enclosed in square brackets. For example, "[Broda]" means Turk Broda registered a shutout that game
- all empty-net goals for and against are recorded
- all overtime goals for and against are recorded
- significant game events are also recorded, as are scorers in all 1–0 games

1917–1918
All home games started at 8:30 p.m.

First half
December
19　Toronto 9 at Wanderers 10 (Brooks (T) replaced Hebert at start of 2nd)
22　Ottawa 4 at Toronto 11
26　Canadiens 5 at Toronto 7
29　Toronto 2 at Canadiens 9

January
2　Toronto 6 at Ottawa 5
5　Wanderers—at Toronto 1 (the only "game" of its kind in the NHL. The Wanderers' building had burned down three days earlier, but team owner Sammy Lichtenstein elected to cut his losses and not send his team to Toronto for the Saturday game at the Arena. The Arenas, about to lose gate receipts, took a legal precaution by "playing" the game anyway. Thus, at 8:30, Holmes took his place in goal—his first game as an Arena—Cameron and Randall lined up on defence, and Skinner, Dennenay, and Meeking played forward. Referee Lou Marsh dropped the puck, and Dennenay skated in and scored. The team left the ice, winning 1–0 by default.)
9　Canadiens 4 at Toronto 6
14　Toronto 6 at Ottawa 9
16　Ottawa 4 at Toronto 5 (game played without any substitutions)

19　Toronto 1 at Canadiens 5
26　Toronto 3 at Ottawa 6
28　Canadiens 1 at Toronto 5 (all goals in 1st) (Joe Hall and Alf Skinner fined $15 and arrested for stick-swinging)

February
2　Toronto 2 at Canadiens 11
4　Ottawa 2 at Toronto 8 (Randall fined $5 for using bad language)

Second half
9　Toronto 7 at Canadiens 3
11　Ottawa 1 at Toronto 3
13　Toronto 6 at Ottawa 1
18　Canadiens 9 at Toronto 0 [Vezina]
20　Toronto 4 at Canadiens 5 (Jack MacDonald 4:50 OT)
23　Ottawa 3 at Toronto 9 (Ken Randall had been temporarily suspended by NHL President Frank Calder. However, he was allowed to play if he paid referee Lou Marsh the $35 in unpaid fines he [Randall] owed. Randall paid $32 in bills and $3 in pennies, but when someone knocked the coins from Marsh's hand onto the ice, the start of the game was delayed some minutes until all the coins could be collected.)

March
2　Canadiens 3 at Toronto 5
6　Toronto 3 at Ottawa 9

1918–1919
First half
December
23　Canadiens 4 at Toronto 3
26　Toronto 2 at Ottawa 5
28　Toronto 3 at Canadiens 6
31　Ottawa 2 at Toronto 4

January
7 Canadiens 7 at Toronto 6
9 Toronto 2 at Ottawa 4
11 Toronto 3 at Canadiens 13
14 Ottawa 2 at Toronto 5 (Cy Dennenay
    and Ken Randall given match penalties
    and fined $15 for fighting; Randall fined
    an additional $10 for calling referee
    Steve Vair a "son of a bitch")
21 Canadiens 3 at Toronto 11
23 Toronto 2 at Ottawa 3 (Crawford given
    major penalty at 6:00 of the first;
    Toronto forced to play one man short
    the rest of the game)

Second half
28 Ottawa 2 at Toronto 1
    (Cameron 16:00 OT)

February
1 Toronto 0 at Canadiens 10 [Vezina]
4 Canadiens 3 at Toronto 6
6 Toronto 1 at Ottawa 3
11 Canadiens 4 at Toronto 6
15 Toronto 2 at Canadiens 8
18 Ottawa 4 at Toronto 3
    (Broadbent 2:30 OT)
20 Toronto 3 at Ottawa 9

1919–1920
December 13, 1919 Arenas changed name to
St. Patricks (although tentatively called the
"Tecumsehs")

First half
December
23 Toronto 0 at Ottawa 3 [Benedict]
27 Bulldogs 4 at Toronto 7
31 Canadiens 1 at Toronto 5

January
3 Ottawa 3 at Toronto 4 (Referee Steve
   Vair injured his shoulder at 18:00 of the
   first; the teams went to the dressing-
   room, and the extra two minutes was
   added to the second period)

7 Toronto 5 at Bulldogs 7
10 Toronto 7 at Canadiens 14
    (first game at Mount Royal Arena)
14 Canadiens 4 at Toronto 3
17 Bulldogs 3 at Toronto 8
21 Toronto 2 at Canadiens 3
24 Ottawa 3 at Toronto 5 (Benedict, Ottawa
    goalie, given a minor penalty)
28 Toronto 0 at Ottawa 7 [Benedict]
31 Toronto 6 at Bulldogs 10 (Joe Malone
    (B) scored 7 goals)

Second half
February
4 Canadiens 6 at Toronto 5
7 Toronto 4 at Ottawa 3 (at the end of the
   first period, the players were promised a
   bonus of $25 if they won the game; they
   did, and were paid the next day)
11 Bulldogs 2 at Toronto 7
16 Toronto 4 at Bulldogs 3
    (Dennenay scores winner at 19:35)
18 Toronto 8 at Canadiens 2
21 Ottawa 5 at Toronto 3
25 Toronto 8 at Bulldogs 2
28 Ottawa 1 at Toronto 0 [Benedict]
    (Nighbor 12:00) (Cy Dennenay (O) and
    Wilson (T) got into a fight. Dennenay
    was penalized and while in the box a
    fan hit him. His brother, Corbett (T)
    came over and then hit the fan)

March
3 Toronto 4 at Ottawa 7
6 Bulldogs 2 at Toronto 11 (Toronto goalie
   Lockhart played for Quebec when regular Bulldogs goalie Brophy was too
   injured to make the trip)
10 Toronto 2 at Bulldogs 7
13 Canadiens 4 at Toronto 11

1920–1921
First half
December
22 Toronto 3 at Ottawa 6
25 Canadiens 4 at Toronto 5
29 Ottawa 8 at Toronto 1

January

3 Toronto 5 at Hamilton 4
8 Hamilton 3 at Toronto 2
   (Couture 5:00 ot)
12 Toronto 4 at Hamilton 2
15 Ottawa 5 at Toronto 2
17 Toronto 5 at Canadiens 9
19 Canadiens 2 at Toronto 7
22 Toronto 5 at Ottawa 4
   (Dennenay 15:30 ot)

Second half

26 Hamilton 3 at Toronto 10
29 Toronto 2 at Canadiens 4

February

2 Toronto 3 at Ottawa 4 (two delays during the game caused by power failures; a line of candles around the rink was set up to augment the lighting)
5 Canadiens 6 at Toronto 10
9 Toronto 5 at Canadiens 3 (Noble fined $50 for arguing with referee Smeaton)
12 Toronto 6 at Hamilton 4
16 Ottawa 3 at Toronto 4 (game delayed three minutes from the end when Forbes (T) in net suffered a bad cut that had to be stitched)
19 Hamilton 4 at Toronto 5
23 Toronto 4 at Hamilton 7 (goal awarded to Hamilton when Dye blocked a shot)
26 Ottawa 2 at Toronto 4
28 Toronto 0 at Canadiens 4 [Vezina]

March

2 Toronto 3 at Ottawa 2
5 Hamilton 3 at Toronto 4
   (Cameron 3:00 ot)
   (Randall fined $25 for stick-swinging)
7 Canadiens 4 at Toronto 6

1921–1922

December

17 Canadiens 2 at Toronto 5
21 Toronto 5 at Ottawa 4
   (Lord and Lady Byng in attendance)
24 Hamilton 4 at Toronto 2
28 Toronto 4 at Hamilton 3
31 Toronto 3 at Canadiens 5

January

4 Ottawa 2 at Toronto 3
   (Stuart wins game in final minute)
7 Hamilton 2 at Toronto 5
11 Toronto 2 at Ottawa 7
14 Ottawa 5 at Toronto 2 (at 9:20 of the 3rd with Toronto trailing 3–2, Dye was given a minor penalty he felt was unwarranted. He began to shove referee Percy LeSueur and was given a five-minute major; he then used abusive language and was given five more. Noble and Randall got minors when play resumed, and with Toronto playing with only two skaters, Ottawa scored two goals. Dye's penalties meant the St. Pats played one man down the rest of the game)
18 Toronto 4 at Hamilton 9
21 Toronto 5 at Canadiens 3 (Dye (T) scored a goal in the 2nd, but after play had resumed for fully two minutes, referee Smeaton disallowed the goal on advice from the goal judge who, reversing his initial decision, said the puck had not crossed the goal line)
25 Canadiens 1 at Toronto 3
28 Ottawa 2 at Toronto 1

February

1 Toronto 5 at Hamilton 4
4 Canadiens 1 at Toronto 3
8 Toronto 4 at Canadiens 6
11 Toronto 4 at Ottawa 4 (20:00 ot)
15 Hamilton 4 at Toronto 6
18 Toronto 4 at Canadiens 6
22 Toronto 3 at Hamilton 4
25 Ottawa 5 at Toronto 7

March

1 Toronto 3 at Ottawa 2
4 Hamilton 4 at Toronto 8 (in an effort to help their chances to make the playoffs, the Canadiens' owners offered all Hamilton players $25 if they beat Toronto. The St. Pats won and the Canadiens missed the playoffs)
7 Canadiens 8 at Toronto 7

1922–1923

December

16 Canadiens 2 at Toronto 7
20 Toronto 2 at Ottawa 7 (game delayed 75 minutes because trains from Toronto were late arriving; players dressed on the train!)
23 Hamilton 4 at Toronto 9
27 Toronto 6 at Hamilton 9
30 Toronto 2 at Canadiens 8

January

3 Ottawa 2 at Toronto 3 (Dye 5:15 OT) (in a pre-game ceremony, the St. Pats presented the Senators' Eddie Gerard with a tie pin to acknowledge their appreciation for his contribution in the Cup-winning 1922 playoffs)
6 Toronto 1 at Ottawa 2 (both teams played 38 minutes without making a single change)
10 Toronto 7 at Hamilton 6 (Dye :40 OT)
13 Canadiens 2 at Toronto 2 (20:00 OT)
17 Hamilton 5 at Toronto 2 (Randall fined $15 for attack on Bouchard (H))
20 Toronto 1 at Canadiens 3
24 Toronto 2 at Ottawa 1 (Noble 1:09 OT)
27 Canadiens 2 at Toronto 4
31 Toronto 1 at Ottawa 2 (all goals in the 1st)

February

3 Hamilton 5 at Toronto 6
7 Toronto 4 at Hamilton 2
10 Toronto 3 at Canadiens 5 (Noble fined $50 for verbal abuse of referee Cooper Smeaton)
14 Ottawa 4 at Toronto 6
17 Toronto 3 at Hamilton 2
21 Toronto 1 at Ottawa 6
24 Canadiens 3 at Toronto 4 (game delayed three times when ceiling lightbulbs burst because of leaks in the roof and glass had to be cleaned from the ice)
28 Toronto 0 at Canadiens 3 [Vezina]

March

3 Hamilton 3 at Toronto 4
5 Ottawa 0 at Toronto 2 [Roach] (both goals in 3rd)

1923–1924

December

15 Canadiens 1 at Toronto 2
19 Toronto 2 at Ottawa 5
22 Hamilton 2 at Toronto 5
26 Toronto 2 at Hamilton 1 (fans pelted ice with eggs when referee Laflamme disallowed a Hamilton goal by Mickey Roach in the last minute of play)
29 Toronto 0 at Canadiens 3 [Vezina]

January

2 Ottawa 4 at Toronto 3
5 Toronto 3 at Ottawa 7
9 Toronto 3 at Hamilton 5
12 Canadiens 3 at Toronto 5
16 Hamilton 1 at Toronto 3
19 Toronto 2 at Canadiens 0 [Roach] (both goals in the 2nd)
23 Ottawa 5 at Toronto 1
26 Canadiens 1 at Toronto 2
30 Toronto 2 at Ottawa 7 (with eight minutes left in the game, referee Art Ross gave Toronto three major or match penalties, leaving them to play 6-on-3 for the rest of the game. Toronto formally protested the outcome, but Querrie was fined $200 for abusing Ross)

February

2 Hamilton 4 at Toronto 2
6 Toronto 4 at Hamilton 6
9 Toronto 3 at Canadiens 5
13 Ottawa 2 at Toronto 4
16 Toronto 2 at Ottawa 1
20 Toronto 1 at Hamilton 3
23 Hamilton 1 at Toronto 2 (game delayed 10 minutes to allow fans to enter)
27 Toronto 1 at Canadiens 6

March

1 Canadiens 4 at Toronto 1
5 Ottawa 8 at Toronto 4

1924–1925

November

29 Toronto 1 at Canadiens 7 (first game at the Forum)

December

3 Boston 3 at Toronto 5 (Noble, trying to buy time during a Boston power play, threw puck into crowd. Puck retrieved, Noble given two-minute penalty)

5 Hamilton 10 at Toronto 3

10 Toronto 6 at Ottawa 3

13 Maroons 3 at Toronto 1

17 Canadiens 5 at Toronto 2

22 Toronto 10 at Boston 1

25 Toronto 1 at Hamilton 8

27 Ottawa 4 at Toronto 3 (Connell, Ottawa's goalie, is penalized. Clancy goes in net, and during the ensuing power play the Senators score a goal short-handed)

31 Toronto 2 at Maroons 1

January

3 Canadiens 3 at Toronto 1

5 Toronto 3 at Boston 2

10 Hamilton 1 at Toronto 3

14 Ottawa 2 at Toronto 3

17 Toronto 1 at Maroons 2

21 Toronto 4 at Canadiens 2

24 Boston 3 at Toronto 4

28 Toronto 0 at Hamilton 4 [Forbes]

31 Toronto 2 at Ottawa 1 (all goals in 3rd)

February

4 Maroons 2 at Toronto 3

7 Canadiens 4 at Toronto 5

10 Toronto 5 at Boston 1 (Dye (T) awarded a goal after goalie threw his stick)

14 Hamilton 1 at Toronto 3

18 Ottawa 2 at Toronto 4

21 Toronto 2 at Maroons 1

25 Toronto 3 at Canadiens 1

28 Boston 1 at Toronto 5

March

4 Toronto 2 at Hamilton 3

7 Toronto 0 at Ottawa 3 [Connell]

9 Maroons 0 at Toronto 3 [Roach]

1925–1926

November

28 Boston 3 at Toronto 2

December

1 Toronto 2 at Maroons 4

5 Americans 3 at Toronto 5

9 Toronto 3 at Pirates 6

12 Canadiens 0 at Toronto 4 [Roach]

19 Pirates 1 at Toronto 1 (20:00 OT)

23 Toronto 2 at Ottawa 4

26 Maroons 2 at Toronto 0 [Benedict]

29 Toronto 0 at Boston 3 [Stewart]

30 Toronto 1 at Americans 2 (Green 8:00 OT)

January

1 Ottawa 0 at Toronto 3 [Roach]

5 Toronto 4 at Canadiens 5

9 Boston 2 at Toronto 3

12 Toronto 2 at Maroons 5

15 Americans 3 at Toronto 4

21 Toronto 4 at Pirates 5

23 Canadiens 2 at Toronto 6

26 Toronto 3 at Canadiens 6

29 Pirates 2 at Toronto 3

February

2 Toronto 2 at Boston 3 (all goals in 1st)

3 Toronto 1 at Americans 1 (20:00 OT) (both goals in the 2nd)

6 Ottawa 1 at Toronto 4

9 Maroons 5 at Toronto 3

11 Toronto 1 at Ottawa 2

13 Boston 7 at Toronto 4

16 Toronto 3 at Americans 2

18 Toronto 2 at Maroons 5

20 Pirates 1 at Toronto 3

22 Toronto 1 at Boston 2 (Hitchman 2:25 OT)

27 Maroons 4 at Toronto 3 (game delayed with 4 minutes left when Babe Dye refused to give the referee the puck; the referee left the ice and did not return for some time) (Corbeau (T) suspended one game after brawl with Babe Seibert (M))

March

4 Toronto 2 at Pirates 7

6 Americans 2 at Toronto 4

11 Canadiens 3 at Toronto 5

13 Ottawa 1 at Toronto 1 (20:00 OT)

16 Toronto 1 at Canadiens 6
17 Toronto 0 at Ottawa 4 [Connell]

1926–1927
November
17 Toronto 1 at Chicago 4
20 Rangers 5 at Toronto 1
25 Ottawa 2 at Toronto 2 (20:00 OT)
30 Pirates 0 at Toronto 6 [Roach]

December
2 Toronto 0 at Canadiens 2 [Hainsworth]
4 Americans 1 at Toronto 0
    (Simpson 7:30 3rd) [Forbes]
9 Chicago 2 at Toronto 5 (St. Pats general
    manager Querrie changed benches, put-
    ting two green blankets on the pine and
    using them for his team)
11 Toronto 1 at Ottawa 2
14 Toronto 0 at Maroons 3 [Benedict]
18 Canadiens 2 at Toronto 0 [Hainsworth]
20 Toronto 0 at Americans 2 (Conacher
    and Bailey fined $15) [Forbes]
21 Toronto 5 at Boston 3
25 Toronto 2 at Pirates 3
30 Boston 1 at Toronto 4 (Art Ross of
    Boston protested Toronto's use of Al
    Pudas, believing Pudas to be ineligible)

January
1 Maroons 3 at Toronto 0 [Benedict]
    (all goals in the 3rd)
4 Toronto 2 at Cougars 1
8 Americans 1 at Toronto 3
11 Toronto 1 at Ottawa 4
13 Toronto 1 at Rangers 1 (20:00 OT)
15 Cougars 1 at Toronto 1 (20:00 OT)
19 Toronto 3 at Chicago 4 (Fraser 2:30 OT)
    (Dye fined $15 for abusive language)
22 Toronto 0 at Canadiens 4 (all goals in
    the 1st) [Hainsworth]
27 Maroons 5 at Toronto 3
29 Chicago 1 at Toronto 6

February
1 Toronto 0 at Boston 1 [Stewart]
    (Frederickson in 2nd)

3 Toronto 0 at Americans 0 (20:00 OT)
    (Roach (T)/Forbes (A)]
5 Boston 0 at Toronto 1
    (McCaffery 14:00 2nd) [Roach]
8 Toronto 0 at Maroons 3 [Benedict]
10 Rangers 3 at Toronto 2
12 Ottawa 1 at Toronto 0
    (Adams 13:15 2nd) [Connell]
16 Toronto 1 at Cougars 5
17 Americans 1 at Toronto 4 (first game
    played as the Maple Leafs)
19 Maroons 2 at Toronto 1
    (Munro 12:40 OT)
22 Toronto 3 at Rangers 2 (Bailey 8:47 OT)
24 Canadiens 3 at Toronto 2
26 Toronto 1 at Pirates 1 (20:00 OT)

March
1 Pirates 1 at Toronto 4
5 Cougars 2 at Toronto 4
10 Toronto 2 at Canadiens 4
12 Toronto 1 at Maroons 0 (Bailey awarded
    goal at 9:55 of 1st when goalie threw his
    stick) [Roach]
19 Ottawa 2 at Toronto 0
    (both goals in the 3rd) [Connell]
21 Toronto 4 at Americans 1
24 Toronto 0 at Ottawa 4 [Connell]
26 Canadiens 1 at Toronto 2

1927–1928
November
15 Rangers 4 at Toronto 2 (W.D. Ross,
    Lieutenant-Governor of Ontario, faced
    off opening puck)
19 Chicago 2 at Toronto 4
22 Toronto 0 at Boston 1
    [Winkler] (Cleghorn in 3rd)
24 Toronto 2 at Americans 1
26 Toronto 2 at Pirates 1 (Bailey :44 OT)

December
3 Maroons 2 at Toronto 1 (all goals in the
    1st) (Day fined $25 after refusing to
    leave the ice when given a penalty for
    charging the goalie)
6 Toronto 0 at Ottawa 0 (10:00 OT)
    [Roach (T)/Connell (O)]

8   Toronto 1 at Canadiens 2
    (Joliat 3:47 OT)
10 Ottawa 0 at Toronto 0 (10:00 OT)
    [Connell (O)/Roach (T)]
14 Toronto 4 at Chicago 2
17 Cougars 1 at Toronto 0
    (Copper 9:00 OT) [Holmes]
20 Americans 2 at Toronto 5
22 Pirates 3 at Toronto 2
    (McKinnon :35 OT)
24 Toronto 1 at Ottawa 1 (10:00 OT)
29 Boston 1 at Toronto 2
    (all goals in the 3rd)

January

2   Toronto 4 at Chicago 1
5   Toronto 1 at Maroons 2
7   Canadiens 9 at Toronto 1 (Carson
    awarded Leafs' only goal, in 3rd, when
    goalie Gardiner (C) threw his stick)
10 Toronto 1 at Americans 2
    (all goals in the 3rd)
12 Toronto 2 at Cougars 1
14 Rangers 1 at Toronto 6
17 Toronto 2 at Rangers 1
21 Ottawa 1 at Toronto 2
26 Toronto 0 at Maroons 1
    (Stewart 15:07 1st) [Benedict]
28 Chicago 1 at Toronto 4
31 Toronto 0 at Ottawa 4 [Connell]

February

2   Toronto 4 at Canadiens 3
4   Cougars 0 at Toronto 2 [Roach]
7   Canadiens 2 at Toronto 1
    (all goals in the 2nd)
11 Americans 2 at Toronto 2 (10:00 OT)
14 Pirates 4 at Toronto 2
16 Toronto 3 at Americans 2
18 Toronto 1 at Maroons 2
21 Toronto 0 at Canadiens 0 (10:00 OT)
    [Roach (T)/ Hainsworth (C)]
23 Maroons 2 at Toronto 2 (10:00 OT)
28 Toronto 0 at Rangers 1
    (Bourgeault 2:49 3rd) [Chabot]

March

1   Toronto 2 at Pirates 4
3   Boston 0 at Toronto 0 (10:00 OT)
    [Winkler (B)/ Ironstone (T)]

6   Toronto 1 at Cougars 3
8   Americans 2 at Toronto 4
13 Ottawa 1 at Toronto 1 (10:00 OT)
17 Canadiens 3 at Toronto 5
    ("Parents' Night" at Arena Gardens)
20 Toronto 6 at Boston 2
    (Herberts (T) presented with a gold
    watch by Boston sports writers)
24 Maroons 8 at Toronto 4

1928–1929

November

15 Chicago 0 at Toronto 2
    (both goals in the 2nd) [Chabot]
17 Canadiens 2 at Toronto 4
20 Toronto 1 at Ottawa 4 (Clancy scored
    Ottawa's first goal while Toronto had
    four men in the penalty box and only
    Chabot and Blair on the ice!)
22 Toronto 0 at Americans 3 [Walsh]
24 Maroons 1 at Toronto 4
27 Toronto 0 at Maroons 4 [Benedict]

December

1   Americans 0 at Toronto 3 [Chabot]
4   Toronto 3 at Canadiens 1
8   Ottawa 2 at Toronto 1
    (Boucher 6:30 OT)
11 Toronto 2 at Rangers 3
15 Boston 0 at Toronto 2 [Chabot]
20 Toronto 3 at Maroons 6
22 Pirates 3 at Toronto 2
25 Maroons 1 at Toronto 4
27 Toronto 2 at Pirates 0 [Chabot]
29 Cougars 3 at Toronto 4

January

1   Rangers 3 at Toronto 2
3   Toronto 2 at Chicago 0 [Chabot]
5   Ottawa 1 at Toronto 3
8   Toronto 2 at Boston 5
10 Toronto 0 at Americans 2 [Worters]
    (Grant replaced Chabot after 16 minutes
    of first period when Chabot was cut
    badly over eye)
12 Americans 1 at Toronto 0
    (Connors 6:00 OT) [Worters]
17 Canadiens 1 at Toronto 1
    (10:00 OT) (both goals in the 2nd)

20 Toronto 1 at Cougars 2
22 Toronto 0 at Rangers 1
(Murdoch 18:46 1st) [Roach]
24 Toronto 1 at Canadiens 1 (10:00 OT)
26 Chicago 0 at Toronto 2 [Chabot]
29 Toronto 2 at Ottawa 4 (Finnigan
7:40/Grosvenor 9:00 OT—both goals
scored with three Leafs in the penalty
box!)
31 Boston 3 at Toronto 1

February
2 Toronto 3 at Boston 0 [Chabot]
3 Toronto 3 at Americans 1
5 Toronto 0 at Pirates 0 (10:00 OT)
[Chabot (T)/Miller (P)]
9 Pirates 1 at Toronto 2
14 Rangers 1 at Toronto 3
16 Maroons 0 at Toronto 3
(all goals in the 3rd) [Chabot]
17 Toronto 0 at Cougars 2 [Dolson]
23 Canadiens 1 at Toronto 2
28 Toronto 4 at Maroons 0 [Chabot]

March
2 Ottawa 1 at Toronto 1 (10:00 OT)
(both goals in the 3rd)
7 Toronto 1 at Chicago 1 (10:00 OT)
(played at Fort Erie)
9 Cougars 0 at Toronto 3 [Chabot]
12 Toronto 1 at Canadiens 2 (all goals in
the 2nd) (Grant replaced Chabot to
start 2nd)
14 Americans 0 at Toronto 5
[Chabot/Grant] (Grant replaced
Chabot in 2nd)
16 Toronto 0 at Ottawa 2 [Connell]

1929–1930
November
14 Chicago 2 at Toronto 2 (10:00 OT) (W.D.
Ross, Lieutenant-Governor of Ontario,
faced off opening puck. Also, a moment
of silence is observed for Shorty Horne,
who drowned during the summer)
16 Boston 6 at Toronto 5
19 Toronto 5 at Pirates 10

21 Toronto 2 at Canadiens 3
(Leduc 7:23 OT)
23 Ottawa 6 at Toronto 2
26 Toronto 4 at Rangers 3
30 Falcons 0 at Toronto 1
(Primeau 11:15 1st) [Chabot]

December
3 Americans 0 at Toronto 6 [Chabot]
5 Toronto 2 at Ottawa 9 (Horner and
Conacher fined $25 for leaving the
bench during a fight)
7 Canadiens 1 at Toronto 0
(Lepine 2:50 2nd) [Hainsworth]
10 Toronto 0 at Americans 1
(Conacher 4:58 1st) [Worters]
14 Rangers 6 at Toronto 7 (Cotton (T)
1:30/Cotton (T) 2:50/Boucher (R)
3:20 OT)
15 Toronto 3 at Falcons 5
17 Toronto 1 at Maroons 3 (Conn Smythe
fined $50 for verbally berating the ref-
eree, Bailey $15 for abusive language
and gestures)
21 Pirates 1 at Toronto 2 (Duncan 3:00 OT)
25 Toronto 2 at Boston 6
29 Toronto 4 at Chicago 3

January
1 Maroons 3 at Toronto 5
4 Canadiens 3 at Toronto 4 (prior to the
game of December 14, 1929, vs.
Rangers, Leaf fan Ivan Mickailoff offered
a watch to the Leaf who scored the winning goal that night. Before the start of
the game, he presented Baldy Cotton
with the timepiece)
7 Toronto 1 at Americans 1
(10:00 OT) (both goals in the 2nd)
9 Ottawa 0 at Toronto 4 [Chabot]
14 Toronto 1 at Maroons 1 (10:00 OT)
16 Toronto 1 at Ottawa 2
18 Americans 1 at Toronto 4
25 Falcons 2 at Toronto 1
30 Maroons 3 at Toronto 0 [Walsh]

February
1 Chicago 0 at Toronto 6 [Chabot]
4 Toronto 1 at Canadiens 3

6   Canadiens 3 at Toronto 3 (10:00 OT)
    (Larochelle (C) tied game at 19:31)
9   Toronto 3 at Americans 2
11 Toronto 5 at Boston 6
    (Conacher (T) 2:18/Clapper (B)
    7:06/Shore (B) 8:20 OT)
15 Boston 5 at Toronto 3
18 Toronto 5 at Rangers 1
20 Toronto 4 at Pirates 0
    (all goals in the 3rd) [Chabot]
22 Ottawa 1 at Toronto 0 [Connell]
    (Finnigan 13:25 1st)
25 Toronto 0 at Ottawa 2 (Finnigan :20/
    Finnigan 2:30 OT) [Connell]
27 Toronto 2 at Canadiens 6

    March
1   Rangers 3 at Toronto 3 (10:00 OT)
4   Americans 1 at Toronto 1 (10:00 OT)
8   Maroons 3 at Toronto 2
9   Toronto 2 at Falcons 1
11 Pirates 2 at Toronto 3
15 Toronto 3 at Maroons 0 [Chabot]
18 Toronto 1 at Chicago 4

1930–1931
November
13 Americans 0 at Toronto 0 (10:00 OT)
    [Worters (A)/Chabot (T)]
15 Quakers 0 at Toronto 4 [Chabot]
18 Toronto 3 at Maroons 0 [Chabot]
    (Bailey awarded Toronto's second goal
    when L. Conacher threw his stick to stop
    a shot)
20 Toronto 0 at Americans 0 (10:00 OT)
    [Grant (T)/Worters (A)]
22 Ottawa 0 at Toronto 2 [Chabot]
25 Toronto 1 at Quakers 2
29 Falcons 2 at Toronto 4

    December
2   Toronto 2 at Boston 3
6   Rangers 2 at Toronto 4
9   Toronto 1 at Canadiens 2
13 Boston 7 at Toronto 3
18 Maroons 2 at Toronto 1
20 Chicago 1 at Toronto 3
23 Toronto 4 at Maroons 4 (10:00 OT)

25 Toronto 1 at Falcons 10
28 Toronto 3 at Chicago 2

    January
1   Americans 0 at Toronto 2
    (both goals in the 3rd) [Chabot]
3   Canadiens 1 at Toronto 2
    (fan threw chair at referee Cleghorn)
6   Toronto 2 at Ottawa 2 (10:00 OT)
8   Maroons 0 at Toronto 1
    (Blair 5:30 3rd) [Chabot]
10 Toronto 1 at Canadiens 6
15 Toronto 1 at Rangers 1 (10:00 OT)
17 Canadiens 1 at Toronto 3
22 Toronto 4 at Maroons 2
24 Ottawa 2 at Toronto 5
27 Toronto 2 at Americans 3
29 Toronto 3 at Ottawa 2
31 Quakers 2 at Toronto 3

    February
1   Toronto 0 at Falcons 2 [Dolson]
3   Toronto 1 at Canadiens 2
7   Americans 0 at Toronto 2 [Chabot]
14 Falcons 1 at Toronto 1 (10:00 OT)
19 Ottawa 2 at Toronto 1
21 Boston 2 at Toronto 4
24 Toronto 1 at Americans 1 (10:00 OT)
26 Toronto 1 at Rangers 4
28 Canadiens 5 at Toronto 5 (Morenz (C)
    4:00/Gagnon (C) 5:05/Blair (T)
    7:30/Conacher (T) 8:10 OT)

    March
3   Toronto 5 at Quakers 1
5   Maroons 6 at Toronto 5
7   Rangers 2 at Toronto 5
10 Toronto 3 at Boston 3 (10:00 OT)
    (Boston scored in the overtime right
    from a faceoff in front of the goal, but
    King Clancy protested to the referee he
    was offside in the faceoff. The referee
    believed Clancy and nullified the goal.
    The Leafs won the next draw and kept
    the score tied!)
15 Toronto 2 at Chicago 1
19 Chicago 2 at Toronto 8
21 Toronto 9 at Ottawa 6

1931–1932
The beginning of the Maple Leaf Gardens era

November

12 Chicago 2 at Toronto 1 (the home opener at the new Maple Leaf Gardens. Puck is dropped by Mayor Stewart for Tommy Cook (C) and Ace Bailey (T). March (C) scored at 2:30 of 1st; Conacher (T) 18:42 of 2nd; Ripley (C) 2:35 of 3rd)
14 Canadiens 1 at Toronto 1 (10:00 OT)
18 Toronto 1 at Chicago 1 (10:00 OT)
21 Rangers 5 at Toronto 3
26 Toronto 2 at Canadiens 3
28 Boston 5 at Toronto 6 (Blair 1:45 OT)

December

 1 Americans 2 at Toronto 2 (10:00 OT)
 3 Toronto 2 at Maroons 8
 5 Maroons 0 at Toronto 4 [Chabot]
 8 Toronto 4 at Rangers 2
12 Falcons 1 at Toronto 3
15 Toronto 2 at Americans 2 (10:00 OT)
19 Maroons 2 at Toronto 4
20 Toronto 0 at Chicago 1 (March 9:10 OT) [Gardiner]
22 Americans 3 at Toronto 9
24 Toronto 2 at Canadiens 1 (H. Jackson 9:55 OT) (Cotton challenged referee Cooper Smeaton to a fight after receiving a penalty late in the 3rd)
26 Canadiens 2 at Toronto 0 (Morenz 2:15/Lepine 2:55 OT) [Hainsworth]
29 Toronto 5 at Americans 0 (Chabot badly cut; game delayed while he was attended to) [Chabot]
31 Maroons 1 at Toronto 3

January

 3 Toronto 2 at Falcons 3 (Sorrell 3:05 OT)
 5 Toronto 3 at Boston 3 (10:00 OT)
10 Toronto 0 at Rangers 2 [Roach]
12 Falcons 4 at Toronto 7
14 Toronto 6 at Maroons 4
17 Toronto 0 at Americans 4 [Worters]
19 Americans 3 at Toronto 11
21 Toronto 1 at Canadiens 3 (Joliat 19:48 en) (the earliest known instance in the

NHL of a team pulling a goalie in the dying seconds for an extra attacker)
23 Canadiens 0 at Toronto 2 [Chabot]
30 Rangers 3 at Toronto 6 (Finnigan :25/ H. Jackson 2:10/Clancy 3:15 OT)

February

 3 Toronto 0 at Chicago 7 [Gardiner]
 6 Boston 0 at Toronto 6 [Chabot]
 7 Toronto 1 at Falcons 3 (Chabot punched goal judge Duke Kennedy and suspended one game)
13 Maroons 0 at Toronto 6 (Clancy, Day, Starr, and Phillips all fined $25 for brawling) [Grant]
16 Toronto 0 at Boston 3 [Thompson]
18 Rangers 3 at Toronto 5 (toward the end of the game, Dick Irvin pulled a clever trick. According to the rules of the day, any player who stepped on the ice while his team was at full strength received an automatic major penalty. Three majors meant an automatic one-game suspension. On his bench were Conacher and Horner, both injured and both with two majors to their credit on the year. Irvin told them both to get on the ice during play and both received majors and one-game suspensions, but as they weren't ready to play anyway, the punishment only served to give them a fresh record when they got healthy.)
20 Toronto 0 at Maroons 3 [Walsh]
23 Toronto 4 at Americans 4 (10:00 OT)
25 Falcons 5 at Toronto 3
27 Chicago 2 at Toronto 4

March

 1 Americans 1 at Toronto 3
 5 Canadiens 1 at Toronto 1 (10:00 OT)
10 Toronto 1 at Maroons 3
12 Boston 3 at Toronto 5 (Horner 8:50/Conacher 9:42 OT)
15 Toronto 2 at Boston 6 (one of the more unique games ever played in the NHL. Shortly after the opening faceoff, Leaf goalie Lorne Chabot was assessed a minor penalty (2 minutes), which he had to serve himself. During the ensuing

Bruin power play, three Leaf defencemen each played goal. Each allowed a goal. Marty Barry scored on Red Horner, then just seconds later against Alex Levinsky. King Clancy then went in goal, only to be scored upon by George Owen)

17   Toronto 6 at Rangers 3

19   Chicago 3 at Toronto 11 (Chicago goalie Gardiner was hurt by a shot at 18:12 of 1st. The referee called for an early inter-mission, but Gardiner couldn't continue and was replaced by Cude. Late in the 2nd, Cude was knocked unconscious by a shot and was carried off. After a delay, he was able to continue)

20   Toronto 3 at Falcons 2

22   Toronto 2 at Canadiens 4

1932–1933

November

10   Boston 1 at Toronto 1 (10:00 OT) (Hon. H.A. Bruce, Lieutenant-Governor of Ontario, dropped the puck, and the 1932 Stanley Cup banner was raised to the rafters)

12   Rangers 2 at Toronto 4

17   Toronto 1 at Chicago 3

20   Toronto 0 at Rangers 7 [Aitkenhead] (New York mayor Joseph V. McKee dropped the puck)

24   Canadiens 0 at Toronto 2 (both goals in the 2nd) [Chabot]

26   Maroons 2 at Toronto 3

27   Toronto 2 at Falcons 1

December

3   Ottawa 1 at Toronto 4

8   Toronto 0 at Maroons 1 (Hayes 11:32 3rd) [Walsh]

10   Americans 2 at Toronto 2 (McVeigh (A) 1:54 (pp)/Bailey (T) 2:56 (pp) OT)

13   Toronto 1 at Boston 5 (Boston manager Art Ross fined $50 for hitting King Clancy (T) during a fracas in the penalty box)

15   Ottawa 1 at Toronto 4

17   Falcons 0 at Toronto 3 [Chabot]

20   Toronto 2 at Canadiens 1

22   Toronto 0 at Americans 1 (Sheppard 16:14 2nd) [Worters]

24   Chicago 2 at Toronto 1 (Young Canada Night)

27   Toronto 4 at Chicago 3

29   Maroons 0 at Toronto 1 (Clancy 19:49 1st) [Chabot]

January

1   Toronto 2 at Detroit 2 (10:00 OT)

3   Toronto 2 at Rangers 4

5   Toronto 2 at Maroons 2 (10:00 OT)

7   Falcons 6 at Toronto 1 (first nationwide broadcast of a Leaf game by Foster Hewitt on CBC Radio)

10   Rangers 2 at Toronto 3

14   Toronto 5 at Ottawa 3 (Bailey 3:20/Cotton 5:00 (pp) OT)

17   Toronto 1 at Americans 3

19   Boston 0 at Toronto 3 [Chabot]

24   Toronto 4 at Ottawa 2

26   Toronto 2 at Boston 4

28   Canadiens 2 at Toronto 4

31   Americans 1 at Toronto 7

February

4   Chicago 2 at Toronto 2 (10:00 OT)

7   Toronto 0 at Canadiens 2 [Hainsworth]

11   Rangers 1 at Toronto 2

14   Toronto 2 at Boston 7

16   Toronto 5 at Rangers 2

18   Falcons 1 at Toronto 4

23   Toronto 3 at Ottawa 0 [Chabot]

25   Americans 1 at Toronto 5

28   Canadiens 2 at Toronto 1

March

2   Toronto 3 at Canadiens 4

4   Maroons 2 at Toronto 4

5   Toronto 2 at Chicago 1

7   Toronto 2 at Maroons 7 (before the game, a fan sent a live black rabbit to the Leaf dressing room with instructions to put it in Cotton's locker. After the loss, Cotton had it removed for good)

11   Boston 6 at Toronto 2

16   Toronto 0 at Falcons 1 (Emms 9:56 1st (pp)) [Roach]

18   Ottawa 2 at Toronto 6

21 Toronto 3 at Americans 4
23 Chicago 2 at Toronto 2 (McFadden (C)
tied game at 19:59) (10:00 OT)

1933–1934
November
9 Boston 1 at Toronto 6 (Hon. H.A. Bruce,
Lieutenant-Governor of Ontario,
dropped the puck)
11 Rangers 3 at Toronto 4
18 Ottawa 1 at Toronto 4 (Ottawa formally
protested, claiming the goal creases were
made too small and that Toronto scored
twice inside what should have been
the crease)
21 Toronto 1 at Rangers 1 (10:00 OT)
25 Canadiens 1 at Toronto 0
(Bourgeault 7:21 1st) [Chabot]
28 Americans 3 at Toronto 7
30 Toronto 1 at Maroons 0 [Hainsworth]

December
2 Maroons 3 at Toronto 8
3 Toronto 3 at Detroit 0 [Hainsworth]
5 Toronto 9 at Americans 1
7 Toronto 1 at Ottawa 4
9 Chicago 0 at Toronto 1 (Conacher
11:08 3rd) [Hainsworth]
12 Toronto 4 at Boston 1 (Ace Bailey's
career ended. Eddie Shore suspended
16 games; Red Horner, who attacked
Shore, suspended six games)
14 Toronto 0 at Canadiens 2 [Chabot]
16 Canadiens 1 at Toronto 3
23 Maroons 2 at Toronto 8
(Young Canada Night)
26 Toronto 2 at Boston 2 (10:00 OT)
28 Toronto 2 at Rangers 2 (10:00 OT)
30 Detroit 1 at Toronto 8

January
1 Toronto 2 at Chicago 1
4 Toronto 1 at Canadiens 4
6 Ottawa 3 at Toronto 7
11 Toronto 1 at Americans 1 (10:00 OT)
13 Americans 2 at Toronto 2 (10:00 OT)
16 Toronto 7 at Ottawa 4 (Doraty 1:35/
Doraty 2:20/Doraty 9:05 OT)

18 Boston 2 at Toronto 6 (as a result of the
Bailey incident, all Bruins wore helmets
for this game as a precaution)
20 Chicago 2 at Toronto 2 (10:00 OT)
21 Toronto 2 at Detroit 4
(Lewis 4:17/Lewis 9:55 OT)
23 Maroons 4 at Toronto 8
25 Toronto 0 at Maroons 6 [Kerr]
27 Detroit 2 at Toronto 2 (10:00 OT)
28 Toronto 0 at Chicago 2 [Gardner]

February
1 Toronto 5 at Rangers 5 (10:00 OT)
3 Ottawa 4 at Toronto 8
4 Toronto 1 at Detroit 2
8 Toronto 3 at Americans 3 (10:00 OT)
10 Canadiens 2 at Toronto 4
17 Boston 4 at Toronto 6
20 Toronto 2 at Canadiens 3
(Joliat 6:27 OT)
24 Rangers 3 at Toronto 8
27 Toronto 2 at Maroons 1
(Thoms 8:06 OT)

March
3 Detroit 4 at Toronto 6
6 Toronto 2 at Boston 7
(Ace Bailey dropped first puck)
8 Toronto 1 at Ottawa 3
10 Americans 5 at Toronto 8
15 Chicago 2 at Toronto 1
17 Rangers 2 at Toronto 3
(King Clancy Night)
18 Toronto 2 at Chicago 3

1934–1935
November
8 Boston 3 at Toronto 5
10 Canadiens 1 at Toronto 2 (Doraty (T)
tied game at 19:50/H. Jackson 5:37 OT)
15 Toronto 1 at Americans 0
(Conacher 19:02 3rd) [Hainsworth]
17 Maroons 1 at Toronto 2
18 Toronto 5 at Chicago 0 [Hainsworth]
20 Toronto 5 at Eagles 2
24 Detroit 2 at Toronto 3

December

1 Eagles 3 at Toronto 4
2 Toronto 0 at Detroit 3 [N. Smith]
4 Toronto 1 at Boston 0
 (Conacher 14:40 1st) [Hainsworth]
8 Rangers 5 at Toronto 2
11 Toronto 8 at Rangers 4
13 Toronto 4 at Maroons 2
 (Conacher 5:09/Boll 7:53 OT)
15 Americans 3 at Toronto 4
20 Toronto 1 at Eagles 1 (10:00 OT)
22 Chicago 0 at Toronto 1 (H. Jackson
 18:18 3rd (pp)) [Hainsworth] (Young
 Canada Night)
25 Toronto 6 at Canadiens 2
27 Toronto 4 at Americans 3
 (Kelly 2:44 OT)
29 Maroons 4 at Toronto 2

January

1 Detroit 1 at Toronto 0
 (Weiland 18:15 1st) [Roach]
5 Canadiens 1 at Toronto 3
 (all goals in the 3rd)
8 Toronto 1 at Boston 3
10 Toronto 5 at Americans 5 (10:00 OT)
12 Chicago 1 at Toronto 5
13 Toronto 2 at Detroit 0 [Hainsworth]
15 Toronto 3 at Chicago 2 (originally
 scheduled for February 26)
17 Toronto 3 at Canadiens 4
19 Eagles 2 at Toronto 6
20 Toronto 1 at Chicago 2
22 Toronto 2 at Eagles 1
26 Detroit 0 at Toronto 0 (10:00 OT)
 [Roach (D)/ Hainsworth (T)]
29 Toronto 5 at Rangers 7
31 Rangers 3 at Toronto 2

February

2 Americans 2 at Toronto 1
7 Boston 4 at Toronto 4 (Barry (B) tied
 game at 19:25) (10:00 OT)
9 Maroons 2 at Toronto 4
12 Toronto 5 at Boston 6 (Kelly (T) 5:05/
 Kaminsky (B) 8:11/Clapper (B) 8:23 OT)
14 Toronto 0 at Rangers 3 [Kerr]
16 Rangers 1 at Toronto 5

19 Toronto 3 at Maroons 1
23 Chicago 1 at Toronto 4
24 Toronto 2 at Detroit 4

March

2 Americans 0 at Toronto 6 [Hainsworth]
5 Toronto 10 at Canadiens 3
9 Boston 7 at Toronto 4
12 Toronto 1 at Maroons 0
 (Kilrea 16:55 2nd (pp)) [Hainsworth]
16 Canadiens 3 at Toronto 5
19 Eagles 3 at Toronto 5

1935–1936

November

9 Americans 5 at Toronto 5
 (puck dropped by Mr. R.S. McLaughlin
 to start season) (N. Metz (T) :37/
 Schriner 7:42 OT)
14 Toronto 1 at Rangers 0 (Boll 10:44 3rd)
 [Hainsworth]
16 Rangers 2 at Toronto 3
19 Toronto 7 at Canadiens 2
21 Toronto 3 at Chicago 4
23 Maroons 5 at Toronto 2
24 Toronto 1 at Detroit 2 (Detroit's Scotty
 Bowman was given a penalty, but Syd
 Howe went to the penalty box. After the
 penalty had elapsed, the Leafs complained the wrong Wing had sat out.
 Howe was then given a minor himself
 for sitting out Bowman's penalty!)
26 Toronto 2 at Boston 1
30 Canadiens 3 at Toronto 8

December

7 Chicago 1 at Toronto 2
 (H. Jackson 2:12 OT)
10 Toronto 2 at Americans 4
14 Detroit 4 at Toronto 2
 (Lewis 4:01/Brûneteau 7:27 OT)
17 Toronto 1 at Maroons 0
 (Davidson 8:07 1st) [Hainsworth]
19 Boston 0 at Toronto 0 (10:00 OT)
 [Thompson (B)/Hainsworth (T)]
21 Americans 3 at Toronto 5
 (Young Canada Night)

26 Toronto 2 at Canadiens 0 (game held up for 20 minutes after fans littered the ice with coins, bottles, and papers to show their displeasure with a penalty call to a Hab) [Hainsworth]

28 Rangers 3 at Toronto 9

January

2 Toronto 2 at Maroons 5 (bench-clearing brawl lasted 20 minutes and had 11 fights)

4 Maroons 1 at Toronto 1 (10:00 OT) (both goals in the 3rd)

11 Canadiens 7 at Toronto 3

14 Toronto 1 at Boston 4

16 Toronto 0 at Rangers 1 (Connelly penalty shot 2nd) [Kerr]

18 Boston 2 at Toronto 5 (Dr. Allan R. Dafoe, the man who delivered the Dionne quintuplets, is in attendance)

19 Toronto 0 at Detroit 4 [N. Smith]

21 Canadiens at Toronto (postponed to February 20 due to death of King George V)

23 Toronto 2 at Americans 3 (Jerwa 3:00 OT)

25 Detroit 1 at Toronto 6

30 Toronto 0 at Canadiens 3 [Cude]

February

1 Chicago 2 at Toronto 3 (N. Metz 8:29 OT)

2 Toronto 0 at Chicago 2 (both goals in the 3rd) [Karakas]

4 Toronto 3 at Boston 0 [Hainsworth]

6 Toronto 3 at Americans 4 (Horner suffers bad concussion after vicious cross-check from Dutton)

8 Americans 0 at Toronto 3 (after calling a penalty shot against the Americans for a Dutton foul, referee Rodden was knocked unconscious "accidentally" by Dutton. Rodden recovered to finish the 1st, but was replaced by Ag Smith for the balance of the game)

13 Toronto 1 at Maroons 2

15 Detroit 2 at Toronto 3 (Thoms 8:15 OT)

20 Canadiens 1 at Toronto 2

22 Maroons 0 at Toronto 1 (Blair 9:00 3rd) [Hainsworth]

23 Toronto 1 at Chicago 5

25 Rangers 2 at Toronto 2 (10:00 OT)

29 Chicago 2 at Toronto 4

March

3 Toronto 0 at Rangers 0 (10:00 OT) [Hainsworth (T)/Kerr (R)]

7 Canadiens 1 at Toronto 8

10 Toronto 2 at Americans 3

12 Toronto 6 at Canadiens 3 (Conn Smythe and Dick Irvin involved in penalty box melee)

14 Maroons 1 at Toronto 0 (Trottier 11:49 2nd) [Chabot]

15 Toronto 2 at Detroit 1 (Conacher 7:30 OT)

17 Toronto 1 at Maroons 2

19 Boston 2 at Toronto 2 (10:00 OT) (Charlie Conacher set NHL record with 13 shots on goal)

21 Americans 1 at Toronto 4

1936–1937

November

5 Detroit 3 at Toronto 1 (Hon. H.A. Bruce, Lieutenant-Governor of Ontario, faced off the opening puck)

7 Americans 3 at Toronto 2

14 Chicago 2 at Toronto 6 (Hawks complained that the blue-lines weren't painted up the boards)

15 Toronto 1 at Chicago 1 (10:00 OT)

21 Boston 4 at Toronto 3

22 Toronto 2 at Detroit 4

24 Toronto 1 at Rangers 5

26 Toronto 4 at Canadiens 2 (early in the 3rd, Seibert broke Boll's arm and got a penalty. Irate Montreal fans threw bottles on the ice, then stormed onto the ice and surrounded the referee. Eight police had to come out to help restore order.)

28 Canadiens 2 at Toronto 4

December
1   Toronto 2 at Maroons 1
5   Maroons 3 at Toronto 1
12 Rangers 5 at Toronto 3
    (Dillon 1:15/Patrick 7:28 OT)
17 Toronto 5 at Americans 1
19 Americans 1 at Toronto 3
    (Young Canada Night)
22 Toronto 4 at Boston 2
26 Boston 2 at Toronto 1
31 Toronto 1 at Maroons 3
    (Ward 4:46/Gracie 6:07 OT)

January
2   Maroons 0 at Toronto 0 (10:00 OT)
    [Connell (M)/Broda (T)]
3   Toronto 2 at Detroit 4
7   Toronto 1 at Canadiens 4
9   Canadiens 1 at Toronto 2
10 Toronto 1 at Chicago 2 (Apps was given
    a penalty by referee Bill Stewart for kick-
    ing the puck. Conn Smythe officially
    protested the call, and two days later,
    President Calder clarified the rule, siding
    with Smythe and Apps)
16 Chicago 2 at Toronto 3
    (N. Metz 2:09 OT)
19 Toronto 6 at Boston 2
21 Toronto 3 at Americans 6
23 Rangers 0 at Toronto 4 [Broda]
24 Toronto 2 at Rangers 4 (Conn Smythe
    became involved in an on-ice fight)
26 Canadiens 3 at Toronto 1
30 Maroons 4 at Toronto 7

February
2   Toronto 1 at Maroons 3
4   Toronto 2 at Americans 1
6   Americans 0 at Toronto 5 [Broda]
9   Rangers 5 at Toronto 1
13 Boston 3 at Toronto 0 [Thompson]
14 Toronto 3 at Detroit 3 (10:00 OT)
18 Detroit 1 at Toronto 3
20 Americans 3 at Toronto 4
21 Toronto 1 at Americans 3
23 Toronto 1 at Rangers 2
25 Toronto 3 at Canadiens 1

27 Maroons 2 at Toronto 3 (John
    McGinnis, a fan, was struck by Lionel
    Conacher during a free-for-all. No
    charges were laid.)

March
6   Canadiens 1 at Toronto 3
    (Jackson 2:05/Fowler 5:40 OT)
7   Toronto 2 at Chicago 2 (10:00 OT)
    ("Presentation Night" at the Gardens.
    Apps received a travelling bag and golf
    clubs; Toe Blake and Babe Siebert each
    received travelling bags)
11 Toronto 2 at Maroons 3
13 Chicago 2 at Toronto 3
16 Toronto 1 at Boston 1 (10:00 OT)
18 Toronto 2 at Canadiens 1
20 Detroit 2 at Toronto 3

1937–1938
November
4   Detroit 2 at Toronto 2 (10:00 OT) (Hon.
    Gordon Conaut, Attorney-General of
    Ontario, dropped the puck) (Barry (D)
    tied game at 19:46)
6   Americans 3 at Toronto 6 (Hap Day,
    now with the Americans, given floral
    horseshoe prior to game)
13 Chicago 3 at Toronto 7
14 Toronto 3 at Chicago 3 (10:00 OT)
18 Toronto 6 at Canadiens 6 (10:00 OT)
    (H. Jackson (T) tied game at 19:54)
20 Boston 3 at Toronto 2
21 Toronto 5 at Detroit 0 [Broda]
23 Toronto 1 at Maroons 2
25 Toronto 3 at Rangers 1
27 Maroons 0 at Toronto 4 [Broda]

December
4   Canadiens 3 at Toronto 3 (10:00 OT)
11 Rangers 6 at Toronto 3
14 Toronto 1 at Boston 3
16 Toronto 4 at Canadiens 2
18 Americans 2 at Toronto 3
25 Detroit 1 at Toronto 1 (10:00 OT) (both
    goals in the 2nd) (Young Canada Night)
26 Toronto 3 at Detroit 1
28 Toronto 3 at Americans 0 [Broda]

January

1 Canadiens 4 at Toronto 6
4 Toronto 3 at Boston 6
6 Toronto 3 at Maroons 6
8 Rangers 2 at Toronto 3 (Moncton mayor
presented a gold watch to native son
Gord Drillon in pre-game ceremonies)
13 Maroons 2 at Toronto 3
15 Chicago 4 at Toronto 4 (10:00 OT)
16 Toronto 7 at Chicago 2
20 Toronto 1 at Americans 1 (10:00 OT)
(both goals in the 2nd)
22 Boston 9 at Toronto 1
29 Detroit 1 at Toronto 4

February

1 Toronto 1 at Canadiens 6
3 Canadiens 0 at Toronto 3 [Broda]
5 Boston 1 at Toronto 3
6 Toronto 1 at Rangers 2 (in the 1st, Conn
Smythe thought an offside call was
missed and came storming onto the ice
to protest to referee Billy Boyd, who
wrestled him to the ice!)
10 Maroons 0 at Toronto 3 (Apps
1:01/Parsons 2:06/Kelly 3:33 OT)
[Broda] (Newmarket Night: Thoms,
Kelly, Herbie Cain (Maroons), and Don
Wilson (Habs) all received gifts from
Newmarket Mayor Boyd)
12 Chicago 2 at Toronto 1
13 Toronto 1 at Chicago 1 (10:00 OT)
17 Toronto 2 at Maroons 1
19 Americans 4 at Toronto 0 [Robertson]
20 Toronto 3 at Americans 2
22 Toronto 0 at Boston 2 [Thompson]
26 Rangers 4 at Toronto 2

March

1 Toronto 5 at Maroons 3
5 Maroons 0 at Toronto 2 (both goals in
the 1st) [Broda] (Toronto Night:
Danforth Businessmen's Association
honoured locals Jim Fowler and Bob
Davidson of the Leafs)
6 Toronto 6 at Canadiens 3
8 Toronto 3 at Rangers 4
12 Canadiens 3 at Toronto 3 (10:00 OT)
(Swansea Night: Honours for Parsons.

Also, Aurel Joliat given lifelong achieve-
ment award from the *Globe* on behalf of
Toronto at his last game in the city)
17 Toronto 7 at Detroit 2
19 Americans 5 at Toronto 8 (Busher
Jackson and Reg Hamilton given silver
chests by West Toronto Businessmen's
Association. Red Horner also received
gifts from friends.)
20 Toronto 2 at Americans 4

1938–1939

November

3 Boston 3 at Toronto 2 (Hon. Albert
Matthews, Lieutenant-Governor of
Ontario, dropped the puck)
5 Chicago 2 at Toronto 0 (both goals
in 2nd) [Karakas]
10 Toronto 2 at Canadiens 0 [Broda]
12 Canadiens 1 at Toronto 4
15 Toronto 1 at Boston 1 (10:00 OT)
17 Toronto 1 at Americans 0
(Kelly 6:06 (pp) 3rd) [Broda]
19 Americans 2 at Toronto 1
(Schriner 3:52 OT)
20 Toronto 1 at Chicago 1 (10:00 OT)
24 Toronto 2 at Rangers 6
26 Detroit 0 at Toronto 5 [Broda]

December

3 Canadiens 3 at Toronto 1
4 Toronto 0 at Detroit 1 (Brûneteau
14:33 3rd) [Thompson]
10 Chicago 1 at Toronto 4
15 Toronto 4 at Chicago 4 (10:00 OT)
17 Rangers 3 at Toronto 2
24 Detroit 0 at Toronto 2 [Broda]
(Young Canada Night)
26 Toronto 2 at Rangers 0 [Broda]
27 Toronto 2 at Boston 8
31 Americans 3 at Toronto 2

January

1 Toronto 1 at Americans 5
3 Canadiens 2 at Toronto 2 (10:00 OT)
7 Boston 0 at Toronto 2 [Broda]
8 Toronto 0 at Chicago 1
(Thoms 14:28 1st) [Karakas]

12   Toronto 9 at Canadiens 4
14   Chicago 1 at Toronto 3 (Chicago's Bill
     Thoms received presents from
     Newmarket and Aurora friends during
     1st intermission)
15   Toronto 0 at Detroit 1 (Giesebrecht
     17:22 (pp) 2nd) [Thompson]
17   Toronto 1 at Boston 2
21   Americans 2 at Toronto 7
24   Toronto 1 at Americans 4
28   Detroit 0 at Toronto 6 [Broda]
29   Toronto 2 at Detroit 2 (10:00 OT)

February
2   Boston 2 at Toronto 1
4   Rangers 4 at Toronto 2
5   Toronto 5 at Rangers 5 (10:00 OT)
    (Smith (R) awarded goal in 3rd after
    thrown stick)
7   Toronto 0 at Boston 2 [Brimsek]
11 Canadiens 3 at Toronto 3 (10:00 OT)
12 Toronto 4 at Canadiens 3 (Cain (C)
    awarded goal when Drillon threw stick)
18 Rangers 1 at Toronto 2
19 Toronto 4 at Chicago 3 (Marker 4:35 OT)
25 Boston 0 at Toronto 1 (McDonald 12:23
    1st) [Broda] (presentations made to Dit
    Clapper, Jack Portland, and Johnny
    Crawford of Boston, and Noel
    McDonald (voted outstanding female
    athlete of 1938))
26 Toronto 1 at Detroit 5
28 Toronto 1 at Americans 1 (10:00 OT)

March
2   Toronto 1 at Canadiens 3
4   Chicago 1 at Toronto 1 (10:00 OT) (ref-
    eree Mickey Ion and Baldy Northcott
    each presented with a silver telephone
    set from Brantford sports fans)
11 Detroit 1 at Toronto 5 (Charlie
    Conacher Night during 1st
    intermission)
14 Americans 3 at Toronto 7
18 Rangers 1 at Toronto 2
19 Toronto 2 at Rangers 6

1939–1940

November
4   Boston 0 at Toronto 5 [Broda]
11 Rangers 1 at Toronto 1 (10:00 OT)
12 Toronto 1 at Rangers 0
    (Drillon 6:55 3rd) [Broda]
18 Detroit 0 at Toronto 3 [Broda]
19 Toronto 7 at Detroit 1
25 Americans 3 at Toronto 4
26 Toronto 1 at Americans 2
    (Wiseman 1:08 OT)
28 Toronto 2 at Boston 6

December
2   Chicago 3 at Toronto 3 (10:00 OT)
3   Toronto 3 at Chicago 1
    (Schriner 3:10/Goldup 8:09 OT)
7   Toronto 1 at Canadiens 4
9   Canadiens 0 at Toronto 3 [Broda]
14 Boston 1 at Toronto 1 (10:00 OT)
16 Americans 1 at Toronto 5
17 Toronto 4 at Americans 1
19 Toronto 2 at Boston 3 (Dumart (B)
    2:28/Bauer (B) 8:07/McDonald (T)
    9:36 OT)
21 Toronto 1 at Chicago 3
23 Detroit 1 at Toronto 5
    (Young Canada Night)
25 Toronto 1 at Rangers 4
28 Toronto 6 at Canadiens 4
30 Chicago 2 at Toronto 4
31 Toronto 3 at Detroit 2

January
4   Toronto 1 at Chicago 2
6   Canadiens 1 at Toronto 3
    (all goals in the 3rd)
9   Toronto 3 at Americans 2
11 Boston 5 at Toronto 2
13 Rangers 4 at Toronto 1
18 Detroit 2 at Toronto 2 (10:00 OT)
20 Americans 1 at Toronto 5
21 Toronto 2 at Detroit 3
23 Toronto 1 at Boston 4
25 Toronto 0 at Rangers 3 [Kerr]
27 Canadiens 1 at Toronto 3

February
3 Chicago 3 at Toronto 2
8 Toronto 1 at Rangers 2
10 Rangers 4 at Toronto 4 (Goldup (T) :09/MacDonald (R) 1:17 OT)
17 Canadiens 1 at Toronto 3
18 Toronto 2 at Canadiens 1
20 Toronto 0 at Boston 5 [Brimsek]
22 Toronto 2 at Detroit 1
24 Boston 1 at Toronto 3
29 Detroit 1 at Toronto 3

March
2 Rangers 1 at Toronto 1 (10:00 OT)
9 Chicago 2 at Toronto 5
10 Toronto 1 at Chicago 2
14 Toronto 8 at Canadiens 4
16 Americans 6 at Toronto 8
17 Toronto 2 at Americans 5

1940–1941

November
2 Rangers 4 at Toronto 1
9 Detroit 0 at Toronto 3 [Broda]
14 Toronto 6 at Canadiens 2
16 Canadiens 2 at Toronto 4
17 Toronto 4 at Boston 1
21 Toronto 2 at Americans 1 (Apps 1:16 OT)
23 Chicago 1 at Toronto 0 (Dahlstrom 10:05 2nd) [Goodman]
24 Toronto 4 at Chicago 2
26 Toronto 4 at Rangers 2
30 Americans 1 at Toronto 6

December
1 Toronto 3 at Detroit 1
7 Boston 2 at Toronto 3
12 Canadiens 3 at Toronto 4
14 Chicago 1 at Toronto 2 (all goals in the 3rd)
15 Toronto 4 at Chicago 1
17 Toronto 2 at Boston 5
21 Americans 2 at Toronto 2 (10:00 OT) (Young Canada Night)
22 Toronto 1 at Americans 2
25 Toronto 2 at Detroit 3

28 Rangers 2 at Toronto 3 (Conn Smythe fined $100 for arguing on ice with the referee)
29 Toronto 2 at Rangers 3 (Conn Smythe fined $100 for stepping on ice to argue with referee Ion)

January
4 Detroit 3 at Toronto 1
7 Toronto 4 at Canadiens 3 (D. Metz 5:23 OT)
9 Rangers 2 at Toronto 3 (Apps 9:57 OT) (originally scheduled for March 13)
11 Americans 0 at Toronto 9 [Broda]
18 Boston 1 at Toronto 0 (Clapper 12:30 3rd) [Brimsek]
19 Toronto 3 at Americans 3 (10:00 OT)
23 Toronto 3 at Canadiens 2
25 Canadiens 2 at Toronto 2 (10:00 OT)
26 Toronto 2 at Detroit 0 [Broda]
30 Detroit 1 at Toronto 2

February
1 Chicago 1 at Toronto 3
2 Toronto 1 at Chicago 4
8 Boston 3 at Toronto 2
15 Rangers 3 at Toronto 4
16 Toronto 4 at Rangers 1
18 Toronto 2 at Boston 2 (10:00 OT)
20 Canadiens 1 at Toronto 2
22 Detroit 2 at Toronto 6
23 Toronto 0 at Detroit 3 [Mowers]
25 Toronto 4 at Americans 4 (10:00 OT)

March
1 Boston 0 at Toronto 0 (10:00 OT) [Brimsek (B)/Broda (T)]
6 Toronto 3 at Canadiens 4
8 Americans 1 at Toronto 6
9 Toronto 5 at Rangers 8
11 Toronto 2 at Boston 3
15 Chicago 1 at Toronto 7
16 Toronto 3 at Chicago 0 [Broda]

1941–1942

November

1 Rangers 4 at Toronto 3
8 Boston 0 at Toronto 2 (both goals in the 2nd) [Broda]
13 Canadiens 2 at Toronto 4
15 Detroit 1 at Toronto 2
18 Toronto 8 at Rangers 6
20 Toronto 4 at Detroit 3 (Goldup (T) :47/Carr (T) 3:18/Abel (D) 9:19 OT)
22 Chicago 0 at Toronto 3 [Broda]
23 Toronto 2 at Chicago 3
29 Brooklyn 2 at Toronto 8
30 Toronto 5 at Brooklyn 1

December

2 Toronto 1 at Boston 3 (Wiseman 6:47/Hamill 7:21 OT)
6 Canadiens 1 at Toronto 3
11 Toronto 1 at Canadiens 2 (Heffernan 6:50 OT)
13 Rangers 1 at Toronto 2
14 Toronto 4 at Detroit 0 [Broda]
20 Chicago 2 at Toronto 0 [LoPresti] (Young Canada Night)
21 Toronto 3 at Chicago 0 [Broda]
25 Boston 0 at Toronto 2 (both goals in the 3rd) [Broda]
27 Detroit 3 at Toronto 5
28 Toronto 1 at Brooklyn 2
30 Toronto 1 at Boston 4

January

1 Toronto 3 at Rangers 3 (10:00 OT)
3 Brooklyn 2 at Toronto 4
10 Detroit 6 at Toronto 4
15 Toronto 3 at Canadiens 2 (N. Metz :31 OT)
17 Chicago 4 at Toronto 2
24 Brooklyn 2 at Toronto 3
25 Toronto 4 at Chicago 6
27 Toronto 0 at Boston 0 (10:00 OT) [Broda (T)/Brimsek (B)]
29 Canadiens 3 at Toronto 7
31 Boston 3 at Toronto 2 (Schmidt 2:54 OT)

February

1 Toronto 2 at Rangers 7
5 Toronto 3 at Detroit 3 (10:00 OT)

7 Rangers 4 at Toronto 6
8 Toronto 4 at Brooklyn 3
12 Toronto 6 at Canadiens 4
14 Detroit 2 at Toronto 4
21 Brooklyn 3 at Toronto 4
22 Toronto 0 at Detroit 3 [Mowers]
28 Chicago 2 at Toronto 8

March

1 Toronto 4 at Chicago 3
3 Toronto 3 at Boston 5
5 Canadiens 5 at Toronto 2
7 Rangers 2 at Toronto 4
8 Toronto 0 at Rangers 2 [Henry]
14 Boston 4 at Toronto 6
15 Toronto 3 at Brooklyn 6
19 Toronto 3 at Canadiens 7

1942–1943

October

31 Rangers 2 at Toronto 7 (Private Alex Chisholm, decorated for his service at Dieppe, dropped the puck)

November

7 Detroit 2 at Toronto 5
12 Boston 1 at Toronto 3
14 Chicago 4 at Toronto 3
15 Toronto 4 at Chicago 5
19 Toronto 7 at Rangers 3
21 Canadiens 0 at Toronto 8 [Broda]
22 Toronto 6 at Boston 7
26 Toronto 1 at Detroit 2
28 Rangers 6 at Toronto 8
29 Toronto 2 at Chicago 3

December

3 Toronto 2 at Canadiens 4
5 Canadiens 1 at Toronto 9
6 Toronto 2 at Detroit 2
10 Chicago 2 at Toronto 7
12 Detroit 4 at Toronto 5
13 Toronto 2 at Chicago 5
17 Toronto 8 at Canadiens 1
19 Boston 3 at Toronto 3
20 Toronto 8 at Rangers 2
22 Toronto 4 at Boston 4
26 Boston 2 at Toronto 7
27 Toronto 1 at Rangers 3

January

2   Canadiens 3 at Toronto 6
3   Toronto 4 at Canadiens 4
9   Detroit 4 at Toronto 0 (all goals in
    the 3rd) [Mowers]
10 Toronto 4 at Boston 5
16 Canadiens 4 at Toronto 8
17 Toronto 0 at Canadiens 2 [Bibeault]
21 Rangers 4 at Toronto 7
23 Chicago 3 at Toronto 5
30 Boston 5 at Toronto 3
31 Toronto 3 at Chicago 3

February

4   Detroit 3 at Toronto 2
6   Rangers 2 at Toronto 3
7   Toronto 3 at Detroit 5
9   Toronto 1 at Boston 3
13 Chicago 2 at Toronto 3
14 Toronto 4 at Rangers 4
20 Boston 2 at Toronto 4
21 Toronto 0 at Chicago 5 [Gardiner]
27 Chicago 4 at Toronto 1
28 Toronto 4 at Canadiens 2

March

2   Rangers 4 at Toronto 0 [Beveridge]
6   Canadiens 2 at Toronto 2
7   Toronto 5 at Rangers 5
9   Toronto 5 at Boston 5
11 Toronto 1 at Detroit 2
13 Detroit 1 at Toronto 3
14 Toronto 5 at Detroit 3

1943–1944

October

30 Rangers 2 at Toronto 5
31 Toronto 4 at Chicago 1

November

4   Toronto 5 at Detroit 5
6   Boston 5 at Toronto 2
    (Carr (T) tied game at 19:42)
7   Toronto 7 at Rangers 4
11 Detroit 2 at Toronto 2
13 Chicago 4 at Toronto 1
18 Toronto 2 at Canadiens 5
20 Canadiens 7 at Toronto 2

21 Toronto 5 at Rangers 2
23 Toronto 5 at Boston 8
27 Boston 4 at Toronto 7
28 Toronto 4 at Detroit 6

December

2   Detroit 5 at Toronto 6
4   Rangers 4 at Toronto 11
11 Canadiens 2 at Toronto 4
12 Toronto 2 at Chicago 3
16 Detroit 4 at Toronto 1
18 Chicago 4 at Toronto 8
19 Toronto 5 at Chicago 2
21 Toronto 5 at Boston 8
25 Rangers 5 at Toronto 3
31 Toronto 4 at Rangers 0 [Bibeault]

January

1   Toronto 5 at Boston 2
4   Toronto 3 at Canadiens 6
7   Chicago 1 at Toronto 6
8   Boston 3 at Toronto 12
11 Canadiens 0 at Toronto 5 [Bibeault]
15 Detroit 6 at Toronto 4
16 Toronto 1 at Detroit 4
18 Toronto 7 at Boston 2
22 Rangers 5 at Toronto 1
    (Young Canada Night)
23 Toronto 3 at Chicago 5
27 Toronto 2 at Canadiens 2
29 Chicago 4 at Toronto 3

February

5   Detroit 1 at Toronto 3
6   Toronto 2 at Detroit 3
12 Canadiens 3 at Toronto 2
13 Toronto 6 at Rangers 3
19 Boston 4 at Toronto 10
20 Toronto 0 at Chicago 0
    [Bibeault (T)/Karakas (C)]
24 Toronto 1 at Canadiens 3
26 Chicago 3 at Toronto 2
29 Toronto 7 at Boston 3 (Bert Gardner (B)
    became first goalie to register an assist)

March

4   Canadiens 5 at Toronto 2
5   Toronto 3 at Canadiens 8
9   Toronto 8 at Rangers 0 [Bibeault]

11   Rangers 0 at Toronto 5 [Bibeault]
12   Toronto 1 at Detroit 4
18   Boston 2 at Toronto 10 (Boston forced
     to use Toronto's spare goalie, Benny
     Grant) (Babe Pratt receives $100 from
     E.W. Bickle as "most popular Leaf")

1944–1945

October

28   Rangers 1 at Toronto 2 (puck dropped
     by J.G. Parker, chairman of Toronto
     National War Finance Committee)
29   Toronto 11 at Chicago 5

November

2   Toronto 4 at Canadiens 1
4   Boston 2 at Toronto 7
9   Toronto 6 at Rangers 3
11   Canadiens 1 at Toronto 3
12   Toronto 2 at Detroit 4
15   Detroit 8 at Toronto 4
18   Chicago 4 at Toronto 5
19   Toronto 4 at Chicago 3
23   Toronto 1 at Boston 5
25   Canadiens 0 at Toronto 2
     (both goals in the 3rd) [McCool]
26   Toronto 1 at Canadiens 4

December

2   Rangers 3 at Toronto 4
3   Toronto 4 at Boston 5
9   Boston 5 at Toronto 3
14   Toronto 2 at Canadiens 2 (special lights
     placed over the goals in Forum to pro-
     vide extra lighting for the benefit of the
     goalies. With 2 minutes left to go and
     the score tied, the lights went out. The
     Leafs refused to play until they were
     turned back on. They were!)
16   Detroit 1 at Toronto 1
23   Detroit 5 at Toronto 4
     (Young Canada Night)
25   Toronto 4 at Detroit 6 (third game
     in a row against same opponent
27   Toronto 8 at Rangers 7
30   Chicago 0 at Toronto 4 [McCool]

January

4   Canadiens 2 at Toronto 4
6   Detroit 5 at Toronto 2
9   Rangers 5 at Toronto 4
11   Toronto 4 at Canadiens 7
13   Boston 1 at Toronto 2
14   Toronto 0 at Detroit 3 [Lumley]
16   Toronto 3 at Boston 5
20   Chicago 4 at Toronto 8 (Conn Smythe
     in attendance for first time since 1942,
     because of war and injuries)
21   Toronto 0 at Chicago 4 [Karakas]
27   Rangers 0 at Toronto 3 [McCool]
28   Toronto 7 at Rangers 0 [McCool]

February

3   Boston 4 at Toronto 2
4   Toronto 4 at Chicago 3
6   Toronto 5 at Boston 1
10   Chicago 2 at Toronto 1
11   Toronto 1 at Chicago 2
17   Canadiens 4 at Toronto 3
18   Toronto 1 at Detroit 6
24   Rangers 4 at Toronto 4
25   Toronto 2 at Canadiens 5
27   Chicago 3 at Toronto 3

March

3   Canadiens 2 at Toronto 3
4   Toronto 6 at Rangers 3
6   Toronto 5 at Boston 2
10   Boston 2 at Toronto 9
11   Toronto 3 at Detroit 2
17   Detroit 4 at Toronto 3
18   Toronto 5 at Rangers 6
     (Warwick wins game at 19:59)

1945–1946

October

27   Boston 1 at Toronto 1 (puck faced off by
     six Victoria Cross holders: Cpl. Fred
     Topham, Pvt. Smoky Smith, Major Fred
     Tilson, Lt. Col. Paul Triquet, Lt. Col.
     D.V. Currie, Maj. J.J. Mahony)

November

1   Toronto 2 at Canadiens 4
3   Rangers 4 at Toronto 1

4   Toronto 4 at Chicago 7
7   Boston 4 at Toronto 3
8   Toronto 2 at Detroit 3
10 Chicago 2 at Toronto 3 (Babe Pratt
    received a silver spoon for being a star of
    the game, but gave the spoon to his
    defence partner, young Jim Thomson)
11 Toronto 3 at Chicago 5
14 Canadiens 6 at Toronto 1
17 Detroit 6 at Toronto 5
18 Toronto 3 at Rangers 1
24 Rangers 3 at Toronto 4
25 Toronto 3 at Boston 5

December
1   Chicago 8 at Toronto 2
2   Toronto 5 at Chicago 3
8   Canadiens 1 at Toronto 0
    (Lamoureux 6:43 3rd) [Durnan]
9   Toronto 1 at Rangers 2
13 Toronto 4 at Canadiens 3
15 Detroit 1 at Toronto 3
16 Toronto 3 at Boston 3
22 Rangers 5 at Toronto 5
    (Young Canada Night)
23 Toronto 4 at Rangers 3
25 Toronto 3 at Detroit 6
26 Canadiens 4 at Toronto 2
29 Boston 4 at Toronto 3

January
1   Toronto 1 at Chicago 3
5   Chicago 3 at Toronto 0 [Karakas]
10 Toronto 5 at Canadiens 4
12 Detroit 3 at Toronto 9
19 Rangers 1 at Toronto 3
20 Toronto 3 at Detroit 1
23 Toronto 1 at Boston 7
26 Chicago 5 at Toronto 6

February
2   Boston 5 at Toronto 3
3   Toronto 6 at Rangers 6
6   Toronto 3 at Boston 3
9   Detroit 1 at Toronto 4
10 Toronto 2 at Detroit 2
16 Canadiens 4 at Toronto 2 (Blake en)
23 Boston 2 at Toronto 7
24 Toronto 2 at Canadiens 6
27 Rangers 6 at Toronto 4 (Laprade en)

March
2   Chicago 4 at Toronto 9
3   Toronto 5 at Rangers 2
6   Toronto 5 at Chicago 2
9   Canadiens 2 at Toronto 1
10 Toronto 3 at Boston 7
14 Toronto 2 at Canadiens 2
16 Detroit 3 at Toronto 7
17 Toronto 11 at Detroit 7

1946–1947
October
16 Toronto 3 at Detroit 3 (Gordie Howe
    scored his first NHL goal; Abel tied game
    at 19:49 with goalie out) (Goldham
    won $50 Savings Bond for scoring first
    Leaf goal of the season)
19 Detroit 3 at Toronto 6 (N. Metz acting
    captain) (Toronto mayor Robert
    Saunders faced off opening puck)
23 Toronto 3 at Boston 3 (Stewart (T) tied
    game at 19:43 with goalie out)
26 Chicago 1 at Toronto 2
30 Toronto 5 at Chicago 2
31 Toronto at Canadiens (postponed to
    November 1 because of "transportation
    uncertainties")

November
1   Toronto 1 at Canadiens 1
2   Boston 5 at Toronto 0 (Schmidt awarded
    goal when Broda threw stick) [Brimsek]
9   Rangers 2 at Toronto 4
10 Toronto 4 at Chicago 2
16 Canadiens 0 at Toronto 3 [Broda]
17 Toronto 5 at Rangers 4
20 Toronto 1 at Boston 4
    (all goals in the 3rd)
23 Detroit 4 at Toronto 2
24 Toronto 5 at Detroit 0 [Broda]
27 Toronto 2 at Chicago 5
30 Chicago 0 at Toronto 11 [Broda]

December
4   Toronto 2 at Boston 2
7   Boston 1 at Toronto 5
8   Toronto 5 at Detroit 4
11 Canadiens 3 at Toronto 2
14 Rangers 2 at Toronto 3

15 Toronto 4 at Chicago 3
19 Detroit 1 at Toronto 3
    (Young Canada Night)
21 Chicago 1 at Toronto 3
22 Toronto 3 at Rangers 1
25 Toronto 2 at Detroit 1
26 Toronto 1 at Canadiens 4
28 Boston 3 at Toronto 4

January
1   Detroit 1 at Toronto 2
2   Toronto 5 at Rangers 4
4   Rangers 2 at Toronto 0 [Rayner]
8   Chicago 4 at Toronto 10
11 Boston 3 at Toronto 4
12 Toronto 2 at Rangers 3
15 Canadiens 1 at Toronto 2
16 Toronto 1 at Canadiens 1
18 Detroit 4 at Toronto 7
19 Toronto 2 at Boston 3
25 Rangers 1 at Toronto 0
    (Hextall 15:58 1st) [Rayner]
26 Toronto 6 at Chicago 6
30 Toronto 0 at Canadiens 2 [Durnan]

February
1   Chicago 5 at Toronto 4
6   Toronto 2 at Canadiens 8
8   Boston 2 at Toronto 5
15 Canadiens 4 at Toronto 4
16 Toronto 2 at Rangers 6
19 Toronto 3 at Chicago 5
22 Rangers 0 at Toronto 2
    (both goals in the 1st) [Broda]
23 Toronto 2 at Canadiens 2 (Reardon (C)
    tied game at 19:53 with goalie out)
26 Canadiens 1 at Toronto 0
    (Peters 5:27 1st) [Durnan]
27 Toronto 3 at Detroit 3

March
1   Detroit 5 at Toronto 4
5   Toronto 4 at Boston 5
8   Chicago 4 at Toronto 12
9   Toronto 4 at Rangers 2
15 Boston 5 at Toronto 5 (Dit Clapper
    Night: Baldy Cotton, E.W. Bickle,
    Weston Adams, and Art Ross present
    him with a silver cocktail service)

16 Toronto 3 at Boston 5
19 Canadiens 4 at Toronto 5
22 Rangers 3 at Toronto 5
23 Toronto 5 at Detroit 3

1947–1948
October
18 Detroit 2 at Toronto 2 (Field Marshal
    Lord Alexander, Governor-General of
    Canada, dropped the puck)
19 Toronto 0 at Detroit 2 [Lumley]
22 Rangers 1 at Toronto 3
25 Chicago 1 at Toronto 5
29 Canadiens 1 at Toronto 3

November
1   Boston 1 at Toronto 1 (Henderson (B)
    tied game at 19:52 with goalie out)
2   Toronto 4 at Rangers 7
6   Toronto 0 at Canadiens 3 [Durnan]
8   Rangers 2 at Toronto 7
9   Toronto 6 at Detroit 0 (McGratton (D)
    replaced Lumley at 12:00 3rd) [Broda]
12 Chicago 5 at Toronto 4
15 Detroit 3 at Toronto 5
16 Toronto 5 at Chicago 4
19 Toronto 2 at Boston 7
22 Boston 3 at Toronto 4
27 Toronto 0 at Canadiens 2 [Durnan]
29 Canadiens 1 at Toronto 3
30 Toronto 0 at Boston 0
    [Broda (T)/Brimsek (B)]

December
3   Toronto 4 at Rangers 1
6   Chicago 5 at Toronto 12
7   Toronto 3 at Chicago 2
10 Toronto 2 at Detroit 2
13 Rangers 4 at Toronto 1
14 Toronto 1 at Boston 1
20 Detroit 4 at Toronto 4
21 Toronto 3 at Chicago 1
25 Toronto 3 at Canadiens 0
    (all goals in the 2nd) [Broda]
27 Boston 1 at Toronto 2
28 Toronto 1 at Rangers 1

January
1   Canadiens 1 at Toronto 2
3   Rangers 5 at Toronto 5
10 Chicago 4 at Toronto 6
11 Toronto 2 at Detroit 2
15 Toronto 4 at Canadiens 8
17 Boston 1 at Toronto 4
18 Toronto 2 at Rangers 2
21 Toronto 1 at Boston 2
24 Chicago 1 at Toronto 2
25 Toronto 4 at Chicago 4
28 Canadiens 3 at Toronto 3
31 Detroit 2 at Toronto 3

February
1   Toronto 0 at Detroit 3 [Lumley] (Johnny
    McCormack gets into a fight with fan)
4   Toronto 4 at Boston 2
7   Rangers 0 at Toronto 3 [Broda]
14 Canadiens 2 at Toronto 4
15 Toronto 4 at Rangers 4 (Watson (T) tied
    game at 19:45 with goalie out)
19 Toronto 1 at Canadiens 3
21 Detroit 2 at Toronto 3
22 Toronto 3 at Chicago 2
25 Boston 2 at Toronto 4
28 Chicago 3 at Toronto 4

March
2   Toronto 0 at Rangers 1
    (Laprade 5:35 1st) [Henry]
3   Canadiens 3 at Toronto 2
6   Rangers 1 at Toronto 2
7   Toronto 1 at Boston 3
11 Toronto 1 at Canadiens 3
13 Boston 2 at Toronto 5
14 Toronto 3 at Chicago 0 [Broda]
20 Detroit 3 at Toronto 5
21 Toronto 5 at Detroit 2

1948–1949
October
16 Boston 4 at Toronto 1 (Brigadier
    General H.D. Crerer dropped the puck)
    (Turk Broda presented with Vezina
    Trophy by Clarence Campbell)
21 Toronto 0 at Canadiens 5 [Durnan]
23 Chicago 1 at Toronto 6

24 Toronto 1 at Detroit 2
27 Canadiens 2 at Toronto 3
30 Detroit 1 at Toronto 2
31 Toronto 1 at Chicago 2 (D. Bentley
    won game at 19:49) (the ice was so bad
    referee Keeling had teams switch ends
    midway through 3rd period)

November
6   Rangers 3 at Toronto 3
13 Chicago 6 at Toronto 3
14 Toronto 4 at Rangers 4
17 Toronto 1 at Boston 2
20 Boston 2 at Toronto 2
21 Toronto 3 at Chicago 3
24 Canadiens 3 at Toronto 3
25 Toronto 2 at Canadiens 0
    (both goals in the 3rd) [Broda]
27 Rangers 0 at Toronto 3 [Broda]
28 Toronto 2 at Boston 6

December
1   Toronto 3 at Detroit 5
4   Chicago 6 at Toronto 4
5   Toronto 2 at Chicago 0
    (both goals in the 2nd) [Broda]
8   Detroit 4 at Toronto 3
11 Boston 2 at Toronto 3
12 Toronto 4 at Boston 3
15 Toronto 1 at Rangers 3
18 Rangers 3 at Toronto 3
    (Young Canada Night)
19 Toronto 1 at Detroit 5
25 Detroit 1 at Toronto 2
30 Toronto 2 at Canadiens 3

January
1   Canadiens 3 at Toronto 5 (Gardner and
    Reardon fined $250 and $200 respec-
    tively and suspended for one game
    against each other for vicious stick-
    swinging incident)
2   Toronto 2 at Rangers 4
5   Boston 0 at Toronto 4 [Broda]
8   Chicago 3 at Toronto 3
9   Toronto 2 at Detroit 2
15 Rangers 1 at Toronto 2
16 Toronto 0 at Rangers 4 [Rayner]
19 Canadiens 4 at Toronto 1

22 Detroit 2 at Toronto 2
23 Toronto 1 at Detroit 2
26 Toronto 3 at Boston 1
29 Chicago 4 at Toronto 4
30 Toronto 2 at Chicago 4

February
3 Toronto 4 at Canadiens 1
5 Rangers 1 at Toronto 1
    (both goals in the 3rd)
6 Toronto 4 at Boston 2
9 Canadiens 2 at Toronto 2
12 Detroit 1 at Toronto 3
13 Toronto 3 at Rangers 0 [Broda]
17 Toronto 0 at Canadiens 3 [Durnan]
19 Boston 2 at Toronto 5
20 Toronto 4 at Chicago 3 (Red Hamill
    fined $250 and suspended one game
    for vicious stick-swinging attack on
    Vic Lynn)
26 Chicago 2 at Toronto 2 (a North Bay
    delegation honoured native son Bill
    Tobin (C) during first intermission)

March
2 Canadiens 2 at Toronto 0 [Durnan]
5 Rangers 1 at Toronto 7
6 Toronto 4 at Rangers 3
9 Toronto 0 at Detroit 5 [Lumley]
12 Boston 2 at Toronto 1
13 Toronto 3 at Chicago 1
17 Toronto 1 at Canadiens 3
19 Detroit 5 at Toronto 2
20 Toronto 2 at Boston 7

1949–1950

October
15 Chicago 4 at Toronto 4
16 Toronto 5 at Detroit 1
19 Canadiens 3 at Toronto 1
22 Rangers 2 at Toronto 2
27 Toronto 2 at Canadiens 0 [Broda]
29 Boston 1 at Toronto 8
30 Toronto 4 at Rangers 2

November
2 Rangers 3 at Toronto 3
5 Detroit 4 at Toronto 3

6 Toronto 4 at Chicago 2
10 Toronto 2 at Canadiens 4
12 Chicago 0 at Toronto 4 [Broda]
13 Toronto 2 at Boston 4
16 Canadiens 0 at Toronto 1
    (Smith 5:20 1st) [Broda]
19 Detroit 5 at Toronto 2
20 Toronto 2 at Detroit 5
23 Toronto 1 at Boston 3
    (Peirson 18:54 en)
24 Toronto 3 at Canadiens 5
26 Boston 3 at Toronto 3
27 Toronto 3 at Chicago 6

December
1 Detroit 2 at Toronto 0 (both goals in the
    first) [Lumley] (Broda benched because
    Conn Smythe said he was too fat—Gil
    Mayer played goal)
3 Rangers 0 at Toronto 2 (both goals in
    the 3rd) (Broda returned for shutout)
4 Toronto 2 at Detroit 1
8 Toronto 4 at Chicago 1
10 Boston 1 at Toronto 2
11 Toronto 0 at Boston 2 [Gelineau]
14 Canadiens 2 at Toronto 2
15 Toronto 1 at Canadiens 4
17 Chicago 7 at Toronto 1
18 Toronto 2 at Rangers 0 [Broda]
21 Toronto 1 at Detroit 7
24 Boston 8 at Toronto 4
    (Rollins replaced Broda start of 2nd)
25 Toronto 1 at Rangers 3
28 Canadiens 1 at Toronto 1
31 Detroit 5 at Toronto 1

January
1 Toronto 0 at Detroit 5 [Lumley]
4 Chicago 4 at Toronto 4
7 Chicago 2 at Toronto 5
11 Toronto 2 at Rangers 1
14 Boston 3 at Toronto 4
18 Canadiens 1 at Toronto 0
    (Lach 2:11 1st) [Durnan]
19 Toronto 4 at Canadiens 2
21 Rangers 1 at Toronto 2
22 Toronto 1 at Detroit 0
    (Smith 14:47 2nd) [Broda]
25 Rangers 1 at Toronto 5

28 Chicago 1 at Toronto 9
29 Toronto 4 at Chicago 0 [Broda]

February
1   Toronto 0 at Chicago 3 [Brimsek]
4   Detroit 3 at Toronto 3
5   Toronto 2 at Boston 1
8   Toronto 3 at Boston 1 (two consecutive road games in the same city)
11 Canadiens 0 at Toronto 2 [Broda]
12 Toronto 1 at Chicago 1
16 Canadiens 3 at Toronto 3
18 Detroit 2 at Toronto 3
19 Toronto 1 at Rangers 2 (with the Leafs pressing and their goalie Turk Broda on the bench, Ranger goalie Rayner got the puck and shot at the empty net, just missing!)
22 Boston 1 at Toronto 3
25 Rangers 2 at Toronto 4

March
1   Toronto 2 at Boston 5
4   Detroit 2 at Toronto 3
5   Toronto 2 at Rangers 5
9   Toronto 1 at Canadiens 1
11 Rangers 0 at Toronto 4 [Broda]
12 Toronto 2 at Boston 2
15 Toronto 0 at Chicago 4 [Brimsek]
18 Chicago 1 at Toronto 2
19 Toronto 0 at Detroit 5 [Lumley]
22 Canadiens 2 at Toronto 1
25 Boston 0 at Toronto 8 [Rollins]
26 Toronto 3 at Rangers 5

1950–1951
October
14 Chicago 2 at Toronto 1 (Brigadier General John Rockingham dropped the puck)
15 Toronto 4 at Detroit 4
18 Toronto 2 at Boston 0 (both goals in the 3rd) [Broda]
21 Rangers 0 at Toronto 5 [Broda]
22 Toronto 5 at Chicago 3
25 Detroit 0 at Toronto 1 (Gardner 11:22 3rd) [Broda]
28 Boston 2 at Toronto 4
29 Toronto 3 at Chicago 3

November
1   Canadiens 3 at Toronto 5
2   Toronto 2 at Canadiens 1
4   Rangers 2 at Toronto 2 (all goals in the 2nd)
8   Toronto 5 at Rangers 3
11 Detroit 3 at Toronto 1
12 Toronto 7 at Boston 0 [Broda]
16 Toronto 2 at Canadiens 5
18 Rangers 4 at Toronto 5
19 Toronto 1 at Boston 3
22 Chicago 2 at Toronto 5
23 Toronto 2 at Detroit 1
25 Canadiens 1 at Toronto 4
26 Toronto 3 at Rangers 2
30 Toronto 0 at Canadiens 0 [Rollins (T)/McNeil (C)]

December
2   Chicago 0 at Toronto 0 (Broda replaced Rollins at 6:50 of 2nd/Lumley [C])
3   Toronto 3 at Chicago 3
6   Canadiens 1 at Toronto 3
9   Boston 1 at Toronto 8
10 Toronto 2 at Detroit 3
13 Detroit 4 at Toronto 3
14 Toronto 7 at Chicago 1
16 Chicago 3 at Toronto 2
17 Toronto 4 at Boston 2
20 Canadiens 1 at Toronto 6
23 Boston 2 at Toronto 2 (Young Canada Night)
27 Toronto 1 at Rangers 3
30 Detroit 3 at Toronto 1
31 Toronto 4 at Detroit 2 (McCormack 19:58 en)

January
6   Rangers 4 at Toronto 2
9   Toronto 3 at Detroit 3
13 Chicago 3 at Toronto 3
14 Toronto 1 at Rangers 2
18 Toronto 5 at Canadiens 2
20 Boston 1 at Toronto 2
21 Toronto 0 at Detroit 0 [Rollins (T)/Sawchuk (D)]
24 Canadiens 3 at Toronto 4
27 Rangers 1 at Toronto 2
28 Toronto 4 at Chicago 3

February

1 Toronto 3 at Canadiens 1
3 Chicago 3 at Toronto 6
4 Toronto 3 at Boston 3
7 Canadiens 1 at Toronto 3
10 Detroit 2 at Toronto 1
11 Toronto 5 at Chicago 3 (Sloan 19:22 en)
15 Toronto 2 at Canadiens 2
17 Rangers 0 at Toronto 2 [Rollins]
18 Toronto 5 at Rangers 2
21 Detroit 2 at Toronto 2
24 Boston 2 at Toronto 6

March

1 Toronto 1 at Canadiens 3
3 Chicago 0 at Toronto 3 [Broda]
5 Toronto 1 at Detroit 3
7 Detroit 3 at Toronto 0 (game delayed when both starting goalies Sawchuk (D) and Broda (T) injured in warmup; Sawchuk played and got a shutout, Broda replaced by Rollins)
10 Boston 3 at Toronto 5
11 Toronto 1 at Boston 3
14 Toronto 3 at Rangers 1 (Thomson 18:52 en)
15 Toronto 5 at Chicago 3
17 Rangers 1 at Toronto 3
18 Toronto 4 at Rangers 1
21 Canadiens 0 at Toronto 2 [Rollins]
24 Boston 1 at Toronto 4
25 Toronto 1 at Boston 0 (Smith 17:05 3rd) [Rollins]

1951–1952

October

13 Chicago 3 at Toronto 1 (Princess Elizabeth and Prince Philip in attendance)
14 Toronto 3 at Detroit 2
17 Boston 2 at Toronto 4 (Gardner 19:40 en)
20 Rangers 3 at Toronto 2
21 Toronto 1 at Chicago 1
27 Detroit 2 at Toronto 1
29 Toronto 2 at Detroit 2

31 Canadiens 0 at Toronto 1 (Bolton 13:46 1st) [Rollins] (M. Richard threatened a railside fan, then swung stick at him, after being taunted)

November

1 Toronto 4 at Canadiens 2
3 Rangers 2 at Toronto 1
7 Chicago 0 at Toronto 1 (Bentley 9:43 2nd) [Rollins]
8 Toronto 3 at Chicago 1
10 Detroit 3 at Toronto 3
11 Toronto 1 at Boston 1
14 Toronto 2 at Rangers 2 (Ronty (R) tied game at 19:18 with goalie out)
17 Boston 1 at Toronto 1 (Schmidt (B) tied game at 19:35 with goalie out)
18 Toronto 0 at Chicago 1 (McFadden 14:44 2nd) [Lumley]
21 Chicago 1 at Toronto 5
24 Canadiens 2 at Toronto 4
25 Toronto 4 at Boston 1
29 Toronto 1 at Canadiens 5

December

1 Rangers 2 at Toronto 8
2 Toronto 2 at Detroit 1
5 Detroit 2 at Toronto 2
8 Chicago 1 at Toronto 3 (Watson 19:44 en)
9 Toronto 2 at Rangers 7
13 Toronto 1 at Detroit 3
15 Rangers 1 at Toronto 4
16 Toronto 3 at Chicago 4
20 Toronto 1 at Canadiens 4
22 Boston 2 at Toronto 3 (Turk Broda Night and Young Canada Night at the Gardens)
23 Toronto 2 at Boston 4
26 Canadiens 3 at Toronto 2
29 Boston 0 at Toronto 4 [Rollins]
30 Toronto 2 at Rangers 2

January

3 Toronto 1 at Canadiens 3
5 Chicago 1 at Toronto 2
9 Toronto 2 at Rangers 1
12 Detroit 3 at Toronto 5
13 Toronto 1 at Detroit 2

15 Toronto 1 at Boston 0
    (Sloan (pp) 12:17 2nd) [Rollins]
17 Toronto 2 at Canadiens 2
19 Boston 2 at Toronto 6
20 Toronto 3 at Chicago 1
    (first afternoon game ever in NHL)
23 Canadiens 4 at Toronto 2
24 Toronto 2 at Detroit 2
26 Rangers 3 at Toronto 3
27 Toronto 3 at Boston 0 [Rollins]

February
 2 Boston 1 at Toronto 1
 3 Toronto 1 at Chicago 3
    (afternoon game)
 6 Rangers at Toronto (postponed to
    February 19 due to the death of King
    George VI)
 9 Canadiens 2 at Toronto 3
10 Toronto 4 at Rangers 3
13 Detroit 3 at Toronto 1 (Howe 19:18 en)
14 Toronto 1 at Canadiens 3
16 Chicago 2 at Toronto 2
19 Rangers 3 at Toronto 3
    (Mortson (T) fined $100 for
    attempting to kick Hy Buller)
21 Toronto 1 at Chicago 5
23 Detroit 3 at Toronto 1 (Abel 19:55 en)
27 Toronto 3 at Rangers 1

March
 1 Boston 1 at Toronto 1
 2 Toronto 2 at Boston 2
 5 Canadiens 2 at Toronto 6
 8 Detroit 3 at Toronto 6
 9 Toronto 1 at Detroit 6
13 Toronto 1 at Canadiens 3
15 Rangers 2 at Toronto 5
16 Toronto 4 at Rangers 2
19 Canadiens 3 at Toronto 0 [McNeil]
22 Chicago 3 at Toronto 2
23 Toronto 2 at Boston 4
    (Rollins replaced Broda at 10:00 2nd)

1952–1953
October
11 Chicago 6 at Toronto 2 (Conn Smythe
    dropped puck to open season)

12 Toronto 4 at Detroit 4 (Kennedy (T)
    scored at 19:15 to tie)
16 Toronto 1 at Boston 2
18 Rangers 3 at Toronto 4
19 Toronto 3 at Chicago 2
22 Detroit 4 at Toronto 5
25 Boston 4 at Toronto 0 [Henry]
29 Canadiens 5 at Toronto 7
    (Kennedy 19:30 en)

November
 1 Boston 2 at Toronto 3 (first Leaf
    telecast on CBC television)
 2 Toronto 4 at Detroit 2
 5 Rangers 1 at Toronto 4
 6 Toronto 1 at Canadiens 3
 8 Detroit 3 at Toronto 3
11 Toronto 0 at Boston 4
    (all goals in the 1st) [Henry]
13 Toronto 3 at Canadiens 1
    (all goals in the 2nd)
15 Chicago 3 at Toronto 1
16 Toronto 6 at Rangers 3
19 Boston 2 at Toronto 1
22 Canadiens 2 at Toronto 2
23 Toronto 5 at Boston 6
26 Toronto 2 at Rangers 4
27 Toronto 3 at Chicago 3 (Smith (T)
    scored at 18:52 with goalie out)
29 Detroit 3 at Toronto 1
30 Toronto 1 at Detroit 4

December
 4 Toronto 2 at Canadiens 1
    (moment of silence observed for
    the passing of James Norris Sr.)
 6 Rangers 2 at Toronto 2
 7 Toronto 2 at Chicago 0
    (both goals in the 2nd) [Lumley]
10 Canadiens 2 at Toronto 1
13 Detroit 3 at Toronto 1
14 Toronto 2 at Rangers 2
18 Toronto 1 at Detroit 1
20 Chicago 1 at Toronto 4
21 Toronto 2 at Chicago 4
24 Canadiens 0 at Toronto 2
    (both goals in the 3rd) [Lumley]
27 Boston 0 at Toronto 3 [Lumley]
31 Toronto 3 at Rangers 3

January

1   Toronto 1 at Boston 5
3   Chicago 1 at Toronto 1
    (both goals in the 1st)
10 Boston 1 at Toronto 3
11 Toronto 2 at Detroit 5
14 Chicago 0 at Toronto 3
    (all goals in the 3rd) [Lumley]
17 Rangers 0 at Toronto 1
    (Maloney 14:57 3rd) [Lumley]
18 Toronto 1 at Boston 2
21 Canadiens 1 at Toronto 0
    (Geoffrion 17:11 1st (pp)) [McNeil]
22 Toronto 1 at Canadiens 4
24 Detroit 0 at Toronto 2 [Lumley]
25 Toronto 4 at Chicago 3
29 Toronto 2 at Boston 2
31 Rangers 0 at Toronto 4 [Lumley]

February

1   Toronto 1 at Detroit 5
5   Toronto 0 at Canadiens 2
    (both goals in the 3rd) [McNeil]
7   Chicago 4 at Toronto 2
8   Toronto 2 at Chicago 4
    (McFadden 19:20 en)
14 Canadiens 2 at Toronto 2
15 Toronto 2 at Rangers 1
18 Detroit 0 at Toronto 2
    (Flaman 19:55 en) [Lumley]
21 Boston 2 at Toronto 2
25 Canadiens 2 at Toronto 1
26 Toronto 1 at Canadiens 4
28 Rangers 0 at Toronto 3 [Lumley]

March

1   Toronto 2 at Rangers 4
    (Kullman 19:49 en)
5   Toronto 1 at Chicago 3
7   Detroit 3 at Toronto 0 [Sawchuk]
8   Toronto 1 at Detroit 3
14 Boston 3 at Toronto 1
    (Dumart 19:25 en)
15 Toronto 1 at Rangers 1
18 Chicago 3 at Toronto 4
19 Toronto 4 at Canadiens 1
21 Rangers 0 at Toronto 5 [Lumley]
22 Toronto 3 at Boston 1

1953–1954

October

10 Chicago 2 at Toronto 6 (Ted Kennedy
    presented with Bickell Cup in a pre-
    game ceremony)
11 Toronto 0 at Detroit 4 [Gatherum]
15 Toronto 4 at Boston 1
17 Rangers 1 at Toronto 1
18 Toronto 2 at Chicago 1
21 Detroit 1 at Toronto 1
24 Boston 3 at Toronto 2 (in pre-game
    ceremony, Gardens associate Henry
    Roxborough presented Ted Kennedy
    with award to acknowledge his 20th
    goal of the season in a previous game.
    Kennedy then scored after just 8 sec-
    onds, tying an NHL record)
25 Toronto 0 at Detroit 2 [Sawchuk]
29 Toronto 1 at Canadiens 3
31 Rangers 1 at Toronto 4

November

1   Toronto 2 at Rangers 2 (Kennedy (T)
    tied game at 18:26 with goalie out)
4   Chicago 1 at Toronto 3
7   Detroit 2 at Toronto 2
8   Toronto 2 at Chicago 1
11 Canadiens 1 at Toronto 4
14 Boston 0 at Toronto 2
    (Horton 19:19 en) [Lumley]
15 Toronto 1 at Boston 1
19 Toronto 0 at Canadiens 1
    (Geoffrion 4:31 2nd) [McNeil]
21 Rangers 0 at Toronto 1
    (Morrison 15:29 3rd) [Lumley]
22 Toronto 5 at Chicago 1
26 Toronto 0 at Detroit 2 [Sawchuk]
28 Canadiens 1 at Toronto 3
29 Toronto 1 at Boston 2

December

3   Toronto 1 at Canadiens 5
5   Detroit 0 at Toronto 3 [Lumley]
6   Toronto 3 at Rangers 3
    (W. Hergesheimer tied game at
    19:32 with goalie out)
9   Canadiens 0 at Toronto 3 [Lumley]
    (dubbed the "War of 1812." At 18:12 of
    the 3rd, a bench-clearing brawl erupted;

when it was over, referee Frank Udvari
handed out 18 misconducts (nine a
side) and two majors (one each), leaving each team with only a goalie and
three skaters (no subs left on the
benches) to play out the final 1:48)

12 Chicago 0 at Toronto 2 [Lumley]
13 Toronto 2 at Rangers 1
17 Toronto 2 at Boston 3
19 Rangers 2 at Toronto 3
    (Young Canada Night)
20 Toronto 1 at Chicago 4
26 Detroit 2 at Toronto 4
30 Canadiens 2 at Toronto 2

January
2   Chicago 0 at Toronto 4 [Lumley]
3   Toronto 0 at Detroit 0
    [Lumley (T)/Sawchuk (D)]
7   Toronto 3 at Canadiens 7
9   Boston 2 at Toronto 3
10 Toronto 1 at Rangers 4
13 Chicago 1 at Toronto 2
16 Rangers 0 at Toronto 4 [Lumley]
17 Toronto 3 at Chicago 1
    (all goals in the 3rd)
23 Detroit 1 at Toronto 4
24 Toronto 0 at Detroit 2 [Sawchuk]
27 Canadiens 2 at Toronto 0 [McNeil]
30 Boston 2 at Toronto 4 (Migay 19:59 en)
31 Toronto 0 at Boston 2 [Henry]

February
4   Toronto 4 at Canadiens 2
    (Smith 19:42 en)
6   Chicago 0 at Toronto 6 [Lumley]
7   Toronto 1 at Chicago 2
10 Boston 3 at Toronto 2
11 Toronto 3 at Boston 1
13 Canadiens 2 at Toronto 2
14 Toronto 3 at Rangers 3
17 Detroit 0 at Toronto 0
    [Sawchuk (D)/Lumley (T)]
20 Boston 2 at Toronto 3
21 Toronto 1 at Rangers 6
25 Toronto 0 at Canadiens 0
    [Lumley (T)/Plante (C)]
27 Chicago 2 at Toronto 4
28 Toronto 1 at Chicago 2

March
3   Rangers 3 at Toronto 3
4   Toronto 3 at Detroit 3
6   Detroit 3 at Toronto 1
    (all goals in the 1st)
7   Toronto 4 at Rangers 0 [Lumley]
11 Toronto 3 at Canadiens 0 [Lumley]
13 Boston 2 at Toronto 1
14 Toronto 0 at Boston 3
    (all goals in the 2nd) [Henry]
17 Canadiens 1 at Toronto 3
    (Migay 19:22 en)
20 Rangers 5 at Toronto 2
21 Toronto 1 at Detroit 6

1954–1955
October
7   Toronto 1 at Detroit 2
9   Chicago 3 at Toronto 3
    (Gus Ryder and Marilyn Bell honoured
    at opening ceremonies)
16 Rangers 4 at Toronto 2
    (Prentice 19:00 en)
17 Toronto 1 at Boston 1 (McKenney (B)
    tied game at 18:43 with goalie out)
21 Toronto 3 at Canadiens 1
23 Boston 3 at Toronto 3
27 Canadiens 3 at Toronto 1
30 Rangers 1 at Toronto 3

November
3   Detroit 1 at Toronto 1
6   Chicago 2 at Toronto 5
7   Toronto 2 at Chicago 1
10 Toronto 2 at Rangers 1
11 Toronto 1 at Detroit 0
    (Smith 19:44 2nd) [Lumley]
13 Detroit 0 at Toronto 1
    (Smith :42 3rd) [Lumley]
14 Toronto 3 at Boston 1
17 Canadiens 2 at Toronto 5
18 Toronto 4 at Canadiens 5 (Béliveau won
    game at 19:46 (pp). Leafs played the last
    two periods under protest because
    Charlie Hodge played for the Canadiens
    even though his name was not on
    the roster.)

20 Boston 1 at Toronto 0
(Ferguson 14:34 1st) [Henderson]
21 Toronto 2 at Rangers 2
25 Toronto 0 at Detroit 2 [Sawchuk]
27 Rangers 1 at Toronto 3
28 Toronto 1 at Chicago 1

December
1   Boston 0 at Toronto 6 [Lumley]
4   Detroit 0 at Toronto 1
(Stewart 3:28 3rd) [Lumley]
5   Toronto 4 at Boston 2
8   Canadiens 1 at Toronto 3
9   Toronto 0 at Canadiens 2 [Hodge]
11 Chicago 2 at Toronto 1
12 Toronto 1 at Rangers 1
15 Toronto 8 at Chicago 3
(played at St. Louis)
18 Rangers 1 at Toronto 3
19 Toronto 3 at Rangers 3
(Lewicki (R) tied game at 19:54)
25 Detroit 3 at Toronto 2
26 Toronto 1 at Detroit 1
29 Canadiens 1 at Toronto 1
30 Toronto 1 at Detroit 4

January
1   Chicago 2 at Toronto 2
2   Toronto 2 at Chicago 3
(played at St. Louis)
5   Boston 2 at Toronto 1
8   Rangers 0 at Toronto 5 [Lumley]
9   Toronto 1 at Boston 1
12 Toronto 0 at Rangers 0
[Lumley (T)/Worsley (R)]
15 Boston 2 at Toronto 4
16 Toronto 4 at Chicago 2
19 Chicago 3 at Toronto 3
20 Toronto 2 at Canadiens 6
22 Detroit 1 at Toronto 3
(Lindsay suspended ten days for hitting
fan with stick when fan tried to grab
Howe's stick)
23 Toronto 0 at Detroit 4 [Sawchuk]
26 Canadiens 1 at Toronto 1
29 Rangers 3 at Toronto 1
30 Toronto 0 at Boston 3 [Henderson]

February
3   Toronto 2 at Canadiens 3
5   Chicago 2 at Toronto 2 (power failure
later in the game ruined TV coverage,
PA system, and penalty clocks)
6   Toronto 4 at Chicago 2
9   Canadiens 1 at Toronto 3
(Lumley penalized for using oversized
stick—too long and blade too high)
12 Detroit 2 at Toronto 1
13 Toronto 3 at Boston 3 (Cullen (T) tied
game at 18:23 with goalie out)
19 Boston 1 at Toronto 1
20 Toronto 1 at Chicago 4
23 Toronto 3 at Rangers 1
(Thomson 19:23 en)
24 Toronto 1 at Canadiens 1
26 Detroit 1 at Toronto 1

March
2   Canadiens 3 at Toronto 2
5   Boston 2 at Toronto 2
6   Toronto 1 at Boston 3
10 Toronto 0 at Canadiens 0 (Zamboni
used for the first time ever in the NHL)
[Lumley (T)/Plante (C)]
12 Rangers 2 at Toronto 1
13 Toronto 1 at Detroit 6
19 Chicago 0 at Toronto 5 [Lumley]
20 Toronto 2 at Rangers 3

1955–1956
Wednesday night games now start
at 8:00 p.m.

October
6   Toronto 0 at Canadiens 2 [Plante]
8   Detroit 2 at Toronto 4
9   Toronto 1 at Chicago 3
12 Toronto 0 at Boston 2 [Sawchuk]
15 Boston 2 at Toronto 2
16 Toronto 0 at Detroit 6 [Hall] (Thomson
(T) threw Lindsay's stick into the crowd
during a last-minute fight. Lindsay
responded in kind; both were given misconducts in a fight-filled game)
19 Toronto 2 at Rangers 6
22 Rangers 2 at Toronto 3

26 Canadiens 1 at Toronto 2
29 Chicago 0 at Toronto 2 [Lumley]

November

2 Detroit 1 at Toronto 3
3 Toronto 3 at Canadiens 3 (Stewart (T)
tied game at 19:52 with goalie out)
5 Rangers 3 at Toronto 0 [Worsley]
6 Toronto 1 at Detroit 4
11 Toronto 0 at Chicago 2 [Rollins]
12 Boston 3 at Toronto 2
13 Toronto 1 at Rangers 4
16 Canadiens 3 at Toronto 2
19 Boston 2 at Toronto 3
20 Toronto 1 at Boston 1
24 Toronto 2 at Chicago 3
26 Chicago 4 at Toronto 7
27 Toronto 2 at Detroit 1
(all goals in the 1st)
30 Detroit 3 at Toronto 3

December

3 Canadiens 3 at Toronto 1
4 Toronto 0 at Boston 5 [Sawchuk]
7 Toronto 1 at Rangers 3
(Bathgate 19:12 en)
8 Toronto 1 at Canadiens 3
10 Rangers 1 at Toronto 6
11 Toronto 3 at Chicago 3
15 Toronto 0 at Detroit 4 [Hall]
17 Boston 1 at Toronto 5
18 Toronto 1 at Rangers 4
24 Chicago 2 at Toronto 5
25 Toronto 1 at Detroit 1
28 Canadiens 0 at Toronto 2 [Lumley]
29 Toronto 2 at Canadiens 5
31 Detroit 2 at Toronto 2

January

4 Chicago 2 at Toronto 4
(Stewart 19:11 en)
7 Boston 2 at Toronto 6
14 Rangers 6 at Toronto 5
15 Toronto 4 at Boston 1
18 Canadiens 3 at Toronto 2
19 Toronto 1 at Canadiens 3
21 Detroit 2 at Toronto 4
22 Toronto 1 at Detroit 4 (When Lumley
(T) was injured at 6:59 of 3rd, Detroit

trainer Lefty Wilson played goal for the
Leafs, shutting out his own team for the
final 13:01 of the game!)
25 Chicago 1 at Toronto 3
28 Rangers 3 at Toronto 1
(Hebenton 19:18 en)
29 Toronto 1 at Boston 3

February

1 Toronto 2 at Rangers 5
4 Chicago 4 at Toronto 2
5 Toronto 2 at Chicago 3
8 Canadiens 1 at Toronto 1
9 Toronto 1 at Boston 1
(both goals in the 1st)
11 Rangers 0 at Toronto 5 [Chadwick]
12 Toronto 1 at Chicago 1
15 Boston 0 at Toronto 1
(Sloan 3:56 3rd) [Chadwick]
16 Toronto 1 at Canadiens 8
18 Detroit 6 at Toronto 1
22 Toronto 4 at Rangers 2
(Hannigan 19:58 en)
24 Toronto 2 at Chicago 1
25 Boston 3 at Toronto 1
(Stasiuk 19:56 en)
29 Canadiens 1 at Toronto 4

March

3 Detroit 2 at Toronto 2
4 Toronto 2 at Boston 2
8 Toronto 3 at Canadiens 4
10 Rangers 2 at Toronto 5
11 Toronto 2 at Rangers 4
17 Chicago 1 at Toronto 1
18 Toronto 2 at Detroit 0 [Lumley]

1956–1957
October

11 Toronto 4 at Boston 4
13 Detroit 4 at Toronto 1 (Kelly 19:35 en)
(pre-game ceremony involved many
Leafs from the 1932 Cup-winning team)
14 Toronto 1 at Chicago 0
(Sloan 14:11 1st) [Chadwick]
18 Toronto 3 at Detroit 3
20 Boston 2 at Toronto 2
25 Toronto 3 at Canadiens 2

27 Chicago 2 at Toronto 5

28 Toronto 1 at Rangers 1

31 Rangers 2 at Toronto 7

November

3 Detroit 2 at Toronto 1 (Toronto pulled goalie and tied game, but referee Udvari disallowed goal because he didn't see the red light come on. NHL president Clarence Campbell later ruled that the goal should have counted.)

7 Canadiens 4 at Toronto 3

8 Toronto 2 at Chicago 5

10 Chicago 1 at Toronto 4

15 Toronto 2 at Detroit 4

17 Chicago 6 at Toronto 3

18 Toronto 3 at Boston 4

21 Toronto 3 at Rangers 3

22 Toronto 2 at Detroit 2 (Barry Cullen (T) tied game at 18:45 with goalie out)

24 Boston 3 at Toronto 2

25 Toronto 1 at Boston 3 (Mohns 19:32 en)

29 Toronto 2 at Canadiens 4

December

1 Detroit 0 at Toronto 4 [Chadwick]

2 Toronto 2 at Rangers 4 (Bathgate 19:04 en)

5 Canadiens 3 at Toronto 1

8 Rangers 0 at Toronto 0 [Worsley (R)/Chadwick (T)]

9 Toronto 2 at Chicago 1

13 Toronto 2 at Canadiens 6

15 Rangers 1 at Toronto 2

16 Toronto 2 at Boston 4

20 Toronto 2 at Canadiens 4

22 Boston 3 at Toronto 2

23 Toronto 3 at Rangers 1 (Migay 19:24 en)

26 Canadiens 0 at Toronto 1 (MacNeil 15:56 (pp) 1st) [Chadwick]

29 Chicago 3 at Toronto 6

30 Toronto 0 at Chicago 2 (Skov 19:57 en) [Rollins]

January

2 Detroit 2 at Toronto 0 [Hall]

5 Boston 2 at Toronto 3

6 Toronto 1 at Detroit 2

9 Toronto 4 at Rangers 3

10 Toronto 1 at Canadiens 2 (Duff (T) tied game at 18:37 with goalie out and M. Richard in penalty box; Richard stormed after referee Udvari and drew a 10-minute misconduct. Marshall (C) won game at 19:54)

12 Chicago 3 at Toronto 4

13 Toronto 1 at Chicago 1

16 Canadiens 3 at Toronto 2

19 Boston 1 at Toronto 4

20 Toronto 3 at Boston 2

23 Rangers 4 at Toronto 4

26 Detroit 4 at Toronto 1

27 Toronto 1 at Detroit 3

February

2 Chicago 3 at Toronto 3

3 Toronto 3 at Chicago 6 (Skov 18:30 en)

6 Canadiens 1 at Toronto 1

9 Rangers 4 at Toronto 4

10 Toronto 1 at Boston 5

13 Boston 2 at Toronto 2

14 Toronto 2 at Canadiens 1

16 Detroit 3 at Toronto 1

17 Toronto 2 at Rangers 3

23 Boston 5 at Toronto 2

24 Toronto 2 at Detroit 1

March

2 Chicago 4 at Toronto 3

3 Toronto 0 at Chicago 0 [Chadwick (T)/Rollins (C)]

6 Canadiens 1 at Toronto 3

9 Rangers 2 at Toronto 1

10 Toronto 3 at Boston 3 (Stasiuk (B) tied game at 19:25 with goalie out)

14 Toronto 4 at Canadiens 8

16 Rangers 1 at Toronto 14

17 Toronto 5 at Rangers 3 (Armstrong 19:40 en)

20 Canadiens 2 at Toronto 1

23 Detroit 5 at Toronto 3 (Lindsay 19:50 en)

24 Toronto 1 at Detroit 4

1957–1958

October

8   Toronto 0 at Chicago 1
    (Lindsay 15:06 2nd) [Hall]
12   Detroit 5 at Toronto 3
17   Toronto 3 at Canadiens 9
19   Boston 0 at Toronto 7 [Chadwick]
20   Toronto 1 at Detroit 3
23   Toronto 0 at Rangers 3 [Worsley]
26   Rangers 0 at Toronto 3 [Chadwick]
30   Canadiens 6 at Toronto 2
31   Toronto 3 at Canadiens 1

November

2   Chicago 3 at Toronto 3
6   Rangers 4 at Toronto 2
    (Bathgate 19:55 en)
7   Toronto 5 at Boston 3
9   Detroit 3 at Toronto 3
10   Toronto 1 at Chicago 3
13   Canadiens 4 at Toronto 2
16   Boston 4 at Toronto 2
17   Toronto 2 at Boston 2
20   Chicago 1 at Toronto 2
23   Detroit 2 at Toronto 1
24   Toronto 5 at Rangers 1
28   Toronto 3 at Detroit 3 (Duff (T) tied
    game at 19:15 with goalie out)
30   Boston 2 at Toronto 3

December

1   Toronto 7 at Chicago 2
4   Canadiens 0 at Toronto 0
    [Plante (C)/Chadwick (T)]
5   Toronto 3 at Canadiens 4
    (Moore wins game at 19:40)
7   Rangers 3 at Toronto 3
8   Toronto 2 at Rangers 1
14   Chicago 1 at Toronto 4
15   Toronto 3 at Boston 1
    (Pulford 19:54 en)
19   Toronto 2 at Detroit 3
21   Boston 3 at Toronto 3
    (Young Canada Night)
22   Toronto 2 at Rangers 5
25   Canadiens 4 at Toronto 5
28   Rangers 1 at Toronto 6
29   Toronto 1 at Chicago 2

January

2   Toronto 2 at Canadiens 5
4   Chicago 4 at Toronto 2
    (Lindsay 19:49 en)
5   Toronto 2 at Detroit 3
8   Toronto 5 at Rangers 5 (Henry (R) tied
    game at 19:35 with goalie out)
11   Boston 2 at Toronto 2
12   Toronto 5 at Boston 3
16   Toronto 2 at Canadiens 5
18   Detroit 1 at Toronto 2
19   Toronto 3 at Chicago 5
22   Canadiens 2 at Toronto 0 [Plante]
25   Rangers 1 at Toronto 7
26   Toronto 3 at Boston 3 (Labine (B) tied
    game at 19:59 with goalie out)
29   Chicago 4 at Toronto 1

February

1   Detroit 2 at Toronto 9
2   Toronto 1 at Detroit 3
8   Boston 7 at Toronto 3
9   Toronto 2 at Boston 0 [Chadwick]
12   Canadiens 5 at Toronto 2
15   Detroit 6 at Toronto 3
16   Toronto 1 at Detroit 4
22   Chicago 1 at Toronto 3
    (Mahovlich 18:48 en)
23   Toronto 2 at Rangers 4
    (Bathgate 19:31 en)
27   Toronto 1 at Canadiens 4

March

1   Rangers 5 at Toronto 4
2   Toronto 6 at Chicago 5
5   Chicago 2 at Toronto 5
8   Boston 3 at Toronto 3
9   Toronto 0 at Boston 7 [Simmons]
12   Canadiens 5 at Toronto 3
15   Detroit 3 at Toronto 1
16   Toronto 2 at Chicago 3
18   Toronto 2 at Detroit 4
20   Toronto 4 at Canadiens 7
22   Rangers 7 at Toronto 0 [Worsley]
23   Toronto 2 at Rangers 3

1958–1959

October

11 Chicago 3 at Toronto 1 (Hap Day dropped first puck)
12 Toronto 2 at Chicago 5
16 Toronto 3 at Canadiens 4
18 Boston 2 at Toronto 3
19 Toronto 1 at Detroit 3
25 Detroit 0 at Toronto 3 [Bower]
26 Toronto 2 at Rangers 3
29 Canadiens 5 at Toronto 0 [Plante]

November

1 Rangers 3 at Toronto 4
2 Toronto 0 at Boston 2 [Simmons]
8 Boston 3 at Toronto 5
9 Toronto 2 at Detroit 0 [Chadwick]
12 Canadiens 4 at Toronto 1
15 Detroit 4 at Toronto 1
16 Toronto 4 at Boston 4 (Coach Imlach threatened players with $200 fine each if they didn't get one road point against both Boston and New York)
19 Toronto 4 at Rangers 7
22 Rangers 2 at Toronto 2
23 Toronto 3 at Chicago 3
26 Detroit 5 at Toronto 2
27 Toronto 2 at Detroit 3 (all goals in the 3rd)
29 Chicago 2 at Toronto 1
30 Toronto 2 at Boston 1

December

4 Toronto 2 at Canadiens 2
6 Boston 1 at Toronto 4
7 Toronto 2 at Rangers 0 [Bower]
10 Toronto 2 at Chicago 2
13 Rangers 4 at Toronto 4 (Duff (T) tied game at 18:38 with goalie out)
14 Toronto 3 at Boston 6 (McKenney 19:15 en)
18 Toronto 1 at Canadiens 4
20 Boston 2 at Toronto 2
21 Toronto 1 at Rangers 5
25 Toronto 2 at Detroit 0 [Chadwick]
27 Chicago 2 at Toronto 2 (all goals in the 1st)
28 Toronto 3 at Chicago 4
31 Canadiens 0 at Toronto 2 [Chadwick]

January

3 Chicago 2 at Toronto 1
4 Toronto 4 at Rangers 2 (Armstrong 19:26 en)
7 Detroit 1 at Toronto 3 (Duff 19:45 en)
8 Toronto 0 at Canadiens 3 [Plante]
10 Boston 1 at Toronto 4
11 Toronto 6 at Detroit 6
14 Rangers 3 at Toronto 2
17 Detroit 1 at Toronto 2
18 Toronto 3 at Boston 4
21 Canadiens 1 at Toronto 3
24 Boston 3 at Toronto 1
25 Toronto 4 at Chicago 1
31 Rangers 5 at Toronto 2

February

1 Toronto 4 at Boston 6 (Gendron 18:56 en)
5 Toronto 6 at Canadiens 3 (Pronovost (C) replaced Plante at start of 3rd)
7 Detroit 1 at Toronto 4
8 Toronto 2 at Chicago 7
11 Canadiens 5 at Toronto 2
14 Chicago 1 at Toronto 5
15 Toronto 2 at Detroit 4
21 Rangers 1 at Toronto 1
22 Toronto 1 at Chicago 5
25 Canadiens 2 at Toronto 3
28 Detroit 4 at Toronto 2 (Kelly 19:21 en)

March

1 Toronto 1 at Rangers 1
4 Chicago 2 at Toronto 5
5 Toronto 1 at Canadiens 2
7 Boston 1 at Toronto 4
8 Toronto 3 at Boston 4
11 Canadiens 6 at Toronto 2
14 Rangers 0 at Toronto 5 [Bower]
15 Toronto 6 at Rangers 5
19 Toronto 6 at Canadiens 3 (Cyr (C) replaced Pronovost at start of 3rd)
21 Chicago 1 at Toronto 5
22 Toronto 6 at Detroit 4

1959–1960

October

10 Chicago 3 at Toronto 6 (puck dropped
by Prime Minister John Diefenbaker)
11 Toronto 3 at Chicago 1
15 Toronto 2 at Canadiens 4
17 Boston 0 at Toronto 3 [Bower]
18 Toronto 0 at Detroit 3 [Sawchuk]
21 Toronto 3 at Rangers 2
24 Rangers 1 at Toronto 1
28 Canadiens 1 at Toronto 1
31 Boston 3 at Toronto 4

November

1 Toronto 3 at Boston 6
4 Rangers 1 at Toronto 4
7 Detroit 2 at Toronto 2
10 Toronto 3 at Chicago 1
(Stewart 19:12 en)
12 Toronto 0 at Canadiens 3 [Plante]
14 Chicago 3 at Toronto 3
15 Toronto 2 at Rangers 2
18 Detroit 2 at Toronto 3
21 Canadiens 4 at Toronto 1
(Marshall 19:15 en)
22 Toronto 2 at Boston 1
26 Toronto 4 at Chicago 3
28 Boston 2 at Toronto 2
29 Toronto 4 at Detroit 1

December

2 Canadiens 0 at Toronto 1
(Mahovlich 8:23 1st) [Bower]
5 Rangers 3 at Toronto 6
6 Toronto 0 at Rangers 6 [Paille]
10 Toronto 3 at Boston 6
12 Chicago 4 at Toronto 2 (Sloan 19:09 en)
13 Toronto 2 at Detroit 4
17 Toronto 2 at Canadiens 8
19 Detroit 2 at Toronto 4
20 Toronto 4 at Chicago 7
26 Rangers 0 at Toronto 4 [Bower]
27 Toronto 6 at Rangers 3
30 Canadiens 3 at Toronto 2 (Pulford
scored at 19:48 with goalie out)
31 Toronto 4 at Detroit 2

January

2 Chicago 4 at Toronto 2
3 Toronto 4 at Chicago 0 [Bower]
6 Detroit 1 at Toronto 3
9 Boston 3 at Toronto 2
10 Toronto 0 at Boston 4 [Simmons]
14 Toronto 1 at Canadiens 3
16 Rangers 1 at Toronto 3
(Pulford 19:47 en)
17 Toronto 3 at Detroit 4
23 Boston 3 at Toronto 3
24 Toronto 2 at Boston 6
27 Chicago 1 at Toronto 2
30 Rangers 2 at Toronto 3
31 Toronto 3 at Chicago 3

February

3 Toronto 4 at Rangers 2
4 Toronto 2 at Canadiens 4
6 Detroit 4 at Toronto 6
(Stewart 19:27 en)
7 Toronto 0 at Boston 3 [Lumley]
10 Canadiens 4 at Toronto 2
(Provost 19:50 en)
13 Detroit 1 at Toronto 7
(Leafs scored all seven in the 3rd)
14 Toronto 3 at Detroit 1
17 Boston 1 at Toronto 3
20 Chicago 1 at Toronto 3
21 Toronto 5 at Chicago 7
24 Canadiens 1 at Toronto 3
27 Detroit 4 at Toronto 3
28 Toronto 5 at Rangers 3 (pay TV was provided to one thousand homes in
Etobicoke for $1 on a trial basis for all
remaining Sunday games)

March

3 Toronto 1 at Canadiens 5
5 Boston 2 at Toronto 5
6 Toronto 3 at Boston 1 (Kelly 19:43 en)
9 Canadiens 9 at Toronto 4
12 Rangers 4 at Toronto 1
13 Toronto 2 at Rangers 2
17 Toronto 6 at Canadiens 2
19 Chicago 0 at Toronto 1
(Kelly 3:20 3rd) [Bower]
20 Toronto 3 at Detroit 2
(Wilson wins game at 18:32)

1960–1961

October

6 Toronto 0 at Canadiens 5 [Plante]
8 Rangers 5 at Toronto 2 (Keiller McKay, Lieutenant-Governor of Ontario, dropped first puck)
9 Toronto 3 at Detroit 3
12 Toronto 0 at Chicago 3 [Hall]
15 Boston 1 at Toronto 1
16 Toronto 7 at Rangers 2
19 Canadiens 1 at Toronto 3
22 Detroit 2 at Toronto 1
23 Toronto 3 at Detroit 1
29 Chicago 4 at Toronto 8
28 Toronto 3 at Rangers 1

November

2 Boston 2 at Toronto 2
3 Toronto 1 at Canadiens 3
5 Rangers 3 at Toronto 7
9 Toronto 0 at Chicago 2 [Hall]
12 Chicago 1 at Toronto 7 (Lou Marsh and Charlie Conacher dropped first puck on night of Maple Leaf Gardens' 29th anniversary)
13 Toronto 4 at Boston 2 (Mahovlich 19:44 en)
16 Detroit 3 at Toronto 3
19 Canadiens 3 at Toronto 6
20 Toronto 3 at Boston 2
24 Toronto 1 at Chicago 2
26 Detroit 3 at Toronto 3 (Pronovost (T) tied game at 19:35 with goalie out)
27 Toronto 0 at Detroit 2 [Sawchuk] (Gordie Howe became first ever in NHL to score 1,000 points)

December

1 Toronto 3 at Canadiens 6 (Imlach fined $200 for public criticism of the referee)
3 Rangers 2 at Toronto 5
4 Toronto 5 at Boston 2
7 Canadiens 6 at Toronto 2
10 Chicago 2 at Toronto 5
11 Toronto 6 at Chicago 1
15 Toronto 4 at Canadiens 2
17 Boston 3 at Toronto 3
18 Toronto 3 at Rangers 2
24 Detroit 4 at Toronto 4

25 Toronto 4 at Boston 1
28 Canadiens 4 at Toronto 1
31 Rangers 1 at Toronto 2

January

1 Toronto 4 at Rangers 1 (all goals in the 3rd)
4 Detroit 4 at Toronto 6
5 Toronto 4 at Detroit 1
7 Boston 1 at Toronto 4
8 Toronto 1 at Chicago 5
12 Toronto 2 at Canadiens 6
14 Chicago 1 at Toronto 4
15 Toronto 6 at Boston 4
18 Rangers 4 at Toronto 4 (Kelly (T) tied game at 19:35 with goalie out)
21 Boston 3 at Toronto 1
25 Canadiens 3 at Toronto 5 (Kelly 19:45 en)
26 Toronto 4 at Boston 5
28 Chicago 1 at Toronto 2
29 Toronto 4 at Rangers 1

February

2 Toronto 5 at Detroit 0 [Bower]
4 Detroit 2 at Toronto 4
5 Toronto 1 at Chicago 1
8 Rangers 3 at Toronto 5
11 Boston 3 at Toronto 6
12 Toronto 4 at Detroit 2 (Keon 18:46 en)
15 Canadiens 3 at Toronto 1 (Marshall 18:55 en)
18 Chicago 2 at Toronto 5
19 Toronto 2 at Rangers 4
23 Toronto 4 at Canadiens 2 (King Clancy behind bench)
25 Detroit 1 at Toronto 3
26 Toronto 2 at Detroit 2

March

1 Canadiens 1 at Toronto 3
4 Rangers 4 at Toronto 5
5 Toronto 1 at Chicago 3
11 Chicago 2 at Toronto 2 (bench-clearing brawl required police to come on ice to restore order)
12 Toronto 5 at Boston 0 [Bower]
16 Toronto 2 at Canadiens 5
18 Boston 2 at Toronto 6
19 Toronto 2 at Rangers 2

1961–1962

October

12   Toronto 4 at Detroit 2 (Duff 19:51 en)
14   Boston 2 at Toronto 3 (first puck
       dropped by former Prime Minister Louis
       St. Laurent)
15   Toronto 1 at Rangers 2
21   Chicago 1 at Toronto 1
22   Toronto 9 at Boston 1
28   Rangers 1 at Toronto 5
29   Toronto 2 at Rangers 4

November

 1   Canadiens 2 at Toronto 3
 4   Chicago 1 at Toronto 2
 5   Toronto 3 at Detroit 2
 7   Toronto 0 at Chicago 6 [Hall]
 9   Toronto 2 at Canadiens 5
11   Detroit 1 at Toronto 5
12   Toronto 3 at Boston 4
15   Canadiens 2 at Toronto 3
18   Detroit 1 at Toronto 6
19   Toronto 3 at Rangers 5
       (Ingarfield 19:10 en)
23   Toronto 5 at Chicago 2
25   Rangers 0 at Toronto 6 [Bower]
26   Toronto 4 at Boston 1
       (Stewart 19:48 en)
29   Canadiens 2 at Toronto 2
30   Toronto 1 at Canadiens 1

December

 2   Chicago 4 at Toronto 6
 3   Toronto 1 at Detroit 3
       (Ullman 19:48 en)
 7   Toronto 1 at Canadiens 4
 9   Boston 2 at Toronto 9
10   Toronto 3 at Rangers 2
16   Rangers 2 at Toronto 4
17   Toronto 4 at Boston 1 (Keon 19:50 en)
23   Boston 7 at Toronto 4
25   Toronto 3 at Chicago 3
27   Chicago 0 at Toronto 0
       [Hall (C)/Bower (T)]
30   Detroit 4 at Toronto 6
31   Toronto 2 at Detroit 4

January

 3   Canadiens 1 at Toronto 3
 6   Chicago 3 at Toronto 6
 7   Toronto 4 at Rangers 3
10   Boston 5 at Toronto 7
11   Toronto 2 at Canadiens 4
13   Detroit 3 at Toronto 4
14   Toronto 2 at Chicago 2
17   Rangers 2 at Toronto 4
20   Boston 5 at Toronto 4
21   Toronto 5 at Boston 1
24   Toronto 1 at Chicago 2
27   Detroit 2 at Toronto 4
28   Toronto 2 at Detroit 2

February

 1   Toronto 2 at Canadiens 5
 3   Rangers 1 at Toronto 4
 4   Toronto 1 at Chicago 2
 7   Boston 2 at Toronto 2
10   Canadiens 4 at Toronto 2
11   Toronto 0 at Detroit 5 [Bassen]
17   Rangers 3 at Toronto 5
18   Toronto 2 at Rangers 6
21   Canadiens 4 at Toronto 2
24   Boston 2 at Toronto 7
25   Toronto 8 at Detroit 2
28   Chicago 2 at Toronto 4

March

 3   Rangers 1 at Toronto 3 (Kelly 19:37 en)
 4   Toronto 5 at Boston 1
 8   Toronto 1 at Canadiens 1
10   Detroit 0 at Toronto 2 [Simmons]
11   Toronto 3 at Chicago 2
14   Canadiens 2 at Toronto 5
17   Chicago 3 at Toronto 1
18   Toronto 2 at Rangers 2
22   Toronto 1 at Canadiens 4
24   Detroit 2 at Toronto 2
25   Toronto 4 at Boston 5

1962–1963

October

10   Toronto 3 at Chicago 1
13   Boston 2 at Toronto 2
14   Toronto 3 at Rangers 5
18   Toronto 2 at Canadiens 4

20 Chicago 1 at Toronto 3
    (Armstrong 19:57 en)
21 Toronto 6 at Boston 4
    (Mahovlich 19:17 en)
27 Rangers 5 at Toronto 1
28 Toronto 0 at Detroit 2
    (Howe 19:27 en) [Sawchuk]
31 Canadiens 4 at Toronto 3

November
1   Toronto 3 at Canadiens 1
3   Detroit 7 at Toronto 3
7   Toronto 5 at Rangers 1
10 Rangers 3 at Toronto 5
11 Toronto 5 at Chicago 3
14 Canadiens 2 at Toronto 4
17 Detroit 2 at Toronto 3
18 Toronto 1 at Rangers 3
22 Toronto 0 at Chicago 1
    (Pilote 11:51 (pp) 2nd) [Hall]
24 Rangers 1 at Toronto 4
25 Toronto 2 at Boston 5
29 Toronto 4 at Canadiens 4

December
1   Boston 2 at Toronto 8
2   Toronto 3 at Detroit 1
    (Pulford 19:54 en)
5   Canadiens 1 at Toronto 2
8   Chicago 1 at Toronto 1
    (both goals in the 2nd)
9   Toronto 3 at Detroit 4
15 Boston 2 at Toronto 8
16 Toronto 6 at Chicago 2
20 Toronto 4 at Canadiens 4
22 Rangers 2 at Toronto 4 (Keon 19:46 en)
23 Toronto 5 at Boston 4
25 Toronto 1 at Detroit 2
26 Detroit 4 at Toronto 5
29 Chicago 1 at Toronto 1

January
1   Toronto 0 at Boston 3 [Johnston]
2   Toronto 2 at Rangers 3
5   Boston 2 at Toronto 4
6   Toronto 5 at Chicago 1
9   Chicago 3 at Toronto 1
12 Detroit 1 at Toronto 2
13 Toronto 2 at Boston 2

17 Toronto 4 at Canadiens 6
19 Chicago 4 at Toronto 1
20 Toronto 2 at Detroit 2
23 Canadiens 1 at Toronto 5
24 Toronto 6 at Boston 3
26 Boston 5 at Toronto 2 (Boivin 18:33 en)
27 Toronto 4 at Rangers 2
31 Toronto 6 at Canadiens 3

February
2   Rangers 2 at Toronto 2
3   Toronto 1 at Chicago 3
9   Canadiens 3 at Toronto 3 (H. Richard
    tied game at 19:02 with goalie out)
10 Toronto 1 at Detroit 2
13 Detroit 2 at Toronto 6
16 Rangers 2 at Toronto 4
17 Toronto 1 at Rangers 4
20 Canadiens 1 at Toronto 2
    (all goals in the 2nd)
23 Boston 4 at Toronto 2
27 Chicago 3 at Toronto 6

March
2   Rangers 3 at Toronto 4
3   Toronto 6 at Boston 3
6   Boston 0 at Toronto 4 [Bower]
9   Detroit 3 at Toronto 5
10 Toronto 1 at Chicago 1
    (both goals in the 3rd)
14 Toronto 3 at Canadiens 3
16 Chicago 0 at Toronto 3 [Simmons]
17 Toronto 2 at Rangers 1
20 Canadiens 3 at Toronto 3 (Keon tied
    game at 19:52 with goalie out)
23 Detroit 2 at Toronto 1
24 Toronto 2 at Detroit 3

1963–1964
October
12 Boston 1 at Toronto 5
13 Toronto 2 at Chicago 4
16 Toronto 4 at Canadiens 2
19 Detroit 1 at Toronto 2
20 Toronto 2 at Detroit 3
26 Rangers 4 at Toronto 6
27 Toronto 0 at Boston 2 [Johnston]
30 Canadiens 3 at Toronto 6

November

2   Chicago 2 at Toronto 0 [Hall]
7   Toronto 4 at Boston 3
9   Chicago 3 at Toronto 3
13 Toronto 2 at Canadiens 2
14 Toronto 5 at Rangers 4
16 Rangers 4 at Toronto 5
17 Toronto 0 at Chicago 6 [Hall]
20 Canadiens 3 at Toronto 1
23 Boston 1 at Toronto 4
24 Toronto 3 at Rangers 3
28 Toronto 0 at Chicago 2 [Hall]
30 Detroit 1 at Toronto 1

December

1   Toronto 4 at Detroit 1
4   Canadiens 0 at Toronto 3 [Simmons]
7   Chicago 0 at Toronto 3 [Simmons]
8   Toronto 5 at Detroit 3
11 Detroit 3 at Toronto 1
14 Rangers 3 at Toronto 5
15 Toronto 4 at Boston 4
18 Toronto 3 at Canadiens 7
21 Detroit 0 at Toronto 2 [Bower]
22 Toronto 1 at Rangers 1
25 Toronto 5 at Boston 1
28 Boston 0 at Toronto 2 [Bower]
29 Toronto 0 at Chicago 2 [Hall]
31 Toronto 5 at Detroit 4

January

4   Chicago 0 at Toronto 3 [Bower] (Howie
    Young (C) suspended five games after
    using filthy language and spitting while
    in the penalty box)
5   Toronto 2 at Rangers 3
8   Canadiens 1 at Toronto 6
11 Boston 1 at Toronto 3
12 Toronto 3 at Boston 6 (Boivin 19:41 en)
15 Rangers 5 at Toronto 4
18 Boston 11 at Toronto 0 [Johnston]
19 Toronto 2 at Chicago 0 [Simmons]
22 Canadiens 3 at Toronto 0 [Hodge]
25 Rangers 1 at Toronto 1
26 Toronto 0 at Boston 2 [Johnston]
29 Toronto 1 at Canadiens 2

February

1   Boston 1 at Toronto 5
2   Toronto 2 at Detroit 2
5   Canadiens 2 at Toronto 0 [Hodge]
8   Chicago 3 at Toronto 3 (Keon tied
    game at 19:12 with goalie out)
9   Toronto 1 at Chicago 2
12 Toronto 0 at Canadiens 4 [Hodge]
15 Chicago 0 at Toronto 4 [Bower]
16 Toronto 2 at Rangers 4
    (Ingarfield 19:32 en)
19 Detroit 1 at Toronto 1
22 Rangers 2 at Toronto 5
23 Toronto 4 at Rangers 3
    (Keon wins game at 19:32)
26 Toronto 0 at Canadiens 1
    (Geoffrion 10:08 2nd) [Hodge]
29 Chicago 1 at Toronto 4

March

1   Toronto 3 at Boston 5
3   Toronto 2 at Detroit 3
4   Boston 4 at Toronto 4 (Kelly tied
    game at 19:39 with goalie out)
7   Detroit 2 at Toronto 4
8   Toronto 3 at Chicago 4
11 Canadiens 0 at Toronto 1
    (Mahovlich 8:46 1st) [Bower]
14 Rangers 3 at Toronto 7
15 Toronto 3 at Rangers 1
18 Toronto 2 at Canadiens 2
21 Detroit 3 at Toronto 5
22 Toronto 4 at Detroit 1

1964–1965

October

15 Toronto 5 at Detroit 3
17 Boston 2 at Toronto 7
18 Toronto 3 at Rangers 3
22 Toronto 2 at Boston 2
24 Rangers 1 at Toronto 1
27 Toronto 3 at Chicago 2
28 Canadiens 5 at Toronto 2
31 Chicago 1 at Toronto 5

November

1   Toronto 2 at Detroit 4
5   Toronto 2 at Canadiens 2

7 Rangers 1 at Toronto 0
   (Henry 19:19 2nd) [Plante]
11 Detroit 1 at Toronto 3
   (Pulford 19:51 en)
14 Boston 3 at Toronto 1
15 Toronto 2 at Chicago 4
18 Canadiens 1 at Toronto 3
21 Chicago 0 at Toronto 1
   (Pulford 18:08 1st) [Sawchuk]
22 Toronto 3 at Boston 1
25 Toronto 3 at Rangers 6
26 Toronto 4 at Chicago 2
28 Rangers 4 at Toronto 1
29 Toronto 1 at Detroit 1

December

3 Toronto 2 at Canadiens 4
5 Detroit 2 at Toronto 10
9 Canadiens 3 at Toronto 2
12 Boston 3 at Toronto 6
13 Toronto 3 at Rangers 3 (Ellis tied
   game at 19:59 with goalie out)
17 Toronto 2 at Canadiens 2
19 Rangers 3 at Toronto 6
20 Toronto 1 at Detroit 3
25 Toronto 3 at Chicago 3
26 Chicago 5 at Toronto 3
30 Canadiens 4 at Toronto 3

January

1 Toronto 0 at Boston 3 [Johnston]
2 Detroit 1 at Toronto 3
3 Toronto 3 at Rangers 3
6 Toronto 3 at Chicago 1
9 Boston 1 at Toronto 2
10 Toronto 6 at Rangers 0 [Bower]
13 Chicago 0 at Toronto 0
   [DeJordy (C)/Bower (T)]
14 Toronto 5 at Canadiens 3
16 Detroit 4 at Toronto 2
17 Toronto 3 at Boston 1
20 Canadiens 2 at Toronto 1
23 Rangers 1 at Toronto 1
24 Toronto 1 at Detroit 4
30 Boston 1 at Toronto 6
31 Toronto 4 at Boston 2

February

4 Toronto 5 at Canadiens 2
6 Chicago 6 at Toronto 3
7 Toronto 2 at Chicago 1
10 Canadiens 2 at Toronto 6
13 Detroit 1 at Toronto 2
14 Toronto 2 at Boston 2
20 Chicago 3 at Toronto 4
21 Toronto 2 at Detroit 3
24 Boston 3 at Toronto 1
27 Rangers 4 at Toronto 3
28 Toronto 2 at Rangers 6

March

4 Toronto 2 at Canadiens 2
6 Chicago 1 at Toronto 4
7 Toronto 3 at Boston 3
10 Detroit 4 at Toronto 2
13 Boston 2 at Toronto 0 [Norris]
14 Toronto 3 at Chicago 5
18 Toronto 1 at Canadiens 4
20 Rangers 1 at Toronto 4
21 Toronto 10 at Rangers 1
24 Canadiens 2 at Toronto 3
27 Detroit 4 at Toronto 1
28 Toronto 4 at Detroit 0
   (Keon 19:57 en) [Bower]

1965–1966

October

23 Chicago 4 at Toronto 0 [Hall]
24 Toronto 0 at Detroit 3 [Crozier]
27 Toronto 2 at Boston 1
30 Detroit 3 at Toronto 4

November

3 Toronto 2 at Rangers 2
4 Toronto 1 at Canadiens 5
6 Rangers 4 at Toronto 2
7 Toronto 0 at Chicago 9 [Hall]
10 Canadiens 3 at Toronto 3
13 Rangers 2 at Toronto 5
14 Toronto 0 at Boston 2 [Parent]
18 Toronto 3 at Canadiens 1
   (Pulford 19:34 en)
20 Chicago 1 at Toronto 3
21 Toronto 7 at Chicago 3
24 Canadiens 2 at Toronto 1

27 Boston 2 at Toronto 1
28 Toronto 4 at Rangers 2
    (Pulford 19:20 en)

December
1 Toronto 2 at Rangers 2
4 Detroit 5 at Toronto 3
   (Henderson 19:58 en)
5 Toronto 1 at Detroit 5
11 Boston 3 at Toronto 8
12 Toronto 1 at Rangers 1
15 Detroit 3 at Toronto 5
16 Toronto 3 at Canadiens 2
18 Rangers 4 at Toronto 8
19 Toronto 3 at Boston 1
25 Chicago 3 at Toronto 5
26 Toronto 1 at Chicago 1
29 Canadiens 2 at Toronto 3

January
1 Boston 3 at Toronto 6
2 Toronto 0 at Detroit 4 [Crozier]
8 Detroit 3 at Toronto 1
9 Toronto 3 at Chicago 5
   (Nesterenko 19:48 en)
13 Toronto 6 at Canadiens 0 [Bower]
15 Boston 1 at Toronto 6
16 Toronto 0 at Detroit 4 [Crozier]
19 Rangers 2 at Toronto 6
22 Chicago 0 at Toronto 4 [Bower]
23 Toronto 1 at Boston 2
29 Boston 3 at Toronto 6
30 Toronto 4 at Rangers 8

February
3 Toronto 4 at Canadiens 5
5 Chicago 2 at Toronto 5
6 Toronto 2 at Chicago 3
9 Rangers 0 at Toronto 3 [Sawchuk]
12 Detroit 3 at Toronto 3 (Henderson (D)
    tied game at 19:59 with goalie out)
13 Toronto 4 at Boston 4
16 Canadiens 1 at Toronto 3
19 Rangers 3 at Toronto 1
20 Toronto 1 at Detroit 4
23 Toronto 3 at Chicago 2
26 Boston 2 at Toronto 3
27 Toronto 2 at Rangers 2

March
2 Canadiens 3 at Toronto 3
3 Toronto 4 at Canadiens 0 [Gamble]
5 Chicago 0 at Toronto 5 [Gamble]
6 Toronto 5 at Boston 3
9 Detroit 0 at Toronto 1
   (Mahovlich 17:24 1st) [Gamble]
12 Boston 0 at Toronto 6 [Gamble]
13 Toronto 1 at Chicago 5
16 Canadiens 7 at Toronto 2
19 Chicago 2 at Toronto 4 (Douglas (T)
    suspended for two games for swinging
    at linesman John D'Amico)
20 Toronto 1 at Detroit 6
24 Toronto 2 at Canadiens 0 [Bower]
26 Detroit 1 at Toronto 3
27 Toronto 5 at Rangers 1
30 Canadiens 3 at Toronto 1
31 Toronto 1 at Boston 3 (Bower and
    Sawchuk alternated in goal many times)

April
2 Rangers 3 at Toronto 3 (Sawchuk and
   Gamble alternated many times in goal)
3 Toronto 3 at Detroit 3 (Leafs used three
   goalies: Bower (1st), Sawchuk (2nd),
   Gamble (3rd). Bower had the "flu" after
   the first, thus allowing a third goalie to
   dress. He was later well enough to coach
   the third period while Punch Imlach
   watched the end of the game from
   the stands)

1966–1967
October
22 Rangers 4 at Toronto 4 (John P. Robarts,
    Premier of Ontario, dropped first puck)
23 Toronto 0 at Rangers 1
    (Hillman 7:14 3rd) [Giacomin]
26 Detroit 2 at Toronto 3
29 Boston 3 at Toronto 3

November
2 Canadiens 2 at Toronto 2
3 Toronto 2 at Detroit 2
5 Rangers 1 at Toronto 3
   (Conacher 19:58 en)
6 Toronto 3 at Rangers 3

9 Toronto 3 at Canadiens 2
10 Toronto 0 at Boston 4 [Cheevers]
12 Toronto 3 at Detroit 3
13 Toronto 1 at Chicago 6
19 Canadiens 1 at Toronto 5
20 Toronto 2 at Chicago 2
23 Chicago 3 at Toronto 6 (Hall (C) replaced Dejordy for penalty shot only)
26 Boston 2 at Toronto 4
27 Toronto 0 at Rangers 5 [Giacomin]
30 Canadiens 2 at Toronto 3

December
3 Detroit 2 at Toronto 5
4 Toronto 8 at Boston 3
7 Toronto 3 at Canadiens 6
10 Chicago 3 at Toronto 5
11 Toronto 1 at Detroit 4 (Howe 19:48 en)
14 Boston 1 at Toronto 2
17 Rangers 3 at Toronto 1
18 Toronto 1 at Chicago 3
21 Toronto 2 at Canadiens 6
24 Boston 0 at Toronto 3 [Bower]
25 Toronto 4 at Boston 2
31 Chicago 5 at Toronto 1

January
1 Toronto 2 at Rangers 1
4 Rangers 1 at Toronto 1
7 Boston 2 at Toronto 5
8 Toronto 1 at Detroit 3
11 Toronto 2 at Canadiens 1
14 Detroit 2 at Toronto 5
15 Toronto 0 at Chicago 4 [DeJordy]
19 Toronto 2 at Detroit 6
21 Detroit 5 at Toronto 4
22 Toronto 1 at Boston 3 (Westfall 19:40 en)
25 Canadiens 3 at Toronto 1
28 Chicago 5 at Toronto 2
29 Toronto 1 at Chicago 5

February
1 Toronto 1 at Canadiens 7
5 Toronto 1 at Rangers 4
8 Detroit 5 at Toronto 2
11 Chicago 4 at Toronto 4
12 Toronto 2 at Boston 1
15 Rangers 0 at Toronto 6 [Bower]

18 Boston 3 at Toronto 5 (King Clancy took over as coach)
22 Canadiens 2 at Toronto 5
23 Toronto 4 at Detroit 2
25 Detroit 0 at Toronto 4 [Sawchuk]
26 Toronto 4 at Rangers 2

March
1 Toronto 1 at Canadiens 1 (Pappin (T) tied game at 19:11 with goalie out)
4 Chicago 0 at Toronto 3 (Sawchuk's 100th career shutout)
5 Toronto 2 at Chicago 5
8 Canadiens 4 at Toronto 6
11 Rangers 2 at Toronto 2
12 Toronto 0 at Chicago 5 (afternoon game) [Hall] (Imlach returned as coach)
15 Detroit 4 at Toronto 2
18 Chicago 5 at Toronto 9
19 Toronto 6 at Detroit 5 (afternoon game)
22 Canadiens 5 at Toronto 3
23 Toronto 5 at Boston 3
25 Boston 3 at Toronto 4
26 Toronto 0 at Rangers 4 [Giacomin]
29 Toronto 3 at Canadiens 5

April
1 Rangers 1 at Toronto 5
2 Toronto 5 at Boston 2

1967–1968
Imlach fined each player $100 for every home loss to an expansion team.

October
14 Chicago 1 at Toronto 5 (The Hon. Robert Stanfield present at opening ceremonies)
15 Toronto 5 at Chicago 3 (Mahovlich 19:05 en)
18 Detroit 3 at Toronto 2
19 Toronto 0 at Canadiens 1 (Cournoyer 5:36 1st) [Worsley]
21 Rangers 5 at Toronto 3
25 Los Angeles 2 at Toronto 4
28 Oakland 2 at Toronto 5
29 Toronto 2 at Rangers 3

November

1 Canadiens 0 at Toronto 5 [Bower]
2 Toronto 9 at Detroit 3
4 Rangers 2 at Toronto 4
5 Toronto 2 at Boston 2
8 Toronto 6 at Oakland 1
9 Toronto 1 at Los Angeles 4
   (Joyal 18:32 en)
11 Toronto 1 at Minnesota 2
15 Boston 2 at Toronto 4
18 Chicago 2 at Toronto 2
19 Toronto 2 at Boston 6
22 Minnesota 0 at Toronto 3 [Gamble]
25 Detroit 2 at Toronto 3
29 Canadiens 1 at Toronto 2
28 Toronto 3 at Detroit 3

December

2 Oakland 0 at Toronto 3 [Bower]
6 Toronto 1 at Minnesota 1
9 Boston 3 at Toronto 3 (Armstrong (T)
   tied game at 19:57 with goalie out)
10 Toronto 1 at St. Louis 2
13 Pittsburgh 2 at Toronto 1
16 Rangers 2 at Toronto 4
17 Toronto 0 at Chicago 2
   (Mohns 19:12 en) [DeJordy]
20 Toronto 0 at Canadiens 5 [Worsley]
23 Detroit 3 at Toronto 5
25 Toronto 3 at Detroit 1
27 Canadiens 2 at Toronto 2
30 St. Louis 1 at Toronto 8
31 Toronto 0 at Rangers 4 [Giacomin]

January

3 Toronto 1 at Canadiens 1
6 Boston 3 at Toronto 3
7 Toronto 2 at Rangers 6
10 Detroit 1 at Toronto 2
12 Toronto 3 at Pittsburgh 4
13 Pittsburgh 0 at Toronto 7
   (afternoon game) [Gamble]
18 Toronto 4 at Boston 2
20 Minnesota 1 at Toronto 5
21 Toronto 2 at Detroit 0 [Gamble]
24 Flyers 2 at Toronto 1
27 Chicago 4 at Toronto 1
28 Toronto 3 at Chicago 1
   (Pulford 19:47 en)
30 Toronto 0 at Canadiens 3 [Vachon]

February

3 Toronto 3 at Pittsburgh 3
4 Toronto 1 at Flyers 4
7 Toronto 2 at Chicago 3
11 Toronto 3 at Oakland 4
12 Toronto 0 at Los Angeles 2 [Rutledge]
14 Canadiens 4 at Toronto 2
   (Beliveau 19:46 en)
17 Rangers 3 at Toronto 2
21 St. Louis 5 at Toronto 1
24 Boston 0 at Toronto 1
   (McKenny 4:33 3rd) [Gamble]
25 Toronto 1 at Rangers 3
   (Goyette 19:59 en) (afternoon game)
28 Chicago 1 at Toronto 0
   (Schmautz 15:48 1st) [DeJordy]
29 Toronto 1 at Boston 4

March

2 Los Angeles 2 at Toronto 5
6 Flyers 2 at Toronto 7
9 Detroit 5 at Toronto 7
10 Toronto 0 at Chicago 4 (Martin 18:28
   en) (afternoon game) [Norris]
13 Toronto 3 at St. Louis 3
16 Boston 0 at Toronto 3 [Gamble]
17 Toronto 4 at Flyers 7 (Sutherland 19:08
   en/Gauthier 19:41 en) (afternoon game)
20 Toronto 2 at Canadiens 3
21 Toronto 5 at Detroit 2
23 Rangers 1 at Toronto 3
24 Toronto 2 at Rangers 4
27 Canadiens 0 at Toronto 6 [Bower]
30 Chicago 0 at Toronto 3 [Bower]
31 Toronto 4 at Boston 1

Note: On March 7, 1968, Boston and
Philadelphia played a game at Maple Leaf
Gardens (the Spectrum roof had been badly
damaged and the arena rendered unusable).

1968–1969

October

13 Toronto 2 at Detroit 1
16 Pittsburgh 2 at Toronto 2
   (William Davis, Minister of Education
   for Ontario, present for opening
   ceremonies)
19 Chicago 3 at Toronto 1

23 St. Louis 4 at Toronto 6
26 Boston 0 at Toronto 2 [Bower]
27 Toronto 5 at Rangers 3
30 Canadiens 5 at Toronto 0 [Vachon]

November
2 Flyers 3 at Toronto 2
6 Toronto 1 at Minnesota 0
   (Henderson 3:30 3rd) [Gamble]
9 Toronto 1 at Los Angeles 3
   (Irvine 19:29 en)
10 Toronto 3 at Oakland 1
13 Boston 1 at Toronto 1
14 Toronto 5 at Canadiens 3
16 Chicago 1 at Toronto 3
17 Toronto 1 at Chicago 1
20 Pittsburgh 2 at Toronto 5
   (Keon 19:38 en)
23 Detroit 5 at Toronto 2
24 Toronto 4 at Boston 7
27 Toronto 3 at Pittsburgh 3
30 Minnesota 3 at Toronto 3

December
1 Toronto 1 at Rangers 3
4 Toronto 4 at Minnesota 2
7 Rangers 2 at Toronto 5
8 Toronto 4 at Pittsburgh 1
11 Canadiens 4 at Toronto 4
12 Toronto 1 at Flyers 0
   (Ellis 15:51 1st) [Bower]
14 St. Louis 2 at Toronto 3
18 Oakland 2 at Toronto 5
21 Detroit 3 at Toronto 8
22 Toronto 2 at Detroit 3
25 Toronto 4 at Chicago 3
26 Toronto 2 at Canadiens 4
28 Los Angeles 4 at Toronto 1

January
1 Oakland 3 at Toronto 7
4 Rangers 3 at Toronto 5
5 Toronto 2 at Flyers 2
8 Flyers 4 at Toronto 4
9 Toronto 2 at Boston 3
11 Los Angeles 2 at Toronto 4
15 Boston 5 at Toronto 5
18 Detroit 1 at Toronto 1

19 Toronto 3 at Boston 5 (afternoon game)
   (Bower replaced Gamble in the 3rd,
   wore a mask for the first time)
23 Toronto 3 at St. Louis 2
25 Toronto 2 at Pittsburgh 0 [Gamble]
26 Toronto 2 at Detroit 3
29 Toronto 1 at Los Angeles 3
31 Toronto 4 at Oakland 5

February
2 Toronto 3 at St. Louis 5
5 Minnesota 5 at Toronto 5
8 Oakland 4 at Toronto 1
9 Toronto 5 at Chicago 3
12 Minnesota 1 at Toronto 7
15 Rangers 2 at Toronto 6
16 Toronto 2 at Rangers 4 (Balon 19:31 en)
19 Canadiens 1 at Toronto 5
20 Toronto 1 at Canadiens 2
22 Chicago 4 at Toronto 2
23 Toronto 2 at Minnesota 7
   (afternoon game)
26 St. Louis 2 at Toronto 3
27 Toronto 1 at Flyers 1

March
1 Pittsburgh 3 at Toronto 3
2 Chicago 1 at Toronto 2
   (afternoon game)
5 Los Angeles 4 at Toronto 6
6 Toronto 3 at Canadiens 5
8 Flyers 2 at Toronto 2
12 Toronto 4 at Los Angeles 0 [Gamble]
13 Toronto 3 at Oakland 1
15 Boston 4 at Toronto 7
16 Toronto 3 at Boston 11
19 Toronto 1 at St. Louis 1
22 Detroit 1 at Toronto 3
23 Toronto 1 at Chicago 4
26 Canadiens 4 at Toronto 6
27 Toronto 4 at Detroit 2
29 Rangers 4 at Toronto 2
   (Stewart 16:35 en)
30 Toronto 0 at Rangers 4
   [Giacomin] (Gamble and Bower
   alternated in goal all game)

1969–1970

October

11   Toronto 2 at Detroit 3
15   Canadiens 2 at Toronto 2
      (Foster Hewitt dropped first puck)
18   Chicago 1 at Toronto 4
19   Toronto 0 at Rangers 1
      (Hadfield 7:33 1st) [Giacomin]
22   Flyers 4 at Toronto 3
25   St. Louis 2 at Toronto 4
29   Boston 2 at Toronto 4

November

1   Rangers 3 at Toronto 2
2   Toronto 4 at Boston 4
4   Toronto 5 at Oakland 2
5   Toronto 2 at Los Angeles 6
8   Toronto 3 at Canadiens 6
9   Toronto 0 at Chicago 9 [Esposito]
12   Pittsburgh 3 at Toronto 0
      (McCreary 19:41 en) [Binkley]
15   Flyers 2 at Toronto 4 (Pulford 19:21 en)
19   Los Angeles 4 at Toronto 4
22   Detroit 0 at Toronto 4 [Gamble]
23   Toronto 3 at Flyers 2
26   Canadiens 3 at Toronto 1
29   Minnesota 2 at Toronto 5
30   Toronto 1 at Boston 4

December

3   Toronto 5 at Minnesota 5
6   Pittsburgh 0 at Toronto 5 [Gamble]
7   Toronto 2 at Pittsburgh 3
10   Toronto 3 at Canadiens 6
      (Provost 19:54 en)
11   Toronto 3 at Flyers 6
13   Detroit 3 at Toronto 1
14   Toronto 3 at Rangers 1
20   Rangers 5 at Toronto 2
21   Toronto 3 at Detroit 0 [Gamble]
24   Los Angeles 1 at Toronto 8
26   Toronto 1 at St. Louis 3
27   St. Louis 1 at Toronto 4
31   Oakland 1 at Toronto 1

January

3   Chicago 2 at Toronto 6
4   Toronto 4 at Pittsburgh 4
7   Minnesota 3 at Toronto 3
10   Boston 3 at Toronto 4

14   Rangers 7 at Toronto 1
15   Toronto 0 at St. Louis 2 [Wakely]
17   Pittsburgh 0 at Toronto 4 [Gamble]
22   Toronto 3 at Los Angeles 2
23   Toronto 3 at Oakland 6
25   Toronto 3 at Chicago 2
28   Toronto 4 at Pittsburgh 4
31   Toronto 4 at Minnesota 2

February

1   Toronto 6 at Boston 7 (afternoon
      game)(wild brawl in 2nd)
4   St. Louis 0 at Toronto 1
      (Walton 6:05 3rd) [Gamble]
5   Toronto 1 at Detroit 4
7   Oakland 1 at Toronto 5
11   Toronto 3 at Canadiens 3
12   Toronto 3 at Flyers 3
14   Flyers 3 at Toronto 4
15   Toronto 4 at Chicago 6
18   Canadiens 3 at Toronto 5
21   Detroit 7 at Toronto 5
22   Toronto 3 at Rangers 5
25   Oakland 1 at Toronto 4
28   Los Angeles 3 at Toronto 3

March

1   Toronto 0 at Minnesota 8
      (afternoon game) [Maniago]
3   Toronto 4 at Oakland 1
5   Toronto 5 at Los Angeles 3
7   Minnesota 8 at Toronto 3
11   Detroit 3 at Toronto 1
14   Boston 1 at Toronto 2
15   Canadiens 3 at Toronto 3
      (afternoon game)
18   Chicago 7 at Toronto 4
21   Toronto 2 at St. Louis 0 [Edwards]
22   Toronto 5 at Rangers 2
      (afternoon game)
25   Toronto 2 at Canadiens 5
28   Chicago 1 at Toronto 1
29   Toronto 0 at Chicago 4 [Esposito]

April

1   Rangers 2 at Toronto 1
2   Toronto 2 at Detroit 4
4   Boston 4 at Toronto 2
5   Toronto 1 at Boston 3

1970–1971

Beginning with the 1970–71 season, teams now wore white uniforms at home, dark uniforms on the road.

October

11 Toronto 3 at Vancouver 5
    (afternoon game)
14 St. Louis 3 at Toronto 7
    (Clarence Campbell, NHL president,
    dropped first puck)
17 Rangers 6 at Toronto 2
18 Toronto 2 at Flyers 4
21 Toronto 2 at Rangers 3
24 Chicago 1 at Toronto 0
    (Maki 3:34 3rd) [Esposito]
28 Canadiens 2 at Toronto 6
31 Minnesota 3 at Toronto 1
    (Burns 19:42 en)

November

1 Toronto 5 at Detroit 4
4 Toronto 2 at Los Angeles 3
6 Toronto 4 at California 8
7 Toronto 2 at Vancouver 3
11 Vancouver 4 at Toronto 2
14 Boston 2 at Toronto 3
15 Toronto 2 at Rangers 4 (Irvine 19:47 en)
18 Buffalo 7 at Toronto 2
19 Toronto 1 at Canadiens 5
21 California 3 at Toronto 5
    (Henderson 19:16 en)
24 Pittsburgh 4 at Toronto 4
26 Toronto 0 at St. Louis 1
    (B. Plager 18:59 2nd) [Wakely]
28 Detroit 4 at Toronto 9
29 Toronto 2 at Boston 4 (Orr 19:54 en)

December

2 Los Angeles 0 at Toronto 7 [Plante]
5 Rangers 1 at Toronto 0
    (Stemkowski :38 2nd)
6 Toronto 2 at Chicago 6
8 Toronto 0 at Pittsburgh 4 [Smith]
9 Canadiens 0 at Toronto 4 [Gamble]
12 Chicago 1 at Toronto 2
13 Toronto 4 at Buffalo 0 [Gamble]
16 Toronto 4 at Pittsburgh 2
19 Buffalo 0 at Toronto 2 [Plante]

20 Toronto 4 at Buffalo 2
    (Ullman 19:46 en)
23 Vancouver 2 at Toronto 7
25 Toronto 3 at Minnesota 6
26 Flyers 1 at Toronto 9
30 California 1 at Toronto 3

January

2 Detroit 0 at Toronto 13 [Plante/Gamble]
5 Toronto 2 at Minnesota 0 [Plante]
6 Minnesota 4 at Toronto 4
9 Pittsburgh 2 at Toronto 5
10 Toronto 3 at Detroit 2
13 California 1 at Toronto 1
14 Toronto 0 at Flyers 3 [Favell]
16 Los Angeles 1 at Toronto 8
17 Toronto 1 at Boston 9
20 Toronto 5 at Vancouver 1
22 Toronto 2 at California 5
23 Toronto 2 at Los Angeles 3
27 Toronto 1 at Pittsburgh 3
    (Pronovost 19:53 en)
30 Toronto 5 at Canadiens 4

February

3 St. Louis 2 at Toronto 6
6 Flyers 2 at Toronto 4
7 Toronto 4 at Buffalo 3
9 Toronto 3 at St. Louis 3
10 Toronto 3 at Chicago 2
13 Los Angeles 1 at Toronto 8
14 Boston 5 at Toronto 1 (afternoon game)
17 Pittsburgh 3 at Toronto 4
20 St. Louis 1 at Toronto 3 (Keon 19:55 en)
21 Toronto 4 at Minnesota 1
25 Minnesota 1 at Toronto 1
27 Buffalo 0 at Toronto 2 [Plante]
28 Toronto 3 at Boston 4 (afternoon game)

March

3 Vancouver 1 at Toronto 3
    (Armstrong 19:46 en)
5 Toronto 1 at St. Louis 3
6 Chicago 2 at Toronto 2
10 Canadiens 1 at Toronto 2
13 Flyers 3 at Toronto 2
14 Toronto 0 at Rangers 1
    (MacGregor 19:16 1st) [Giacomin]
18 Toronto 1 at Canadiens 4

20 Rangers 1 at Toronto 3
21 Toronto 1 at Flyers 1
24 Toronto 6 at California 0 [Plante/Parent]
25 Toronto 3 at Los Angeles 5
    (Howell 19:24 en)
28 Toronto 1 at Detroit 2 (afternoon game)
31 Detroit 2 at Toronto 2 (Gordie Howe
    Night at Maple Leaf Gardens)

April
3 Boston 8 at Toronto 3
4 Toronto 3 at Chicago 2

1971–1972
October
8 Toronto 3 at Vancouver 2
10 Toronto 3 at California 3
13 Detroit at Toronto (postponed to
    November 1 due to death of
    Stafford Smythe)
16 Rangers 5 at Toronto 3
17 Toronto 2 at Boston 2
20 Buffalo 7 at Toronto 2
22 Toronto 2 at Detroit 5
23 Flyers 3 at Toronto 5
27 Vancouver 0 at Toronto 0
    [Wilson (V)/Parent (T)]
30 Minnesota 1 at Toronto 1
31 Toronto 3 at Rangers 3

November
1 Detroit 1 at Toronto 6
   (game from October 13)
3 Toronto 1 at Minnesota 2
6 Toronto 3 at Los Angeles 2
7 Toronto 1 at California 8
10 Canadiens 5 at Toronto 2
13 Vancouver 2 at Toronto 2
14 Toronto 3 at Flyers 3
17 Los Angeles 1 at Toronto 5
20 California 1 at Toronto 5
21 Toronto 4 at Buffalo 3
24 Toronto 2 at Pittsburgh 1
27 Chicago 3 at Toronto 3
28 Toronto 1 at Chicago 4

December
1 St. Louis 2 at Toronto 4
4 Boston 5 at Toronto 3
8 Minnesota 1 at Toronto 3
11 Chicago 3 at Toronto 1
12 Toronto 4 at Buffalo 2
14 Toronto 4 at St. Louis 2
15 Pittsburgh 2 at Toronto 3
18 Buffalo 1 at Toronto 8
19 Toronto 4 at Flyers 0 [Plante]
22 Toronto 2 at Canadiens 4
25 Detroit 3 at Toronto 5
26 Toronto 1 at Boston 3 (Hodge 19:37 en)
28 Toronto 4 at Pittsburgh 2
    (Ullman 19:42 en)
29 St. Louis 6 at Toronto 3

January
1 Canadiens 2 at Toronto 5
5 Boston 2 at Toronto 0 [Johnston]
8 Flyers 2 at Toronto 2
9 Toronto 2 at Buffalo 1
12 Los Angeles 1 at Toronto 1
15 Rangers 3 at Toronto 4
16 St. Louis 4 at Toronto 3
19 Toronto 0 at Canadiens 1
    (P. Mahovlich 19:58 3rd) [Dryden]
22 Toronto 1 at Minnesota 4
23 Toronto 0 at Chicago 4 [Esposito]
26 Toronto 3 at Los Angeles 5
    (Widing 19:12 en)
28 Toronto 0 at California 3 [Meloche]
29 Toronto 2 at Vancouver 5

February
1 Toronto 0 at Detroit 4
   (Berenson 19:43 en) [Al Smith]
2 Minnesota 2 at Toronto 3
5 Flyers 3 at Toronto 1
6 Toronto 2 at Rangers 2
8 Toronto 2 at St. Louis 1
9 Pittsburgh 4 at Toronto 1
12 California 0 at Toronto 3 [Plante]
13 Toronto 1 at Chicago 3
16 Toronto 2 at Pittsburgh 4
    (Pronovost 19:56 en)
19 Buffalo 1 at Toronto 4
20 Toronto 1 at Flyers 3
22 Toronto 4 at Detroit 5

23 Pittsburgh 0 at Toronto 2 [Parent]
26 Vancouver 1 at Toronto 7

March
1 Toronto 3 at St. Louis 1
4 Los Angeles 2 at Toronto 3
8 Detroit 1 at Toronto 5
11 California 1 at Toronto 2
12 Toronto 2 at Minnesota 2
(afternoon game)
15 Canadiens 5 at Toronto 2
18 Chicago 2 at Toronto 2
19 Toronto 3 at Rangers 5
22 Toronto 3 at Canadiens 3
24 Toronto 3 at Vancouver 5
(Schmautz 19:26 en)
25 Toronto 4 at Los Angeles 0 [Parent]
29 Boston 1 at Toronto 4

April
1 Rangers 1 at Toronto 2
2 Toronto 4 at Boston 6 (Bailey 19:25 en)

1972–1973
October
7 Chicago 3 at Toronto 1
(King Clancy dropped first puck)
11 Canadiens 2 at Toronto 2
14 Los Angeles 4 at Toronto 6
15 Toronto 2 at Buffalo 3
18 Pittsburgh 3 at Toronto 4
21 Detroit 3 at Toronto 1
22 Toronto 2 at Detroit 6
25 Toronto 4 at Minnesota 3
28 Boston 3 at Toronto 2
29 Toronto 2 at Flyers 5

November
1 Buffalo 1 at Toronto 7
4 St. Louis 2 at Toronto 4
5 Toronto 2 at Atlanta 2
8 Toronto 2 at Canadiens 5
(P. Mahovlich 19:12 en)
11 Toronto 0 at St. Louis 1
(Unger 15:22 2nd) [Stephenson]
15 Atlanta 1 at Toronto 2
18 Minnesota 4 at Toronto 4
19 Toronto 5 at Boston 6

22 Toronto 1 at Minnesota 3
25 California 0 at Toronto 11 [Plante/Low]
26 Toronto 4 at Rangers 7
28 Toronto 2 at St. Louis 4
29 Toronto 4 at Pittsburgh 7

December
2 Flyers 2 at Toronto 2
3 Toronto 3 at Detroit 0 [Plante]
5 Toronto 5 at Vancouver 2
9 Vancouver 5 at Toronto 5
10 Toronto 2 at Flyers 5
13 Rangers 4 at Toronto 3
16 Detroit 4 at Toronto 1
17 Toronto 0 at Buffalo 4 [D. Dryden]
20 Toronto 3 at Atlanta 5
23 Chicago 3 at Toronto 5
24 Toronto 1 at Chicago 5
(afternoon game)
27 Pittsburgh 3 at Toronto 3
29 Toronto 4 at Pittsburgh 0 [Plante/Low]
30 St. Louis 4 at Toronto 5

January
3 Canadiens 8 at Toronto 4
6 Los Angeles 2 at Toronto 4
(Keon 19:54 en)
7 California 0 at Toronto 4 [Low]
10 Islanders 2 at Toronto 4
12 Toronto 0 at Atlanta 1
(Romanchych 3:31 3rd) [Bouchard]
13 Boston 4 at Toronto 1
16 Toronto 4 at Vancouver 6
17 Toronto 3 at California 3
20 Toronto 6 at Los Angeles 2
24 Toronto 2 at Pittsburgh 5
27 Toronto 2 at Canadiens 4
28 Toronto 2 at Rangers 5
31 Islanders 3 at Toronto 5

February
1 Toronto 2 at Boston 5
3 Vancouver 2 at Toronto 1
6 Toronto 2 at Islanders 4
7 California 3 at Toronto 5
(Ellis 19:00 en)
10 Los Angeles 4 at Toronto 2
14 Buffalo 3 at Toronto 2
17 Islanders 2 at Toronto 6

18 Canadiens 2 at Toronto 1
    (afternoon game)
21 Atlanta 2 at Toronto 2
24 St. Louis 2 at Toronto 4
28 Vancouver 2 at Toronto 7

March
 3 Chicago 3 at Toronto 3
 4 Toronto 0 at Flyers 10 [Favell]
 7 Toronto 1 at Canadiens 4
 8 Toronto 4 at Islanders 1
10 Minnesota 3 at Toronto 4
11 Toronto 2 at Rangers 4
    (afternoon game)
14 Flyers 1 at Toronto 5
15 Toronto 2 at Minnesota 5
17 Rangers 5 at Toronto 7
18 Toronto 1 at Buffalo 5
21 Toronto 1 at Los Angeles 5
23 Toronto 4 at California 7
25 Toronto 4 at Vancouver 7
    (afternoon game)
27 Detroit 8 at Toronto 1
29 Toronto 6 at Detroit 4
31 Boston 3 at Toronto 7

April
 1 Toronto 4 at Chicago 4

1973–1974
October
10 Buffalo 4 at Toronto 7 (to acknowledge
    the first Swedes to play for the Leafs—
    Borje Salming and Inge Hammar-
    strom—Swedish Ambassador to Canada
    Ake Malmaeus dropped the first puck)
11 Toronto 0 at Philadelphia 2 [Parent]
13 Los Angeles 3 at Toronto 6
17 Toronto 5 at Canadiens 3
    (Jarry 19:55 en)
20 Rangers 2 at Toronto 3
21 Toronto 3 at Buffalo 4
23 Minnesota 2 at Toronto 2
27 Boston 3 at Toronto 2
28 Toronto 1 at Chicago 1
30 Detroit 0 at Toronto 7 [Johnston]

November
 1 Toronto 2 at Islanders 2
 3 Pittsburgh 0 at Toronto 6 [Wilson]
 7 Canadiens 4 at Toronto 1
10 Islanders 3 at Toronto 3
11 Toronto 4 at Detroit 5
14 Toronto 4 at California 1
16 Toronto 3 at Vancouver 3
17 Toronto 4 at Los Angeles 3
20 Toronto 4 at Islanders 2
    (Keon 19:55 en)
22 Pittsburgh 4 at Toronto 2
    (Pronovost 19:42 en)
24 Chicago 3 at Toronto 1
28 Toronto 4 at Pittsburgh 3
29 St. Louis 1 at Toronto 5

December
 1 California 2 at Toronto 3
 2 Toronto 4 at Rangers 6
 6 Toronto 4 at Minnesota 1
 8 Flyers 3 at Toronto 1
 9 Toronto 2 at Buffalo 5
11 Toronto 3 at St. Louis 7
13 Toronto 6 at Atlanta 1
15 Rangers 2 at Toronto 2
19 California 3 at Toronto 5
22 Vancouver 6 at Toronto 4
    (Lever 19:27 en)
23 Toronto 3 at Boston 4
26 Canadiens 2 at Toronto 9
29 Atlanta 3 at Toronto 3
30 Toronto 4 at Chicago 3

January
 2 Detroit 3 at Toronto 4
 5 Toronto 3 at Los Angeles 5
    (Goring 19:46 en)
 7 Atlanta 2 at Toronto 6
 9 Toronto 6 at Pittsburgh 4
12 St. Louis 2 at Toronto 4
15 Toronto 2 at Vancouver 4
16 Toronto 5 at California 5
19 Toronto 3 at Minnesota 5
23 Toronto 3 at Canadiens 4
26 Toronto 3 at St. Louis 3
27 Toronto 5 at Atlanta 2
31 Minnesota 1 at Toronto 3

February

2 Boston 2 at Toronto 6
3 Toronto 3 at Buffalo 3
6 Detroit 2 at Toronto 2
9 Minnesota 1 at Toronto 4
13 Flyers 3 at Toronto 1
16 Atlanta 2 at Toronto 7
17 Toronto 1 at Chicago 4
20 Buffalo 2 at Toronto 4
23 Vancouver 4 at Toronto 3
24 Los Angeles 3 at Toronto 3
26 Toronto 3 at Detroit 7
28 Toronto 6 at Islanders 4
    (Henderson 19:31 en)

March

2 Islanders 2 at Toronto 5
3 Toronto 6 at Boston 4
7 Pittsburgh 2 at Toronto 2
9 Flyers 2 at Toronto 1
12 Toronto 1 at St. Louis 2
14 Islanders 1 at Toronto 2
16 Boston 5 at Toronto 2 (afternoon game)
17 Toronto 2 at Flyers 2
19 Toronto 1 at Los Angeles 1
22 Toronto 3 at California 2
24 Toronto 2 at Vancouver 3
    (afternoon game)
27 Chicago 5 at Toronto 3
    (Pappin 19:49 en)
30 Rangers 3 at Toronto 7
31 Toronto 3 at Rangers 3
    (afternoon game)

April

3 Toronto 5 at Canadiens 3
6 Buffalo 1 at Toronto 3 (Sittler 18:38 en)
7 Toronto 4 at Boston 6 (Cashman 19:33
   en) (Keon fought with Greg Sheppard,
   the only fight of Keon's career)

1974–1975

October

9 Kansas City 2 at Toronto 6 (broadcaster
   Gordon Sinclair dropped first puck)
12 Rangers 3 at Toronto 7
13 Toronto 2 at Boston 2
16 Los Angeles 1 at Toronto 1

19 Vancouver 5 at Toronto 4
20 Toronto 5 at Buffalo 5
23 Canadiens 3 at Toronto 2
26 Chicago 9 at Toronto 3
27 Toronto 4 at Washington 3
29 St. Louis at Toronto
    (postponed to November 25)

November

1 Toronto 2 at Atlanta 5
2 Buffalo 6 at Toronto 3
6 Minnesota 4 at Toronto 7
9 Toronto 5 at Minnesota 7
13 Toronto 0 at Los Angeles 4 [Vachon]
15 Toronto 5 at California 3
16 Toronto 2 at Vancouver 5
20 Pittsburgh 8 at Toronto 5
22 Toronto 0 at Islanders 6 [B. Smith]
23 Flyers 6 at Toronto 3
25 St. Louis 2 at Toronto 2
    (from October 29)
27 Toronto 1 at Rangers 4
30 Washington 1 at Toronto 7

December

1 Toronto at Detroit (postponed because
   of snowstorm to February 9)
4 Toronto 2 at Pittsburgh 4
   (Arnason 19:57 en)
5 Toronto 3 at Islanders 3
7 Detroit 3 at Toronto 3
8 Toronto 4 at Chicago 1
   (Stoughton 19:21 en)
11 Los Angeles 4 at Toronto 1
14 Atlanta 2 at Toronto 4
15 Toronto 1 at Washington 3
18 Pittsburgh 4 at Toronto 6
19 Toronto 1 at Flyers 5
21 Boston 4 at Toronto 8
22 Toronto 0 at Chicago 3 [Esposito]
28 Islanders 1 at Toronto 3
30 Toronto 5 at Pittsburgh 7

January

1 California 3 at Toronto 3
4 Chicago 3 at Toronto 6
   (Thompson 19:18 en)
5 Toronto 1 at Detroit 0
   (McDonald 10:43 2nd) [Favell]

7 Toronto 3 at Islanders 5
8 Vancouver 4 at Toronto 6
11 Los Angeles 7 at Toronto 5
   (St. Marseille 19:59 en)
12 Islanders 3 at Toronto 4
15 Toronto 4 at St. Louis 1
   (McDonald 19:52 en)
18 Toronto 5 at Canadiens 3
   (Flett 19:28 en)
19 Toronto 3 at Boston 6
23 Toronto 0 at Los Angeles 8 [Vachon]
24 Toronto 1 at California 6
26 Toronto 4 at Vancouver 6
   (afternoon game)
29 California 2 at Toronto 4
30 Toronto 1 at Flyers 3

February
1 Boston 2 at Toronto 3
4 Toronto 5 at St. Louis 3
6 Toronto 2 at Kansas City 3
8 St. Louis 3 at Toronto 3
9 Toronto 3 at Detroit 5
   (from December 1)
12 Canadiens 2 at Toronto 2
15 Pittsburgh 8 at Toronto 3
16 Toronto 5 at Rangers 5
19 Toronto 3 at California 3
22 Rangers 2 at Toronto 5
23 Toronto 1 at Buffalo 4
25 Toronto 9 at Minnesota 2
26 Kansas City 2 at Toronto 4

March
1 Washington 4 at Toronto 5
2 Toronto 5 at Detroit 4
5 Detroit 3 at Toronto 4
8 Minnesota 3 at Toronto 5
9 Toronto 4 at Washington 2
12 Canadiens 3 at Toronto 3
15 Flyers 4 at Toronto 4
16 Buffalo 11 at Toronto 3
19 Toronto 7 at Atlanta 8 (Ecclestone 19:09
   en) (Salming 19:40 with goalie out)
22 Toronto 6 at Canadiens 4
24 California 3 at Toronto 5
   (Keon 19:57 en)
26 Toronto 2 at Kansas City 2
29 Boston 1 at Toronto 1
30 Toronto 5 at Buffalo 4

April
2 Atlanta 3 at Toronto 0 [Bouchard]
5 Buffalo 4 at Toronto 2
6 Boston 4 at Toronto 4

1975–1976
October
11 Chicago 1 at Toronto 2 (The Hon.
   Pauline McGibbon, first female lieutenant-governor of Ontario, present at
   opening ceremonies)
12 Toronto 3 at Buffalo 8
15 Pittsburgh 8 at Toronto 4
18 Rangers 1 at Toronto 4
19 Toronto 0 at Boston 3 [Gilbert]
22 Vancouver 2 at Toronto 3
24 Toronto 6 at Washington 3
   (Ashby 19:58 en)
25 California 2 at Toronto 2
29 Buffalo 2 at Toronto 3
30 Toronto 2 at Flyers 6

November
1 Kansas City 0 at Toronto 3 [Thomas]
5 Detroit 3 at Toronto 7
7 Toronto 3 at Kansas City 3
8 Toronto 3 at St. Louis 3
11 Toronto 2 at Vancouver 3
14 Toronto 4 at California 2
   (Neely 19:06 en)
15 Toronto 1 at Los Angeles 1
18 Washington 2 at Toronto 4
22 Canadiens 4 at Toronto 2
   (Wilson 19:49 en)
23 Toronto 3 at Boston 3
26 Toronto 4 at Chicago 4
28 Toronto 3 at Atlanta 6
29 Flyers 1 at Toronto 1

December
3 Toronto 1 at Minnesota 3
6 Boston 4 at Toronto 2
7 Toronto 3 at Pittsburgh 6
10 Toronto 3 at Canadiens 3
13 Islanders 5 at Toronto 3
14 Toronto 6 at Rangers 1
17 St. Louis 2 at Toronto 6
18 Toronto 2 at Islanders 4
20 Kansas City 1 at Toronto 5

22 Los Angeles 3 at Toronto 4
27 Chicago 4 at Toronto 1
29 Atlanta 2 at Toronto 6
31 California at Toronto
    (postponed to January 1)

January
1 California 1 at Toronto 5
   (from December 31)
   (afternoon game)
3 Detroit 1 at Toronto 0
   (McKechnie 17:51 2nd) [Rutherford]
4 Toronto 8 at Rangers 6
7 Flyers 7 at Toronto 3
8 Toronto 5 at Islanders 3
10 Los Angeles 3 at Toronto 4
11 Toronto 0 at Canadiens 2 [Dryden]
14 Toronto 6 at Minnesota 5
15 Toronto 6 at Kansas City 4
17 Toronto 4 at Detroit 4
22 Toronto 3 at Los Angeles 6
   (Murphy 19:35 en)
24 Toronto 5 at Vancouver 5
25 Toronto 3 at California 5
28 Islanders 3 at Toronto 2
31 Rangers 4 at Toronto 6

February
1 Toronto 1 at Pittsburgh 7
   (afternoon game)
4 Washington 4 at Toronto 4
7 Boston 4 at Toronto 11
8 Minnesota 1 at Toronto 4
11 Toronto 2 at Atlanta 5 (Bennett 19:17
    en/Ecclestone 19:47 en)
14 Vancouver 4 at Toronto 3
16 Toronto 5 at Washington 1
18 Canadiens 7 at Toronto 5
19 Toronto 5 at Pittsburgh 7
21 Buffalo 4 at Toronto 6
    (Thompson 19:40 en)
23 Atlanta 1 at Toronto 7
25 Detroit 0 at Toronto 8 [Thomas]
26 Toronto 2 at Buffalo 5
28 California 2 at Toronto 4

March
1 Minnesota 2 at Toronto 4
3 Toronto 4 at St. Louis 1

6 Toronto 4 at Los Angeles 1
7 Toronto 7 at California 7
10 St. Louis 2 at Toronto 2
11 Toronto 2 at Boston 6
13 Islanders 2 at Toronto 2
17 Toronto 5 at Chicago 6
20 Washington 3 at Toronto 7
21 Toronto 2 at Philadelphia 4
    (Barber 19:59 en)
24 Toronto 2 at Canadiens 1
27 Buffalo 4 at Toronto 2 (Martin 19:36 en)
29 Pittsburgh 4 at Toronto 5
31 Toronto 4 at Detroit 4

April
3 Boston 4 at Toronto 2
4 Toronto 2 at Buffalo 5

1976–1977
October
5 Toronto 2 at Colorado 4
9 Boston 5 at Toronto 7 (McDonald 18:54
   en) (Joe Primeau dropped first puck)
13 Los Angeles 4 at Toronto 4
15 Toronto 3 at Boston 5
16 Flyers 5 at Toronto 5
20 Pittsburgh 4 at Toronto 4
21 Toronto 3 at Canadiens 5
    (Lemaire 19:36 en)
23 Islanders 5 at Toronto 2
27 Minnesota 5 at Toronto 3
28 Toronto 3 at Detroit 1
30 Toronto 5 at Minnesota 1

November
1 Toronto 6 at Cleveland 3
3 St. Louis 6 at Toronto 2
5 Toronto 4 at Atlanta 2
6 Toronto 2 at St. Louis 3
10 Toronto 2 at Los Angeles 2
13 Toronto 3 at Vancouver 0 [Palmateer]
17 Canadiens 0 at Toronto 1
    (McDonald 8:26 1st) [Palmateer]
20 Minnesota 3 at Toronto 8
21 Toronto 5 at Canadiens 9
24 Toronto 3 at Detroit 4
27 Boston 2 at Toronto 4
28 Cleveland 1 at Toronto 5
30 Toronto 4 at Islanders 2

December

1   Los Angeles 3 at Toronto 6
4   Chicago 2 at Toronto 2
5   Toronto 5 at Rangers 5
8   Vancouver 4 at Toronto 3
11 Rangers 1 at Toronto 4
12 Toronto 4 at Flyers 7
15 St. Louis 1 at Toronto 4
17 Toronto 2 at Washington 3
18 Colorado 2 at Toronto 4
20 Atlanta 2 at Toronto 6
22 Pittsburgh 5 at Toronto 2
23 Toronto 2 at Buffalo 4
    (Ramsay 19:04 en)
26 Toronto 2 at Pittsburgh 4
29 Toronto 6 at Cleveland 2

January

1   Washington 1 at Toronto 3
2   Toronto 4 at Chicago 6
5   Colorado 4 at Toronto 6
    (McDonald 19:51 en)
8   Buffalo 4 at Toronto 2
    (Martin 19:29 en)
11 Toronto 2 at Pittsburgh 0 [Thomas]
12 Los Angeles 2 at Toronto 3
15 Chicago 4 at Toronto 1
18 Toronto 3 at Los Angeles 6
21 Toronto 3 at Vancouver 1
23 Toronto 5 at Minnesota 2
    (afternoon game)
27 Toronto 2 at Islanders 1
29 Toronto 3 at Boston 3 (afternoon game)
31 Toronto 3 at Atlanta 7

February

2   Detroit 1 at Toronto 9
5   Flyers 7 at Toronto 5
7   Toronto at Buffalo (postponed to
    February 14 due to snowstorm)
9   Atlanta 1 at Toronto 5
12 Washington 0 at Toronto 10 [Palmateer]
13 Toronto 3 at Rangers 8
14 Toronto 2 at Buffalo 7 (from February 7)
16 Toronto 5 at Cleveland 3
17 Toronto 2 at Detroit 2
19 Pittsburgh 6 at Toronto 6
20 Toronto 10 at Chicago 8
23 Rangers 5 at Toronto 4

25 Toronto 2 at Washington 4
26 Buffalo 6 at Toronto 5

March

2   Cleveland 4 at Toronto 1
5   Vancouver 4 at Toronto 4
7   Toronto 4 at Flyers 2
    (Turnbull 19:55 en)
9   Canadiens 2 at Toronto 2
12 Detroit 0 at Toronto 6 [Palmateer]
13 Toronto 1 at Buffalo 6
15 Toronto 4 at St. Louis 1
16 Toronto 4 at Colorado 4
19 Atlanta 4 at Toronto 5
21 Cleveland 7 at Toronto 2
23 Islanders 1 at Toronto 1
26 Boston 7 at Toronto 5 (Smith 19:29 en)
27 Toronto 4 at Washington 7
30 Toronto 3 at Canadiens 3

April

2   Buffalo 1 at Toronto 1
3   Toronto 4 at Boston 7 (Sheppard 19:21
    en/Marcotte 19:55 en)(Jean Ratelle
    scores 1,000th point)

1977–1978

October

13 Toronto 3 at Detroit 3
15 Buffalo 5 at Toronto 2 (Ramsay 19:56
    en)(Clarence Campbell, NHL president,
    dropped first puck)
19 Colorado 4 at Toronto 5
22 Flyers 1 at Toronto 6
23 Toronto 6 at Flyers 3
26 Canadiens 2 at Toronto 2
29 Detroit 4 at Toronto 7

November

2   Toronto 5 at Vancouver 1
3   Toronto 2 at Los Angeles 4
    (Murphy 19:45 en)
5   Toronto 5 at Colorado 2
9   Toronto 4 at Atlanta 0 [Palmateer]
11 Toronto 3 at Washington 1
12 Toronto 0 at Canadiens 5 [Dryden]
16 Washington 2 at Toronto 5
17 Toronto 2 at Buffalo 1

19 Boston 3 at Toronto 1
23 Toronto 3 at St. Louis 2
26 Washington 4 at Toronto 4
29 Cleveland 2 at Toronto 3
30 Toronto 3 at Cleveland 5

December
3 Detroit 2 at Toronto 4
4 Toronto 1 at Boston 3
7 Minnesota 3 at Toronto 6
9 Toronto 3 at Colorado 2
10 Toronto 3 at Los Angeles 0 [Palmateer]
14 Islanders 2 at Toronto 3
16 Toronto 8 at Minnesota 5
17 Chicago 1 at Toronto 7
19 St. Louis 4 at Toronto 4
21 Canadiens 3 at Toronto 2
23 Toronto 6 at Pittsburgh 2
26 Pittsburgh 5 at Toronto 4 (McDonald
   (T) tied game at 19:06 with goalie
   out/Chapman (P) scored winner at
   19:34)
28 Toronto 0 at Chicago 4 [Veisor]
30 Toronto 5 at Cleveland 0 [Palmateer]
31 Atlanta 3 at Toronto 0 [Belanger]

January
4 Colorado 0 at Toronto 5 [Palmateer]
5 Toronto 1 at Detroit 2
7 Vancouver 4 at Toronto 6
9 Atlanta 5 at Toronto 2
   (MacMillan 18:43 en)
11 Toronto 4 at Minnesota 3
13 Toronto 2 at Cleveland 5
   (MacAdam 19:45 en)
14 Chicago 3 at Toronto 3
17 Toronto 2 at St. Louis 2
19 Toronto 3 at Vancouver 3
21 Toronto 1 at Los Angeles 2
25 Toronto 4 at Rangers 3
26 Toronto 2 at Islanders 4
28 Toronto 7 at Atlanta 5 (Ellis 19:03 en)

February
1 Buffalo 2 at Toronto 2
4 Detroit 2 at Toronto 2
5 Toronto 3 at Boston 3
8 St. Louis 4 at Toronto 5
11 Rangers 2 at Toronto 3

13 Toronto 4 at Buffalo 2
   (Thompson 19:46 en)
15 Boston 4 at Toronto 2
18 Minnesota 4 at Toronto 5
22 Cleveland 3 at Toronto 5
25 Washington 0 at Toronto 4 [McRae]
26 Toronto 5 at Chicago 3 (Sittler 19:17 en)
   (Leafs wore their names on the back of
   their sweaters for the first time, but the
   lettering was the same colour as the blue
   sweater, thus making the names indis-
   tinguishable. Team owner Harold
   Ballard fined $10,000 by the NHL for
   the prank)
28 Toronto 3 at Islanders 4

March
1 Flyers 2 at Toronto 3
4 Vancouver 3 at Toronto 4
5 Toronto 4 at Rangers 1
8 Los Angeles 5 at Toronto 1
9 Toronto 1 at Canadiens 4
11 Cleveland 2 at Toronto 5
12 Toronto 7 at Pittsburgh 1
15 Toronto 5 at Washington 2
18 Pittsburgh 3 at Toronto 2
19 Toronto 4 at Boston 6
22 Islanders 6 at Toronto 2
23 Toronto 1 at Flyers 4
25 Rangers 5 at Toronto 2
27 Los Angeles 0 at Toronto 3 [Palmateer]
29 Toronto 4 at Atlanta 7

April
1 Buffalo 2 at Toronto 3
2 Toronto 3 at Pittsburgh 6
5 Canadiens 6 at Toronto 3
8 Boston 3 at Toronto 1 (Miller 19:54 en)
9 Toronto 1 at Buffalo 2

1978–1979
October
11 Toronto 3 at Pittsburgh 2
14 Islanders 7 at Toronto 10 (Whipper Billy
   Watson, former wrestling champion,
   present at opening ceremonies)
15 Toronto 2 at Boston 4
18 Buffalo 0 at Toronto 2 [Palmateer]

19 Toronto 0 at Buffalo 1
(Ramsay 9:57 1st) [Edwards]
21 Flyers 0 at Toronto 2 [Palmateer]
22 Toronto 2 at Rangers 5
25 Canadiens 4 at Toronto 4
26 Toronto 0 at Flyers 5 [Parent]
28 Boston 5 at Toronto 3

November

1 Toronto 4 at Los Angeles 2
3 Toronto 3 at Vancouver 1
4 Toronto 4 at Colorado 4
7 Toronto 5 at St. Louis 0 [Harrison]
8 Toronto 1 at Chicago 2
11 Toronto 2 at Canadiens 3
15 Buffalo 2 at Toronto 2
16 Toronto 6 at Boston 4
(Maloney 18:50 en)
18 St. Louis 1 at Toronto 3
21 Toronto 4 at Atlanta 3
22 Toronto 3 at Rangers 3
25 Colorado 6 at Toronto 3
(Pierce 19:41 en)
26 Pittsburgh 2 at Toronto 8
29 Toronto 5 at Minnesota 3

December

2 Rangers 2 at Toronto 5
3 Toronto 2 at Flyers 7
5 Boston 5 at Toronto 1
6 Toronto 4 at Pittsburgh 6
9 Islanders 3 at Toronto 2
10 Toronto 3 at Buffalo 5
13 Vancouver 1 at Toronto 5
16 Detroit 2 at Toronto 4
17 Toronto 6 at Washington 7
20 Minnesota 2 at Toronto 4
22 Toronto 1 at Atlanta 3
23 Toronto 6 at St. Louis 1
26 Toronto 1 at Islanders 5
27 Boston 1 at Toronto 1
30 Washington 5 at Toronto 5

January

3 Atlanta 4 at Toronto 1
6 Chicago 5 at Toronto 3
(Mikita 19:57 en)
8 Vancouver 5 at Toronto 1
10 Minnesota 2 at Toronto 2
13 Colorado 2 at Toronto 4

14 Toronto at Chicago (postponed until
February 12 due to snowstorm)
16 Toronto 3 at Colorado 2
19 Toronto 3 at Vancouver 3
20 Toronto 3 at Los Angeles 2
24 Toronto 2 at Minnesota 2
26 Toronto 2 at Atlanta 4
28 Toronto 2 at Washington 2
31 St. Louis 1 at Toronto 5

February

2 Canadiens 6 at Toronto 3
4 Toronto 4 at Minnesota 6
12 Toronto 5 at Chicago 2
(from January 14)
14 Flyers 2 at Toronto 2
17 Los Angeles 2 at Toronto 5
(McKechnie 19:27 en)
19 Toronto 6 at Detroit 2
21 Toronto 1 at Minnesota 5
24 Rangers 4 at Toronto 2
26 Toronto 1 at Buffalo 3
28 Atlanta 6 at Toronto 4

March

1 Toronto 1 at Canadiens 2
3 Flyers 3 at Toronto 4
4 Toronto 4 at Rangers 2
(Boutette 19:49 en)
7 Vancouver 0 at Toronto 2 [Palmateer]
10 Los Angeles 4 at Toronto 9
11 Pittsburgh 0 at Toronto 4 [Palmateer]
14 Buffalo 4 at Toronto 1
15 Toronto 2 at Islanders 6
(Potvin 19:46 en)
17 Minnesota 4 at Toronto 6
(Williams 19:39 en)
19 Toronto 3 at Boston 4
21 Detroit 4 at Toronto 2
24 Chicago 3 at Toronto 3
25 Toronto 1 at Detroit 2 (afternoon game)
28 Washington 2 at Toronto 6
31 Minnesota 2 at Toronto 6

April

1 Toronto 6 at Buffalo 3
4 Boston 3 at Toronto 3
7 Buffalo 2 at Toronto 6
8 Toronto 3 at Boston 6

1979–1980

October

10 Rangers 6 at Toronto 3 (Nilsson 19:39 en) (season opened by His Eminence G. Emmett Cardinal Carter)
13 Colorado 1 at Toronto 2
14 Toronto 3 at Flyers 4
17 Minnesota 2 at Toronto 6
19 Toronto 5 at Washington 3 (Sittler 19:08 en)
20 Vancouver 0 at Toronto 2 [Palmateer]
24 Toronto 1 at Vancouver 5
26 Toronto 2 at Colorado 2
27 Toronto 5 at Los Angeles 7 (Simmer 19:48 en)
31 Hartford 4 at Toronto 2

November

2 Toronto 3 at Hartford 5
3 Buffalo 4 at Toronto 3
7 Toronto 7 at St. Louis 4 (Williams 19:32 en)
10 Toronto 8 at Winnipeg 4
11 Toronto 6 at Edmonton 3 (Butler 19:26 en) (afternoon game)
14 St. Louis 2 at Toronto 7
17 Boston 2 at Toronto 0 (Marcotte 19:30 en) [Cheevers]
18 Toronto 2 at Quebec 4
21 Edmonton 4 at Toronto 4
24 Chicago 2 at Toronto 1
25 Toronto 4 at Rangers 3
27 Toronto 5 at Atlanta 3
28 Toronto 4 at Washington 2

December

1 Flyers 4 at Toronto 4
5 Canadiens 2 at Toronto 3
7 Islanders 6 at Toronto 1
12 Colorado 3 at Toronto 5
15 Atlanta 1 at Toronto 8
17 Toronto 1 at Minnesota 5
19 Los Angeles 4 at Toronto 4
20 Toronto 0 at Boston 10 [Cheevers]
22 Detroit 1 at Toronto 2
23 Toronto 4 at Canadiens 8
26 Washington 8 at Toronto 2
27 Toronto 3 at Buffalo 5 (Gare 19:12 en)
29 Winnipeg 1 at Toronto 6

January

2 Islanders 3 at Toronto 1
5 Quebec 7 at Toronto 3
7 Pittsburgh 5 at Toronto 9
9 Canadiens 5 at Toronto 3
12 Vancouver 4 at Toronto 6
16 Toronto 4 at Pittsburgh 6 (Lonsberry 19:28 en)
17 Toronto 6 at Islanders 9
19 Toronto 2 at Canadiens 7
22 Toronto 4 at Atlanta 2
24 Toronto 4 at Los Angeles 5
26 Toronto 3 at Edmonton 8
27 Toronto 5 at Vancouver 2
30 Detroit 4 at Toronto 6

February

2 Chicago 5 at Toronto 4
3 Toronto 2 at Chicago 4 (afternoon game)
7 Toronto 6 at Boston 8 (Redmond 19:50 en)
9 Los Angeles 7 at Toronto 2
10 Toronto 4 at Detroit 1
13 Pittsburgh 4 at Toronto 2
16 Hartford 3 at Toronto 5 (Butler 19:58 en)
17 Toronto 6 at Rangers 4 (Williams 19:57 en)
19 Toronto 6 at Islanders 4
20 Toronto 2 at Chicago 4
23 Toronto 9 at Winnipeg 3
26 Toronto 2 at St. Louis 5
27 Toronto 4 at Colorado 3

March

1 Flyers 3 at Toronto 3
2 Toronto 6 at Detroit 3 (Sittler 19:42 en)
5 Toronto 5 at Pittsburgh 3 (Sittler 19:37 en)
7 Quebec 2 at Toronto 3
9 Toronto 4 at Quebec 5
12 St. Louis 3 at Toronto 2 (a streaker interrupted play; the first such occurrence at Maple Leaf Gardens)
15 Rangers 8 at Toronto 4
17 Atlanta 5 at Toronto 1
19 Winnipeg 1 at Toronto 9
20 Toronto 3 at Flyers 0 [Palmateer]

22 Buffalo 5 at Toronto 1
24 Washington 1 at Toronto 6
25 Toronto 2 at Minnesota 7
29 Edmonton 8 at Toronto 5 (game inter-
    rupted when three mice were thrown
    onto the ice)

April

1 Toronto 5 at Hartford 4
2 Boston 5 at Toronto 2
5 Minnesota 1 at Toronto 2
6 Toronto 3 at Buffalo 7

1980–1981

October

11 Rangers 8 at Toronto 3 (Harold
    Adamson, former Toronto police chief,
    dropped first puck)
12 Toronto 4 at Flyers 2 (Paiement 19:46
    en) (Paiement's goal was the 100,000th
    goal scored in NHL history)
15 Detroit 4 at Toronto 6
18 Flyers 2 at Toronto 6
19 Toronto 4 at Buffalo 2
21 Pittsburgh 5 at Toronto 8
23 Toronto 5 at Calgary 4
25 Toronto 4 at Los Angeles 5
26 Toronto 5 at Vancouver 8
29 Toronto 4 at Edmonton 4

November

1 Colorado 5 at Toronto 4
5 Toronto 2 at Pittsburgh 1
8 Toronto 3 at Colorado 3
9 Toronto 7 at Winnipeg 4
12 Islanders 4 at Toronto 2
    (Bourne 19:20 en)
15 Edmonton 2 at Toronto 4
19 Canadiens 5 at Toronto 4
22 Los Angeles 5 at Toronto 2
    (Simmer 18:22 en)
23 Toronto 5 at Boston 5
26 St. Louis 6 at Toronto 4 (Patey 19:52 en)
28 Toronto 2 at Washington 6
29 Washington 7 at Toronto 3

December

3 Pittsburgh 4 at Toronto 4
6 Quebec 2 at Toronto 5
7 Toronto 4 at Quebec 4
10 Vancouver 8 at Toronto 5
    (Rota 19:11 en)
11 Toronto 2 at Canadiens 5
13 Buffalo 5 at Toronto 4
15 Toronto 6 at Minnesota 3
    (Vaive 19:37 en)
17 Minnesota 2 at Toronto 4
    (Ellis 19:10 en)
18 Toronto 3 at Detroit 5
    (Foligno 19:48 en)
20 Chicago 5 at Toronto 2
23 Hartford 7 at Toronto 2
27 Boston 6 at Toronto 3
28 Toronto 6 at Chicago 3
30 Toronto 3 at St. Louis 5

January

3 Toronto 1 at Edmonton 4
    (McCreary (T) hit Gretzky with
    devastating open-ice check)
4 Toronto 5 at Calgary 8
6 Toronto 3 at Islanders 6
    (Tonelli 19:18 en)
7 Winnipeg 8 at Toronto 2
10 Flyers 4 at Toronto 4
11 Toronto 5 at Rangers 3
14 Edmonton 7 at Toronto 4
17 Canadiens 5 at Toronto 6
18 Toronto 5 at Winnipeg 4
20 Toronto 2 at Vancouver 2
22 Toronto 3 at Los Angeles 3
24 Hartford 4 at Toronto 7
26 Detroit 4 at Toronto 2
28 Islanders 6 at Toronto 4
30 Toronto 5 at Hartford 5
31 Winnipeg 2 at Toronto 0 [Mattsson]

February

3 Toronto 3 at Detroit 5
5 Toronto 4 at St. Louis 8
8 Toronto 6 at Colorado 6
    (afternoon game)
12 Toronto 4 at Minnesota 3
14 Rangers 3 at Toronto 6

17 Toronto 8 at Islanders 5
    (Saganiuk 19:52 en)
18 Toronto 3 at Rangers 8
21 Minnesota 3 at Toronto 5
    (Paiement 19:23 en)
22 Toronto 7 at Chicago 4
    (T. Martin 19:41 en)
25 Colorado 5 at Toronto 9
28 Toronto 3 at Canadiens 5

March

2   Los Angeles 1 at Toronto 0
    (St. Laurent 10:33 2nd) [Lessard]
4   Vancouver 5 at Toronto 2
7   Calgary 6 at Toronto 4
8   Toronto 3 at Washington 7
11 Boston 4 at Toronto 4
14 Washington 3 at Toronto 5
    (Sittler 19:48 en)
15 Toronto 4 at Flyers 4
18 St. Louis 2 at Toronto 6
19 Toronto 4 at Buffalo 14
21 Buffalo 6 at Toronto 2
22 Toronto 3 at Hartford 3
25 Toronto 2 at Pittsburgh 5
26 Toronto 3 at Boston 2
28 Calgary 5 at Toronto 9

April

1   Chicago 2 at Toronto 2
4   Quebec 5 at Toronto 5
5   Toronto 4 at Quebec 2
    (Derlago 19:11 en)

1981–1982

October

6   Toronto 6 at Winnipeg 1
8   Toronto 3 at Minnesota 3
10 Chicago 8 at Toronto 9
14 Minnesota 2 at Toronto 1
17 Toronto 4 at Quebec 6
21 Colorado 4 at Toronto 4
23 Toronto 2 at Buffalo 6
24 Rangers 5 at Toronto 3
27 Toronto 5 at St. Louis 7
28 Toronto 5 at Pittsburgh 3
31 Winnipeg 6 at Toronto 5

November

1   Toronto 4 at Chicago 9
4   Toronto 4 at Edmonton 6
    (Gretzky 19:56 en)
6   Toronto 4 at Colorado 4
7   Toronto 9 at Los Angeles 4
11 Islanders 4 at Toronto 3
14 Flyers 0 at Toronto 4 [Tremblay]
18 Toronto 5 at Hartford 8
20 Toronto 3 at Pittsburgh 3
21 Boston 5 at Toronto 3
24 Toronto 3 at Flyers 6
25 Toronto 3 at Rangers 3
28 Buffalo 4 at Toronto 4
29 Toronto 6 at Detroit 3

December

2   Hartford 5 at Toronto 3
5   Washington 4 at Toronto 9
6   Toronto at Boston (postponed because
    of snowstorm to January 21)
9   Winnipeg 3 at Toronto 3
11 Toronto 2 at Washington 11
12 Canadiens 6 at Toronto 2
16 Toronto 6 at Vancouver 6
19 Toronto 8 at Winnipeg 4
20 Toronto 3 at Chicago 1
23 Pittsburgh 4 at Toronto 4
26 Detroit 3 at Toronto 8
27 Toronto 3 at Hartford 7
30 St. Louis 6 at Toronto 4
31 Toronto 5 at Detroit 2

January

2   Minnesota 6 at Toronto 2
6   Toronto 3 at Minnesota 3
7   Toronto 4 at Calgary 4
9   Los Angeles 3 at Toronto 5
    (Vaive 19:55 en)
11 Toronto 2 at Boston 5
13 Colorado 1 at Toronto 2
15 Toronto 2 at Buffalo 8
16 Edmonton 1 at Toronto 7
18 Rangers 2 at Toronto 6
20 Calgary 4 at Toronto 4
21 Toronto 2 at Boston 4
    (rescheduled from December 6)
23 Toronto 2 at St. Louis 6
25 Minnesota 9 at Toronto 2

27 Winnipeg 4 at Toronto 3
30 Quebec 2 at Toronto 2
31 Toronto 5 at Chicago 2 (Vaive 19:04 en)

February
3 Toronto 1 at Vancouver 3
   (Williams 19:55 en)
6 Toronto 1 at Edmonton 5
7 Toronto 2 at Calgary 8
10 Vancouver 4 at Toronto 1
13 Chicago 6 at Toronto 4
   (Secord 19:35 en)
15 Minnesota 3 at Toronto 3
17 Detroit 3 at Toronto 3
18 Toronto 3 at Detroit 4
20 St. Louis 5 at Toronto 8
23 Toronto 2 at St. Louis 3
24 Toronto 5 at Minnesota 7
27 Toronto 3 at Canadiens 3

March
1 Islanders 9 at Toronto 5
3 Los Angeles 4 at Toronto 1
   (Kelly 19:53 en)
4 Toronto 1 at Islanders 10
6 Canadiens 6 at Toronto 1
10 Chicago 7 at Toronto 6
13 Winnipeg 10 at Toronto 2
17 Quebec 3 at Toronto 6
20 Toronto 0 at Winnipeg 7 [Staniowski]
22 Chicago 5 at Toronto 8 (Vaive 18:59 en)
24 St. Louis 3 at Toronto 4
27 Detroit 2 at Toronto 1
28 Toronto 4 at Detroit 6
30 Toronto 3 at St. Louis 5

April
3 Washington 6 at Toronto 4
4 Toronto 1 at Flyers 7

1982–1983
October
6 Toronto 3 at Chicago 3
7 Toronto 2 at St. Louis 3
9 New Jersey 5 at Toronto 5
13 Washington 5 at Toronto 3
14 Toronto 2 at Minnesota 6
16 Chicago 3 at Toronto 2

20 Minnesota 2 at Toronto 5
23 Calgary 5 at Toronto 5
26 Toronto 4 at Quebec 9
27 Boston 1 at Toronto 4 (Korn 19:15 en)
30 Buffalo 3 at Toronto 3

November
3 Toronto 2 at Los Angeles 6
6 Toronto 3 at St. Louis 3
7 Toronto 3 at Chicago 7
10 Detroit 2 at Toronto 8
13 Minnesota 3 at Toronto 4
17 Toronto 1 at Rangers 6
20 Rangers 6 at Toronto 3
24 Toronto 3 at Pittsburgh 4
26 Toronto 3 at Washington 5
27 Winnipeg 6 at Toronto 3
   (Deblois 19:32 en)

December
1 Toronto 3 at New Jersey 7
4 Islanders 1 at Toronto 4
5 Toronto 5 at Rangers 6
7 Toronto 3 at Islanders 6
8 Vancouver 7 at Toronto 3
11 Detroit 6 at Toronto 2
14 Toronto 4 at Quebec 4
15 St. Louis 4 at Toronto 2
18 Chicago 8 at Toronto 5
22 Toronto 3 at Chicago 4
23 Toronto 3 at St. Louis 7
28 Toronto 4 at Canadiens 4
29 Canadiens 5 at Toronto 6

January
1 Hartford 5 at Toronto 7
   (Poddubny 19:15 en)
2 Detroit 3 at Toronto 6
5 Toronto 4 at New Jersey 4
6 Toronto 3 at Washington 1
8 Los Angeles 5 at Toronto 7
12 Boston 6 at Toronto 4
   (Pederson 19:47 en)
13 Toronto 1 at Minnesota 2
15 Toronto 3 at Detroit 4
17 St. Louis 4 at Toronto 4
19 Toronto 3 at Winnipeg 6
22 Chicago 3 at Toronto 2
24 Pittsburgh 2 at Toronto 8

26 Toronto 6 at Edmonton 6
27 Toronto 1 at Calgary 3
29 Buffalo 3 at Toronto 5
    (T. Martin 19:59 en)
31 Minnesota 4 at Toronto 2

February

2 Hartford 1 at Toronto 7
5 Vancouver 4 at Toronto 6
6 Toronto 0 at Detroit 3 [Micalef]
13 Toronto 3 at Hartford 5
16 St. Louis 3 at Toronto 6
17 Toronto 6 at St. Louis 3
    (Harris 18:39 en)
19 Calgary 3 at Toronto 5 (Vaive 19:13 en)
21 Pittsburgh 2 at Toronto 4
23 Toronto 3 at Minnesota 2
25 Toronto 4 at Vancouver 1
    (Terrion 18:47 en)
26 Toronto 2 at Los Angeles 6
28 Toronto 3 at Boston 6

March

2 Flyers 2 at Toronto 2
3 Toronto 1 at Islanders 5
5 Edmonton 6 at Toronto 3
8 Toronto 3 at Canadiens 3
9 St. Louis 2 at Toronto 5
    (Salming 19:01 en)
12 Chicago 2 at Toronto 4
13 Toronto 5 at Detroit 2
16 Detroit 4 at Toronto 3
18 Toronto 3 at Winnipeg 7
20 Toronto 3 at Chicago 7
21 Edmonton 4 at Toronto 1
    (Messier 19:28 en)
23 Minnesota 3 at Toronto 6
24 Toronto 4 at Flyers 7
26 Quebec 1 at Toronto 2
29 Toronto 4 at Minnesota 2
    (T. Martin 19:42 en)
30 Toronto 4 at Detroit 2

April

2 Flyers 6 at Toronto 3
3 Toronto 4 at Buffalo 3

1983–1984

October

5 Toronto 4 at Edmonton 5
8 Toronto 6 at Los Angeles 3
    (Terrion 19:10 en/Vaive 19:50 en)
9 Toronto 4 at Vancouver 7
12 Buffalo 4 at Toronto 4 (5:00 OT)
15 Chicago 8 at Toronto 10
16 Toronto 4 at New Jersey 1
19 Quebec 8 at Toronto 1
22 Canadiens 3 at Toronto 5
23 Toronto 5 at Flyers 8
26 Edmonton 3 at Toronto 8
28 Toronto 5 at Rangers 3 (Gavin 19:37 en)
29 Los Angeles 5 at Toronto 5 (5:00 OT)

November

2 Toronto 5 at Minnesota 8
4 Toronto 2 at Winnipeg 8
5 Toronto 3 at Calgary 5
    (Hindmarch 19:48 en)
9 New Jersey 1 at Toronto 2
11 Toronto 1 at Buffalo 3
12 Flyers 5 at Toronto 3
16 Toronto 3 at Pittsburgh 2
17 Toronto 1 at Boston 4
19 Detroit 4 at Toronto 5
22 Toronto 4 at St. Louis 7
    (Hickey 19:50 en)
23 Toronto 6 at Minnesota 4
26 Minnesota 7 at Toronto 6
    (Broten 1:42 OT)
30 Toronto 5 at Detroit 3

December

3 Vancouver 5 at Toronto 5 (5:00 OT)
7 St. Louis 4 at Toronto 3
8 Toronto 8 at Hartford 6
10 Calgary 3 at Toronto 3 (5:00 OT)
14 Winnipeg 8 at Toronto 4
17 Washington 3 at Toronto 1
    (Gustafson 19:32 en)
18 Pittsburgh 3 at Toronto 3 (5:00 OT)
21 St. Louis 4 at Toronto 5
23 Toronto 2 at Detroit 9
26 Detroit 2 at Toronto 6
28 Toronto 6 at Minnesota 8
29 Toronto 1 at St. Louis 3

31 Los Angeles 3 at Toronto 5
(T. Martin 19:17 en)

January

3 Toronto 3 at St. Louis 8
4 Toronto 1 at Chicago 5
7 Toronto 2 at Quebec 4
(Paiement 19:03 en)
8 St. Louis 5 at Toronto 2
11 Canadiens 6 at Toronto 4
(Carbonneau 19:53 en)
12 Toronto 4 at Minnesota 5
(McCarthy :35 OT)
14 Chicago 2 at Toronto 2 (5:00 OT)
18 Minnesota 4 at Toronto 9
21 Rangers 6 at Toronto 3
23 Chicago 6 at Toronto 2
24 Toronto 3 at St. Louis 6

27 Toronto 1 at Washington 6
28 Washington 8 at Toronto 0 [Riggin]

February

1 Toronto 2 at Chicago 7
4 Toronto 6 at Detroit 3 (Derlago 19:09
en/Derlago 19:52 en)
5 Toronto 0 at Flyers 7 [Froese]
8 Boston 4 at Toronto 6
9 Toronto 6 at Boston 3
11 Quebec 2 at Toronto 5
13 Islanders 1 at Toronto 3
15 Minnesota 3 at Toronto 1
18 Hartford 8 at Toronto 2
19 Detroit 6 at Toronto 2
21 Toronto 2 at Calgary 2 (5:00 OT)
25 Toronto 3 at Edmonton 8
26 Toronto 4 at Vancouver 4 (5:00 OT)

Borje Salming

29 Rangers 1 at Toronto 3
(Derlago 19:34 en)

March

3   Islanders 11 at Toronto 6
4   Toronto 4 at Chicago 5
7   New Jersey 4 at Toronto 8
8   Toronto 5 at Islanders 9
10 Detroit 3 at Toronto 4 (Gavin :29 OT)
12 Winnipeg 8 at Toronto 7
(MacLean 3:12 OT)
14 Minnesota 3 at Toronto 3 (5:00 OT)
15 Toronto 3 at Hartford 5
17 Toronto 1 at Canadiens 6
21 Toronto 1 at Pittsburgh 3
24 Chicago 3 at Toronto 7
25 Toronto 4 at Chicago 5
28 Toronto 2 at Detroit 4 (Gare 19:14 en)
31 St. Louis 4 at Toronto 6

April

1   Toronto 2 at Buffalo 4

1984–1985

October

11 Toronto 1 at Minnesota 0
(Frycer 2:51 OT) [Bester]
13 Buffalo 3 at Toronto 4 (Benning 2:41 OT)
14 Toronto 2 at Winnipeg 5
(Arniel 19:22 en)
17 Hartford 5 at Toronto 3
19 Toronto 1 at New Jersey 4
20 Quebec 12 at Toronto 3
24 Detroit 1 at Toronto 6
26 Toronto 2 at Quebec 2 (5:00 OT)
27 Calgary 5 at Toronto 3
31 Toronto 5 at St. Louis 6
(Brian Sutter 1:08 OT)

November

3   Toronto 0 at Los Angeles 7 [Janecyk]
5   Toronto 3 at Minnesota 5
(Payne 19:43 en)
7   Vancouver 4 at Toronto 4 (5:00 OT)
10 Chicago 4 at Toronto 4 (5:00 OT)
11 Minnesota 7 at Toronto 6
14 Los Angeles 4 at Toronto 3

17 Winnipeg 5 at Toronto 3
(Picard 18:59 en)
19 Toronto 6 at Canadiens 4
(Derlago 18:51 en)
21 Toronto 1 at Minnesota 7
23 Toronto 5 at Detroit 6
24 Minnesota 4 at Toronto 2
27 Edmonton 7 at Toronto 1
30 Toronto 3 at Rangers 3 (5:00 OT)

December

1   Rangers 4 at Toronto 1
4   Toronto 6 at Detroit 7
5   Detroit 4 at Toronto 2
8   Toronto 3 at St. Louis 3 (5:00 OT)
9   Toronto 2 at Chicago 7
12 Flyers 3 at Toronto 6
14 Toronto 4 at Winnipeg 6
15 Pittsburgh 5 at Toronto 2
17 St. Louis 3 at Toronto 2
21 Toronto 3 at Chicago 4
22 Boston 4 at Toronto 6
26 Toronto 0 at Buffalo 6 [Barrasso]
27 Toronto 1 at New Jersey 4
29 Chicago 5 at Toronto 4

January

2   Pittsburgh 2 at Toronto 1
5   Vancouver 4 at Toronto 1
7   Hartford 7 at Toronto 4
9   Boston 5 at Toronto 3
13 Toronto 5 at Vancouver 3
16 Toronto 4 at Los Angeles 3
19 St. Louis 1 at Toronto 6
22 Toronto 2 at Quebec 2 (5:00 OT)
24 Toronto 1 at Islanders 4
(Diduck 19:13 en)
26 Chicago 5 at Toronto 2
27 Toronto 6 at Chicago 2
30 Toronto 6 at Pittsburgh 5

February

1   Toronto 3 at Washington 3 (5:00 OT)
2   Minnesota 5 at Toronto 2
5   Washington 4 at Toronto 1
(Langway 19:58 en)
6   Toronto 2 at Chicago 3
9   Toronto 6 at Canadiens 2

10   Canadiens 2 at Toronto 3
     (Vaive 3:38 OT)
14   Toronto 3 at St. Louis 5
16   New Jersey 6 at Toronto 3
17   Toronto 5 at Hartford 4
     (Daoust 1:30 OT) (afternoon game)
19   Edmonton 9 at Toronto 4
21   Toronto 1 at Flyers 4
23   Toronto 4 at Detroit 2 (afternoon game)
25   Chicago 4 at Toronto 3
     (D. Wilson 3:46 OT)
27   Minnesota 1 at Toronto 6

     March
2   Islanders 2 at Toronto 4
     (Terrion 19:07 en)
5   Toronto 2 at St. Louis 7
6   Detroit 5 at Toronto 3 (Foster 19:14 en)
9   Toronto 2 at Islanders 4
     (Tonelli 18:46 en)
13   Calgary 5 at Toronto 3
     (Risebrough 19:49 en)
14   Toronto 0 at Washington 4 [Jensen]
16   Flyers 6 at Toronto 1
18   St. Louis 3 at Toronto 4
     (J. Anderson 1:45 OT)
20   Toronto 4 at Calgary 7
22   Toronto 3 at Edmonton 3 (5:00 OT)
24   Toronto 5 at Detroit 3
27   St. Louis 2 at Toronto 4
     (Derlago 18:50 en)
30   Detroit 9 at Toronto 3
31   Toronto 5 at Rangers 7

     April
3   Toronto 7 at Minnesota 9
6   Buffalo 5 at Toronto 2
     (Perreault 19:39 en)
7   Toronto 1 at Boston 5

1985–1986
October
10   Toronto 1 at Boston 3
12   Quebec 4 at Toronto 0 [Gosselin]
13   Toronto 5 at Chicago 1
16   Washington 6 at Toronto 5
     (Duchesne :47 OT)
19   Winnipeg 4 at Toronto 3

23   Pittsburgh 5 at Toronto 4
24   Toronto 4 at Pittsburgh 6
26   Minnesota 7 at Toronto 5
30   Toronto 3 at Vancouver 5

     November
2   Toronto 2 at Calgary 4
3   Toronto 1 at Edmonton 7
6   Islanders 5 at Toronto 4
8   Toronto 3 at Detroit 3 (5:00 OT)
9   St. Louis 2 at Toronto 2 (5:00 OT)
12   Toronto 3 at St. Louis 4
     (Mullen 2:57 OT)
14   Boston 6 at Toronto 6 (5:00 OT)
16   Chicago 4 at Toronto 6
17   Toronto 5 at Buffalo 3
20   Toronto 3 at Rangers 7
23   Detroit 3 at Toronto 9
26   Toronto 1 at St. Louis 5
27   Toronto 1 at Pittsburgh 7
30   Buffalo 2 at Toronto 3 (Thomas :26 OT)

     December
4   New Jersey 7 at Toronto 10
5   Toronto 6 at Flyers 3
7   Canadiens 6 at Toronto 3
10   Toronto 2 at Washington 3
11   St. Louis 4 at Toronto 6
14   Toronto 6 at Minnesota 6 (5:00 OT)
     (afternoon game)
15   Toronto 3 at Winnipeg 3 (5:00 OT)
18   Toronto 3 at Los Angeles 4
20   Toronto 3 at Vancouver 5
     (Smyl 18:44 en)
26   Toronto 5 at Detroit 4
28   Hartford 6 at Toronto 3

     January
1   Canadiens 2 at Toronto 3
4   Los Angeles 6 at Toronto 4
5   Detroit 6 at Toronto 5
8   Edmonton 9 at Toronto 11
10   Toronto 7 at Buffalo 9
11   Quebec 5 at Toronto 1
13   Detroit 4 at Toronto 7
15   Toronto 1 at St. Louis 10
18   Minnesota 5 at Toronto 2
19   Calgary 9 at Toronto 5
22   Rangers 4 at Toronto 2

23 Toronto 1 at Hartford 4
25 Toronto 2 at Canadiens 3
(B. Smith 3:38 OT)
28 Toronto 2 at Islanders 9
29 Washington 2 at Toronto 5

February
1 Chicago 7 at Toronto 4
2 Toronto 4 at Chicago 3
(afternoon game)
6 Toronto 7 at Minnesota 8
(Rouse 4:15 OT)
8 St. Louis 2 at Toronto 3
(Courtnall 3:32 OT)
11 Minnesota 4 at Toronto 2
(Acton 19:23 en)
13 Toronto 4 at Chicago 5 (Fraser 3:29 OT)
15 Chicago 3 at Toronto 4
16 Vancouver 4 at Toronto 4 (5:00 OT)
19 Toronto 5 at Edmonton 9
20 Toronto 7 at Calgary 6 (Fergus 1:41 OT)
23 Toronto 3 at Minnesota 4
(afternoon game)
25 Rangers 3 at Toronto 7
28 Toronto 7 at Detroit 3

March
1 Detroit 6 at Toronto 4
3 Winnipeg 1 at Toronto 6
5 Toronto 3 at Minnesota 5
6 Toronto 4 at Flyers 7 (Sinisalo 19:14 en)
8 Chicago 3 at Toronto 4
13 Toronto 7 at New Jersey 4
15 Flyers 6 at Toronto 5
(Crossman 2:43 OT)
17 Los Angeles 6 at Toronto 7
19 Toronto 2 at Quebec 5 (Gillis 19:52 en)
20 Islanders 7 at Toronto 1
22 New Jersey 6 at Toronto 3
26 Minnesota 6 at Toronto 1
29 St. Louis 1 at Toronto 4
30 Toronto 5 at Chicago 4 (Frycer 2:02 OT)

April
1 Toronto 2 at St. Louis 2 (5:00 OT)
3 Toronto 2 at Boston 4
5 Toronto 1 at Hartford 7
6 Toronto 2 at Detroit 4

1986–1987
October
9 Canadiens 4 at Toronto 7
(Fergus 19:41 en)
11 Buffalo 5 at Toronto 5 (5:00 OT)
14 St. Louis 1 at Toronto 1 (5:00 OT)
17 Toronto 3 at New Jersey 2
18 Chicago 2 at Toronto 3
22 Quebec 7 at Toronto 1
25 Toronto 3 at Quebec 4
26 Toronto 3 at Rangers 3 (5:00 OT)
28 Chicago 1 at Toronto 2
30 Hartford 2 at Toronto 6

November
1 Detroit 0 at Toronto 2 [Bester]
5 St. Louis 4 at Toronto 6
(Kotsopoulos 19:31 en)
6 Toronto 1 at Minnesota 4
(Bellows 19:36 en)
8 Vancouver 5 at Toronto 3
(Skriko 19:56 en)
12 Toronto 2 at St. Louis 4
15 Detroit 0 at Toronto 6 [Bester]
16 Toronto 7 at Chicago 3
19 Flyers 2 at Toronto 2 (5:00 OT)
20 Toronto 4 at Islanders 6
(Brent Sutter 19:22 en)
22 Toronto 1 at Flyers 6
24 Boston 3 at Toronto 2
26 Toronto 3 at Detroit 1
28 Toronto 3 at Minnesota 6
29 Minnesota 7 at Toronto 2

December
4 Toronto 3 at Los Angeles 4
7 Toronto 3 at St. Louis 5
10 Washington 2 at Toronto 8
12 Toronto 3 at Pittsburgh 8
13 Pittsburgh 2 at Toronto 3
(Thomas 4:36 OT)
17 Toronto 2 at New Jersey 3
(Sulliman :35 OT)
18 Minnesota 6 at Toronto 5
(Broten 2:10 OT)
20 Buffalo 4 at Toronto 5 (Thomas 4:55 OT)
23 Toronto 4 at Minnesota 3
(Vaive 4:02 OT)

26 Toronto 2 at Detroit 4
27 Detroit 5 at Toronto 5 (5:00 OT)
31 Winnipeg 1 at Toronto 6

January
3 New Jersey 2 at Toronto 7
4 Toronto 3 at Hartford 8
6 Toronto 3 at Detroit 1
(M. Ihnacak 19:48 en)
7 Toronto 4 at Chicago 6
(Savard 19:22 en)
10 Toronto 2 at Islanders 3
12 Toronto 1 at Canadiens 2
14 Minnesota 3 at Toronto 2
15 Toronto 3 at Detroit 1 (Frycer 19:35 en)
17 Edmonton 7 at Toronto 4
(Gretzky 18:43 en)
21 St. Louis 2 at Toronto 4
(P. Ihnacak 19:54 en)
23 Toronto 5 at Winnipeg 7
(Hamel 19:59 en)
24 Hartford 3 at Toronto 0 [Weeks]
26 Calgary 6 at Toronto 5
(Patterson 1:30 OT)
28 Toronto 0 at Chicago 5 [Sauve]
29 Toronto 2 at St. Louis 4
31 Detroit 4 at Toronto 2

February
2 Flyers 4 at Toronto 8
4 Los Angeles 4 at Toronto 5
7 Toronto 5 at Boston 8
8 Toronto 5 at Rangers 4
14 Boston 5 at Toronto 4
16 Toronto 1 at Los Angeles 1 (5:00 OT)
18 Toronto 2 at Edmonton 9
20 Toronto 2 at Calgary 7
22 Toronto 2 at Vancouver 3
25 Rangers 4 at Toronto 2
28 Vancouver 6 at Toronto 8

March
3 St. Louis 4 at Toronto 3
5 Pittsburgh 2 at Toronto 7
7 Islanders 2 at Toronto 7
9 Toronto 2 at St. Louis 3
(Paslawski 4:01 OT)
11 Toronto 4 at Minnesota 2
13 Toronto 2 at Washington 10

14 Calgary 4 at Toronto 6
18 Chicago 6 at Toronto 3
20 Toronto 4 at Quebec 5
21 Toronto 4 at Canadiens 9
24 Toronto 6 at Buffalo 5
25 Minnesota 6 at Toronto 2
28 Edmonton 2 at Toronto 4
29 Toronto 6 at Winnipeg 2
31 Toronto 2 at Washington 4

April
4 Chicago 1 at Toronto 3
5 Toronto 2 at Chicago 5

1987–1988
October
8 Toronto 7 at Chicago 5
10 New Jersey 2 at Toronto 5
14 Toronto 3 at Minnesota 4
16 Toronto 2 at Detroit 3
17 Detroit 4 at Toronto 7
21 Canadiens 10 at Toronto 3
24 Minnesota 7 at Toronto 4
28 Islanders 2 at Toronto 5
29 Toronto 4 at Pittsburgh 0 [Bester]
31 Chicago 5 at Toronto 6

November
4 Winnipeg 3 at Toronto 7
5 Toronto 7 at Boston 6
7 St. Louis 4 at Toronto 3
9 Toronto 1 at Canadiens 3
11 Boston 3 at Toronto 2
14 Toronto 6 at Flyers 0 [Wregget]
15 Toronto 4 at Buffalo 5
18 St. Louis 6 at Toronto 3
19 Toronto 3 at St. Louis 3 (5:00 OT)
21 Los Angeles 6 at Toronto 6 (5:00 OT)
24 Toronto 4 at Islanders 3
25 Toronto 3 at Rangers 5
28 Hartford 4 at Toronto 2

December
1 Toronto 2 at Minnesota 3
(Bellows 1:20 OT)
3 Toronto 3 at Calgary 5
5 Toronto 2 at Edmonton 5

 7 Detroit 4 at Toronto 5
    (Courtnall 2:21 OT)
12 Rangers 3 at Toronto 4
13 Toronto 1 at Chicago 5
15 Washington 3 at Toronto 5
    (Olczyk 19:51 en)
18 Toronto 2 at Washington 4
    (Christian 18:33 en)
19 Chicago 6 at Toronto 2
21 Minnesota 0 at Toronto 0 (5:00 OT)
    [Takko (M)/Bester (T)]
23 Toronto 5 at St. Louis 1
26 Canadiens 4 at Toronto 2
28 Washington 4 at Toronto 4 (5:00 OT)
30 Toronto 1 at Hartford 3

January
 2 Buffalo 6 at Toronto 4
 4 Vancouver 7 at Toronto 7 (5:00 OT)
 6 Minnesota 5 at Toronto 5 (5:00 OT)
    (Dino Ciccarelli attacked Leaf defence-
    man Luke Richardson with his stick. He
    was suspended ten games, fined $1,000,
    and later sentenced to one day in jail
    after being convicted on assault charges)
 8 Toronto 3 at Chicago 7
10 Toronto 3 at Winnipeg 4
13 Toronto 3 at Minnesota 3 (5:00 OT)
15 Toronto 3 at New Jersey 7
16 Pittsburgh 4 at Toronto 3
18 Toronto 3 at Detroit 4
21 Quebec 5 at Toronto 4
23 Chicago 3 at Toronto 2
25 Calgary 11 at Toronto 3
27 Los Angeles 2 at Toronto 5
    (Osborne 19:04 en/Leeman 19:44 en)
29 Toronto 3 at Detroit 3 (5:00 OT)
30 Detroit 5 at Toronto 5 (5:00 OT)

February
 1 St. Louis 5 at Toronto 4
 4 Toronto 1 at Flyers 6
 5 Toronto 2 at Buffalo 5
    (Ruuttu 19:12 en)
 7 Toronto 2 at Hartford 4
11 Islanders 3 at Toronto 4
13 Flyers 4 at Toronto 7 (Olczyk 19:19 en)
14 New Jersey 7 at Toronto 2
17 Toronto 4 at Edmonton 4 (5:00 OT)

19 Toronto 5 at Vancouver 0 [Wregget]
20 Toronto 0 at Los Angeles 3 [Melanson]
22 Toronto 2 at Minnesota 4
24 Minnesota 2 at Toronto 4
27 St. Louis 6 at Toronto 2
    (Borje Salming Night)

March
 2 Quebec 4 at Toronto 3
 3 Toronto 3 at Boston 5 (Neely 19:54 en)
 5 Winnipeg 10 at Toronto 1
 8 Toronto 2 at St. Louis 3
 9 Toronto 3 at Chicago 4
12 Chicago 4 at Toronto 6
15 Toronto 2 at Quebec 3
16 Toronto 2 at Pittsburgh 5
19 Rangers 4 at Toronto 3
22 Toronto 3 at Vancouver 5
24 Toronto 1 at Calgary 7
26 Toronto 2 at St. Louis 3
    (Paslawski 2:07 OT)
28 Edmonton 6 at Toronto 4
    (Gretzky 19:44 en)

April
 1 Toronto 3 at Detroit 7
 2 Detroit 3 at Toronto 5

1988–1989
October
 6 Toronto 1 at Boston 2
 8 Chicago 4 at Toronto 7
    (Hap Day dropped first puck)
 9 Toronto 8 at Chicago 4
12 St. Louis 4 at Toronto 2
14 Toronto 3 at Washington 1
15 Detroit 5 at Toronto 3
    (Yzerman 19:37 en)
17 Toronto 6 at Canadiens 2
19 Buffalo 2 at Toronto 4
    (Olczyk 19:52 en)
21 Toronto 4 at Detroit 2
22 Calgary 3 at Toronto 3 (5:00 OT)
25 Toronto 4 at Islanders 3
26 Toronto 3 at Minnesota 2
29 Toronto 2 at St. Louis 3

November

2 Boston 7 at Toronto 2
5 Los Angeles 6 at Toronto 4
   (Nicholls 19:46 en)
10 Toronto 1 at Pittsburgh 5
12 Edmonton 6 at Toronto 2
14 Minnesota 5 at Toronto 4
16 Pittsburgh 5 at Toronto 8
   (Laxdal 19:37 en)
18 Toronto 0 at Winnipeg 3 [Chevrier]
19 Toronto 1 at Edmonton 9
21 St. Louis 0 at Toronto 4 [Bester]
23 Chicago 3 at Toronto 4
25 Toronto 3 at Minnesota 5
26 Minnesota 6 at Toronto 3

December

1 Toronto 3 at Los Angeles 9
3 Toronto 0 at St. Louis 3
   (Tuttle 19:11 en) [Millen]
9 Toronto 3 at Detroit 4
10 Detroit 8 at Toronto 2
12 Calgary 4 at Toronto 4 (5:00 OT)
14 Edmonton 8 at Toronto 2
15 Toronto 3 at New Jersey 6
17 Flyers 7 at Toronto 1
19 St. Louis 3 at Toronto 4
21 Pittsburgh 6 at Toronto 1
23 Toronto 2 at Buffalo 5
26 Islanders 4 at Toronto 3
29 Toronto 6 at Quebec 5
31 Quebec 1 at Toronto 6

January

1 Toronto 3 at Chicago 3 (5:00 OT)
6 Toronto 0 at Washington 3 [Peeters]
7 Buffalo 6 at Toronto 1
9 Vancouver 0 at Toronto 3
   (Fergus 19:54 en) [Bester]
11 Washington 3 at Toronto 2
14 Canadiens 5 at Toronto 3
   (Walter 19:51 en)
16 Hartford 3 at Toronto 5
19 Minnesota 3 at Toronto 3 (5:00 OT)
21 Toronto 3 at Canadiens 4
25 Boston 2 at Toronto 1 (Brickley 1:57 OT)
27 Toronto 1 at Detroit 8
28 Rangers 1 at Toronto 1 (5:00 OT)
30 Toronto 1 at Chicago 7

February

2 Toronto 4 at Islanders 1
   (Laughlin 19:24 en)
4 Chicago 3 at Toronto 1
11 Flyers 3 at Toronto 4
13 Toronto 1 at New Jersey 8
15 Hartford 4 at Toronto 2
   (Tippett 19:42 en)
17 Toronto 10 at Rangers 6
18 New Jersey 3 at Toronto 5
20 Toronto 4 at Los Angeles 5
22 Toronto 4 at Calgary 3 (Leeman 4:11 OT)
23 Toronto 1 at Vancouver 2
   (Sandlak 4:42 OT)
25 Toronto 4 at Minnesota 2
27 St. Louis 7 at Toronto 5 (Vesey 19:26 en)

March

1 Toronto 4 at Rangers 7
4 Chicago 3 at Toronto 3 (5:00 OT)
5 Toronto 0 at Hartford 3 [Sidorkiewicz]
7 Toronto 6 at Quebec 4
9 Toronto 1 at St. Louis 4
11 Detroit 3 at Toronto 5
   (Osborne 19:43 en)
12 Toronto 7 at Winnipeg 9
14 Toronto 5 at Minnesota 3
18 Winnipeg 10 at Toronto 2
19 Toronto 6 at Flyers 8
22 Vancouver 3 at Toronto 5
24 Toronto 2 at Detroit 6
25 Detroit 5 at Toronto 6 (Olczyk 19:19 en/
   Kocur (D) 19:55 with extra attacker)
29 Minnesota 1 at Toronto 3

April

1 Toronto 3 at St. Louis 4 (G. Cavallini
   4:10 en OT—in an effort to catch
   Chicago in the standings for the final
   playoff spot, the Leafs pulled goalie
   Allan Bester during the 5-on-5 overtime,
   resulting in the first-ever empty-net goal
   in overtime)
2 Toronto 3 at Chicago 4 (T. Murray :48 OT)

1989–1990

October

5 Toronto 2 at Los Angeles 4
7 Toronto 8 at St. Louis 5

11 Buffalo 7 at Toronto 1
12 Toronto 6 at Chicago 9
14 Winnipeg 5 at Toronto 1
17 Toronto 5 at Pittsburgh 7 (Lemieux
    19:17 en/Iafrate (T) 19:27 with
    goalie out/Lemieux 19:47 en)
18 Vancouver 3 at Toronto 4
21 Washington 4 at Toronto 8
23 New Jersey 5 at Toronto 4
25 Toronto 8 at Pittsburgh 6
    (Franceschetti 19:34 en)
27 Toronto 5 at Buffalo 6
    (P. Turgeon 2:30 OT)
28 Detroit 4 at Toronto 6
31 Toronto 6 at Minnesota 4

November
3   Toronto 1 at Washington 2
4   Flyers 7 at Toronto 4
6   Minnesota 1 at Toronto 2
9   Toronto 4 at Flyers 1
11 Detroit 2 at Toronto 4
12 Toronto 3 at Minnesota 6
15 St. Louis 2 at Toronto 5
16 Toronto 2 at Islanders 6
18 Toronto 3 at Canadiens 4
    (Naslund 3:25 OT)
22 Toronto 3 at Minnesota 6
    (Gavin 19:35 en)
23 Toronto 0 at Boston 6 [Moog]
25 Rangers 4 at Toronto 7
29 Toronto 3 at Vancouver 2
    (Damphousse 3:48 OT)

December
2   Toronto 4 at Calgary 7
3   Toronto 3 at Edmonton 5
6   Toronto 4 at Chicago 6
    (Wilson 19:32 en)
7   Toronto 5 at St. Louis 2
    (Franceschetti 19:47 en)
9   Canadiens 4 at Toronto 7
11 St. Louis 1 at Toronto 3
    (Leeman 19:06 en)
13 Toronto 4 at Detroit 2
16 Minnesota 4 at Toronto 3
18 St. Louis 3 at Toronto 6
20 Toronto 2 at Detroit 4
22 Toronto 5 at Chicago 3
    (Leeman 19:37 en)

23 Chicago 7 at Toronto 5
26 Toronto 4 at Boston 6
27 Detroit 7 at Toronto 7 (5:00 OT)
30 Boston 6 at Toronto 7 (Clark 3:19 OT)

January
3   Quebec 4 at Toronto 5
6   Los Angeles 4 at Toronto 7
    (Franceschetti 18:28 en)
8   Washington 6 at Toronto 8
10 Islanders 3 at Toronto 1
13 Calgary 5 at Toronto 6
15 Chicago 6 at Toronto 7
18 Toronto 4 at St. Louis 1
24 Minnesota 3 at Toronto 7
26 Toronto 5 at New Jersey 1
27 Canadiens 5 at Toronto 3
31 Toronto 5 at Winnipeg 5 (5:00 OT)

February
2   Toronto 2 at Detroit 5
    (Yzerman 19:33 en)
3   Pittsburgh 4 at Toronto 8
6   Toronto 4 at St. Louis 6
7   St. Louis 1 at Toronto 7
10 Toronto 2 at Hartford 6
12 Los Angeles 3 at Toronto 5
    (Leeman 19:15 en)
14 Hartford 6 at Toronto 6 (5:00 OT)
15 Toronto 0 at Flyers 3
    (Tocchet 19:32 en) [Peeters]
17 New Jersey 4 at Toronto 5
22 Toronto 2 at Calgary 12
23 Toronto 6 at Edmonton 5
26 Toronto 2 at Vancouver 5
28 Quebec 4 at Toronto 5

March
2   Toronto 2 at Detroit 3
    (Yzerman 3:44 OT)
3   Detroit 5 at Toronto 2
8   Toronto 7 at Hartford 6
10 Edmonton 2 at Toronto 3
12 Minnesota 4 at Toronto 1
14 Rangers 8 at Toronto 2
16 Toronto 4 at Buffalo 3
17 Winnipeg 5 at Toronto 4
    (Taglianetti 4:52 OT)
19 Chicago 3 at Toronto 2

21 Toronto 5 at Rangers 5 (5:00 OT)
24 Toronto 4 at Quebec 3 (Osborne :49 OT)
26 Toronto 4 at Minnesota 5
28 Islanders 6 at Toronto 3
    (Don Maloney 18:52 en)
29 Toronto 2 at Chicago 4
31 Chicago 4 at Toronto 6

1990–1991

October

4   Toronto 1 at Winnipeg 7
6   Toronto 1 at Calgary 4
7   Toronto 2 at Edmonton 3
10 Quebec 8 at Toronto 5 (Sakic 19:18 en)
13 Detroit 3 at Toronto 3 (5:00 OT)
17 Hartford 3 at Toronto 1 (Cyr 19:18 en)
18 Toronto 0 at Chicago 3 [Belfour]
20 Chicago 2 at Toronto 6
22 Toronto 1 at Rangers 5
24 St. Louis 8 at Toronto 3
25 Toronto 5 at St. Louis 8
    (Bassen 19:24 en)
27 Buffalo 3 at Toronto 1
30 Minnesota 4 at Toronto 5

November

1   Toronto 4 at Detroit 5
3   Calgary 7 at Toronto 3
4   Flyers 7 at Toronto 1
6   Toronto 3 at Islanders 4
8   Vancouver 5 at Toronto 3
10 Chicago 5 at Toronto 1
12 Winnipeg 2 at Toronto 5
    (Reid 19:24 en)
14 Washington 3 at Toronto 5
17 Detroit 8 at Toronto 4
19 Boston 5 at Toronto 2
21 Toronto 3 at Washington 5
23 Toronto 1 at Flyers 4 (afternoon game)
24 Edmonton 4 at Toronto 1
    (Simpson 19:40 en)
27 Toronto 4 at St. Louis 3
    (Clark 3:58 OT)
29 Toronto 1 at Vancouver 2

December

1   Toronto 4 at Los Angeles 3
5   Minnesota 3 at Toronto 2

6   Toronto 2 at Minnesota 1
8   Chicago 2 at Toronto 1
12 Canadiens 1 at Toronto 4
15 St. Louis 4 at Toronto 2
18 Toronto 2 at Islanders 2 (5:00 OT)
19 Toronto 4 at Rangers 1
    (Deblois 19:52 en)
22 Toronto 5 at Washington 2
    (afternoon game)
23 Toronto 2 at New Jersey 4
27 St. Louis 4 at Toronto 6
29 Pittsburgh 3 at Toronto 6

January

3   Toronto 3 at Minnesota 3 (5:00 OT)
5   Los Angeles 4 at Toronto 2
8   Calgary 5 at Toronto 3
10 Toronto 2 at Chicago 7
12 Hartford 2 at Toronto 2 (5:00 OT)
14 Buffalo 9 at Toronto 3
17 Pittsburgh 6 at Toronto 5
    (Young 3:31 OT)
22 Toronto 4 at Quebec 4 (5:00 OT)
23 Toronto 3 at Canadiens 7
26 Toronto 1 at Chicago 5
28 Minnesota 0 at Toronto 4 [Ing]

February

1   Toronto 1 at Detroit 4
    (Ysebaert 19:55 en)
2   Detroit 5 at Toronto 2
4   St. Louis 5 at Toronto 6
    (Hannan 3:58 OT)
6   Toronto 5 at Winnipeg 5 (5:00 OT)
7   Toronto 2 at Minnesota 4
9   Islanders 2 at Toronto 3
13 Flyers 6 at Toronto 3
16 Edmonton 2 at Toronto 3
17 Toronto 3 at Buffalo 0 [Reese]
19 Toronto 2 at St. Louis 3
21 Toronto 4 at Pittsburgh 11
23 Toronto 3 at Canadiens 3 (5:00 OT)
25 Toronto 4 at Detroit 5 (Racine 1:26 OT)
27 New Jersey 3 at Toronto 7

March

2   Rangers 5 at Toronto 2
3   Toronto 4 at Hartford 4 (5:00 OT)
5   Boston 3 at Toronto 6

7   Vancouver 3 at Toronto 3 (5:00 OT)
9   Toronto 0 at Boston 2
    [Moog] (afternoon game)
12 Toronto 4 at Quebec 3
13 Toronto 2 at New Jersey 3
16 Minnesota 3 at Toronto 4 (Petit 2:44 OT)
17 Toronto 3 at Minnesota 4
20 Toronto 4 at Los Angeles 4 (5:00 OT)
22 Toronto 3 at Detroit 1
    (Damphousse 19:33 en)
23 Detroit 1 at Toronto 4 (Gill 19:47 en)
    (Leafs honour Gulf War veterans Master
    Corporal Don Andrea, Leading Seaman
    Gerry Ross, and Master Corporal
    Louise Williams)
26 Chicago 2 at Toronto 2 (5:00 OT)
28 Toronto 3 at Chicago 5
    (Goulet 19:52 en)
30 Toronto 2 at St. Louis 5 (Tilley 19:54 en)

1991–1992

October

3   Toronto 3 at Canadiens 4
5   Detroit 5 at Toronto 8
7   St. Louis 0 at Toronto 3
    (Loiselle 19:16 en) [Fuhr]
9   Washington 5 at Toronto 4
12 Vancouver 2 at Toronto 1
15 Toronto 1 at St. Louis 5
17 Toronto 4 at Calgary 6
19 Toronto 2 at Winnipeg 4
21 Toronto 1 at Vancouver 4
    (Valk 19:52 en)
25 Toronto 0 at Detroit 4 [Cheveldae]
26 Detroit 1 at Toronto 6
28 St. Louis 1 at Toronto 1 (5:00 OT)

November

1   Toronto 0 at Washington 4 [Liut]
2   Los Angeles 5 at Toronto 2
4   San Jose 1 at Toronto 4
6   Minnesota 3 at Toronto 4
8   Toronto 3 at Rangers 3 (5:00 OT)
9   Calgary 6 at Toronto 1
12 Toronto 0 at Minnesota 7 [Casey]
14 Toronto 0 at Chicago 3
    (Roenick 19:57 en) [Belfour]
16 Chicago 2 at Toronto 2 (5:00 OT)

17 Hartford 3 at Toronto 1
20 Toronto 2 at St. Louis 5
22 Toronto 3 at San Jose 1
26 Toronto 4 at Los Angeles 4 (5:00 OT)
29 Toronto 3 at Minnesota 2
30 Minnesota 4 at Toronto 3

December

4   Toronto 3 at Hartford 0
    (Zezel 19:58 en) [Reese]
7   Vancouver 3 at Toronto 6
9   Canadiens 4 at Toronto 1
    (Corson 19:37 en)
11 Islanders 5 at Toronto 4
12 Toronto 1 at Flyers 1 (5:00 OT)
14 Toronto 3 at Boston 4
18 Edmonton 7 at Toronto 5
20 Toronto 3 at Washington 4
21 Buffalo 4 at Toronto 1
23 Winnipeg 1 at Toronto 3
26 Toronto 1 at Pittsburgh 12
28 Detroit 5 at Toronto 4
30 Toronto 2 at Quebec 5
    (Paslawski 19:56 en)

January

3   Toronto 4 at Detroit 6
    (Ysebaert 19:24 en)
4   Chicago 4 at Toronto 2
6   St. Louis 2 at Toronto 3 (Ellett 4:51 OT)
9   Toronto 0 at Chicago 2 [Hasek]
11 Toronto 4 at New Jersey 3
16 Toronto 0 at Chicago 4 [Belfour]
22 Boston 5 at Toronto 2
    (Neely 18:26 en)
23 Toronto 4 at Islanders 3
25 Flyers 4 at Toronto 6 (Zezel 19:52 en)
29 Quebec 2 at Toronto 5

February

1   New Jersey 4 at Toronto 6
    (Clark 18:58 en)
3   Toronto 2 at Minnesota 4
    (Johnson 19:29 en)
5   Minnesota 2 at Toronto 3 (Clark :18 OT)
7   Toronto 4 at Detroit 3
8   Canadiens 4 at Toronto 6
11 Detroit 3 at Toronto 4
    (Bradley wins game at 19:58)

15 Winnipeg 3 at Toronto 1
16 Edmonton 5 at Toronto 7
    (Gilmour 18:45 en)
18 Toronto 1 at Pittsburgh 7
20 Toronto 2 at Detroit 3
22 Toronto 3 at St. Louis 4
25 New Jersey 5 at Toronto 5 (5:00 OT)
27 Toronto 2 at Boston 4
29 Chicago 5 at Toronto 6 (Clark 1:02 OT)

    March
1   Minnesota 2 at Toronto 6
4   Toronto 5 at Edmonton 2
5   Toronto 5 at Calgary 5 (5:00 OT)
8   Toronto 1 at San Jose 4
    (afternoon game)
9   Toronto 1 at Los Angeles 4
11 Toronto 3 at Minnesota 0 [Fuhr]
14 Pittsburgh 3 at Toronto 6
    (G. Anderson 19:18 en)
17 Quebec 3 at Toronto 4
    (G. Anderson 2:08 OT)
21 Chicago 3 at Toronto 1
    (Goulet 19:52 en)
23 St. Louis 2 at Toronto 3
25 Toronto 2 at Buffalo 5
    (Mogilny 19:53 en)
28 Toronto 3 at St. Louis 2
29 Toronto 1 at Chicago 5

    April
1   Islanders at Toronto
    (cancelled due to players' strike)
4   Rangers at Toronto
    (cancelled due to players' strike)
5   Toronto at Flyers
    (cancelled due to players' strike)
12 Islanders 6 at Toronto 2
    (make-up game for April 1)
13 Rangers 2 at Toronto 4
    (make-up game for April 4)
15 Toronto 2 at Flyers 6
    (make-up game for April 5)

1992–1993

To celebrate the NHL's 75th anniversary, all
Original Six teams wore their dark sweaters at
home in games against each other.

October
6   Washington 6 at Toronto 5
10 Toronto 2 at Calgary 3
11 Toronto 3 at Edmonton 3 (5:00 OT)
15 Tampa Bay 3 at Toronto 5
17 Chicago 3 at Toronto 4
18 Minnesota 5 at Toronto 1
20 Ottawa 3 at Toronto 5
    (Gilmour 19:39 en)
    (played at Hamilton)
22 Toronto 5 at Tampa Bay 2
24 San Jose 1 at Toronto 5
28 Buffalo 4 at Toronto 4 (5:00 OT)
30 Toronto 1 at Detroit 7
31 Detroit 1 at Toronto 3

November
5   Toronto 0 at Chicago 1
    [Belfour] (Ruuttu 7:38 2nd)
7   Pittsburgh 2 at Toronto 4
    (Clark 19:16 en)
9   Toronto 3 at Ottawa 1
14 Toronto 4 at Boston 1
16 St. Louis 2 at Toronto 2 (5:00 OT)
17 Toronto 1 at Quebec 3
    (played at Hamilton)
19 Toronto 2 at San Jose 0 [Fuhr]
21 Toronto 4 at Los Angeles 6
    (Granato 19:50 en)
24 Tampa Bay 3 at Toronto 2
26 Quebec 5 at Toronto 4 (Nolan :23 OT)
28 Los Angeles 2 at Toronto 3

December
1   Toronto 3 at New Jersey 8
3   Toronto 3 at Chicago 4
5   Chicago 2 at Toronto 2 (5:00 OT)
6   Toronto 0 at Rangers 6 [Vanbiesbrouck]
9   Detroit 3 at Toronto 5
11 Calgary 6 at Toronto 3
15 Toronto 5 at Minnesota 6
19 Ottawa 1 at Toronto 5
20 Toronto 4 at Buffalo 5
22 Toronto 4 at Detroit 4 (5:00 OT)
26 Detroit 5 at Toronto 1
27 Toronto 6 at St. Louis 3 (Ellett 18:33 en)
29 Toronto 3 at Islanders 2
31 Toronto 3 at Pittsburgh 3 (5:00 OT)

January

2 St. Louis 2 at Toronto 2 (5:00 OT)
4 Toronto 4 at Detroit 2
   (Osborne 19:57 en)
6 Vancouver 5 at Toronto 2
8 San Jose 1 at Toronto 5
9 Toronto 5 at Canadiens 4
11 Tampa Bay 2 at Toronto 4
13 St. Louis 3 at Toronto 4
16 Chicago 5 at Toronto 3
   (Larmer 19:41 en)
17 Toronto 3 at Chicago 5
19 Toronto 5 at St. Louis 1
21 Toronto 6 at Tampa Bay 1
23 Canadiens 0 at Toronto 4 [Potvin]
26 Minnesota 2 at Toronto 1
30 Rangers 1 at Toronto 3

February

1 Toronto 1 at St. Louis 1 (5:00 OT)
3 Islanders 3 at Toronto 2
9 Toronto 1 at Tampa Bay 3
   (Zamuner 19:31 en)
11 Vancouver 2 at Toronto 5
13 Minnesota 1 at Toronto 6
14 Toronto 6 at Minnesota 5
17 Calgary 2 at Toronto 4
19 Tampa Bay 1 at Toronto 4
20 Boston 4 at Toronto 4 (5:00 OT)
22 Toronto 8 at Vancouver 1
25 Toronto 5 at San Jose 0 [Puppa]
27 Toronto 5 at Los Angeles 2

March

3 Minnesota 1 at Toronto 3
5 Toronto 1 at Detroit 5
6 Winnipeg 2 at Toronto 4
9 Toronto 1 at Washington 3
   (Hatcher 19:58 en)
10 Hartford 3 at Toronto 5
12 Tampa Bay 2 at Toronto 8
15 Toronto 2 at Quebec 4
   (Cavallini 19:14 en)
18 Toronto 4 at Tampa Bay 2
20 Edmonton 2 at Toronto 4
23 Toronto 5 at Winnipeg 4
25 Toronto 3 at Minnesota 3 (5:00 OT)
27 Toronto 6 at Edmonton 2
28 Toronto 4 at Calgary 0 [Puppa]
31 Los Angeles 5 at Toronto 5 (5:00 OT)

April

1 Toronto at Philadelphia
   (postponed to April 4)
3 New Jersey 0 at Toronto 1
   (Gilmour 16:22 3rd) [Potvin]
4 Toronto 0 at Flyers 4 [Soderstrom]
8 Toronto 3 at Winnipeg 5
10 Flyers 4 at Toronto 0 [Soderstrom]
11 Toronto 4 at Hartford 2
13 St. Louis 1 at Toronto 2 (Zezel 1:46 OT)
15 Toronto 2 at Chicago 3

1993–1994

October

7 Dallas 3 at Toronto 6 (Clark 19:09 en)
9 Chicago 1 at Toronto 2
10 Toronto 5 at Flyers 4
13 Washington 1 at Toronto 7
15 Detroit 3 at Toronto 6
   (Gilmour 18:18 en)
16 Toronto 2 at Detroit 1
19 Hartford 2 at Toronto 7
21 Toronto 4 at Florida 3 (Pearson 2:17 OT)
23 Toronto 2 at Tampa Bay 0 [Potvin]
28 Toronto 4 at Chicago 2
30 Toronto 2 at Canadiens 5

November

1 Toronto 3 at Dallas 3 (5:00 OT)
3 Florida 3 at Toronto 6
4 Toronto 3 at Detroit 3 (5:00 OT)
6 Flyers 3 at Toronto 5
9 Toronto 2 at San Jose 2 (5:00 OT)
11 Toronto 2 at St. Louis 3
13 Chicago 3 at Toronto 2
15 Edmonton 5 at Toronto 5 (5:00 OT)
17 Toronto 4 at Anaheim 3
18 Toronto 3 at Los Angeles 2
20 Toronto 3 at Edmonton 2
22 Toronto 5 at Vancouver 2
   (Osborne 19:11 en)
24 Toronto 3 at Calgary 5 (Kisio 19:32 en)
27 Boston 2 at Toronto 4
29 Buffalo 3 at Toronto 0 [Hasek]

December

1 St. Louis 2 at Toronto 4
2 Toronto 5 at St. Louis 4
4 Rangers 4 at Toronto 3

8   Winnipeg 5 at Toronto 4
11 Calgary 1 at Toronto 3
    (Andreychuk 19:25 en)
12 Toronto 3 at Winnipeg 3 (5:00 OT)
15 Anaheim 1 at Toronto 0
    (Sweeney 6:15 3rd) [Hebert]
17 Toronto 2 at Islanders 6
18 Los Angeles 1 at Toronto 4
22 San Jose 2 at Toronto 2 (5:00 OT)
23 Toronto 2 at New Jersey 3
27 Toronto 2 at Chicago 5
29 Toronto 0 at Dallas 4 [Wakaluk]

January
1   Los Angeles 7 at Toronto 4
2   Toronto 3 at Buffalo 3 (5:00 OT)
4   Tampa Bay 1 at Toronto 0 (played at
    Hamilton) (Elyniuk 5:34 2nd) [Puppa]
6   Ottawa 3 at Toronto 6
8   Vancouver 3 at Toronto 5
10 Toronto 3 at Boston 0 [Potvin]
11 Toronto 2 at Washington 1
13 Dallas 3 at Toronto 4
    (G. Anderson 4:46 OT)
15 Toronto 5 at Winnipeg 1
18 Anaheim 3 at Toronto 3 (5:00 OT)
19 Toronto 3 at Hartford 3 (5:00 OT)
26 Islanders 3 at Toronto 4
29 Pittsburgh 4 at Toronto 4 (5:00 OT)

February
1   Toronto 4 at St. Louis 4 (5:00 OT)
5   Detroit 4 at Toronto 3
7   Tampa Bay 2 at Toronto 1
11 Toronto 3 at Winnipeg 1
12 Toronto 2 at Calgary 3
15 Detroit 4 at Toronto 5 (Clark 2:55 OT)
17 New Jersey 1 at Toronto 2
19 Edmonton 2 at Toronto 3
21 Toronto 6 at Los Angeles 4
    (Berg 19:54 en)
23 Toronto 3 at Edmonton 6
26 Canadiens 3 at Toronto 0 [Roy]
28 Toronto 4 at Ottawa 1

March
4   Toronto 6 at Detroit 5 (Clark :53 OT)
5   Toronto 1 at Quebec 4
7   St. Louis 3 at Toronto 2
9   Dallas 2 at Toronto 4

10 Toronto 4 at Pittsburgh 2
12 Winnipeg 1 at Toronto 3
16 Vancouver 4 at Toronto 1
    (Bure 19:24 en)
18 St. Louis 2 at Toronto 4
20 Calgary 6 at Toronto 3
    (Roberts 19:37 en)
23 Toronto 1 at Florida 1
    (5:00 OT) (played at Hamilton)
24 San Jose 2 at Toronto 1
26 Quebec 3 at Toronto 6 (Gartner 17:18 en)
28 Toronto 2 at Vancouver 3
    (Clark tied game at 19:33 with
    goalie out) (Craven 3:57 OT)
31 Toronto 3 at San Jose 5

April
2   Toronto 1 at Anaheim 3
5   Toronto 6 at Dallas 4
    (Osborne 18:54 en)
8   Toronto 3 at Rangers 5
10 Winnipeg 0 at Toronto 7 [Potvin]
12 Chicago 4 at Toronto 3
14 Toronto 6 at Chicago 4

1994–1995
An owners' lockout forced the 1994–95
season to be revised to a 48-game schedule.

January
20 Toronto 3 at Los Angeles 3 (5:00 OT)
21 Toronto 2 at San Jose 3
25 Vancouver 2 at Toronto 6
27 Toronto 1 at Chicago 4
28 Calgary 1 at Toronto 2
30 Toronto 2 at Dallas 1

February
1   Toronto 4 at Vancouver 4 (5:00 OT)
3   Toronto 3 at Edmonton 5
    (Corson 19:46 en)
4   Toronto 1 at Calgary 4 (Titov 19:55 en)
6   San Jose 3 at Toronto 7
8   Dallas 3 at Toronto 3 (5:00 OT) (Sundin
    tied game at 19:58 with goalie out)
10 Toronto 2 at Detroit 1
11 Los Angeles 5 at Toronto 2
    (Granato 19:29 en)
13 Chicago 2 at Toronto 4

15 Edmonton 4 at Toronto 1
18 St. Louis 1 at Toronto 3
20 Detroit 4 at Toronto 2
    (Ciccarelli 19:23 en)
22 Toronto 1 at Detroit 4
    (Johnson 19:38 en)
23 Anaheim 1 at Toronto 3
25 Winnipeg 2 at Toronto 5
    (Eastwood 18:39 en)
27 Toronto 2 at St. Louis 3

March

2 San Jose 4 at Toronto 3
4 Calgary 2 at Toronto 3
8 Dallas 2 at Toronto 3
11 Chicago 2 at Toronto 2 (5:00 OT)
13 Los Angeles 4 at Toronto 1
    (Gretzky 19:33 en)
15 Toronto 2 at San Jose 1
17 Toronto 3 at Anaheim 3 (5:00 OT)
18 Toronto 5 at Los Angeles 3
    (Sundin 19:26 en)
21 Toronto 1 at Vancouver 3
    (Ruuttu 19:59 en)
24 Winnipeg 2 at Toronto 3
25 Toronto 3 at Winnipeg 3 (5:00 OT)
27 Edmonton 3 at Toronto 4
31 Toronto 3 at Chicago 3 (5:00 OT)

April

3 Toronto 2 at St. Louis 5
    (Laperrière 19:14 en)
5 St. Louis 6 at Toronto 4
7 Detroit 4 at Toronto 2
8 Winnipeg 3 at Toronto 4
14 Dallas 1 at Toronto 2
15 Toronto 1 at Winnipeg 5
17 Toronto 3 at Chicago 1
    (Gartner 19:39 en)
19 Anaheim 2 at Toronto 3
21 St. Louis 3 at Toronto 1
22 Toronto 4 at Dallas 6
26 Vancouver 2 at Toronto 5
29 Toronto 2 at Calgary 2 (5:00 OT)

May

1 Toronto 6 at Edmonton 5
3 Toronto 1 at Anaheim 6

1995–1996

October

7 Toronto 3 at Pittsburgh 8
10 Islanders 3 at Toronto 7
14 Rangers 2 at Toronto 0
    [Richter] (Domi suspended eight
    games for punch on Samuelsson)
17 San Jose 2 at Toronto 7
20 Calgary 3 at Toronto 4 (Craig 1:31 OT)
21 Toronto 3 at Canadiens 4
    (Turgeon scored winner at 19:59)
24 Florida 6 at Toronto 1 (Bob Davidson
    presented with the Bickell Cup)
26 Toronto 2 at Chicago 1
28 Los Angeles 2 at Toronto 2 (5:00 OT)
29 Toronto 2 at Rangers 3

November

1 Toronto 4 at Winnipeg 2
3 Toronto 4 at Vancouver 4 (5:00 OT)
4 Toronto 3 at Edmonton 3 (5:00 OT)
7 Anaheim 3 at Toronto 6
    (Gilmour 19:42 en)
10 Washington 1 at Toronto 6
11 Toronto 3 at Boston 1 (Gartner 19:41 en)
14 Toronto 2 at Florida 5
16 Toronto 5 at Tampa Bay 4
    (Hogue :32 OT) (Hogue tied game
    at 19:05 with extra attacker)
18 Winnipeg 1 at Toronto 2
21 St. Louis 2 at Toronto 5
    (Clancy and Horton #7 become
    Honoured Numbers)
24 Hartford 4 at Toronto 0 [Reese]
25 Toronto 2 at St. Louis 2 (5:00 OT)
28 Toronto 3 at Winnipeg 4
30 Toronto 2 at Flyers 3

December

2 Anaheim 4 at Toronto 4 (5:00 OT)
5 Ottawa 1 at Toronto 4
7 Toronto 2 at New Jersey 1
9 Dallas 1 at Toronto 3
11 Colorado 5 at Toronto 1
14 Toronto 4 at San Jose 1
16 Toronto 6 at Los Angeles 3
    (Wood 19:11 en)
17 Toronto 3 at Anaheim 2
    (Andreychuk 2:05 OT)

20 Chicago 4 at Toronto 2
21 Toronto 3 at Chicago 3 (5:00 OT)
(Murphy tied game at 19:10 with
extra attacker)
23 Edmonton 1 at Toronto 6 (Gilmour
scored 1,000th point on a goal, but
video judge ruled the net was off before
the puck crossed the line. Minutes later,
he assisted on a Mats Sundin goal to
officially register his 1,000th)
27 Toronto 0 at Calgary 4 [Kidd]
29 Toronto 2 at Colorado 3 (coach Burns
missed 3rd period with bad flu)
30 Toronto 4 at St. Louis 3 (Sundin :06 OT)

January

1 Toronto 1 at Dallas 0 (afternoon game)
[Potvin] (Sundin 2:53 2nd)
3 Boston 4 at Toronto 4 (5:00 OT)
(Gilmour honoured for 1,000th point)
5 Toronto 1 at Buffalo 3
6 Colorado 2 at Toronto 5 (first 6:50
played without a whistle)
10 Los Angeles 4 at Toronto 5
11 Toronto 3 at Islanders 4
13 Vancouver 5 at Toronto 2
17 Winnipeg 4 at Toronto 2
24 Chicago 2 at Toronto 2 (5:00 OT)
27 Toronto 2 at Ottawa 2 (5:00 OT)
(Alfredsson tied game at 19:50 with
extra attacker)
30 Toronto 2 at Detroit 4
(Yzerman 18:59 en)
31 St. Louis 4 at Toronto 0 [Fuhr]
(MacInnis 19:06 en)

February

3 Canadiens 4 at Toronto 1
(Rucinsky 19:31 en)
5 Toronto 4 at San Jose 6
7 Toronto 2 at Anaheim 1
8 Toronto 3 at Los Angeles 4
10 Buffalo 2 at Toronto 2 (5:00 OT)
12 Pittsburgh 1 at Toronto 4
14 San Jose 3 at Toronto 4
16 Toronto 3 at Washington 4
18 Detroit 3 at Toronto 2 (afternoon game)
21 Tampa Bay 3 at Toronto 2
(Bellows 1:42 OT)

22 Toronto 3 at Detroit 5
24 Dallas 3 at Toronto 2
28 Toronto 3 at Winnipeg 4

March

2 Toronto 1 at Dallas 5
3 Toronto 0 at Colorado 4 [Roy]
6 New Jersey 2 at Toronto 2 (5:00 OT)
8 Toronto 4 at Hartford 7
9 Calgary 3 at Toronto 4
13 Winnipeg 3 at Toronto 3 (5:00 OT)
15 Dallas 0 at Toronto 3
(Gilmour 19:01 en) [Potvin]
17 Vancouver 2 at Toronto 4
(afternoon game)
19 Toronto 5 at Detroit 6
20 Detroit 4 at Toronto 3 (McCarty 2:41 OT)
23 Flyers 4 at Toronto 0 [Hextall]
25 Toronto 4 at Calgary 2
27 Toronto 6 at Vancouver 2
(Murphy scored 1,000th point)
30 Toronto 4 at Edmonton 3

April

3 Chicago 5 at Toronto 2
(Probert 18:53 en)
4 Toronto 3 at St. Louis 1
6 St. Louis 1 at Toronto 5
11 Toronto 2 at Chicago 5
13 Edmonton 3 at Toronto 6 (Gagner 19:51
en) (Murphy honoured for 1,000th
point and received Horton Trophy)

1996–1997

October

5 Anaheim 1 at Toronto 4
(opening attended by 28 members of
Canada's medal-winning team from
1996 Summer Olympics)
8 Edmonton 4 at Toronto 2
(Smyth 19:52 en)
12 Tampa Bay 7 at Toronto 4
(Gratton 19:59 en)
15 Chicago 3 at Toronto 1
(Amonte 19:17 en)
17 Toronto 1 at St. Louis 6
19 Toronto 0 at Dallas 2 [Moog]
22 San Jose 3 at Toronto 4

24 Toronto 2 at Boston 1
26 Phoenix 2 at Toronto 5 (Craig 19:53 en)
29 Los Angeles 5 at Toronto 2
    (Perreault 19:45 en)
31 Toronto 5 at Islanders 3

November

2 Detroit 2 at Toronto 6 (65th anniversary
   of Maple Leaf Gardens; Red Horner and
   Mush March in attendance, and both
   teams wore vintage sweaters)
5 St. Louis 3 at Toronto 6
7 Toronto 2 at Ottawa 6
9 Edmonton 3 at Toronto 7
10 Toronto 1 at Flyers 3 (goalies Potvin and
    Hextall fight in end-of-game melee)
13 Toronto 2 at Anaheim 3
14 Toronto 1 at Los Angeles 4
16 Toronto 2 at Phoenix 3
19 Buffalo 3 at Toronto 4
21 Toronto 3 at Buffalo 6
    (Barnaby 19:58 en)
23 Canadiens 4 at Toronto 3
    (Borje Salming Night)
26 Vancouver 2 at Toronto 3
    (Roberts (V) 19:14 with extra attacker)
27 Toronto 2 at Detroit 5
30 Toronto 2 at Dallas 5

December

3 St. Louis 0 at Toronto 2
   [Cousineau/Potvin]
6 Toronto 5 at Rangers 6
   (Berg wins game at 19:33)
7 Rangers 4 at Toronto 0 [Healy]
9 Toronto 3 at Chicago 1
   (Warriner 19:48 en)
10 New Jersey 5 at Toronto 2
14 Phoenix 5 at Toronto 3
    (Tkachuk 19:59 en)
15 Toronto 1 at Detroit 3
17 Toronto 6 at San Jose 3
    (Sundin 19:15 en)
20 Toronto 2 at Phoenix 5
21 Toronto 6 at Colorado 2
23 Pittsburgh 6 at Toronto 5
    (Modin (T) 19:32 with extra attacker)
27 Toronto 3 at St. Louis 2
    (Brett Hull honoured in pre-game
    ceremonies to mark 500th goal)

28 Chicago 4 at Toronto 5
30 Islanders 0 at Toronto 2 [Cousineau]

January

3 Toronto 3 at Edmonton 4
   (Leafs wore white sweaters)
4 Toronto 3 at Vancouver 7
   (Leafs wore white sweaters;
   Canucks wore third sweaters)
7 Toronto 3 at Calgary 4 (Fleury (C) tied
   game at 19:29 with extra attacker;
   Gagner 4:00 ot) (clock stopped at 9:54
   of 3rd for 21 seconds of play, but was
   never altered)
11 Colorado 3 at Toronto 2
13 Toronto 3 at Washington 6
15 Los Angeles 3 at Toronto 2
    (six OHL players from Canada's
    gold medal–winning World Junior
    Championship team dropped the puck)
20 Toronto 1 at Hartford 3
    (Cassels 19:53 en)
22 Calgary 3 at Toronto 5
    (Sundin 19:59 en) (national anthem
    sung by Michael Schade)
24 Toronto 2 at Chicago 1 (Muller 2:07 ot)
    (Toronto wore white sweaters; Chicago
    wore third sweaters)
25 Dallas 5 at Toronto 1
27 Colorado 5 at Toronto 2
29 St. Louis 4 at Toronto 0 [Fuhr]
31 Toronto 3 at New Jersey 3 (5:00 ot)

February

1 Ottawa 2 at Toronto 1
5 Anaheim 2 at Toronto 4
8 Vancouver 2 at Toronto 4
12 Toronto 2 at Anaheim 5
13 Toronto 4 at Los Angeles 4 (5:00 ot)
15 Toronto 0 at Calgary 3 [Kidd]
18 Toronto 6 at Vancouver 5
19 Toronto 5 at Edmonton 6
22 Toronto 5 at Canadiens 1 (Leafs wore
    65th anniversary sweaters)
26 Washington 3 at Toronto 1

March

1 San Jose 2 at Toronto 3
3 Boston 2 at Toronto 4

5   Detroit 4 at Toronto 4 (5:00 OT)
8   Hartford 1 at Toronto 1 (5:00 OT)
10 Dallas 3 at Toronto 3 (5:00 OT)
    (Hendrickson (T) tied game at 19:18
    with extra attacker)
12 Chicago 3 at Toronto 2
15 Toronto 3 at Florida 3 (5:00 OT)
16 Toronto 3 at Tampa Bay 1
19 Flyers 6 at Toronto 3 (Lindros 19:12 en)
20 Toronto 3 at Pittsburgh 6
22 Phoenix 3 at Toronto 0 [Khabibulin]
26 Toronto 2 at San Jose 1
27 Toronto 1 at Phoenix 1 (5:00 OT)
29 Toronto 3 at Colorado 2

April

2   Florida 1 at Toronto 3
3   Toronto 2 at Detroit 2 (5:00 OT)
5   Detroit 4 at Toronto 2
9   Toronto 2 at Dallas 3
10 Toronto 1 at St. Louis 5
12 Calgary 1 at Toronto 4 (opening cere-
    monies honoured Canada's Women's
    World Championship team) (Clark
    19:05 en—the puck never went in the
    net. Albelin of Calgary jumped off the
    bench to stop the puck, thus the goal
    was automatically awarded)

1997–98

October

1   Washington 4 at Toronto 1(Don Cherry
    and Ken Dryden face off opening puck)
4   Toronto 0 at Islanders 3 [Salo]
7   Toronto 2 at Calgary 1
9   Toronto 2 at Vancouver 2 (5:00 OT)
11 Toronto 1 at Edmonton 2
14 Detroit 3 at Toronto 2
15 Toronto 4 at Detroit 3
18 Dallas 5 at Toronto 4
22 Ottawa 6 at Toronto 2
25 Calgary 3 at Toronto 4
28 Anaheim 2 at Toronto 2 (5:00 OT)

November

1   Toronto 1 at Canadiens 5
4   Toronto 0 at San Jose 0 [Healy-
    Cousineau/Vernon] (5:00 OT)

5   Toronto 4 at Calgary 3
8   Phoenix 3 at Toronto 0 (Tkachuk 18:49
    en) [Khabibulin] (Jamie Macoun hon-
    oured for playing 1,000th game)
11 Chicago 2 at Toronto 5 ("O Canada"
    played with bagpipes for Remembrance
    Day) (Hendrickson 19:42 en)
13 Toronto 2 at Chicago 1 (all goals in 1st)
15 Pittsburgh 5 at Toronto 0 (Mario
    Lemieux, Bryan Trottier, and Glen
    Sather, newest inductees to the Hockey
    Hall of Fame, face off opening puck)
    [Barrasso]
17 St. Louis 3 at Toronto 2
    (MacInnis scored winner at 19:58 of
    3rd from centre ice)
19 Philadelphia 1 at Toronto 3 (Pinball
    Clemons, Paul Masotti, and Doug Flutie,
    from Grey Cup champion Argos, face off
    opening puck)
21 Toronto 1 at Colorado 3
    (Sakic 19:35 en)
22 Toronto 0 at Phoenix 2
    (Roenick 19:37 en) [Khabibulin]
25 San Jose 1 at Toronto 3
    (McCauley 19:44 en)
29 Vancouver 4 at Toronto 2

December

2   Anaheim 3 at Toronto 3 (5:00 OT)
4   Toronto 3 at St. Louis 4 (D. King 19:34
    with extra attacker)
6   Los Angeles 2 at Toronto 7
8   Dallas 0 at Toronto 3 (Toronto's 5,000th
    NHL game) [Potvin] (Sundin 18:49 en)
10 Colorado 2 at Toronto 2 (5:00 OT)
13 New Jersey 3 at Toronto 0 [Brodeur]
15 Toronto 2 at Colorado 3
17 Toronto 6 at Anaheim 2
18 Toronto 2 at Los Angeles 5
20 Toronto 3 at Phoenix 2
23 Edmonton 4 at Toronto 5
26 Toronto 1 at Detroit 4
27 Detroit 8 at Toronto 1
31 Boston 2 at Toronto 2 (5:00 OT)

January

1   Toronto 3 at Chicago 3 (5:00 OT)
3   Toronto 2 at New Jersey 4

6   Toronto 3 at Washington 5
7   Toronto 5 at Tampa Bay 2
10 Chicago 4 at Toronto 3
12 Toronto 2 at Rangers 3
14 Buffalo 4 at Toronto 1
21 Toronto 3 at Detroit 0
    (Smith 19:59 en) [Potvin]
22 Toronto 3 at Chicago 0
    (Schneider 18:38 en)[Potvin]
24 Tampa Bay 2 at Toronto 5
26 Toronto 1 at Dallas 5
29 Toronto 0 at St. Louis 2 [Fuhr]
31 Phoenix 5 at Toronto 2

February
2   Dallas 5 at Toronto 1
4   St. Louis 2 at Toronto 3
5   Toronto 2 at Ottawa 3
7   Florida 2 at Toronto 3 (afternoon
    game)(four players—Schneider
    and Sundin (T) and Svehla and
    Vanbiesbrouck (F) honoured prior
    to game in recognition of their par-
    ticipation in Nagano Olympics)
25 Toronto 2 at Buffalo 2 (Sundin 19:55
    with extra attacker) (5:00 OT)
26 Rangers 5 at Toronto 2 (ceremony to
    honour medalists from Nagano)
28 Canadiens 0 at Toronto 4 (banners to
    honour George Armstrong and Charlie
    Conacher raised to rafters) [Potvin]

March
2   Toronto 1 at Pittsburgh 3
    (all goals in 1st)
4   Colorado 5 at Toronto 3
    (Deadmarsh 19:50 en)
7   Edmonton 1 at Toronto 4
9   Toronto 2 at San Jose 3 (all goals in 3rd)
    (Gill (SJ) 19:23 en)
11 Toronto 3 at Anaheim 1
    (Sundin 19:54 en)
12 Toronto 2 at Los Angeles 1
14 Calgary 1 at Toronto 2
16 Toronto 1 at Philadelphia 4
18 Detroit 5 at Toronto 2
    (Draper 19:09 en)
19 Toronto 0 at Boston 4 [Dafoe]
21 Vancouver 1 at Toronto 1 (5:00 OT)

24 Toronto 2 at Phoenix 4
    (all goals in 3rd) (Tocchet 19:44 en)
26 Toronto 1 at Dallas 0
    (Berezin 3:42 3rd) [Potvin]
28 Islanders 3 at Toronto 4 (D. King 19:09
    with extra attacker) (Côté 4:56 OT)
30 Los Angeles 3 at Toronto 2 (Clark 19:45
    with extra attacker)

April
1   St. Louis 6 at Toronto 4
4   San Jose 5 at Toronto 3
6   Toronto 2 at Dallas 4
7   Toronto 3 at Florida 1
9   Toronto 2 at Carolina 5
    (Roberts 19:33 en)
11 Carolina 1 at Toronto 5
    (Schneider 17:37 en)
15 Chicago 2 at Toronto 3
18 Toronto 3 at Edmonton 4
19 Toronto 2 at Vancouver 1

1998–99
October
10 Detroit 1 at Toronto 2 (final home
    opener at Maple Leaf Gardens)
    (Leafs wore Original Six sweaters)
13 Toronto 3 at Edmonton 2
16 Toronto 7 at Calgary 3
17 Toronto 1 at Vancouver 4
19 Nashville 2 at Toronto 2 (5:00 OT)
23 Toronto 5 at Detroit 3
    (Leafs wore Original Six sweaters)
24 Toronto 6 at Pittsburgh 4
    (K. King 19:33 en)
26 Pittsburgh 2 at Toronto 0 [Skudra]
30 Toronto 1 at Buffalo 4
31 Buffalo 6 at Toronto 3

November
4   Colorado 0 at Toronto 3
    (all goals in 2nd) [Joseph]
5   Toronto 1 at Boston 4
7   Rangers 6 at Toronto 6 (5:00 OT)
    (Leafs wear Original Six sweaters)
9   Islanders 3 at Toronto 1
    (all goals in 3rd)
11 Edmonton 2 at Toronto 3

12 Toronto 10 at Chicago 3
    (Leafs wore Original Six sweaters)
14 Ottawa 1 at Toronto 2
18 Toronto 1 at Washington 4
20 Toronto 1 at Buffalo 4
21 Buffalo 1 at Toronto 2
23 Calgary 2 at Toronto 3
25 Vancouver 1 at Toronto 5 (Yushkevich
    10:58 en 3rd, on Vancouver power-play)
27 Toronto 3 at Philadelphia 4
28 Ottawa 2 at Toronto 3 (D. King :42 OT)

December

 2 Los Angeles 1 at Toronto 3
 5 Toronto 4 at Canadiens 3
    (Kaberle :34 OT)
 7 Toronto 2 at Rangers 6
11 Toronto 3 at Chicago 2
12 Philadelphia 3 at Toronto 0
    [Vanbiesbrouck]
16 Phoenix 2 at Toronto 5
19 Rangers 4 at Toronto 7
    (last game at MLG for Gretzky)
21 Pittsburgh 1 at Toronto 7
23 Dallas 5 at Toronto 1
26 Canadiens 2 at Toronto 1 (moment of
    silence to remember the passing of Syl
    Apps) (Leafs wore Original Six sweaters)
30 Anaheim 1 at Toronto 4
31 Toronto 4 at Detroit 2

January

 2 Washington 5 at Toronto 2
    (Johansson 19:37 en)
 4 Tampa Bay 4 at Toronto 5
    (Modin 1:54 OT)
 7 Toronto 1 at Boston 2
    (Leafs wore Original Six sweaters)
 9 Boston 3 at Toronto 6
    (Bobby Orr and George Armstrong
    faced off opening puck)
12 Toronto 4 at Tampa Bay 3
13 Toronto 3 at Florida 3 (5:00 OT)
16 Toronto 4 at Philadelphia 3
18 Toronto 2 at Carolina 4
20 Toronto 6 at Dallas 4
21 Toronto 4 at St. Louis 2
28 Toronto 0 at Pittsburgh 6 [Skudra]
30 Washington 3 at Toronto 5
    (Sundin 19:53 en)

February

 2 Toronto 3 at Tampa Bay 0 [Joseph]
 3 Toronto 2 at Florida 5
    (Niedermayer 19:35 en)
 6 Toronto 3 at New Jersey 2
10 Carolina 6 at Toronto 5
13 Chicago 6 at Toronto 2 (last game at
    Maple Leaf Gardens—final goal scored
    by Bob Probert at 11:05 of 3rd; last Leaf
    goal by Derek King at 8:15 of 2nd)
    (Leafs wore Original Six sweaters)
15 Toronto 3 at New Jersey 3 (5:00 OT)
17 Toronto 3 at Buffalo 2 (Sundin 4:04 OT)
20 Canadiens 2 at Toronto 3 (Thomas 3:48
    OT—first game at Air Canada Centre)
22 Toronto 3 at Washington 4
24 Carolina 2 at Toronto 2 (5:00 OT)
25 Toronto 4 at Islanders 1
27 Florida 1 at Toronto 4

March

 3 New Jersey 5 at Toronto 2
    (Elias 19:16 en)
 4 Toronto 4 at St. Louis 0 [Joseph]
    (Leafs record just nine total shots on
    goal, the lowest total for a winning
    team in NHL history)
 6 Toronto 1 at Ottawa 3
 8 Toronto 2 at Rangers 3 (Nedved 4:46 OT)
 9 Tampa Bay 1 at Toronto 6
11 Toronto 2 at Islanders 1
13 Toronto 1 at Canadiens 2
    (all goals in 2nd)
17 Boston 4 at Toronto 1 (Carter 19:54 en)
20 New Jersey 1 at Toronto 3
22 Philadelphia 3 at Toronto 1
24 San Jose 8 at Toronto 5
    (Murphy 19:57 en)
26 Toronto 7 at Carolina 2
27 Boston 2 at Toronto 2 (5:00 OT)
    (Leafs wore Original Six sweaters)
31 Toronto 6 at Vancouver 5

April

 1 Toronto 5 at Edmonton 1
 3 Toronto 5 at Calgary 1
 5 St. Louis 2 at Toronto 2 (5:00 OT)
 7 Ottawa 2 at Toronto 4
 8 Toronto 1 at Ottawa 3
10 Florida 1 at Toronto 9

14   Islanders 2 at Toronto 3 (Berard :42 OT)

17   Toronto 2 at Canadiens 3 (Leafs wore Original Six sweaters)

1999–2000

October

2   Toronto 4 at Canadiens 1 (Bruny Surin faced off opening puck)

4   Boston 0 at Toronto 4 [Joseph]

6   Colorado 1 at Toronto 2

9   Toronto 3 at Ottawa 4

11   Nashville 4 at Toronto 2

13   Florida 2 at Toronto 3

15   Toronto 2 at Chicago 1

16   Toronto 2 at St. Louis 4

20   Carolina 3 at Toronto 3 (5:00 OT)

23   Canadiens 2 at Toronto 3

25   Dallas 0 at Toronto 4 [Joseph]

27   Atlanta 0 at Toronto 4 [Healy]

30   Calgary 1 at Toronto 2

November

3   Toronto 6 at Carolina 0 [Joseph]

5   Toronto 3 at Washington 5

6   Toronto 3 at New Jersey 3 (5:00 OT)

9   Anaheim 2 at Toronto 0 (Kariya 19:47 en) [Hebert]

11   Toronto 3 at Boston 4 (Axelsson 3:58 OT)

13   Detroit 1 at Toronto 1 (5:00 OT)

15   San Jose 2 at Toronto 4

17   St. Louis 3 at Toronto 2

20   Rangers 3 at Toronto 4 (Korolev 1:16 OT) (Hockey Hall of Fame Game—new inductees Scotty Morrison, Andy Van Hellemond, and Wayne Gretzky dropped opening puck, accompanied by many previous Hall of Famers. Players of the Game replaced the Three Star selection: Rangers—Adam Graves; Toronto—Yanic Perreault)

23   Toronto 1 at Pittsburgh 3 (Titov 19:38 en)

26   Toronto 2 at Philadelphia 3 (Berezin 19:48 with extra attacker) (Recchi 4:08 OT)

27   Edmonton 2 at Toronto 5

29   Washington 1 at Toronto 3 (Thomas 19:40 en)

December

2   Toronto 2 at Carolina 2 (5:00 OT)

4   Pittsburgh 2 at Toronto 3 (Sundin :27 OT)

6   Buffalo 2 at Toronto 3 (Thomas 1:05 OT)

9   Toronto 2 at Philadelphia 4

11   Philadelphia 4 at Toronto 6 (Hoglund 19:48 en)

13   Ottawa 3 at Toronto 1

15   Islanders 1 at Toronto 5

18   Canadiens 1 at Toronto 2 (Canada Post unveiled Hockey Night in Canada stamps; Foster Hewitt's daughter attended ceremony)

20   Toronto 6 at Florida 4

21   Toronto 4 at Tampa Bay 2

23   New Jersey 1 at Toronto 4

29   Toronto 2 at Islanders 1 (Hoglund 19:11 en)

January

1   Toronto 1 at Buffalo 8

3   Buffalo 2 at Toronto 6

5   Toronto 2 at Rangers 3 (Graves 4:26 OT)

7   Toronto 2 at Pittsburgh 5 (Straka 18:56 en)

8   Rangers 5 at Toronto 3

11   Toronto 3 at Boston 2

14   Toronto 3 at Edmonton 2 (Sundin 2:59 OT)

15   Toronto 0 at Calgary 4 [Brathwaite]

17   Toronto 5 at Vancouver 4 (Thomas 4:55 OT)

22   Washington 5 at Toronto 5 (5:00 OT)

24   Ottawa 3 at Toronto 3 (5:00 OT)

26   Toronto 2 at Detroit 4

27   Toronto 4 at Rangers 3

29   Los Angeles 2 at Toronto 3

February

1   Toronto 5 at Tampa Bay 3 (Korolev 19:21 en)

3   Toronto 2 at Boston 4

9   Philadelphia 4 at Toronto 2

12   Vancouver 4 at Toronto 1 (Bertuzzi 18:41 en)

14   Carolina 5 at Toronto 2

16 Boston 3 at Toronto 3 (5:00 OT)
19 Toronto 1 at Canadiens 2
23 Phoenix 3 at Toronto 5
    (Perreault 19:07 en)
25 Toronto 3 at New Jersey 1
26 Buffalo 2 at Toronto 5
29 Toronto 4 at Atlanta 0 (assistant coach
    Rick Ley assumed head coaching duties
    while Pat Quinn attended general man-
    ager meetings) [Healy]

March
1 Toronto 1 at Florida 3
4 Canadiens 3 at Toronto 4
6 Toronto 6 at Vancouver 5
   (Sundin 3:13 OT)
7 Toronto 2 at Edmonton 0
   (both goals in 1st) [Joseph]
9 Toronto 6 at Calgary 2
11 Toronto 4 at Ottawa 2
15 Chicago 5 at Toronto 2
16 Toronto 4 at Detroit 3 (Sundin 1:38 OT)
18 Atlanta 4 at Toronto 1
22 Islanders 5 at Toronto 2
23 Toronto 2 at Ottawa 3
25 New Jersey 3 at Toronto 5
29 Toronto 3 at St. Louis 2
30 Toronto 0 at Chicago 4 [Thibault]

April
1 Toronto 4 at Washington 3
3 Toronto 2 at Buffalo 3 (all goals in 1st)
5 Pittsburgh 4 at Toronto 2
7 Toronto 2 at Islanders 1
8 Tampa Bay 2 at Toronto 4

2000–01
October
7 Canadiens 0 at Toronto 2 [Joseph]
   (Wendel Clark dropped opening puck)
9 Dallas 3 at Toronto 1
11 Islanders 2 at Toronto 3
14 Ottawa 4 at Toronto 0 [Lalime]
16 Toronto 2 at Vancouver 5
   (Naslund 18:53 en)
19 Toronto 4 at Edmonton 1
21 Toronto 2 at Calgary 1
25 Wild 1 at Toronto 6

27 Toronto 1 at Buffalo 2
28 Toronto 2 at Boston 1 (Sundin 3:36 OT)
31 Toronto 3 at Ottawa 4

November
2 New Jersey 3 at Toronto 5
4 Toronto 0 at St. Louis 0 (5:00 OT)
   [Joseph (T)/Turek (St.L.)]
5 Boston 1 at Toronto 7
8 Carolina 0 at Toronto 5 [Joseph]
10 Toronto 1 at Carolina 3
11 Chicago 3 at Toronto 3 (Daze (C) tied
   game at 19:54 with extra attacker) (5:00
   OT) (Hockey Hall of Fame Game—new
   inductees Denis Savard, Joe Mullen, and
   Walter Bush honoured in pre-game ceremony. Three Star selection replaced by
   Players of the Game: Chicago—Daze;
   Toronto—Berezin)
15 Philadelphia 2 at Toronto 1
   (Recchi 3:26 OT)
17 Tampa Bay 2 at Toronto 2 (5:00 OT)
18 Toronto 6 at Canadiens 1
21 Toronto 3 at Rangers 1
22 Edmonton 3 at Toronto 4
25 Ottawa 4 at Toronto 2
29 St. Louis 6 at Toronto 5 (Khavanov
   (St.L.) tied game at 19:35 with extra
   attacker) (Hecht 0:18 OT)
30 Toronto 6 at Islanders 4
   (Tucker 19:45 en)

December
2 Rangers 2 at Toronto 8
4 Florida 4 at Toronto 4 (5:00 OT)
6 Toronto 3 at Detroit 0 [Joseph]
9 Pittsburgh 1 at Toronto 5
13 Toronto 7 at Pittsburgh 4
15 Toronto 2 at Islanders 3
16 Calgary 6 at Toronto 5 (Bure :34 OT)
20 Nashville 3 at Toronto 1
   (Walker 19:48 en)
21 Toronto 0 at Boston 4 [Dafoe]
23 Toronto 5 at Canadiens 2
26 Toronto 3 at Thrashers 5
   (Audette 19:54 en)
27 Toronto 0 at Pittsburgh 5
   [Snow] (Mario Lemieux's first game
   in three and a half years)

30 Toronto 4 at Florida 1

31 Toronto 3 at Tampa Bay 2

January

3 Buffalo 1 at Toronto 1
(both goals in 3rd) (5:00 OT)

5 Toronto 3 at Buffalo 3 (5:00 OT)

6 Washington 3 at Toronto 2

10 Tampa Bay 3 at Toronto 1
(Modin 19:58 en)

12 Phoenix 2 at Toronto 3

13 Toronto 4 at New Jersey 4 (5:00 OT)

17 Los Angeles 2 at Toronto 1

18 Toronto 1 at Rangers 2 (Leetch 4:33 OT)

20 Buffalo 0 at Toronto 2 [Joseph]

24 Boston 2 at Toronto 1

25 Toronto 2 at Thrashers 1
(McCabe :39 OT)

27 Rangers 1 at Toronto 3

29 Toronto 1 at St. Louis 2

31 Toronto 4 at Carolina 3

February

1 Toronto 4 at Washington 5

7 Thrashers 1 at Toronto 7

8 Toronto 1 at Detroit 2

10 Detroit 3 at Toronto 3 (Hoglund (T) tied
game at 19:16 with extra attacker) (5:00
OT) (Leaf trainer Brian Papineau honoured in pre-game ceremony for 1,000
games with club)

14 Columbus 2 at Toronto 2 (5:00 OT)

15 Toronto 2 at Philadelphia 5

17 Colorado 5 at Toronto 5 (5:00 OT)

19 New Jersey 2 at Toronto 0 [Brodeur]

22 Vancouver 1 at Toronto 4

24 Canadiens 1 at Toronto 5

25 Toronto 4 at Chicago 6
(Sullivan 19:52 en)

28 San Jose 1 at Toronto 2

March

1 Toronto 3 at Washington 2
(Roberts 1:21 OT)

3 Ottawa 3 at Toronto 2 (Yashin 0:42 OT)

6 Toronto 3 at Calgary 1
(Thomas 19:38 en)

7 Toronto 0 at Edmonton 4 [Salo]

10 Toronto 3 at Vancouver 3 (5:00 OT)

14 Anaheim 2 at Toronto 3

15 Toronto 2 at Tampa Bay 3

17 Toronto 5 at Florida 3
(Sundin 19:52 en)

20 Toronto 0 at Buffalo 3 [Hasek]

21 Florida 3 at Toronto 1 (near end of
game, disgruntled fan with a broken leg
threw one of his crutches onto the ice)

24 Philadelphia 3 at Toronto 5
(Tucker 19:59 en)

28 Boston 3 at Toronto 0
[Dafoe] (penalty-free game)

29 Toronto 2 at Philadelphia 1 (Domi and
a fan got in mixup in penalty box)

31 Toronto 1 at Montreal 4
(Darby 19:06 en)

April

4 Islanders 2 at Toronto 4

6 Toronto 1 at Chicago 0
(Thomas 6:35 2nd) [Joseph]

7 Toronto 3 at Ottawa 5

Complete List of Entries

THE ESSENTIAL BLUE AND WHITE BOOK'S GUIDE TO MAPLELEAFS.COM

Just as the The Blue And White Book is your source of information on everything you would want to know about what's happened with the Leafs, the team's official Web site, MAPLELEAFS.COM, has all the news and info on what is happening and what's going to happen with your favourite team. It's updated regularly with breaking news and features, analysis and game coverage, history and kids sections and a whole lot more. There are also exclusive columns from our Leafs.commentators who have the inside scoop on what's happening with the team. Here are just some of the features for you to enjoy at MAPLELEAFS.COM:

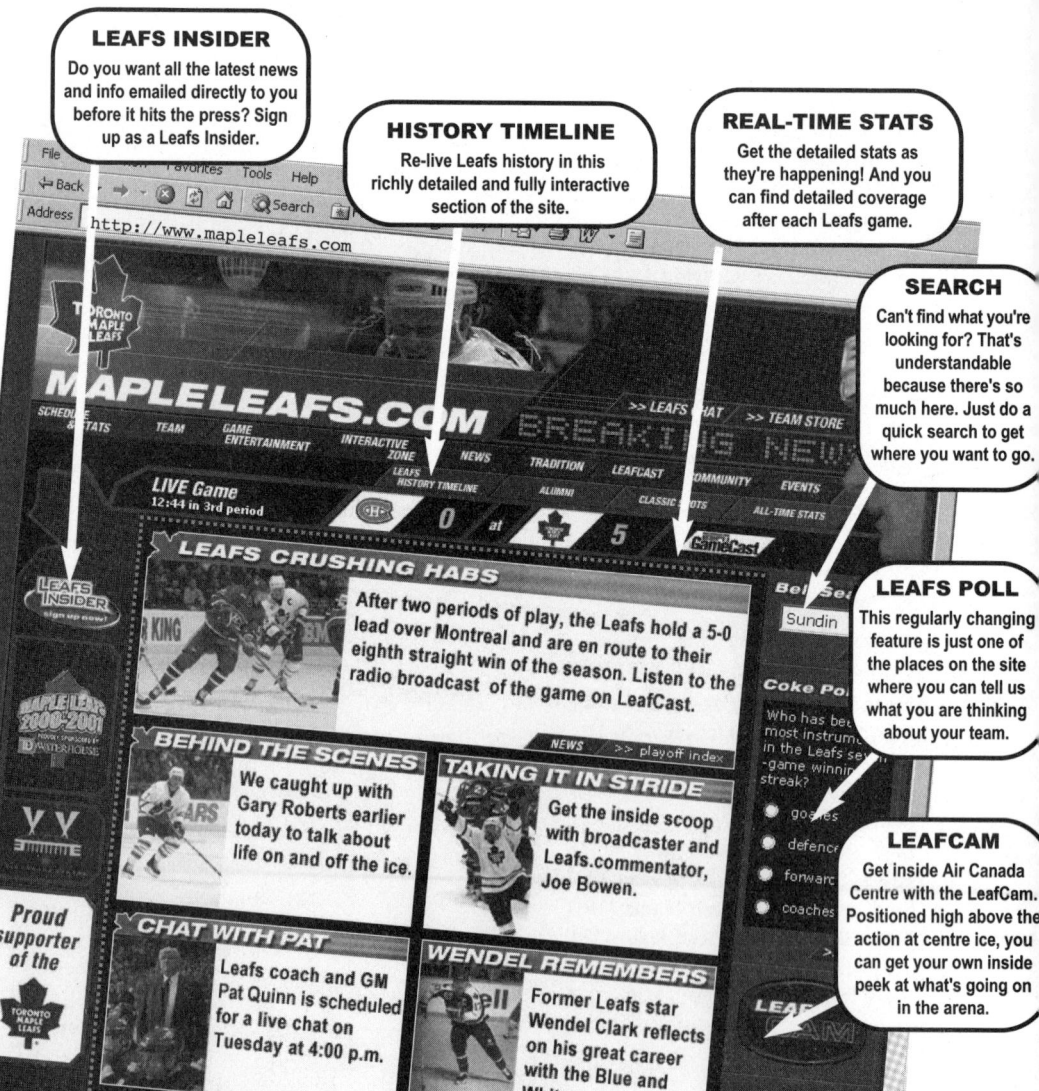

LEAFS INSIDER
Do you want all the latest news and info emailed directly to you before it hits the press? Sign up as a Leafs Insider.

HISTORY TIMELINE
Re-live Leafs history in this richly detailed and fully interactive section of the site.

REAL-TIME STATS
Get the detailed stats as they're happening! And you can find detailed coverage after each Leafs game.

SEARCH
Can't find what you're looking for? That's understandable because there's so much here. Just do a quick search to get where you want to go.

LEAFS POLL
This regularly changing feature is just one of the places on the site where you can tell us what you are thinking about your team.

LEAFCAM
Get inside Air Canada Centre with the LeafCam. Positioned high above the action at centre ice, you can get your own inside peek at what's going on in the arena.

LEAFS CRUSHING HABS
After two periods of play, the Leafs hold a 5-0 lead over Montreal and are en route to their eighth straight win of the season. Listen to the radio broadcast of the game on LeafCast.

BEHIND THE SCENES
We caught up with Gary Roberts earlier today to talk about life on and off the ice.

TAKING IT IN STRIDE
Get the inside scoop with broadcaster and Leafs.commentator, Joe Bowen.

CHAT WITH PAT
Leafs coach and GM Pat Quinn is scheduled for a live chat on Tuesday at 4:00 p.m.

WENDEL REMEMBERS
Former Leafs star Wendel Clark reflects on his great career with the Blue and White.

75 YEARS OF WATCHING THE MAPLE LEAFS JUST GOT BETTER!

LEAFS TV

Introducing Leafs TV...the digital channel dedicated to fans of the Blue and White. It's all Leafs... all the time!

As the nation's most popular hockey team, the Toronto Maple Leafs is a franchise built on a history and commitment to excellence, both on and off the ice. Rooted in their respect for the traditions of the game, the fabled Blue and White are prepared to offer their fans a progressive new initiative in Leafs TV that promises to position the Toronto Maple Leafs at the forefront of the sports and entertainment industry.

Leafs TV will have the distinction of being the only specialty channel in North America dedicated exclusively to one sports club. The ultimate in wrap-around programming, Leafs TV will offer an authentic, insider all-Leafs environment with an in-depth look at the Leafs community involvement, compelling analysis of the franchise, punctuated with insightful, insider commentary.

Leafs TV...looking to change the way people watch hockey!